D1233453

THE AMERICAN POLICE STATE

The Government Against the People

THE
AMERICAN
POLICE STATE
The Government
Against the People

DAVID WISE

Vintage Books
A Division of Random House
New York

FIRST VINTAGE BOOKS EDITION, February 1978
Copyright © 1976 by David Wise

All rights reserved under International and Pan American Copyright
Conventions. Published in the United States by Random House, Inc.,
New York, and simultaneously in Canada by Random House of Canada
Limited, Toronto. Originally published by Random House, Inc.,
in November 1976.

Library of Congress Cataloging in Publication Data
Wise, David.
  The American police state.

  Bibliography: p.
  Includes index.
  1. Intelligence service—United States. 2. Civil rights—United States.
3. United States—Politics and government—1933-1945. 4. United States
—Politics and government—1945-   I. Title.
[JK468.16W49 1978]   323.4'0973   77-12582
ISBN 0-394-72498-4

Manufactured in the United States of America

To K.P.W. and R.L.W.

Contents

THE
AMERICAN
POLICE STATE
The Government
Against the People

> *"Though I am accused of something, I cannot recall the slightest offense that might be charged against me."*
>
> —Joseph K., in Franz
> Kafka, *The Trial*

1
CATO

The short gray-haired man atop the telephone pole behind the George-town home of Washington columnist Joseph Kraft looked like a tele-phone-company repairman: test set on hip, screwdriver in hand, casual clothes. His name was John J. Ragan.

In the box at the top of the pole Ragan located two little bolts that were the terminals of Kraft's telephone line. To these he wired a small battery-powered transmitter. A miniature FM radio station was now in operation; when anyone used the phone in Kraft's red brick home on N Street, the conversations were broadcast to a voice-acti-vated tape recorder locked in the trunk of a car parked nearby.

At fifty-five, Ragan was getting a little old to be shinnying up telephone poles. He was, however, no ordinary tapper; not only was Ragan on a mission for the White House, he had also served, until quite recently, as personal electronics expert for the President of the United States. And a member of the White House staff had told him "the top man" wanted this job done; Ragan understood the phrase to mean President Richard M. Nixon.

Looking back at what he did that day, Ragan was able to ration-alize that a different political atmosphere existed in 1969. "It's not like today when everybody is distrustful of the White House. It's a new

Administration. The top man is concerned and he's got troubles. What are you going to do, say 'Go fuck yourself'?"

Some 250 miles away, on the wall of Ragan's home on Long Island, there hung a map of the United States with a maze of crisscrossed lines connecting the cities where Nixon had campaigned in 1968 in his quest for the Presidency. After his election, Nixon had sent the map as a memento to the members of his staff. Ragan had his copy framed. His role in the campaign had been unique; in each of the cities, Ragan had arrived one day ahead of Nixon and had carefully performed electronic sweeps of his hotel rooms. Richard Nixon, whose White House tapes later brought about his downfall, did not want anyone eavesdropping on him.

Although in the campaign Ragan's task was to *find* bugs, not to install them, as he did in the case of Joseph Kraft, the distinction may be less significant than the fact that in the electronic age a candidate for President believed that he required his own wiretap expert, much as medieval kings had employed official tasters.

In using Ragan as his personal wireman, Nixon had chosen with discretion. During twenty-four years with the FBI, Ragan had earned the reputation, inside the half-lit world of the government's secret agents, as "the best wireman to come out of the Bureau." For years he had been in charge of all FBI wiretapping in New York City. At the time he climbed up Joseph Kraft's telephone pole, in June of 1969, Ragan had left the FBI and was working as a private investigator in New York. He also held another job in Washington—director of security for the Republican National Committee.

Ragan's name was mentioned during the televised Senate Watergate hearings only once, by John Dean, and quickly forgotten. Dean, testifying under the television lights before the Watergate committee, was destroying a President, and testimony about the bugging of a newspaper columnist seemed peripheral. So Ragan's background as an expert wiretapper and his unusual relationship to President Nixon never really emerged. He was a marginal character in the Watergate drama. Marginal, yet symbolic of how far America had come in creating its own version of a police state.

In summary form, the facts sound rather like something that might happen in a small Central American country under a military dictatorship: a skilled wiretapper, trained by the federal police, is employed by a presidential candidate as his personal electronics assistant. After the election, and while director of security for the President's political party, he is secretly dispatched by the President's staff to intercept and tape the conversations of a citizen, a newspaperman, whose columns have in some manner disturbed the President.

Yet that is only a part of what happened to Joseph Kraft, one facet of a complex story of intrigue that came to be identified in the files of the federal government by a single code name: Cato.

Georgetown is more than a place to live; it is a symbol. If the most powerful men in Washington lunch at the Metropolitan Club, they go home at night to Georgetown. Rows of brick town houses, some authentic Federal homes, others modern imitations, line its narrow tree-shaded streets. John F. Kennedy lived in Georgetown before he moved into the White House. Senators and Cabinet members reside there, as do foreign service officers with money, a number of high CIA officials, Old Washington society, and those journalists who can afford it.

But even within Georgetown, some parts are better than other parts, and if one had to select the most prestigious block in the area, it would doubtless be N Street between 30th and 31st streets. Joseph Kraft lived there, at number 3021, across the street from Averell Harriman. Next door to Kraft was the exquisite home once owned by Abe Fortas, and immediately to the east, at 3017, was the mansion occupied by Jacqueline Kennedy after Dallas. For a time the tourists used to stand across the street, gawking at the house, hoping to catch a glimpse of Mrs. Kennedy. But they were gone after 1965; the President's widow had moved to New York, and the mansion was purchased by Michael Straight, the wealthy former publisher of the *New Republic*.

By 1969, when Kraft's telephone was bugged—a fact he was unaware of until four years later—it was entirely suitable that he lived where he did, for he was one of a handful of the most eminent nationally syndicated columnists in the United States. He ranked somewhere in the pantheon occupied by James Reston, Tom Wicker, Marquis Childs, and Anthony Lewis. No one had inherited the mantle vacated by the retirement and death of Walter Lippmann, and perhaps no one would, but Kraft was trying.° He worked prodigiously, turning out books and numerous magazine articles in addition to his three-times-a-week syndicated column. He traveled the globe, dropping in on prime ministers and chatting with them, he hoped, as equals.

In Washington, Kraft moved easily in the higher circles of power, of which he was a part. He called Secretary of State Kissinger "Henry." So did many others in Washington to display their importance, but Kraft was entitled; he really *knew* Kissinger as Henry. And, rare among Washington newsmen, Kraft was a member of the Council on Foreign Relations, sometimes caricatured as the New York office of the Eastern establishment.

Kraft was forty-five and doing very nicely; socially and professionally he had come a considerable way from South Orange, New

---

° Lippmann had termed Kraft "the most promising commentator of his generation."

Jersey, where he was born into a comfortable upper-middle-class family. The son of a New York businessman, Kraft grew up on the West Side of Manhattan, living in one of those large apartment houses that line Central Park West in the Eighties. He attended private school and then Columbia College, where he was valedictorian of his class. He spent a year at Princeton after that, at the Institute for Advanced Study, and in 1951 went to work writing editorials for the Washington *Post.* He moved next to the Week in Review section of the *New York Times* for six years, then struck out on his own. He covered the war in Algeria, wrote a book about it, and became a speech writer for John F. Kennedy in the 1960 presidential campaign. In the early sixties he was Washington correspondent for *Harper's* magazine, and in 1963 he launched his syndicated column; by 1975 it appeared regularly in the Washington *Post* and some 180 other newspapers.

Kraft married well—to Polly Winton, a red-haired, attractive, and rich woman whose family owned timberlands in Minnesota and other Midwestern states.° Joe and Polly spent their summers in the Hamptons.

Kraft, a pleasant and unfailingly courteous man, had definite tastes that were reflected in his elegant life style; in a column he wrote in March 1975, he could hardly conceal his astonishment at California Governor Jerry Brown's calculatedly informal manner (no limousine, no private plane), and he reported with some dismay that the governor had been carrying around his laundry in a bundle while Kraft interviewed him, a task presumably made more difficult by the presence throughout of an unidentified "young woman dressed in faded blue jeans" who had with her "a little girl of about six." Kraft wrote: "We drove—he in his Plymouth, I in a borrowed car—to a small restaurant on Fairfax Avenue. The young woman and little girl were there. The fare was 'macrobiotic.' All of it tasted to me like broccoli."

That same year Kraft was criticized in the *Washington Monthly* magazine for preserving too close a relationship with his establishment sources. "Respecting them," wrote James Fallows, an editor of the magazine, "he seeks their respect in return."

And Kraft thought he *had* earned their respect; he was bewildered and at first disbelieving when he first heard, in 1973, that he had been wiretapped by the Nixon White House.

"I had rather good relations with the Nixon Administration," Kraft said somewhat wistfully during an interview in his office, in the basement of his home on N Street. "My reaction is still one of incredulity. I'm baffled as to why they did it. I just can't fit it into the life in Wash-

° He had even married well within the upper reaches of the Washington news media; Polly Kraft's second cousin is Kay Evans, the wife of syndicated columnist Rowland Evans; like Bourbon kings, the two columnists were related by marriage.

ington that I know and that I lead." Kraft said he was confident he had good relations with the Nixon people because "I had all kinds of fairly good evidence. Solid evidence in payoffs," by which he meant leaks and stories from the White House.

"I was pretty hostile, pretty critical on Vietnam from the beginning, but I would see Haldeman and Ehrlichman and Henry and they were rather friendly to me, and the President was fairly friendly. He kept reminding me that I used the term 'Middle America,' and he had drawn on that theme heavily in the 1968 campaign. I was one of the people he kept asking to see throughout the 1968 campaign."

So the tap had come as a great surprise to Kraft and that shock was soon followed by another, for when the White House Enemies List was disclosed, it included an entry that read: "Kraft, Joseph (Polly) 3021 N Street, N.W. Washington D.C."

"You check to see that you have the right line in the first place. In other words, you put the clips on any line and you get the dial tone. You dial the phone that you're interested in, then you rake the board—its called raking."

John Ragan was explaining in his friendly way how to tap a telephone, what to do when you open the terminal box on the top of the pole. First, he said, you must have a test set—a portable phone that can be attached to any line with metal alligator clips. Then you rake. You take a screwdriver and run it down the double rows of bolts, or "pairs," in the terminal box; each pair represents someone's telephone line. When you hear a click on the test set, it means you have touched the screwdriver to the line you wish to tap. "When you get the click, you go to that line; you take the clips off and put them on that line and dial the number you're interested in. If you get a busy tone, that proves you're on it."

We were sitting in a hotel room in mid-Manhattan, and Ragan was talking at length about his profession and the services he had rendered unto Richard Nixon. He discussed the Kraft tap gingerly, he would only talk around the edges of that; not that he faced criminal prosecution for the tap, the federal statute of limitations had run out, but still, it was a touchy business. He found comfort in euphemisms. He preferred to call the Kraft tap a "test," or a "survey."

He was a genial man, rather handsome, with a quick smile; he might be the affable older man wearing a cardigan and hound's-tooth slacks in a four-color beer ad in a magazine; or perhaps an auto mechanic, a bartender, or an insurance salesman. Everyman as wireman. Justice Oliver Wendell Holmes called wiretapping "a dirty business," and clearly it is, dirty and illicit, outrageous and often illegal, so it was all the more difficult to accept the fact that this man was *likable*. John Ragan might not be at home with Joe and Polly in the Hamptons, but he did not appear very different from anyone else one might encounter on the 7:45 from Massapequa.

He was a professional, and he did not question the values of his profession. If people were going to talk on the telephone, there would be John Ragans to listen in. He had worked for the FBI for twenty-four years. He was serving his government, and he had learned not to question. He was only obeying orders.

Ragan was born in 1913, the same year as Richard Nixon, in Fall River, Massachusetts. He had switched from engineering school to law school, and earned a degree at Southeastern Massachusetts Law School. "But my natural inclination," he explained, "is toward the mechanical or electronic type of thing." He noted with a touch of pride that he had taken aptitude tests much later that showed he would have made a good engineering executive. "But the nearest I came was to being supervisor in charge of technical operations for the FBI in New York."

He joined the FBI in 1940 and spent two years in Missouri and Illinois. Then he was transferred to New York City in 1942, during World War II. "I was doing mostly criminal work, bank robberies, stolen cars, white-slave traffic, deserters, the usual gamut." Because it was wartime, he also got involved in some espionage and internal security cases; and he set up some of the technical equipment shown in *The House on 92nd Street*, a movie about a wartime Nazi spy ring in New York. "I helped them make the movie," Ragan recalled. "I met Lloyd Nolan."

"Around 1943," he said, "because of my aptitude for the electronic or mechanical type of thing, they sent me to their sound school in Virginia, in Quantico. I became qualified for telephone-microphone surveillance." After that, for more than a decade, he was assigned to the FBI section that handled electronic activity in the Greater New York area; the unit operated a radio station, radio cars, and wiretaps. Ragan headed this squad for five years, directing all wiretapping and other forms of electronic eavesdropping not only in Manhattan but in the four other boroughs of New York, as well as Westchester and Long Island.

"It was a full-time operation. When I was in charge of the squad there were like thirty-five men on the squad, either monitoring or some of the men putting the things in, and, you know, taking care of them."

Putting the things in was, of course, the most delicate part of the FBI operation. While a wiretap often does not involve entering a home or office, implanting a microphone without a court warrant may mean an illegal entry in violation of both the Fourth Amendment of the

United States Constitution and local law. And Ragan made it clear his squad had performed both "microphone and telephone surveillance."°

Ragan had done some of the most difficult jobs himself. "I used to get the tough ones, but, uh, you know, it takes expertise and the nerve to go into a place. If you were caught, you were doing it on your own."

According to Ragan, the FBI during this period ran its wiretap and electronic-surveillance operations out of a secret plant located in mid-Manhattan. Who was tapped? "Spies, double agents. People that you wouldn't trust too much, you know." Ragan declined to provide names, but the targets are not difficult to imagine. This was the early fifties, the height of the McCarthy years, a time of fear. It was the era of congressional investigations, of federal prosecution of Communist party leaders under the Smith Act. The FBI gathered the evidence, one way or another.

A few years later Ragan switched over to investigating crime on the high seas and general criminal work, but periodically he continued to wiretap for the FBI in New York. He spent the last four years of his Bureau career as resident agent at Babylon, Long Island, near his home. In 1964, at the age of fifty, he retired from the FBI. For two years thereafter he handled security for the Pinkerton detective agency at the New York World's Fair; then he joined the New York branch of E. J. Charters Associates, a Philadelphia-based investigative agency. In his new job Ragan got a license as a private eye and operated from an office in the Graybar Building in Manhattan. But it was dull work, mostly following around laundry trucks to make sure the drivers weren't goofing off or stealing shirts.

Consequently, Ragan was in a receptive mood when in 1967 or 1968, he does not remember precisely, he received a telephone call from Louis B. Nichols, executive vice president of Schenley Industries, Inc., in New York, and former assistant to the Director of the FBI. Nichols' was a powerful name in the Bureau, and among retired FBI agents; for a time he was considered a likely successor should Hoover ever give up his directorship. Some measure of Lou Nichols' devotion to the Director can be perceived from the fact that he named the first of his two sons John Edgar.

"Nichols said he had a friend in the political area who was going to declare his candidacy," Ragan said. "He was hemming and hawing.

° In May 1975 the Justice Department under Attorney General Edward H. Levi took the startling position that the federal government may make "physical entries into private premises" without a warrant in cases involving foreign espionage or intelligence. But as of that date, the Supreme Court had not agreed that the Fourth Amendment allowed the government to commit burglary in the name of national security.

Everybody in the Bureau knew that Nichols and Nixon were friends, so I said, 'Lou, if it's any consolation to you, I have been a registered Republican all my life, and I think I know what you are talking about.' "

At Nichols' request, Ragan began exploring Nixon's offices in New York and Washington for bugs. He was paid by personal check, signed by Louis B. Nichols, at $75 a sweep. "I started by checking out Nixon's law offices, when he was with Nixon, Mudge down on Broad Street, and his Washington offices, which were on Pennsylvania Avenue almost across from the White House." But Ragan did not get to meet very many other Nixon campaign workers; he performed most of his work at night.

At times Ragan encountered Nixon during his sweeps of the Nixon, Mudge offices in Manhattan. Early on, during one such occasion, Ragan introduced himself, explaining, " 'Lou Nichols asked me to make checks of the premises, and so forth.' He [Nixon] said, 'Great idea, great idea,' and nothing else, and that was the conversation." But Ragan saw Nixon more frequently as time went on.

When Nixon opened his New York campaign headquarters at 450 Park Avenue, Ragan performed electronic sweeps of these offices as well, and it was there that he first met John J. Caulfield. A former detective in the New York City Police Department, where he had once served as Nixon's bodyguard, Caulfield was security officer in the Nixon campaign by the late spring of 1968.

The Republican National Convention was scheduled to open in Miami Beach on August 5, and Ragan, who must have realized that opportunity was knocking, that there might be more than laundry trucks in his future, volunteered his services for the convention. He took a two-week vacation from E. J. Charters and flew with Caulfield to Miami. Nixon and his staff were at the Hilton Plaza in Miami Beach, and there Ragan and Caulfield had lunch with John D. Ehrlichman. It was Ragan's first meeting with Ehrlichman, who instructed the two men to provide overall security for Nixon and his staff at the convention. Ragan electronically swept the staff's rooms, including those of Ehrlichman and Haldeman, and helped to guard the Nixon communications trailer outside the convention hall.°

After Nixon was nominated and had selected Spiro T. Agnew as his running mate, Ragan and Caulfield were invited along with the

---

° Two of Nixon's rivals for the Republican presidential nomination, Nelson A. Rockefeller and Governor Ronald Reagan of California, also had communications trailers outside the convention hall. Ragan asserted, however, that his duties were entirely defensive: to make certain that no one penetrated the Nixon trailer or the cable leading from the trailer to the convention floor. "Everybody was guarding that particular cable," he said, "to be sure nobody sabotaged it."

rest of the staff to accompany the Nixons, the Agnews, and the press on a jet flight to San Diego. There, at Mission Bay, a seaside resort, the Republican nominee rested and planned his campaign. "Jack [Caulfield] and I would check out the living quarters of the various people, Nixon's and Haldeman's and Ehrlichman's, and also any meeting rooms they had. We might check them several times a day, just to make sure there were no transmitters dropped in there, because these things could be put in in a matter of seconds."

It is fascinating in retrospect to realize that as far back as the 1968 campaign—fully four years before the Watergate burglars broke into the Democratic National Committee's offices and planted transmitters there—Nixon and his staff were taking steps to make sure that no one wiretapped or bugged *them*. It revealed the nature of their thinking, for men who constantly had their own bedrooms and offices swept for transmitters must have acted on the premise that their political opponents would, as a matter of normal practice, attempt to eavesdrop on their conversations. From such a mindset it was only a short step further to wiretap one's opponents. The fact that Nixon, Haldeman, and Ehrlichman had Ragan wielding his electronic broom at Miami Beach, San Diego, and across the country during the 1968 campaign was a symptom, a faint harbinger of the future and of the disasters that lay ahead.

Although the Nixon camp lived in fear of being overheard, at no time did Ragan discover any offensive electronic devices aimed at the candidate, his staff, or his campaign. "But they were very concerned, they wanted to make sure that there wasn't." Most of the time Ragan used what he called "a regenerative feedback receiver" to search for bugs. "If there's a transmitter in the room, it'll create a feedback squeal—a real loud squeal—because it's picking up stuff from the air and sending it back to the transmitter in the room." With this equipment, Ragan explained, it was not necessary to be tuned in on the same frequency as the hidden room transmitter, because the receiver acted like an electronic blanket that "covers everything up to nine hundred megacycles" on the FM band. But Ragan never got any squeals.

It was in San Diego, after the convention, that Ragan formally joined the 1968 Nixon campaign. "We were in Mission Bay and it was interesting and a kind of fascinating thing to be close to such a big operation, presidential campaign, big deal. I went to Ehrlichman and said that I would like to work with the campaign when it started, after Labor Day. But I couldn't do it for free; I said I needed about two hundred dollars a week and we agreed that would be the figure.

"When the campaign started, Ken Cole [later a White House official] would have the itinerary of the campaign party. And from week to week he would tell me where they were going. They gave me an airlines charge card, and I would arrange my own itinerary. Like at the Blackstone Hotel in Chicago or the Muehlebach in Kansas City, and they would crisscross something terrible, back and forth, not in any kind of sequence. My job was to be one day ahead of the campaign party. Ken would tell me who the advance men were, what hotel they were in, and I would go there, and I would check out the rooms."

Ragan's presidential campaign was unlike anyone else's—a wild cross-country jet scramble to stay one jump ahead of the candidate's chartered plane. Often, since Ragan was traveling by commercial airline, he barely got to a city ahead of Nixon. "I remember one time it took me fourteen hours to get from St. Louis down to Houston. But I always made it." Occasionally on two-night stopovers, Ragan would overlap with the candidate and the rest of the campaign staff.

Besides examining Nixon's suite in each city and sweeping the rooms with his feedback receiver, Ragan made general recommendations on electronic security. "I know I used to drive hotel engineers crazy; there wasn't time to fool around. You know: 'Nail that door shut,' which was leading into a telephone room, and 'Nail those windows shut,' which was leading from a parapet."

After Nixon's election Ragan, like other members of the campaign staff, was invited to Washington for the inauguration. He was in the audience at the United States Capitol when the President took the oath of office. "My wife and I went down there; we had tickets for the Inaugural Ball, breakfast at the White House on the morning after, and oh, the whole bit. It was great." Ragan had his invitation to the Inaugural framed and hung it on the wall near the map of the 1968 campaign.

By now Ragan had moved closer into the inner circle of the new Administration and the Republican party. During the campaign he had met Robert J. Hitt, an official of the Republican National Committee, and after the election Hitt paid him $1,000 to sweep the committee's headquarters in Washington at 1625 I Street. From that initial assignment, Hitt hired Ragan on a monthly basis to perform electronic sweeps of the committee offices and serve as security director for the national committee, a part-time post Ragan held from 1969 to 1971. He commuted from New York six days a month in this capacity, at a salary of about $200 a week; in all, the Republican National Committee paid Ragan $34,000 over three years.

The national committee was moving to its new headquarters on Capitol Hill, and much of Ragan's work related to the new building; he recommended a lock system, unbreakable glass for the first two floors, and closed-circuit television. As part of his job, he also did background investigations on a number of persons. Some, although not all of these, were prospective employees of the Republican National Committee. In at least one instance, the Senate Watergate committee was told, Ragan investigated an official of the Democratic National Committee. He also joined the Washington Credit Bureau under his own name, a device that enabled the Republican party, without showing its hand, to have access to credit information about persons in the Washington area.°

It may be that Ragan has described his personal relationship with Richard Nixon too modestly; someone, in any event, must have spread the word about his special talents, because during the 1968 campaign and thereafter, he swept the homes and offices of an astonishing number of high officials and Nixon friends. They included John N. Mitchell, Nixon's campaign manager, whose home in Rye, New York, Ragan swept in 1968; Charles G. (Bebe) Rebozo, whose bank office in Key Biscayne, Florida, he swept the same year; Donald M. Kendall, president of Pepsi-Cola, a Nixon intimate whose company was a major client when Nixon was a lawyer in New York in the mid-sixties; and Robert H. Abplanalp, the inventor of the valve used in aerosol sprays.† Ragan also swept the homes of a number of officials of the International Telephone and Telegraph Corporation, including Dita Beard, whose famous memo became entangled in the folds of Watergate, and William R. Merriam, formerly ITT's Washington lobbyist.

Early in April 1969, after Nixon's election, John Caulfield, Ragan's sponsor, was hired by Ehrlichman, then counsel to the President, to be a member of his staff. Caulfield's overt White House role was to act as liaison with federal law-enforcement agencies, but his covert function was to handle political intelligence investigations for the White House. To carry out this assignment, he proposed to use his friend Anthony T. Ulasewicz, who had served with him in the intelligence bureau of the New York City Police Department, and who was nearing retirement. The following month Ulasewicz was hired, and paid clandestinely not by the White House but by Herbert W. Kalmbach, the President's personal lawyer. Caulfield and Ulasewicz were

° Through Ragan's ties with Caulfield, the Republican National Committee was apparently also able to obtain information from the files of the Washington police department. Over a two-year period Ragan paid Caulfield approximately $800; Ragan said the money was paid to Caulfield to make background checks with the Washington police, at $5 to $8 a head, on new employees of the RNC.

† Ragan said he checked Abplanalp's home in Westchester at the request of a mutual friend; he said the job did not come to him through his work for Nixon. "I found a transmitter in Abplanalp's house," Ragan said, "but the transmitter operated a door on a cabana."

Nixon's first "Plumbers"; the political intelligence-gathering operations that exploded in the Watergate scandal in 1972 and 1973 had begun, much earlier, at the very start of the Nixon Administration, with their employment.

About six weeks after Caulfield joined the White House staff, he was called in by Ehrlichman and asked to place a wiretap on the home of Joseph Kraft. At the time, Richard Nixon had been President of the United States for about four months.

In an interview at his home in the suburbs of northern Virginia, Caulfield said he never learned precisely what triggered the wiretap request; Ehrlichman had not explained the specific reason, although he had made a reference to "Cambodia." "Ehrlichman told me it was a national security undertaking of the highest priority," Caulfield said. Wary of the assignment, Caulfield urged Ehrlichman to have the FBI do it: "I said, 'For Chrissakes, John, that belongs with the Bureau.'" But, as Caulfield later explained it to the Senate Watergate committee, Ehrlichman said the FBI was a "sieve," and could not be trusted to keep the matter secret.

Caulfield contacted Ragan and told him, according to Ragan, that "the top man is concerned about security leaks. Which to me is the President . . . There was one line in Georgetown that they wanted to put surveillance on and could it be done? Not that I was to do it, but could it be done?" Only later, Ragan said, did he learn that the telephone was Joseph Kraft's.

But the name of the citizen to be tapped was of little importance; Ragan was accustomed to carrying out his instructions. "At that point," Ragan said, "I didn't know who it was, I didn't care who it was. In the Bureau, you get used to working on a need-to-know basis; if they want a line on somebody at 23 Smith Street, you do it, you know, it doesn't really matter who it is, you are relying on top authority to have made the determinations that are necessary."

Together, Caulfield and Ragan drove to Georgetown and parked near Kraft's home, and Ragan got out. Along the west side of the house, a wooden gate and a brick archway led into a garden area in the rear, but an eight-foot wall that ran completely around the property inhibited easy access to the back of Kraft's house. As it happened, however, there was no telephone pole in the enclosed area; the wires from Kraft's house led to a pole about fifty feet to the east, at the rear of Michael Straight's house. Ragan's trained eye must immediately have seen that this was the vulnerable point where a transmitter might be placed. Ragan returned to the car and reported to Caulfield. As Ragan remembered it, "I said it could be done."

Caulfield, however, reported back to Ehrlichman that the tap would be difficult to install "because Mr. Kraft lived in a very prestigious area of Georgetown." Ehrlichman, Caulfield later testified, told him "it would have to be done." And Ehrlichman was in a hurry; he wanted it done, Caulfield said, "like yesterday."

Caulfield also testified that Ragan wanted some sort of credentials to carry if he were to do the tap, and "I arranged to have Mr. Ragan supplied with a telephone company card, installer credentials, as I recall." Caulfield said he was able to obtain the card through John Davies, a White House official. Davies' job was to handle the tourists and other visitors who flock through the White House—he had nothing whatever to do with telephones—but Caulfield knew that Davies had formerly been an official of AT&T, so Ehrlichman arranged for him to see Davies about getting the card. According to Caulfield, Davies obtained the card on the understanding that it was needed in a "national security matter." Caulfield said he gave it to Ragan.

Caulfield testified that Ragan indicated he would need the pair and cable numbers of Kraft's telephone.° These identifying numbers are confidential. But Caulfield testified he was able to obtain them through a friend in the Secret Service, whom he declined to name.

Whether Caulfield gave the pair and cable numbers to Ragan is not clear; in an interview Ragan insisted he would not have needed them, in any event. Because, as he had explained, the target number can be located by "raking the board," using a screwdriver to find the telltale click.†

But an awkward problem soon developed for Caulfield. In the midst of all these arrangements John Ehrlichman called him in and tried to stop the Kraft wiretap. "I indicated to Mr. Ehrlichman that I hoped it hadn't gone too far," Caulfield later told the Watergate committee.

He elaborated in an interview: "I had impressed on Ragan it was

° These are the markings that enable a telephone-company employee to identify and work on a customer's line that legitimately needs repair.
† When Ragan explained how he could locate a given telephone by this method, I asked him what would happen if he encountered the unexpected—if the person he was tapping picked up the phone.

Q. When you first take a pair at random and clip on, when you dial the number you are interested in, what happens if someone answers? Do you have to move [off the line] before there's an answer?
A. No, you make a pretext call, and ask for Joe.
Q. And while you are doing that you can still be testing.
A. That's right.
Q. With the screwdriver.
A. And even after they hang up for about a minute, that line is still connected as long as you keep your instrument open. And you can still rake. And you do it almost every time within that period. That's why the business of needing pair numbers . . . you don't need 'em.

a high national security purpose. He went out with someone from the Bell System and put on a transmitter on the damn pole. Ehrlichman called me and said, 'We're going to have the FBI do it.' I attempted to contact Ragan. I met him at the Congressional Hotel. He handed me a tape and said, 'It's done.' I blew my cork."

Caulfield tried to persuade the Watergate committee that he had never specifically ordered Ragan to go ahead with the wiretap. His surprise at its accomplishment could not have been overwhelming, however, since he had personally escorted Ragan to Kraft's house and had provided Ragan with telephone-company credentials to do the job.

Ragan never testified before the Watergate committee, but Michael J. Hershman, a committee investigator, questioned Ragan during the summer of 1973. In an interview Hershman said that Ragan had attached a battery-powered transmitter to Kraft's phone line.* "It transmitted to a receiver in the trunk of an automobile parked a block from the house. A voice-activated tape recorder was located in the trunk. The car was left parked on the street and did not need to be monitored. This was standard operating procedure."

The reel of tape Ragan handed to Caulfield at the Congressional Hotel, Caulfield testified, "allegedly contained some conversations. He [Ragan], as I recall, indicated that Mr. Kraft was not on the wiretap, his voice was not on the wiretap, there was some conversation. As I recall it, it might have been a maid."

As it turned out, the bug that the counsel to the President had ordered placed on Kraft's telephone had been installed while Kraft was in Paris with his family, en route to a vacation in Italy.†

Caulfield took the tape back to his office in the Executive Office Building and unwound about thirty to fifty feet, which he then put

* Michael Hershman said Ragan had initially denied performing the wiretap to the Watergate committee investigators, then admitted it under dramatic circumstances. On the morning of June 25, 1973, Hershman was watching John Dean testify before the Senate committee, headed by Senator Sam J. Ervin, Jr. Dean told of the Kraft wiretap; his testimony was the first public mention of it. "Dean testified that Ragan had tapped the Georgetown number," Hershman said, "and I called him [Ragan] on the phone and said, 'Don't you think it's time we had a little talk, because it's just been testified to.' And he said, 'Well, let me call you back.' And he called back and admitted it."

Ragan himself declined to go into details, but conceded in an interview that a transmitter placed on Kraft's line "probably would have been" battery-operated and would "only last twenty-four, forty-eight hours at the most. . . . If somebody was going to do that, it would just be a test, and that's what it was—a test."

† Kraft later concluded, "I assume that the reason that they took out the bug was that they were getting nothing on it. They were just getting our Spanish maid, Argentine maid, who talked a kind of broken English."

in his burn bag to be destroyed. He insisted he never listened to the tape; he testified that Ragan told him the recorded conversation was short, so he assumed he had unwound enough to destroy that portion of the tape. He said he kept the rest of the tape and the reel for several weeks, then put those into his office burn bag as well. "I never mentioned to Mr. Ehrlichman that the tap had been implemented," he added.

When Ehrlichman eventually appeared before the Watergate committee he was asked whether he had approved any wiretaps. In 1969, he said, "I authorized an attempt which never came to anything." Did he know about a wiretap on Joseph Kraft? "That was the one that I was talking about in 1969, that, so far as I know, never happened." He had authorized the tap, Ehrlichman said, for "a national security purpose."

Even while bobbing and weaving about his own responsibility, Ehrlichman provided the first evidence that John Ragan had not misunderstood the phrase "top man," and that Nixon himself had ordered or approved the wiretap on Joseph Kraft.

"Did you ever discuss that tap with the President?" Samuel Dash, chief counsel to the Watergate committee, asked Ehrlichman.

"I am sure I did," Ehrlichman replied.

In an interview with the author, Ehrlichman went further than in his Senate testimony. "The President ordered the Kraft tap," he said.

The interview took place in the summer of 1975 at a time when Ehrlichman—who did not have the benefit of a presidential pardon—faced prison. He had been convicted on charges resulting from the burglary of Daniel Ellsberg's psychiatrist, and in a separate case, for his role in covering up the Watergate break-in. A federal court had turned down his plea that he be given a lighter sentence so he could work with Indians in New Mexico, but he had gone to live in Santa Fe anyway.

He had, after many months, agreed to an interview, and it was held in the conference room of his lawyer's office in Washington. Physically, at least, Ehrlichman had changed. He had grown a beard and he had a deep tan. His right eyebrow arched up characteristically when he answered difficult questions, as it had on television during the Ervin hearings, but the arrogance, the intensely combative style he had displayed on television, had given way to a mellower and more subdued manner.

"I don't know the President's motive" in ordering the Kraft tap, Ehrlichman said. But, he added, the President told him in a general way that it was to be done for reasons of "national security." And, Ehrlichman said, "the President didn't want the FBI used." Ehrlichman then added that while he could not be sure of the specific purpose of the Kraft tap, he could recall one possibility. "Either the President, or Haldeman in his presence, explained it was because of Kraft's relationship with the North Vietnamese."

Other journalists were in touch with North Vietnamese officials during this period, so it was not at all clear from Ehrlichman's account why Kraft should have been singled out for such extraordinary attention. But it might explain why the effort to eavesdrop on Joseph Kraft now moved into a new, international phase; astonishingly, the White House reached across the Atlantic to eavesdrop on an American citizen.

A request by the President's counsel to wiretap a prominent American newsman in another country was not an everyday occurrence; it is highly unlikely that J. Edgar Hoover would have acted without first satisfying himself that the President wanted it done. Hoover must have concluded this was indeed the case, for he sent no ordinary FBI agent to follow Kraft to Paris. He called in William C. Sullivan, assistant director of the FBI in charge of the Domestic Intelligence Division, whose job it was to watch groups that were considered a threat to the Republic, and to catch spies. A thin, wiry New Englander, Sullivan did not dress in the neat-as-a-pin, Efrem Zimbalist, Jr., FBI style that was all but obligatory under Hoover. Sullivan was a rather incongruous figure for the nation's counter-espionage chief; he looked more like a farmer come to town for the day, uncomfortable in his city clothes and anxious to get back home. In fact, Sullivan grew up on the farm his parents had run for fifty years in Bolton, Massachusetts, near the New Hampshire border. But he was a former schoolteacher with a master's degree in education and a reputation as something of a house intellectual within the FBI.

In 1975 Sullivan was retired and living in the White Mountains in the little town of Sugar Hill, New Hampshire. He recalled very well what had happened in 1969. "One day the Director called me in. And he said, 'You have good contacts among the French, particularly with a couple of French generals.' And I said, 'Yes, reasonably good contact.' He said, 'I want you to go to Paris immediately and arrange through your contacts to have electronic coverage made of Joseph Kraft, who is in Paris.' I was astonished and I said, 'Mr. Hoover, why?' I said, 'I know of nothing that would warrant a coverage of Joseph Kraft. But of course I'll review the files. But,' I said, 'offhand I don't remember anything about Kraft. He's a reputable journalist.' He said, 'That may be, but he's talking to the Viet Cong, and from Paris he's going into Russia.'"

Sullivan said he told Hoover that Kraft had a right to go to

Russia; lots of journalists did. "Hoover said, 'Kraft may be the source of a leak. I want you to go to Paris and arrange a coverage and stay there and bring back the results.'"

J. Edgar Hoover, although it was not generally known, had never been outside the United States. He expected Sullivan to leave within the hour for Paris; he seemed only vaguely aware that the assistant director would have to find his passport and make plane reservations. Sullivan arranged to leave the next day, and in his broad New England accent, he described how the trip got off to a bad start: "I went to Paris. And I daahn near got killed. We flew from Dulles to Logan Airport and it was a terrible night when I left, foggy. We overshot the airport three times because of the daahn clouds and fog, and the fourth time the pilot came on and said, 'Landing conditions are extremely wet, and we've missed the field three times, but there's nothing to worry about, we have gas for one more try.' Can you imagine the pilot saying that? Everyone was petrified, including myself."

In Paris, Sullivan made arrangements for the Direction de la Surveillance du Territoire, the French equivalent of the FBI, to bug Kraft's hotel room. Kraft, who was accompanied by Polly and their sons, Mark, then eighteen, and David, fifteen, was staying at the George V, probably the most elegant hotel in the French capital, and certainly one of the more expensive. The family occupied two rooms.

Apparently the DST planted a hidden microphone in Kraft's bedroom at the George V; there is some indication that the French security service considered it too difficult to tap his telephone. The hotel has 312 rooms, which meant that there were as many extensions running off the main switchboard, and it may have been too complicated to install a tap. In any event, the House Committee on the Judiciary, which compiled the impeachment evidence against President Nixon, referred explicitly to "microphone coverage" of Kraft's hotel room in Paris, rather than to a wiretap.°

Sullivan said he did not know the precise form of electronic surveillance directed at Kraft, and did not wait around Paris for the results. Instead he arranged with Norman W. Philcox, the FBI legal attaché in the American embassy, to forward the reports to him when they were received from the DST. Philcox had been stationed in Paris

---

° In one of the thirty-nine volumes of evidence and testimony compiled by the Judiciary Committee there is a summary of sensitive FBI documents dealing with "microphone coverage of Kraft in a foreign country." The guarded reference to a "foreign country" was phraseology adopted by the committee in deference to the French, who were extremely annoyed when reports of their role surfaced during the Watergate scandal. For the same reason, the committee summary refers to unnamed "local authorities" rather than the DST.

for fifteen years because Hoover liked him and let him stay in that choice, and coveted, foreign post.

Sullivan, after spending two days in Paris, flew back to Washington. "Hoover was very disgruntled. 'I told you to stay there and bring the reports back,' he said. I said I saw no need to do that. And so he was unhappy over that, but the results came in and they didn't prove a daahn thing. They proved nothing wrong about Kraft."

In the files of the FBI are nineteen pages of material produced by the DST microphone in Kraft's Paris hotel. Microphones cannot discriminate, however; as Kraft and his wife later realized, the DST presumably picked up pillow talk as well as conversations of any political content, remarks by visitors, or meetings Kraft may have had with news sources.

Later, when the Justice Department turned over the FBI wiretap reports from Paris to Kraft and his attorneys, the columnist, after reading them, said he did not know "whether to laugh or cry." The contents were all useless political gossip. Sullivan, working from tapes and transcripts provided by the DST, prepared the report. One entry read: "The subject then dialed another number, 5236, and asked for John Monay"—undoubtedly the FBI's phonetic version of Jean Monnet, the distinguished father of European economic unity and the Common Market.° Another entry read: "The subject and his wife have been in contact with Mrs. Kay Graham (phonetic) and [names deleted] whose identities at this time are not known." If the FBI did not know that Mrs. Graham was the publisher of the Washington *Post*, it was probably the only agency in town that lacked this knowledge.

Another FBI report from Sullivan to Hoover included this bugged quote from one of Kraft's telephone conversations: "I think he [Nixon] sent Rockefeller to South America because you know he had nothing else to do ... Rumania is a little complicated. I think partially he wanted to be nice to them because they had been nice to him in the wilderness." That month, Nixon was preparing to visit Rumania, whose President, Nicolae Ceausescu, had given him a red-carpet welcome in 1967—in contrast to other Communist countries—at a time when Nixon was a private citizen.

Rose Kennedy's name came up in the FBI wiretap reports because while in Paris, Kraft called on Sargent Shriver, Jr., the American ambassador, and his wife, Eunice Kennedy Shriver. The name of Presi-

---

° In March of 1970 the Justice Department finally agreed to destroy these summaries and transcripts and other results of the FBI's surveillance of Kraft. Attorney General Levi apologized to Kraft for the bugging and added that "the surveillance did not indicate that Mr. Kraft's activities posed any risk to the national security."

dent Kennedy's press secretary, Pierre Salinger, also appears frequently in the FBI file.

But most curious of all in the Kraft file were FBI documents about Mehdi Ben Barka, the leftist Moroccan political figure who was kidnapped in Paris in 1965 and presumably murdered, apparently with the complicity of French intelligence. After examining his file, Kraft concluded that the FBI "made up a story out of whole cloth that I was connected with Ben Barka to get the French secret service interested in me." Kraft based his conclusion in part on one document suggesting that the FBI told the French that Kraft might be in touch with someone whose name was blanked out; the next two documents in the file, both dated March 1969, related to Ben Barka and his brother, then living in Paris. On the top of each of the Ben Barka documents appeared the handwritten notation "Joseph Kraft."°

Hoover, the bureaucratic fox, always built a shield of paper to protect himself. In the files of the FBI is a copy of a letter Hoover wrote to Jean Rochet, then head of the DST, thanking him for his cooperation. Ostensibly a courteous international thank-you note, it also created a record on paper; it was the French, not the FBI or Hoover, who had installed the microphone in Paris.†

Two letters were sent by the FBI to Ehrlichman reporting on the Paris bug. One, dated July 15, enclosed the nineteen pages of transcript. In the files of the FBI this letter and transcript were in a folder bearing the code name Cato.†

Sullivan said he could shed no light on the significance of the code name. "I didn't coin it and I don't know why they selected that rather than Plato or Aristotle or somebody else."‡

The FBI sent another report on Kraft to Ehrlichman on November 7, 1969. By this time Kraft was back in Washington. Much later, during Watergate, after Kraft learned of the various surveillance

° Sullivan, who presented the request for electronic eavesdropping to the French authorities, told the author that he did not "recall mentioning the Ben Barka case or his brother to the French or to anybody else in connection with Joseph Kraft."

† In the manner of two diners fighting over a restaurant check, Hoover and the French battled over who should pay for the bugging of Kraft at the George V. The French insisted. After much back-and-forth, Hoover lost and sent the DST an autographed picture.

† Kraft was not certain whether he was supposed to be Cato the Elder (Marcus Porcius Cato, 234–149 B.C.), or Cato the Younger (95–46 B.C.). Cato the Elder, the Roman statesman, detested luxury. The first Latin writer of importance, he was, incongruously, a censor and sort of bluenose opposed to new ideas. His great-grandson, Cato the Younger, was a Roman philosopher and opponent of Caesar; he was known as an outspoken enemy of graft and government corruption.

‡ Did the FBI often use Roman or Greek philosophers for code names? I asked Sullivan. "No," he replied, "they weren't that familiar with them."

operations directed against him, he talked to friends in the FBI and learned that "what apparently triggered that [November 7] report was that through coverage of the Polish embassy [in Washington], they picked up a call to me from Ambassador [Jerzy] Michalowski in which I was invited to come by the embassy for a drink." In other words, the renewed interest in Kraft resulted this time from an FBI tap not of Kraft, but of the Polish embassy.[*] Given the "top man's" presumed interest in Kraft, the FBI apparently considered it important to alert the White House to the otherwise unelectrifying news that Kraft was having a drink with the Polish ambassador.

This must have been considered suspicious behavior, because Attorney General Mitchell asked the FBI to recommend what form of surveillance on Kraft would be most effective. Sullivan sent a memo to Cartha D. (Deke) DeLoach, Hoover's top assistant, discussing Mitchell's request. In answer to Mitchell, the FBI replied that close physical surveillance of Kraft was too dangerous, "but that a selective spot surveillance in the evenings to check on his social contacts would be safe and productive."

The Bureau's Washington field office was asked to determine the feasibility of a wiretap on Kraft's home and office, and reported back on November 5 that it was technically feasible. Mitchell never signed the authorization for a tap, however, and there is no evidence that the FBI installed one.

But for a period of about six weeks, from early November to December 12, Kraft was under spot physical surveillance in Washington. He was tailed by FBI agents in the evenings to dinner parties, to the homes of friends and associates.

Sullivan, according to the impeachment evidence, reported that "the spot physical surveillance of Kraft had been unproductive from an intelligence standpoint" and recommended that it be terminated, which it was, on December 12, 1969.

John Ragan continued to serve as security director for the Republican National Committee on a part-time basis, and he remained in fairly close contact with Caulfield and Ulasewicz. The three men met at the Roger Smith Hotel in Washington late in July 1969, and at times, when Ragan came down from New York, they would get together for lunch at the Black Steer restaurant, a block from the White House. Ragan characterized these as "social luncheons." Most of the time, he said, they discussed Caulfield's plan to set up a private

---

[*] Sullivan reported to Ehrlichman on November 7: "Washington Field Office reports Michalowski has indicated friendship with other Washington newspapermen in addition to Kraft. These include Charles Bartlett, Chalmers Roberts, Murrey Marder, and Max Frankel."

investigative agency to work for political campaigns and private industry. "I would have the electronic part of it, and Tony and Jack, probably, the investigative part of it."°

The plan did not come to fruition, but Ragan—who had met Ulasewicz through Caulfield—said he used Ulasewicz for one investigation in New York unrelated to White House political intelligence-gathering. And Ragan got other interesting assignments. In May 1971 he was contacted by Russ Tagliareni, deputy director of security for ITT, and like Ragan, a former FBI man. At a fee of $200 a day, Ragan went to Chile with Tagliareni for eleven days, ostensibly to teach anti-bugging, defensive electronic procedures to officials of the Chilean government. In Chile, Ragan met Marxist President Salvador Allende and conducted an electronic sweep of his summer residence; by one account, he also swept the presidential palace. Since ITT had collaborated with the CIA in 1970 in a variety of schemes to prevent Allende's election—at one point ITT board chairman Harold S. Geneen offered the CIA $1 million for this purpose—some federal investigators in Washington were, to say the very least, skeptical of the explanation that ITT had sent Ragan to Chile to help Allende and his government discover electronic bugs; they thought it more logical that Ragan might have gone through Allende's homes for an opposite purpose, to plant transmitters, but Ragan has denied this.†

By the fall of 1971 Ragan, still at the Republican National Committee, found himself dealing with a new boss, Barry Mountain. In September, Mountain called Ragan in; he told him the committee was gearing up for the 1972 campaign, and had to consider its financial resources. Ragan said Mountain told him "not to come down every week as I had been doing, but they would call me when they needed me. And they never called me. I think I still have the master key to their building."

Ragan also kept his building pass, a laminated plastic identification card with his photograph in color alongside a red, white, and blue Republican elephant. What he did not learn was that John Caul-

---

° In 1971 Caulfield put his proposal in written form in a memorandum outlining Project Sandwedge, a plan to create a private security company—with a budget of $511,000 and the capacity to conduct covert operations—to serve Nixon in the 1972 presidential campaign. The White House turned down Caulfield's plan; instead the President's Plumbers were sent into the Watergate.

† Senate Watergate committee investigators learned that in April 1973 Ragan was paid $150 a day to sweep the Washington hotel room occupied by ITT chairman Geneen. At the time, Geneen was testifying before a Senate subcommittee on multinational corporations, headed by Senator Frank Church, the Idaho Democrat, which was investigating ITT's involvement with the CIA in efforts to stop Allende's election. The CIA was authorized to spend $8 million in Chile between 1970 and 1973 to work against Allende, who died in a military coup on September 11, 1973.

field had recruited a former CIA agent for his job. As far as Ragan knew, he was still in charge of security for the Republican National Committee.

"I didn't know anything different until the spring of 1972," Ragan said, "when I picked up a paper and read about James McCord being arrested in the Watergate. It said he was security director for the Republican National Committee. I thought I was."

In the spring of 1973 Richard Nixon's attempt to cover up the Watergate burglary was coming unstuck. His counsel, John Dean, had begun talking to the federal prosecutors. Each day brought new disclosures that burst like star shells over the land. In Los Angeles the case against Daniel Ellsberg, who was on trial for leaking the Pentagon Papers to the press, collapsed; it was thrown out of court when the government was forced to admit that the White House had burgled the office of Ellsberg's psychiatrist and that Ellsberg had been overheard on an FBI wiretap. The wiretap had been put on the home telephone of Dr. Morton H. Halperin, a former assistant to Henry Kissinger. By May 15 the press was able to report that the Halperin tap was one of seventeen wiretaps secretly authorized by the White House on four journalists and thirteen officials, most of them members of Kissinger's National Security Council staff. These were to become known as "the Kissinger taps." The President claimed he had authorized the taps for "national security" reasons, to plug news leaks.

Time magazine, late in February, had printed the fact that news reporters had been wiretapped by the White House. "I began to hear rumors," Joseph Kraft said, "that I was one of them. I checked with my own sources in the FBI and was told that I was not one." Kraft could not imagine that the Administration would do such a thing to him, and he was pleased to learn that the reports were untrue. But on May 17, after the White House admitted the seventeen wiretaps, the Associated Press moved a story on its wires naming five newsmen whose telephones had been tapped by the White House, and identifying one of these as "syndicated columnist Joseph Kraft."

Kraft was sure it was wrong, and he did not wish to get publicity as a wiretap victim if he had not been one. He called an editor at the Washington *Post*. "I was convinced that this was not true because of my own Bureau connections and I was able to have it taken out of at least the Washington *Post* version of the AP story. I told the people at the *Post* that I had checked that thoroughly and was sure that it was wrong."

But reports persisted that Kraft was one of the newsmen tapped, and early in June, Kraft called another source in the FBI. This time he found out that the rumors were true, after all. Kraft was told that

his folder had turned up among FBI wiretap files that had been retrieved from the White House.

By now the Senate Select Committee on Presidential Campaign
Activities, better known as the Watergate committee, had begun its
televised hearings. The star witness, John Dean, appeared before the
TV cameras on June 25. The scene was sharply etched in the memory
of the millions who watched him that day: Dean, in a crisp summer
suit and round horn-rimmed glasses, sipping ice water, which apparently also flowed in his veins, and indicting Richard Nixon beyond
redemption in a flat monotone. It is difficult to say with precision
when Richard Nixon began the long slide to the weed-covered purga-
tory of San Clemente and his shattering disgrace, but the descent was
inevitable after June 25, 1973.

Early in his long opening statement to the committee, Dean testified that Joseph Kraft's telephone had been tapped. "Caulfield told
me that it was performed by Mr. Ulasewicz, Mr. John Ragan, and
himself.° He later repeated the story to me telling me that it had been
a rather harrowing experience when he was holding the ladder in a
back alley of Georgetown while also trying to keep a lookout as another member of the group was working at the top of the ladder."

It was the first official confirmation that Kraft had been tapped.
"Polly's first reaction on hearing the Dean testimony," Kraft said, "was
'Oh, so that's what happened to the ladder.' Because we had a ladder
that was missing. And we then assumed that they used our ladder
and walked out with it to gain cover as workmen. Our ladder is still
missing."†

Ragan was indignant over any suggestion that he stole Joseph
Kraft's ladder. "There was no ladder, no entry" into the house, he insisted. He was "never in the house." Ragan added, "I will say this,
too. If those nuts who went into Watergate had used their heads,
there's no need to go into that place, into the premises. Those lines
are in the basement. You can pick them up there. Why go into the
place, expose yourself? It was dumb in conception and dumb in execution. It was a dumb operation. I wouldn't get caught that way."

Even before Dean testified, Kraft had written a column about
the bugging of his telephone. "At first I didn't believe the reports,"
he wrote, but now he did. The column, Kraft later concluded, contained inaccurate information, including the statement that "the bug
was removed by men who entered my home through a second-story
window." But, understandably, Kraft became determined to find out

---

° There is no evidence that Ulasewicz participated in the Kraft wiretap, however.
† Polly Kraft said the ladder was aluminum, about fifteen feet in height, and could
be folded up. "I used it to prune the ivy," she said. "I kept it inside the garden
wall. One day I noticed it wasn't there any more."

more about how he had been wiretapped and why. It was the why that was particularly nagging. What could he have done to merit this?

Kraft searched his memory and recalled an incident early in the Nixon years. It had happened after the wiretap, but perhaps it shed light on the situation. He had been having lunch one day with Charles W. Colson, whose title was special counsel to the President, but whose role was that of hatchet man and dirty trickster; he later became celebrated for proclaiming that "I would walk over my grandmother if necessary" in the interests of Richard Nixon.* They had been spotted by another Nixon aide, Lyn Nofziger. "He'll probably report this lunch to Haldeman," Colson remarked.

Kraft had not seen Colson again since that day. But in June 1973, in his search for the reasons why, Kraft sought him out and arranged another lunch with him. Colson confirmed that after their earlier luncheon, Haldeman had ordered him to stay away from Kraft. Colson said, "He called me in and said, 'You'd better stop seeing Kraft. I've got stuff on him that would curl your hair.'"

Kraft continued his inquiries; he talked next to the Senate Watergate committee, which eventually questioned John Caulfield and developed more information about the Georgetown wiretap. And he went to the Watergate Special Prosecutor, Archibald Cox. "I did take it up with Archie," Kraft said.† Cox indicated it would be all right if Kraft conferred with members of his staff, and Kraft did. The Special Prosecutor's office investigated and developed considerable information about the case, although it did not bring any indictments.

Kraft was no closer to knowing why he had been tapped. Actually, he recalled, Nixon had reason to be friendly toward him. "In 1968," he said, "I broke the story that Johnson canceled his summit meeting with the Soviets because of the Czech invasion. Nixon himself called me to congratulate me on the story." The story, in fact, had come from a source in the Nixon organization.

Indeed, Kraft was in very close to Nixon then. The telephone call had come while Kraft was in Chicago covering the Democratic National Convention. When Nixon called he had even offered Kraft a job working in his campaign. Nixon had another reason to be grateful to Kraft in 1968. President Johnson and Soviet Premier Alexei Kosygin had agreed that summer to begin strategic arms limitation talks, and, Kraft said, "someone in the Soviet embassy asked me about

* One of Colson's grandmothers traced her ancestry back to George Washington's mother.

† The familiarity was based on long acquaintance. "I had worked for Cox as a speechwriter in the Kennedy campaign of 1960," Kraft later wrote in the *New York Review of Books*, "and so I had no difficulty arranging dinner at a Georgetown restaurant."

Nixon's attitude toward SALT. I said I didn't know. But I said they ought to arrange for a Nixon visit to Moscow." Kraft did more than that; he put Robert Ellsworth, a senior Nixon campaign adviser, in touch with Anatoly F. Dobrynin, the Soviet ambassador in Washington. In due course an understanding was reached that Nixon would visit the Soviet Union during 1968. Kraft was well aware that when Nixon went to Moscow in 1967 as a private citizen, he had been snubbed by the Soviet leaders, who refused to meet with him. If anything, that rebuff made Kraft's services as a behind-the-scenes intermediary even more valuable to Nixon.°

So, in 1973, Kraft racked his brains, trying to find the key to what transgression had led to his fall from grace. He wondered whether the trouble might have stemmed from his friendship with Ellsworth, or with John P. Sears, who had played a key role in managing Nixon's campaign for the Republican nomination in 1968, but who had incurred John Mitchell's displeasure. Sears left the Nixon White House after only eight months, but not before he, too, was tapped. Sears may have fallen under suspicion because he was known to have many friends in the Washington press corps—including Joseph Kraft.

But there was no way to prove that these associations and friendships were responsible. Since he had allegedly been tapped for vague reasons of "national security," Kraft reread his columns from the spring of 1969. He could find none containing information that had come from the NSC or that could be considered a national security leak. Several of the columns did deal with the war in Vietnam, however, and with the peace negotiations then dragging on unproductively in Paris. Perhaps, Kraft thought, the key was Jean Sainteny, a French banker and former government official in Indochina who had been close to Ho Chi Minh for more than two decades. Kissinger had brought Sainteny to the White House to see Nixon; Sainteny had agreed to deliver a letter from the President to Ho, dated July 15, proposing new contacts. Three weeks later Kissinger slipped away to his first secret peace talk with Xuan Thuy, the North Vietnamese

° As it turned out, Nixon did not go to the Soviet Union in 1968, but the Russians were annoyed at news reports saying Nixon was considering the trip. "I had all kinds of trouble getting into the Soviet Union," Kraft said, "because they [the Russians] thought I had leaked the story. I didn't. Nixon leaked it from Montauk, where he was just before the Republican convention." The *New York Times* of August 5, 1968, reported in a dispatch from Montauk, Long Island, that if Nixon won the Republican nomination later that week, he might go to Moscow. The story carried a terse "No comment" from the Soviet embassy. It quoted Nixon as saying he had received suggestions of a Moscow trip from his staff but did not want to discuss it until after his nomination. "Ask me about it on Thursday morning," he added.

negotiator, in Sainteny's Paris apartment. "I used to see Sainteny," Kraft said, "and that may have scared the Administration." Perhaps, Kraft reasoned, the President thought he was too close to finding out about Kissinger's secret peace talks.

Indeed, this possibility tied in with what ultimately emerged as Kraft's favorite theory about the motives behind the wiretapping. "My guess is that this was part of an inside operation against Kissinger. The things that are special about this is, first, they didn't go through Kissinger the way they have for all the other journalists, they went through Ehrlichman instead, and second, Nixon knew that I was a friend of Henry's. In fact, he once spoke to me here when he was calling Henry [who was at a dinner party at Kraft's home]. And third, my lawyer, Lloyd Cutler, at one point went and talked to John Ehrlichman's attorney and got the impression from them that Nixon wanted to know who Henry was talking to."[*]

Kraft also advanced this theory in 1974 when he testified at a Senate hearing on wiretapping. It was "only a hypothesis," Kraft told the senators, but "the one theory that keeps coming back is that perhaps there was internal concern about Dr. Kissinger. He was a friend of mine . . . Maybe they thought that Dr. Kissinger was leaking."

Kissinger as wiretap victim! Kissinger, who played a central and crucial role in the most widespread program of secret government wiretapping ever to be uncovered, might he also have been a target? If it had happened, it would of course have been the supreme irony: the eavesdropper eavesdropped upon.

Kraft was quick to say that "there is no shred of real evidence" that Kissinger was the actual target of the operation directed at Kraft. But Kraft added that "he [Kissinger] likes to encourage me in that belief."

In their book, *Kissinger*, Marvin Kalb and Bernard Kalb report that after the controversial "Christmas bombing" of Hanoi in 1972—which took place after Kissinger had announced in October that "peace is at hand"—his enemies in the White House tried to force him out. "In the book," Kraft said, "they have Henry telling a columnist: 'Haldeman nearly got me.' That columnist was me, but I never took it very seriously."

At one point the whole matter of wiretapping even strained diplomatic relations between Kraft and Kissinger; but the falling-out was brief. The problem arose over a column in which Kraft had suggested that Kissinger "helped arrange for" the wiretapping of some of his National Security Council staff. "The column enraged him,"

---

[*] Ehrlichman said in his interview in 1975 that he did not know whether Kissinger was a target of the Kraft bugging, but he could make the general observation that "there was such a concern" by Nixon about Kissinger.

Kraft later wrote, "and in a phone conversation he said some things which, I felt, obliged me not to attend a fiftieth-birthday party given for him by old friends at the Colony Club in New York. But subsequently we did get together."

The truth is often elusive, and neither Kraft nor any of the official inquiries discovered a wholly satisfying answer to the mystery, but for what it may be worth, Nixon's own explanation finally surfaced, on tape. When the President released the edited transcripts of forty-six of his conversations, they showed that even as the Watergate dam was bursting, the President was desperately trying to cover up the Kraft wiretap. When Nixon met with John Dean on the morning of April 16, 1973, he knew that Dean was talking to the prosecutors, but he got Dean to agree that the Kraft and other wiretaps were not to be mentioned because they were done for reasons of "national security."

The President told Dean that "what we call the electronic, uh, stuff ... is in the leak area, national security area, uh, that I consider privileged." As to "the Kraft stuff," the President told Dean, "there were some done, some done through, uh, private sources. Most of it was done by the Bureau after we got going." Nixon added, "Hoover didn't want to do, uh, to do Kraft. But what it involved, John, apparently was this: there were leaks in the NSC. They were in Kraft and other columns. We were trying to plug the leaks."

It was clear that the President was coaching Dean; he hoped his counsel would not mention the Kraft wiretap to the federal prosecutors. "I consider that privileged," Nixon repeated.

"I have no intention of raising that ..." Dean replied.

"Have you informed your lawyers about that?" Nixon asked.

"No."

"I think you should not. ... I do think it's privileged. But it's up to, up to you, I mean, I—"

"No, I think its privileged, also."

The President's sense of relief was only temporary. On July 30, 1974, the House Committee on the Judiciary completed action on a resolution to impeach President Richard M. Nixon for high crimes and misdemeanors. Article II of the three articles approved by the committee accused Nixon of abuse of power, of misusing federal agencies and personnel "in violation or disregard of the constitutional rights of citizens, by directing or authorizing such agencies or personnel to conduct or continue electronic surveillance or other investigations for purposes unrelated to national security ..."

In its report to the House of Representatives, the committee listed as paragraph two of the evidence to support this article the "Joseph Kraft wiretap and surveillance." Summarizing the case, the committee concluded: "The President discussed the Kraft tap with Ehrlichman. Although Ehrlichman has testified that the wiretap was authorized for a national security purpose, there is no evidence of this in FBI records or in any other evidence before the Committee. The Attorney General did not sign an FBI authorization for the Kraft wiretap. It was not authorized by court order."

In his testimony to the United States Senate in 1974, Kraft said, "To this day I do not understand why I was made the subject of the wiretapping, the bugging, or the surveillance, or whether the purpose was really to entrap me or perhaps someone inside the government who might be speaking to me.

"I am only sure that a monster has been allowed to grow up, and unless it is subject to regular control by impartial persons I think all of us will be the victims."

Kraft also reflected on the meaning of his experience in an interview. "We came a hell of a lot closer to a police state," he said, "than I thought possible."

"You talk about police state. Let me tell you what happens when you go to what is really a police state. You can't talk in your bedroom. You can't talk in your sitting room. You don't talk on the telephone. You don't talk in the bathroom. As a matter of fact . . . you can't even talk in front of a shrub."

—President Richard M. Nixon,
April 16, 1971

2
JUNE:
"Destroy Whoever Did This"

The sand was soft underfoot, and palm trees fringed the beach. But as the two men in bathing suits walked along, following the curve of the ocean, the beauty of the tropical surroundings mocked the unpleasant subject of their conversation.

The older man, Dr. Henry A. Kissinger, had not yet become, on this Friday afternoon of May 9, 1969, a global celebrity, within the government second in power only to Richard Nixon. But at forty-five, he was assistant to the President for national security affairs, and as such, the central figure in the new Administration's efforts to negotiate an end to the war in Vietnam. He had accompanied Nixon to Key Biscayne this weekend to work on the major speech on Vietnam policy that the President would deliver a few days hence.

As he walked along the beach, however, Kissinger had only bad news for his thirty-year-old deputy, Morton H. Halperin, one of the several bright young men whom Kissinger had hired for the staff of the National Security Council. Halperin, too, had come to Florida to work on the draft of the Vietnam speech.

"We were in the swimming pool together," Halperin recounted, "and suddenly he said, 'Let's take a walk.'" The two men had left the hotel, the cabanas, and the other staff members and walked down the beach. They knew each other well, for they had been colleagues on the faculty at Harvard, where they had even taught a government course together.

That morning, as both men knew, the *New York Times* had published a page-one story by William Beecher, the newspaper's Pentagon correspondent, disclosing that American B-52 aircraft had recently bombed North Vietnamese base camps in Cambodia for the first time. The story caused surprisingly little reaction in the country, but inside the White House it struck like a thunderbolt. For the bombing of Cambodia was a dark secret, highly classified, and known only to a handful of government officials, including the two men walking along the beach at Key Biscayne. Within the government, the bombing had the code name Operation Menu. It had begun in March; before it was over fourteen months later, the giant B-52s had flown 3,800 missions and dropped more than 108,000 tons of bombs on a country toward which the Administration officially professed a policy of neutrality. The devastating air raids were kept secret not from the Cambodians, who could hardly have failed to notice the cratering of their country by the B-52s, but from the American people, some of whom— had they been permitted to know—might presumably have objected, in the belief that the Constitution vested the power to declare war in the Congress, and not in the President or his national security adviser.*

Now the secret was out, and all sorts of alarums were sounding inside the White House. According to Halperin, Kissinger said that since suspicion had fallen on a member of the NSC staff, he, Kissinger, was on the spot, under pressure from Attorney General John Mitchell, Secretary of Defense Melvin R. Laird, and the twin guardians of the palace gates, H. R. Haldeman and John D. Ehrlichman. Kissinger, Halperin continued, said that Laird and Secretary of State William P. Rogers "had both called the President to say that I was the source of that story. And that they both said that I had done it, that they had great suspicion that I had done it."

To these men, Halperin was a natural locus of mistrust, for he had all the wrong credentials: he was to the left of center politically; he was born in Brooklyn and thus came from New York, an ethnically polyglot and therefore suspect city; he had worked for a Democratic

---

* The deliberate deception of the American people extended as well to the rest of the American government; the Air Force used a system of false bookkeeping to conceal the Cambodian raids. In 1973 General Creighton W. Abrams, the top U.S. commander in Vietnam, told a Senate hearing that at his headquarters in Vietnam there was "a whole special furnace" to burn records of the Cambodia bombing targets. "We burned probably twelve hours a day," Abrams said. He also testified that the reporting system for the bombing raids "had become too complicated. I could not keep these things in my mind, so I had to have specialists . . ." Specialists, as it were, in lying.

President, serving in the Johnson Administration under Robert Mc-Namara and Clark Clifford as a Deputy Assistant Secretary of Defense for Policy Planning and Arms Control; he was a Vietnam expert who opposed military escalation in Vietnam, and finally, because of his political views, he was a favorite security target of FBI chief J. Edgar Hoover. Indeed, Kissinger later claimed he had hired Halperin over Hoover's strenuous objections.

Still, on the beach at Key Biscayne, Halperin believed he had successfully persuaded Kissinger that he was not the source of the *Times* story. For one thing, he pointed out, he was not privy to many of the details contained in the story. It was then that Kissinger made a proposal, and presented it so smoothly, so plausibly, that Halperin did not fully know what was happening to him. "He proposed that he cut off my access to very sensitive material so that if something like this happened again, he could say, look, it wasn't Halperin, he didn't even know about it. It was only by accident that I knew about the Cambodian bombing. I had not been involved in the operation, but I happened to be in Henry's office when [Colonel Alexander M.] Haig rushed in with the first report of the bombings."

Al Haig was then Kissinger's military assistant. He controlled the flow of paper in and out of Kissinger's NSC office, and it would be physically very simple, no trouble at all, to keep highly secret documents away from Halperin. "So it was very easy to do," Halperin recalled, "and I agreed to it."

Halperin did not know it, but he would never again during the Nixon Administration have access to highly classified material, and he would soon be out of the government. Under the palm trees, Morton Halperin had just had his head chopped off. But Kissinger had done it so skillfully that Halperin never felt the blade pass through his neck. There was no blood on the sand.

At 6:20 P.M. the telephone rang in a split-level brick home in Bethesda, Maryland, a bedroom suburb of Washington. Mort Halperin, having returned from his stroll along the beach with Kissinger, had a good deal of news to share with his wife, Ina, and he called her long distance as soon as he was alone. He thinks he may have placed the call from Kissinger's cabana, he cannot be sure of that, but in any event, he reached his wife.

At the precise moment that Ina Halperin lifted the receiver in their home at 8215 Stone Trail Drive, a red light blinked on ten miles away on a telephone switchboard in the Old Post Office Building in downtown Washington. An FBI agent seated at the switchboard quickly plugged in a cord, which automatically powered a tape recorder, and clamped on a set of earphones. He began listening in to the long-distance conversation between Mort and Ina Halperin and taking careful notes.

Through a series of secret connections that had been made earlier that afternoon by the Chesapeake and Potomac Telephone Company, the conversation between man and wife was being circuitously piped from the house on Stone Trail Drive, through the local telephone-company substation in Bethesda, south to the C&P's central office in downtown Washington, and from there, by special cable, to the Washington field office of the FBI in the Old Post Office Building on Pennsylvania Avenue at 12th Street. It was, for all practical purposes, as though the Halperins, without their knowledge of course, had an extra bedroom extension ten miles away in the offices of the FBI.

When the red light flickered, it was an exciting moment for Ernest Belter. In his twenty years of supervising national security wiretaps for the FBI there had never been anything quite like this before. He had been told by his superiors that the tap on Halperin had been ordered by the White House and that extraordinary measures were to be taken to keep it secret even within the FBI. "We all figured there was a big spy ring somewhere," Belter said later, "or a big leak somewhere, and I immediately got busy to hook up Dr. Halperin's line."

A few hours earlier, about the time that Kissinger and Halperin were walking along the beach in Key Biscayne, Ernie Belter had gone over to the rows of telephone pairs, or terminals, in the FBI listening post, and personally connected Halperin's line to the special FBI switchboard. At least he believed, from what the telephone company had said, that Halperin's calls would come in on that line, but one could never be sure until the first conversation actually took place, and on this one he had to be sure, because William Sullivan himself, the assistant director of the FBI for intelligence, had sent word to Belter to "let me know the instant you have them."

So Belter waited, although it was getting past his normal departure time. "I waited around, waiting for some sign of traffic on this line." But it was early evening "before we actually got proof that we were on Dr. Halperin's telephone," when one of the monitors signaled Belter. "I remember one of them telling me that he had received a call and he was pretty sure it was Dr. Halperin. I believe the first call was to Dr. Halperin's wife."

At the time, of course, Halperin had no knowledge that an FBI agent wearing headphones was listening in on his home telephone, taking notes, and often tape-recording his conversations. There was a good deal more he did not know; he did not know, for example, that as he walked along the beach that afternoon his former faculty colleague and friend, Henry Kissinger, had already spoken several times that day with J. Edgar Hoover in Washington, who had set the wiretap machinery in motion.

According to the late FBI Director's log, which it was his custom to keep precisely, when the Beecher story broke in the *Times* on May 9, Kissinger was on the phone to Hoover at 10:35 that morning. Since Kissinger himself has disclosed relatively little about his several conversations with Hoover that day, we are forced to rely on the memoranda that Hoover wrote. These, it must be cautioned, are notoriously self-serving documents, designed primarily to protect J. Edgar Hoover, and they may or may not be accurate in many respects, but at the same time, they might be presumed to bear at least some relationship to actual events, however filtered through the political prejudices and bureaucratic requisites of the Director.

And the memorandum of the 10:35 A.M. call said that Kissinger had telephoned from Key Biscayne to advise that the Beecher story in that morning's *New York Times* was "extraordinarily damaging and uses secret information." Kissinger asked for a "major effort" to find the source, and Hoover said he promised to try. Kissinger asked the FBI Director to put "whatever resources I need to find who did this ... Dr. Kissinger said to do it discreetly of course, but they would like to know where it came from." All this according to Hoover's memo.°

At 11:05 A.M. Kissinger called again, referred to two earlier articles by Beecher, and asked that these be included by Hoover in the FBI's investigation of the leak. Hoover promised to call back the next morning if not sooner.

Two hours later, at 1:05 P.M., Kissinger was on the long-distance phone a third time to the FBI Director to ask that the inquiry be handled discreetly "so no stories will get out." By this time Kissinger's calls must have become rather trying. But Hoover soothingly assured Kissinger he would be back to him the next morning.

Even before that, however, at 5:05 the same afternoon, Hoover telephoned Kissinger in Key Biscayne with some background information about William Beecher, who, Hoover said, "frequents" the Department of Defense press office, which was not entirely startling

---

° In memorandum, as sanitized by the House Judiciary Committee during impeachment proceedings against President Nixon, Beecher's name was masked out and the letter Q substituted. At the request of the Justice Department, the letters A through Q were used by the committee in place of the names of all seventeen targets of the Kissinger wiretaps, which makes analyzing these documents rather like a giant crossword puzzle. But as will be seen, it is not impossible to deduce the actual identities.

information, since Beecher was the *Times* Pentagon correspondent. According to Hoover's memo of the call, the press office employees "freely furnish him information inasmuch as they are largely Kennedy people and anti-Nixon." Hoover also warned Kissinger that in the Pentagon's Systems Analysis branch, a majority of the employees "are still McNamara people and express a very definite Kennedy philosophy."

Hoover added that there was "speculation all the way through tying it into this man Halperin."* He solemnly assured Kissinger that there was adverse information about Halperin in the FBI files; when Halperin had applied for government work he was investigated by the FBI, in 1962 and again in 1969, and the investigation reflected that Halperin and others "are of the opinion that the United States leadership erred in the Vietnam commitment." Even more ominous was Hoover's next disclosure: "I said that the Royal Canadian Mounted Police in 1965 advised that Halperin's name was on a list of Americans who had reportedly received the World Marxist Review, 'Problems of Peace and Socialism,' a communist publication."

The Mounties! This was serious indeed. Kissinger's reaction to this cataclysmic news is not recorded, but Hoover pressed on, mentioning a friend of Halperin's who worked for the Defense Department, "and both are so-called arrogant Harvard-type Kennedy men." Halperin knew Beecher, Hoover added, and accepted him as a fellow member "of the Harvard clique." The Director of the FBI was presumably not unaware that Henry Kissinger was a Harvard graduate and on leave from Harvard as a professor of government, so it may be assumed that Hoover took an especial glee in this, his fourth phone conversation of the day with Kissinger.

Hoover included a paragraph near the end of his memo that was later to come back to haunt Kissinger: "I said that is as far as we have gotten so far. Dr. Kissinger said he appreciated this very much and he hoped I would follow it up as far as we can take it and they will destroy whoever did this if we can find him, no matter where he is."

In all four of these conversations, there was in the written record no specific mention of the word "wiretaps," but Kissinger understood what he and J. Edgar Hoover were talking about; Kissinger was later to tell the Senate Foreign Relations Committee that at the time he had recently met with Nixon, Hoover, and Mitchell, and that "I was told—I do not remember by whom—that wiretapping was necessary" to track down leaks that had been upsetting the Administration. "I was not naïve," Kissinger added. "There has never been any dispute that

* In the House Judiciary Committee documents, Halperin's name has been deleted from Hoover's memo and the letter N substituted.

when my office submitted names I knew that an investigation was certain and a wiretap probable."

Hoover well knew what special "resources" the FBI would use to pursue the Beecher story. During the afternoon he had telephoned William Sullivan (who would follow Joseph Kraft to Paris a month later), and Sullivan in turn called Courtland J. Jones, a supervisor in the Washington field office.

According to Ernie Belter, this is what happened next: Jones came to his office and said, "I just got a call from Bill Sullivan, and he got a call from the White House, and he wants us to put on this coverage right away." Jones handed Belter a list of four names, including that of Morton Halperin. Belter knew exactly what to do; the machinery for tapping a citizen of the United States is amazingly simple and incredibly swift. Just a handful of men, three or four, really, could install the wiretap within hours.°

Belter spoke with James J. Gaffney, a special agent of the FBI whose job it was to serve as FBI liaison with the C&P Telephone Company. Belter told Gaffney that he had a request from the White House through William Sullivan, "and need I say more about the urgency." As was his custom in such matters, Gaffney paid a personal visit to the main office of the C&P Telephone Company close by the FBI in 'downtown Washington. He went directly to the office of Horace R. Hampton, whose title was director of Government Communication Services. Horace Hampton was a man whose name, outside certain highly specialized circles, was unknown in Washington,

---

° It is unlikely, although possible, that the FBI has elaborate listening centers, such as Ernie Belter's command post, in cities outside of Washington and New York, the two major areas for "national security" wiretapping. But through the same technique of using leased lines, the FBI can quickly install a wiretap almost anywhere. Michael J. Hershman, who served as chief investigator for the National Wiretap Commission, said, "The vast majority of federal wiretaps are done through leased lines. The government is technically capable of wiretapping any citizen's telephone. I can think of no instance where they could not. It's just like getting a phone line put in and it can be done in minutes."

Determining if one's phone is tapped is difficult. "The telephone company will do a perfunctory but honest check," Hershman explained. "If an illegal tap is found, they will tell you. Some telephone companies will even tell you if there's a legal tap. Nationwide, the telephone company gets approximately ten thousand complaints a year from people who say, 'My phone is tapped.' They find about two hundred taps a year. But they don't do a thorough check of the inside of the telephone and they can't find anything that's even half sophisticated."

What if a citizen is not satisfied with the phone company's check? "You're up the creek. You have to get a competent electronic countermeasures firm, and very few do a competent job. At forty dollars an hour per man—and usually two men come out. The problem is that the field is shot through with charlatans. Some have idiot boxes that light up and tell you everything from a bug to the best vintage wine. It's a great ripoff and it might cost you five hundred dollars."

but whose importance in the capital could hardly be overestimated. When the FBI wanted to tap a phone without a warrant, they went to Horace Hampton; he was the phone-company executive officially assigned to make the surreptitious arrangements.*

Gaffney and Hampton had dealt with each other over the years and developed a mutual bond of trust. The particular Government Communication Service that Horace Hampton was to provide on this afternoon in May was secretly to hook up a wiretap on Morton Halperin's telephone in Bethesda and to do it fast. He was not shown, and did not ask for, any written authorization from the FBI, or for a court order, which did not exist, or even for evidence that the tap had been approved in writing by the Attorney General of the United States, which, at the time, it had not. It was all done by word of mouth, with the easy familiarity of two old friends who knew the routine.

"Mr. Hampton had worked with us for many years," Belter later explained. "He is a highly patriotic person, and felt that his work with the FBI was a contribution on the part of himself and the phone company."

Gaffney brought with him to Hampton's office a 3 x 5 card with Halperin's telephone number: 469–7818. That was all Hampton needed; American telephone companies are efficient, so he required no name or address. As Hampton later laconically explained it, in cases of this sort "I would call the particular offices involved and tell them to make the necessary connections. And the facility would be provided." Usually, Hampton seemed to suggest, the wiring was done in the dead of night, "by a supervisor after hours."

But the telephone company could not wait until dark on this occasion, there was too much urgency. Hampton could not remember the details, but if the tap coming from Bethesda ran through several phone company offices, "I'd have to call each one of those offices and tell them to make the connections between the wires... to get it downtown."

Hampton got it downtown; he assigned a set of pair numbers in the FBI cable for the Halperin tap. The cable terminating in Belter's wiretap center contained dozens of such pairs that could be wired to the special FBI switchboard. The cable, the tape recorders, the red lights, and the earphones were always there and ready; it was a permanent installation and only the people had to be selected for wiretapping.

* At the time, the Chesapeake and Potomac Telephone Company did not charge the FBI for the special cable running to the Old Post Office Building. After Hampton's retirement in 1971, the phone company started billing the FBI for the wiretap cable. Business is business.

Even before the telephone company completed its secret wiring that afternoon, Belter had got everything hooked up and ready at his end. If you dial your own telephone number on your own phone, you get a busy signal; it was Belter's practice, once a tap was in place, to test it by using the same line to dial the telephone number being tapped, rather in the manner of a snake eating its own tail. He would then hang up, and dial again a few minutes later. If the phone was busy each time, it was a pretty good indication "you are on the right line." This was the only moment of risk for the FBI, the only time when a person tapped might sense that something odd was happening, for, as Belter explained, "If while you were on his line he picked up his phone and tried to use his phone, he'd hear it was busy too. He would hear someone else using this line. He would hear someone else dialing on his line." Contrary to popular belief, except for this one moment of test-dialing, an FBI wiretap of this type produces no clicks or other noises on the telephone.*

In this instance, however, Belter had a technical problem that prevented him from test-dialing Halperin's house. Because Halperin lived in the Maryland suburbs, the tap stretched over several miles, and the telephone company had to use amplifiers to prevent a suspicious drop in volume at Halperin's end. Because of the amplifiers, Belter said, "there was no way I could raise a dial tone and make a check." So Belter waited, waited until 6:20 P.M., when the red light flashed as Ina Halperin picked up the telephone.

In the FBI's eavesdropping center, Belter explained, each listening agent or monitoring clerk sat at "an ordinary library table. At his command, he had a minimum of two tape recorders." Before him was a switchboard "quite similar to a telephone company switchboard. . . . When he saw the light come on . . . he could plug in his tape recorder, start it up, and record the entire conversation." Or he might just listen in. The monitors were busy men, Belter noted, for there were many wiretaps going at once, and if one conversation was not fasci-

---

* Belter himself confirmed this in a deposition he gave in a lawsuit brought by Morton Halperin over the wiretaps:

Q. Do any of these pluggings in, switchings out, produce clicks on the telephone line?

A. No, no.

Belter explained that the special FBI switchboard was so constructed electronically that any activity on the FBI end "does not feed back . . . These units are condenser protected. They protect the line from any kind of activity. This is the reason we have it."

Halperin sued Nixon, Kissinger, Mitchell, several federal officials, and the C&P Telephone Company. His attorneys questioned Belter, Gaffney, Hampton, and others; and details of how the FBI actually tapped wires, and the helpful role of the phone company, emerged for the first time.

nating, "he would let that one go and turn to something else. Maybe the one he turned to was even less interesting or less pertinent, and he might go back to the first one. He had the facility, too, of flipping back and forth between conversations. There was just a flip switch, you know, that would permit him to go instantly from Conversation 1 to Conversation 2, and a good monitor could cut back and forth between conversations and still pick up the gist of it. And remember, too, he could be recording both of them at the same time. So if in the listening of part of it he missed something, he could go back on his tape."

Until Halperin brought suit over the wiretap and forced the details into the daylight, no outsider knew whether the FBI recorded phone calls, listened in, or, as it turned out, both. Even William D. Ruckelshaus, who served briefly as FBI Director, and who played a heroic role in unearthing the hidden logs of the Kissinger taps, was not sure. At one point he was asked by Halperin's attorney:

Q. Just to make sure we understand the procedure, is there a little man sitting somewhere in a little room listening to everything that is being said or is there a tape?

A. I really don't know. I have never been over there to where they are listening to find out how it is done. I don't know whether they actually listen or whether it is transcribed off the tape to the log. I don't know.

As it turned out, there *was* a little man, a score of them in fact, a point that Halperin later found particularly offensive. "The fact it was done live I find somehow upsets me more than the notion of a tape recorder," he said. "There was actually a guy sitting there listening with earphones taking notes and turning on the tape recorder when he thought it was an important conversation."

Like Dickensian bookkeepers, the listening FBI men would carefully log each call, writing the identity of the caller on the left-hand side of a ledger, the name of the person called on the right side of the page. And, as Belter explained it, "under the name of the caller, he'd jot down . . . some of the high points of the things of what he said." From this ledger, the FBI monitor would then type up his summaries; if the conversation seemed important enough, the summary might consist of the entire conversation, or at least some portions, verbatim. These summaries, or "logs," as they were also known, would then—under normal practice—be read by FBI officials and then sent to the FBI's confidential files.

It was essential, of course, that the listeners be able to identify the people talking on the tapped lines, and to help in this, the monitor would have spread out before him the *Congressional Directory*, lists of names, newspaper clippings, and other reference material. They kept little file boxes of 3 x 5 index cards on which they would jot down first names or last names, or other fragments that might help to identify callers; in that way the listener on the night shift could go through the cards and see who had been added to the file by the day man, and, as Belter put it, "in many instances, through the cumulative observations of the monitors, you end up being able to identify the fellow."

Once a person overheard by the FBI was identified, his name, again under normal circumstances, was typed up on an ELSUR (electronic surveillance) card and entered in the FBI's main wiretap index. Thus, if an FBI agent wished to check on whether anyone had ever been overheard and identified on a wiretap, he had but to consult the ELSUR index.

That was under normal circumstances. But on May 9, 1969, Ernie Belter was told to forget the rules. His superior, Courtland Jones, informed him that "this coverage was to be on a strictly need-to-know basis; that I was to assign only old and trusted employees to it; that we were to keep the knowledge of the thing limited to an absolute minimum ... that we were to generate no paper on the installation; that we were to keep no copies of the log summaries ... that the log summaries should be hand-carried to Mr. Sullivan's office first thing in the morning of each regular work day."

In addition, the monitors were told not to number the logs, as was the usual practice, not to type their initials at the end of each log, to keep no copies of the logs, and to prepare no ELSUR cards. In short, from the inception, what eventually became known as the Kissinger wiretaps were carried out in extraordinary secrecy, completely outside of normal Bureau procedures.

It was the first time that Ernie Belter had been told not to keep the usual written records, and he and Jones were worried. Since they were tapping "people still in the White House ... it made us a little bit nervous," Belter said. "At that time Mr. Sullivan was feuding with Mr. Hoover and things were rather tense between them." So the thought occurred to both Belter and Courtland Jones that Sullivan might have been acting on his own in ordering the taps. "Court," Belter recalled asking Jones, "you don't suppose that son of a gun was freewheeling on us?" Jones said he hoped not, but he would try to find out. (The assistant FBI director had indeed not been acting on his own, but Belter and Jones had no way of knowing that, or about Kissinger's four conversations with Hoover that day.)

The next morning, Saturday, May 10, Colonel Alexander Haig called on Sullivan at the FBI. A handsome, intense man of rigid military bearing—he seemed perpetually coiled and ready to spring

—Haig was quietly but rapidly becoming Henry Kissinger's indispensable staffman; ultimately, when Watergate flooded in, he was commissioned Nixon's last general, the stage manager for Götterdämmerung. Power-driven, enigmatic, and politically conservative, Haig had risen to the top from a Depression boyhood in Philadelphia. He grew up poor on the Manayunk line, the son of an attorney who died of cancer at age thirty-eight, when Haig was ten. His death left Haig's mother with three children and very little money, and Haig with a cold ambition to succeed. His brother Frank became a Jesuit priest, an astrophysicist with his eyes on the stars, but Al went to West Point, served on Douglas MacArthur's staff during the Korean War, and emerged in the mid-sixties as one of the promising younger officers in Robert McNamara's orbit at the Pentagon.

In 1969, he was just what Henry Kissinger needed as a pacifier for the Joint Chiefs of Staff and a political counterbalance to the young liberals with whom Kissinger had surrounded himself at the White House. Bob Haldeman might instinctively distrust Mort Halperin and the other intellectuals on Kissinger's staff, all those long-haired kids wearing glasses, but no one could doubt Al Haig's loyalty. Haig's uniform, his West Point ring, his military *machismo*, provided useful insulation for Kissinger against Nixon's staff Junkers, the brush-cut centurions of Southern California. And Haig was more than a buffer; he had the added virtue of being a skillful, obedient bureaucrat who kept the papers flowing smoothly.*

After Haig visited the FBI on May 10, Sullivan wrote a memorandum for the record reporting that Haig had asked "on the highest authority" that "technical surveillance"† be placed on four government officials. "He stressed that it is so sensitive it demands handling on a need-to-know basis, with no record maintained." Haig, the memo

---

* One story from Haig's Korean service demonstrates the qualities that so endeared him to his superiors. Haig was aide-de-camp to General Edward Almond, commander of X Corps, in Hungnam, North Korea. An active field commander, Almond spent much of his time with his front-line troops accompanied by Haig. But Haig was also responsible for administering Almond's mess and headquarters billets. The villa that Almond used as his headquarters wasn't much, but "I had a bathtub put together for him out of tile by local North Korean labor," Haig recalled. "That damn thing was a labor of love." When the Chinese crossed the Yalu in October 1950, Almond's troops withdrew from Hungnam. Haig had already left the villa when he started thinking: *A Chinese general might take a bath in General Almond's tile tub!* Braving enemy fire, and at considerable risk to life and limb, Haig went back to the villa, dropped a grenade in the tub, and blew it up "so no commissar would have an opportunity to wallow in it." As always, Al Haig was the perfect staffman.

† Hoover was more specific; in reporting the White House request to Attorney General Mitchell, he said Haig had asked for "telephone surveillance."

made clear, did not want any wiretap logs floating around the White House. "Instead, he will come to my office to review the information developed, which will enable us to maintain tight control of it." Sullivan even ordered that his own memorandum of Haig's visit not be placed in the regular FBI files. At the top of Sullivan's memo, the code word JUNE was typed in capital letters.

On Kissinger's orders, when Haig visited the FBI, he handed Sullivan four names. They included Morton Halperin and two other members of Kissinger's staff, Helmut Sonnenfeldt and Daniel I. Davidson. Sonnenfeldt was born in Berlin, and like Kissinger, had fled Nazi Germany in 1938; they had met briefly in Germany in 1946 while both were serving in the United States Army. Sonnenfeldt's parents were both physicians, and Sonnenfeldt, heavy-set and dark-visaged, was a sober, serious man, somewhat pedantic in style. In 1953 he married Marjorie Hecht, of the department-store family, an attractive blonde who made an effervescent contrast. Sonnenfeldt had joined the State Department a year earlier, and by the mid-sixties he was the top Soviet analyst for the Department's Bureau of Intelligence and Research. Although a registered Democrat, Sonnenfeldt was decidedly conservative in foreign affairs, particularly in policies relating to the Soviet Union; despite these hard-line political credentials, the FBI and Otto F. Otepka, the State Department's security hound, suspected him of leaking classified information to the press. He was placed under surveillance, interrogated, and eventually cleared; but no one in Washington is ever really cleared because the charges, and the memos, and the investigative reports remain in the files. Moreover, Marge Sonnenfeldt was active in local Democratic politics in Maryland, and this did not please the Nixon loyalists in the White House.

The story circulated that when Sonnenfeldt was hired by Kissinger for the Nixon NSC staff, he came home proudly that night, told his wife, and remarked, "Maybe I'll get to swim in the White House pool." And according to the story, Marge replied, "Do you want to use the same pool as that man?"

By Monday, May 12, the C&P and the FBI had wired up their special cross-connections to the Sonnenfeldts' home on Thornapple Street in Chevy Chase, and the family's telephone conversations were being overheard in the Old Post Office Building on Pennsylvania Avenue, only four blocks from the White House. So the logs of Sonnenfeldt's conversations or those of his family did not have to travel far to reach Kissinger, who had also fled a totalitarian system to enjoy the protections of constitutional democracy.

The Sonnenfeldt tap created a particularly uncomfortable problem for Al Haig. "He used to come in and tell me he was sure he was being tapped, almost weekly," Haig later testified. Haig, who of course knew that Sonnenfeldt was correct in his suspicions—since he had brought his name over to the FBI—said nothing to Sonnenfeldt.

Daniel Davidson, the other Kissinger aide on Haig's list, was a young lawyer who had rather unexpectedly become a foreign policy expert. Like Mort Halperin, he was born in Brooklyn and grew up in Bensonhurst, a middle-class Jewish-Italian neighborhood, where "the Jews lived in the corner apartment houses and the Italians lived in the single-family residences." Davidson lived in an apartment house. But he escaped from Bensonhurst; he was an outstanding student at Columbia Law School, graduating third in his class, and as a result he made the great leap forward to Cravath, Swaine & Moore, one of the old-line WASP law firms in the canyons of lower Manhattan. Davidson was handling litigation and might have ended up in Scarsdale like some other successful young lawyer but for the fact that early in 1965 William P. Bundy, the Assistant Secretary of State for Far Eastern Affairs, telephoned an old friend at Cravath, Swaine. The government had just issued a White Paper trying to prove the Johnson Administration's case in Vietnam, it was being criticized, and Bundy was embarrassed. He needed a bright young man in order, as Davidson put it, "to alert him to traps."

So Davidson signed on, moved to Washington, and worked for a year as Bundy's special assistant for Vietnam policy, then performed the same job for Averell Harriman, who was Ambassador at Large. He became a protégé of Harriman's and was named one of six delegates to the Paris peace talks on Vietnam that began in May of 1968. Davidson had met Kissinger during the Johnson years, "and we became close friends, I thought. He'd been to my house for dinner; I fixed him up with a date, et cetera." After Nixon's election Davidson, then job-hunting, telephoned Kissinger and was hired.

But Davidson was a Democrat, and the FBI files, Hoover later reported to John Mitchell, contained an allegation that while in Paris, Davidson had leaked information about the peace negotiations to a newsman.° So Davidson was another in the nest of suspect Democrats working for Kissinger, and Horace Hampton's men made their cross-connections to the Potomac Plaza apartments, near the State Department, where Davidson and his wife, Susan, then lived.

In many ways the fourth name on Haig's list was the most intriguing. A few hours after Haig's visit to the FBI, Sullivan telephoned Hoover. Hoover's secretary, Helen W. Gandy, typed up a memoran-

° Davidson in an interview denied that he had leaked any information in Paris. He confirmed, however, that he had occupied adjoining rooms at the Hôtel Crillon with Hedrick L. Smith of the New York Times, who occasionally walked into the bathroom connecting the two suites and shared his shaving mirror.

dum of the call; Sullivan, she wrote, had reported that Haig "visited him this morning and made certain requests re a Colonel in the Pentagon."

The colonel was Robert E. Pursley, but he was not, despite the vagueness of Miss Gandy's memo, just any old colonel; he was the military assistant to Melvin Laird, Nixon's Secretary of Defense. By dispatching Haig to the FBI and thereby triggering a tap on Pursley, Kissinger, was, in effect, tapping Laird. Here the plot of the seventeen wiretaps becomes truly Byzantine.

Pursley, like Haig a graduate of West Point, had flown fifty bombing missions in the Korean War. He had earned a master's degree at the Harvard School of Business, and in 1966 became military assistant to Secretary of Defense Robert McNamara. He stayed in the job, after McNamara left, first under Clark Clifford, then Laird.

Laird was confident his own phone was not bugged because he regularly called in the National Security Agency to check his telephones and was always assured they were clean. But he was outraged when, much later, he learned of the tap on Pursley, since Laird would customarily talk by phone with his assistant several times in the evening.

In the deliberations of the National Security Council, Laird said in an interview, he had recommended the bombing of Cambodia but had urged that the decision be made public. "I recommended hitting the sanctuaries; I took the position in the NSC that this could get public support, and that it would be impossible to keep it secret." As a result, he said, when Beecher's story appeared on May 9, the President and Kissinger suspected him as the source. "They thought we had leaked that. That is why they put the tap on Pursley's phone in my office, and also the phone in his home. They thought I leaked the story to Beecher, that I tried to prove myself right, that the bombing could not be kept secret. Those [wiretap] instructions came directly out of— from the White House. They were madder than hell about the story. Henry was mad, and so was the President.

"I denied it," Laird said. "I said I had nothing to do with the story. I told the President, too."[*]

Laird did not know in 1969, of course, that Kissinger, via Haig, had turned over the name of his assistant to the FBI for wiretapping. When Laird left the government in 1974, he suggested in a farewell press conference that the Beecher story, which marked the beginning of the whole wiretap program, had not resulted from a leak at all but from a news story published in the *Times* of London forty-eight hours

---

[*] Pursley, now a business executive in Meriden, Connecticut, also denied any role in the leak in a telephone interview with the author.

earlier. "A correspondent had flown over the border," Laird said, "and he saw certain craters in Cambodia and the London *Times* came out with this particular story. Bill Beecher, being an enterprising young reporter, went out and started checking this out and he couldn't get denials because I wouldn't deny it."

It would be a marvelous irony if the wiretapping and the paranoia within the Nixon White House, with all of the attendant internal rivalries, finger-pointing and suspicion, began with an effort to track down a leak that had, in fact, never occurred. There was some difficulty with Laird's explanation, however, in that no news story published in London precisely fit his description, or at least, one has not been found.°

Beecher was particularly annoyed at the implication that he had merely been rewriting the British press. Sometime later Laird and Beecher were both guests at a party at the home of Bob Schieffer, then the CBS Pentagon correspondent. "Mel," Beecher told Laird, "you've been repeating this, and it isn't what happened." Beecher then claimed that he had pieced together the Cambodia bombing story, in mosaic fashion, over a long period of time.

By Monday, May 12, three days after Beecher's story appeared, Mitchell had returned to the Justice Department from Key Biscayne. Waiting for him was a memo from Hoover summarizing the wiretap requests that had come from Kissinger's office. At 5:48 P.M. Mitchell signed Hoover's memorandum, and by so doing gave his approval to the four wiretaps.

But the tap on Morton Halperin's home on Stone Trail Drive was already in place and had been since 6:20 P.M. on Friday, when the red light appeared on Ernie Belter's switchboard. And the evidence suggests that some or all of the other three taps may also have been

° The alleged *Times* story on the bombing of Cambodia has become a sort of Flying Dutchman of news stories, an elusive legend that has never sailed into harbor. A check in the *Times* of London for April and May of 1969 disclosed no such article. Nor did the *Sunday Times* publish such a story in the five weeks preceding Beecher's story of May 9, 1969. However, Fred A. Emery, the *Times* correspondent in the Far East at the time, did take a picture from a helicopter of bomb craters in Vietnam along the Vam Co Dong River, on the Cambodian border. The photograph was published in the *Times* of London on March 13, 1969, two months, not two days, before the Beecher story was published, under a headline reading: "Saturation Bombing on the Vam Co Dong." The caption explained that the photograph showed the effects of B-52 bombing in Vietnam, not Cambodia. So it may or may not be what Laird had in mind. Laird told the author that the story he remembered was among a batch of newspaper clippings shown to him each day at the Pentagon. When he saw it, Laird said he exclaimed, "'Oh, hell, here it comes.' I knew there would now be stories in the American press about the bombing."

working before Mitchell signed the authorization. In all of the subsequent investigations no one, neither Kissinger, Haig, or Mitchell, nor any of the FBI officials, was able to explain how it happened that Morton Halperin's telephone had been tapped three days before the Attorney General of the United States signed the authorization.°

The power to eavesdrop on the private lives of one's closest associates, to read their confidential comments in classified transcripts, is heady wine, sweet, secret knowledge to those playing the game of politics in Washington. Did they smile inwardly when they greeted their unsuspecting colleagues each morning?

Certainly they knew what Halperin was saying about them, for Hoover pointedly included Halperin's remarks about his superiors in the FBI wiretap reports. One report of a conversation Halperin had with a colleague noted that Halperin had referred to Haig as "that God-damn gossip." The FBI summary said the two men agreed that Haig was "the big gossip—he knows everything about everybody." Another FBI summary, in the form of a letter from Hoover to Kissinger, reported that Halperin "said that the Attorney General was an ignoramus."

The FBI noted that Ina Halperin had boasted to a friend over the telephone that her husband was important because "he has Henry Kissinger's ear." And it reported verbatim a conversation in which a visitor to Halperin's house, using the phone, told a friend that Halperin "really is an ace." Yes, the friend agreed, Halperin was "the best guy they've got . . . He's about three times as good as HENRY."†

After one week the list increased. On May 20 Haig asked the FBI to tap the telephones of two more of his colleagues on the NSC staff, Richard M. Moose and Richard L. Sneider. Moose had the distinct disadvantage around the Nixon White House of having worked for, and being a known admirer of, his fellow Arkansan, Senator J. William Fulbright, then chairman of the Senate Foreign Relations Committee (which would ultimately, but lightly, question Kissinger about the wiretapping of, among others, Richard Moose). He had resigned from the foreign service to work on the NSC staff under Walt W. Rostow during the Johnson Administration, left, and had been brought back by Kissinger.

Soon after he joined the White House staff, Moose had bumped

° During Halperin's walk on the beach on Friday, he and Kissinger had passed by a cabana where a meeting was under way of Ehrlichman, Haldeman, Mitchell, and other staff aides. Unaware that Kissinger and Mitchell were about to tap his phone, Halperin was suitably impressed when Kissinger stopped and made a point of introducing his assistant to the Attorney General. "It was the first time I met Mitchell," Halperin recalled.

† The FBI customarily uses upper-case letters for names in its memos.

into Fulbright in the corridor outside the Oval Office, and while they were chatting for a few moments, Haig happened by and stared at them. It was said around the White House that in a conversation with Moose soon afterward, Al Haig referred to Fulbright as a "traitor" and a "menace," infuriating Moose and causing raised voices.[*] Moose was politically unreliable; the wiretap machine, geared and ready, hummed into action once more. Hoover obtained Mitchell's signature, and Courtland Jones and the C&P Telephone Company did the rest. Moose lived on Glasgow Road in Alexandria, Virginia, and within hours, through the miracle of modern communications, the conversations over the family's home telephone were being piped across the Potomac into the Old Post Office Building, where the men with earphones were waiting. The grid of tapped wires now stretched over two state lines, Maryland and Virginia, into the District of Columbia.

Richard Sneider, tapped the same day as Richard Moose, was a shrewd bureaucrat, a foreign service officer and expert on Japanese affairs who had joined Kissinger's NSC staff as a senior assistant for the Far East. (In 1974 Sneider was to become President Gerald Ford's ambassador to Korea.)

There is every reason to believe that Haig and Kissinger personally brought over the names of Moose and Sneider to the FBI, for on May 20, the day that these two taps were requested and approved, William Sullivan wrote a memo to Hoover which said: "Dr. Kissinger and Colonel Haig came to my office this morning around 11:45. Dr. Kissinger read all the logs. On doing this he said, 'It is clear that I do not have anybody in my office that I can trust except Colonel Haig here.'"

Sullivan later said he could not recall Kissinger's ever coming to his office to read the logs, but neither did he disavow his memo, which was very specific about who had come to see him, the time of day, and what was said. Presumably the assistant director of the FBI was not in the habit of inventing details of this sort in his official memoranda.

Severe cases of amnesia developed over this incident, however, when the existence of the Kissinger wiretaps was finally disclosed four years later. "I have no recollection of having been in Sullivan's office to read logs," Kissinger told the Foreign Relations Committee. He thought it was "extraordinarily unlikely" but would "certainly not deny" that he might have made the "semisarcastic" remark about trusting only Haig.

Haig, in his own Senate testimony, could not recall such a visit

---

[*] In an interview, Haig remembered the encounter. "I think I may have referred to him [Fulbright] as a menace," he said. Could Haig have used the word "traitor"? "No, I don't think so. I don't think of him as that in any sense of the word. But I disagree with his views in general."

either, but he added—quite unnecessarily, Kissinger must have thought —that "it would not surprise me if there had been one." Haig said he had gone over to the FBI four or five times to read transcripts of the wiretaps and might easily be confused "as to whether Henry was with me or not." But Haig "vividly" recalled that he and Kissinger had twice gone to the FBI together to see Hoover. "I did participate with Henry in those two discussions," he said.

Eight days after the Moose and Sneider taps, Al Haig was back to the FBI with a request to wiretap a newspaper reporter. The stakes were escalating now, the game becoming even more risky for the government. It must have occurred to the Administration that the tapping of the press might abridge the First Amendment to the Constitution, and that even if it did not, politically the bugging of reporters was a potentially explosive step.

The name Haig submitted to the FBI appears in the House Judiciary Committee impeachment evidence simply as "P." P was Henry Brandon, probably the best-known foreign correspondent in the capital. Since 1950 he had been representing the *Sunday Times* of London in Washington. Urbane, well-tailored, distinguished-looking, Brandon retained a slight trace of a continental accent, for he was born a Czech, in Prague. He came to London in 1938 (the same year that Henry Kissinger arrived in Washington Heights) and joined the staff of the *Sunday Times* a year later. He was a war correspondent during World War II, and opened the *Sunday Times* Paris bureau on the day the city was liberated.

He was regarded as one of the most perceptive interpreters of America, and of U.S. foreign policy, to British audiences, and he had over the years developed an extraordinarily wide range of sources and friends in official Washington.

This fact did not escape the eye of J. Edgar Hoover, or of William Sullivan, his counterintelligence chief. Hoover regarded Brandon with deep suspicion; he was, first of all, a foreigner, which was bad enough, and second, he knew a great deal about what was going on inside the American government. As far back as the Kennedy Administration, during the early sixties, it was whispered in Washington that Brandon worked for MI-6, the British equivalent of the CIA.

Kissinger's explanation of the Brandon tap in his testimony to the Senate Foreign Relations Committee was heavily censored. But it is delicately noted in the impeachment documents that Kissinger testified that the name of one newsman "was presented by FBI Director Hoover to the President as a man who had connections with an allied foreign intelligence service and the decision to place a tap resulted from that presentation."

"I assume Kissinger, was referring to me," Brandon said in an interview in which he simultaneously denied the allegation. "I have never had anything to do with the British secret service in any form or shape," he said. Moreover, he said, Justice Department officials who had read the FBI files had assured him that there was no such evidence about him; and during the Kennedy Administration McGeorge Bundy, one of Kissinger's predecessors as national security adviser, also told him he had checked the files with negative results. Bundy, Brandon said, added that British and American intelligence had an agreement not to spy on each other.

"No newsman should have a connection with an intelligence organization," Brandon said. "I personally feel I could not carry out my profession in good conscience unless I had nothing to do with any intelligence agency."

There were other crosscurrents swirling around Brandon. During the impeachment inquiry James D. St. Clair, the Boston lawyer imported by Nixon to manage his defense, presented a lengthy brief in behalf of the President to the House Judiciary Committee. To complicate matters even further, St. Clair used his own set of code letters (different from that of the Judiciary Committee) to mask the identity of the persons wiretapped. Attempting to justify the taps, St. Clair said the FBI had reported that two NSC employees, "X and L, discussed many aspects of the internal workings of the NSC with Y, a newsman." Decoded, this means that St. Clair was asserting that Davidson (X) and Halperin (L) had talked to Brandon (Y). Then St. Clair wrote: "Various FBI documents suggest that Y may have aided foreign governments in gathering intelligence information in the past."

It must be assumed that James St. Clair, who earned a six-figure income as a senior partner of Hale & Dorr, was a man of precision, and that when he referred to the FBI reports, his use of the words "foreign governments" in the plural was not accidental. Possibly this reflected the xenophobia in the upper echelons of the FBI toward Brandon's Czech origins; one can also hear Hoover saying, "If the sonofabitch has been around for twenty years, he must be working for *somebody*."

So the FBI's vigilance in regard to Brandon extended to the East, too; if he was not reporting to Whitehall, perhaps he was reporting to the damn Commies. And the fact that the FBI leaders could prove neither theory only added to their frustration. Brandon was not unaware of all this; he had heard intimations that he was rumored to be connected with an East European intelligence service, but he repeated the same blanket denial he had made of his supposed link to MI-6.

When Brandon was tapped he was a bachelor living on Rodman Street in the residential area of northwest Washington. In 1970, while the tap was still in place, he married. He and his wife, Muffie, and her three children by a previous marriage, moved into a house on Whitehaven Street. The FBI wiretap followed Brandon to his new home.

The tap remained on Brandon's telephone for a very long time— one year and eight months, to be precise. As a foreign correspondent, Brandon said, he would perhaps expect an occasional spot check on his telephone by American security. "I don't mind a short tap," he said, "but a long one . . ." He could only conclude, Brandon said, that "the Nixon Administration wanted to know who my sources were."

They did indeed. The interest in Brandon rose to a crescendo in August 1969, when the FBI learned that he had eaten lunch with Morton Halperin. Brandon and Halperin together! J. Edgar Hoover must have fairly quivered with excitement, for the FBI covered the meeting as though John Dillinger had been spotted dining with Bonnie and Clyde.

The FBI report of this lunch, sanitized by the use of code letters for names, is worth reproducing in its entirety:

P, Washington correspondent for the —— and N lunched at the Occidental Restaurant on August 6, 1969. P arrived at about 1 P.M., and N joined him at a table in the West Room at 1:10 P.M. They engaged in a continuing conversation while they lunched and departed the restaurant at 2:45 P.M. They walked to the vicinity of the Executive Office Building, during which time they continued in conversation. They parted in the vicinity of the Executive Office Building about 3 P.M.

Enclosed are photographs of N and P taken as they departed the West Room of the Occidental Restaurant, leaving the entrance to the restaurant and walking thereafter toward the White House.

Six clandestine photographs of Brandon and Halperin were taken by FBI agents as they left the restaurant and walked past the Treasury Building back toward the White House.° When questioned under oath by Halperin's attorneys, Alexander Haig later had difficulty

---

° Even before the Occidental luncheon, the FBI was carefully logging contacts between Brandon and Halperin. Late in May, the FBI reported, Brandon had asked Halperin's help in tracking down a memo on Vietnam written by Secretary of State Dean Rusk. "Subsequently, Halperin spoke to a Dr. Gilm (phonetic)" about the memo, the FBI reported. The Bureau concluded that "Dr. Gilm" was "probably identical with Dr. Leslie H. Gelb . . . who is now connected with the Brookings Institution."

remembering whether he had seen the photographs; even with the great amount of material that crossed Haig's desk, six clandestine FBI photographs of a colleague leaving a restaurant might be expected to make some impression, to stand out even a little from the humdrum, routine paperwork, but Haig said he could "not recall" seeing the pictures.

As the wiretap program continued, it generated hundreds of pages of transcripts of conversation, and there was a steady flow from the FBI to the White House of the summaries of Brandon's phone conversations, and of the others who were tapped. The original arrangement, for Haig to come over and read the take, was too much trouble. Soon summaries were being delivered to the President and Kissinger; some went directly and personally to Kissinger, but more often, they were handed to Haig. "I would open them," Haig later testified, "and then pass them to Henry, if they were significant."° The wiretapping program took on a life of its own. Such was the climate within the Nixon White House that even in October 1974, after Nixon had resigned to avoid certain impeachment, Alexander Haig could argue that the wiretaps were justified. Morton Halperin, he said, had been in touch with a "prime suspect for espionage activity." It was obvious whom Haig had in mind.

The tap on Henry Brandon remained in place until February 10, 1971. Two weeks later Brandon went to see someone who knew a good deal more than he realized about the intimate details of his personal and private life. He was granted an interview with President Nixon.

It was, needless to say, a busy time in 1969 down at the Old Post Office Building. After the Halperin tap had been on for a time, Ernest Belter assigned two of his best clerks, George Ross and James Barnhardt, to listen to the Halperins' conversations. Eavesdropping is fatiguing, so Belter also assigned Raymond Broz, Jr., as a relief man to spell them. Jimmy Barnhardt, or someone, clipped out an article in *Newsweek* that detailed the organization of Kissinger's staff along with capsuled biographies of key members. He tacked it up over the switchboard as an aid to better listening.

There were no manuals or written instructions to the wiretappers. As Belter explained, even within the FBI "the whole activity of electronic surveillance has sort of been kept in a closet." So technique developed informally. If Belter was briefing a new man he might say "this fellow is a suspected spy . . . or we think this fellow is leaking

---

° Haig testified in the Halperin lawsuit that he would also receive the President's sets of logs and send them to Ehrlichman for the President. But Ehrlichman disputed this; he said he did not recall seeing the logs as they came in.

information to some spy . . . Be alert for anything that looks suspicious and for any contacts, luncheons, any unexplained activity."

If a "known spy" was being tapped, Belter said, the FBI's interest became total. "Sometimes I tell the boys if he calls for weather, put it in. We want to know everything." In such cases, Belter said, "we want to know if he gets along with his wife, or if he doesn't. We particularly want to know if he has some extramarital affair going."

Belter made it clear that wives and children and friends were recorded and logged, too. When a tap was first placed on a telephone, he explained, it was essential to learn the identities of everyone who would be heard on that phone over many months, "who they are and where they work, their particular relationship to the subject of the surveillance. And this includes the friends of the wife; if there are children, friends of the children."

There was, in addition, Belter explained candidly, a problem peculiar to the profession of wiretapping: after a while, some of the FBI clerks would lose interest. "Sometimes," he said, "questions arise on the part of the people who read the traffic as to whether you are really paying much attention to it, or whether . . . your monitors are sitting there reading the paper." So from time to time, Belter said, "I get on the monitors and I say, look, turn out some kind of log. I don't like to see a whole day go by and at the end of the day a blank page."

Blank pages might also mean the tap had somehow been lost by technical difficulty, Belter said, so he would tell the listeners "that I would prefer to have three or four what we call, you know, no-value calls in there rather than a blank page. At least I can look at it and know we are still on that telephone line, and the monitor at least was paying some attention to it."

There was no special rule about tape-recording calls; if the monitor thought a conversation sounded intriguing, he would push the record button. Often, when making a call, the person being tapped would dial some office and be put on a hold button. There was no sense recording *that*, Belter said. (It was only minor comfort to know that the listening FBI men were just as irritated as the wiretap victim at being put, vicariously, on hold.)

"On the other hand," said Belter, if a Mr. Smith was being tapped and his telephone rang, the monitor "might start the recorder when he finds out the caller wants Mr. Smith. It's the garage, let's say. Shucks, he [the monitor] might say; I know what that's all about; that's of no consequence whatever. He won't start the recorder again."

About one thing Ernie Belter's men were careful; if a C&P customer being wiretapped reported any trouble on his line, the FBI would immediately take the tap off. Rarely, Belter said, "was a problem on the line due to our tap." The telephone company would repair the line, since it always wanted to provide the best possible service to its customers. "When it was cleared up, Mr. Hampton would say, 'Okay, it can go back on.' "

Washington began digging in the streets for a new subway during the period of the Kissinger wiretaps, and it apparently caused unexpected technical difficulties for the White House. For Belter noted that trouble on the tapped lines "was quite prevalent in all of the latter years, with all the construction downtown, because of the cables being cut and the necessity to transfer cables. So the whole phone company was driven crazy by all of these changes and plenty of opportunity for things to go wrong."

Under questioning by Walter Slocombe, a brilliant young attorney who represented Halperin in his lawsuit against the government, Belter conceded that there were really no conversations that the FBI might not listen to or record.*

If his men overheard "pure scandal" or "gutter gossip" about "sex or you name it," Belter said, he might tell the monitors to leave it out of the logs. But then again, he said, he might not tell them to leave it out.

Not only the persons tapped but their friends and associates were of interest. Slocombe pursued the point with Belter: "Did you give any instructions with respect to visitors to the house ... that is, people other than Dr. Halperin or members of his family who might be using the Halperins' phones?"

"I gave no instructions about not entering those [in the] logs. My instructions, in fact, would have been the other way around. Visitors to Dr. Halperin's home were matters of legitimate interest in any investigative case of this nature."

What about the personal politics of the people being tapped, Slocombe asked; were the monitors told to look for material on active Democratic presidential candidates?

Well, Belter said, they were "not told specifically to look for any political-type material" but when you listen for leaks it may involve

* The FBI, for example, found it significant that during a conversation with a cemetery-lot salesman, "Halperin's wife volunteered the information that he was working at the White House on the President's speech." In May of 1969 Hoover reported to Kissinger that "information received from our extremely sensitive sources shows that [deleted] and Halperin are associates of I. F. Stone and his family. I. F. Stone is a former member of the Communist Party who publishes 'I. F. Stone's Weekly.' He is well known for his attacks on prominent Government officials and on United States policy." The FBI also reported to the White House that "During a conversation with Jeremy Stone, the son of I. F. Stone, Halperin's wife invited the Stones to their home and said that Halperin was working all weekend on the North Vietnam peace program." Mrs. Halperin, the FBI reported, sympathized with the Stone family's opposition to the Administration's Vietnam policies.

people in the opposition political party. For example, he told Slocombe, a monitor would definitely be expected to log "a contact with a staunch McGovern supporter."

By the morning of Wednesday, June 4, 1969, seven wiretaps had been placed on telephones in the homes of Morton Halperin, Helmut Sonnenfeldt, Daniel Davidson, Robert Pursley, Richard Sneider, Richard Moose, and Henry Brandon; only the tap on Pursley had been removed.

On that morning the *New York Times* carried another story that disturbed Henry Kissinger. On page one under the by-line of Hedrick Smith of the Washington Bureau, the *Times* correctly reported that the first reduction of United States forces in Vietnam would be announced a few days later when Presidents Nixon and Nguyen Van Thieu of South Vietnam met on Midway Island.

At 9:30 A.M. Kissinger was sitting in the office of J. Edgar Hoover at the FBI. There is no question that this meeting took place, only the substance remains somewhat elusive. Kissinger testified before the Senate Foreign Relations Committee in July 1974: "I did express to Mr. Hoover at a June 4 meeting the view that the taps in general should be stopped as soon as possible."

Since the taps were not terminated until one year and eight months later, Kissinger had lamentably little success if this was his purpose in going to Hoover's office. The documentary evidence suggests, however, that aside from any other possible reasons, Kissinger had gone to Hoover's office to ask that a *new* tap be placed—on Hedrick Smith.

In the fine print of the hearings of the Senate Foreign Relations Committee there is a small portion of a memo written by William Sullivan to Deke DeLoach on the day of the meeting: "Today Dr. Kissinger requested that a telephone surveillance be placed on [deleted] who has been in contact with the individuals on whom we have had telephone coverage in this case." Deleted was clearly Rick Smith of the *New York Times*, because on the same date Hoover sent a memo to John Mitchell: "Dr. Kissinger has requested that a telephone surveillance be placed on Hedrick Smith."[*]

Thus far, at least, the White House had wiretapped officials of the NSC and the Defense Department who dealt with national security affairs, and two newsmen who wrote primarily about foreign policy. However doubtful the legality of these acts, the President could make

---

[*] According to evidence cited in the House Judiciary Committee's impeachment inquiry, the FBI had already overheard the *New York Times* correspondent on its wiretap of Kissinger's assistant Daniel Davidson, his neighbor at the Hôtel Crillon the previous year.

the claim, as he later did, that he acted to protect the "national security." But in July, with the selection of the ninth person to be tapped, all pretense of "national security" was cast aside.

On July 22, 1969, Richard Nixon, by all external signs, should have been a happy man, secure in his power and his Presidency. He was poised to leave on a triumphant journey around the world. Forty-eight hours earlier, the Apollo 11 astronauts had walked on the moon, and Nixon had shared in the reflected glory of that monumental achievement. Two days before the moon walk, the one man whose popularity might represent a threat to Nixon's re-election, Senator Edward M. Kennedy of Massachusetts, had been effectively removed from the 1972 presidential race. Kennedy, the news tickers reported, had been driving a car that went off a bridge on Chappaquiddick Island, and a young woman who was a passenger, Mary Jo Kopechne, had drowned.

Shortly after 10 P.M. on July 22 Nixon left Washington. He flew west toward the Pacific, where he would greet the astronauts aboard the carrier *Hornet* at splashdown two days later. Then on to Southeast Asia and Rumania, in a 24,000-mile global tour designed to focus world attention on American power, and America's President.

At 5:15 P.M., five hours before Nixon's jet took off for San Francisco and the Pacific, Attorney General Mitchell telephoned Deke De-Loach. According to the memo that DeLoach wrote the next day to Hoover's deputy and long-time companion, Clyde A. Tolson, Mitchell first asked whether DeLoach was familiar with "the wiretapping business at the White House." DeLoach was, of course, and Mitchell then reported that the President "was extremely exercised and very aggravated." The cause of Nixon's discontent was his twenty-nine-year-old deputy counsel, John P. Sears, whom Nixon apparently suspected of being too friendly with the press.

For almost two years Sears had been one of Nixon's closest aides in his drive for the Republican presidential nomination. During that time he held various titles, but his basic task was to organize the primary states, win delegates, and help manage the campaign to secure the 1968 presidential nomination for Richard Nixon.°

And now the President—as DeLoach reported his conversation with Mitchell—had ordered his Attorney General to tell the Director of the FBI that Nixon wanted "a 24-hour surveillance and a tap" placed on John Sears. The results were to be sent to John Ehrlichman, on whose staff Sears served. Moreover, the President had a plan to trap Sears. Mitchell said the President wanted "to set Sears up" and

° In 1976 Sears served as director of Ronald Reagan's campaign against President Ford for the Republican presidential nomination.

"planned to send material from Guam this coming Thursday night which Sears would definitely see."

The implication was clear: from the far Pacific, the day after the President had greeted the astronauts returning from the moon, as the world marveled at the reach and vision of mankind, the President of the United States would attempt to ensnare and destroy the young man who, as much as anyone, had helped to put him in the White House. His phone would be tapped and he would be followed around the clock by FBI men so that if he slipped the sensitive documents to a newsman, the President would know, and could pounce.

Mitchell might have been acting on his own, of course, there was always that possibility, but the FBI did what it was told; within a day the tap had been placed on Sears's home in Falls Church, Virginia, where he lived with his wife, Carol, and their three young children. "Instructions have also been issued to conduct the 24-hour surveillance requested," DeLoach reported.

Perhaps it is too easy to say that John Sears had looked upon Nixon like a father, but Sears grew up on a dairy farm near Syracuse, New York, and his own father burned to death in a fire on the farm when he was ten. Sears was only twenty-six, a young lawyer working under Leonard Garment in Nixon's New York law firm, when Nixon asked him to take a leave of absence and join his political staff.

Sears had accepted. Nixon was then campaigning for Republican candidates in the 1966 congressional elections, earning due bills, and politics seemed more exciting to Sears than the litigation department of Nixon, Mudge. After the 1966 elections, Sears and Robert Ellsworth began organizing for the 1968 nomination. The "Nixon for President" committee had trouble finding a chairman; Nixon ran through two of them before Leonard Garment suggested John Mitchell, who had joined the Nixon law firm early in 1967. In the spring of 1968 Mitchell took charge of the campaign.

Friction soon developed between Mitchell and Sears. "You didn't have to be around Nixon more than five minutes," Sears said, "before you understood that one way you could always 'get' someone with Nixon was to tell him the fellow was too close to the press. I was pretty close to the press; we didn't have a press secretary then, we didn't even have Ziegler until June of 1968, and meanwhile you had all these guys hanging around looking for stories. I guess I always believed that newspapermen have to write stories. They can get a story either from you or your worst enemy. You're not helping yourself if you just stonewall them. Nixon would pick up a paper and see something he didn't like; Mitchell would attempt to blame it on me."

Despite the campaign rivalries, after Nixon's election Sears was invited to join the White House staff. Although he was attached to Ehrlichman's office as deputy counsel, his duties were really those of a political adviser. He worked on patronage, and liaison with the national party.

By May of 1969, however, Harry Dent, former South Carolina Republican chairman and a protégé of Senator Strom Thurmond's, had taken on a major political role within the White House. Sears felt his own job was not working out and he said he let it be known that he planned to leave, which he did in October.

Sears never found out precisely why he was tapped and placed under twenty-four-hour surveillance. It seems likely, however, that Nixon or Mitchell suspected that Sears was the unidentified White House official quoted by Brandon in a tapped conversation: "The President is weak. He has difficulty saying no. He wants to please all and he dislikes having to make a choice ... With a man like this, Henry Kissinger, of course, has great influence."

That seemed a deadly accurate assessment of the Nixon White House, and one can see why, for that very reason, if Nixon suspected Sears as the author, it would have driven him up the wall. Sears said he recalled no such conversation with Brandon, but did have dinner with him at the Hay-Adams Hotel in June 1969, during the period Brandon was being wiretapped.

One of the collateral mysteries in all of this is what happened to the documents from Guam. "I never got anything from Guam," Sears said. "If I'd ever gotten anything that said 'classified' on it, I would have had a heart attack. To my knowledge, I've never seen a document in my life that contained any secrets."

During the summer the FBI wiretap logs of Sears's conversations were sent to Mitchell and Ehrlichman, but the impeachment inquiry found that "none of the summaries reported on discussions of classified material." It must have been frustrating to Nixon that even with the wiretapping and the physical surveillance, he could not catch Sears leaking information. Despite this, according to Ehrlichman, Nixon ordered that Sears be banished from the White House.

Ehrlichman insisted, in a 1975 interview, that he did not know why Sears had been tapped, that he was not involved in the decision to place the tap. "The Sears thing had been going on for a while," he said. "I was given a copy of the surveillance log and was told the President wanted to discuss it with me. . . . The President wanted him fired." Apparently Nixon professed to Ehrlichman to be offended by Sears's personal life style; he expected his assistants to spend less time partying and socializing and more time at their desks. Much later, when the wiretaps became part of the impeachment evidence against the President, the members of the House Judiciary Committee were informed in closed session that the reports on "Mr. E," who was Sears, "deal entirely with the question of him having social engagements with a woman other than his wife, visiting female dancer establishments, some of his drinking habits, and his contacts with Republican Party officials."

There was astonishing irony in the fact that Richard Nixon, who lied to the American people for two years about his role in the Watergate cover-up, who could in the Oval Office discuss with his counsel a million-dollar payoff to buy the silence of a Watergate burglar, whose expletives were deleted, who was the first American President in history to resign his office, and who then required a criminal pardon, could summon up great clouds of moral outrage over the fact this his young assistant had visited a go-go bar.

In any event, Ehrlichman said the President began sending him memos: " 'Sears is still here. What are you doing about Sears? I want him out of here. Quickly.' I was sort of the buffer and I took a lot of heat. It went on and on. Finally Sears left."

And toward the end, the whole business was getting to be an expensive and bothersome administrative burden to Hoover—the twenty-four-hour surveillance, the three eight-hour shifts, all those FBI agents shuffling back and forth between Falls Church and the White House. "On September 15, 1969," it is noted in one of the impeachment documents, "Hoover told Mitchell that the surveillance of Mr. E. [Sears] required 10 men per day and 'consideration should be given to the discontinuation of these surveillances at this time.' " Two weeks later Sears left the White House, and the following day the wiretap on his home was removed.

On August 4, 1969, the day after Nixon returned from his global tour, Hoover wrote to Mitchell reporting that Haig had asked for another wiretap: "He requested that a telephone surveillance be placed on William Safire of the White House staff." Mitchell approved, and the memo bearing his signature, as in the case of the other wiretap documents, was classified "Top Secret, Group 1," which meant that it was excluded from automatic downgrading and declassification so that it might remain a state secret indefinitely.*

As a presidential speech writer, Safire did not have national security responsibilities—any more than John Sears did. But in wiretapping

---

* Under the executive order then in effect, material could be stamped "Top Secret" only if its unauthorized disclosure "could result in exceptionally grave damage to the Nation such as leading to a definite break in diplomatic relations affecting the defense of the United States, an armed attack against the United States or its allies, a war, or the compromise of military or defense plans, or intelligence operations, or scientific or technological developments vital to the national defense."

Henry Brandon, the FBI monitors had heard Safire talking to the *Sunday Times* correspondent. A memorandum by Thomas J. Smith, an FBI inspector in the Domestic Intelligence Division, sheds further light on the Safire tap. As sanitized in the impeachment documents, Safire in Smith's memo is F and Brandon is P: "...the rationale used by Colonel Haig was that the coverage on P revealed that P and F were friends and that F told P what would be in a speech by the President."

Safire, who became a Washington columnist for the *New York Times* early in 1973 when he left the White House, was an author and public relations man who had worked on five campaigns for Nixon. When Nixon was Vice President, Safire had maneuvered him and Soviet Premier Nikita Khrushchev into the kitchen of a model home at the American exhibition in Moscow, where their celebrated "kitchen debate" took place. At the time, Safire was publicizing the kitchen. In 1968 he left his own public relations firm to work for Nixon as a campaign speech writer and then moved with him into the White House.

In retrospect, Safire said he doubted the official explanation that he was tapped because he discussed a presidential speech with Brandon. "At the time," he said, "I was working on a speech, but it was the welfare reform speech that the President gave on August 8 and we were told to leak the hell out of it."* Safire said he could "vaguely recall talking about welfare reform with Brandon," but he said he could not remember promising to show him Nixon's speech, or the substance of their conversation. Safire said he believed he was wiretapped for a more general reason—"because I was talking to the press."

Later Kissinger told the Senate that he had not personally ordered the tap on Safire and was "astonished" when he learned about it four years later. General Haig in his testimony to the senators said he, too, did not know how Safire came to be tapped. "I do not have a recollection that I brought the name over there," Haig said.

But the FBI records clearly state that Haig requested the tap. "Al Haig," Safire said, "wouldn't go to the bathroom without first raising his hand and asking Henry Kissinger's permission. And Henry did not always give his permission. The suggestion that Haig asked for this wiretap without the knowledge of Henry Kissinger is patently ridiculous."

In July 1973 Safire, seeking satisfaction, telephoned his former colleagues at the Western White House, in San Clemente. Haig, Safire later wrote in his newspaper column, explained he had only been

---

* The FBI wiretap summaries substantiate the fact that the speech Safire was overheard discussing dealt only with domestic affairs; namely, welfare reform and revenue sharing.

carrying out "somebody's orders." Kissinger was audible in the background, Safire indicated, instructing Haig: "Tell him it wasn't me, make sure he knows it wasn't me."

When Haig appeared before the Senate Foreign Relations Committee in 1974, he confirmed that he and Kissinger were having breakfast when Safire telephoned asking about the wiretap, "and I think Henry denied knowing it." Safire said Kissinger not only denied knowledge of the tap, but suggested to him that perhaps Haig had not been involved in it either, despite the FBI documents.

Safire said he believed that the reason Kissinger and Haig had so much trouble remembering anything about his wiretap was that "of all the taps, the one that could get Henry in the greatest trouble, because it had no national security rationale, was the one on me." The tap on John Sears also had no national security basis, Safire noted, but that had been requested by Mitchell, not Kissinger.

According to FBI records, the tap on Safire's home was removed on September 15, after one month and eleven days. Oddly, however, wiretap reports on Safire were sent to Nixon in November, to Kissinger on January 15, 1970, and to Haldeman in May and June of 1970. Why these reports were sent to the White House eight months after the tap on Safire was supposedly removed has never been made clear.

Safire himself said he asked Kissinger why he had been "astonished" to learn of the tap in 1973 if he had received a report about it in January 1970. "At that point," Safire said, "he stopped talking to me directly and had his lawyer talk to me. The answer his attorney gave me was that he [Kissinger] thought the report he saw was part of a Brandon report."

When the tap was put on his home telephone in August 1969, Safire lived in Chevy Chase with his British wife, Helene, and their two young children. He sometimes talked to the President from his home; and if that happened while the tap was in place, it must have given Ernie Belter's men some excruciatingly nervous moments.

Apparently it did happen. In 1974 a joint report on wiretapping by three Senate subcommittees concluded: "The President himself was overheard talking on the telephone to one of the persons tapped." The basis of this conclusion was an exchange during a hearing on May 9, 1974 between Senator Edward Kennedy and William Ruckelshaus, then Acting Director of the FBI:

SENATOR KENNEDY: Do you know if the President was overheard on any of the 17 taps?
MR. RUCKELSHAUS: Yes, I think he was overheard once.
MR. KENNEDY: Could you tell us about that?
MR. RUCKELSHAUS: Well, it was simply a discussion he was having with one of his employees who had been tapped.

Ruckelshaus declined to identify the employee; he would not discuss the names of any of the seventeen persons tapped. But Kennedy pressed, and Ruckelshaus obliquely confirmed that the President had been overheard on a wiretap of William Safire.

On the afternoon of September 10, 1969, Mitchell telephoned DeLoach again, this time to say that the President wanted an immediate wiretap put on Marvin Kalb, the diplomatic correspondent of CBS. According to the memo that DeLoach sent Clyde Tolson, Mitchell said the tap should of course be "accompanied by the other business." DeLoach replied that if "by the other business" Mitchell meant that Nixon wanted a tail put on Kalb, "such a surveillance tied up six men on a 24-hour basis. The AG thought for a moment and then stated he thought the electronic surveillance would be sufficient at this time."[*] The logs, Mitchell added, should go only to himself and John Ehrlichman.[†] Mitchell signed the approval the same day, and the C&P obligingly wired the tap into Kalb's spacious home in Chevy Chase.

As it happened, Madeleine Kalb, a red-haired beauty who might have stepped out of a Botticelli painting, and Marge Sonnenfeldt were good friends and frequently talked to each other on the phone. So did their husbands. "For the most part we were talking about social occasions more than business," Kalb said. "Mrs. Kalb and Mrs. Sonnenfeldt did a great deal of car pooling together, so the government wasted a great deal of money on that one."

Moreover, when Kalb had served as CBS bureau chief in Moscow from 1960 to 1963, he assumed he was wiretapped and got in the habit of being very cautious. "In the Soviet Union I developed a journalistic practice never to discuss genuinely sensitive issues on the telephone," he said. "I didn't then, and I maintain that practice in Washington. If there is anything important that I would discuss with an official, it would be done in person."

Kalb's Moscow training must have disappointed Ernie Belter's squad, the President, and John Mitchell; the summary of the FBI's wiretaps on Kalb in the impeachment evidence reads as follows:

"Reports were sent to Attorney General Mitchell on October 9, 1969 and to the President on October 10, 1969 with respect to electronic surveillance of the residence of Mr. M [Kalb], a newsman. The summaries reported only personal family matters, news coverage of

---

[*] Hoover, it will be recalled, said the twenty-four-hour surveillance of John Sears took ten men. It is not clear why Kalb would have rated only six.

[†] Ehrlichman said in an interview that he never received the Kalb summaries, did not know why Mitchell would have asked that they be sent to him, and did not recall knowing at the time that Kalb was being wiretapped.

future events, and a discussion of criticism of the President by the media. None of the summaries reported on discussions of classified material."

Kalb's crisp reports and commentaries on international affairs had made him a familiar face to millions of Americans. He had a master's degree from Harvard, was fluent in Russian, and was the author of several books. For two years in the early fifties he held a high security clearance in Army intelligence. Before joining CBS in 1957, Kalb had worked for the State Department for a year, at the American embassy in Moscow.

In November 1969 Kalb was one of the network correspondents whose "instant analysis" of Nixon's November 3 speech on Vietnam triggered Vice President Spiro Agnew's diatribe against the networks ten days later. Nixon, in his speech, had announced that President Ho Chi Minh of North Vietnam had "flatly rejected" his peace proposals. In the hours just before the televised address, Kalb had read Nixon's exchange of letters with Ho, talked to half a dozen high Administration officials, and concluded that the contents of Ho's letter did not support Nixon's characterization of the letter as a total rejection. Kalb said so in his comments over the CBS television network immediately after the President's speech.

Kalb's analysis touched off a zany sequence of events in the White House. Jeb Stuart Magruder, the Nixon campaign official who went to jail for his role in the Watergate cover-up, writes in his book, *An American Life*, of a meeting held in the Oval Office two days after the Vietnam speech. Magruder says the President, exulting over public reaction to his speech, turned to his conservative speech writer Pat Buchanan to ask about the television reports; Buchanan replied they were all good except one, and named "a network correspondent" whom the White House considered to be anti-Administration. Magruder's account continues:

> Henry Kissinger broke in.
> "Well, Mr. President, that man is an agent of the Rumanian government."
> He explained that the correspondent was on a retainer to provide Washington reports to the Rumanian government, which is, of course, a Communist government.
> "That's right," the President said angrily. "That guy is a Communist."

According to Magruder, Nixon asked him to spread this word on the network correspondent, and when he did so, the correspondent heard about it and stormed into the office of Herbert Klein, Nixon's

Director of Communications, to denounce Magruder. Klein then supposedly apologized to the correspondent.

Magruder has declined to identify the network correspondent whom he said Kissinger had called an agent. Kalb said he had been led to believe by his own sources that "Magruder is talking about me." But Kalb added exasperatedly, "I never had anything to do with Rumanians. I never worked there, I've never been there, I never talked to them. I never in any way worked anywhere for Rumanians. No Rumanians!"

Kissinger privately assured Kalb that he had never made the statement attributed to him by Magruder. Herb Klein, a television executive in 1975, said he hazily remembers *Nixon*, not Kissinger, making some remark about Marvin Kalb, something about a reporter being on a Communist payroll. But Klein said he could not remember any reference to Rumania

Marvin Kalb said he never went to Klein's office to complain about any reports concerning Rumanians. And Klein said no correspondent ever came to his office to complain about the reports, as Magruder had claimed. But Stephen Hess, a former White House assistant to Nixon, said that early in the Administration he was visiting Herb Klein one day, and Klein told him that Marvin Kalb was "a Rumanian spy." Hess, a political scientist and author, also happened to be a good friend of Marvin Kalb's. He immediately passed this startling news on to Kalb. "Hey, Marvin," he said, "Herb Klein says you're a Rumanian spy."*

The alleged Rumanian spy is presumably still at large on the television networks, broadcasting the nightly news and periodically slipping over to the dimly lit cafés of Bucharest to plot new Balkan intrigues. At any rate, he has never been caught, and none of the officials involved in the incident can agree on who said what to whom.

The entire incident would be hilarious but for the fact that the conspiratorial mindset and the paranoia that ran rampant in the Nixon White House ultimately led to political and national tragedy. Inexplicably, the tap on Kalb was removed on November 4, the day after the instant analysis that had brought him so much White House attention.

"When I learned I had been tapped, and that my wife had been tapped," Kalb said, "we were both shocked in a very profound way. We talked deep into the night many, many times about how could

---

* John Ehrlichman, when asked by the author if he had ever heard any such reference to Kalb around the Nixon White House, laughed and said he had not. "I've had some experience with Rumanian spies," he said, "and they don't amount to much. They put a couple of ham-handed ones on me when I was in Bucharest to prepare the President's trip there. They followed me everywhere, real Keystone Cops."

they do this; we reviewed our calendar, we went through all of the people we had talked to, had dinner with, who had been to our home. I went through all of my broadcasts; had I done anything different from what I had done before, could anything that I said on the air, in the most convoluted way, be interpreted as a violation of America's interests? And the answer was in every case no.

"We were personally, and as Americans, deeply offended that a President could resort to that kind of activity without a real justification. I would like to believe that if a President of the United States intrudes into your privacy, running against every tradition in this country, he has a very good reason for doing so. But in all of my research I came upon no reason. It just could very well be that I was one of those people that Nixon just didn't like."

About the time that Horace Hampton's men were wiring Marvin Kalb's home telephone in Chevy Chase into the Old Post Office Building, an interesting pattern was developing within the Nixon Administration's subterranean world of wiretaps. In some instances the White House was keeping the taps on even after the tapped officials had left the government. The ostensible justification was that officials who had dealt with secrets still carried the information in their heads, and so bore watching. But in two of these cases, former Kissinger aides whose home telephones remained tapped went to work for Senator Edmund Muskie, the Maine Democrat who was then emerging as a potential major rival to Nixon in the 1972 presidential campaign. Thus, the Nixon White House gained valuable partisan political intelligence from wiretaps supposedly required to protect the national security.

In late September, Halperin left Kissinger's staff. He remained a consultant until May 1970, but he had no access to classified information and actually worked as a consultant for only one day. Not long after Halperin left Kissinger's staff, he became associated with the group of foreign policy advisers forming around Muskie.

Late in December, Hoover wrote to Nixon to report that something interesting had been overheard on the tap of Halperin's home telephone. The FBI Director knew a juicy political tidbit when he heard one; he informed Nixon that Halperin had recently had a conversation with someone, not identified, who told him of receiving a telephone call from Clark Clifford. "Clifford," Hoover deadpanned, "is probably identical with the former Secretary of Defense." (Hoover's literary style somehow suggests either that Clark Clifford was an alias or that he was wanted for some sort of dubious activity, interstate transportation of stolen vehicles, perhaps, or safecracking.) The FBI chief said it was apparent from the conversation with Halperin that Clifford was "sharpening up his attack on Nixon" and worse yet, preparing an article for *Life* magazine that would use potentially embarrassing statements Nixon had made on Vietnam. The statements, Hoover wrote, included Nixon comments "to the effect that President Thieu is one of the five greatest men of our time," and that "Vietnam is one of the finest hours in United States history." Halperin's unidentified caller had also dropped a clue to his identity; he mentioned that on December 29 he was supposed to attend a meeting on Vietnam with "Henry."

Hoover's letter caused a great flurry of memo-writing in the White House; Alexander P. Butterfield, a deputy assistant to Nixon (who later revealed the existence of the White House taping system), suggested that Magruder go to Haig to try to figure out who the person was who had met with Kissinger on Vietnam on December 29. He also urged that the embarrassing Nixon statements that Clifford had unearthed also be located by the White House so they could be put in the best possible light.* "The name of the game, of course, is to get ourselves springloaded to a position from which we can effectively counter whatever tack Clifford takes . . . Al Haig can get you squared away on at least a preliminary scheme."

Ehrlichman was particularly pleased with the political benefits of the "national security" tap on Mort Halperin. In a handwritten note to Haldeman he said: "This is the kind of early warning we need more of. Your game planners are now in an excellent position to map anticipatory action." Haldeman passed the memo along to Magruder with a covering note: "I agree with John's point. Let's get going."

On April 30, 1970, Nixon launched his Cambodia gamble, sending thousands of U.S. troops across the border into the "Fishhook." The invasion triggered massive campus demonstrations across America, and led to the tragedy at Kent State, where four students were shot and killed by national guardsmen. Within the White House, several of the younger members of Kissinger's staff were sick at heart over what the President had informed the nation, with characteristic duplicity, was "not an invasion of Cambodia."

The reaction, within and without the White House, touched off the last paroxysm of wiretapping—as though the Nixon men thought that by splicing into enough telephone wires and ringing the White House with enough buses, to act as barriers against antiwar demonstrators, they could somehow insulate themselves against the rising tide of public anger. In rapid succession, six wiretaps were placed in the thirteen days after Cambodia. JUNE was busting out all over.

---

* Two Nixon statements closely paralleling those overheard by Hoover's agents on the Halperin tap were duly tracked down by James Keogh, Nixon's chief speech editor, and incorporated by him in a memorandum.

It began on the night of May 2, when the White House learned that Bill Beecher would publish a story in the *Times* the next day revealing that American planes had carried out a heavy bombing attack on North Vietnam for the first time since President Johnson stopped the bombing in November 1968. Haig got in touch with Robert H. Haynes, the FBI agent who was the Bureau's liaison with the White House. Haynes knew of the wiretapping, of course, since he was the one who had been hand-delivering the logs to the White House for the President and Kissinger. According to an FBI memo, Haig said the President had called him about the Beecher leak, which, Haig said, had been "nailed down to a couple of people." But perhaps it had not been nailed down, because Haig requested that the tap on Pursley be reimposed, and that taps be placed on Beecher and two State Department officials, Richard F. Pedersen and Ambassador William H. Sullivan. For the first time, Haig asked that the taps be put on the office as well as the home of each man.

It is one of the anomalies of the entire Kissinger wiretap story that Beecher, whose article in May 1969 on the secret bombing of Cambodia had seemingly begun the tapping, was not himself wiretapped until a year later. The fact that Beecher was not tapped immediately suggests that the first three persons selected were tapped primarily for their personal political views, and not because they may also have been suspected of leaking to Bill Beecher.°

Now, if the tap approved by Mitchell was in fact wired into the Washington bureau of the *New York Times*, or even to Beecher's telephone in the Pentagon press room—and it is reasonable to assume that one or more of Beecher's office telephones was tapped as ordered—it meant that the President was in a position to eavesdrop on at least some of the operations of the most influential newspaper in the world, and significantly, one that opposed his policies in Southeast Asia. If Beecher's office telephone was tapped, then Richard Nixon had in effect, despite the First Amendment to the Constitution, wiretapped the *New York Times*. (He had, of course, already wiretapped the home telephones of correspondents for the *Times*, CBS, and the *Sunday Times* of London.)

Beecher, a native of Massachusetts and a Harvard graduate, had joined the *Times*' Washington bureau in 1966. Such are the interconnections in the worlds of journalism and government in Washington

---

° A further incongruity is that Beecher, whose name formed a continuing thread running through the Kissinger wiretaps, was appointed by Nixon in 1973 to be Deputy Assistant Secretary of Defense for Public Affairs. He was recruited by then Secretary of Defense Elliot L. Richardson, who had not met Beecher but admired his work in the *New York Times*, including, presumably, the same news stories that had so disturbed the White House.

that as it happened, Beecher, his wife, Eileen, and their four small daughters lived near the Halperins, in Bethesda. The two families were friendly, and about once a month the Halperins and the Beechers would drive together to see a play at the Arena Stage, which overlooks the Potomac in Washington, and during intermission they would stroll together on the grass across from the theater. They could have said anything to each other, without much chance of being overheard, and in retrospect, to Halperin, it made the taps seem even more preposterous.

The next wiretap, on the State Department's Richard Pedersen, bore a close parallel to that on Pursley (which was renewed), in that Pedersen, the counselor of the Department (and later ambassador to Hungary) was the right-hand man of Secretary of State William Rogers—just as Pursley served Laird. William H. Sullivan, the fourth name on Haig's list, had been U.S. ambassador to Laos, and at the time he was wiretapped he was Deputy Assistant Secretary of State for Asian affairs. During the early sixties Sullivan had caught the eye of Averell Harriman, and owed much of his rapid advancement within the foreign service to Harriman's patronage.

The day before the President announced that he was sending combat troops into Cambodia, two young members of Kissinger's staff, Anthony Lake and Roger Morris, had resigned in protest. Both were extremely bright and highly articulate, and later on, both became vocal and public critics of American policy in Indochina. But now they quietly handed in a "Dear Henry" letter of resignation marked "Eyes Only."*

Tony Lake, one of the bright young lights of the foreign service in the mid-sixties, grew up in New Canaan, Connecticut, and went to all the right Eastern schools—Middlesex, Harvard, then off to England on a year's fellowship at Cambridge, then to Princeton's Woodrow Wilson School for a Ph.D. In another, Achesonian era, Lake would have prospered in the foreign service, slowly graying at the temples as he patiently served out his time in various remote outposts, making it to career ambassador in his early fifties. He had in fact started on that traditional path. Lake and his attractive wife, Antonia, went to Vietnam in 1963; he worked as staff assistant to Ambassador Henry Cabot Lodge in Saigon, and then he became vice counsel in Hué. But

---

* The letter said in part: "As you know, we have grave reservations about the value of using U.S. troops in Cambodia. We believe the costs and consequences of such an action far exceed any gains one can reasonably expect. But the reasons for our resignations, involving an increasing alienation from this Administration also pre-date and go beyond the Cambodian problem. We wished to inform you now, before public reaction to our Cambodian policy, so that it will be clear that our decision was not made after the fact and as a result of those consequences."

disenchantment with U.S. policy in Vietnam began to set in after he returned to the State Department and it had intensified by 1969, when Lake was working for Kissinger inside the White House and Antonia was demonstrating outside the gates.

About a week before the Cambodian invasion, Kissinger called in several aides, including Lake, Morris, Winston Lord, William Watts (who was also to quit over Cambodia), and Laurence E. Lynn, Jr. "He called in Larry as his defense systems analyst," Lake said, "and Winston, Roger, Bill, and I as his doves. Kissinger outlined the possibility of an invasion of Cambodia by South Vietnamese troops, with American forward air controllers, and asked what we thought of that. I picked up an argument I had been having with Kissinger for a year about Vietnam. I argued that it was simply extending the war once you got bogged down in Cambodia, that when the South Vietnamese troops got into trouble, the American troops would have to go in also. It was a moment of personal difficulty for me. At the end Kissinger said, 'Well, Tony, I knew what you were going to say.' And I remember thinking that, well, I am out of the effectiveness trap; if I am predictable, then there is no point in my staying on, and I decided to resign then if they did it."

On May 12, two weeks after Lake handed in his resignation, Al Haig contacted the FBI. A letter from Hoover to Mitchell the next day said Haig advised "that Dr. Henry A. Kissinger of the White House staff" had requested taps on the home telephones of Tony Lake and Win Lord, a former foreign service officer who had worked on the Pentagon's foreign policy staff before joining Kissinger at the White House. Only four months earlier, Kissinger had made Lord his special assistant.

Lake was still on the staff; he stayed for about a month after turning in his formal resignation, but the tap on the Lakes' Lowell Street home in Washington remained in place for nine months, until February 1971, by which time Lake was already working on the campaign staff of Senator Muskie.° Now the Nixon White House was

° The Nixon Administration twice spied on Tony Lake during the period he worked for Muskie. "One of my loyal assistants," Lake said, "as it turned out, was hired by Howard Hunt." The aide was Thomas Gregory, a college student whom Hunt recruited to infiltrate Muskie headquarters under the code name Ruby II. "He appeared to be a very innocuous guy from Brigham Young and said he was in foreign policy and wanted to volunteer," Lake said. "He didn't really have enough experience to do research but you treat volunteers nicely, so I put him to work reorganizing my files. I can remember now walking into the outer office and there would be Tom with all my files spread around." Unknown to Lake, Gregory was meeting once a week with Hunt at a drugstore at 17th and K streets in downtown Washington, and turning over typed reports of what was happening in Muskie's headquarters.

secretly listening in on the conversations of both Halperin and Lake, at a time when they were advising Muskie.

Lake and his wife were outraged when they learned in the spring of 1973 that they had been wiretapped, but Lake, who personally liked Haig, telephoned him and obtained an appointment. Lake spent ten minutes in his office—Haig was by now a four-star general and Nixon's chief of staff—but Haig expressed no regrets over the tapping of his former colleague.

Lake also telephoned Kissinger to express his feelings, but from neither man did he get what he wanted. "I was hoping," Lake said in his terse way, "that someone would say that it was wrong." No one would tell Tony Lake that it was wrong.

The tap on Winston Lord also remained on for nine months, with one ludicrous result. Lord's wife, the former Betty Bao, was Chinese and a gourmet cook. She was in the habit of telephoning her mother each morning to discuss complex recipes in Chinese. Ernie Belter's monitors were baffled; they recorded the conversations and had them translated. According to William Safire, the logs were even turned over to cryptographic experts to see if a code was hidden among the bean sprouts. "All the computer ever ground out," Safire has reported, "was Moo Goo Gai Pan."

On May 13, 1970, the same day that Lake and Lord were wiretapped, Nixon met with Hoover at the White House, and apparently Nixon expressed concern that there might be leaks about the wiretaps; from now on the logs were to go only to Haldeman. Haldeman told Bob Haynes to hand the logs to him personally from then on, or to his assistant, Larry Higby, in his absence. And Haldeman said he would take care of advising Kissinger about the change. A DeLoach memo following up this decision said Hoover had ordered that henceforth any requests by Kissinger or Haig for wiretaps or "super secret technical surveillance" must first be cleared with Haldeman.*

Something like a state of siege pervaded the atmosphere in the White House in early May; even much later to hear the President's men discussing the antiwar protesters who gathered in Washington that May is to understand that the buses pulled up in a circle around the White House were more than symbolic; the men inside the gates, or some of them, feared not only for the safety of the Republic and its President, but for their own skin. During the demonstration on the Ellipse on May 9, there were troops in the basement of the White House.

Only a siege mentality could explain what went on during this

---

* It was the only evidence that the Nixon Administration may have used secret and highly sophisticated eavesdropping or surveillance equipment against White House staff members and newsmen.

period. As one of the nation's most distinguished diplomats and elder statesmen, Averell Harriman hardly qualified as a subversive character; but when the FBI learned from the tap on Ambassador Sullivan's telephone that there was to be a meeting at Harriman's home of persons opposed to the Administration's policy in Cambodia, the Bureau responded in classic secret-police fashion: it placed Harriman's Georgetown home, at 3038 N Street, under surveillance. (N Street was a busy place; had it been some months earlier, the FBI agents might have tripped over Caulfield and Ragan reconnoitering the home of Joseph Kraft, who, it will be recalled, lived across the street.)

The report Haldeman received about the meeting at Harriman's house identified several of those who attended; he talked with J. Edgar Hoover and later received a second report. The surveillance of Harriman's home was also noted by the FBI's William Sullivan in a memo of May 18, to which Hoover responded by scribbling a note that said: "An excellent job. I talked to Haldeman at Key Biscayne."

Later the Senate Foreign Relations Committee asked Bernard Wells, who had been Sullivan's assistant in the FBI and handled the paperwork for the wiretaps, about the surveillance of the meeting at Harriman's house. Wells said yes, he had actually written the report signed by Sullivan. "They wanted to identify the people who came," Wells testified.

"Just see who came and went?" Senator Fulbright asked.

"Yes, sir," Wells replied. Were the names of those who attended the meeting in the report? "Yes, sir, the ones we identified."

Haldeman, emerging in 1970 as a more active participant in the wiretapping, telephoned Hoover in mid-October to ask that the tap on Sonnenfeldt, which had been discontinued after six weeks in 1969, be reinstated. In a memo of October 15 Hoover wrote: "Mr. Haldeman said they have some concern on B [Sonnenfeldt] they may have a bad apple and have to get him out of the basket. . . . I told him I would take care of it right away." So back went the tap on Sonnenfeldt's home on Thornapple Street in Chevy Chase.

In mid-December, the Christmas spirit notwithstanding, Haldeman again contacted the FBI, according to Hoover's files, and this time asked that a tap be put on the home telephone of James W. McLane, the third White House official tapped whose responsibilities were entirely in the domestic arena.

A tall Ivy Leaguer (Yale, Harvard Business School), Jamie McLane had the appearance of one of those classic East Coast patricians, of whom not too many had been admitted to the inner precincts of the Nixon White House. He came to Washington in 1969 and soon became executive assistant to Robert H. Finch, the Secretary of Health, Education and Welfare. McLane had married the daughter of Francis

W. Sargent, the Republican governor of Massachusetts, and in mid-1970 he left Finch to direct his father-in-law's successful re-election campaign. By December, when McLane was wiretapped, he had returned to Washington to join the staff of John Ehrlichman's Domestic Council, where he worked on programs for youth, old age, and revenue sharing.

McLane does not know why he was selected to be wiretapped. His first reaction when he learned about it was that someone in the White House had made a mistake. "I thought they had me mixed up with somebody else," he said. "I thought it was a case of mistaken identity." But, in retrospect, McLane leaned toward the conclusion that "my Finch-Sargent ties might have done it. They were both considered to be a little more 'liberal' Republican than the Administration."

It was to be the last of the seventeen wiretaps. On February 10, 1971, Hoover abruptly sent a handwritten note to Clyde Tolson and a memo listing the nine taps then in place.° "Inquire of Col. Haig," Hoover wrote, "if any may be taken off." Hoover had finally had enough. Haig, who was still Kissinger's deputy, quickly got the message; he agreed, and the same day all the taps were removed.

The reason for the sudden end became clear two years later, when the Senate Foreign Relations Committee investigated the fitness of Henry Kissinger to serve as Secretary of State. The committee delicately appointed a subcommittee of two senators to review the FBI report on the wiretapping; the subcommittee, consisting of John Sparkman of Alabama and Clifford P. Case of New Jersey, inquired of William Ruckelshaus, the acting head of the FBI, how it came to pass that the taps were all dismantled on February 10, 1971. The report of the two senators explained: "Mr. Ruckelshaus stated that this date was significant only because it had been the practice of Mr. Hoover to discontinue wiretaps just prior to his Congressional appearances so that he could report minimum taps in effect if he were questioned. The first appearance of Mr. Hoover after February 10, 1971 was on March 17, 1971 before a House Subcommittee on Appropriations for the FBI."

In 1975 James Barnhardt, one of the FBI wiretap monitors, was being questioned by Mort Halperin's lawyers in the presence of a Justice Department attorney, and he, too, was asked about the removal of the tap on Halperin on February 10, after more than twenty months. The transcript reads as follows:

° At the time, the FBI was still tapping Halperin—after one year, eight months and twenty-eight days, his was the longest—as well as Brandon, Beecher, Pedersen, Sullivan, Pursley, Lord, Lake, and Sonnenfeldt.

Q. Do you recall these taps being removed, the tap on Dr. Hal perin being removed?

A. No, it was on my weekend. I came back and everything was gone. . . . It was just the first I knew about it. I came in and there was nothing there.

Q. Like losing an old friend?

(General laughter.)

So it was over in February 1971, but in a sense it had just begun, because the ugly secret of the wiretapping was there, just below the surface, like a dark and dangerous reef that might be exposed at any moment by the receding tide. The President knew it, Kissinger knew it, Haig knew it, and J. Edgar Hoover knew it. So did several others in the White House and the FBI. After Watergate the tide went out rapidly for Nixon, and the reef, at least its jagged tip, was exposed. In time, the seventeen wiretaps were incorporated into the impeachment articles that forced Nixon from the White House. (Ironically, on February 14, 1971, four days after the last of the seventeen taps was finally removed, Nixon installed the secret taping system in the Oval Office. Having ceased the tapping of his subordinates, he tapped himself.)

And it was all so futile; the seventeen wiretaps were so unnecessary, so ultimately worthless. But their political cost was enormous. In February 1973, the Wategate cover-up was in full swing. How to keep wiretaps hidden was the subject of a considerable portion of the President's conversation on the morning of February 28 with his counsel, John Dean. Nixon was clearly frightened that the secret of the wiretapping was about to surface. At the same time he was rueful, not over what had been done, but that it had been of so little value.

"Lake and Halperin," he said. "They're both bad. But the taps were too. They never helped us. Just gobs and gobs of material; gossip and bull shitting [unintelligible]."

*"Henry [unintelligible] . . . I know that he asked that it
be done, and I assumed that it was."*

—Richard Nixon, discussing wiretaps
with John Dean, February 28, 1973

3
Henry:
"I Find Wiretapping Distasteful"

The Situation Room in the White House basement is early Dr. Strange-
love in style, a euphemistically named communications center where
the President and his highest aides attempt to cope with the most
dangerous and volatile military crises.

During the period when Dr. Henry Kissinger was receiving wiretap reports on the private conversations of his assistants and of newsmen, there was one little safe in the Situation Room that was wired
to an alarm and stood apart from the others. A duty officer was
stationed constantly next to this special safe, for it contained the
nation's most highly classified nuclear codes.* Only Kissinger and
Alexander Haig had the combination.

Roger Morris, who in 1970 resigned from Kissinger's staff with
Anthony Lake over the Cambodian invasion, remembered that once
Lake had pointed out the little safe in the Situation Room and
wondered aloud, in a semi-joking way, whether it contained wiretap
logs of their conversations.

* The precise nature of these materials was and is classified but it is reasonable
to assume that they included the coded orders by which the President could authorize a nuclear attack. Wherever the President goes, a warrant officer is always
nearby, carrying one set of these orders in a locked briefcase known as "the football," or "black box." These orders constitute the "nuclear button."

It did.

Along with the classified nuclear documents, in what was certainly the most protected safe in the government this side of Fort Knox, Henry Kissinger kept some of the summaries of the wiretapped conversations of his assistants. When special agent Robert Haynes delivered the summaries of the FBI logs, Haig would read them, put them in a red folder, and place it in Kissinger's in-basket.° At least some of the FBI reports ended up in the nuclear safe.

It was an entirely fitting storage point, for Kissinger knew how explosive the wiretaps could be, and how dangerous to his own reputation, if they became known. The initial burglary and bugging of the Democratic National Committee offices in the Watergate on May 28, 1972, and the capture of the burglars during their re-entry on June 17, triggered a chain reaction that ultimately exposed a whole interlocking net of secret activities by the Nixon White House—break-ins, political investigations, misuse of the CIA, the FBI, and other federal investigative agencies, enemies lists and illegal campaign contributions, payoffs and cover-ups, high crimes and low crimes, misdemeanors and felonies, and abuse of power too extensive to be catalogued in any one volume. The fact that the CIA had engaged in illegal surveillance of domestic dissidents, wiretaps, and break-ins, and had opened mail in violation of the law, details of FBI break-ins and the Bureau's disruptive activities in the name of "counterintelligence"—all these came to light as the press and congressional committees, aided in some cases by disillusioned members of the federal bureaucracy, continued to probe in the aftermath of Watergate.

There seemed to be no end to the chain reaction, but back in the fall of 1972 and the early months of 1973, the Nixon White House was desperately attempting to contain it, to jam safety rods into the unstable nuclear core. The chain reaction reached out toward Kissinger, and began to contaminate him—although no one knew it yet—on February 26, 1973, when *Time* magazine accurately reported that the FBI had wiretapped reporters and White House officials. Three or four days earlier, the news weekly had queried the White House press office for comment, and the press office turned to John Dean for guidance. Dean contacted the FBI, and then Mitchell, who said he was denying the story. Dean said he then called Ehrlichman, who instructed him to have Ziegler "flatly deny it—period."†

The President met with Dean two days later to discuss the trouble-

° The red folder indicated special sensitivity. This was designed to distinguish it from other, less important material awaiting Kissinger's attention.

† When the *Time* story was published it quoted Mitchell calling the wiretapping report "a pipe dream," and a White House spokesman saying, "No one at the White House asked for or ordered any such taps."

some *Time* story, which, Dean assured him, "we are stonewalling totally." ("Oh, absolutely," Nixon agreed.) They spent a good deal of time speculating on how the leak had occurred (which is ironic, since the wiretapping had ostensibly been ordered to stop leaks). Dean suspected that William Sullivan, since he had managed the wiretapping for the FBI, might have been the source, but that was very delicate because both Nixon and Dean were hoping that Sullivan might provide them with juicy details of political misuse of the FBI by Lyndon Johnson or John F. Kennedy, which could be used to distract public attention from Watergate, to bolster the "they all do it" argument. So Sullivan was being played like a particularly large but slippery rainbow trout who might be causing great trouble, but who would be a sensational catch if only he could be gotten into the creel.*

But the brazen lie to the press and public, in which the President personally concurred, the flat denial that the wiretapping had taken place, would not work. Too many people knew, and the chain reaction continued.

On March 1 L. Patrick Gray III, the Acting FBI Director—who later admitted he had destroyed Watergate evidence on White House orders—was twisting slowly in the wind before the Senate Judiciary Committee, which was holding hearings on his nomination to be FBI Director. Gray testified that he "checked the records and indexes of the FBI" and could find no record of the wiretapping of newsmen and White House officials. Of course he couldn't; Ernie Belter had been told to keep no normal records, no copies of the logs, and no index cards.

But the bureaucracy was churning within the FBI. Four days earlier E. S. Miller, an assistant director of the FBI, had sent a memo to W. Mark Felt, a high official of the Bureau, briefly summarizing the wiretap program. Miller attached an even more detailed description that he had prepared in October 1971, which concluded, with admirable foresight: "It goes without saying that knowledge of this coverage represents a potential source of tremendous embarrassment to the Bureau and political disaster for the Nixon administration. Copies of the material itself could be used for political blackmail and the ruination of Nixon, Mitchell, and others of this administration." The details of the story could not hold much longer, and early

---

* Sullivan protested his innocence of the leak and offered a complicated alternative; according to Dean, Sullivan postulated that it had come from Hoover, who had told Patrick Coyne, the executive secretary of the President's Foreign Intelligence Advisory Board, who had told Nelson Rockefeller, a member of the board, who had told Kissinger, who had presumably told *Time.* Nixon was intrigued with this labyrinthine explanation and, the White House transcripts indicate, accepted it as true, although Dean offered no evidence to support it.

in May the Washington *Post* and the *New York Times* began publishing more bits and pieces. On May 4 William Ruckelshaus, who had by now replaced the discredited Gray as Acting FBI Director, launched his own investigation of the taps. Who was tapped, for how long, and where were the logs and summaries? It was by no means certain they still existed, for there were two handwritten notes by Hoover in the FBI files indicating that according to Mitchell, the wiretap records had been destroyed. The story Ruckelshaus pieced together, as it emerged from his inquiries and other testimony and evidence, was as serpentine as any aspect of the Watergate scandal. What had happened was this:

In July 1971, when the infighting between William Sullivan and Hoover was nearing its climax, Sullivan approached Assistant Attorney General Robert Mardian in a bold gamble for the President's favor. He informed Mardian that he had FBI wiretap records in his possession.° He wanted to turn them over to the President because Hoover could not be trusted with them. As Mardian recalled this conversation when interviewed by FBI agents at his home in Phoenix, Arizona, Sullivan had said "that Mr. Hoover had used wiretap information to blackmail other Presidents of the United States and was afraid that he could blackmail Mr. Nixon with this information."†

Things were getting sticky. Mardian flew to San Clemente on an Air Force courier jet and met with Nixon on July 12. Nixon instructed Mardian to get the logs from Sullivan and deliver them safely to the White House. Mardian immediately flew back to Washington and contacted Sullivan. What happened next in this frantic cross-country scenario is best told in the dry language of the FBI report of the Mardian interview:

"Mr. Mardian said shortly thereafter Mr. Charles Brennan, Assistant director of the FBI, appeared in his office with an old beat up satchel, as best he could recall olive drab in color, measuring approximately 8 inches by 12 inches by 17 inches. He said he also specifically remembered that this satchel had William C. Sullivan's initials on it. He said he cannot specifically recall a middle initial but he is sure that W.S. was on the satchel."‡

° Sullivan had the original wiretap reports because the FBI had periodically received them back from Haig and had then recovered most of the remainder from the White House after the last of the taps was removed in February 1971.

† In later testimony to the Senate Watergate committee, Mardian was more precise about the nature of the alleged blackmail that Sullivan feared; he said Sullivan indicated "that Mr. Hoover might use these tapes for the purpose of preserving his position as Director of the FBI."

‡ It sounds very much as though the wiretap logs were being transported around Washington in something one might expect to find in a 25-cent locker at the bus depot. Brennan, however, had a recollection of somewhat more elegant luggage.

Mardian knew a hot satchel when he saw one, and he stuck it in his closet at the Department of Justice until two days later, the FBI report said, when "he got a call from the White House to bring it over and to deliver it to Dr. Kissinger and General Haig. Mr. Mardian said he responded to the White House request right away.* He said when he went into the White House he went directly to Dr. Kissinger's office. Dr. Kissinger and General Haig were present."

Mardian said he was sure Kissinger was there, because when he walked in, Kissinger said something like "Do you have what I said on the phone?," implying to Mardian that the wiretap material included Kissinger's own conversations. Mardian did not think that was funny, so he remembered it. With Kissinger and Haig watching, Mardian opened the satchel, which was "crammed full" of wiretaps.

The satchel also contained a chronological list, or index, of the summaries that had previously been sent to Kissinger, and Mardian told the FBI "that he and Dr. Kissinger checked by date and satisfied themselves that Dr. Kissinger's material matched with the cover sheet which Mr. Mardian was using."†

Satisfied that everything was in apple-pie order, Mardian said he left the satchel briefly with Haldeman, who also went over the list. "After Mr. Haldeman completed his check, Mr. Mardian said he retrieved the bag with all its contents and walked into the Oval Room of the White House and left the bag. He was specifically asked to whom he gave the bag. He said he preferred not to answer because of the President's order concerning employees talking about national

---

He said the wiretaps were carried in a "briefcase" that was made of "black cowhide and had straps on it."
* Mardian was relieved to get rid of the wiretap reports, according to Ehrlichman, who has testified to an extraordinary meeting with him that summer: "He [Mardian] asked me to come to his house, he lived five or six miles from my house in Virginia. So, after church, I drove to his house, parked my family in the driveway in the car, and I went into Mardian's house, and we went downstairs into his den." Mardian explained that he was worried about the wiretap files in his office at the Justice Department. "He told me that he was very afraid of not only the integrity of these files, but also of his own personal safety, that he felt he was being surveilled by Hoover through his agents, and it was only a matter of time before Hoover caused agents of the FBI to break into his files and recover the various records of this activity which Sullivan had turned over to him."
† The record is confused, but apparently the purpose of this meeting, which Haig characterized as "quick and dirty," was to make sure that Kissinger did not still retain any of the wiretap reports in his files. At this point the White House was anxious to scoop up all originals or copies of any wiretaps. Apparently, when Mardian's master list was checked over, it was determined that Kissinger had returned his copies to the FBI, except for those that had been squirreled away in the special safe in the Situation Room.

security information. Mr. Mardian was specifically asked 'Did you give the bag to Mr. Nixon, the President of the United States?'

"He sat back in his chair, shrugged his shoulders, hesitated, and said, 'I cannot answer that question.' "

So the question was not answered, but John Ehrlichman later testified that ultimately, he received the logs. "The President asked me to take custody of them, which I did." Ehrlichman said he recalled "sampling" the material, leafing through the reports at random, before placing them in a two-drawer combination file in his office. There they remained until April 30, 1973, when Ehrlichman resigned and the wiretap records were moved once again, to the Executive Office Building.

While Ruckelshaus' FBI agents were trying to follow the circuitous trail of the satchel in May of 1973, the trial of Daniel Ellsberg was in progress in Los Angeles, forming an insistent obbligato to the search for the wiretaps. The *New York Times* had begun publishing the Pentagon Papers in June 1971. Ellsberg, who had leaked the classified history of the Vietnam war to the *Times*, was indicted two weeks after publication of the papers began. In preparation for the trial, the Justice Department asked the FBI to review its files to see if Ellsberg had been overheard on any government wiretaps; in due course the FBI reported he had not, and this assurance was given to the court.

Now with Ruckelshaus turning the FBI upside down to find the missing wiretap logs, George Ross, the clerk whom Ernie Belter had assigned to listen to Mort and Ina Halperin's telephone, remembered that Ellsberg had been overheard on Halperin's telephone. In fact, Ross now volunteered, Ellsberg had stayed with Halperin over the weekend and had called someone—Ross did not know whom—"to set up a pot-smoking party."

Ruckelshaus immediately notified the Justice Department that Ellsberg had been overheard, after all, and he recommended that the court be informed without delay.° The next day, May 10, the Justice

---

° As it turned out, Ellsberg had been overheard not once but fifteen times on Halperin's telephone. And it was entirely possible that Kissinger knew and remembered that Ellsberg had been overheard; he was informed of that fact in a letter from Hoover dated September 3, 1969. "Daniel Ellsberg, not further identified, was a recent house guest of Morton H. Halperin," Hoover's letter said. "Ellsberg, during a contact with one Harry, not further identified, but who may be his brother, discussed sitting up with Harry while Harry went on a 'trip.' From their conversation, it was obvious that they were discussing the use of drugs. Ellsberg recommended that Harry not take the 'trip' at the same time his wife takes one. Ellsberg subsequently mentioned to another individual that he had left a satchel filled with 'stuff' at his friend's house and during a contact with Pat Marks [*sic*]

Department disclosed the tap to Judge William Matthew Byrne, Jr., who was presiding over the Ellsberg trial. Both the government's position and Byrne's had already been compromised a week earlier when it was disclosed that the President had offered Byrne the job of FBI Director and that Byrne had twice discussed this with Ehrlichman while the Ellsberg trial was in progress.

On the same day that Byrne was told that Ellsberg had been overheard, the FBI agents learned from Mardian in Phoenix that the wiretap logs had been delivered in a satchel to the White House and had perhaps not been destroyed after all. At 6 P.M. on Friday, May 11, Ehrlichman was interviewed in Washington, and confirmed he had received the wiretap reports and stored them in the White House. The discovery came too late to affect the government's case in California; an hour earlier Judge Byrne—who had by now been informed not only of the wiretap but of the burglary of Ellsberg's psychiatrist by agents of the White House—dismissed the case because of the government's improper conduct.

The next morning Ruckelshaus, accompanied by FBI inspector Thomas J. Smith, went to Room 128 of the Executive Office Building across the street from the White House. Presidential attorney J. Fred Buzhardt escorted them into a vault and turned over two sealed boxes. Buzhardt insisted on a receipt—bureaucracy is wonderful and it was three and a half hours before an inventory could be completed and the wiretaps returned, by car, to the FBI. Even so, there was resistance to the removal of official records from the White House. "When we took the papers out," Ruckelshaus later recalled, "it was the most difficult thing I've ever had to do. We almost had an arm wrestle with the Secret Service."

About the same time that morning Kissinger was holding a press conference at the White House, in the course of which a reporter asked about the tap on Halperin: "Were you aware at the time it was taking place that the home of one of your staff members was being wiretapped and did you get any information from those wiretaps?"

So there it was. Kissinger launched nervously into a long, double-talking explanation of which a few excerpts will suffice to give the flavor: "The agencies concerned with intelligence in our government, that is to say, the Central Intelligence Agency and the Federal Bureau of Investigation, submit reports through my office when they concern national security. In the overwhelming majority of cases, these reports are always at the direction of the director of the agency or the head

---

of Scarsdale, New York, she told him that the 'stuff' Harry had was all right although it was disorienting."

of the agency and follow duly constituted processes. My office has not handled or been aware of any activities that were conducted by other processes. The overwhelming majority of reports that come through my office from both of these agencies concern matters of foreign intelligence. In a very few cases where it concerns allegations of the mishandling of classified information . . . I would receive summaries of reports from agency heads concerning these activities."

Reporters' heads must have been spinning as they tried to absorb Kissinger's answer, but from a standpoint of technique his next comment was such a classic example of official deception that the sheer artistry of it must almost be admired: "I must say in fairness," Kissinger declared, "I will not go into individual cases, but we have asked the Director of the Federal Bureau of Investigation to make a full report of these investigations and he will do so early next week." Kissinger was going to get to the bottom of the wiretapping! The clear implication was that the FBI would be hauled on the carpet to give an accounting of a program about which Kissinger was disturbed and knew very little if anything.

And the FBI did give a report. On Monday, Ruckelshaus held a press conference to disclose that the missing wiretaps had been found and recovered. In answer to questions, he said the effort to stop leaks by using wiretaps had stemmed from a discussion in 1969. Between whom? Hoover and Henry Kissinger. It was the first official mention of Kissinger as a participant in the original decision to wiretap. The wiretaps had, like an unwelcome foundling, been placed on the doorstep of the President's assistant for national security. Kissinger quickly disclaimed paternity.

He bobbed and weaved; yes, he remembered meeting with Hoover and expressing his "great concern" over leaks of national security information. But he added, "My conversation with J. Edgar Hoover concerned the safeguarding of classified information and not the initiation of any particular form of investigation." Yes, a few summaries of wiretaps had been brought to his attention.

Kissinger's modest explanation of his role did not satisfy anyone; the drumfire of news stories began. Two days later Seymour M. Hersh of the *New York Times* reported that Kissinger had personally provided the FBI with the names of a number of his aides whom he wanted wiretapped. "The request came from Kissinger," Hersh quoted an unidentified Justice Department source as saying. "Henry wanted some of those guys bugged himself. If Henry didn't approve of all this, he could have said so."

On May 22, with the Senate Watergate committee hearings under way, Nixon issued a lengthy statement attempting to defend the activities of his Plumbers, his own actions in Watergate, and the wiretaps. The taps, Nixon said, were undertaken "to find and stop serious national security leaks . . . I authorized this entire program."

Nixon's statement briefly relieved the pressure on Kissinger, but the cloud over Kissinger's head, and the questions over his role, continued to grow. In August, Nixon nominated Kissinger to be Secretary of State (in addition to his existing job as national security adviser to the President). Over the summer, more names of wiretapped officials and reporters leaked out; by September, when the Senate Foreign Relations Committee opened hearings on Kissinger's nomination, all of the names of those tapped were known. Kissinger's role in the wiretapping loomed as the major issue at the Senate hearings.

When the hearings opened on September 7, the first question asked by Senator Fulbright, the committee chairman, concerned the wiretaps. Kissinger launched into the first of many explanations he would give to the committee. In May of 1969, he said, Nixon had consulted Hoover and Mitchell about news leaks; the President had been told the best method was to use wiretaps, as had been done in previous Administrations; Mitchell had assured the President the taps were legal. Kissinger had only been in the government for four months at the time; he would not dream of questioning the judgment of the Director of the FBI and the Attorney General (who had also been in the government for only four months).

Kissinger not only minimized his own role; as the hearings progressed he left the impression that he was a champion of civil liberties who had frowned on the whole business. "The issue of wiretapping," he solemnly assured the committee, "raises the issue of the balance between human liberty and the requirements of national security. I would say that the weight should be on the side of human liberty and that if human liberty is to be ever infringed, the demonstration on the national security side must be overwhelming. That would be my general attitude."

In a closed hearing on his nomination, later released by the committee, Kissinger sought to distance himself even more strongly from the wiretapping. Without conceding that the tapping had been wrong, or illegal, Kissinger nevertheless said he wouldn't do it again. "What will be my attitude in the future?" he asked rhetorically. "I cannot conceive a circumstance in which I would recommend a wiretap on a subordinate in the State Department. . . . I cannot foresee a circumstance in which I would recommend a wiretap, and certainly not for newspaper leaks."

Kissinger knew just the right way to caress the Senate Foreign Relations Committee; he knew how to tell the senators what they wanted to hear. In the same executive session, he deprecated his own role in a statement that captures the tone and thrust of his Senate testimony: "First, I never recommended the practice of wiretapping. I was aware of it, and I went along with it to the extent of supplying the names of the people who had had access to the sensitive documents in question. Despite some newspaper reports, I never recommended it, urged it, or took it anywhere." Kissinger sounded rather like a divinity student who had, over his protests, been transported by a group of fun-loving friends to a bordello where he had taken part in the festivities because he did not want to seem square, and had really had a rather good time, in fact, but would certainly never do it again.

On September 19, after five days of hearings, the committee reported to the Senate. The "Members noted with approval" Kissinger's views on the requirements of liberty over national security, and the report quoted the nominee's ringing testimony on this point. The committee also thought the fact that the Administration had permitted two of its members to peek at the FBI report summarizing the wiretapping program was a "good omen" for the development of mutual trust between the Administration and the Congress. The committee, however, was deeply concerned over "the pattern of casual and arbitrary infringement of individual rights" evidenced by the wiretapping. But the committee concluded that Kissinger's role "did not constitute grounds to bar his confirmation as Secretary of State."

The process was tribal; rather like a ceremonial dance in which both Kissinger and the Foreign Relations Committee acted out their roles. The committee would question him, yes, and he would reply, gourds would be shaken and rattled, and a report would be issued. What an outsider might not understand was that the senators *wanted* to approve Kissinger's nomination; they were eager to do so, flattered to be there under the television lights in the same room with the illustrious nominee. Both Kissinger and the senators sought mutual support in the camaraderie of famous men; they would play their parts, but in the end they were all members of the same establishment team, and what's a little wiretapping among friends? The ritual came to its preordained end two days later, when the Senate, following the recommendation of the Committee on Foreign Relations, voted 78–7 to approve the nomination.

In the ensuing months some rumblings of dissatisfaction over Kissinger's role in the wiretapping continued to be heard, but there were more important distractions. First, Spiro Agnew copped a plea for income-tax evasion, then came the "Saturday night massacre," in which Nixon fired Watergate Special Prosecutor Archibald Cox, thereby losing his Attorney General Elliot Richardson, and also William Ruckelshaus, who was by now Richardson's deputy, and touching off the firestorm of public reaction that led to the start of impeachment proceedings in the House.

Attempting to stave off his ruin, Nixon, in a gamble that his public relations men, incredibly, half believed would work, issued the expurgated edition of the White House transcripts on April 29, 1974. The nation was both repelled and fascinated, horrified and transfixed by what it read. But there was more to come. A conversation of February 28, 1973, made public by the House Judiciary Committee, shed new light on Kissinger's role in the wiretapping: Nixon told Dean, "Henry's staff— He insisted on Lake, you see after working . . . for Muskie." It wasn't perfectly clear, but the sentence might be construed to mean that Kissinger had insisted on wiretapping Anthony Lake. "Incidentally," the President asked, "didn't Muskie do anything bad on there? [Unintelligible] Henry [unintelligible]. At least I know not because I know that, I know that he asked that it be done, and I assumed that it was. Lake and Halperin. They're both bad."

The conversation was garbled, but it seemed that the President was saying either that Kissinger had asked for the wiretapping program or that Kissinger, for reasons of his own, had caused certain individuals to be tapped, which was not at all what Kissinger had said in his sworn testimony to the Senate Foreign Relations Committee.

The Washington *Post* published this portion of the Judiciary Committee's transcript on June 6, the same day that Kissinger, fresh from a breakthrough in his Middle East shuttle diplomacy, held what was to have been a triumphal news conference. Only six days earlier, as a direct result of his efforts, Israel and Egypt had signed an agreement to disengage their forces on the Golan Heights. Kissinger was at the peak of his popularity and prestige; that very week he was on the cover of both *Time* and *Newsweek*, appearing on the latter as "Super K," a brightly colored cartoon figure in tights and a cape.

The press conference went smoothly enough, sailing along safely on NATO and the Middle East, until someone asked whether new evidence did not contradict Kissinger's statements that he knew nothing of the Plumbers, even though one of his own assistants, David Young, had been assigned to that unit. Kissinger stood by his previous denials. Another questioner noted that the Nixon impeachment hearings were generating news reports that Kissinger had, after all, asked that the seventeen wiretaps be installed. "I have attempted to serve the government in an honorable manner for five and a half years," Kissinger began with a pained expression. He had testified at length on the subject; he would answer no more questions from the press about wiretaps.

Things were not going at all well, but the worst was still to come. Peter Peckarsky, a young correspondent for a college newspaper, noted that Kissinger had sworn to the Senate Foreign Relations Committee that he did not know that David Young was a Plumber working on internal-security and news leaks. But Kissinger had later testified before the Senate Armed Services Committee that he had listened to a tape of an interview conducted by David Young, and the tape concerned the theft of documents by a Navy yeoman from Kissinger's office.° Could the Secretary reconcile these two statements, and had he "retained counsel" to prepare for "a possible perjury indictment"?

Kissinger, sputtering with anger by now, replied he had not retained counsel and "I am not conducting my office as if it were a conspiracy." At that, Clark Mollenhoff of the Des Moines *Register and Tribune*, a very large man with a voice as gentle as a sheriff's bullhorn, began bellowing questions at Kissinger about the wiretaps, and the triumphal press conference disintegrated into a shambles.

Four days later Nixon and Kissinger flew to Salzburg, Austria, en route to the Middle East. On the next day, June 11, with no warning of what was coming, reporters were loaded on buses and taken to Kavalier Haus, one of the palace buildings in Salzburg. They were seated in a large drawing room at 1 P.M. when Kissinger strode in scowling. With none of the usual preliminary bantering, he announced that he had summoned the newsmen to reply to articles stemming from his press conference in Washington, an appearance at which some had commented that "I seemed irritated, angered, flustered, discombobulated. All these words are correct." The reason was that in Washington he had been taken by surprise; he had been prepared to talk about the Middle East, not about wiretaps. Now he was ready to discuss the subject.

He repeated the familiar litany about how the tapping had begun: he had been ordered to provide the names of those tapped, and he had done so using three agreed criteria—persons with adverse information in their security files, or with access to information

---

° As a member of the White House Plumbers, Young had been investigating what became known as the "Pentagon spy" case, triggered when highly secret documents relating to the India-Pakistan war were published by columnist Jack Anderson in December 1971. The investigation centered on Yeoman Charles E. Radford, a Pentagon liaison man assigned to Kissinger's staff who admitted he had been removing documents and slipping them to the Joint Chiefs of Staff. Radford conceded he knew Jack Anderson but denied giving classified information to him.

that had leaked, or whose names "had appeared" as the investigation progressed. (The last category really meant people who had been overheard, or whose names had been mentioned, in conversations with officials whose telephones were already being tapped.) But it was "totally incorrect and outrageous to say that these tapes that were submitted to my office involved a description of extramarital affairs or pornographic descriptions." He had read no verbatim transcripts of tapped conversations; he had seen some wiretap summaries, but perhaps only one or two a month. He would not apologize for his role, for "it is not a shady affair." He knew nothing about any Plumbers.

"This is a question of my honor," Kissinger declared. "I have attempted, however inadequate, to set some standards in my public life. If I cannot set these standards, I do not wish to be in public life."

"I find wiretapping distasteful," he said. It was "extremely painful" to tap "individuals with whom I had been closely associated."* And in the statement that sent shock waves back to Washington and around the world, Kissinger concluded, "I do not believe that it is possible to conduct the foreign policy of the United States under these circumstances when the character and credibility of the Secretary of State is at issue. And if it is not cleared up, I will resign."

But, Kissinger quickly added, he would withdraw his threat if the Senate Foreign Relations Committee reopened its hearings and cleared his name. He had written a letter to the committee formally requesting that it review the entire record; he would be happy to appear as a witness.

It was a bold move, shrewdly timed. For more than a year, American politics had been dominated by Watergate. Richard Nixon was a tarnished leader, an unindicted co-conspirator, the target of an impeachment investigation then nearing its climax in the House.

---

* Some of Kissinger's former close associates whose home telephones had been wiretapped with his knowledge and assistance were amused at Kissinger's indignant reaction in July 1975 when a reporter for the tabloid *National Enquirer* went through his garbage. A spokesman for Kissinger said the episode had caused "grave anguish" to Mrs. Kissinger and had "really revolted" the Secretary of State, who "considers at least the privacy of his house should be respected." The Kissinger trash included Secret Service documents, some of which bore teeth marks, indicating the presence of a dog in the Kissinger household, the newspaper reported. The Secret Service, which guarded Kissinger, launched an official inquiry to discover why the documents had been thrown out with Kissinger's garbage.
The Kissinger tappees were further amused in October, when Kissinger's indiscreet remarks about world figures were picked up on an open microphone at a banquet in Ottawa and subsequently published to the world. "He was a very odd man," Kissinger said of Richard Nixon, "... an unpleasant man. He was so nervous ... He was an artificial man ... he didn't enjoy people ... What I never understood is why he became a politician."

The cloud of corruption at home had sullied America's reputation abroad; millions of ordinary citizens, even many who had voted for Nixon, were embarrassed and angry over a President who found it necessary to proclaim he was not a crook. As with a black sheep in the family, the President's growing disgrace reflected, to some extent, upon each citizen, illogical as that might be.

In such a climate, the country was leaderless and drifting. Americans longed for someone to respect, to follow, to lessen the sense of national shame. Only one high official had emerged almost untouched by the scandals, and that was Henry Kissinger. He must not now be implicated. The prevailing attitude in Washington was summed up by Representative Trent Lott of Mississippi, a Republican member of the House Judiciary Committee. Of Kissinger, Lott declared, "Even if he did order them [the wiretaps], what's so big about it? Is it important enough when we might lose one of the best men in government?"

Only crusty George Aiken of Vermont reacted sharply to Kissinger's *son et lumière* performance at Salzburg. "Can't he take it?" Aiken snapped. "Why, that's part of the business, being criticized." But the Foreign Relations Committee immediately acquiesced to Kissinger's wishes and agreed to review his role. Its members practically vied with one another to be first to praise Kissinger. Even Muskie, whose campaign aides had been wiretapped, called him "a brilliant servant" deserving of public support. Hubert Humphrey, another member of the committee, put it directly: "We obviously do not want Dr. Kissinger to resign. I want to say to him as a friend, 'Stay with it—cool it.'" Within twenty-four hours of the Salzburg explosion, and before any new review of the facts, forty-one senators had signed and introduced a resolution in the Senate supporting and expressing "deep gratitude" to Kissinger, a man "whose integrity and veracity are above reproach," and pleading with him to remain in office.

The Foreign Relations Committee held five days of closed hearings during July, and it questioned Kissinger again, but its conclusions were predictable. On August 6 the Senate panel unanimously cleared Kissinger of deceiving the committee about his role in the wiretapping. The committee found the controversy was "a question of semantics." The Foreign Relations Committee report drew only passing attention; this was the same week that President Nixon resigned.

The questions remained, however; they were not dispelled by the official findings of the committee. Much of the debate turned on the question of whether Kissinger had "initiated" the program of wiretaps or the requests for the wiretapping of individual officials and newsmen—the garbled Nixon tape seemed to suggest one or the other—or whether he had acted in a subordinate clerical capacity, merely supplying the names to the FBI. The real question, however, was whether in Kissinger's public statements and 1973 testimony he had so minimized his own role as to deliberately mislead and deceive the press, the public, and the Congress. The overwhelming burden of the evidence is that he did precisely that.

In September 1973, when Kissinger first appeared before the Foreign Relations Committee during hearings on his nomination to be Secretary of State, he had testified that "the first time I heard of the wiretapping" was the day the Beecher story about the bombing of Cambodia was published in the *New York Times*. That article had appeared on May 9, 1969. On the day the story ran, Kissinger testified, he attended a meeting in the White House of the President, Hoover, Mitchell, and Haldeman. At this meeting, Kissinger said, the President ordered the use of wiretaps.

Kissinger could not specifically remember the May 9 date, but the meeting took place "on whatever the day was that that [Beecher] leak occurred." He added, "Now, I think the easy way to check it is to find out when that Beecher story appeared that dealt with Cambodia, and whenever that story appeared was the date that my knowledge of the program begins. I was unaware of any wiretapping prior to that story."

But after Salzburg, in July of 1974, with the ugly details of the wiretapping seeping out in the press, and with Nixon dancing on the knife edge of impeachment, Kissinger changed his testimony. He could not have been in two places at once; since he had, after all, been in Key Biscayne on May 9, walking along the beach with Mort Halperin, Kissinger corrected his earlier testimony. He now said the initial meeting had "most likely" taken place in the Oval Office on April 25, 1969, before Nixon, Hoover, and Mitchell had gone off by helicopter to have dinner at Camp David.

"The meeting I refer to took place in the Oval Office, and it was in progress when I was called in. The President, the Attorney General and Mr. Hoover were present. They were discussing the problem of stopping leaks and I was told—I do not remember by whom—that wiretapping was necessary, that the practice and procedures were well established, and that I should cooperate by supplying the names of key individuals having access to sensitive information which had leaked."*

---

* William Ruckelshaus, who investigated the origins and operations of the wiretap program in detail when he headed the FBI, believed that more than the date

In a sworn statement in the Halperin wiretap suit, Kissinger said that at the Oval Office meeting, "President Nixon authorized an electronic surveillance . . . of Morton Halperin" and three others. The four names, Kissinger said, had been suggested by Hoover at the meeting, and "President Nixon directed surveillance of the persons then suggested by Director Hoover." The four names, it is plain from the various FBI documents and testimony, were Halperin, Davidson, and Sonnenfeldt, of Kissinger's staff, and Henry Brandon.

But Richard Nixon, questioned at San Clemente by Halperin's attorneys in January 1976, gave a different version of how the first four names were selected. "I of course did not select the names myself because I did not know," he said. "I told Dr. Kissinger that he should inform Mr. Hoover of any names that he considered to be prime suspects . . . That was Dr. Kissinger's responsibility." Had Nixon directed the FBI to tap Halperin? "No," he replied. "I have no recollection of so doing." Nixon said he did not even recall "Morton Halperin's name coming up." Later in his testimony, Nixon said Halperin was wiretapped because *both* Kissinger and Hoover wanted it done.°

Nixon and Kissinger agreed only that after the Beecher story was published on May 9, Nixon had instructed Kissinger to telephone Hoover to launch an investigation. Although Kissinger insisted that "My role in this program was substantially passive," events contradicted his testimony. Repeatedly Kissinger testified that "a journalist" had been among the first four names selected at the meeting in the Oval Office. But there was no journalist's name on the list of four names that Haig handed to Sullivan when the program of wiretaps began. The names of Kissinger's three assistants appeared, but the fourth name was that of Laird's assistant, Colonel Pursley. Who had put Pursley's name on the list? One of the first rules taught at West Point is to protect one's flank, and when Haig was questioned by the Senate

---

of the meeting might be open to question. In an interview with the author, Ruckelshaus expressed doubt that such a meeting had ever taken place. "Kissinger has several times referred to such a meeting," Ruckelshaus said, "and I've never seen any record that the meeting took place. That doesn't mean it didn't."

° Although he contradicted Kissinger, Nixon in his testimony may have shed new light on the FBI's lengthy surveillance of Henry Brandon. "Within two days" after he became President, Nixon said, he received a top-secret memorandum from Hoover about "a British correspondent." Nixon said he called Hoover and "he said, 'We have been surveilling him for years because our information is that he is probably an intelligence agent for the British . . .' When I saw this memorandum, I recall calling Dr. Kissinger into my office and I handed it to him. I knew the individual. He knew the individual. I said, 'As far as this kind of memorandum is concerned, I don't want to see any of them in the future. I have not the time to look at them. That is your job.' "

Foreign Relations Committee, he made it clear that he had gotten all four names from Kissinger.

"He [Kissinger] asked me to go over and see Mr. Sullivan," Haig said. "... He also at that time gave me the names of four individuals who were to be surveilled and I at that time assumed that surveillance would probably include wiretaps..."

But no senator asked how it came to pass that Kissinger had sent Pursley's name to the FBI, when Hoover had selected Brandon as the fourth name. There were many other, stronger indications that Kissinger's role in selecting the persons to be tapped was much more active than he cared to admit; that he had not been a mere conveyor belt of names, or a clerk for J. Edgar Hoover. In fact, Kissinger's meetings and contacts with Hoover are highly revealing in themselves, for their frequency suggests a high degree of interest and personal participation by Kissinger in the wiretapping.

The evidence indicates that Kissinger met with Hoover a total of three times between April 25 and June 4, 1969. The meetings took place on April 25, according to Kissinger's testimony; at 4:27 P.M. on May 5, according to Hoover's office log; and at 9:30 A.M. on June 4, according to FBI records. In addition, Kissinger spoke with Hoover four times on May 9, the day the Beecher story was published, and personally went to the FBI to read wiretap logs on May 20, according to Sullivan's memo dated the same day.

Haig twice accompanied Kissinger on visits to Hoover's office; during one of these, the FBI Director regaled the Assistant to the President for National Security Affairs with details of the sexual exploits of a female spy for a foreign power who had slept in a number of official beds in Washington. Describing this meeting with Hoover, Haig testified that "the security problem was discussed" in general, "and Mr. Hoover went through a particular case file of an espionage agent who had been very successful here in Washington with a number of highly placed people. It happened she was a [deleted] national, a very attractive gal who I guess spread her favors around rather loosely and [deleted]."

Kissinger's personal meetings and telephone conversations with Hoover, and his visits to the FBI, are inconsistent with the picture he painted for the complaisant senators of himself as an innocent bystander, an ingenuous Harvard professor initiated unwillingly into the secret world of wiretaps.

Moreover, the FBI files record that in the case of fourteen of the seventeen persons wiretapped, the names were provided to the FBI by Haig, acting for Kissinger.* Haig's own testimony on his subordinate

* The three exceptions were Sears and Kalb, both requested by John Mitchell;

role is explicit: "I never viewed myself as anything but an extension of Dr. Kissinger, an agent of Dr. Kissinger. . . . I never would have submitted a name that I did not get from Dr. Kissinger or from the President with Dr. Kissinger's knowledge." Only once, Haig testified, had the President given him a name, and even then "I checked with Henry before I went to Mr. Sullivan. All other names that I ever conveyed were names given to me by Henry." Kissinger himself told the Foreign Relations Committee that "it would be inconceivable to me that Haig would go off on his own."

So Kissinger had direct, intimate knowledge of who was being wiretapped, although he was reluctant to admit it. At one point in his Senate testimony, Kissinger waffled: "I would not say that I ever said to the FBI, please tap this individual. My perception is that I would not have said anything to the FBI. That was done by Haig. I would have said to Haig, we have had this leak, give the names of the people who have had access to the information."

Yet, as already noted, the evidence strongly indicates that Kissinger personally brought over to Hoover the name of Hedrick Smith of the *New York Times* when he met with Hoover on June 4, 1969, and the record is clear that Haig *always* checked with Kissinger and discussed each name before sending it to the FBI.

When the wiretap story began to emerge, Kissinger publicly denied that he had supplied the names of any newsmen who were wiretapped. Furthermore, at a press conference on May 29, 1973, Kissinger said he did not know who had. But in 1974 Haig was testifying that Kissinger was aware of *all* the names that Haig took to the FBI, including newsmen.

Kissinger also misled the committee and the public about the extent of his interest in, and knowledge of, the results of the wiretapping. At Salzburg, Kissinger had made much of how he saw only summaries of taps, not verbatim transcripts, which was technically true, but Haig testified that on his visits to the FBI *he* saw "raw taps," i.e., actual conversations.* Haig—who both men agreed never acted without Kissinger's knowledge—testified that he went to the FBI four or five times to read wiretaps; Sullivan placed the number of Haig's visits rather higher, at "12 to 18 times."

---

and McLane, requested by Haldeman; Haldeman also requested the second wiretap on Sonnenfeldt.

* Testifying in the Halperin lawsuit, Haig described these visits to Sullivan's office to read the logs:

A. He would sometimes show me the raw taps. He would give me a folder, and I would sit down and read it.
Q. Can you describe what the papers which were in the folder looked like?
A. They were onion skin transcripts of telephone conversations.

In the Halperin lawsuit, Haig testified: "Henry always knew before I went. I would never go over there unless he authorized me to do so, and when I would come back ... I would tell Dr. Kissinger about it."

In all, according to FBI records, Kissinger received thirty-seven wiretap summaries from the FBI over a period of twelve months. And Kissinger was well aware of the value of logging and taping telephone calls, for he did both; at first he ordered that his staff monitor his own telephone conversations, a common practice in Washington. Often a secretary would do this, listening in and taking notes. Sometimes Kissinger would ask Haig or another staff member to listen in. The mini-logs of Kissinger's conversations were then typed up.[*]

Later, however, Kissinger switched to taping his telephone conversations, even those with President Nixon, and the transcripts were typed by secretaries working into the night. "The reason taping was instituted of telephone conversations," Kissinger testified in the Halperin lawsuit, "—I don't remember when it was, that it was instituted. It was a technical device, because too much of the time the secretaries during the day was consumed in listening to the conversations. The tapes were then transcribed in the evening and destroyed that same evening. No tapes were ever kept."

The aides whose job it was to listen in on Kissinger's telephone calls often heard an earful. William Watts, Kissinger's staff secretary, regularly monitored the calls. About a week before the Cambodian invasion, Watts was listening and taking notes when Nixon and his crony Bebe Rebozo telephoned Kissinger from a helicopter en route to Camp David. Nixon spoke to Kissinger for a moment about the invasion plans and then said, "Wait a minute—Bebe has something to say to you."

Rebozo got on the line. "The President wants you to know, if this doesn't work, Henry, it's your ass."

Although Kissinger testified he had nothing to do with *removing* any wiretaps, the record is by no means clear on this point, either. "I

---

[*] From an administrative viewpoint, the memos of conversations were a convenience for Kissinger, in that his aides could follow up on various points without further instruction. But presumably they would also be useful as raw material for Kissinger's diary. Kissinger kept the diary during his years in the White House; he would customarily dictate entries at the end of the day. His staff assumed that the diary would form the core of his personal memoirs, which would be an extremely valuable literary property.

Before Roger Morris and Anthony Lake quit Kissinger's staff, one of their assigned tasks was to edit and work on the diary, which Morris described as "very, very frank, very detailed and very caustic." The diary, Morris said, was "a very intimate reflection on the United States government ... we caught glimpses of Nixon, Laird, Rogers, and Kissinger very much in action."

never had any knowledge of when a tap was terminated," Kissinger told the senators. "That was done by a decision that I was not involved in."

But General Haig was fuzzy on this question; when he testified before the Senate after the Salzburg press conference, Senator Fulbright read to him an FBI memo of June 20, 1969, from Sullivan to DeLoach. The memo reported that the existing taps had produced "nothing of late relevant to the leaks. I have suggested to Colonel Haig that he might want to consider discontinuing some of them. He agreed."

After reading the memo, Fulbright noted that Kissinger had sworn to the committee he was not involved in the removal of wiretaps. Was that Haig's recollection, too?

Confronted with the memo, Haig rapidly backpedaled away from Kissinger's position. Haig said he could not be sure that after conversations with the FBI he might not have "suggested to Henry that we should take a tap off." But, Haig added, "I would never on my own [have] given them approval without getting it from Dr. Kissinger." The more Haig thought about it, the more he thought it was entirely possible that he might have discussed the termination of wiretaps with Kissinger. Haig said he might have told Kissinger that the FBI wanted to take some off, "and he may have said OK." Haig added, "I must say, my own memory is sharpened by what you have read to me and it may have been that way."

It may indeed, for June 20, when Sullivan noted Haig's agreement to discontinue some taps, was the date that taps were removed on Sonnenfeldt, Sneider, and Moose. In the FBI files there is a top-secret letter from Sullivan to Hoover, dated July 8, 1969, which reads in part: "In regard to our very sensitive coverage on N of the National Security Council Staff, et cetera, as I have previously stated nothing has come to light that is of significance from the standpoint of the leak in question. I am suggesting to Colonel Haig that some of this coverage be removed. I had previously suggested the removal of the coverage of G, I, C, and B, and he agreed." Translated from the code, the letter meant that Sullivan was saying that the tap on Halperin (who was N) had proved useless, and that it should be taken off, as Haig had already agreed to do in the case of Pursley, Moose, Sneider, and Sonnenfeldt.°

° The letter code, devised by the Judiciary Committee at the request of the Justice Department, is employed in this FBI letter and all other documents published in the impeachment inquiry. During 1973 the names of all seventeen persons wiretapped leaked out to the press. Analysis of the impeachment documents shows that the Judiciary Committee used a simple letter-substitution code. The code can be broken, and the seventeen names matched correctly to the letters, by

But apparently Kissinger, who later claimed a "passive" role, would not agree to removing the tap on Halperin. A September 15, 1969, memo from Hoover to Mitchell states: "According to Col. Alexander Haig, Dr. Kissinger has now advised that he desires all such surveillances installed at his request discontinued except the ones with reference to Morton Halperin . . ."°

Kissinger's testimony to the Senate was artful, but even he tripped up occasionally. This happened in his first appearance when he assured the senators that when the tapping began, he had been told by Hoover that it "had been a common practice in every previous administration." Then Kissinger added, "I do not from my own knowledge know that this program was carried out in previous administrations."

But Kissinger must have forgotten that earlier in his testimony he had told the senators that one of his assistants had been "a bone of contention between me and the FBI ever since I put him on my staff . . . *I know for a fact* [he] *had been tapped on many occasions prior to my hiring him, because I was given the wiretaps on him* when there was a discussion about his suitability for appointment to my staff." (Italics added.) It is clear from Kissinger's later testimony that this assistant had been hired early in 1969, so the wiretaps Kissinger saw must have taken place prior to the Nixon Administration.

On almost every crucial point Kissinger attempted to conceal the extent of his own role in the wiretapping from the Senate Foreign Relations Committee and the public. It is true that there is no evidence

---

the following process: first, arrange the seventeen published names in alphabetical order, beginning with Beecher and ending with Sullivan. Assign each a letter, A to Q. Then reverse the alphabet, so that $A = Q$, $B = P$, and so on. Thus, William Beecher, the first name on the list in alphabetical order, becomes Q. The full list of code letters used for each tappee is as follows:

A.	William Sullivan	J.	James McLane
B.	Helmut Sonnenfeldt	K.	Winston Lord
C.	Richard Sneider	L.	Anthony Lake
D.	Hedrick Smith	M.	Marvin Kalb
E.	John Sears	N.	Morton Halperin
F.	William Safire	O.	Daniel Davidson
G.	Robert Pursley	P.	Henry Brandon
H.	Richard Pedersen	Q.	William Beecher
I.	Richard Moose		

° Testifying in the Halperin lawsuit, Mitchell was asked by Halperin's attorney, Walter Slocombe, whether this meant "that it was up to Dr. Kissinger to decide when the wiretaps came off?" Mitchell replied, "I think I would have to answer the question the way you put it, yes, Dr. Kissinger, having initiated the taps, that it would be his determination as to when they came off."

Nixon, in his deposition, also swore that Kissinger had the "obligation" to inform Hoover when a tap was no longer needed. "It was Hoover who removed the taps," Nixon said, but the FBI chief "would give very great weight to Dr. Kissinger's recommendation that a tap be removed."

that the original idea of installing the taps was proposed by Kissinger, even though the unclear Nixon tape might be read that way, and even though Kissinger gave conflicting testimony about the origins of the program. But the record indicates that Kissinger met Hoover three times, conferred with him by telephone, sent Haig to the FBI with the names of fourteen of the seventeen persons wiretapped, always knew when Haig went to the FBI to read raw taps, went himself to read taps on at least one occasion, received thirty-seven letters summarizing wiretapped conversations, and was involved in terminating wiretaps despite his denial that he had done so. In sum, Kissinger was deeply implicated and intimately involved in the program of wiretaps on his aides and newsmen, despite his sworn testimony to the contrary.

It is not an unimportant matter when the Secretary of State misleads the public and the committee of the Senate considering his nomination, even when the committee is willing to be waltzed. But beyond Kissinger's role, and his attempts to cover it up, there was a broader question: Does the President or his national security adviser have the right to wiretap American citizens at will in the name of "national security"? Were the seventeen wiretaps justified to protect secrets? Were they legal and constitutional?

Probably no murkier area has existed within the American politico-legal system than that of government eavesdropping. First, the extent of wiretapping by the FBI and other federal police agencies, and the various exotic techniques used, have been enveloped in secrecy; the uninvited ear of the government hears but is not often seen. Much is now known about official wiretapping, but it must be presumed that much remains hidden from view.

Through Supreme Court and lower-court decisions, legislation, and changing practices in the executive branch, the rules governing what Mr. Justice Holmes called a "dirty business" have constantly shifted, resulting in a legal and administrative tangle that has often defied any cohesive meaning. Legal scholars and jurists alike have disagreed on what the law provides and the Constitution requires.

The whole issue of government wiretapping involves a complex mix of legal, constitutional, and political factors. At its center for decades stood the enigmatic figure of J. Edgar Hoover, whose own power rested in no small measure on the fact that he did the tapping and controlled the results. Hoover used his power to intimidate and titillate a series of Presidents. Ostensibly a subordinate official within the Department of Justice, Hoover in fact more closely resembled a fourth branch of government. No President dared fire him.

Francis Biddle, whom Franklin D. Roosevelt appointed Attorney

General in 1941, and who was nominally Hoover's boss, soon learned that the FBI Director possessed astonishing information about the private lives of high officials. He wrote:

> Lunching alone with me in a room adjoining my office, he began to reciprocate by sharing some of his extraordinarily broad knowledge of the intimate details of what my associates in the Cabinet did and said, of their likes and dislikes, their weaknesses and their associations.... Edgar was not above relishing a story derogatory to an occupant of one of the seats of the mighty, particularly if the little great man was pompous or stuffy. And I confess that, within limits, I enjoyed hearing it. His reading of human nature was shrewd, if perhaps colored with the eye of an observer to whom the less admirable aspects of behavior were being constantly revealed.

Biddle suggests that Roosevelt was not overly disturbed by Hoover's wiretapping. On one occasion an FBI agent in New York City was forced to make a hasty exit when he was spotted tapping the telephone of Harry Bridges, the left-wing union leader. The embarrassing story was publicized and Biddle asked Hoover to explain the facts directly to the President:

> We went over to the White House together. F.D.R. was delighted; and, with one of his great grins, intent on every word, slapped Hoover on the back when he had finished. "By God, Edgar, that's first time you've been caught with your pants down!" The two men liked and understood each other.

Hoover's unique position aside, wiretapping has, over the years, offered a tempting tool of secret power to successive Presidents. Obviously, its use and abuse did not begin with Richard Nixon, even though he employed it extensively and became the first Chief Executive to be brought down by eavesdropping on himself.

From a legal and constitutional point of view, much of the difficulty centered on the fact that the Constitution was written eighty-nine years before Alexander Graham Bell invented the telephone, and therefore contained no protection against electronic trespass.*

* In any discussion of electronic eavesdropping, the distinction—often misunderstood—must be made between *wiretapping*, which means the clandestine interception of a telephone conversation and *bugging*, the secret overhearing of room conversations by use of a hidden transmitter or microphone. (When a bug is attached to a telephone or telephone wire so that it intercepts the conversation, it is considered a wiretap. A room bug may of course transmit one side of a telephone conversation, but it is not a wiretap.) Government policy, and until 1968,

The issue did not reach the Supreme Court until 1928. In that year the Court decided the *Olmstead* case, in which Prohibition agents had wiretapped and recorded the telephone conversations of a Seattle bootlegger. The Justices held that wiretapping, when no illegal break-in had occurred, did not violate the Fourth Amendment's prohibition against unreasonable search and seizure.

Despite this constitutional interpretation, Congress was free to legislate against wiretapping, and it did. The Communications Act of 1934 provided that "no person not being authorized by the sender shall intercept any communication and divulge or publish" the contents to anyone else. This language, in Section 605 of the act, seemed clear enough; wiretapping was outlawed. In a series of decisions that followed, the Supreme Court ruled that it was illegal for anyone, including federal agents, to wiretap and divulge the contents, and that wiretap evidence obtained from taps was tainted and could not be used in the federal courts. The Court also ruled that the law, while barring telephone wiretapping, did not apply to electronic bugs.

The government did not allow itself to be inhibited by anything so prosaic as the law. For the next three decades the Justice Department interpreted the 1934 act to mean that wiretaps could not be divulged *outside the federal government*, a view that permitted the FBI, the CIA, the National Security Agency, the IRS, and other agencies to wiretap as long as they did not tell anybody what they were hearing.

Not until 1967 in the *Katz* case did the Constitution catch up with the electronic age. In that year the Supreme Court overruled *Olmstead* and finally held that a conversation was tangible and could be "seized" within the meaning of the Fourth Amendment. Specifically, the Court ruled that placing a bug or tap did not have to involve physical trespass to violate the Fourth Amendment. The unlikely instrument of this historic conclusion was one Charles Katz, a Los Angeles bookie whose habit it was to make cross-country calls from his favorite phone booth on Sunset Boulevard. He did not know that the FBI had taped a microphone to the top of the phone booth. By holding in *Katz* that the Constitution protected citizens against illegal wiretapping, the Supreme Court said in effect that henceforth police could wiretap only after obtaining a court warrant that met the requirements of the Fourth Amendment. (The Court did not get into the question of national security wiretapping.)

In 1968, with public concern over crime increasing and "law and

---

federal law, varied for each practice. To complicate matters even further, the two terms, wiretapping and bugging, are so similar that they are often used interchangeably.

order" emerging as a presidential campaign issue, Congress passed the Omnibus Crime Control and Safe Streets Act. In part, the 1968 act was designed to meet the changed legal situation after *Katz*. The new law permitted wiretapping with a court-authorized warrant by federal, state, and local law-enforcement authorities, and it outlawed private wiretapping or bugging. The act was ambiguous, however, on the question of whether federal wiretapping for "national security" purposes required a court warrant.

To follow the complicated thread of national security wiretapping, one must go back to the Roosevelt Administration. In a confidential directive to Biddle's predecessor, Attorney General Robert H. Jackson, dated May 21, 1940, Roosevelt said he agreed with the Supreme Court's recent ruling declaring wiretapping illegal, but he was certain the Court never meant to apply this standard to "grave matters involving the defense of the nation." It was well known, FDR wrote, that certain nations had established "fifth columns" in other countries to prepare for sabotage; it was too late to do anything about it after "sabotage, assassinations" and similar activities had taken place. Therefore, in cases where the Attorney General approved, he was authorized "to secure information by listening devices directed to the conversation ... of persons suspected of subversive activities against the Government of the United States, including suspected spies." Roosevelt added that this should be limited "insofar as possible to aliens."

Thus, Roosevelt used the Nazi threat to justify illegal wiretapping by the government.° This was the beginning, and in one sense the Kissinger wiretaps thirty years later were lineal descendants of the Roosevelt order. Roosevelt, however, acted under the threat of a world war that had already begun in Europe. He directed that the tapping be limited as far as possible to aliens, and there is no indication that he expected the practice to continue after the war.

° Ironically, one of those apparently wiretapped during World War II was Mrs. Eleanor Roosevelt. In 1965 Willis R. Adams of Arlington, Virginia, a former Army intelligence agent, said that when he was stationed in Chicago during the war he had tapped Mrs. Roosevelt "several times." Whenever the President's wife was "in our area—Michigan, Illinois, Wisconsin and a few counties of Indiana—we had occasion to put listening devices on her phone from a national security standpoint," Willis said. "We were more or less tapping her for her own protection." Mrs. Roosevelt apparently was never aware of the taps, he said, but the last time it was done it "created a storm" when someone in Washington did learn about it. Adams said he also tapped and bugged scientists building the atomic bomb in Chicago. Microphones were placed inside telephones or on poles, or sometimes switchboards were tapped. "Other times," he said, "we would put bugs in beds or chairs."

But in 1946 Attorney General Tom C. Clark obtained President Truman's approval of an even broader wiretap directive. Clark cited Roosevelt's directive in a memo to Truman, but he left out the reference to aliens, and subtly modified its wartime cast. With the Cold War under way, Clark stressed that "subversive activities" at home were increasing, and he urged that tapping be permitted in cases "affecting the domestic security." Truman bought it; a directive originally aimed principally at catching enemy spies in wartime became, in revised and expanded form, a justification for wiretapping domestic radicals in time of peace. The government could now freely tap those whose political opinions or activities were suspect. Yet three years later, Clark claimed that there had been no change in the wiretapping rules established by Roosevelt.

For three decades the Roosevelt and Truman directives served as the basis of official policy. Under that policy the Attorney General could "authorize" wiretapping by federal agents, in violation of existing law, and without a court warrant, in cases that involved whatever was interpreted to be domestic or national security.* Under such a broad grant of authority, there were inevitable abuses, of which the most notable before Nixon was the bugging and tapping of Dr. Martin Luther King, Jr., the leader of the civil rights movement, during the Kennedy and Johnson Administrations.

When Congress passed the Omnibus Crime and Safe Streets Act of 1968 it appeared, on the surface at least, to promise a change in the rules for national security wiretapping and to prevent its political misuse. The new law permitted wiretapping with a court warrant for specified offenses, including atomic spying, espionage, treason, sabotage, kidnapping, and activities of organized crime. Police and federal authorities were required to make a case to a judge as to why the tap was needed, and to state probable cause for their belief that the person to be tapped was committing a crime.

But the law contained a confusing disclaimer. It said that nothing in the act limited the President's constitutional power to take such actions as he deemed necessary to protect the nation against foreign

---

* In 1965 President Johnson issued a memorandum to department heads in which he declared himself "strongly opposed to the interception of telephone conversations as a general investigative technique." Johnson said this should be done "only where the national security is at stake" and subject to the approval of the Attorney General. The memo thus left the basic policy unchanged. Johnson also noted that bugs presented "an even more difficult problem" than wiretaps; he suggested that federal agencies using bugs consult with the Attorney General. In 1967 Johnson's Attorney General, Ramsey Clark—perhaps doing penance for his father's quickstep with Truman that broadened the Roosevelt order—issued a memo designed to curtail the government's use of wiretapping and bugging. But Clark's memo did not apply to "national security" cases.

attack, to obtain essential foreign intelligence information, "or to protect national security information against foreign intelligence activities." Read one way, the language might mean that the President did not need a warrant to wiretap in cases involving national security, despite all the warrant provisions of the new law. Construed another way, it simply meant that Congress was saying it had not attempted to legislate in the area of wiretapping for national security.

John Mitchell chose to read it the first way. In June of 1969, about one month after the first four Kissinger taps had been installed, the Justice Department asserted that it had the power, without a warrant, to tap domestic groups regarded as a threat to the government. So it was back to square one, with the government—despite the safeguards of the new law—asserting again the blanket right to wiretap in "national security" cases.[*]

On June 19, 1972 (two days after the Watergate burglars were caught inside Democratic headquarters where they had gone to adjust a telephone bug), the Supreme Court ruled 8–0 in the *Keith* case that the government could not tap domestic groups without a warrant, as Mitchell had claimed the right to do. The case involved three members of the White Panther Party who were accused of conspiracy in the September 1968 dynamiting of an office in Ann Arbor used by the Central Intelligence Agency to recruit students at the University of Michigan. The government acknowledged it had overheard one of the defendants, Lawrence Plamondon, on a wiretap.

While ruling that the government could not tap *domestic* groups without first going to court and obtaining a warrant, the Supreme Court explicitly noted that it was not ruling on wiretaps involving the "activities of foreign powers or their agents."[†]

Two years later, in defending the Kissinger wiretaps against Morton Halperin's lawsuit, the government sought to justify them as having just such a foreign intelligence connection. On behalf of Kis-

[*] Mitchell took this regressive position in papers filed in a federal court in Chicago disclosing that the government had eavesdropped on the "Chicago Seven," the antiwar activists indicted (under Mitchell) for allegedly inciting disorders at the 1968 Democratic National Convention.

[†] The Supreme Court defined domestic groups as those having "no significant connection with a foreign power, its agents or agencies." In the *Keith* case, therefore, the Court did not rule on either the question of government wiretapping to protect information against spies or taps designed to gather foreign intelligence. But in June 1975 the Court of Appeals for the District of Columbia further restricted the government's wiretapping power, holding that a domestic group could not be tapped without a warrant even when the stated purpose was to obtain foreign intelligence information. The case involved FBI taps on the headquarters of the Jewish Defense League in New York City during 1970–71.

singer and other defendants, the Justice Department argued that when national security information leaked out, the nation's enemies "for the price of a daily newspaper, could become privy to the innermost deliberations of the Executive" and obtain classified information without spying. The publication of classified information, the government argued, was "clearly tantamount to 'foreign intelligence activity' ... as surely as if the same information had been obtained through direct covert intelligence activities by agents of that foreign power."

What the government was saying was, put simply, that reporters and officials could be wiretapped because the *New York Times* is read in Moscow. It was a startling and dangerous doctrine because it virtually asserted that U.S. officials who talk to the press, and the reporters, too, are accessories of the KGB, the Soviet secret intelligence service. Carried to its logical conclusion, it would mean that the government was free to spy, tap, bug, and put any news reporter under surveillance who covered foreign or defense policy, or any government employee. If so, freedom of the press and the First Amendment would have very little meaning, and the flow of information to the public would be drastically reduced and substantially controlled by the government.

It is true that when the seventeen wiretaps were carried out under Nixon, the Supreme Court had not yet ruled in the *Keith* case, and that when it did so, the Court did not reach the question of wiretapping in the area of foreign intelligence. It is also true that the "disclaimer" in the 1968 law is ambiguous and might be interpreted as permitting a President to wiretap without a warrant in national security cases.°

Having said this, and granted the fuzzy state of the law governing national security wiretaps, the seventeen taps were nevertheless unjustified, and some or all arguably illegal, for a number of reasons. First, whatever is meant by national security surely cannot include the wiretapping of someone like Jamie McLane, whose apparent danger to the Republic consisted of the fact that he had a liberal Republican for a father-in-law.† All three White House officials tapped

---

° On the other hand, if the Nixon Administration *really* suspected espionage in the case of the news leaks in 1969–71, it could have gone to court under the 1968 law and obtained a warrant to wiretap, since this is one of the specific crimes for which the warrant procedure is provided and required. But the 1968 law also required that court-approved wiretaps be disclosed to the person tapped within ninety days after they were removed, a provision that the Administration preferred to circumvent.

† The wiretap summaries on McLane, which the FBI sent to Haldeman, reported that McLane, dissatisfied with his job, was planning to join the campaign staff of his wife's father, Governor Sargent of Massachusetts.

—Sears, Safire, and McLane—had no access to national security information and were obviously selected for Byzantine reasons related to the internal politics of the White House.

Even in the case of those officials who *did* handle secret information, there is ample evidence throughout the record that many of those tapped were selected because of their personal political views —they had worked for Democratic Administrations, or were considered suspiciously liberal. A program ostensibly designed to prevent and track down leaks vital to the nation's safety was reporting personal gossip to the White House, social chitchat, conversations of wives and children, and the political opinions of newsmen and officials. Not insignificantly, the FBI reported to the White House at one point that Winston Lord, Kissinger's special assistant, was overheard in a tapped conversation saying that someone who had spoken to Kissinger recently was an admirer of Angela Davis and the Black Panthers.

Similarly, there is written evidence that Nixon and Kissinger had been receiving political information produced by the tap on Morton Halperin. In May of 1970, after the Cambodian invasion, Nixon met with Hoover; an FBI memo written for Hoover in preparation for the meeting reported that the FBI had learned through the wiretap that because of the invasion, Halperin planned to resign as a consultant to the NSC. It added: "During conversations with other individuals Halperin indicated that he feels the President intends to attack North Vietnam and Laos and agreed to work with Senator Fulbright (D-Arkansas) in opposing the war.... The above are the highlights received from this coverage during the past few days. It has received very limited dissemination going only to the President and Dr. Kissinger."*

To the secret police in a totalitarian system, the political views and personal lives of government officials or other citizens are of course of great interest, for such knowledge gives the state great power over the individual. It is the essence of Orwellian government. In many respects the Kissinger wiretaps fit the identical pattern of secret surveillance used for political and social control.

The taps on two persons, Halperin and Lake, were maintained at a time when they were advising Edmund Muskie, a political opponent of the President. The argument that these taps were kept on for reasons of national security is discredited by the fact that the White House made political use of the information about Clark Clifford's

---

* At the same meeting Nixon directed that in the future, all wiretap reports be sent to Haldeman rather than Kissinger.

plans for a magazine article that it picked up on the Halperin tap.

The taps were ended abruptly in February 1971 because J. Edgar Hoover was about to testify before Congress, and as was his custom, wanted low numbers to report. If the taps were truly required in the interest of "national security," this was hardly sufficient reason to remove them.

Nor was the government able to demonstrate that the news stories which supposedly caused the tapping had in fact damaged national security. The bombing of Cambodia, for example, was a secret only from the American people, not the Cambodians. Kissinger later argued that the matter was sensitive because Cambodia's chief of state, Prince Norodom Sihanouk, had given his tacit approval of the bombing, which Sihanouk denied; but no matter, the fact is that even *after* the Beecher story appeared, the bombing of Cambodia went right on for four years.

Beyond the question of whether a particular news story embarrassed or inconvenienced the Administration in power, the wiretapping of newsmen threatens First Amendment values. For it is difficult to see how there can be a free press when the government is listening in on the home telephones of reporters and their families.

Perhaps the most devastating evidence of the impropriety of the Kissinger taps is the fact that the officials who conducted them acted like guilty men. The normal FBI procedures were not followed; Belter and his men were told to keep no regular records, no ELSUR cards, no copies of logs. Under FBI procedures, the Attorney General reviews each national security wiretap every ninety days; Mitchell did not do this in the case of any of the seventeen taps. The Halperin tap, and perhaps others, was installed before Mitchell had signed any authorization.

The wiretap records were concealed, buried in a White House vault after being transported about Washington in an old satchel, like the hot merchandise they were. When the existence of the wiretaps was first revealed in the press, Mitchell denied everything; the President later approved of his lie. Henry Kissinger misled the press, the public, and the Congress, and successfully to a point, attempted to conceal his own pivotal role in the wiretapping. If tapping was legal, proper, and necessary, why did Kissinger go to such risky lengths to disguise his own participation?

The officials responsible for the wiretapping knew full well that what they were doing was wrong, otherwise William Sullivan would hardly have feared that Hoover would use the wiretap reports to blackmail Nixon. Perhaps the most explicit admission in this regard was a statement Mitchell made to the FBI in May 1973. He said he had at one point discussed the taps with either Haig or Kissinger, and they agreed that the taps could become "explosive" and that the whole operation was a "dangerous game we were playing."

In short, the evidence leads to the conclusion that at least some and perhaps all seventeen of the taps were illegal and unconstitutional. They were carried out by men who acted as though they knew it, and who made every effort to cover up their conduct. But wholly aside from the question of whether the taps were illegal, they were certainly improper, and constituted a gross abuse of power.

The irony of it all is that despite the full resources of the FBI, the physical surveillance employed in several instances, the hundreds of logs and thousands of man-hours frittered away at taxpayer expense, the taps produced nothing. When Senator Clarborne Pell of Rhode Island asked Kissinger whether the taps had ever uncovered the source of Beecher's Cambodia bombing story, Kissinger replied "No." Kissinger also informed the Senate that "no source of a previously published leak was uncovered."

There are documents indicating that as a result of the wiretaps, Daniel Davidson was forced out of the government by J. Edgar Hoover, with Kissinger's consent and complicity, even though Davidson had not leaked any classified information. On May 29, 1969, Sullivan wrote to Hoover that "they are releasing O [Davidson] today. At least this is one leak that will be stopped." In a later letter Sullivan referred to the "removal" of Davidson. According to one impeachment document, in a tapped conversation Davidson mentioned that his employment as an NSC assistant was being terminated because he had been seeing reporters. And Haig testified that "Mr. Hoover insisted, in writing to Dr. Kissinger" that Davidson "be removed from the staff based on the surveillance."

Davidson said in an interview that he left in July 1969 after Haig "intimated to me that they would be happier if I was anywhere else in government other than the NSC." The wiretaps were not mentioned by Haig, of course; they were still a secret at the time. Davidson said he was not aware that Hoover had written to Kissinger about him. He left, he said, "because I was being treated as a Democratic spy or something. It was a very uncomfortable atmosphere and it was clear that Haig would have been happier without me."*

So that was the sum of it; after twenty-one months of clandestine eavesdropping by the White House and the FBI, after all the ex-

---

* The House Judiciary Committee staff, which reviewed all the wiretap summaries, said that most of those about Davidson reported contacts with journalists. But the committee document concluded: "Although some of the discussions involved foreign policy negotiations, none of them revealed classified information."

pense, time, and effort, the grand result was the easing out of the government of one staff assistant who had *not* violated security. No leaks were found. No sources uncovered. No national security protected.

If anything, the national security was weakened because the disclosure of the wiretapping diminished public trust in the government. National security, if that term can be defined at all, is not strengthened when the President, his adviser, as well as the Director of the FBI and other high officials conspire to abuse the great power that is vested in them by the people.

Richard Nixon was not the first President to engage in secret wiretapping in the name of national security. The tapping that Nixon did surfaced because of the accident of Watergate and the impeachment inquiry by the House. Examples of wiretapping by other Presidents had been reported in the press prior to the Nixon years and were documented by the Senate intelligence committee headed by Senator Frank Church that began its inquiries early in 1976. Some—such as the surveillance of Dr. Martin Luther King, Jr., during the Kennedy and Johnson Administrations—are outrageous and shocking.

In one sense, comparisons are not really necessary. To recognize that other Presidents wiretapped is not to exonerate Richard Nixon of the abuses of power that finally drove him from office. What one President, Richard Nixon, did is now known in considerable detail, and sufficiently chilling in and of itself.

"More than our privacy is implicated," Justice William O. Douglas wrote in the *Keith* case. "Also at stake is the reach of the Government's power to intimidate its critics."

But apparently the misuse of the police power of the state, the danger to free thought and a free press, was not something that disturbed anyone in the government during the period of the Kissinger taps. The prevailing police-state mentality was perhaps best typified by an exchange that occurred when the Senate Foreign Relations Committee reopened its hearings after Kissinger's press conference at Salzburg. In July 1974 Bernard Wells, who had been William Sullivan's mechanic, handling the paperwork on the wiretapping within the FBI, was being questioned by Chairman Fulbright and Senator Muskie. Wells had read the hundreds of wiretap logs, but he told the Senators he found not a single leak:

THE CHAIRMAN: There is nothing that occurred...that caused you to say "This is a leak"?
MR. WELLS: No, no, sir.
SENATOR MUSKIE: ... Is wiretapping useful in the interest of national security?...

MR. WELLS: I think in national security cases ... it is one more tool.

SENATOR MUSKIE: In this case, you were digging sand, you did not get any gold?

THE CHAIRMAN: Did not even get a clam?

MR. WELLS: It shows some loose talk and some potential leaks. I think if I was in the White House I would like to know so-and-so said this. I think I might like to know that from a national security standpoint. ...

SENATOR MUSKIE: This is a country where loose talk is encouraged by the Constitution.

It can happen again; perhaps it is happening. By 1975 Ernie Belter had retired and was reluctant to talk about his wiretapping career ("I'm still FBI all the way"), but there is no reason to think that the C&P telephone cable, the rows of pairs, and the switchboard in his old shop are not still available, waiting to be hooked up again. The red lights may be blinking even now.

4
The Political Police

In July of 1969, after Senator Edward M. Kennedy's accident at Chappaquiddick, in which Mary Jo Kopechne drowned, one of the summer residents of Martha's Vineyard who visited the scene was Robert Crichton, the novelist and author of *The Secret of Santa Vittoria*. Crichton was not the sort of person normally drawn to such disasters, but he was a friend of the Kennedy family, particularly of Robert Kennedy.* So he took the ferry over to Chappaquiddick.

"I was standing and talking with a group of friends," Crichton recalled, "when this fellow came over and began asking me leading questions. He said he was from the Philadelphia *Inquirer*. He was tough-looking. He looked more like a truckdriver than a reporter, short and heavy-set. I said, 'That's some Philadelphia accent you've got. That's New York if I ever heard it.' I had a feeling I should shut

---

* Crichton's connection with the Kennedys was casual but went back many years. Crichton had grown up in an Irish-Catholic working-class neighborhood in Queens. "Suddenly my father had some money and we moved to Bronxville. The only other Irish Catholics in Bronxville were the Kennedys." Crichton attended Portsmouth Priory, possibly the best Catholic prep school in the country, with Robert Kennedy, and then they went to Harvard together, so he had gotten to know Bobby fairly well and had mourned his death a year earlier.

up, but I had known Bobby Kennedy and so I talked to him. I was talking more than I probably should have." Crichton, six-foot-six, towered over the inquisitive reporter from Philadelphia. A breezy, open man, with a great zest for life, Crichton is gregarious and approachable, and the man did say he needed all kinds of details about the Kennedys to round out his story.

Crichton tried to help. The inquiring reporter "acted as though he were pro-Kennedy," he recalled. "Very sympathetic and understanding." Crichton gave his name to the reporter but not his telephone number, and since as a summer resident he was not listed in the Martha's Vineyard phone book, he was quite surprised and puzzled when the man telephoned him. "When I got home he called, and he kept calling. I realized I was being seriously used." The reporter from Philadelphia was becoming a pest and after a few such calls, Crichton stopped coming to the phone.

Four years later, in May 1973, Crichton was back on the Vineyard watching the Senate Watergate hearings on television at his summer home when Anthony T. Ulasewicz was sworn in as a witness. Crichton sat bolt upright. "Hey," he said, "I know him. That's the guy from the Philadelphia *Inquirer!*"

Ulasewicz was a twenty-six-year veteran of the New York City Police Department. He had left to become an undercover operator for the White House. Street-wise in the way that only a New York City detective becomes, Ulasewicz also had the physique, deadpan expression, and perfect timing of a borscht-belt comedian. In his appearance as a star witness before the Senate Watergate committee, he had the senators and spectators laughing. As Senator Lowell P. Weicker of Connecticut pointed out, however, there was nothing funny about what he did.

Beneath the boffo manner, Ulasewicz was a shrewd cop, and he had been no ordinary detective. He had served in the elite corps of the New York City Police Department, the Bureau of Special Services and Investigations, or BOSSI (pronounced to rhyme with flossy). The detectives assigned to this unit guarded foreign dignitaries who visited New York, but mainly BOSSI served as a mini-FBI or domestic intelligence unit. It worked closely with various federal intelligence agencies, including the FBI and the CIA, and it built up extensive and controversial dossiers on domestic political groups and individuals, as well as on foreign and émigré organizations in the New York area.

In his work for the police department, Ulasewicz investigated and infiltrated various political groups, and trained persons who were paid to infiltrate dissident organizations. In 1966 he had received a commendation for undercover work in helping to break up a plot by black extremists and a French Canadian woman to blow up the Washington Monument, the Liberty Bell, and the Statue of Liberty—"that damned old bitch" in the words attributed to one of the plotters.

Ulasewicz was born in December 1918 on the Lower East Side of Manhattan, the son of a Russian-speaking father and a Polish-speaking mother. He went to parochial school and Stuyvesant High, joined the police department during World War II, served in the Navy for a while, and returned to the force. He married and moved to Flushing, in Queens, the borough where most New York cops seem to prefer to live.

When Soviet Premier Nikita S. Khrushchev visited Manhattan in 1960 for his shoe-pounding appearance at the United Nations, Ulasewicz, because he spoke Russian, was assigned as a bodyguard. Once they were stuck between floors in the Waldorf, and Ulasewicz, stalling while a repairman was found, had a long chat with Khrushchev in Russian, although he later claimed to a reporter that he could not remember a word they said to each other.

One of Ulasewicz' fellow detectives in BOSSI was John J. Caulfield, who had also won a commendation in the Statue of Liberty case. In 1960, it will be recalled, Caulfield was assigned as presidential candidate Richard Nixon's bodyguard when Nixon campaigned in the city. Mostly, however, Caulfield and his partner, Frank Bianco, watched Cuban exile groups in New York.

Caulfield did not really get to know the Republican nominee during the campaign; he was, he said, "just running alongside Nixon's car," but he did become friendly with Jack Sherwood, the Secret Service agent guarding Nixon, and that contact in turn led to Haldeman's recruitment of Caulfield for the 1968 campaign.

After Nixon's election Caulfield tried to promote himself to the job of chief United States marshal, but John Mitchell vetoed that. In March of 1969, however, Ehrlichman, then counsel to the President, telephoned Caulfield and asked whether he would be interested in setting up a private security unit in Washington to conduct secret investigations for the White House. Caulfield countered with his own proposal that would put him closer to the power: he would join the White House staff and serve as liaison with law-enforcement agencies but also conduct the confidential investigations that Ehrlichman wanted.

Ehrlichman agreed to this, and Caulfield was hired on April 8, 1969. Caulfield told Ehrlichman that he knew just the man to handle the sensitive investigative work: Anthony Ulasewicz. In May an unusual meeting took place in the VIP lounge of LaGuardia Airport in New York. Present were Ehrlichman, Caulfield, and Ulasewicz.

The setting was cinematic: the counsel to the President of the

United States, and his staff assistant, meeting clandestinely in an airport lounge with a New York City detective to hire him to conduct secret political investigations, planes roaring overhead as they talk, and the public address system droning out metallic announcements of flight arrivals and departures.

Ehrlichman quickly made clear what sort of investigations he had in mind. According to a staff memo of the Senate Watergate committee, "Ehrlichman explained to Ulasewicz that he wanted some investigation of political figures . . . Ehrlichman emphasized that all of Ulasewicz' activities were to be very discreet."

It was decided that Ulasewicz would receive a salary of $22,000 a year plus expenses. As Ulasewicz later recounted the meeting to Senate investigators, he set certain other terms; he demanded that he report to only one person and put nothing in writing. The counsel to the President agreed.

In retrospect Terry Lenzner, who served as assistant chief counsel of the Ervin committee and became steeped in the details of Watergate, regarded the LaGuardia meeting as a seminal, and symbolic, event. "While some Administrations may in time have grown into states of paranoia," he said, "the most significant event of Watergate in my mind was Ehrlichman and Caulfield meeting with Ulasewicz at the VIP lounge in May of 1060. Hiring a gumshoe as almost a first act. Before the seat was even warm, they were off and running."

When Ehrlichman returned to Washington, he arranged—in time-honored espionage fashion—for a cut-out, or go-between, to handle and pay Ulasewicz. The man he turned to was Herbert Warren Kalmbach, who had risen from modest Midwestern beginnings to become bagman to the President of the United States. Kalmbach, tall, and oil-smooth, had the bland, crinkly-eyed good looks of a man who inspires misplaced confidence in elderly widows. He smiled a lot. One had only to look at Kalmbach to know that he could do an effortless fox trot on a very small dance floor. He was born in Michigan, but he was a creature of California; he went to college there at the University of Southern California (like a great number of other Watergate figures) and at the USC law school he became close to Robert H. Finch, who later served Nixon in various high-level capacities and who introduced Kalmbach to Nixon in 1964.

Kalmbach's fortunes improved after he became known as a confidant of Nixon; by 1967 he was a partner in the Newport Beach law firm of Kalmbach, DeMarco, Knapp and Chillingworth. He became deputy finance chairman under Maurice H. Stans in the 1968 Nixon presidential campaign, and he displayed a golden touch in soliciting large campaign contributions from top-ranking corporate executives. After the election, word went out that Kalmbach was the President's personal attorney, and his law firm's business burgeoned; some of America's largest corporations found that they needed a lawyer in Newport Beach, California. At the same time, Kalmbach emerged as a power in the Lincoln Club of Orange County, the ultimate in fat cats, an exclusive organization of Republicans whose members are almost all millionaires, conservative, and owners of yachts. It was the treasurer of the Lincoln Club, one Robert F. Beaver, who provided one of the more memorable pronunciamentos on Watergate. "Political espionage," he announced at the height of the Ervin committee revelations in 1973, "is as American as apple pie."

Be that as it may, after Nixon moved into the White House, Kalmbach had custody of trustee accounts containing more than $1 million left over from the 1968 campaign, and it was arranged that Tony Ulasewicz would be paid out of these funds.° (Over the next three years Kalmbach disbursed more than $130,000 in Nixon campaign money for the operations of Ulasewicz and Caulfield.)

To arrange the details of their operation, Kalmbach met with Caulfield and Ulasewicz at the Madison Hotel in Washington at eight o'clock on Sunday morning, June 29, 1969. In addition to Ulasewicz' basic salary, it was agreed that he would receive $1,000 a month in expenses; the checks were to be sent to his home every two weeks. Ulasewicz informed Kalmbach he would use the alias Edward T. Stanley in his work, and would always give that name when telephoning Caulfield at the White House to receive his assignments. All communication with Kalmbach was to go through Kalmbach's secretary.

Ulasewicz had his own American Express credit card, but Kalmbach instructed him to apply for a second card in the name of Edward T. Stanley, which he did, and Kalmbach also arranged somehow to obtain telephone credit cards for Ulasewicz in both his real name and that of Edward T. Stanley. It was a pleasant, if conspiratorial conference—the Madison is a glittering, luxurious hotel—and his work done, Herbert Warren Kalmbach, having just completed the enormous step of hiring a secret-police agent for the President of the United States, concluded the meeting and went to church.

A few weeks later, on Saturday morning, July 19, John Caulfield was playing golf at the Fairfax Country Club, near his home, when he was summoned to a telephone. Socially and geographically, the

---

° In the 1972 campaign Kalmbach *personally* raised an astonishing $10.6 million, most of it before the new campaign finance law went into effect on April 7, a sum that amounted to more than one third of the anticipated campaign budget. Almost all of the money was in amounts of $100,000 or more, from leaders of the oil, steel, automotive, banking, and other industries.

country club was far from the Ryer Avenue precinct in the Bronx, where he had started out walking a beat sixteen years earlier.

By the summer of 1969, chance—the Nixon bodyguard assignment in 1960—and ambition had carried Caulfield, who had just turned forty, higher and faster than might have been expected. He was born in the Bronx, the son of an Irish immigrant father, went to parochial school, and attended Wake Forest University in North Carolina on a basketball scholarship. But there was not enough money; he dropped out after two years and worked as a bank teller and then as a draftsman for the New York Telephone Company. He was drafted during the Korean War, and served in the Army Signal Corps. He joined the police department in June 1953, made some good arrests in the Bronx and caught the eye of Frank Robb, a high-ranking and sophisticated police officer, who recruited him for BOSSI. From there the path, in time, led to the White House.

And it was the White House calling to summon Caulfield off the golf links that morning. Some hours before, Senator Kennedy's car had plunged off the bridge at Chappaquiddick. Miss Kopechne, twenty-eight, one of the young women who had worked for Robert Kennedy in the 1968 campaign, had drowned. The tragedy was for the moment overshadowed by another news event; most of the world's attention was focused on the Apollo 11 spaceship then nearing its destination and on the two American astronauts who, on the evening of Sunday, July 20, would for the first time in man's history walk on the moon.

"Ehrlichman called me," Caulfield recounted.* "I went right over to the White House. Ehrlichman said, 'Have Tony go up and find out what's to it.'"

It was Ulasewicz' first assignment. President Nixon was personally interested in being kept up to the minute on Chappaquiddick. Over the next four years, the Nixon White House carried out a dozen

---

* Caulfield had avoided public statements, but he agreed to be interviewed two years after Watergate; the talk took place on the backyard patio of his home in the Virginia suburbs. He lived in a ranch house on a pleasant, wide street of middle-class brick homes, neatly kept. There was a basketball hoop out front. A tall man, over six feet, Caulfield seemed heavier than he had looked on television when he testified before the Watergate committee. His hair was shorter and his face much puffier. He smoked cigarettes almost constantly as he talked. The pressure had taken its toll, and it was obvious that as in the case of most Watergate figures, his life had changed for the worse. He had been hospitalized for ulcers, then had a major stomach operation, and had not worked for two years. There were endless legal entanglements, depositions, lawyers, and prosecutors; but he had his police pension to live on and his wife had a job at a nearby university. They had, he explained, three sons in college.

clandestine investigations of Senator Kennedy. Most, although not all, were conducted by Ulasewicz.

On July 19 Ulasewicz flew on an Eastern Airlines shuttle to Boston, where he rented a car for the trip to Martha's Vineyard and Chappaquiddick. Posing sometimes as "James Ferguson from the Magazine Writers of America" and at other times as a newspaperman, Ulasewicz interviewed a wide variety of people, as Robert Crichton ruefully had reason to recall, and spent almost a week—eventually months—investigating the accident. He took pictures and drew diagrams of the scene at the Dike Bridge, where Kennedy's black four-door Oldsmobile had fallen upside down into eight feet of water in a tidal pond.

The accident had suddenly turned a weekend cookout of drinking, dancing, and reminiscing into a tragedy. Kennedy and five other men friends, all but one married but none with their wives, had gathered in a cottage on Chappaquiddick for a party in honor of the "boiler-room girls," six young single women who in 1968 had kept count of Democratic delegates for Robert Kennedy in a rear office in his presidential headquarters on L Street in Washington—unglamorous but essential work. Kennedy said he had two rum drinks at the party and left at 11:15 P.M. to drive with Mary Jo Kopechne to the ferry back to Edgartown, but he said he had mistakenly turned right toward the beach instead of left toward the ferry slip; the car, traveling at 20 miles an hour, went off the bridge, which angled sharply away from the road and had no guardrails, and fell into the swift, dark water. Kennedy said he had the sensation of drowning but somehow struggled to the surface; he said he dived repeatedly in attempts to rescue Miss Kopechne, failed, returned to the cottage, got his cousin Joseph Gargan and a friend, Paul Markham, both lawyers, who returned with him to the bridge, where more attempts were made to rescue Mary Jo. His two friends then took him to the ferry landing, but the *On Time*, the little ferry to Edgartown, stops running at midnight, and it was well after that, so Kennedy said he impulsively jumped into the water, swam the 500-foot channel, and collapsed in his hotel room near the harbor. Not until the next morning did he report the accident to police, a delay which he later called "indefensible," explaining that he had been overcome by "grief, fear, doubt, exhaustion, panic, confusion and shock." Whatever Kennedy's reasons, his failure to report the accident meant that no rescue efforts could be made by police or firemen during the night, at a time when, Kennedy's critics maintain, Miss Kopechne might conceivably still have been alive in an air pocket in the overturned car. Kennedy denied he had been drunk or that he had any romantic liaison with, or intentions toward, Miss Kopechne. The accident left many unanswered questions, clouded Kennedy's political career, and cast doubt on whether he could be elected President.

No outsider knew, of course, that Anthony Ulasewicz, the President's agent, was mingling with the reporters swarming over Chappaquiddick in the days after the accident. Three times a day Ulasewicz telephoned reports to Caulfield at the White House. He also dispatched to Caulfield several of the photographs he had taken at the scene of the accident. "It was clear to him [Ulasewicz]," Caulfield said, "the story of the wrong turn on the road wasn't going to hold, that it was flimsy at best." When Ulasewicz called in, he said, "if the information was important, I would pass it on to Ehrlichman." Ulasewicz made many visits to Chappaquiddick and Martha's Vineyard, returning there twenty times.°

John Ehrlichman claimed in an interview that he could "not recall" ordering Caulfield to send Ulasewicz to Chappaquiddick. Did Nixon direct that someone be sent to the scene of the accident? "I doubt it," Ehrlichman replied. Did the President know of Tony Ulasewicz? "I think he knew there was such a person," Ehrlichman said. And did Nixon know that this person was at Chappaquiddick? Yes, Ehrlichman said, he thought the President did know that.† Ulasewicz was sent, he added, because within the White House there was "a feeling there was going to be a whitewash."

Before dawn, Washington time, on July 25, one week after Chappaquiddick, Richard Nixon landed halfway across the world on Guam, having greeted the Apollo 11 astronauts at splashdown the day before as the highlight of his global tour. Later that day, in a local court in Edgartown, Massachusetts, Senator Kennedy pleaded guilty to leaving the scene of an accident; his driver's license was revoked for one year, and he received a two-month suspended jail

° Over a three-year period Ulasewicz made an astonishing 47 trips to Boston, or the Cape Cod–Martha's Vineyard area, an analysis of his travel records shows. The breakdown is as follows: 1969: Boston, 14, Martha's Vineyard, 7; 1970: Boston, 13, Martha's Vineyard, 5; 1971: Martha's Vineyard, 8.

† In this connection it may be noted that at least some of the money paid to Caulfield and Ulasewicz was sent to Kalmbach by the President's closest friend, Bebe Rebozo, who withdrew campaign funds from a special account in his Key Biscayne Bank in Florida. Kalmbach has stated that Rebozo knew the money was being used to pay for Ulasewicz' activities, because they had discussed the subject a number of times. Rebozo sent a $1,000 check to Kalmbach the day before the Chappaquiddick accident to cover Ulasewicz's first two weeks' salary; since this was during the period when Ulasewicz first traveled to Martha's Vineyard, it would be accurate to say that Rebozo provided the initial cash to finance the White House investigation of Chappaquiddick, a point that was not explicitly brought out in the Watergate investigations.

sentence. He then prepared to make a nationally televised address that evening, in which he gave his explanation of the long night of Chappaquiddick.

That afternoon, with the President out of the country, John Ehrlichman was traveling to New York City for a short holiday. On board the northbound Metroliner, Ehrlichman received a call from the President in the western Pacific. (The resourceful White House telephone operators had tracked Ehrlichman down and switched Nixon's call to the radiotelephone circuits on the Metroliner.)

It was on Guam that the President first enunciated what became known, rather grandiosely, as the "Nixon Doctrine," a policy that seemed to suggest more limited U.S. involvement in future overseas adventures. But less lofty thoughts prompted the call to Ehrlichman.

"The subject of the call was Chappaquiddick," Ehrlichman said. "It was the day of Kennedy's speech." The President, Ehrlichman added, "had a lively interest in Chappaquiddick." The purpose of the call, he said, "was just to bring Nixon up to date, since he was away." Ehrlichman, of course, was receiving Ulasewicz' clandestine reports via Caulfield, and one assumes he briefed Nixon guardedly on the open phone line. He left the train hurriedly when it arrived in New York and got to his hotel just in time to see Kennedy's speech on television.°

Political Washington is really a small town, with all sorts of interlocking relationships, and one of the first things that E. W. Kenworthy, a veteran correspondent in the *New York Times* Washington bureau, did after Chappaquiddick was to try to reach Margaret Carroll. She had been one of Mary Jo Kopechne's roommates in a house on Olive Street in Georgetown, along with Nance Lyons, another of the young women at the cookout in Chappaquiddick. Margaret Carroll, a tall red-haired young woman with a pleasantly direct manner, was the daughter of Wallace Carroll, the *Times'* former Washington news editor who had left to become publisher of the Winston-Salem *Journal*. Kenworthy, a good friend of Wally Carroll, was almost a second father to Margaret.

"I knew Margaret from the time she was three years old," Kenworthy explained. "I immediately tried to call her and couldn't get her. She'd been out shopping. When she came back to the house that morning, of course the place was surrounded by reporters and tele-

° Ehrlichman has a vivid recollection of the call, because he retained the image in his mind of the President jetting westward on *Air Force One* at 500 miles an hour, as he traveled north on the Metroliner at 100 miles an hour. If Nixon did call from *Air Force One*, however, it is doubtful that the plane was airborne; allowing for the time difference on Guam, Nixon would not yet have left the island.

vision crews. I knew Mary Jo Kopechne from dinner with Margaret or whatever. She was a very plain string, Mary Jo. Very shy, painfully shy kid. Anyway, I couldn't reach Margaret but when she got back I got her on the phone and I said, 'Margaret, get the hell out of there and get over to our house and stay at our house until its over. Your life is gonna be miserable.' So she did for a couple of days."

Margaret Carroll went to Wilkes-Barre, Pennsylvania, for Mary Jo's funeral. When she returned to Olive Street she noticed two un usual occurrences. First, a nondescript, unmarked panel truck, sometimes two, was parked on the street outside her house for long periods of time. The van's windows were cloudy and it was not possible to look inside. Second, the telephone in the house on Olive Street began acting very strangely—there were clicks and whirring noises, and the voices of the people with whom she talked on the telephone would fade away. Before the weekend of Chappaquiddick, there had been no panel trucks and no telephone peculiarities.

The Carrolls were good friends of Richard M. Helms, Director of the CIA—Wally Carroll and Helms had been newsmen together in Europe before World War II—and later in the summer of 1969 Margaret Carroll's mother, visiting Washington, saw Helms at a dinner party. She described to the CIA Director the strange behavior of her daughter's telephone, and Helms observed that the fading voices would be consistent with a wiretap that took its power from the telephone line.

Margaret Carroll was then all the more convinced that the telephone at Olive Street had been tapped after Chappaquiddick, but she did nothing about her suspicions until 1973, after John Dean testified that Anthony Ulasewicz had been sent to Martha's Vineyard to investigate. She then told Kenworthy about her telephone and the vans. As it happened, a senior member of the staff of the Senate Watergate committee lunched at the *Times* Washington bureau around this time, and according to Kenworthy, said that Mary Jo Kopechne's house on Olive Street had been wiretapped. On July 6 the *Times* published a front-page story by Kenworthy. Attributed to a source close to the Senate Watergate committee, the article said the Georgetown house had been wiretapped by, or under the direction of, Caulfield and Ulasewicz.[*]

"I had nothing to do with it," Caulfield said of the alleged wiretap. He said he also had no knowledge of any van or truck parked outside. "I know nothing about Kopechne's house or anything about

---

[*] After the story appeared, Margaret Carroll filed a lawsuit against Ehrlichman, Caulfield, and Ulasewicz. All three denied any knowledge of any tap and Margaret Carroll, who had no independent evidence to support her suit, eventually dropped it.

a tap of Kopechne's house," he said. "But being in this business, I can tell you that the possibility of that phone being wiretapped is considerable." If the phone was tapped, Caulfield added, it would have been by some other agency or person. "Ehrlichman never asked me to do it, and I never did it and Tony did not do things on his own, so he never did it."°

So there was no proof of a tap, and the supposition that it took place arose from a combination of circumstances, including the intriguing if apparently coincidental role of CIA Director Richard Helms, the leak to the *New York Times*, and the fact that Senator Edward Kennedy was indeed the target of a number of White House investigations, including many conducted by Ulasewicz and Caulfield.

In 1971 the White House investigations of Kennedy intensified, obviously reflecting Nixon's fear, and that of his advisers, that Kennedy might—despite Chappaquiddick—emerge as the 1972 Democratic nominee.

In August of 1971 Kennedy stopped off in Hawaii on his return from an Asian trip. Ulasewicz flew into Honolulu soon afterward, according to a Senate Watergate committee summary of sixty-one investigations undertaken by Ulasewicz for the Nixon White House at Caulfield's direction. A separate list of the investigations, compiled by the staff of Senator Weicker, was explicit; it states: "Kennedy trip to Hawaii—allegations of a wild party attended by Kennedy. [Ulasewicz] Talked to bartenders and proprietors of hideaway night spots. Charges found to be false. Kennedy did contact Japanese businessmen."†

Ulasewicz must have reported exhaustively on the results of his gumshoeing in Hawaii, for his findings formed the basis of a lengthy report from Caulfield to John Dean.‡ The memo was as detailed as a classified report the CIA might have produced on the movements of a Soviet spy:

° Caulfield also speculated that the allegation of a wiretap on Miss Kopechne may have resulted from confusion with the tap on Joseph Kraft, in which Caulfield was involved and which also took place in Georgetown—only two blocks away from the Olive Street address, as it happened.

† Both lists have the same origin; the committee list of sixty-one investigations was pieced together by the staff of the Senate Watergate committee from interviews with Caulfield, Ulasewicz, and other witnesses. It provides few details. The Weicker list contains additional data in some cases, and varies somewhat from the committee list because it was compiled by a Weicker aide who interviewed Terry Lenzner and Marc Lackritz, the Watergate staff attorneys who conducted the investigation of Caulfield and Ulasewicz.

‡ Caulfield reported to Ehrlichman until about July 1970, when John Dean was hired to replace Ehrlichman as counsel to the Preisdent. From that time on, Caulfield reported to Dean.

EMK arrived in Honolulu alone aboard Pan American Flight #2 from India via Tokyo (he didn't get off plane in Tokyo) at 11:00 A.M. August 17th . . . He departed the airport quickly with two friends identified as follows: A) John W. Goemans, Attorney, Resides in Waialua City, close to Honolulu Former EMK classmate and Aide to both Jack and Robert Kennedy B) John Carl Warnecke Architect Friend of Kennedy family Designer of JFK gravesight [sic].

Ostensibly, EMK's visit was for the purpose of evaluating the creation of a National Park at the site of a black coral reef island off the Honolulu coast. The reef bears an identifiable likeness to the profile of the late JFK. It was determined that a local Democratic Councilman, Joseph E. Bulgo (Maui Island) is handling the project on behalf of EMK.

EMK made no public appearances during his stay in Honolulu. Inquiry ascertained that he occupied the private estate of one J. Otani, located at Diamond Head Road, Honolulu. Otani is initially described as a wealthy Japanese industrialist (attempts will be made to identify him further).

Discreet inquiry determined that Kennedy used the estate solely for sleeping purposes, took only his breakfast meal at that location and quietly visited friends at other locations on the island. . . . An extensive survey of hotels, discreet cocktail lounges and other hideaways was conducted with a view towards determining a covert EMK visit. *The results were negative.* . . . In conclusion it is believed that EMK activity during his stay in Honolulu was adequately covered. No evidence was developed to indicate that his conduct was improper.

Hyannisport sources indicated EMK will remain in that area until after Labor Day and then return to Washington when Congress reconvenes. A discreet inquiry at Hyannis is programmed by our source during this period. [The last sentence, despite the *Mission: Impossible* phraseology, simply meant that Tony Ulasewicz would get to spend Labor Day weekend in Hyannis, which his travel records indicate that he did.]

Caulfield's report also informed the counsel to the President that Senator Kennedy had played tennis on August 18, and it even listed his tennis partners. It was basically a very disappointing report; quite obviously the White House had hoped to catch Kennedy with a girl —chasing a topless hula dancer around a coconut tree, perhaps, or loudly singing "The Rose of Tralee" in one of those discreet cocktail lounges—and instead all he did was sleep on the estate of that damn Japanese businessman, eat breakfast, and play tennis.

A few months later, in October, Haldeman received information from one of his assistants indicating that, as Caulfield relayed it in a memo to John Dean, "Kennedy people have engineered a regional Toyota franchise in New England." Something must have clicked in Caulfield's mind. Japs!

"My memo of August," he informed Dean, "indicating EMK visited with an asserted Japanese industrialist (J. Otani—not further identified) during a two day layover enroute from India now suggests a follow-up on J. Otani. Such inquiry is underway."

A week later Caulfield solemnly reported that Otani was "a multi-millionaire Democrat with extensive real estate and business holdings in Hawaii." Not only was Otani the proprietor of "a successful whole-sale seafood enterprise," Caulfield added, but he "significantly controls local politics in Honolulu to the extent that he is referred to as the 'Mayor Maker.' He is a frequent visitor to Honolulu's Customs area, *particularly when important Japanese visit the island.*"

Then, in the anticlimactic style that characterized many of the Caulfield-Ulasewicz operations, Caulfield added: "U.S. Customs sources contacted in this regard were unaware of any relationship between Otani and Toyota." The whole episode might have been scripted by the Marx Brothers; needless to say, nothing further was heard about the sinister doings of the Hawaiian shrimp magnate.

But more serious and nastier schemes were afoot. That same fall, as Dean later remembered it, he received a call from Haldeman's assistant, Larry Higby, "who told me that Haldeman wanted 24-hour surveillance of Senator Kennedy and regular reports on his activities."

Dean, testifying before the Senate Watergate committee about the request, added, "I passed this on to Caulfield and we discussed it. He told me that he thought that this was most unwise, because it would require several men, and also could uncover his activities in that Senator Kennedy was bound to realize he was under surveillance, and given the fact that it could easily be misinterpreted as someone who was planning an attack on his life, and the police or the FBI might be called in to investigate."

Dean said he agreed with Caulfield, convinced Higby that twenty-four-hour surveillance was an impractical idea, "and it was called off. Instead, Caulfield was to keep a general overview of Senator Kennedy's activities and pursue specific investigations of activities that might be of interest." Throughout this discussion, there is no indication that Dean expressed any shock or surprise that the counsel to the President had been asked to place a United States senator under round-the-clock physical surveillance. Implicit in Haldeman's chilling request once again was the rationale that Kennedy should be watched solely because he might run against the President in 1972, and thus represented a threat to Nixon's power and the power of the men who served him.

Ulasewicz continued to investigate Kennedy in other locales.

Senator Weicker's list includes this entry: "Phoenix-Tuscon—allegations of a wild party at a ranch in the area, attended by Senators Kennedy and Tunney—determined that the charges were unfounded." The reference is to Kennedy's close friend Senator John V. Tunney of California.

Another item states: "Hollywood, Calif. allegations of a wild party with misbehavior by leaders of both parties: Regan [undoubtedly a misspelling of Governor Ronald Reagan of California], Kennedy, Tunney." It was Honolulu all over again; there is no evidence whatever that Ulasewicz was able to document any senatorial orgies.

The black-and-white engraving depicted a pastoral eighteenth-century idyll. There was a buxom girl on a swing, a milkmaid perhaps, wearing a low-cut dress and displaying generous cleavage; nearby, in front of a castle, another full-bosomed woman was being serenaded by a man playing the flute. Trees and flowers abounded, sheep were grazing and cherubs gazed benevolently down upon the scene.

This enticing bucolic motif appeared on the wallpaper covering one side of the living room and a portion of the ceiling of a high-rise apartment on Manhattan's East Side. In October of 1971 a man who called himself Thomas A. Watkins, but who used many other names as well, rented this three-room apartment, number 11-C, at 321 East Forty-eighth Street, for $370 a month.

It was a small apartment. The living room, about fifteen by thirty feet, had as its most distinctive feature a very dark, highly polished parquet floor with a white shag rug. The room was furnished with red velour chairs, a black sofa, and a large mirror with a rococo gilt frame. There were several paintings on the walls, including some dark, brooding oils that seemed vaguely Spanish. The small bedroom had one wall completely covered in dark-brown corkboard, a double bed with a gold brocade spread, another gilt-edged mirror, and a bright-orange carpet. The bathroom was adequate, the kitchen tiny.

The wallpaper, the dark floor, the gilded mirrors, and the other furnishings made the apartment a strange mixture of mock Versailles and contemporary—as though Louis XIV had decorated a pad for a Playboy bunny. It certainly did not look at all like a place where clandestine activities would be conducted on behalf of the President of the United States with funds raised for his presidential campaign and disbursed by his personal attorney. But it was all of these things.

The canopy on the sidewalk downstairs read "Continental Apartments," and a uniformed doorman stood guard in the lobby. He wore white gloves but lacked hauteur; there was a busy garage across the street, it was far from Fifth Avenue, and the total effect was one of bogus elegance gone to seed. The setting was, nevertheless, perfect for the man who called himself Watkins. It was the sort of apartment building where there was a fairly frequent turnover in tenants and where no one inquired too closely into his or her neighbor's business.

The new tenant was a heavy-set middle-aged man, but he moved gracefully in the deceptive manner of some fat men, and he was well dressed. Mr. Watkins apparently traveled a great deal; he was not around very much. He did not seem to have a checking account, for he paid his rent and his ultilities with money orders. He met his December rent, for example, with a money order drawn on Manufacturers Hanover Trust Company, but the money order for the January rent was drawn on the Chemical Bank. The telephone company and Con Edison were paid with money orders purchased at two other banks. In addition to the name Thomas A. Watkins, he sometimes used the alias Edward T. Stanley, and at various other times, Tom Kane, Frank Rice, Tom H. Smith, James Ferguson, and John Rivers.

His real name, of course, was Anthony Ulasewicz. In August of 1971, the same month that Ulasewicz flew to Hawaii on the trail of Edward Kennedy, he had received an advance of $12,000 from Herbert Kalmbach to cover the cost of renting the apartment in New York and other expenses. Over the next several months, according to the Watergate committee records, Kalmbach paid out $50,000 in cash to finance present and planned activities by Ulasewicz.

There is no doubt that Ulasewicz, as Thomas A. Watkins, rented the apartment on East Forty-eighth Street. What remains a matter of dispute, and considerable mystery, is the purpose for which he did so.

On January 10, 1972, a meeting of Caulfield, Ulasewicz, and G. Gordon Liddy took place in apartment 11-C. With his guards mustache, fanatic expression, and views to match, Liddy later became a central figure in the Watergate scandal. The Liddy stories were legion: as a young prosecutor he had fired a gun in a courtroom to impress a jury; he once held his hand over a burning candle to demonstrate his bravado; and he liked to tell women how to kill a man with a pencil. After his team of bunglers was caught in the Watergate, he refused to talk to the prosecutors and went silently to jail. He told his White House superiors they could shoot him if that would help. G. Gordon Liddy gave *machismo* a bad name.

A former FBI man and local prosecutor in Dutchess County, New York, Liddy had joined the Nixon Administration in 1969, worked in the Treasury Department, and was recruited to the White House Plumbers unit in July 1971. In September, along with fellow Plumber E. Howard Hunt, Jr., Liddy and two of the Cuban-Americans who later broke into the Watergate participated in the burglary in Los Angeles of the office of Daniel Ellsberg's psychiatrist. In December, Liddy was named counsel to the Committee for the Re-Election of the President (CRP or CREEP, as it became better known). From that time on, he was placed in charge of developing a political intelligence plan, code-named Gemstone, that seven months later culminated in the Watergate break-in.

So in January, when Liddy flew to New York with Caulfield for the meeting in the apartment on East Forty-eighth Street, he had already been named Nixon's chief covert operative, outranking both Caulfield and Ulasewicz. Caulfield's version of the meeting is that it took place for the purpose of going over Ulasewicz' financial records. "We were going up at my insistence that Ulasewicz' accounts be totally correct," he said. Caulfield said he had asked John Dean to come to New York for this worthy fiscal purpose, but Dean was too busy and "had Gordon go up with me. It was a half-hour, forty-five-minute meeting. He checked the books and everything was in order."

While it may be that the meeting was, in effect, a gathering of accountants beneath the gilded mirrors, a further explanation was offered by Watergate staff attorney Marc Lackritz: "Ulasewicz and Caulfield claimed that the White House was not using Ulasewicz much in late 1971, so Caulfield went to Dean and urged him to go to New York City to check up on Ulasewicz, to check his books, make sure everything was running smoothly. But this was a ploy to bring Ulasewicz back into White House attention more."

On the plane en route to New York, Liddy had asked Caulfield, "What are you fellows doing, what type of activity?"

Caulfield said he replied, "We are trying to determine if Esther Newberg is working for Muskie." Esther Newberg had worked in the boiler room for Robert Kennedy in the 1968 campaign. She was one of the women who attended the cookout at Chappaquiddick.

Many months later Howard Hunt was being questioned by investigators for the Senate Watergate committee; he said that Liddy had told him the New York apartment was to be used in a scheme to seduce one of the girls who had been at the Chappaquiddick party; she would be photographed, and then blackmailed to reveal details of what had happened the night that Mary Jo Kopechne died.

Both Caulfield and Ulasewicz have vehemently denied this version. Hunt, in an autobiographical book published after Watergate, stuck to his story.[*] He said he asked what was involved in New York, and Liddy replied: "Something about one of the broads who was at the Chappaquiddick party—you know one of the survivors. I gather they've set up some sort of fabulous pad and it's run by another ex-New York cop. The idea seems to be to have the broad fall in love

[*] *Undercover: Memoirs of an American Secret Agent* (New York: Berkley, 1974).

with the ex-cop, and while they're in bed together, automatic cameras are supposed to whir and buzz like *From Russia With Love*."

When Liddy returned from New York, Hunt wrote, he telephoned and said, "The setup's unbelievable. This middle-aged guy who's in charge of the 'operation' has an accent I can't place. And the pad! It's got to be a cop's idea of an East Side bordello in the 1880's—secondhand furniture, red plush sofas—and the Golden Greek's trying to build a fake wall—a partition—so he can get cameras behind it." In a footnote Hunt added: "Not until the Ervin televised hearings was I able to identify ex-New York policeman Anthony Ulasewicz as Liddy's 'Golden Greek.' "*

By January 1972, when Caulfield told Liddy on the flight to New York that they were investigating whether Esther Newberg was working for Muskie, Miss Newberg had in fact already been located by another former New York City police detective hired by Ulasewicz. The new recruit was Anthony LaRocco, a twenty-one-year veteran of the New York City Police Department who for much of his career had done squad work in the South Bronx, in an area now known by the police as "Fort Apache" because of the high crime rate.† He lived in northern Westchester County, where he had helped to organize a police fraternal organization known as the Westchester and Putnam County Shields. In June of 1970, as the new president of the group, LaRocco pledged his organization's support of Nixon's Cambodian invasion, and in an Agnewesque speech he attacked demonstrating students and "weak-kneed school and public officials" who give in "to mangy, malingering radicals and oftentimes side with them in criticizing their own police forces."

LaRocco retired from the police force that year, and Ulasewicz hired him to work in four or five White House investigations in December 1971 and January 1972. He was paid about $1,500.

His first major assignment was to find out surreptitiously whether

---

* According to other versions of the story that circulated among Watergate investigators, the alleged scheme involved the hiring of a handsome man to do the seducing. As for Hunt's identification of Ulasewicz as the "Golden Greek," it was rather improbable on the face of it; Anthony Ulasewicz was neither Greek nor likely to be mistaken, even in the dark, for a Hollywood star.

In an interview with the author in Washington in November of 1974, Howard Hunt reiterated this version, and this exchange took place:

Q. Were the "boiler-room girls" the target of the apartment?
A. One girl was the target. I don't know the girl's name. She was one of the girls who worked for Kennedy . . . no operation was conducted.

† Of minor historical interest, it may be noted that LaRocco's beat included Hunts Point, a section of the Bronx that Howard Hunt claims was named for one of his ancestors.

Esther Newberg was working at Muskie headquarters in Manhattan. Asked how he was expected to carry out that task, since he had not met Miss Newberg, LaRocco said in an interview that he had been given a "magazine picture" of her. It was from "a local magazine in the Boston area," he said. "Tony showed me the picture." He went to Muskie headquarters at Fifty-ninth Street and Park Avenue and was able to pick out Miss Newberg from the photo. "She was a pretty, dark-haired girl, sort of on the short side," he said, adding that he had no idea why Ulasewicz wanted to locate Esther Newberg.

LaRocco said he had been in the apartment on East Forty-eighth Street, but he denied knowledge of any plan to attempt to seduce Miss Newberg or the other young woman in the apartment. "They weren't going to use me," LaRocco said. "I have a wife and six kids, and as a matter of fact, my wife was with me, doing some Christmas shopping that day." It was while his wife was shopping, LaRocco said, that he strolled into Muskie headquarters and spotted Miss Newberg.

Esther Newberg was born in Middletown, Connecticut, of a political family with Kennedy roots: "My mother was part of the John Bailey machine." When Miss Newberg got out of college it was not too difficult to place her as a chief clerk of Senator Abraham Ribicoff's Subcommittee on Government Operations. Robert Kennedy was a member of the subcommittee, and in 1967 Miss Newberg joined his staff. She worked in the boiler room in 1968, and at the time of Chappaquiddick, was employed at the Urban Institute in Washington.

By 1976 Miss Newberg, an articulate woman with a quick intelligence, had moved further ahead in her successful career in politics; she was executive director of the New York State Democratic Committee, with offices at the committee's headquarters in Manhattan. Until informed by the author, she said, she had been unaware that Ulasewicz' agent had gone to Muskie headquarters to locate her. She had heard of the apartment, of course, because a story had been published about it in the newspapers.

She found it astonishing, crazy, that the White House would have had to run a covert operation to find her. "It was very easy to locate me," she said. "I was Muskie's campaign manager for New York State, and the first woman to head a state campaign for a major presidential candidate. The *New York Times* ran a big story about it with a picture in the summer of 1971. So it was not difficult to find me."

Miss Newberg said she had never been in the apartment at 321 East Forty-eighth Street. "During that period of time I was seeing one person," she said, and it would have been very unlikely that anyone working for the Nixon Administration had asked her for a date. But she saw a lot of people politically, and very occasionally, someone in politics might ask her out for a drink at the end of the day, so it was always possible. "So I went over that in my head. I keep a weekly calendar. I went back over my calendar. There was no one."

Still, just to be sure, Esther Newberg took a look at the building. "After the address became known," she said, "I walked by the apartment building to see if I had ever been there, and I hadn't."

She had checked with Nance Lyons, the only other member of the group who had been living in New York City at the time, and "she had not been approached either." Susan Tannenbaum, another of the young women at Chappaquiddick, had dated the same man for seven years, Miss Newberg said, and would not have gone out with someone else. In short, Miss Newberg said, she was sure that if any of the other women had been approached, she would have heard about it.

On the other hand, she had learned to be careful. "I was convinced along with Margaret that my phone was tapped, there was so much clicking and noise. So I used pay phones to talk to any of the other girls."

John Caulfield has characterized as nonsense Howard Hunt's story of the plan to use the apartment as a seduction nest. "Ulasewicz did in fact rent the apartment, but the only females that I know were there were his wife and daughter on their hands and knees to clean it up. There was never any boiler-room-girl seduction plan. That was leaked purposefully to discredit Ulasewicz or myself . . . The name of the game in Washington at that time was to destroy the guy who can destroy you." Ulasewicz rented the apartment, Caulfield said, "with a view that he would start his own detective agency there." But Caulfield also conceded that the apartment would have served as the New York base for Project Sandwedge, the ill-fated intelligence plan Caulfield had proposed for Nixon's 1972 campaign. The $511,000 budget for Sandwedge that Caulfield submitted to John Dean allocated $210,000 for operations in New York, including $50,000 for "Special Projects," $5,000 for "Headquarters, N.Y.C. (Apartment, false identities, mail drops, telephone, etc.)," and $15,000 for "Equipment-Electronic-Surveillance)."

Caulfield confirmed that Ulasewicz had given him a key to the apartment, and said he had slept there once. Caulfield said he could not explain how Liddy might have come away from their meeting at the apartment with the impression that it was to be used for seducing women in an operation ultimately aimed at discrediting Teddy Kennedy. "The only way I can figure it out is the type of apartment, and the mention of Esther Newberg [on the flight to New York] all created in Gordon's mind's eye this idea. But Gordon's sitting up in the can, so I don't want to guess at what was in his mind. The last thing Caulfield and Ulasewicz would be involved in is to take broads up there and seduce them. We were too smart for that. If there was anything to it, the prosecutors would have jumped on it. It never happened. Sure Tony said to the prosecutors, 'I did it.' 'You did what?' they said. Tony said he had rented the apartment as a seduction nest and then he said, 'I was going to knock off one a month.'" And everyone laughed at that, Caulfield said.*

Why, then, the covert surveillance of Esther Newberg at Muskie headquarters? Caulfield said the assignment came from Dean through Colson. Caulfield claimed he did not know the purpose, but had assumed that Colson suspected "it might be an intelligence coup for Muskie—a Chappie girl now working for Muskie." Perhaps, Caulfield indicated, Miss Newberg would talk to her new employer and "Muskie would be able to break the Chappaquiddick thing."

As for the apartment, Ulasewicz said, it was rented "as an office for a New York agency headed by myself." Did he mean as the New York City base for Sandwedge? No, Ulasewicz said, he had never heard of Sandwedge at that time. "In the type of work I do," he continued, "I wouldn't take an office in a building. A lot of it is after hours. People don't like to sign a book, like you have to do in an office building. They don't want that. In the building where I rented the apartment, there were other people in businesses, real estate, girl Fridays, what not, a lot of people coming and going."

But neither Caulfield nor Ulasewicz, nor the Watergate investigators, ever explained why the White House, through Kalmbach, paid for an East Side apartment that Ulasewicz planned to use, or was using, "for a New York agency headed by myself."

The Kennedy seduction plot, if it existed, was not proven. Nor is there any evidence that any of the women who were present at Chappaquiddick were ever lured to apartment 11-C. The seduction story, ultimately, rests upon evidence given only by Howard Hunt.

On the other hand, it is entirely possible that the scheme was thought of and discussed but not carried out. It is a matter of record that Ulasewicz rented the apartment with Nixon campaign funds provided by Kalmbach. It is also a matter of record that Ulasewicz rented the apartment under a false name, that he gave the key to Caulfield, a presidential assistant, that G. Gordon Liddy attended a meeting in the apartment while serving as chief burglar and head of secret political operations for Nixon's 1972 re-election campaign, and

---

* Ulasewicz, too, shrugged off the seduction plot. "My age is fifty-five," he said. "I'm not Clark Gable, although I'm pretty rugged. Anyone who would credit me with seducing five women in a political homicide to make them tell the truth is giving me a lot of credit. I don't know how my wife would feel about it, but it's giving me a lot of credit.

"A good investigator I was. For three years, nobody even knew I existed. As far as the apartment is concerned, it is a figment of the imagination of Hunt and Liddy."

that soon after the apartment had been rented, a third New York City police detective was hired with Nixon campaign funds to slip up to Muskie headquarters and locate Esther Newberg, a woman who had been at Chappaquiddick with Senator Kennedy.

And of all the women at Chappaquiddick, Esther Newberg would have been of the most interest to Nixon's secret-police agents. In the first place, she was the only one who talked to reporters and who was widely quoted after the accident. In the second place, she had been Mary Jo Kopechne's roommate in the motel at Edgartown. According to the report issued by Judge James A. Boyle, who presided over the inquest, when Miss Kopechne left the cottage at Chappaquiddick with Kennedy she did not ask Esther Newberg for the key to her motel room, and she did not take her own purse. The inquest report with these findings was released in April of 1970, and published in the Washington *Post* and other newspapers. Ulasewicz and Caulfield certainly read the inquest report (there is some reason to think that the White House obtained a copy before it was officially released), and they could have been expected to conclude that of all the young women at the cookout, Esther Newberg might know the most.

When the story of the apartment surfaced during the Watergate investigations, Esther Newberg said, "it frightened me. I thought, suppose I *had* met someone, and gone back to the apartment. Who knows what might have developed, with photographs and cameras and what not. All those thoughts went through my head. I guess I'm just lucky that it didn't happen."

On January 27, 1972, seventeen days after G. Gordon Liddy met with Caulfield and Ulasewicz in the New York apartment, Liddy unveiled his $1 million Gemstone plan to Attorney General Mitchell in Mitchell's office.

Liddy's plan called for the use of mugging squads to rough up anti-Nixon demonstrators, kidnapping teams to spirit demonstrators at the Republican National Convention (then planned for San Diego) across the border to Mexico, buggings and break-ins at various targets, and prostitutes stationed on a floating brothel which would be anchored offshore in Miami Beach during the Democratic convention.[*] Liddy, John Dean testified, had explained that "The prostitutes could be used at the Democratic convention to get information as well as compromise the persons involved. I recall Liddy as saying that the girls would be high class and the best in the business." The plan had a familiar ring: the yacht would be wired for sound, and secret cameras

---

[*] Liddy's plan, considerably scaled down and presented at two subsequent meetings, was finally approved on March 30, 1972, with a budget of $250,000. It called for a break-in and bugging of Democratic National Committee headquarters in the Watergate.

installed. The photographs and tapes of prominent Democrats *in flagrante delicto* with the high-class call girls would then be used for blackmail.

There were various other Caulfield-Ulasewicz investigations directed at or involving Kennedy; at one point, in 1971, a team of *Newsday* reporters, headed by Robert Greene, was preparing a highly enlightening series on Nixon's friend Bebe Rebozo. The members of the White House palace guard got into their heads that "the Kennedy Foundation"—presumably the Robert F. Kennedy Memorial Foundation—was financing the investigation. Caulfield wrote a memo to Dean entitled "Newsday Article Assertedly Financed by Kennedy Foundation."

Caulfield conceded that "Proving this assertion may not be possible. As you know it is based upon Bebe's observation that Greene and Guthman are Kennedy loyalists and that Moyers is now with the Kennedy Foundation." The references were to reporter Greene, Edwin O. Guthman, former press secretary to Robert Kennedy and national editor of the Los Angeles *Times*, which owns *Newsday*, and Bill Moyers, *Newsday*'s former publisher, who had—no easy feat—remained friendly with Robert Kennedy while serving Lyndon Johnson.

There were various desperate efforts to find out in advance about the contents of the Rebozo series and afterward to retaliate against Greene, *Newsday*, and its editors. Caulfield testified that Rebozo had told him of the upcoming article, which Caulfield had already heard about from his friend Pat Henry, an FBI agent in New York. The FBI was pushing hard to find out what was in the series and when it was being published; and the government was clearly watching Greene, because in September, before the series ran, Caulfield had reported to Dean that Greene "has been in both Washington and Florida within the past two weeks."*

At an executive session of the Watergate committee, Caulfield said he thought the information about Greene's travel movements had also come from Pat Henry. Caulfield was asked whether the information might have come from another source—had there been any wiretaps or physical surveillance of the *Newsday* reporter? No wiretaps, Caulfield said, but as for physical surveillance, he had a "vague recollection" of Dean having told him "that the Secret Service was

---

* In the same memo Caulfield reported that "A discreet look at the newspaper's publication calendar has been accomplished," on the basis of which it did not appear that the Rebozo series would be published that month. But, Caulfield wrote, extraordinary security measures were being taken within *Newsday* to prevent employees from learning the contents of the series. Caulfield testified that all this had come from FBI agent Henry.

taking a look at the newspaper reporter team that was in Key Biscayne putting together this story."

The most ominous development was that John Dean ordered a tax audit of Robert Greene. Dean testified that he had been instructed that the *Newsday* reporter "should have some [tax] problems." Caulfield confirmed to the senators that Dean had ordered him to see how an audit might be accomplished; he said he spoke to IRS and it was indicated to him that the audit had been set in motion. Greene was in fact audited by the New York State tax department under a federal-state audit program.* (Caulfield was involved in a number of other efforts by the White House to misuse the Internal Revenue Service, as will be detailed in chapter 10.)

But Caulfield and Ulasewicz never strayed far from the main political target. Any mention of the name Kennedy, however peripheral, apparently triggered a Pavlovian reaction within the White House. In one case Ulasewicz was turned loose to investigate the wife of the chauffeur for Mrs. Rose Kennedy.† The chauffeur, John Ryan, lived in quarters above the garage at Ambassador Joseph P. Kennedy's home in Palm Beach; his wife Rebecca, thirty, died there in January 1972. The local medical examiner, Dr. Hugh Dortch, listed the cause of death as an apparent overdose of Darvon, a painkilling drug which he said Mrs. Ryan had been taking for a recent back injury which she had suffered in her work as an airline stewardess. The medical examiner said Mrs. Ryan had been hit in the back by a suitcase that had shot from an overhead rack when the plane went though some turbulence. The record does not show who in the White House ordered Ulasewicz to inquire into the death of Mrs. Ryan, but Caulfield confirmed that the investigation did take place.

The Ulasewicz-Caulfield investigations fell into distinct categories: many were designed to gather damaging personal information about the social life, sexual activities, or drinking habits of prominent Democrats; some involved the misuse and attempted misuse of IRS and other agencies against political enemies; and still others were defensive, designed to head off trouble in advance. In this category, for

* Both David Laventhol, the editor of *Newsday*, and William Attwood, the publisher, were audited after the series ran, and the Long Island newspaper was plagued by a series of other problems. The paper's White House correspondent, Martin Schram, did not get a seat on the plane to China when Nixon visited Peking in February 1972, and when his typewriter in the White House pressroom broke, he was unable to get a repairman past the gate to fix it.

† The Watergate committee's list of political investigations included this as "Investigation into the causes of death of Rebecca Ryan, personal secretary to Mrs. Rose Kennedy; date unknown." Edward Martin, administrative assistant to Senator Kennedy, said that Mrs. Ryan was not Rose Kennedy's secretary and "had no connection with the Kennedys in any way, shape or form."

example, was one entitled "Investigation into allegations of a White House official being involved with call girls." Liddy had proposed using call girls against Democrats, but it would not do at all, and ran counter to the prim image of the Nixon White House, if an assistant to the President were caught in a cathouse. Fortunately, Caulfield said, the report, when checked out, proved to be false.

A number of the investigations were ludicrous, including Ulasewicz' inquiries into the background of Richard M. Dixon, a comedian and mimic of the President whose sole claim to fame was a rough resemblance to Nixon. Some of the more idiotic investigations had titles that sounded vastly more intriguing than their substance, i.e., "Investigation into the House of Mercy Home for Unwed Mothers, Washington, D.C.; date unknown." The title conjures up marvelous Victorian images: perhaps the White House suspected that an unwed mother, more to be pitied than censured, had been cruelly abandoned by some Democratic scoundrel who would—through the noble efforts of Caulfield and Ulasewicz—be held up to public obloquy.

Caulfield gave a different explanation. "They had some fruit that came into the White House," he said in the interview at his home, "and asked us to check to be sure that this was a legitimate charity." Apparently the White House wanted to get rid of the fruit, someone (Nixon?) had suggested the home for unwed mothers, and—in a fit of caution—Caulfield had been assigned to make sure that the institution was an appropriate repository for the foundling fruit.

One Ulasewicz investigation that might have come straight out of *Alice in Wonderland* is entitled "Investigation into the lessor of the apartment to the Nixon family in 1945 in New York City." Watergate investigators were stumped on why the White House would be digging into the background of someone who had rented an apartment to the Nixons more than *two decades* before.° However, John Ehrlichman provided the key to the mystery in an interview with the author:

"One day Richard Nixon began reminiscing about how he and Pat had lived in a nice apartment in New York. The President said, 'I

° Something of a mystery surrounds Nixon's brief experience as a New Yorker in 1945 and early 1946. That Nixon lived in New York City during this period is nowhere listed in standard biographies of Nixon, nor in official biographical sketches, such as *Who's Who in America*. However, the Department of the Navy, in answer to an inquiry, confirmed that Nixon was stationed in the "Bureau of Aeronautics, New York, New York," for about a year, from the spring of 1945 to March 1946. Nixon, a lieutenant, served in the Navy from 1942 to 1946, much of the time in the South Pacific. After the war he was transferred first to Washington and then to New York to wind up naval aircraft contracts. When he returned to New York to practice law in the mid-sixties, it was in higher style, as a resident of 810 Fifth Avenue, overlooking Central Park at Sixty-second Street.

wonder whatever became of that nice lady who was our landlady?'"
It was the sort of musing that comes to nothing when engaged in by
ordinary mortals, but the whims of kings are indulged; the more Nixon
thought about it, Ehrlichman said, the more he concluded that the
President of these United States ought to be able to find his old
landlady; surely the vast resources of the federal government were
equal to the challenge. "Rather than tax the FBI with the task,"
Ehrlichman said, "I had Caulfield send Ulasewicz to find the landlady.
But he never did. Nixon couldn't remember where he had lived."

There were ludicrous aspects as well to secret investigations of
two films that annoyed the President or his aides. In the summer of
1971 the White House learned that someone was commercially ex-
hibiting Nixon's 1952 Checkers speech; Caulfield wrote a memo to
Dean about the showing of the "uncut film," which made it sound
as though the Checkers speech were obscene, which may be closer
to the truth than actually intended. Dean instructed Caulfield to
investigate. Caulfield, appearing at an executive session of the Watergate committee, was questioned about how this was done:

A. I believe I asked my secretary to go and view the film.
Q. Your secretary being whom?
A. Miss Anne Dawson.
Q. What did Miss Dawson report to you after she had seen the
film?
A. She reported to me her observations . . . that it was an uncut
film of Richard Nixon's 1952 Checkers speech, and I recall her
indicating that the audience was chuckling throughout the entire
speech.

Despite this indignity, Caulfield said no further action was taken.
In a somewhat similar episode, the White House gumshoes even
investigated the Smothers Brothers. Early in 1972, memos began flying
in the White House about another alarming film, and Caulfield was
unleashed again. In due course an investigative report, dated January
17, 1972, was produced. It is worth quoting:

SUBJECT: RUMOR SMOTHERS BROTHERS ARE PRODUCING
A DEROGATORY FILM ABOUT RICHARD NIXON

A pretext inquiry at the offices of SmoBro International Produc-
tions, Inc., Los Angeles developed the following information:
SmoBro has just completed production of a film to be entitled
"Another Nice Mess." It will be distributed to nationwide theatres
beginning in March.
The film is described as a satirical spoof. According to Lanny
Scher, SmoBro's press agent, Richard Nixon will be portrayed as
Oliver Hardy and Spiro Agnew as Laurel . . .

But most of the investigations were less hilarious; many, as Ulasewicz admitted under questioning by Senator Weicker, were designed to dig up dirt on political opponents. When the Senator from Connecticut expressed some wonderment about how Ulasewicz was able to gather such information, Ulasewicz led Weicker gently below stairs: "I would develop my leads by interviewing bartenders, patrons, whatever time it might take, how long— if it were a hotel, hotel employees, waiters. Those kind of people are the most talkative."

Although Senator Kennedy occupied a major share of Ulasewicz' time, other potential presidential candidates were not overlooked; a Watergate committee staff memo of an interview with Ulasewicz states: "Ulasewicz went to Maine to look into Muskie's background and was directed to look at the printed record to discover if there were any scandals or other skeletons in Muskie's closet." The memo said Ulasewicz was assigned to conduct "a similar investigation into the background of Hubert Humphrey."

In the spring of 1971 Charles Colson urged that John Dean have Caulfield investigate Muskie's alleged connections with a Maine sugar company that had received a government loan and was in financial difficulty. Caulfield endorsed Colson's suggestion that the White House obtain backdoor information on the matter from a certain Commerce Department official who was regarded as politically loyal so there would be "minimal White House exposure." Muskie was among the senators whose lists of campaign contributors were checked by Ulasewicz, and there were various other inquiries and operations directed at the Maine Democrat.

One such operation took place in New York City at the Dakota, one of the oldest luxury apartment houses in Manhattan. The building, located on Central Park West at Seventy-second Street, was the setting for the film *Rosemary's Baby*, and many of the exterior shots were taken there. A number of celebrities are among the building's tenants.

Muskie had named Morris B. Abram, the distinguished attorney and civic leader, to head his task force on domestic issues. Abram had been a prosecutor at the Nuremberg trials of Nazi leaders after World War II; he had also been president of the American Jewish Committee, and of Brandeis University. Abram's task force met in his spacious, high-ceilinged apartment on the second floor of the Dakota. At a meeting on November 17, 1971, one member of the task force discussed a possible $30 billion cut in defense spending to free more funds for social programs. Abrams was astonished, and angered, when a column later appeared by Rowland Evans and Robert Novak, reporting the precise figure and blasting the idea as irresponsible.

"The thirty-billion-dollar figure had been mentioned," Abram said. "We never made any recommendation with respect to it and we wondered how in the hell did Evans and Novak get it. I didn't know how they got it, but I realized after Watergate broke that they, the Republicans, were purloining stuff from Muskie headquarters in Washington." According to Novak, the source of the story was a disaffected Muskie contributor.

What Abram was referring to was Ruby I, a separate political espionage operation developed in the summer of 1971 by Jeb Stuart Magruder, a former cosmetics salesman who became Mitchell's deputy in the 1972 campaign, and Ken Rietz, who headed the campaign's youth division. Rietz recruited John R. Buckley, an ex-FBI man and head of the investigation division of the Office of Economic Opportunity who gained notoriety during Watergate under the alias "Fat Jack."[*] Buckley in turn recruited one Elmer Wyatt, a taxi driver who insinuated himself into Muskie headquarters and ended up delivering interoffice mail in his cab. En route, Wyatt fed documents to Buckley, who photographed them (while still working for OEO), and passed them to Rietz, and later to Howard Hunt. At least some of the documents, including a staff recommendation that a Muskie subcommittee hold hearings on' property taxes in California, were sent to Evans and Novak and quoted by them in columns.

On January 11, 1972, Abram's task force held another meeting at his apartment in the Dakota. Abram was unaware that this time the White House attempted physical surveillance of the Muskie advisers. Ulasewicz had dispatched Anthony LaRocco to the Dakota and arranged to rendezvous with him there. But the assignment proved to be more formidable than they had imagined.

As anyone who has ever strolled past the Dakota knows, the entrance is a small fortress guarded by a man in a sentry box who checks all visitors; a grilled iron gate bars the way to an inner courtyard. "We were supposed to sit in the lobby and observe who went

---

[*] Although Ruby I was run separately from the Caulfield-Ulasewicz operations, there was some overlap in one respect. Apparently the White House checked out "Fat Jack" with John Caulfield before he was recruited. On September 21, 1971, Buckley was the subject of a Caulfield memo to Dean:

> During Donald Rumsfeld's tenure at O.E.O., John Buckley was his Director of Inspection and Investigation, therefore, I touched based [*sic*] with Donald and he advised the following: A) Buckley is a Republican and he is considered trustworthy. In addition, he can be counted upon to respect a confidence. B) While Buckley can be considered intelligent, Rumsfeld states that he is not "quick smart." Further, in matters of sensitivity it is Rumsfeld's judgment that he should be led and the specific details of an assignment should be clearly spelled out.

[*] The Nixon family was hamburger-prone. As a Navy lieutenant on Green Island during World War II, Richard Nixon operated "Nixon's Snack Shack," which may have been the only hamburger stand in the South Pacific.

in to the Muskie meeting," LaRocco said in an interview. "But there was no way to get in and do surveillance. There was no place to sit. There is no lobby in the Dakota."

By far the most sensitive assignment given Caulfield was to oversee a Secret Service wiretap of the President's troublesome brother, F. Donald Nixon. The burly Donald, two years younger than the President, had an unerring instinct for financial disaster and a knack for getting into business deals that carried a high potential for political embarrassment to his brother. As far back as 1956, when Nixon was Vice President, Donald accepted a secret $205,000 loan from industrialist Howard Hughes; he sank the money into a string of fast-food restaurants in Southern California that sold Nixonburgers and went broke.°

Donald, a Newport Beach neighbor of Herbert Kalmbach, was vice president of Ogden Foods when his brother moved into the White House in 1969; the company catered to the same airlines whose international routes were subject to presidential approval. The President dispatched Ehrlichman to a summit meeting with the head of the Ogden corporation in New York to see whether less sensitive work could be found for brother Donald; ultimately the President asked his friend J. Willard Marriott, owner of the Hot Shoppes restaurant chain, to hire his brother, and he did.

The President breathed easier, but then in the fall of 1969 Donald broke free and visited the Dominican Republic with John Meier, a Howard Hughes lieutenant, and Anthony Hatsis, a mining promoter. The idea later gained currency that Nixon's two traveling companions were using their pudgy friend's name to try to extract valuable mineral rights from the Dominican Republic, but Donald, in his W. C. Fieldsian manner had a different explanation:

"Mr. Meier had a group of big investors," he told the Watergate committee, ". . . they wanted to build hotels for Marriott. . . . these key guys, $400 million they had to invest in hotels any place in the world, South America, Canada, United States, Europe—anyplace. . . . this guy John Meier, he was always dangling this stuff and always trying— this one trip with Hatsis and Meier to the Dominican Republic, on the return trip of that they were offering me, God, fabulous amounts here, $250,000 a year just to join them and join this organization."

When news of the Dominican trip filtered to the White House, it must have particularly alarmed Kalmbach, who had been delegated to keep his neighbor away from Johnny Meier. Apparently the U.S.

° The Nixon family was hamburger-prone. As a Navy lieutenant on Green Island during World War II, Richard Nixon operated "Nixon's Snack Shack," which may have been the only hamburger stand in the South Pacific.

ambassador to the Dominican Republic was acquainted with Ehrlichman, and got word back to the White House about Donald's escapade. According to one knowledgeable source, Nixon then ordered Ehrlichman to have his own brother wiretapped.

"I've got to know what he's up to," Nixon told Ehrlichman by this account. "I don't want to use Hoover—he can use it against me. See if the CIA will do it."

Ehrlichman telephoned General Robert E. Cushman, Jr., Deputy Director of the CIA, who balked at having the CIA tap the President's brother (although a year later, Cushman acceded to another Ehrlichman request that the CIA assist Howard Hunt, and in due course the Agency gave Hunt his famous red wig and other spy paraphernalia used in the break-in of Ellsberg's psychiatrist).

With the CIA backing off, Nixon then asked Ehrlichman whom Lyndon Johnson had used to keep an eye on *his* troublesome brother, Sam Houston Johnson. The Secret Service, Ehrlichman reported; whereupon Nixon instructed Ehrlichman to have the Secret Service tap Donald. Caulfield was ordered by Ehrlichman to monitor the wiretap on Donald and report back anything interesting. The tap was installed sometime in 1970 on Donald's home in Newport Beach. Caulfield said the Secret Service reported the results to him orally; but nothing very juicy was being overheard, and Caulfield said that after three weeks he recommended, and Ehrlichman agreed, to remove the tap on the President's brother.°

The Secret Service also conducted physical surveillance of Donald Nixon—Caulfield recalled some "in the vicinity of the residence" at Newport Beach—and apparently took surreptitious photographs at Orange County Airport, California, of Donald with Meier and Hatsis.

As if Donald Nixon were not giving his brother enough headaches —what with Nixonburgers, and selling food to the airlines and consorting with Howard Hughes's people in Santo Domingo—in the fall of 1969 Ulasewicz was assigned to investigate unsettling reports that Donald's son, Donald Nixon, Jr., was living in a commune. *The President's nephew might be a hippie.*

According to Ehrlichman, the alarms sounded when police stopped young Donald in California, and the Secret Service sent a report of the incident to Haldeman. The report must have been dismaying to the straight-laced Haldeman, for the Weicker list of Ulasewicz in-

° At a news conference on November 17, 1973, Nixon confirmed that the Secret Service had wiretapped his brother "for security reasons," and he claimed that "my brother was aware of it" at the time his phone was being tapped. Donald, his fraternal loyalty apparently unstrained, testified, "I did find out, of course, and it was approved by me, didn't bother me at all, my phone being tapped, because I had nothing to hide."

vestigations reported allegations that Donald Nixon, Jr., had engaged in "improper conduct, that drugs were involved, and love-making groups, at Three Forks, Sierra Madre." Ulasewicz, like Bogart, made his way to the Sierra Madre. He was apparently true to form in investigating these disturbing reports, for the list notes, "spoke to bartenders."

Ehrlichman's recollection is that it all turned out happily in the end. "He was living in some way, it was not clear if it was a commune or what, that it was felt might be a political liability. I think he was living with a woman. He got very straight thereafter, and wore a blazer and Gucci loafers."

Most of the Ulasewicz operations appear to have ended around January 1972, as Liddy and CREEP began cranking up their felonious Gemstone plan. Most, but not all. Weicker's list contains this entry for Ulasewicz investigation number 42: "Allegation that Carl Albert was involved in improper behavior at the Zebra Room. Spoke to bartenders, etc."

The Zebra Room is a neighborhood bar and grill in a residential section of northwest Washington, and the Democratic Speaker of the House lived a few blocks away. On September 9, 1972, Albert (later insisting "I was not drunk") hit two parked cars with his white Thunderbird outside the bar. According to newspaper accounts of the accident, when police arrived, the Speaker began pushing at them and yelling, "Leave me alone, I'm Carl Albert, Speaker of the House . . . you can't touch me . . . I just got you your raises," which was true enough, since Congress had recently passed a pay raise for police and firemen in the nation's capital. Albert paid the driver of one of the other cars on the spot to settle the dispute, and no charges were filed against him.

The incident might have aroused relatively little attention but for a young couple, Paul Leiman, twenty-two, and his wife, Andrea, both graduate students at George Washington University. The Leimans had left their apartment just before midnight to get some pizza when they saw a crowd and a police car. Drawing near, they recognized Albert. The Speaker, said Leiman, "was plastered." The Leimans did not say anything publicly until they read in the Washington *Post* that Albert had denied he was drunk. Outraged, the couple called the *Post*, which then printed their version.

But the most fascinating aspect of this Ulasewicz investigation is that the Zebra Room incident took place in September almost three months *after* the Watergate break-in. Even as the President and his fellow co-conspirators were contriving to cover up the Watergate burglary, another arm of Nixon's secret police was trying to get something on the Speaker of the House. And there is strong evidence that the investigation was retaliatory and personally ordered by Nixon.*

In any event, the order could not have come through Caulfield. Four months earlier, Caulfield had moved to the Treasury Department, after a brief and disappointing interlude at CREEP, where he was given the ignominious job of serving as John Mitchell's bodyguard. It was back to Ryer Avenue, toting a gun. His dream of heading covert intelligence operations for Nixon in 1972 had been crushed.

Not that Caulfield hadn't tried. In the spring of 1971, sensing that the coming presidential election would be where the action was, Caulfield had told John Dean that he was thinking of leaving the White House to set up his own security consulting firm; it would do work for big corporations and for the Republicans in 1972. Caulfield also discussed his plan, Sandwedge, with Ulasewicz and many others, including Joseph I. Woods, the brother of the President's secretary, Rose Mary Woods. Caulfield's proposal called for Woods to head the Chicago office of Sandwedge, a brilliant stroke, since Woods, the former sheriff of Cook County, also had the advantage of being Rose Mary's brother, which might serve to curry favor within the White House.†

Dean asked Caulfield to put his proposal in writing, and Caulfield prepared a twelve-page memo entitled "Operation Sandwedge." As Caulfield explained, this agency, "surfacely disassociated from the administration by virtue of an established business cover," would be able to perform "offensive intelligence and defensive security" for the entire campaign and the Republican convention and would make "a significant and perhaps crucial contribution towards the reelection of Richard Nixon." As a selling point for his plan, Caulfield warned that Intertel, the mysterious and powerful private intelligence and security agency formed in 1970 and serving, among other corporate clients,

---

* In a conversation with John Dean and H. R. Haldeman on September 15, 1972—four days after Albert's accident had been publicized—Nixon was informed that a General Accounting Office auditor was snooping around the White House on orders of Carl Albert.

HALDEMAN: Well, God damn the Speaker of the House. Maybe we better put a little heat on him.

PRESIDENT: I think so too.

HALDEMAN: Because he's got a lot worse problems than he's going to find down here. . . .

PRESIDENT: I know . . . [Unintelligible] let the police department [unintelligible].

HALDEMAN: . . . What we really ought to do is call the Speaker and say, "I regret to see you ordering GAO down here because of what it's going to cause us to require to do to you."

† Ironically, Woods was in charge of security for the Armored Express Company and its corporate parent, Purolator Security, Inc., in October 1974, when thieves gained access to Armored's airtight vault in Chicago and made off with nearly $4 million—the biggest cash theft in the nation's history.

Howard Hughes, had close ties to Lawrence O'Brien and Kennedy Democrats. "Should this Kennedy mafia dominated intelligence 'gun for hire' be turned against us in '72," Caulfield warned, "we would, indeed, have a dangerous and formidable foe."

The New York office for Sandwedge, which Caulfield expected his friend Ulasewicz to head, would, the memo explained, plant undercover agents in rival candidate headquarters, have "black bag" capability, and engage in surveillance of Democratic meetings. It would also offer something called "Derogatory information investigative capability, world-wide," which sounds a great deal like Tony Ulasewicz broadening his horizons beyond the Zebra Room and the Vineyard and talking to bartenders in Zurich, Gstaad, Paris, and Tokyo. In his Watergate testimony, Caulfield claimed that "black bag" capability meant operatives to carry political money, not agents to perform "bag jobs," FBI slang for clandestine burglaries. However, Caulfield's memo also referred to former FBI man Jack O'Connell, who, he said, was known "to have been a 'black bag' specialist while at the Bureau." Under questioning Caulfield conceded that "black bag" in this instance did not mean carrying around political cash, but "breaking and entering" to place microphones for national security purposes.

Caulfield insisted in his interview with the author that he had opposed any illegal acts, including break-ins. The Senate Watergate committee, however, reached a different conclusion. In its final report the committee said: "it appears that the capability to which Caulfield was referring in his Sandwedge proposal was one of surreptitious breaking and entering for the purpose of placing electronic surveillance, quite similar in nature to the Gemstone operation which ultimately evolved."

Regardless of the meaning of "black bag," Sandwedge was an obvious philosophical harbinger of Gemstone and Watergate. But Caulfield could not sell his scheme to Dean and Mitchell; he was not the man for the job, but it was awkward to say that, so they put him off, stalled, ducked and let it die—fortunately, as it turned out, for Caulfield.

But dreams die hard, and years later, paradoxically, the disappointment was still there. Caulfield arose and paced up and down his patio. "Sandwedge did not fly," he said. He looked off into the distance. "Sandwedge did not fly."°

° I asked Caulfield how he had chosen the code name Sandwedge for his plan. "The answer is right there," he said, pointing to a golf net resting against the rear of his house, which his sons use for practice shots. "I used to be a good golfer, in the low seventies. Sand wedge is the name of a club you use in a sand trap."

The cold-eyed men, who in Senator Weicker's words "almost stole America," had other plans to subvert the political process, and this time they did not include Jack Caulfield. Someone else had been selected. On December 2, 1971, Haldeman received a memo advising him of various political developments, and it included this information:

"The Attorney General discussed with John Dean the need to develop a political intelligence capability. Sandwedge has been scrapped. Instead Gordon Liddy, who has been working with Bud Krogh, will become general counsel to the Committee for the Re-Election of the President, effective December 6, 1971. He will handle political intelligence . . ."

Anthony Ulasewicz conducted clandestine political investigations for the President and his staff for four years, throughout Nixon's first term, working under Caulfield's direction for most of that time. In the course of his investigations Ulasewicz traveled to twenty-three states. Because the Watergate break-in and cover-up and the impeachment of the President became the focus of the drama in Washington, no official body delved deeply into the activities of Caulfield and Ulasewicz.

What celebrity came to both men was for other and later roles: Caulfield for delivering promises of executive clemency to James McCord in secret meetings on the second overlook of George Washington Parkway in Virginia; Ulasewicz for his Runyanesque description of how, working with Kalmbach, he distributed $220,000 in payoffs to the original Watergate defendants and their attorneys, stashing the money in airport lockers and laundry bags. Ulasewicz had to spend so much time in phone booths making calls to Kalmbach to arrange delivery of the money that to carry the change, he testified, he finally acquired a coin holder, "one of these things the bus drivers have."

Ulasewicz' performance on television is difficult to forget, particularly the contrast in style between Ulasewicz and Herbert Kalmbach, who was engaged in the same illicit business but was ever so much more elegant. Poor Ulasewicz; Kalmbach could never quite get the hang of it. The President's attorney learned to say "This is Mr. Novak calling" when he telephoned Ulasewicz, and he even instructed Ulasewicz to use the name "Mr. Rivers." But Kalmbach was never really hip; when Ulasewicz in one phone conversation explained guardedly that "the laundry was in the icebox," Kalmbach seemed confused.

"What was his response to that?" Ulasewicz was asked by the Watergate inquisitors.

"Well, kind of a long pause and I said, 'Well, you know the money is in the vault in New York.' [Laughter]."

So Kalmbach was really hopeless, and Ulasewicz, realizing the delicacy of their mission, especially as the defendants kept raising the ante, tried to warn him. "Well, Mr. Kalmbach," he said, "I will tell you something here is not kosher. . . . it's definitely not your ball game, Mr. Kalmbach."

But as the laughter faded, the danger that the Caulfield-Ulasewicz investigations represented became clear. They had served as the President's secret police long before the Plumbers were formed and long before the Plumbers metamorphosed into the Watergate burglars. Political police, operating in secret from and directed by the White House, had been turned loose against political opponents. Ulasewicz, it is true, was paid with misapplied campaign funds, by the President's own lawyer, but Caulfield was on the White House payroll, and to the extent that he engaged in political investigations, they were financed by federal funds, by all of us.

Moreover, Caulfield was able to call upon the resources of the federal government—the Secret Service, the IRS, and the FBI, for example—in pursuit of political information. Initially through Caulfield and Ulasewicz, later through others, the Nixon Administration used the police power of the state against its political opponents. By using *government* power to serve the interests of the *party* (or, more accurately, the head of the party), the White House was moving America in a familiar and ominous direction. For as it happens, in a totalitarian system, party and government are indistinguishable. To serve one is to serve the other.

By hiring his own secret police, as well as using the existing federal police and intelligence agencies for political ends, Richard Nixon used the power of the state to preserve his own political power, and to ensure his own re-election.

In the interview on the patio of his home, Caulfield used an intriguing metaphor to re-create the atmosphere of the Nixon White House. There was, he said, tremendous pressure to come up with what he called "the plum," the piece of irresistibly useful political intelligence about the enemy. "If you could come up with political intelligence," he said, "it increased your own power. A lot of people were scurrying around for the plum. That was the name of the game."

What Caulfield did not realize, of course, is that there was no plum. Whatever morsel Tony Ulasewicz might wheedle or bribe from a bartender in Edgartown, whatever vice or weakness might be discovered among powerful adversaries only generated insatiable pressure for more. No burnt offering could satisfy the gods of power. The plum could never be found for the reason that it did not exist.

The right of the people to be secure in their persons, houses, papers, and effects, against unreasonable searches and seizures, shall not be violated, and no Warrants shall issue, but upon probable cause, supported by Oath or affirmation, and particularly describing the place to be searched, and the persons or things to be seized.

—The Fourth Amendment
to the Constitution

5
Break-ins

On the evening of October 1, 1969, Annie Fields, the long-time cook and housekeeper for J. Edgar Hoover, was almost certainly working late. Normally the FBI Director dined in or at a restaurant with his close friend and companion Clyde Tolson, but tonight Hoover had a special guest coming for dinner at his home on 30th Place near Rock Creek Park; with his fussy bachelor's eye, he would want to be sure the silver was gleaming, the linen stiffly starched.

Although the guest was the President of the United States, the dinner attracted little notice; Nixon's visit merited only a one-paragraph story in the *New York Times*. The squib reported that the President had gone to Hoover's home "for a private dinner and what was described as 'a social evening' with the director of the Federal Bureau of Investigation."

Accompanying Nixon to dinner were Attorney General John Mitchell and John Ehrlichman, the counsel to the President. The nature of a "social evening" with J. Edgar Hoover, then seventy-four, can be pretty well imagined—the Jack Daniel's flowing, Hoover and Nixon expansively swapping Cold War stories, retelling tales of subversives they had unmasked. At that very time, the White House-ordered FBI wiretaps of officials and newsmen stretched underground in an electronic web of cables beneath the capital, a dank secret shared, as it happens, by Hoover and his three dinner guests.

And what subject did these four men, all of them lawyers, turn to as the evening wore on and the mood grew mellow? Government burglaries, according to John Ehrlichman. "For hours," Ehrlichman said in an interview with the author, "Hoover regaled us with stories of 'black bag' jobs, hair-raising escapes, and so on. 'Wonderful,' the President kept saying. 'How about that, John?' At the end of that evening, Hoover would have had every reason to think he was authorized to do 'black bag' jobs."

It was, of course, an account consistent with Ehrlichman's argument that the President has the right to burglarize at will in the national interest. That theory was rejected by the federal district court that sentenced Ehrlichman to twenty months to five years for the burglary—by White House Plumbers who worked under him—of the office of Dr. Lewis Fielding, Daniel Ellsberg's psychiatrist.

But Ehrlichman's recollection, however convenient for him, need not necessarily be discounted, for in 1975 what had long been suspected was officially acknowledged: the FBI had for years engaged in hundreds of burglaries and break-ins in the name of "national security." Hoover would have had every reason to reminisce.

The public confession came from none other than Clarence M. Kelley, the Kansas City police chief whom Nixon had named FBI Director in 1973 to replace the disastrous L. Patrick Gray III, who—not a creature was stirring all through the house—had burned vital Watergate evidence with his Christmas trash at the suggestion, he said, of the President's assistants. Unlike Gray, Kelley at least *looked* the part of FBI Director. He was bluff and square-jawed, and projected vast amounts of small-town integrity; put him in a white coat and he could be the friendly druggist in a television denture commercial. Alas, appearances deceive, and in the act of confessing the FBI burglaries, Kelley compounded the felony by throwing large amounts of sand in the eyes of the reporters who attended him; he implied the break-ins had all but stopped after 1966, and they had not.

"Yes, the FBI has conducted surreptitious entries in securing information relative to the security of the nation," Kelley told a press conference on July 14, 1975. "However, in 1966 all such activity was terminated with the exception of a small amount of actions which were conducted in connection with foreign counterintelligence investigations which we felt had a grave impact upon the security of the nation."

The phrase "surreptitious entry," is, of course, markedly more distingué than "bag job," "burglary," or "break-in," although it comes down to much the same thing: the government had broken the law and violated the Constitution. The FBI is a unit of the Department of Justice, which is the agency of the federal government responsible for enforcing the law, not breaking it. Yet, so conditioned had Americans become to abuse of power by government police agencies that Kelley's extraordinary confession aroused relatively little public reaction; that the government had become a burglar in the night was almost ho-hum news.

Kelley contended that the FBI agents and officials who had conducted and approved the break-ins had "acted in good faith with the belief that national security interests were paramount." The FBI Director did not think there had been "any gross misuse of authority," because the burglaries were "well-intentioned." He added, "I do not feel that it was a corruption of the trust that has been placed in us." There was, he insisted, "no illegality" involved.

The FBI break-ins confirmed by Kelley occurred within the United States, beginning on the eve of World War II. Although Kelley did not say so, they were of two basic types: break-ins to plant a microphone, and burglaries to steal, photograph, or copy something—an embassy code book or other documents, for example, or the files of a domestic organization.

And Kelley conceded, in effect, that in order to plant a microphone, an agent must break in or gain access by subterfuge.° "Inherent in the request for a microphone installation there is the matter of surreptitious entry," was the way Kelley delicately phrased it.

Many FBI break-ins of embassies and foreign missions have been undertaken at the request of the highly secret National Security Agency, which has its headquarters at Fort Meade, Maryland, and is in charge of making and breaking codes and gathering electronic intelligence around the globe. Because the most sophisticated modern codes work on a random principle, and are computerized, they are as a rule impossible to break without access to a code book or code machine. So the FBI has stolen code materials for NSA. But Kelley side-stepped a question about embassy bag jobs for NSA; although he did not deny that such break-ins had taken place, he said "it's better for them [NSA] to comment than I."†

Kelley was at his friendly-druggist best in implying that the break-ins were all ancient history; in this area, his performance was a public relations triumph. When a reporter asked why "the procedure changed in 1966," Kelley replied that Hoover, in the climate of the

---

° The FBI favors the word "microphone," but the term in this context is synonymous with the words "bug" or "transmitter."

† In court papers filed in December 1975, in the course of a civil suit, the Justice Department officially and formally admitted that the government taps and bugs foreign embassies to gather intelligence.

times, felt that "this was not a viable procedure—they were stopped."

Well, not quite. Earlier in his remarks Kelley had said the break-ins stopped except for a "small amount," and when one of his questioners reminded him of this phraseology he said yes, there "may have been some after 1966" in the field of "foreign counterintelligence." Did he mean embassies? Kelley would not say, but this could be inferred from his comments. There had been "a few" after 1966, he said, concerned with counterintelligence and "foreign in nature."

"How few is a few?" he was asked.

"Not many."

Were all the break-ins after 1966 in Washington, or did they take place in other cities as well? "I don't think that all of the few were confined to Washington, D.C.," Kelley replied carefully, "but I can't tell you absolutely that that is true." Behind all this elliptical language was the fact, which the government preferred to obscure, that only break-ins for purposes of burglary were curtailed to some extent after 1966; bag jobs to plant microphones continued. And so, for that matter, did the broader burglaries.

Kelley was greatly embarrassed a year after his press conference when it developed that contrary to his assurances, the FBI had performed numerous burglaries in the early seventies. The evidence was discovered in the FBI's New York field office in 1976 in the personal file of John F. Malone, who had retired some months before after heading the office for a dozen years. Malone, known to his colleagues as "Cement Head," had left a list of the bag jobs behind in his safe.

The Justice Department began investigating dozens of FBI agents who had reportedly committed burglaries in New York and several other cities. Then, on July 7, 1976, during the Ford Administration and three days after the nation's Bicentennial, an FBI informer, Timothy J. Redfearn, broke into the offices of the Socialist Workers party in Denver. Within hours he had shown the boxes of stolen documents to his FBI case officer, John V. Almon, who examined them but claimed he had not taken possession of them. But the FBI did not notify the Denver Police Department about the burglary for one week.

At the time, the Socialist Workers party, a frequent target of FBI burglaries, was suing the government for damages. A federal judge forced the FBI to release the Redfearn file, and it revealed that the informant had also committed two burglaries against the party in Denver in 1973, and had turned over the stolen files to the FBI office in that city.

Even before Kelley's assurances had been discredited by the new disclosures, it was obvious that he had not been telling the whole story. When Attorney General Levi testified before the Church committee in November 1975, he revealed that between 1940 and October 29, 1975, there had been 2,465 microphones "installed" by the FBI, of which no fewer than 206 were installed since 1966. Kelley's definition of "a small amount" of break-ins after 1966 was gradually becoming clearer.°

Levi did not say that each of the microphones required a break-in; presumably some could have been placed inside common walls from adjoining premises, or planted by agents who used some ruse to gain access to an embassy or other target. ("People redecorate," one official familiar with such matters said cryptically.) Bugs are also installed at times by accomplices or infiltrators who are cooperating with the FBI and who have normal access to the place to be bugged. And, of course, on occasion, the FBI is able to install bugs in a building before the person or organization to be tapped moves in.† But the implication of Levi's testimony was that many, perhaps most of the microphone installations required break-ins. Levi even coined a new term,

---

° Attorney General Levi's figures on FBI microphone installations provide the best indicator of the pattern of Bureau bag jobs, assuming at least a rough correlation between the number of microphones installed and the number of break-ins required to install them. Levi gave annual figures for "national security" telephone taps and microphone installations; he avoided any overall totals. But an analysis of the testimony shows that at least according to Levi, the government installed 8,239 national security telephone taps from 1940 to October 1975, and 2,465 microphones.

Since 1966, when Kelley said that break-ins had largely stopped, the figures for hidden microphones were as follows: 1966: 10; 1967: 0; 1968: 9; 1969: 14; 1970: 19; 1971: 16; 1972: 32; 1973: 40; 1974: 42; and 1975, through October 29: 24; for a total of 206. In addition, the FBI told the Church committee that "at least" fourteen "domestic subversive targets were the subject of at least 238 entries from 1942 to April, 1968." Three such domestic targets were the subject of "numerous entries," the FBI said; so many that apparently the Bureau lost track, for it confessed "we are unable to retrieve an accurate accounting of their number." In one case, however, the FBI burglarized the offices of the Socialist Workers party in New York City 92 times in the early sixties, on the average of once every three weeks. The FBI burglars took some 10,000 photographs of documents.

Levi provided no breakdown by Administrations, but the approximate number of microphones installed under each President since 1940, during their varying terms of office, would be: Roosevelt: 510; Truman: 692; Eisenhower: 616; Kennedy: 268; Johnson: 192; Nixon: 163; Ford: 24 (covers only first ten months of 1975). The annual totals for 1945 and 1974 have been allocated to Truman and Nixon, respectively, although each served less than a full year. The comparable figures for national security telephone wiretaps during the same period were: Roosevelt: 1,369; Truman: 2,984; Eisenhower: 1,574; Kennedy: 582; Johnson: 862; Nixon: 747; Ford: 121.

† The CIA was so worried that someone might plant bugs in its walls that it developed a network of paid informers among the construction workers who built the Agency's $46 million headquarters in Langley, Virginia, in 1960 and 1961.

"trespassory microphone surveillance," a subtle and insidious euphe-mism that rivals the Newspeak and Doublethink of George Orwell's *1984*.°

The Attorney General also explained that President Ford had established new procedures for electronic surveillance without a war-rant; all requests for taps or bugs must be made in writing to the Director of the FBI, and each request "receives my personal attention," which was not entirely reassuring, since Levi, while stating that na-tional security eavesdropping would only be used against those "con-sciously assisting a foreign power or foreign-based political group," failed to explain how such conscious assistance would be determined by him *before* the parties had been overheard by the government. Levi also established in his office a committee on tapping and bugging —he preferred to call it a "special review group"—to consider each request to install a wiretap or transmitter without a warrant. The Attorney General also assured the senators that there would be "the minimum physical intrusion necessary to obtain the information sought." Finesse had become the standard; and the nation's chief law-enforcement officer seemed to be saying that henceforth only *small* burglaries will be committed by the government, mini-rapes, delicately executed, so that the FBI agents will not disturb us as we sleep in the night.

No matter, Levi's testimony was valuable. It is better to know where we stand than to delude ourselves into thinking that the Bill of Rights somehow protects us from all but the misguided actions of lower-level officials who have not got the word from the top. Levi, expounding upon President Ford's wiretap policy, at least made clear the nature of the word from the top.

The myth that all bag jobs had somehow been stopped after 1966 has its roots in a memo dated July 19, 1966, and sent, according to its heading, from the FBI's William Sullivan to Cartha DeLoach.† The memo is also the best documentation of how the FBI concealed its break-ins for more than three decades. Sullivan's Domestic Intelligence

---

° Howard Hunt provided another classic example when, testifying before a fed-eral grand jury, he was asked to define the burglary of the office of Ellsberg's psychiatrist. He replied, "I would simply call it an entry operation conduct[ed] under the auspices of competent authority."

† Sullivan has claimed he never wrote or saw the memo, and that it was drafted by Fred J. Baumgardner, a section chief in his office. Although Sullivan's initials appear on the memo, he said the initials were placed there by one of his other assistants, Inspector Joseph A. Sizoo. It is a common practice in the bureaucracy for a subordinate to draft a memo for a superior. Nevertheless, the memo went out over Sullivan's name, and as chief of the Domestic Intelligence Division, he was responsible for it.

Division had been asked to write a background memo on FBI bur- glary procedures, and in proper bureaucratic fashion, the paper is headed: *"Black Bag" Jobs*.

"We do not obtain authorization for 'black bag' jobs from outside the Bureau," the memo said. "Such a technique involves trespass and is clearly illegal; therefore, it would be impossible to obtain any legal sanction for it. Despite this, 'black bag' jobs have been used because they represent an invaluable technique in combating subversive ac- tivities of a clandestine nature aimed directly at undermining and de- stroying our nation."

The document then reviewed the mind-boggling internal proce- dure used by the FBI for break-ins. The Special Agent in Charge (SAC) of a field office "must completely justify the need for the use of the technique" and at the same time "assure that it can be safely used without any danger or embarrassment to the Bureau." The special agent would do so in a memo either to Hoover or Tolson. The memo was then filed in the office of the assistant director of the FBI under— literally—the heading "Do Not File."

In September 1975 Charles Brennan, who had been Sullivan's deputy and succeeded him as assistant FBI director for domestic intelligence (the same Charles Brennan who carried that old beat-up satchel full of wiretaps over to Robert Mardian), patiently tried to explain to the Church committee° how to file a "Do Not File" memo. Brennan, a heavy-set, well-barbered and jowly Irishman with glasses, was trying to be a helpful witness, but the panel was understandably confused.

"The memorandum was not recorded in the usual record-keeping functions of the FBI," Brennan testified, "but would return to the assistant director and would be filed in his office under a 'do not file.'" Senator Richard Schweiker, the Pennsylvania Republican, did not seem at first to understand:

> SENATOR SCHWEIKER: If it had been filed in the normal procedure, and then somebody subsequently removed it from the normal file and destroyed it—why wasn't it done that way?
> MR. BRENNAN: [Incredulously] There would have been a record of it.
> SENATOR SCHWEIKER: In other words, each file of the FBI was serialized, and as new information is put in a serial number is

---

° In September 1975 the Senate Select Committee to Study Governmental Opera- tions with Respect to Intelligence Activities, headed by Frank Church, the Idaho Democrat, began hearings on federal intelligence and police agencies. The com- mittee is hereinafter referred to as the Church committee or the Senate intelligence committee.

assigned, so . . . if it had been filed in the normal procedure and then removed, there would have been a gap as far as the number is concerned?

MR. BRENNAN: Yes sir.

Filing a memo under "Do Not File" has distinct overtones of Lewis Carroll, but it is by no means as loony as it sounds. Senator Schweiker noted that it was "really the perfect cover-up," because it permitted FBI officials to swear in affidavits or in court that "we've searched our files and records and there is nothing to indicate . . . we did a 'black bag' job." So the officials, Schweiker observed, "would be technically telling the truth . . . yet in fact it would be nearly total deception."

Schweiker then asked Brennan how FBI agents in the field learned how to follow this procedure: "Was this in the manuals of rules and regulations?"

"I frankly can't answer that, Senator," Brennan replied. "I don't believe there was any reference in any manual or the like that referred to 'black bag' jobs . . . I just don't know how they knew."

Somehow they knew, for Sullivan's 1966 memo also explained the separate steps required at the field level to make sure that no trace of a bag job showed up in the FBI files: "In the field, the Special Agent in Charge prepares an informal memorandum showing that he obtained Bureau authority and this memorandum is filed in his safe until the next inspection by Bureau Inspectors, at which time it is destroyed."

The Sullivan memo said that the FBI had used break-ins on a wide range of targets, including "several cases in the espionage field." But it made clear that foreign spies were not the only persons burglarized; through break-ins, "we have on numerous occasions been able to obtain material held highly secret and closely guarded by subversive groups and organizations which consisted of membership lists and mailing lists of these organizations."

And the memo indicated that "black bag" jobs had a valuable spinoff for the Bureau's COINTELPRO* operation of sabotaging groups and individuals whose political views the Bureau regarded as suspect. Through a recent "black bag" job, the memo said, the FBI had obtained the financial and membership records of three high officials of such an organization, "which we have been using most effectively to disrupt the organization and, in fact, to bring about its near disintegration. . . . In short, it is a very valuable weapon which we have used to combat the highly clandestine efforts of subversive elements seeking to undermine our nation."

* COINTELPRO stands for Counterintelligence Program and is pronounced "co-in-tel-pro."

Unfortunately, Sullivan's paean of praise for government second-story jobs met with an unexpected and irascible response from Hoover. In a quavering hand, he scrawled a note at the bottom of the memo in his characteristic blue ink: "No more such techniques must be used. h."

Sullivan's devastation may have been eased by the fact that the ukase was not enforced, and at least some bag jobs continued, as Clarence Kelley was to admit a decade later.

Hoover realized that his order was not being taken very seriously, for on January 6, 1967, he wrote a memo to Tolson noting that requests "are still being made by Bureau officials for the use of 'black bag' techniques." He had already indicated he would not approve these, he wrote, and wanted to see no more such requests. "This practice, which includes also surreptitious entrances upon premises of any kind, will not meet with my approval in the future."

Why Hoover ordered an end to bag jobs in 1966, even though the order was not strictly enforced, is subject to varying interpretations. Charles Brennan has argued that it is best understood as one more move in a series of steps by Hoover that curtailed the activities of the FBI's Domestic Intelligence Division. According to Brennan, the downtrend began during the Kennedy Administration when the Justice Department concentrated its efforts in the divisions dealing with organized crime and civil rights. Interviewed by Senator Weicker during the Senate Watergate investigation in 1973, Brennan argued that this shift in emphasis had drained FBI manpower from the intelligence field; for years, he said, Sullivan had been fighting against cutbacks in his division. Then, by Brennan's account, during the Johnson Administration the FBI chief retrenched even further in wary reaction to the Senate wiretap and invasion-of-privacy hearings held by Senator Edward V. Long of Missouri in 1965 (hearings which disclosed that technology was then so far advanced that it was possible to bug a martini, or more accurately, the conversation taking place around it, by hiding a transmitter in the olive; the toothpick sticking up acted as an antenna).

Brennan's view dovetailed with a widely held belief in Washington that Hoover's reluctance to burglarize was not based upon a newly found concern for civil liberties but on a growing caution and a desire to protect his own image, and that of the FBI, in his twilight years. There were important bureaucratic considerations as well—why risk embarrassment to the Bureau to gather intelligence for NSA or the CIA?

Further insight into Hoover's thinking surfaced in 1973 during hearings before the Senate Judiciary Committee on Nixon's firing of Archibald Cox, the first Watergate Special Prosecutor. Attorney General Elliot Richardson, who had resigned to protest Cox's dismissal, told of constant telephone calls from Nixon's counsel, J. Fred Buzhardt, complaining about Cox's zeal. In one conversation, Richardson recalled, Buzhardt had mentioned that "Hoover's only objection" to the 1970 Huston Plan, which called for embassy break-ins and other police-state actions, "was because he didn't want any FBI used to get into embassies, that he thought they were too well protected."

In the swirling events of those days, scant attention was paid to Richardson's testimony, but it had about it the sure ring of truth: J. Edgar Hoover didn't want his men going into embassies because they might get caught. He worried even though the bag jobs were carried out by specially trained agents who knew they would be disavowed if anything went wrong. And precautions were taken, of course, to ensure that the FBI burglars were not caught. One technique used was simple but effective; according to William W. Turner, a former FBI man fired by Hoover for criticizing the Bureau in public, when a bag job was in progress the FBI would station an agent in local police headquarters to listen to the police radio and "shortstop" any complaint by a citizen that a burglary was taking place.

"We would just tell the police we have an operation in this area, and we want to make sure nothing happens," Turner told the Washington *Post*. Turner also said he could usually tell when the Bureau's top "black bag" operator had committed a successful burglary "because you would read in the house organ that he got another meritorious award. That's the only way they could pay him." Turner said he was trained in surreptitious entry in an attic classroom in the Justice Department in Washington, where FBI agents were instructed on how to make their own lock-picking tools.

The seepage, the gradual publicity about FBI break-ins that began surfacing during the Watergate scandal, was particularly disturbing to Brennan, since it obviously was bad for business. When stories of alleged FBI break-ins were published in the *New York Times* and the Washington *Post* in 1973, Brennan complained to Weicker: "I could just see every embassy in town going, 'Gustav, set the alarm, get some dogs, change the locks.'"

From the very start, the necessity of breaking and entering to plant a microphone caused nagging intellectual and legal problems for the Department of Justice. There were various ways to gain access to an embassy, a private home, an apartment or an office, other than by breaking in, but often illegal entry was required to plant a bug. And the Fourth Amendment, not to mention local law, frowned on burglary. But microphones were so *useful*. Various Attorneys General coped with the problem in their own fashion, but it was always there, an electronic skeleton beeping away in the moral luggage of a succession of the nation's highest lawmen.

Roosevelt's order of May 21, 1940, was the basic document that permitted Presidents to wiretap. But Roosevelt's directive did not speak of wiretaps; it authorized the Attorney General to use "listening devices." As Edward Levi noted to the Church committee, that language was "sufficiently broad" to include bugs, and the Justice Department "construed it as an authorization to conduct trespassory microphone surveillance as well as telephone wiretapping in national security cases."

But Hoover wanted to protect himself; on October 6, 1951, he wrote to President Truman's Attorney General, J. Howard McGrath, informing him that the FBI had used microphones for intelligence purposes. In certain instances, Hoover wrote, "it has been possible to install microphones without trespass." But, he went on, "As you know, in a number of instances it has not been possible to install microphones without trespass." Information "highly pertinent to the defense and welfare of this nation is derived through the use of microphones," Hoover said. But he needed "a definite opinion from you" as to whether the FBI should continue breaking in to plant microphones. Hoover was, as usual, building his protective paper fortress and putting the Attorney General on the spot. Did McGrath really want to take responsibility for ending a practice so vital to the nation's safety? But without the Attorney General's approval, in writing, Hoover would not move.

McGrath, in riverboat-gambler style, called Hoover's bluff and raised. The use of microphones that do not require trespass "would seem to be permissible under the present state of the law," he blandly wrote back on February 26, 1952. But break-ins violated the Fourth Amendment, he told Hoover, and evidence obtained from a microphone that required a trespass would not be admissible in court. "Please be advised that I cannot authorize the installation of a microphone *involving a trespass* under existing law." McGrath had not told Hoover that the FBI was barred from using bugs, but he was not about to approve any break-ins to plant them.

What happened next is revealed in a 28-page top-secret memorandum drafted by Attorney General Nicholas deB. Katzenbach in 1966 when vicious internal warfare broke out between Hoover and Katzenbach over the bugging by the FBI of the hotel room of Washington lobbyist Fred B. Black, Jr.° Katzenbach, in defending the

---

° In 1975 Katzenbach said to the Church committee that his bitter exchange of correspondence with Hoover over the Black case "persuaded me I could no longer effectively serve as Attorney General because of Mr. Hoover's resentment towards me."

manner in which the Justice Department had disclosed that bug to the Supreme Court, traced the secret history of the negotiations between Hoover and the Justice Department over microphones and break-ins.

Katzenbach's classified memorandum disclosed that Hoover would not take McGrath's no for an answer, and kept pushing the Justice Department to approve bag jobs. On April 10, 1952, the Department responded to another Hoover inquiry by warning the FBI chief that installing a mike in a hotel room would invade the privacy "of the guest and his guests."

Hoover was temporarily losing the burglary battle, but with Eisenhower's election in 1952, there was a chance for a more flexible approach. Herbert Brownell took over as Attorney General.

Early in 1953 FBI representatives met with officials of the Justice Department's internal security division to see whether they might arrive at "a less restrictive interpretation of the law pertaining to microphone surveillances." The meeting resulted in an ingenious, if illegal, solution.

"It appears that these representatives agreed upon a new legal approach under which a microphone installed through trespass would be seen as the result of an *illegal entry*," the Katzenbach memo noted, "but not for the purpose of a search and seizure, and thus, not within the proscriptions of the Fourth Amendment..." In other words, the government officials agreed to break the law but to avoid violating the Constitution.

Fred Baumgardner, the FBI's "black bag" theorist, also urged Justice Department officials to change the policy so that the Attorney General could approve each bug in advance. It was, after all, still a risky business, and the FBI wanted company. Katzenbach quoted from a memorandum summarizing a meeting between Baumgardner and Department officials in July; Baumgardner had warned that if anything went wrong, and a bag job was disclosed, "it would precipitate considerable adverse publicity in the press and result in embarrassment publicly, both to the Bureau and the Department."

The lower-level officials were massaging the question nicely now, and in December, Hoover extracted a new memo from Assistant Attorney General Warren Olney III summarizing the tricky new approach to break-ins. It was still not good enough for Hoover. Alan Belmont, a high-ranking FBI official, agreed that the new policy was an improvement, but he still fretted over publicity if agents were caught in mid-burglary; he pushed for authority to install microphones "where the security of the country was at stake."

The Justice Department said the Attorney General still could not authorize a trespass, but there might just be a way: perhaps in emergencies, break-ins would be permitted when the facts were fuzzy enough so it was not certain that the entry would "legally constitute trespass." Hoover saw the hole in the line and charged.

Belmont drafted a proposed memorandum from Brownell to Hoover freeing the FBI Director to plant bugs; it was reviewed and revised in the Justice Department and signed by Brownell on May 20, 1954. Hoover had won; he had outlasted McGrath and brushed aside any vestigial squeamishness over the approval of burglaries by the Attorney General of the United States. He now had virtual carte blanche to break and enter. The key sections of Brownell's memo were:

"It is clear that in some instances the use of microphone surveillance is the only possible way of uncovering the activities of espionage agents, possible saboteurs and subversive persons. In such instances I am of the opinion that the national interest requires that microphone surveillance be utilized by the Federal Bureau of Investigation . . .

"It is realized that not infrequently the question of trespass arises in connection with the installation of a microphone." The Department would review each case. But Brownell said it would be his policy to "permit microphone coverage." He concluded that "internal security and the national safety . . . may compel the unrestricted use of this technique . . ."

Hoover had won blanket permission to break in to plant bugs, which meant that prior approval of the Attorney General was not required for each microphone or transmitter installed. On March 30, 1965, however, Katzenbach changed the rules, requiring advance approval of the Attorney General for each bug. While this gave Hoover and the FBI an even greater bureaucratic shield, it also made it at least somewhat more difficult for the FBI to get such permission to burglarize. Ramsey Clark testified in 1974 that when he served as Attorney General during the Johnson Administration, he had turned down repeated requests by Hoover "to break and enter into a foreign mission at the United Nations" to steal code books.* Clark said Hoover

---

* Clark did not identify the foreign mission but stated elsewhere he thought it was a "North African country." Clark also testified that he had cut back on national security wiretaps, and had denied requests by Hoover to tap Abba Eban, the Foreign Minister of Israel, while he was on a visit to the United States, and to wiretap the Tanzanian mission to the UN. However, Pulitzer Prize-winning correspondent Seymour M. Hersh reported in the *New York Times* on May 22, 1973, that during the Johnson and Nixon Administrations the FBI had wiretapped the Israeli embassy in Washington under a program code-named Scope. Hersh quoted one source as saying that Scope had picked up such material as a 1970 conversation in which Israeli Prime Minister Golda Meir was discussing Secretary of State William P. Rogers with Israel's ambassador in Washington, General Yitzhak Rabin.

acted "apparently at the request of the National Security Agency." He said Hoover kept coming back to him "on perhaps several occasions" to press the request, but that it was never approved. Clark said it was "the only request of that kind" he had received from Hoover.

In August of 1973, with Richard Nixon clinging precariously to his Presidency, James Deakin of the St. Louis *Post-Dispatch* pointed out at a press conference that Mr. Nixon had approved the 1970 Huston Plan permitting burglaries and other crimes, even if he had not approved the burglary of Dr. Fielding, Ellsberg's psychiatrist. If a President sworn to uphold the law had violated his oath of office, was that not grounds for impeachment? Nixon lashed back. In the Kennedy and Johnson years, he said, "burglarizing of this type did take place" and "it was authorized on a very large scale," and "it was quite well known."

Nixon's charge, which was essentially correct—except for the allegation that the practice was well known—touched off a spate of denials. "I never heard of it," Ramsey Clark said. "I do not believe it. I never authorized any burglaries."

Katzenbach struck a similar note. "Here's one guy who didn't know of it," he said. "I have no knowledge of any such burglarizing and I don't believe it ever occurred."

Since Katzenbach had detailed the entire history of FBI break-ins to plant bugs, in the long top-secret memo during his feud with Hoover, and since by Levi's figures nearly two hundred microphones were installed during the Johnson years when Clark and Katzenbach served as Attorney General, the denials seem disingenuous at first glance. But semantics as much as politics may explain the conflict. Nixon, replying to a question about the Fielding break-in and the Huston Plan, was probably talking about burglaries to steal or photograph documents; Clark and Katzenbach were apparently denying knowledge of that type of burglary, but they did not mention break-ins to plant microphones.

When the Church committee investigated the matter of FBI bag jobs, the FBI would not admit to any burglary later than one in 1968. But it was soon disclosed publicly that FBI burglaries had, after all, taken place in the seventies. And the FBI did not—could not—deny that break-ins to plant bugs in embassies had continued all along.

Under Nixon, an attempt was made to institutionalize burglary as an instrument of presidential policy. On July 23, 1970, Tom Charles Huston, a twenty-nine-year-old staff assistant to President Nixon, wrote a two-page memorandum that amounted to nothing less than a blueprint for a police state in America. Although signed by Huston, the memo listed a series of decisions by Nixon and was cast in the form of a presidential order to federal intelligence agencies. The memo summarized more detailed proposals by Huston that had, nine days earlier, received Nixon's full approval. An important element in the plan was labeled "Surreptitious Entry." Under this heading, Huston's memo said: "Restraints on the use of surreptitious entry are to be removed. The technique is to be used to permit procurement of vitally needed foreign cryptographic material and against other urgent and high priority internal security targets." An interagency report relating to the Huston Plan had discussed burglary, pointing out to the President: "Benefits accruing from this technique in the past have been innumerable."

Huston sent the interagency report along to Haldeman, together with his own top-secret recommendations, in which he waxed positively lyrical over the advantages of state burglaries. He recommended that Nixon lift restrictions on bag jobs against both embassies and domestic subversives, whom Huston saw everywhere.

He warned Nixon of the legal and political risk in a chilling phrase that floats back through the national memory long after Watergate: "Use of this technique is clearly illegal: it amounts to burglary." Huston added: "It is also highly risky and could result in great embarrassment if exposed. However, it is also the most fruitful tool and can produce the type of intelligence which cannot be obtained in any other fashion.

"The FBI, in Mr. Hoover's younger days, used to conduct such operations with great success and with no exposure. The information secured was invaluable.

"NSA has a particular interest since it is possible by this technique to secure materials with which NSA can break foreign cryptographic codes. We spend millions of dollars attempting to break these codes by machine. One successful surreptitious entry can do the job successfully at no dollar cost."

Burglaries of "facilities occupied by subversive elements"—by which Huston presumably meant the homes and offices of persons who did not happen to agree with the Administration's policies in Vietnam, for example—could turn up "invaluable" information, the memo assured the President. The technique, Huston added, would be particularly useful against Weathermen and Black Panthers.

Huston's plan also called for NSA eavesdropping on international communications, bugging and wiretapping, illegal opening of first-class mail, and development of campus informants on college campuses, and all of these were approved by Nixon. But Hoover opposed burglary and other features of the plan; Huston, in his youthful zeal, had sadly underestimated Hoover's power. Like an old crocodile dozing in the sun, too sleepy to be bothered, Hoover finally disposed of Tom Charles Huston with one dreadful flick of his tail; he went to

Mitchell, and Mitchell then persuaded Nixon to pull back the memo, which was done five days after it had been issued.

The irony of all this, of course, is that most of the illegal and other activities that Nixon thought he was approving in the Huston plan were already going on. The National Security Agency was already reading and listening in on international communications, the FBI was tapping and bugging, developing campus informants, and breaking and entering—at least to plant bugs, if not to steal things—and the CIA was opening first-class mail. Nor did these activities stop when Nixon rescinded the Huston memo. The importance of the Huston Plan was not that it approved new techniques, but that it gave a presidential imprimatur to police-state methods, centralized the practices in a single document, and sought to institutionalize these abuses of power by creating an interagency group on domestic intelligence to act as a kind of continuing board of directors for secret-police activity in America.*

As later became spectacularly clear, the Nixon Administration's proclivity for burglarizing did not end because of the thwacking that Hoover dealt Huston. On June 13, 1971, the *New York Times* had begun publishing the classified history of the Vietnam war known as the Pentagon Papers. Nixon reacted by forming the Plumbers unit, and instructing Egil "Bud" Krogh, Jr., to find out everything he could about the man who had leaked the documents to the press, Daniel Ellsberg. Ehrlichman, assisted by Charles Colson, was given authority over the Plumbers, David Young was borrowed from Kissinger to work with Krogh, and Hunt and Liddy were recruited to the Plumbers staff.

Soon after the Plumbers were ensconced in Room 16, in the basement of the Executive Office Building across the street from the White House, Caulfield visited John Dean. Caulfield, Dean testified, reported "that Mr. Colson had called him in . . . and instructed him to burglarize the Brookings Institute" to steal documents. Dean said Caulfield had told him that Ulasewicz had already cased the building, made contact with a friendly security man, and reported back that "it would be very difficult to break in." Caulfield, said Dean, reported this to Colson who told him "he should plant a firebomb in the building and retrieve the documents during the commotion that would ensue."

The Brookings Institution (misnamed "Institute" by the Watergate witnesses) is a nonprofit public policy center in Washington, which the Nixon White House regarded as a nest of pipe-smoking, treeful-of-owls Democrats. Caulfield testified that Colson told him the burglary or firebombing at Brookings was necessary "to obtain papers from the

---

* Even though the Huston Plan was suspended, the interagency group was created and operated for nearly three years.

office of a gentleman named Leslie Gelb." The gentleman named Leslie Gelb was the Pentagon official who directed the Vietnam war study for Robert McNamara.

It was one thing to send Ulasewicz to Chappaquiddick, but a firebombing by a "law and order" Administration sounded much more serious. Caulfield, alarmed by Colson's instructions, testified that he "literally ran into the office of Mr. Dean and advised him that if he was not going to take the next plane out to San Clemente, I was." Caulfield told Dean that Colson's orders were "insane," and Dean, who agreed, flew to California to warn Ehrlichman. The idea was then dropped.° But within a few weeks another burglary was being planned in connection with the leak of the Pentagon Papers.

Late in July Dr. Lewis Fielding turned away FBI agents who came to his office in Beverly Hills and attempted to question him about his patient. In August, Krogh and Young sent a memo recommending that "a covert operation be undertaken to examine all the medical files still held by Ellsberg's psychoanalyst covering the two-year period in which he was undergoing analysis." The memo included two spaces marked "Approve" and "Disapprove." Ehrlichman scribbled his big "E" next to "Approve" and wrote underneath: "If done under your assurance that it is not traceable."

On the evening of September 3, 1971, three Cuban Americans, Bernard Barker, Eugenio Martinez—who was on a CIA retainer of $100 a month at the time—and Felipe DeDiego, broke into Dr. Fielding's office to look for Ellsberg's medical records while Hunt and Liddy played lookout. The mission failed; at least the three men testified they did not find Ellsberg's records, and there is no firm evidence that they did, although Dr. Fielding swore that his papers "including those pertaining to Dr. Ellsberg, appeared to have been thoroughly rummaged through" and that Ellsberg's records had been removed from the envelope in which he had left them.† Ehrlichman later argued in

---

° By coincidence, Dean flew to California on the same military courier plane with Assistant Attorney General Robert Mardian. Mardian told Dean he was going to see the President about an important matter he could not discuss. Mardian, as it happened, was flying to San Clemente to ask Nixon what on earth to do with the satchel full of hot wiretaps that he had obtained from the FBI's William Sullivan. Dean was flying to San Clemente to try to stop a firebombing by the White House; somehow the vignette symbolized the Nixon era.

† There was a peculiar and less publicized sequel to the burglary of Dr. Fielding. Less than three months later, in November 1971, unknown burglars broke into the penthouse office at 697 West End Avenue, in Manhattan, of Dr. Robert Akeret, a psychoanalyst who had been treating Mrs. Daniel Ellsberg. The office was left in disorder, but only some blank checks were taken. The checks had been kept inside an unlocked file cabinet that also contained the records of Patricia Ellsberg's treatment. The federal government somehow knew that Mrs.

court that his approval of a covert operation did not necessarily mean a burglary, but the jury did not believe that and he was convicted.*

Nine months later, on June 17, 1972, Bernard Barker, Eugenio Martinez, Virgilio Gonzales (a locksmith), Frank A. Sturgis, and James W. McCord, Jr., were arrested inside the sixth-floor offices of the Democratic National Committee in the Watergate office building. Hunt and Liddy, monitoring the operation with walkie-talkies from their room in the Watergate hotel next door, were arrested later. There were four attempts to break into the Watergate; the first two, on May 26 and 27, had failed, but those on May 28 and June 17 succeeded.

During the first successful break-in, McCord, a former CIA man, placed miniature transmitters in the telephones of chairman Lawrence O'Brien and another DNC official, Spencer Oliver, and Barker and his men photographed documents from the national committee's files. Alfred C. Baldwin III, a former FBI man, monitored the bugged conversations from a room in Howard Johnson's motel across the street. But the transmitter on O'Brien's phone was not working properly— Oliver's office was right behind the balcony facing the motel but O'Brien's office was tucked away in the southeast corner of the office building, as far as it could be from Baldwin's receiver, and the intervening walls may have interfered with the transmission. So a second break-in was conducted in June to repair the bug.

Nowhere in the reams of testimony about Watergate is there any lucid or convincing explanation of precisely why the President's burglars went into the Watergate, other than for the general purpose of gathering political intelligence under the Gemstone plan. There was some effort after the fact to find a national security rationale; stories were leaked claiming that the break-in was carried out because the Administration suspected that Fidel Castro was sending money to the Democratic party. There were other theories, including one developed by the Senate Watergate committee that the White House wanted to know how much O'Brien, who was on a public relations retainer from Howard Hughes, knew about $100,000 that Hughes had given Bebe Rebozo. But the Watergate investigations provided no ultimate answer to the burglary of the century.

In an interview with the author in November 1974, Howard Hunt claimed that his men were looking for evidence of campaign contributions from both Cuba and North Vietnam. The questions, and Hunt's answers on this point, were as follows:

Ellsberg had been seeing Dr. Akeret, because the day after the *New York Times* began publishing the Pentagon Papers, FBI agents also came to his office asking about Mrs. Ellsberg. Dr. Akeret sent them away.

* The convictions of Martinez and Barker were set aside on appeal.

Q. Why did you go into the Watergate? Was it to get a specific piece of information or general intelligence from the DNC?

A. It was a flow, a process, and this was part of it. We were looking for both general and specific information. The specific information was the contribution lists. By going over these we hoped to find, and tracing back the names, a source of foreign funding.

Q. Foreign funding from Cuba?

A. And from Hanoi, that was the specific target. The contribution lists. I know nothing about the Hughes-O'Brien motive.

Hunt also indicated he was unaware of whose phones were being bugged during the break-in. "The way the operation was set up," he said, "I had responsibility for photography only." Hunt said he had nothing to do with placing bugs; his men were there to photograph the documents. He said this with a professional air, in a tone and manner that suggested he still regarded himself very much the technician; after more than twenty years in the CIA it could hardly be otherwise. Hunt obviously did not think of himself as any old White House burglar; he was a *specialist*.

Throughout the history of government-sponsored break-ins, whether the FBI's bag jobs under seven Presidents, or the crimes committed by President Nixon's private team of burglars, there is a common thread—a consistent effort to justify illegal acts under the protective cloak of "national security."

The most graphic illustration comes in a moment on the celebrated White House tape of March 21, 1973, when Nixon was meeting with Dean and Haldeman. It is suggested to Nixon, by Dean, that the burglary of Ellsberg's psychiatrist might be explained on grounds of national security.

Nixon likes that. "National security," he replies, savoring the phrase. "We had to get the information for national security . . . the whole thing was national security."

"I think we could get by on that," Dean replies.

But Nixon knew it wouldn't work; he never publicly invoked that defense. Rather, at a press conference he called the Fielding break-in "illegal, unauthorized as far as I was concerned, and completely deplorable."

Ehrlichman in his defense argued that the break-in was justified for reasons of national security and therefore legal, an argument eloquently rejected in a pre-trial opinion handed down by Federal District Judge Gerhard A. Gesell. Although the Supreme Court in 1972 had left open the constitutionality of warrantless wiretaps, Gesell said that did not mean "an intention to obviate the entire Fourth Amendment whenever the President determines that an American citizen, personally innocent of wrongdoing, has in his possession information that may touch upon foreign policy concerns."

When Ehrlichman appealed his conviction, the Watergate Special Prosecutor filed a brief arguing that there is no presidential right to burglarize; whatever the unsettled state of the law regarding electronic surveillance without a warrant, the prosecutor said, the Supreme Court had always in its long history prohibited the violation of the Fourth Amendment by "physical entry into private premises to conduct a physical search" without a warrant.

The filing of this brief by the then Special Prosecutor, Henry S. Ruth, Jr., brought about an extraordinary step by Attorney General Levi. Levi took exception to the brief in a letter filed with the court on May 9 and signed not by Levi but by Assistant Attorney General John C. Keeney. The letter argued that the Ellsberg break-in was unlawful simply because it was not properly authorized. Break-ins, the Justice Department argued in the astonishing letter, must be carefully controlled, involve "foreign espionage or intelligence," be conducted with "minimum" intrusion, and receive the advance approval of the President or the Attorney General.

"The Department believes that activities so controlled are lawful under the Fourth Amendment," the letter said. It added: "It is and has long been the Department's view that warrantless searches involving physical entries into private premises are justified under the proper circumstances when related to foreign espionage or intelligence."

In his testimony before the Church committee, Levi never came right out and said he thought some government burglaries were legal, but the letter did. The nation's highest legal officer, through a letter signed by a subordinate, had publicly—albeit very quietly—informed the American people that the Bill of Rights notwithstanding, he or the President had the power to decide when to break and enter.

On April 20, 1972, Dr. Constantine D. J. Generales, a distinguished pioneer in space medicine and a practicing cardiologist in Manhattan, received a mysterious telephone call from a young woman who "wanted to talk about something very personal." A few days later the woman telephoned again; she made some cryptic reference to space medicine and again asked to see the doctor. She was given an appointment for May 1 at his office at 8 West Seventy-second Street, in the Majestic Apartments.*

Dr. Generales, born in Athens of American parents, was a stocky,

---

* Dr. Generales' office was directly across the street from the Dakota, where White House agents had attempted, three months earlier, to place a meeting of Muskie advisers under surveillance.

bespectacled man of sixty-three with graying hair and a long string of medical honors. Educated at Harvard and at European medical schools, he was an Air Force veteran of World War II, a member of the staff of Mount Sinai Hospital in New York, and an internationally recognized authority on space medicine. He frequently wrote and lectured on that subject and had been a consultant for the Stanley Kubrick film *2001: A Space Odyssey*. He was a fellow of several medical and scientific societies, and past president of the New York Cardiological Society. While a student at Zurich in 1931, he had become interested in the biomedical aspects of space flight. With a friend and fellow student, Wernher von Braun, he had performed the first experiments demonstrating the effects of centrifugal force on mice.

On May 1, as scheduled, the young woman who had telephoned came to Dr. Generales' office, which is entered from the street. "She was a little bit of a thing," Dr. Generales recalled, "very petite with more or less auburn-colored or dirty-blond hair. She was about twenty, twenty-five years old, very pleasant." She identified herself as an employee of the Central Intelligence Agency.

There was no question that she was, he said. "She showed me her CIA identification, and it said 'CIA' and the picture matched her appearance." When the woman from the CIA began explaining what she wanted, Dr. Generales reached back unobtrusively and turned on a tape recorder behind his desk. The woman knew that Dr. Generales was planning to attend an international conference on space medicine in Miami later that month. "She said, 'There's going to be a lot of Russians down there.' She wanted me to take them out for cocktails and find out as much as possible about what they do and what they think."

Dr. Generales declined to spy on the Soviet delegates. Nor was he impressed with his visitor. The young woman struck him as "completely unprofessional as to carrying out any CIA activities—she looked like a high school girl."

Before leaving his office, the woman "left her little card, her visiting card." It read: "Miss Sharyn L. W. Beers 212 758-2950." In the upper right-hand corner was an address: "P.O. Box 1294, Grand Central Station, New York NY 10017." Above it Dr. Generales noted in ink: "CIA."

Disturbed by the request that he engage in espionage at a scientific meeting, Dr. Generales decided not to go to Miami "because of her approach." The next time he heard from the woman was on October 2, 1972, when his secretary received a telephone call. "Sharyn Beers" wanted to know if Dr. Generales had attended an international congress on space medicine in Nice on September 19–21. But Dr. Generales said the woman seemed to know that he had not in fact gone to the meeting in France. He had decided not to go, for the same reason he had avoided Miami.

By now Dr. Generales was angry. On October 11 he wrote a letter and mailed it to the post-office box at Grand Central. It said:

> Dear Miss Beers:
> On October 2, my secretary informed me that you had called my office asking whether I had attended the conference on space medicine in Nice this summer. I take this opportunity to inform you and your superiors at the Central Intelligence Agency that such queries as this as well as your request of me to observe and report to you about the private conversations of Russian aerospace scientists . . . you made last May are really counterproductive and if I may be so bold as to say, highly distasteful. The mere fact that an intelligence agency approaches any individual of known integrity as myself leaves a stigma of suspicion which is no way rewarding. It is after some thought that I decided to put these remarks on paper and firmly ask you as well as your superior officials to refrain from contacting me.
>
> Sincerely yours,

Four months later, on February 4, 1973, Dr. Generales' secretary noticed, and remarked on the fact, that "the bushes were trampled" outside his office window. It struck him as "very odd, because the men who clean the windows don't do that." That night Dr. Generales worked late, until about midnight. Then he locked up and left.

Sometime in the early morning hours of February 5, his office was broken into. The burglar or burglars took a set of his keys on a ring, a television set, and from the shelf behind his desk, a small cassette tape recorder that still contained the tape of his May 1 conversation with CIA agent Sharyn Beers. The burglars had entered through the window by the bushes on the sidewalk; they did not, apparently, use a flashlight because "the place was all full of matches," Dr. Generales recalled. Police investigated and filed a routine report.

Early in May, after the Watergate revelations had begun, Dr. Generales wrote to General Alexander Haig, Nixon's chief of staff, reporting that he had been approached by "a federal security representative" with a request that "I perform certain functions." He added: "Shortly after the last call, my office was mysteriously burglarized." Dr. Generales apologized; he would not be "calling this matter to your attention had it not been accentuated by certain disclosures in the Watergate affair."

On May 17 Haig wrote back, thanking Dr. Generales for his letter and saying that he turned it over to the Justice Department with a request for an immediate investigation. Five days later the FBI telephoned the physician asking to interview him; not unreasonably, considering his experiences, Dr. Generales asked that the request be made in writing. The next day, however, two men, one displaying an FBI card, showed up at the street door. Dr. Generales politely turned them away, since he was in the midst of his office hours and had asked to see something in writing from the FBI. That was the end of the FBI investigation, he said.

Time passed, Nixon resigned, and on September 10, 1974, from the little town of Schröcken, Austria, Dr. Generales wrote to President Ford: "Mindful of your opening remarks upon assuming the presidency . . . encouraging citizens to communicate with you," he wished "to report to you personally the efforts of the CIA to engage me in despicable espionage activities." The letter then reviewed the entire sequence of events for the President, including the burglary. This "unsettled affair," Dr. Generales wrote, had caused him personal "anguish," and "has resulted in cancellation of active participation in specific international space meetings." He appealed to Ford to investigate.

Receiving no answer, Dr. Generales sent the President a telegram in December. Two weeks later, on January 15, 1975, he received a note on White House stationery signed by Roland L. Elliott, director of correspondence, the White House: "President Ford has asked me to reply to your telegram of December 31. Since the President assumed office there has been a tremendous volume of mail coming to the White House and unfortunately our backlog at this time is so great that it is not possible to locate your previous correspondence. We shall, you may be sure, continue our search and as soon as it is found we will be in touch with you. With best wishes."[*]

The burglary of the office of Dr. Generales was only one of an extraordinary number of unsolved break-ins of the offices or homes of

---

[*] After interviewing Dr. Generales at his office I telephoned from a pay phone the number on Sharyn Beers's visiting card, 758-2950 (which is not the listed number for the CIA in New York City). The conversation went as follows:

DW: Sharyn Beers, please.
Woman with British Accent (hereinafter WBA): Who's calling please?
DW: David Wise.
WBA: (*Long pause*) She's not at her desk. Can I have her call you?
DW: I'm not where she can reach me. I can call back later. Will she be there?
WBA: I'm sure she'll be back later.
DW: What office is this?
WBA: I couldn't give out any information. I only answer the phone.

Later in the day I called again. Sharyn Beers was still out. I left my telephone number, but she never called.

That same afternoon, however, a man telephoned my office wanting to know if I was writing another book; he did not leave his name but said he would like to talk to me about the CIA. I was out, and he was told he could call back. He never did.

individuals, some prominent, who were regarded as enemies of the Nixon White House or who were of interest to federal or local investigative agencies. None of these break-ins has been solved.° Some, of course, may have been ordinary nonpolitical crimes, but almost every one had a common denominator that suggests something more—the burglars seemed interested in files, file cabinets, and documents, often passing up items that one might think would interest ordinary burglars, such as television sets, jewelry, and other valuables.†

In June 1971 Potomac Associates, a liberal public policy research center in Washington, released a survey indicating that many Americans believed the country was in deep trouble and had slid further into difficulty under the Nixon Administration. The report was widely publicized; for example, on June 27, it appeared on page one of the *New York Times*.

Nine days later, on July 6, Caulfield wrote a memo to John Dean about Potomac Associates, which, he noted, was located in Suite 500

° Among the first to perceive the pattern of unsolved burglaries that may have been carried out by government agents was Robert Fink, who described the break-ins in a brilliantly detailed article published in *Rolling Stone* on September 24, 1974.

† There seemed to be no end to the mysterious burglaries; in August 1975, thieves broke into the Washington home of Senator Howard H. Baker, of Tennessee, a member of the Church committee then investigating government intelligence agencies. Baker, who had previously issued a report on CIA links to the Watergate affair, was in the habit of taking home staff summaries of classified documents. He reported no papers missing in the burglary, in which the intruders passed up thousands of dollars' worth of valuables. The incident occurred while Baker was out of town. Both the CIA and the FBI denied they had anything to do with causing the break-in. Nick Stames, head of the FBI's Washington field office, said it was "certainly unusual, because the motive for the break-in wasn't robbery. So somebody was obviously looking for something."

Early in November a second member of the Senate select committee on intelligence was burglarized. This time the Chevy Chase home of Senator Charles McC. Mathias of Maryland was broken into. The burglars, passing up television sets, silverware, China, and expensive figurines, "just rummaged through my personal papers," the senator reported. Mathias, too, was out of town when his home was ransacked.

A few days earlier someone had broken into the Manhattan apartment of author Thomas Kiernan and stolen the only copy of a 382-page handwritten manuscript of a book he was completing on Bebe Rebozo. Also taken were supporting documents and sixteen cassettes of interviews the author had tape-recorded while researching the book. The thieves broke in one day after Kiernan told his typist that the manuscript was ready for her, so Kiernan assumed the burglars were tapping his telephone. Kiernan, who has published fourteen books, had a contract for the Rebozo book with Farrar, Straus & Giroux. His editor, Thomas Stewart, said Kiernan had left Manhattan for an undisclosed location where he was starting to write the book all over again. But Kiernan expected to lose six months at least because of the burglary.

at 1707 L Street, in the ITT Building. "Space is subdivided into four offices which include a storeroom, center alcove and reception room," Caulfield reported. "Building appears to have good security with guard present in lobby during day and evening hours. However, a penetration is deemed possible if required." Caulfield later explained to Watergate investigators that the inquiry into Potomac Associates was the result of interest expressed by Tom Charles Huston.

The president of Potomac Associates was William Watts, the former National Security Council staff secretary who left Kissinger over the Cambodian invasion (and who heard Bebe Rebozo warn Kissinger just before Cambodia, "If this doesn't work, Henry, it's your ass"). A tall Yale graduate and specialist in Soviet affairs, Watts had been a foreign service officer for a decade and then a member of Governor Rockefeller's staff in New York before he went to work for Kissinger on the NSC. After Watts quit the Nixon Administration in 1970, he became president of Potomac Associates. From the point of view of the Nixon White House, Watts had all the wrong credentials—not only was he a Rockefeller man, but Potomac Associates was financed by Indiana industrialist J. Irwin Miller, board chairman of the Cummins Engine Company, who had headed Rockefeller's 1968 presidential campaign, and who was the leading financial angel for New York Mayor John V. Lindsay. By 1971, both Watts personally and Potomac Associates had made Nixon's Enemies List.

Two years later, on June 26, 1973, John Dean revealed the existence of the Enemies List in his testimony to the Ervin committee. On the morning of June 27 the Washington *Post*, in a story by Bob Woodward and Carl Bernstein, quoted Caulfield's memo about Potomac Associates, which stated that "a penetration is deemed possible if required."

"That evening," said Watts in an interview, "I was dining with some friends at home when the telephone rang. It was the building security system reporting that there had been a break-in at my office." Watts's dinner guests, an Argentine diplomat and an official of the American Bicentennial Commission, "thought it was a put-on."

But on the fifth floor of Watts's building, sirens were wailing. Caulfield's view of Potomac Associates' security had become obsolete. Four weeks earlier the research center had signed up with a private security system offered to tenants in the office building; access to the Potomac Associates suite now required a special key to switch off a burglar alarm. Police found no one inside when they arrived, but someone had been there, all right; Watts said that a screw had been replaced on the plate that received the special key and a hole had been drilled in the doorknob in an effort to neutralize the alarm system.

Nothing, apparently, was missing from the office, but Watts contacted his attorney, Mitchell Rogovin, who suggested that the intruders might have been seeking to remove an electronic bug.° Rogovin said he warned Watts not to search the premises, for if a transmitter was found, "we would have to spend the rest of our time defending against the charge we had planted the bug there." Rogovin contacted the staff of the Watergate Special Prosecutor and asked the FBI to search the office. Early in July, FBI agent Robert Tittle called on Watts but declined to search the premises; he urged Watts to let him know if *he* found anything.

Fourteen days later, on the night of July 20, the alarm system was tripped again, and once more police responded. No one was caught, and nothing was taken. A third break-in attempt occurred at Potomac Associates in the early-morning hours of March 2, 1974. Police reported that someone had sought to pry open the door from the bottom. Washington burglars during this period apparently had highly specialized tastes. At the time of the third break-in attempt at Potomac Associates, none of the other tenants who subscribed to the burglar-alarm system in the ten-story office building had reported any break-ins or attempted break-ins.

"Dan," Jean Rather whispered to her husband, "I think there's somebody in the house."

"Go back to sleep. There's nobody in the house."

A few moments later Mrs. Rather shook her husband awake again. "I'm telling you," she repeated fiercely, "there's somebody in the house— My God, the lights just went out!"

It was one o'clock in the morning on Sunday, April 9, 1972, and the Rathers had been asleep for two hours in their home on 33d Street in Georgetown. As the White House correspondent for CBS News, Rather's tough-minded reporting had already so annoyed Nixon that a full year earlier, John Ehrlichman had approached CBS in an effort to have Rather transferred from the White House beat. In an Administration that loathed the networks, Rather occupied a special place in the pantheon of hated media enemies.

It was only by chance that the Rathers were in town that Sunday. The CBS correspondent had made arrangements with the White House

---

° Rogovin, a partner in the prestigious Washington law firm of Arnold and Porter, represented a number of clients who were suing the government in wiretap and surveillance or other cases. Over the years he had earned a reputation as an outstanding civil-liberties attorney in defending the rights of newsmen and other individuals against the government. In 1975, in a move that surprised some of his clients, Rogovin agreed to serve as special counsel to CIA Director William E. Colby during the Senate hearings held by the Church committee.

transportation office to take his family with him on the press plane to Key Biscayne, where Nixon was spending the weekend. There was a last-minute change in plans—one of the children may have felt sick— and Rather flew down alone on Friday, returning home on Saturday evening.

By now Rather was awake and sitting up. "At about that time," he later recalled, "my daughter came in from her bedroom and said, 'Dad, I thought I heard you down in the kitchen.' I heard something myself about then. I got up quickly; I remembered that I had a shotgun in the closet. Sevareid, who's a very good bird shot, hunts up in his place in Virginia and had invited me to go up there the preceding week, and I had this twenty-gauge shotgun in the closet. I got the shotgun and fumbled around and got three shells, and went to the landing of the stairwell outside my bedroom. I heard the door from the basement open. I threw a shell in the chamber very quickly and rammed it back and forth, knowing that a shotgun makes a very distinctive sound, and called to the person below, 'I don't know who you are, but if you don't get out of here I'm going to blow your ass off.' The person—I did see him briefly—was at the top of the stairs coming up from the basement. I saw him move toward the back of the house. My wife picked up the phone to call the police and said to me, 'The phones are dead.' At this point, I've got my daughter and wife in the front bedroom, my son sleeping in the middle bedroom. I've got a dark house, phone dead, somebody below. My daughter got our son, and they all went to the front bedroom. I told my wife to open the window of the front bedroom and see if she could find a passer-by and ask them to go to the police station. There were two passers-by and in a calm voice she said, 'My name is Rather, we're in some trouble here, could you please go to the precinct station and ask the police to come.' The two passers-by took off in a run and shortly after, ten minutes at the most, a police officer arrived at the front door."

Soon afterward, two detectives arrived. In the basement the fuses had been pulled out; two unlocked file cabinets there had been opened and two file folders removed. "Unquestionably the person who was down there took out the files," Rather said. "I never go to those files. They contained very old notes and scripts from the Johnson years, late '66 and '67."

According to Rather, "The only thing the police said, and they said it three times, is 'This is very strange.'" Presumably the police in Georgetown are more accustomed to burglars who grab TV sets and run than to burglars who browse through old television scripts. Rather's burglars left undisturbed two television sets, a hi-fi, and Mrs. Rather's purse containing $100 in cash. Whoever broke in had done so professionally; they had carefully stripped the molding from a pane of glass in the back door, removed the glass, reached in, and unlocked the door. They had also worn gloves, for the police found no prints on the pane that had been taken out.

"This," Jean Rather announced to her husband, "has something to do with politics." Rather at first discounted that idea, but later his opinion began to change during the Watergate hearings, and he called the chief of police in Washington, Jerry Wilson. After three attempts to reach Wilson, Rather received a call back from one of the chief's assistants.

" 'I know what you're thinking, and I don't blame you for thinking it,' " Rather quoted the officer as saying, " 'but frankly I can't help you with that.' " The break-in at the Rather home is described in perfunctory fashion in Crime Complaint Report number 174-812, on file in the Central Records Division of the Metropolitan Police Department, Washington, D.C. The case is listed as "Open."

Marvin Kalb, the CBS diplomatic correspondent who had been wiretapped by the FBI for almost three months in 1969, and on whom John Mitchell had requested physical surveillance, was the target of two break-ins during the summer of 1973. Both took place within a two-week period in Kalb's small broadcast booth and office overlooking the State Department auditorium.

On the weekend of July 7–8, 1973, around the same time that Potomac Associates was having difficulties with burglars, someone gained access to the CBS booth in the State Department. "When I came back it looked like a cyclone had hit the place," Kalb said. "Clearly, someone had gone through it." There were only press releases and speech texts in the office, no important papers, but Kalb reported the incident to State Department security.

Two weeks later, on the same weekend that Potomac Associates experienced its second burglary attempt, someone was back in Kalb's office at the State Department. "It was messed up, but not as bad," Kalb said. "I complained again, and they put a lock on the door."

At the time, Kalb and this brother Bernard were writing their book about Henry Kissinger. "I had a lot of Kissinger tapes and transcripts for the book," Kalb said, "but they were at my home, not at the State Department." Still, after the office break-ins, Kalb installed a burglar system in his home.

State Department security officials investigated the Kalb break-ins, which had occurred in the main building of the Department, even though it is heavily guarded at all times by security forces of the General Services Administration, the GSA. But they discovered no clues. The only lead that Kalb had came from a colleague. "Darius Jhabvala of the Boston *Globe* used the booth down the hall from mine," Kalb said. "At the time my office was ransacked, and I had been talking about it, he told me that once two men had been seen going through the papers in his office. He said they were wearing GSA uniforms."

On August 13, 1971, Nixon's head Plumbers, Egil Krogh and David Young, wrote a memo to John Ehrlichman. To it, they attached an article by Tad Szulc from that morning's edition of the *New York Times*. The memo said the story had prompted a telephone call from CIA Director Richard M. Helms "this morning indicating that this is a direct leak of information from a clandestine source and it puts the source's life in danger."

The Plumbers urged that the CIA be turned loose "to nail down the source of this leak." The FBI "has been out of the clandestine business for five years," the memo said—an apparent reference to Hoover's effort to curtail bag jobs in 1966—and it would therefore take much too long for the FBI to "gear up for such an operation." In fact, it would be better, the memo added, if Hoover were not even told that the CIA was going after the source, "as Hoover is most sensitive about CIA encroachment on the domestic preserve."

Szulc's story cited as its source "intelligence reports" that had been submitted to Nixon only three days earlier. The article reported that the Soviet Union, by signing a friendship treaty with India, had persuaded New Delhi to delay recognition of the government in Bangladesh. It was not too difficult to deduce that this intelligence had been acquired by the CIA from a highly placed source within the Indian government.*

Whether the CIA was in fact unleashed against Szulc is not clear, but if so, it probably would not have fazed him. A tall heavy-set man who smoked Kents, Szulc (pronounced Schulz) had a Paul Lukas accent and distinctly European manners; he was born in Warsaw, left Poland at age twelve ahead of the Nazis. He attended school in Switzerland and France; then in 1940 the family settled in Brazil. He grew up in Rio, where his father was sales director for Mercedes-Benz in Brazil. After World War II he got a job with United Press in New

* There is no evidence that Helms's dire prediction came true. When Secretary of State Kissinger appeared before the Senate Foreign Relations Committee in January 1974, Senator Hugh Scott asked him about the leak that reportedly endangered the life of an agent. "Well, Senator, I must say honestly I do not know whether it cost the life of some agent," Kissinger replied. Scott pressed the point: "He did lose his life? . . . I mean, did he?"

"I do not know," Kissinger answered.

York; he was about to be deported for lack of a visa when he met a tall girl from Akron; five days later they were married. Szulc was able to remain in New York and became a U.S. citizen.°

Szulc worked for the *Times* for almost twenty years, beginning in 1953, serving in Southeast Asia, Latin America, and Spain. He was in Czechoslovakia in 1968 when the Russians invaded the country and he was expelled from Prague at Christmas; he reported from Vienna for a time and then joined the paper's Washington bureau in 1969. The article that upset the White House two years later was one of a series of stories written by Szulc that summer and based on access to intelligence reports.

In a conversation with Nixon on March 27, 1973, Ehrlichman reviewed the wiretapping and other steps taken to find news leaks, and mentioned "the whole Szulc group" as one of three "very serious breaches" (the others being the Pentagon Papers and columnist Jack Anderson's publication of the India-Pakistan papers).† Later in the conversation Ehrlichman noted that "a lot of things" were done "in the national interest . . . they involved taps, they involved entry. . . ."

A little more than a month earlier, on the night of February 10, 1973, Szulc and his wife were dining with Pakistani friends in Maryland. There was no one at home at the Szulc residence in the Forest Hills section of northwest Washington. "Our son Tony came home earlier than he normally would, around ten o'clock, and he telephoned us," Szulc said. "He said something very strange has happened and you better come home. He asked why the bedroom door was locked from the inside. We said we didn't know. My dog, Jason, was in the house. He's a golden retriever, no defense against anything. He rolls over."

The Szulces sped home, and broke down the bedroom door. "The room was in total disarray, all the drawers pulled out, my shirts, Marianne's clothing, on the floor. Marianne had quite a bit of jewelry and the jewels were strung on the bed and on the floor. But nothing was taken, except for six dollar bills from Marianne's wallet, a diamond stickpin, and perhaps an old English coin." The television set was untouched, and no other jewels were missing. "The surprising thing is that nothing of value was taken, and yet such an enormous effort was

---

° Marianne Szulc became her husband's salaried assistant after he left the *Times* in 1972 to work as an independent author and journalist.

† It is reasonably clear from the context that Ehrlichman meant a "group" of stories, and not a group of people of which the White House assumed Szulc to be the ringleader. In an interview with the author Ehrlichman said that the word "group" might be an error in the White House transcript, but that if he used it he meant "a group of stories," not a group of people.

made to go through every drawer, where presumably someone might hide classified documents." The police came, dusted for prints, and wrote up a report. But no one was ever arrested for the break-in.

In June the Washington *Post* reported that Szulc had been wiretapped and that the White House Plumbers had regularly received the transcripts for several months during 1971. In 1974 Szulc and his wife filed suit against the government, the Plumbers, Hunt, Liddy, Caulfield, Ehrlichman, Mitchell, and others, charging that his telephone at his home and at the *New York Times* Washington bureau had been tapped, and alleging that one or more of the defendants had been responsible for the burglary of his home. The tapping and burglary charges were denied by all the defendants, but the government admitted overhearing Szulc and his wife on the telephones of other persons who were wiretapped.

Szulc had engaged Mitchell Rogovin as his attorney. On the day that Nixon resigned as President, Rogovin was in the District of Columbia jail interviewing G. Gordon Liddy on Szulc's behalf. According to Rogovin, Liddy was quite different from his public persona: "He seemed remote and detached, with no animus for anyone. He even spoke well of Judge Sirica." Liddy insisted that the Plumbers "didn't do anything with Tad," and he "didn't put any taps on Tad's phone or request it." As for the burglary, Liddy pointed out that he was already in jail in February 1973, at the time of the Szulc break-in, and had no responsibility for that. While Liddy was of little help in the Szulc case, he did relate one fascinating tidbit about surveillance techniques. It was even possible, he assured Rogovin, to wire a street corner for sound; the FBI had done it by attaching a microphone to a mailbox or a trashcan.

In a separate interview in Rogovin's office, Howard Hunt also claimed he could recall nothing about Szulc.* So Szulc was unable to find out who broke into his home and ransacked it, spurning the expensive jewelry and apparently looking for something else. A federal court permitted Marianne Szulc to look at the log of the single wiretap on which she had been overheard. But Szulc was not allowed to see the logs of the taps on which he had been overheard; they were sealed

---

* As it happened, Szulc knew a good deal about Hunt; he wrote a book about him—*Compulsive Spy: The Strange Career of E. Howard Hunt* (New York: Viking, 1974). After the interview Rogovin took Hunt to lunch, and Hunt told him of his first encounter with Watergate Special Prosecutor Archibald Cox. On the day the new grand jury was sworn in, Hunt was already in the room about to be questioned when Cox strode in. He went around shaking hands, saying, "I'm Archie Cox and I hope this won't be too distressing an experience for you."

Hunt stuck out his hand and said, "I'm Howard Hunt and I'm sure it will be."

by the court at the request of the Department of Justice, on the familiar grounds of "national security."

Among the organizations and individuals on the White House Enemies List was another liberal research center, the Institute for Policy Studies, and its co-directors, Marcus Raskin and Richard Barnet, both former officials of the Kennedy Administration. In October of 1973, IPS's attorney Mitchell Rogovin filed an affidavit stating that the institute had evidence that the FBI and Washington police had infiltrated, burglarized, and wiretapped the research center.*

Some of the information had been provided by Robert Merritt, who told Rogovin that under the name of Robert Chandler he had worked for many months as an informant of the intelligence unit of the Metropolitan Police Department, and later for agents Terry O'Connor and William Tucker of the FBI. Merritt said he was instructed by the police in August 1971 to infiltrate IPS, to attend meetings, to get to know the people there.†

Later, Merritt said, he was transferred to undercover work for the FBI. On one occasion, he said, the FBI learned that a former agent, Robert N. Wall, who had spoken out publicly against the Bureau, was to attend a meeting at IPS. Merritt said that Tucker wanted to know whether Wall had revealed any FBI techniques; particularly whether he had said anything about a boom microphone which, Tucker explained, could be lowered from above, apparently to bug a meeting. And Merritt also said that Tucker had told him the FBI had equipment that could pick up conversations off windows. Finally, Merritt said that the FBI had a suite at the Dupont Plaza Hotel overlooking Dupont Circle, a gathering place for antiwar activists in the early seventies, and used it to photograph the park below. He said the FBI also used another suite in the hotel to monitor IPS, which at the time had offices in a building next door.

Raskin said that he well remembered a room in the hotel across the alley "where people would look down at me." On one occasion he

---

* In July 1975 Representative Otis G. Pike of New York was named chairman of a House counterpart to the Senate intelligence committee. During hearings of the Pike committee it was disclosed that over a period of time the FBI had no fewer than fifty-two informants reporting on the activities of the Institute for Policy Studies.

† In an interview published in an underground newspaper in Washington in October 1973, Merritt said he was recruited into undercover work for the Metropolitan Police Department in 1970 by Officer Carl M. Shoffler, whom he had met around Dupont Circle and thought to be a street person. Shoffler, Officer John B. Barrett, and Sergeant Paul W. Leeper were the three police officers who arrested the Watergate burglars in the sixth-floor offices of the Democratic National Committee.

looked up and saw "a microphone sticking out" of this window. And, he said, participants at an IPS seminar did see a boom microphone extending from the window and aimed at the institute.

IPS sued John Mitchell and a number of other former officials charging that they had wiretapped and burglarized the institute. Rogovin was not shooting in the dark, for in an August 11, 1971 memo from the White House Plumbers to Ehrlichman, which dealt with the Pentagon Papers investigation, Krogh and Young speculated that the grand jury would not be likely to call Barnet and Raskin, "because they have been overheard."

Subsequently the FBI admitted that conversations of Raskin, Barnet, and Ralph Stavins, a third IPS official, had been "intercepted by electronic surveillance conducted by this bureau."

But then the case took a peculiar turn. A federal judge agreed that the institute's attorneys were entitled to receive from the FBI any materials taken from IPS without the institute's knowledge. But to both Rogovin and his associate Patrick F. J. Macrory, it seemed as though the government attorneys were hemming and hawing about turning over the documents; there seemed to be some problem in defining the nature of the material taken.

Finally a red-faced Justice Department attorney explained what was going on. "The FBI has surveilled IPS," Rogovin said, "watched a private garbage truck arrive and take away the trash, and followed the truck out to a dump on the outskirts of the city where the FBI recovered six plastic bags of garbage. Among the garbage were eight carbon ribbons.° The FBI reconstructed the documents from the ribbons. The eight ribbons represented sixteen weeks of typing at IPS, so it was a tremendous job. But it was done; the FBI retyped the documents." Eventually the FBI turned over several pages of reconstructed documents to IPS.

On May 5, 1972, James McCord, the security director for CREEP, rented room 419 of Howard Johnson's motel, across from the Watergate office building. After the Democratic National Committee offices were bugged later that month, McCord's assistant, former FBI agent Alfred Baldwin, used the room as a listening post to monitor the telephone conversations that were being broadcast from the Watergate. Two days before McCord rented the motel room, Howard Hunt's

° Unlike cloth or nylon ribbons, carbon ribbons are used only once and then discarded. Since each typed character makes but a single impression and is not typed over, as in the case of a cloth ribbon, a used carbon ribbon can be read. Depending on the typewriter model, however, it is not always easy; for example, on an IBM Selectric, the ribbon must be deciphered like an encoded message—a slow and painstaking process.

Cubans had made their first trip to Washington. On White House orders, Bernard Barker and half a dozen other Cubans had flown in from Miami to disrupt an antiwar demonstration that was held on the Capitol steps while inside, the body of J. Edgar Hoover lay in state. Daniel Ellsberg participated in the demonstration, and the Cubans had orders, as one of them later put it, "to call him a traitor and punch him in the nose, hit him and run." They failed in that mission, but the Cubans traded punches with some of the demonstrators, and two of the White House counter-demonstrators were seized by police, but then quickly released. The Cubans apparently flew back to Miami on May 4.

Sometime during the weekend of May 6–7, unknown persons broke into the Bank Operations Division of the Federal Reserve Board, located at that time in Room 805 of the Watergate office building, two floors above the Democratic headquarters. How the burglars got in is a mystery, for the door was not forced and it is normally locked after hours. When the break-in was discovered on Monday morning, May 8, officials of the Fed summoned police. Officer Kerry E. White of the Washington police, who responded, interviewed the two officials whose offices had been burglarized, Harry A. Guinter and Walter A. Althausen.

Officer White's report reads: "Compl. [complainant] reports office entered in an unk. [unknown] manner and Mosler safe forced open with unknown tool, and nothing missing. Also five locked filing cabinets forced open; two locked desks forced open. Nothing missing at this time."

The Bank Operations Division of the Fed is a closely guarded and little-known unit that deals with the security of all federal reserve banks. Burglars who photographed plans in the division's safes and files might be in a position to rob a federal reserve bank. The New York Federal Reserve Bank contains more gold than Fort Knox—$16.8 billion in 1975.

There was a peculiar aspect of the break-in: officials of the Fed disputed virtually every point in the police report. Joseph Coyne, the Fed's spokesman, said that the burglars tried to get into the Mosler safe, the file cabinets, and the desk drawers, "but they didn't get into anything." Coyne said the safe had contained "records of currency among federal reserve banks and no security plans." He said the burglars did try to force open a file cabinet in the office of Walter Althausen, the Fed's chief architect, which contained the plans of federal reserve banks planned or under construction. Security plans for existing banks were also kept in the Room 805 area, he said.

Harry Guinter said he had provided information about the burglary to the police: two or three file cabinets had been broken into—

the lock bars had been cut—but no files were missing. He conceded that records could have been photographed, but there was "no evidence that the Mosler safe or any [desk] drawers were forced open."°

Six weeks later, early on the morning of June 17, Watergate security guard Frank Wills discovered tape across the latch of a door leading from the garage level into the office building. He removed the tape, but a few moments later found the door taped again. He called police, and when the officers arrived, they went first to the eighth floor, remembering that there had been a recent burglary there. They met a federal guard assigned to the Federal Reserve Board offices and together they checked the various offices on the floor. They found the door on the stairwell of the eighth floor taped in the same manner as the garage-level door. The police went down to the seventh and then the sixth floor, and caught the Watergate burglars.

On June 16, 1972, a couple of hours before the Watergate break-in, a man checked in at the guard desk in the lobby, signed the book at 10:50 P.M., and wrote down he was going to Room 805, the Bank Operations Division of the Federal Reserve Board. The man signed the name "E. Warren," which was an alias sometimes used by James Mc-Cord (and sometimes by Howard Hunt). The break-in at Room 805 the previous month has never been solved.

On the weekend following the break-in at the Fed, the Chilean embassy in Washington was burglarized and its offices ransacked. According to the official police report, the break-in occurred sometime between Saturday afternoon, May 13, and Monday morning, May 15, when it was discovered.† The story in the Washington *Post* was brief

---

° A follow-up police report filed on June 7 states that comparisons of fingerprints taken at the scene were being made, and the report refers to "fingers and palms of value." Yet Guinter said that Detective Richard Womble had told him on the phone soon after the break-in that the prints police had taken were not usable.
† One week earlier, on the same weekend as the break-in at the Fed, there was an attempt to break into the home in Washington of Chilean press attaché Andrés Rojas. At about two o'clock in the morning on May 8, Rojas was awakened by a noise, looked out the window, and saw three men trying to get into the house. He shouted, and the men ran to a dark-blue car and sped away.

In all, there were six burglaries or attempted break-ins of Chilean officials during 1971–72. On April 5, 1971, the New York hotel suite of UN Ambassador and Mrs. Humberto Diaz-Casanueva was burglarized; a week later, burglars struck the Manhattan apartment of Javier Urrutia, director of the Chilean Development Corporation. About the same time, Patricio Rodriguez, chancellor of the Chilean embassy in Washington, was awakened by noises outside his home in Bethesda; he fired two shots in the air and saw some men run. On February 10, 1972, the New York residence of Victor Rioseco, the economic counselor for the Chilean UN mission, was burglarized.

and attracted little attention. Under a small headline, "Chile Embassy Burglarized," the account read:

> The Chilean Foreign Ministry has described as a "serious matter" the burglary over the weekend at the Chilean Embassy in Washington.
>
> Embassy press attaché Andrew Rojas-Wainer said yesterday that the embassy at 1736 Massachusetts Ave. NW was burglarized sometime between Friday night and Monday morning.
>
> The press attaché said that "so far nothing important is missing" and that the thieves took only "four or five transistor radios," some books and documents.
>
> The State Department issued a statement expressing its deep regret over the incident.

At the time, Salvador Allende, a Marxist, was the duly elected President of Chile. President Nixon, as became known much later, had given direct orders to the Central Intelligence Agency in 1970 to try to organize a military coup to prevent Allende's election. That plan failed, but the CIA spent $8 million in Chile between 1970 and 1973 in an effort to topple Allende. Allende died in a military coup that brought down his government in September 1973.

The Chilean embassy stood on the south side of Massachusetts Avenue, across the street from the Brookings Institution, and two doors from the graceful old mansion occupied by the Canadian embassy.° There was easy access to the rear parking lot of the Chilean embassy from the public alley that ran behind the building. On that weekend in May 1972, the burglar or burglars climbed the east side of the building—the police later found the scuff marks—and entered through an unlocked bay window on the second floor.

Nothing was taken from an administrative office on this floor, but a passport belonging to Andrés Rojas was stolen from the desk in his office in the rear of the building. The burglars also entered the third-floor office of Ambassador Orlando Letelier, which overlooked Massachusetts Avenue and was clearly identified with a bronze marker that said "Ambassador." The intruders also entered the office on the fourth floor of Fernando Bachelet, the embassy's first secretary. In these of-

---

° The mansion was bought by the Canadian government from Mrs. Aksel Wichfeld, an heiress to the Swift meat fortune, whose husband, Clarence Moore, built the house for her; he later perished when the *Titanic* went down. The New York *Daily News* reported on May 29, 1973, that a 1970 White House plan (presumably the Huston Plan) included a proposal to break into the Canadian embassy to determine if the Canadian government was aiding American draft resisters. Richard O'Hagan, the information minister for the embassy, said no break-in had occurred there.

fices, documents were taken from the files and spread around on the floor, the couches, and on the furniture. Four portable radios and an electric razor were stolen, according to a subsequent police report, which placed the total value of the stolen property at $50.

When the robbery was discovered, Pablo Valdes, the minister-counsel, telephoned Ambassador Letelier at his residence on Sheridan Circle. "I instructed Valdes not to touch anything," Letelier said in an interview, "and to immediately call the State Department and the police, which Valdes did." Valdes spoke to John W. Fisher, head of the Chile desk, who dispatched Lewis Girdler, another State Department official. Girdler arrived within the hour, Letelier said, but the police, who had been called about nine-thirty on Monday morning, did not drop by until about noon.

There were a number of unusual aspects to the break-in. According to police, it was the first burglary that had been reported on the block in several years. Although the thieves did take four radios, they passed up cash and office equipment in the second-floor administrative office. And they appeared very interested in the embassy's documents, most of which were written in Spanish. Despite this, according to one embassy official, the police kept insisting the burglary was the work of a teen-ager.

"It was not a normal robbery," Letelier said in an interview in 1975. "For months I pushed the State Department for information. I was always told the police were working on it."

Letelier, a distinguished and aristocratic diplomat, had red hair, a trim mustache, warm brown eyes, and a long, rather sad but friendly face; there was a hint of Fernandel in his expression. He knew it was no teen-ager who had pored over his official files. A lawyer and economist from an old Chilean family—although the name is originally French—Letelier came to Washington in 1960 with the Inter-American Development Bank. After a decade in Washington with the bank, he resigned to become ambassador to the United States. Of his four children, all boys, one was born in America.

In May of 1973 he returned to Santiago to become a member of Allende's Cabinet; he was Minister of Defense at the time of the coup. He was arrested, taken to a prison camp on Dawson Island, and held under brutal conditions for eight months. "After my arrest, the first thing I was forced to do was to watch a firing squad execute twenty-nine persons," he said. Sentenced to forced labor on Dawson Island, Letelier lost forty pounds. In 1974 he was taken to a basement interrogation center in Santiago. "They played rock-and-roll music constantly and shined bright reflector lights in my eyes, so it was not possible to sleep. Every once in a while they would have to change the tape. Changing the tape took seven minutes, and during these seven minutes that they changed the reel I could hear the screams of the other people being tortured in the cells nearby." He was released in September, and with his family returned to Washington on a scholar's visa to work and write at the Institute for Policy Studies.°

In May of 1972, when the Chilean embassy was burglarized, Letelier was not entirely surprised; six or eight months before, he had gone through a somewhat similar experience. He had been vacationing with his family in Virginia and returned unexpectedly to his home on Sheridan Circle. When he entered the residence, he heard a noise and encountered a young man and a woman in their twenties who said they had gotten in by mistake. "We hear you have beautiful chandeliers here," they said before they bolted from the house.

The break-in at the embassy aroused no interest in the press until January 7, 1973, when Martin Schram, the Washington bureau chief of *Newsday*, wrote a story suggesting that the Watergate break-in was part of a larger project that included the photographing of embassy documents. The story said that three men participated in the burglary, and it also said the Watergate defendants "were behind the burglary at the Chilean embassy." The story was attributed to an unidentified source close to the defendants.

At the time, one of the defendants, Frank Sturgis, was talking to some reporters, as was Andrew St. George, a free-lance writer working with Sturgis. A week later Seymour M. Hersh reported in the *New York Times* that St. George was circulating a book outline in New York based on Sturgis' adventures. Hersh said that Sturgis had, in general, corroborated reports that targets in addition to the Watergate had been bugged, but had refused to discuss any specifics. He quoted Sturgis as saying he would not be "a stoolie." On February 9 James Schlesinger, then Director of the CIA, received a telephone call from John Dean at the White House. In a memorandum of their conversation Schlesinger wrote that Dean "mentioned there is a hot story being passed about in the press, primarily instigated by Seymour Hersh of the *New York Times*. The story suggests that Sturgis, who sometimes goes by the code name Federini,† was the individual responsible for the burglarizing of the Chilean Embassy in Washington." Schlesinger's memo added: "Shortly thereafter I discussed these matters with Bill Colby, who indicated that Sturgis has not been on the payroll for a number of years and that whatever the allegations about the Chilean Embassy, the Agency has no connection at all."

The obvious corollary of the fact that Sturgis "has not been on the payroll for a number of years" is that at some earlier point he was

---

° Letelier was killed when a bomb blew up his car in Washington in Sept. 1976.
† The CIA Director (or Dean) did not have his information straight. Sturgis was born Frank Fiorini in Norfolk, Virginia, but later took the name of his stepfather.

indeed on CIA's payroll. According to published accounts of Sturgis' background, he was an ex-Marine, an adventurer who originally joined Castro in the hills of Oriente province in 1958. But later, the stories said, Sturgis broke with Castro and became active among the Cuban exiles in Miami in various anti-Castro plots.

On May 30, 1975, ABC broadcast a one-hour TV special on the CIA. Frank Sturgis was interviewed, and identified as a "former CIA employee" and as "one of Fidel Castro's trusted security men but an agent working for the CIA." On the program Sturgis said he had participated in plots to kill Castro—although he did not say he had done so for the CIA. Asked if he knew of break-ins within the United States by persons on CIA assignment, Sturgis said yes, he did; he had, he said, participated in some of these himself.

William Colby, who succeeded Schlesinger as CIA Director in mid-1973, may have forgotten about Schlesinger's memo saying Sturgis had not been on CIA's payroll for "a number of years." Because the day the ABC special was broadcast, Colby's press spokesman released a statement flatly denying that "Mr. Frank Sturgis" had "ever been connected with the Central Intelligence Agency in any way."

During the Watergate revelations in June 1973, a 1972 memo written by Lieutenant General Vernon A. Walters, Deputy Director of the CIA, was published. It was dated June 28, 1972, which was during the period that Nixon was attempting to cover up the burglary of the Watergate by ordering the CIA to block the FBI investigation of the crime. Walters, summarizing a visit with John Dean, wrote: "He believed that Barker had been involved in a clandestine entry into the Chilean embassy. I said that I was sure none of the [Watergate] suspects had been on the [CIA] payroll for the past two years."

At about the time that Martin Schram suggested that the Watergate burglars were behind the Chilean break-in, Jack A. Blum, associate counsel to Senator Church's subcommittee on multinational corporations, also got a tip that Cubans had broken into the embassy. The subcommittee was investigating the links between ITT, the CIA, and the efforts to block Allende's election.

Without indicating what was on his mind, Blum summoned to his office Detectives Ronald Levers and Thomas Whitehead, the two police officers who had investigated the Chilean break-in. The detectives did not try to tell Blum it had been done by a teen-ager; just the opposite, they said—usually a teen-ager turns to vandalism if he does not find enough valuable items, and there was no sign of destruction in the embassy. The detectives said that several sets of fingerprints had been taken and were available for comparison, but they said they never ran the prints and checked them against their files unless they had a suspect. Blum handed them a copy of Schram's story.

"We have seven suspects," Blum told them. "Run the Watergate burglars." The detectives seemed surprised to see the story, although it had been published in the Washington *Post*, and said they would check the prints against the Watergate burglars. "That's the last we ever saw of them [the detectives]," Blum said. "We couldn't get them on the phone. 'Oh, he's working on the night shift' . . . 'Oh, he's working late today.' Every excuse you ever heard of."

So the Senate subcommittee was unable to pin down the reports that Cubans or Watergate burglars had also broken into the Chilean embassy.* And after a time, the speculation tying the embassy break-in to the Cubans faded away.

In 1975, however, this theory was replaced by a new and even more intriguing possibility. In January of that year John Dean was interviewed by NBC's Carl Stern. Stern noted that Dean had heard a number of things from Charles Colson, with whom he had recently shared a prison barracks. Stern asked if Dean "had knowledge of a CIA break-in into the Chilean embassy, the planting of a bug, and so on. Is that true? Did you talk about it with Colson?" Dean replied that Colson had read "the CIA file on Watergate" and learned that "the CIA had arrangements to have the FBI go in and remove the device that was in the Chilean embassy . . ."

The following month Colson was released from prison and went on the *Today* show. Barbara Walters asked him about Dean's allegation that the CIA had bugged the Chilean embassy and then had the FBI remove the bug. "That's correct," Colson replied. "That's in the— that was in the CIA files that I have read."

The Washington police officers who investigated the embassy burglary, officials of the State Department, and others involved, were interviewed by the author about the embassy break-in, but all were reluctant to talk about it or professed ignorance.

The final report on the break-in by the Watergate Special Prosecutor stated that no "evidence which would form the basis for criminal charges" had been found. An official familiar with the Special Prosecutor's investigation said that all this really meant was that the Special

---

* Barker, Sturgis, and various Cubans were frequently in Washington during the month of May 1972. They were first in Washington on May 3–4 to participate in the counter-demonstration at the Capitol. They returned to Washington on May 22, and began their attempts to break into the Watergate on May 26. There is, however, no available evidence that the Miami group was in the capital on May 13–15, the weekend of the burglary of the Chilean embassy.

The Watergate Special Prosecutor investigated the embassy break-in in 1974 and asked the Washington police and the FBI to compare the fingerprints taken at the embassy with those of the Watergate burglars. "They were inconclusive or didn't match," an investigator who saw the results said. "They were very weak prints."

Prosecutor had not been able to clear up the mystery. But he quickly added that if the FBI had broken in, "we didn't investigate it." A national security burglary, he said, would have been outside the authority of the Special Prosecutor.° A spokesman for the FBI declined all comment on the break-in at the Chilean embassy.

The Senate intelligence committee under Frank Church investigated the Chilean break-in but was eventually persuaded by the Ford Administration not to dig into burglaries or break-ins of specific foreign embassies. But before the committee had agreed to back away from the subject of embassy break-ins, the CIA privately admitted to the committee that there had been an electronic eavesdropping operation directed at the Chilean embassy, involving both the CIA and the FBI. This fact was not disclosed by the committee.

By the CIA's account, it first proposed that the FBI bug the embassy in April 1971, but Hoover refused. On April 23 Helms wrote Attorney General Mitchell requesting that he reverse Hoover's decision, which Mitchell did. The CIA delivered sophisticated bugging equipment to the FBI three days later, and between April 27 and mid-May the FBI got into the embassy and installed several mikes.

The bugs worked, and for more than eight months the government listened in to conversations taking place inside the embassy. But in February 1972 Hoover, still smarting over being reversed by Mitchell, threatened to tell Congress that the FBI was bugging the embassy at the CIA's request. The CIA hastily asked that the eavesdropping be stopped, and the FBI either went in and pulled out the miniature transmitters or turned them off by remote control.

Again by the CIA's account, it asked the FBI to "reinstitute coverage" of the embassy on December 8, action that the State Department also strongly urged, according to the CIA. By the day after Christmas the bugs were broadcasting again, although there is some evidence they may have been turned off or removed again in February 1973.

The CIA's version is fascinating because, by coincidence or design, it claimed that the bugging stopped in February of 1972 and resumed in December, neatly straddling the period during which the known burglary took place, in May. The chronology is almost too good to be true, for it has both agencies messing around with the Chilean embassy at almost every time *except* several months on either side of the May 1972 date.

After the break-in in May, the CIA claimed to have launched a

° The Watergate Special Prosecutor did ask the FBI, the CIA, and the State Department whether they knew anything about who had committed the burglary. All three disclaimed any knowledge of, or responsibility for, the break-in.

detailed in-house investigation to see if the burglary had been committed by CIA agents. CIA officials said that this self-investigation showed that the Agency had no knowledge of who had committed the break-in.

In March of 1974, when the Watergate Special Prosecutor was investigating the unsolved burglary of the Chilean embassy, Nick Akerman, a staff attorney assigned to the investigation, was flipping through some unrelated FBI reports when, much to his surprise, he found one mentioning the embassy break-in: on June 18, 1972, one day after the Watergate burglary, the report said, an informant walked into the FBI's office in Miami and stated that Bernard Barker had been involved in the break-in at the Chilean embassy. The informant, according to Akerman, mentioned no other names, "he just told the FBI that Barker had been involved."

Intrigued, Akerman asked the FBI to check out the report by finding and interviewing the informant's source, a Cuban exile in Miami. Akerman did not recall whether the informant had revealed his source originally, but if not, he must have divulged it under further questioning because the FBI got the name of the Cuban source "and was looking for the man."

In mid-April the FBI reported back that it was too late. "The FBI searched for the guy at my request," Akerman recalled. "He was very active in Cuban exile affairs. They [the FBI] almost got to him in time, it was very close, but he was murdered a few days before." The Cuban had been shot.

"It looked," Akerman said, "like a political assassination."

"We do not target on American citizens."

—Richard Helms,
April 14, 1971

6
CIA:
The Spying Comes Home

"An intelligence service is the ideal vehicle for a conspiracy," Allen Dulles once wrote. "Its members can travel about at home and abroad under secret orders, and no questions are asked. Every scrap of paper in the files, its membership, its expenditure of funds, its contacts, even enemy contacts, are state secrets."

Dulles was writing about the World War II German Abwehr, but by 1976, the year of America's Bicentennial, Americans reading that passage might understandably have assumed that Dulles had in mind the Central Intelligence Agency, which he headed for nearly a decade. For in the space of a few years, the American people learned that:

• The CIA provided disguises, false identities, and other spy paraphernalia to the White House burglars who broke into the Watergate and the office of Dr. Lewis Fielding.

• In blatant violation of its charter, the CIA prepared a psychological profile of an American citizen, Daniel Ellsberg.

• On President Nixon's orders, the CIA attempted to obstruct the FBI investigation of the Watergate burglary.

• The CIA went into the pornographic-movie business, financing a porno film, *Happy Days*, starring an actor who resembled President Sukarno of Indonesia.*

• The CIA procured women for King Hussein of Jordan and other leaders, reimbursing them for their services with federal funds.

• During four Administrations, the CIA plotted the assassination of, or encouraged coups against, eight foreign leaders, five of whom died violently.

• The CIA hired two mobsters, Sam Giancana and Johnny Rosselli, to murder Cuban Premier Fidel Castro, provided them with lethal poison for that purpose, and offered $150,000 for the job.

• In direct defiance of a presidential order, the CIA failed to destroy its stocks of deadly poisons, including cobra venom and enough shellfish toxin to kill 55,000 people.

• Under pressure from Presidents Johnson and Nixon, the CIA, in Operation CHAOS, illegally spied on American citizens inside the United States and infiltrated antiwar and other dissident groups, and compiled a computerized index of more than 300,000 persons and organizations.

• The CIA experimented with mind-altering drugs on persons who did not know that the hallucinogens were being given to them; one victim, Frank R. Olson, a civilian researcher for the Army, committed suicide by jumping out the window nine days after the CIA had laced his after-dinner Cointreau with LSD.

• In violation of strict federal law, the CIA for twenty years secretly opened, read, photographed, and resealed first-class mail; in New York City alone the CIA opened 215,820 letters.

• Although Congress established the CIA to spy overseas, and prohibited it from conducting domestic operations, within the United States the CIA followed and in some cases photographed 96 American citizens, carried out at least 12 break-ins, 32 wiretaps, and 32 buggings, and secretly obtained the federal-income-tax returns of at least 16 persons from the IRS. Three newsmen were among those wiretapped, and the CIA also placed reporters under physical surveillance.

And this is by no means a complete list of the outrages committed by the CIA in the name of the American people, with their tax money. In some instances the CIA acted out of control, on its own. In other cases it followed presidential orders. The Rockefeller Commission, in an official report to President Ford, provided the bottom line; it found that the CIA had taken actions that were "plainly unlawful" and in-

---

* This gem was uncovered by the House intelligence committee, which reported, without elaboration, that the film had been produced around 1957 "for blackmail" purposes, with Howard Hughes lieutenant Robert Maheu serving as "casting director, make-up man, cameraman and director." At the time, Sukarno was still in power.

fringed "the rights of Americans." A powerful, secret agency of the United States government was thus *officially* found to have committed crimes against its own citizens.

It was a shocking and bewildering series of disclosures to those Americans, surely in the majority, who wanted to believe in their government and in the democratic system. Yet it was not altogether surprising that a secret agency, spending billions in hidden funds, and operating outside normal constitutional and political controls, had become a corrupt force in American society.

The historical framework that gave rise to the CIA is familiar enough. The United States, emerging from World War II as a world power, created an enormous national security bureaucracy and military establishment, including an elaborate secret intelligence apparatus with the CIA at its center. In a book published in 1964, Thomas B. Ross and I called this intelligence structure "the invisible government." By 1976 the CIA and other American intelligence agencies were spending an estimated $12 billion a year and— as official investigations had made clear—wielding a frightening degree of secret, sometimes illegal, and often uncontrolled power.° The role of secret intelligence agencies in a democracy had become an issue of major public concern.

Congress established the CIA in 1947. In part it acted in response to Pearl Harbor; both the legislative and executive branches were persuaded that the United States needed a central intelligence organization to guard against another surprise attack. But beyond that, the nation's leaders believed that America's new status as a world power required a central agency within the government to gather and analyze the information that the President needed to make complex foreign policy and military decisions.

The CIA was proposed and presented to Congress primarily as an agency for research and analysis; reading over the congressional testimony at the time, one gets the impression that the CIA would be a collection of elderly ladies clipping *Pravda* and poring over Soviet railroad timetables. Sam Giancana is nowhere mentioned.

Intelligence is another word for information. A basic function assigned to the CIA was to gather intelligence, either openly, or secretly by means of espionage.† Within a short time, technology had a far-

° In 1975 the entire CIA budget was hidden within a $2 billion appropriation for "Other Procurement, Air Force." The $12 billion total for all U.S. intelligence, much higher than previous estimates, was indicated in the report of the Senate intelligence committee.
† The 1947 act did not even give the CIA explicit authority to *collect* intelligence openly, or to spy. In executive sessions of congressional committees considering the act, Administration witnesses indicated that the CIA would engage in espionage, but Congress as a whole was not informed of this. The law empowered the

reaching impact. By the seventies, most intelligence was being collected not by human spies but by electronic ears or overhead reconnaissance satellites.

Once gathered, intelligence is of little use unless it is analyzed, evaluated, summarized, and distributed to the policy makers. In addition to these responsibilities, the CIA was expected to provide estimates or predictions of possible future events.

Within a year of its creation, however, the CIA was secretly given presidential authority to conduct covert political operations. This was done despite the lack of any clearly stated, specific basis in the law. Thus, almost from the start, the CIA was in the business not merely of reporting on events but of attempting to manipulate events in favor of the United States, to cause history to happen, as it were.

This split personality was reflected in the CIA's basic organization. The Directorate of Intelligence was responsible for the research, analysis, and estimating functions; the Directorate of Operations conducted espionage and engaged in secret political operations, from assassinations to overthrowing governments.°

Through its secret political operations the CIA became a powerful instrument of the Cold War. For two decades, Americans were warned by their leaders of the perils of a monolithic international Communism. To preserve the Free World, we were told, it was necessary, as Allen Dulles put it, to "fight fire with fire." Not many Americans appeared to realize that the United States, by adopting the methods of totalitarian systems, would change the nature of the very institutions it was attempting to preserve. The implacable external enemy was the justification for the establishment of a vast intelligence apparatus, its size and budget secret by law, its operations subject to none of the usual checks and balances that the system required of more plebeian government agencies.

In retrospect, it is easy to see where clandestine political operations overseas would lead. To a considerable degree, the Watergate trauma represented a transfer of the psychology, rationale, and agents of the Cold War into the domestic political arena. It is hardly accidental that both the CIA and the FBI were deeply involved in, and ultimately compromised by, Watergate.

Given the existence and growth of a powerful federal intelligence machine, it was only a matter of time before there was a "spillover"

CIA only to "correlate and evaluate" intelligence. But the statute also permitted the CIA to perform for existing intelligence agencies "additional services of common concern," language that the Agency relied upon as its authority to collect intelligence.

° Prior to 1973, the Directorate of Operations was known as the Directorate of Plans. Both names were euphemisms for cloak-and-dagger operations.

into domestic politics. It was inevitable that the tools and techniques of international espionage would be unleashed at home. The corrosion had begun long ago.

From the beginning, a few wary members of Congress feared that the CIA would become an American Gestapo. The question was raised—in precisely those words—at the House hearings on President Truman's bill to create the CIA. On April 25, 1947, Secretary of the Navy James V. Forrestal, testifying before a House committee on expenditures, was questioned by Republican Congressman Clarence J. Brown of Ohio:

> BROWN: How far does this Central Intelligence Agency go in its authority and scope? ... This is a very great departure from what we have done in the past in America. ... I am very much interested in seeing the United States have as fine a foreign military and naval intelligence as they can possibly have, but I am not interested in setting up here in the United States any particular agency under any President ... and just allow him to have a Gestapo of his own if he wants to have it.
> FORRESTAL: The purposes of the Central Intelligence Authority are limited definitely to purposes outside of this country.

In June, at a hearing of the same House committee, Representative Henderson Lanham of Georgia asked Dr. Vannevar Bush, an Administration witness, if there was any danger of the CIA "becoming a Gestapo." Bush replied soothingly, "I think there is no danger of that. The bill provides clearly that it is concerned with intelligence outside of this country, that it is not concerned with intelligence on internal affairs ... We already have, of course, the FBI in this country."

Concerned over the Gestapo issue, however, the House committee inserted language in the final version providing that the CIA "shall have no police, subpoena, law-enforcement powers, or internal-security functions." But the same law also gave the CIA responsibility for protecting "intelligence sources and methods from unauthorized disclosure." In the broadest loophole of all, it provided that the CIA would perform "other functions and duties" as directed by the National Security Council.

Relying in part on these latter two sections of the law, the CIA was soon operating inside the United States in ways never contemplated by Congress. In 1964 the author and Thomas B. Ross reported in *The Invisible Government* that the CIA was heavily involved in domestic activities, that it had financed academic centers, including the Center for International Studies at the Massachusetts Institute of Technology, that it operated through business and foundation fronts in the United States, and had offices throughout the country. In 1967 we disclosed that the CIA had a few years earlier established a Domestic Operations Division one block from the White House, the very name of which flouted the intent or letter of the 1947 law.° The division then operated at 1750 Pennsylvania Avenue under the cover name "U.S. Army Element, Joint Planning Activity, Joint Operations Group (SD 7753)."

The Domestic Operations Division was created on February 11, 1963, and given responsibility, in the words of the CIA order establishing it, for "clandestine operational activities of the Clandestine Services conducted within the United States against foreign targets."†

In fact, the division was only one, although the most secret, of a grid of half a dozen CIA divisions operating domestically inside the United States and controlled from the CIA's $46 million headquarters in Langley, Virginia. CIA Director William E. Colby, testifying before the Senate Appropriations Committee in January 1975, disclosed that the various domestic CIA units had at least sixty-four offices in American cities. Colby said the Domestic Operations Division recruited foreigners, gathered intelligence inside the United States, and worked from cover offices in eight cities.

Its agents operated clandestinely, just as they would in a foreign country. Typically, for example, an agent of the DOD would wear a disguise when he approached a foreign student in the United States; if the recruiting backfired, the student would be unable to give an accurate description of the suspected CIA operator. In 1972 James A. Everett, a veteran CIA agent in Europe, was reassigned to the Chicago office of the Domestic Operations Division. He was given a hairpiece, different glasses, and a wart. The wart was a stick-on type, for use, with the rest of the disguise, in approaching foreign students. Everett had operated in Stockholm ostensibly as a regular employee of the Robert R. Mullen Company, a public relations firm that provided the CIA with commercial cover in Washington and five foreign cities. Howard Hunt was employed by the Mullen firm when he and his confederates conducted the Watergate burglary on June 17, 1972. With the Mullen Company's cover exposed, Everett was caught in the under-

---

° David Wise and Thomas B. Ross, *The Espionage Establishment* (New York: Random House, 1967), pp. 144–47. The same year *Ramparts* magazine disclosed that the CIA was subsidizing a broad range of U.S. student, business, labor, church, and cultural groups through an intricate maze of foundation fronts. A presidential committee then recommended that the CIA end its covert financial relationship with colleges and foundations. President Johnson ordered the recommendations put into effect. Nine years later the House intelligence report revealed that the CIA still had contracts with "a small number of universities."

† By 1972 the name Domestic Operations Division had become an embarrassment and it was changed to the Foreign Resources Division.

tow. He never went to Chicago; he was rewarded for his long service in the CIA by being fired in July 1972. He then worked for two years as a conventional employee of the Mullen Company, not as a CIA operator. His name surfaced publicly during hearings of the House Armed Services subcommittee that investigated the links between the Central Intelligence Agency and the Watergate affair.

In addition to the Domestic Operations Division, the CIA had at least four other units operating domestically:

The Domestic Collection Division, with offices in thirty-six U.S. cities, gathers intelligence from residents of the United States "on foreign areas and developments," Colby testified. However, the Rockefeller report disclosed that for four years, the division had participated in the program of domestic spying on American citizens. The division, Colby said, also resettles defectors and provides them with new identities. Agents of the division are supposed to identify themselves as CIA employees, but there is no way to be sure of that, since they operate from offices with cover names.

Until 1973, the division was called *The Domestic Contact Service.* According to a 1972 memo from Colby to CIA employees, the service "establishes discreet but overt relationships with American private citizens, commercial, academic, and other organizations and resident aliens" to collect foreign intelligence information or help the CIA in its overseas mission. But a different, more innocuous description was offered by Richard Helms in 1973 during hearings on his nomination to be ambassador to Iran.

When Senator Clifford P. Case of New Jersey asked Helms to explain the CIA's Domestic Operations Division with a "headquarters downtown," Helms replied, "Sir, that is what we call the domestic contact service. You will recall that back even as far as World War II when Americans returned from overseas, from trips they had taken for one purpose or another, they were interviewed by Army intelligence, Navy intelligence, by State Department officers, and others. After the founding of the Central Intelligence Agency in 1947, this business of interviewing American travelers was vested in one place, that was domestic contact service . . . so there was only one office in these cities that was approaching people for this kind of information."[*]

---

[*] Helms added, "It is simply a device whereby if the President of some steel company in New York travels to the Soviet Union and returns and has seen certain metallurgical plants in the Soviet Union it is of interest to this Government to know how big those plants are, what they do, and all the rest of it. And individuals from this office who go to see that gentleman and interview him about it. There is no pressure involved. There is no payment of money. There is no effort to twist anybody's arm. We simply are giving them an opportunity as patriotic Americans to say what they know about this."

Colby's memo and Helms's testimony conflicted, and the relationship and degree of overlapping between the Domestic Operations Division, the Domestic Collection Division, and its predecessor, the Domestic Contact Service, remained enveloped in clouds of confusion —which is the way the CIA wanted it.

The Office of Security, with eight field offices inside the United States, is the CIA unit that conducted the surveillance, break-ins, wiretaps, and buggings revealed by the Rockefeller Commission. The office did not confine itself to checking on potential or current CIA employees, but also investigated newsmen and other citizens. Investigators for this office do *not* normally identify themselves as CIA employees.

The Counterintelligence Staff, long headed by the CIA's mysterious, reclusive James Angleton, is responsible for uncovering efforts by other intelligence services to penetrate the CIA. Operation CHAOS, the unit that spied on antiwar dissidents inside the United States, was administratively, at least, part of the Counterintelligence Staff.

The Office of Personnel has twelve listed recruitment offices inside the United States. Various other CIA units operate domestically; the Central Cover Staff, for example, is in charge of setting up CIA proprietaries, which are business firms owned by the CIA that serve as shells for espionage operations. The cover specialists also arrange with real American businesses to plant CIA agents in their companies. Much of this activity is conducted inside the United States.

The CIA has also trained local police in a dozen U.S. cities, and has sometimes lent agents and equipment to police forces. The CIA offered local police courses in lock picking, safe-cracking, burglary, covert photography, surveillance, and bugging.* For example, twenty-four students from police departments in Washington, D.C., and the Virginia suburbs graduated from a secret CIA course in safe-cracking. Police in Boston, Chicago, New York City, and several California

---

* It became somewhat awkward for the CIA to be teaching a bugging course after Watergate. On September 7, 1972, the CIA director of security, Howard J. Osborn, wrote a memo to Helms recommending that the CIA continue to train local police, but that the bugging classes be temporarily suspended while the Watergate burglary and bugging were still receiving publicity. "If you approve," the memo stated, "I would like to continue these courses (in covert photography and 'locks and picks') quietly and discreetly.

"All police representatives attending are given a strong briefing on the agency's passion for anonymity, and I know that you know that our friendly police departments have always respected this, and we have never had a leak of any kind.

"I have some reservations about offering them a basic course in audio surveillance at this time. If you agree, we can defer this aspect of police training to some future date after the Watergate incident has been put to bed one way or another."

communities also got CIA training.* Some of the classes were held at "the Farm," a secret CIA installation at Camp Peary, near Williamsburg, Virginia. Local police also received training in explosives and disarming bombs at a remote CIA facility at Harvey Point, near Elizabeth City, North Carolina.†

Among the exotic equipment lent by the CIA to local police were a mine detector, bugged lamps, and other sophisticated eavesdropping equipment. The CIA has enjoyed a cozy relationship with many local police forces—and in return it has on occasion received local police badges for use by CIA agents. To help maintain its relations with police, the CIA has oiled its friendship with money and gifts. One police official on vacation in Los Angeles had his $800 car-rental bill paid by the CIA. Similarly, when William L. Durrer, the police chief of Fairfax, Virginia, vacationed in Puerto Rico in 1971, he was met by a CIA representative and provided with a free rental car. Cash gifts have also been bestowed upon friendly local police officers, and one police inspector had the free use of a CIA house in Miami for a week's vacation.

The CIA has also secretly provided agents and equipment to other federal agencies. The practice has ranged all the way from CIA agents serving undercover as U.S. sky marshals to such minutiae as the manufacture by the CIA of the small color-coded lapel buttons worn by the Secret Service agents guarding the President.‡

The House intelligence committee found that CIA agents were assigned to many federal departments and agencies "and in the White House itself." In most cases their CIA identities were known only to one or two top officials of the department concerned. The committee found a number of CIA officials detailed to the National Security Council. Some officials, whose true status as CIA agents was

* Among them the police force of San Clemente, California.
† George Stein, a reporter for the Burlington (North Carolina) Daily Times-News, found the CIA base at Harvey Point and got as far as the front gate after the Rockefeller Commission had said the facility was located somewhere in North Carolina. The sign on the chain-link fence read: "Harvey Point Defense Testing Activity." Stein quoted a local resident as saying, "The explosions come from there." He also interviewed an unidentified former CIA man who said the base was code-named Isolation, and that he and other CIA agents who trained there had been taught a wide range of demolition skills. They worked, among other explosives, with something known as "Super Alice," which could be shaped "into ordinary looking objects. You could make a lamp out of it, set a timing device and cause a delayed fire."
‡ The CIA drew the line, however, at a request by the Treasury Department's Alcohol, Tobacco and Firearms unit that it provide infrared aerial photography, presumably by means of U-2 aircraft, to locate moonshiners. The Treasury wanted CIA's help in pinpointing stills in the mountains of North Carolina. The CIA declined to chase the moonshiners.

highly secret, even made recommendations to the NSC—on CIA proposals for covert operations.

In one publicized instance, the CIA thoroughly penetrated another federal agency. In 1970, the director of the Bureau of Narcotics and Dangerous Drugs (later the Drug Enforcement Agency) asked the CIA to infiltrate the narcotics bureau to spot agents suspected of taking payoffs from drug dealers. Through a business cover firm, the CIA recruited nineteen persons to work as counterintelligence agents inside the BNDD. In July of 1973 Colby closed down the operation. In a secret memo that is no less astonishing for its laconic language, Colby wrote: "CIA will not develop operations to penetrate another Government agency, even with the approval of its leadership."*

That the CIA was conducting domestic operations had been reported for a decade, and was dramatically demonstrated again during Watergate when the Agency lent equipment to Howard Hunt and prepared a personality profile on Daniel Ellsberg. But the fact that the CIA directly spied on American citizens in the United States and the existence of Operation CHAOS, a supersecret unit to carry out that mission, was not known. On December 22, 1974, correspondent Seymour M. Hersh revealed, in the lead story on the front page of the New York Times, that the CIA had conducted "a massive illegal domestic intelligence operation" against political dissidents, compiled files on at least 10,000 American citizens, conducted break-ins, tapped wires, and opened mail.

From Iran, Ambassador Helms "categorically denied" the charges, but within a week James Angleton, chief of counterintelligence, and his three top aides had abruptly resigned, and the timing of their departures appeared to lend support to Hersh's story.

* Despite Colby's assurances, the CIA penetrated at least one other government agency. It is painful to report, but even Smokey the Bear is a CIA agent. Until 1974 the CIA had its own air base at Marana Air Park near Tuscon, Arizona, in the guise of a company known as Intermountain Aviation, Inc. Intermountain's "cover" was that it provided aircraft and equipment to the U.S. Forest Service for its "smokejumpers," fire fighters who parachute into remote areas to battle forest fires.

In 1974 Ronald Ridenhour linked Intermountain to the CIA in an article in New Times magazine. Soon afterward Intermountain vanished. If Smokey the Bear, the official symbol of the Forest Service's fire-prevention program, was not aware that he had been providing cover for the CIA, some of his colleagues did seem to know. Bill Monroe, a Forest Service official, said in 1976 that "Intermountain Aviation operated an air base and had facilities for a fire training program at Marana Air Park. We contracted for some aircraft, equipment and personnel. Intermountain severed their connection with CIA two years ago, so we've heard," Monroe added, "although it's not official. Intermountain sold out to a legitimate, ordinary company called Evergreen Helicopters."

Secretary of State Kissinger skittered for cover, announcing through his press spokesman that he knew nothing of any illegal CIA domestic spying. But President Ford, skiing in Vail, Colorado, during the Christmas holidays, said he would tolerate no illegal spying and ordered CIA Director Colby to report on the *Times'* allegations. Then, on January 5, Ford named Vice President Nelson A. Rockefeller to head an eight-member commission to investigate the charges.

The President's action should have been a tip-off that Hersh's story was accurate, because the reflex response of any Administration to an embarrassing story is to deny it as quickly as possible. The fact that Ford appointed a commission suggested that in this case the White House did not dare to deny the story.

Despite these signals, there was a peculiar reaction to Hersh's article within the Washington press corps and in political circles in the capital. It was whispered that the story was overplayed, or incorrect, and that Hersh had put himself and the *Times* out on a limb that was about to be chopped off. Some of this was professional jealousy; Hersh, who broke the story of the My Lai massacre in Vietnam, is a brilliant and extraordinarily energetic reporter who does not bother to hide his talent behind a shield of false modesty. For three weeks Hersh was in a lonely and difficult position; he had published spectacular charges against a powerful secret agency and no substantive official comment was forthcoming.

Then, on January 15, Colby went before the Senate Appropriations Committee and confirmed everything—the infiltration of peace groups, the spying on antiwar activists, and the dossiers on 10,000 Americans.

Feebly, Colby fell back on the only defense available; although the list of CIA's improprieties required forty-five pages, he assured the committee that while the CIA had strayed, its sins were not "massive," which was rather like the old saw about the captain of the *Titanic* assuring the passengers that the ship had merely stopped to take on ice.

If Hersh needed any further vindication, it came in June when the Rockefeller Commission issued its 299-page report. Although the commission had been criticized for its establishment make-up—its members included Ronald Reagan and General Lyman L. Lemnitzer, former Chairman of the Joint Chiefs of Staff—the final report pleasantly surprised those who had expected a whitewash.

The Rockefeller report detailed a broad range of CIA abuses and law-breaking, and disclosed in some detail the workings of the Agency's domestic spying program, Operation CHAOS. Operating from a "vaulted basement area" at the CIA under supersecret security,

CHAOS had begun in 1967 during the Johnson Administration and lasted seven years, through most of the Nixon Administration, until March 1974.* Eventually there were fifty-two agents working out of the CIA basement under the direction of Richard Ober, a large hulking man with reddish hair, a Harvard degree, and a reputation among his colleagues as a skilled clandestine operator.

Demands that the CIA provide information about the peace movement had first come from Lyndon Johnson, who pressured Helms, then the CIA Director, to find foreign links to domestic dissidents. Helms sent two reports to Johnson, but to the President's disappointment, the CIA discovered little foreign involvement and virtually no foreign money flowing in to support the peace movement. A third study, entitled "Restless Youth," was begun under Johnson and delivered to Henry Kissinger in February 1969, after Nixon's inauguration. The paper concluded that student protest arose from social and political alienation at home and not from some foreign conspiracy.†

By the middle of 1969 Operation CHAOS was in full swing, its existence and activities kept secret from much of the rest of the CIA. One of its major programs was called "Project 2." Under it the CIA recruited students, trained them in "New Left" jargon (a process known as "sheepdipping"), and then sent them abroad on espionage missions in the guise of student radicals. CHAOS also recruited agents and used them in similar fashion to penetrate dissident groups at home. In addition, CHAOS collected information from CIA's mail-opening operation in New York, from the Agency's overseas stations, and from the offices of the Domestic Collection Division in cities across the United States. Although the CIA claimed that these domestic offices only gathered foreign intelligence, the Rockefeller report disclosed that beginning in 1969, the division fed "purely domestic information" about American citizens to the CHAOS operators. The CIA men in U.S. cities spied on radical students, on the underground press, and on groups supporting draft evaders and military deserters. A tremendous volume of reports flowed into the CIA's vaulted basement. Eventually 300,000 names were indexed on the CIA's computers.

The elaborate security surrounding CHAOS extended to the CIA's

---

* The operation did not get the name CHAOS until mid-1968. The cryptonym was almost a parody of espionage code names. It was no doubt chosen to reflect the CIA's view of the goals of the peace movement, but the CIA officials who selected it may not have realized that the name was already in use on a popular television spy spoof, *Get Smart*. Maxwell Smart, the boobish secret agent in the series, constantly battled the evil agents of an organization known as K.A.O.S.
† In a covering note to Kissinger, Helms explained that the section on American students was "not within the charter of this Agency, so I need not emphasize how extremely sensitive this makes the paper. Should anyone learn of its existence it would prove most embarrassing for all concerned."

computers, which required a special "password" to print out CHAOS data. The information was banked in several computerized "streams," a system known within CIA as the "Hydra," to which access was based on need to know. In all, the CIA had 1,000 organizations in its CHAOS files, including Women's Strike for Peace, the Student Non-Violent Coordinating Committee (SNCC), and the Women's Liberation Movement. The CIA even opened a file on Grove Press because it had published a book by Kim Philby, the former British intelligence agent who was a spy for the Soviet Union. Since Grove Press had also distributed the film *I Am Curious Yellow,* the CIA agents, the Rockefeller report noted, "dutifully clipped" and filed reviews of the movie.

Within the CIA a number of officials had begun to worry about the legality of CHAOS, so much so that Helms felt it prudent to send a memo to his deputies in 1969 assuring them that the operation was within the law. In 1974, with the agency already in trouble over its Watergate links, Colby ended Operation CHAOS. The Rockefeller Commission expressed concern over the fact that CHAOS had become a "repository for large quantities of information on the domestic activities of American citizens." And it concluded that Operation CHAOS had broken the law.

The Rockefeller report also reviewed the CIA's mail-opening activities, and the physical surveillance, wiretapping, bugging, and break-ins committed by the intelligence agency. "The unauthorized entries into the homes and offices of American citizens were illegal," the report said.

The details of one CIA break-in, mentioned only obliquely in the Rockefeller report, surfaced soon afterward when a Fairfax, Virginia, police officer said that Murray Kutner, the chief of police in that city, together with CIA agents, had personally broken into a photographic studio to take pictures of documents they hoped to find inside. Neither the CIA nor the police had a search warrant.*

The break-in had occurred in February 1971. At the time, the CIA was investigating a former employee, Deborah Fitzgerald, and her partner in the photo studio, Orlando Nunez, whom she later married. Nunez, who had fought with Castro in Cuba, became the deputy director for propaganda in the National Waterworks Department in Havana. He left Cuba and came to the United States in 1965.

Apparently Fitzgerald attempted to find out what the CIA had in its files about Nunez. In January 1975 Colby told a Senate committee that an ex-employee "became involved with a person believed to be a foreign intelligence agent." He said the two were attempting to

---

* The Justice Department investigated the possible prosecution of Helms in connection with the break-in, but in February 1976 Attorney General Levi announced that Helms and others would not be prosecuted.

"elicit information from agency employees." Colby conceded that a "surreptitious entry" had taken place with "negative" results.

Robert L. Fleck, the police officer who talked about the break-in at the couple's photo studio, said he had acted as a lookout in the operation that began around one o'clock in the morning. Several hours went by, and Fleck began to needle the young CIA agent sitting in the car with him, for it was apparent that the Agency's lock-picking expert was unable to get into the studio. Finally, just before dawn, Fleck said, Chief Kutner and a group of CIA agents emerged from the studio. They had been working on the door. "What took us so long," he quoted the police chief as saying, "was that the lock man couldn't get through the lock, so I removed the hinge pins."°

The Rockefeller report provided details of one CIA break-in against a CIA employee who had attended a meeting of an organization that the Agency suspected of foreign ties. "Physical surveillance of the employee was conducted for almost one year," the report said. "A surreptitious entry was made into the employee's apartment by cutting through the walls from an adjacent apartment so that microphones could be installed. Seven microphones were placed so that conversations could be overheard in every room of the apartment. A cover was placed on the employee's mail ... Several of the subject's tax returns were also reviewed. This investigation yielded no evidence of disloyalty."

Some types of CIA domestic activities were not mentioned in the Rockefeller report. For example, in a number of cases the CIA has approached major New York publishing houses in an effort to suppress or alter books about the Agency.

And it has managed to obtain outlines and manuscripts by subterranean means. On April 17, 1972, Robert P. B. Lohmann filed an affidavit in federal court in Alexandria identifying himself as "an employee of the Central Intelligence Agency, presently assigned to the Agency's offices in New York City." Lohmann swore that on March 12 he had received a magazine article and outline for a book about the CIA by Victor L. Marchetti, a former CIA employee. Marchetti's literary agent had circulated copies of the outline to half a dozen New York publishers, but he did not send a copy to the CIA. So the clear

---

° There is evidence that the CIA also conducts break-ins in the United States as part of the training of its agents. In 1974 an attorney for Watergate burglar Bernard Barker said that in the sixties his client, in a training exercise, had conducted a "penetration" of the Radio City Music Hall. Barker was in New York City in September 1964 for a CIA "tradecraft" course. Apparently he was ordered to gain access to the theater's security office, which contained closed-circuit TV cameras. He was later questioned by CIA agents to see if he could describe the office, as proof that he had been there. The lawyer, Daniel Schultz, said Barker had also participated in two CIA-related break-ins in Miami.

implication of Lohmann's affidavit is that a source in one of the publishing houses slipped a copy to the Agency's New York station, unless the CIA obtained it by some other surreptitious means such as a mail intercept or burglary.

The fact that the CIA was able to obtain the Marchetti outline by domestic espionage, and that the Agency apparently had sources of information, perhaps even its own agents, planted in New York publishing houses, was one of the most fascinating, albeit little-noticed aspects of the case. In 1972 a federal court granted an injunction against the Marchetti book, based on secrecy agreements that the author had signed while a CIA employee. Marchetti was required to submit the manuscript to the CIA for clearance before it could be published.

Marchetti and John D. Marks, a former State Department intelligence analyst, wrote the book and duly submitted the manuscript to the CIA in 1973. The Agency designated 339 portions to be deleted, but the number was negotiated down to 168. The authors filed suit, challenging the CIA's censorship, and *The CIA and the Cult of Intelligence* was published by Alfred A. Knopf in 1974 with blank spaces for the 168 deletions.

Federal Judge Albert V. Bryan, Jr., held that the government had shown that only twenty-six of the deleted portions and parts of two others actually had been classified, but an appeals court overruled Bryan and the Supreme Court declined to review the case. So the deletions stood.

But some of the material sliced from the book by the CIA appeared to have been deleted less for reasons of security than out of fear by the Agency that publication would make it look ludicrous. In one of the deleted portions Marchetti and Marks described efforts by the Agency's scientists to wire a cat to serve as a living transmitter. Machines cannot easily discriminate between sounds, tune out background noises, and listen only to conversation, but someone at the CIA got the inspiration that a cat, if properly trained, could do so. A wired cat could be the perfect eavesdropper! Whether accurate or not, reports circulated within the CIA that the Agency was cutting up great quantities of cats and putting batteries inside them.

In an interview in *Harper's* magazine in January 1974, Marchetti sailed close to the wind. He said that the CIA had censored from the book its experiments to develop a bug that could be "surgically implanted" inside the body of "an ordinary house pet." Marchetti did not mention the forbidden word "cat," but the CIA was nevertheless upset.

That same month, on a Canadian television documentary, Marchetti said that Willy Brandt, then the Chancellor of West Germany, and Jomo Kenyatta, the President of Kenya, had worked for the CIA.

It was too much. The CIA stormed into federal court, and in a top-secret document, complained about Brandt, Kenyatta, and the cats. The Agency seemed tacitly to be inviting the court to hold Marchetti in contempt. Judge Bryan declined to support the CIA's classified complaint, politely indicating that the two-year-old injunction against Marchetti might not apply to material already deleted from his book. But the Great Cat Fight in federal court was conducted in total secrecy.

In 1972 Cord Meyer, Jr., a senior official of the CIA's Plans, or "dirty tricks," directorate, and later the Agency's London station chief, paid a visit to the offices of Harper & Row in New York. He came to complain about *The Politics of Heroin in Southeast Asia*, by Alfred W. McCoy. The book, then nearing publication, charged that CIA officials had been involved in the drug traffic in Indochina. Meyer's visit was followed by a formal letter from Lawrence R. Houston, CIA's general counsel, asking to see the manuscript. Over McCoy's anguished protest, Harper & Row made the manuscript available to the CIA, with the publisher reserving the right to decide whether any changes would be made. The CIA delivered an eight-page critique of the book, but Harper & Row decided no changes were justified and published the book as scheduled. But a secret government agency had, over the author's objections, succeeded in screening a book before the public was permitted to read it, which may not be precisely what the Founding Fathers had in mind when they wrote the First Amendment.

In 1975, former CIA agent Philip B. F. Agee described his experiences in Latin America in *Inside the Company: C.I.A. Diary*. The book, an exposé highly critical of the Agency, was originally published by Penguin Books in England and Canada, outside the legal reach of the CIA. Agee claimed that an American girl moved into the hotel in Paris where he lived while writing the book, expressed great interest in the project, gave him money, and lent him a typewriter. But Agee said he noticed his radio made funny sounds whenever he used the typewriter. He examined the case, pulled out a piece of plywood, and found a miniature electronic device behind it; he assumed it was a bug or some kind of beeper to indicate his whereabouts to the CIA. Several American publishers, perhaps wary of an expensive legal battle with the CIA, declined to buy the U.S. rights, but eventually Agee's book was published in the United States by Stonehill, a small New York house.

In 1964, just before Random House was scheduled to publish *The Invisible Government* by this writer and Thomas B. Ross, CIA Director John A. McCone contacted the publisher in an unsuccessful effort to suppress the book or bring about changes in its content. The CIA had, without authorization, obtained a copy of the bound galleys. The

Agency's legal division actually ran a study to see if the CIA had power to buy up the first printing to keep the book out of the hands of the public. The CIA broached the idea to Bennett Cerf, president of Random House. Cerf responded that he would be delighted to sell the first printing to the CIA, but added that he would then immediately order another printing for the public, and another, and another. McCone and the CIA abandoned the plan. The CIA also considered prosecuting the authors under the espionage laws but decided against it.

The CIA even appointed a formal Task Force to draw up plans on how to deal with the book. The Task Force recommended that the CIA use its agents or contacts in the news media and publishing circles to attempt to bring about hostile reviews of the book. This was the principal recommendation of the Task Force. A CIA document entitled "Report of the Chairman of the Task Force" states in part: "Recommendation: That such assets as the Agency may have to secure unfavorable book reviews of *The Invisible Government* be used at the proper time to lessen the book's impact and to cast doubt on the validity of its claims."°

The book was published without any change, despite the CIA's intense pressure on Random House, and became the nation's number-one best seller.

The CIA, however, prepared a lengthy, detailed analysis of the book, designed to discredit it and the authors, and circulated the document within the CIA and the State Department. The CIA also prepared a document which it classified "secret," summarizing world-wide reaction to the book and reporting information about it collected by CIA agents in numerous foreign capitals. "President Kwame Nkrumah of Ghana has told intimates that he had read the book and 'is much impressed' by it," the CIA station in Accra reported. From Asia came this dispatch: "President Ayub Khan of Pakistan told American Ambassador that he had been reading *IG* and was shocked by it, and added he hoped nothing like the things described was going on in Pakistan." The CIA learned—possibly from a wiretap or NSA intercept—that the "Indonesian Embassy, Washington, instructed to pouch 20 copies" of the book "directly to Foreign Minister Subandrio" in Jakarta. Early in December, the CIA reported, President Sukarno had ordered that copies "be circulated among cabinet members." A few weeks later, the CIA station reported, Sukarno called in the U.S. ambassador, lectured him at length about the CIA and quoted from

---

° "Assets" is a term used by the CIA to refer to persons employed by or willing to assist the Agency. In this instance it might apply, for example, to journalists or other individuals working under cover for the CIA, or to editors or others in a position to influence the content of book reviews.

the book to prove his points. (Since the book disclosed that the CIA had provided B-26 bombers to the rebels fighting to overthrow Sukarno, the Indonesian President's ire was understandable.) William Attwood, the U.S. ambassador to Kenya, reported that the book "is regarded as the Bible for Kenya, for everyone has read it." Colonel Enrique Peralta, the head of the government of Guatemala, "told a CIA representative that he considered the sections of the *IG* which concern Guatemala as essentially correct."

The Agency also kept a careful watch on plans for foreign publication of the book. On July 11 it reported: "*Stern*, popular German weekly, reportedly has purchased rights to publish excerpts of *IG*." On September 16 the CIA station in Copenhagen weighed in: "Representative of Danish publishers, Bilman and Eriksen, advised U.S. ambassador they planned to publish *IG* in Danish in mid-October." One way or another, the CIA appears to have spent hundreds of man-hours attempting to stop or alter the book, and when that failed, collecting intelligence about it around the globe.°

The CIA's contacts with the publishing world were not confined to attempts to suppress books. Through the U.S. Information Agency as a "cut-out," the CIA subsidized major publishers to produce books, some of which were then sold in the United States bearing no government imprint to warn the unsuspecting purchaser. In 1967 publisher Frederick A. Praeger conceded he had published "fifteen or sixteen" books for the CIA. By the mid-sixties, more than $1 million had been spent by the government on its "book development" program. The Senate intelligence committee estimated that by 1967, the CIA had produced, sponsored, or subsidized "well over 1,000 books" here and abroad. One of these, the committee noted, was the best seller *The Penkovsky Papers*, published by Doubleday in 1965. The committee said the publisher was "unaware" of the U.S. government's hand in the book.

A decade later, the Senate and House committees investigating intelligence agencies confirmed what Colby had already privately

---

° After the book's publication in June 1964, conservative editor William F. Buckley Jr. wrote a column rancorously attacking the book and its authors, "who verge close to unpatriotism." Buckley did not reveal to his readers that he was a former CIA agent, and that the column was based on a memorandum he had received from his former boss in the CIA, then still working for the Agency, but later to become famous—E. Howard Hunt, Jr. Hunt's 1964 memo to Buckley listed alleged errors and "security violations" in the book. Buckley had served under Hunt in the CIA's Mexico City station after he graduated from Yale in 1950; Hunt assigned Buckley to translate into English a book entitled *The Yenan Way*, by Eudocio Ravines, a Chilean Marxist who had become disenchanted with Communism. Hunt and Buckley became close friends and Buckley was the godfather of Hunt's children.

admitted to editors of the Washington *Star*—that the CIA had agents abroad posing as journalists. The House committee found that in 1975 the CIA had eleven full-time officers overseas using journalistic cover. Until 1973, five such agents represented major news organizations reporting back to the United States. In addition, the CIA paid numerous "stringers" and free-lancers as Agency informants. The Senate committee reported that about fifty United States journalists, or other employees of news organizations, were employed by, or had some covert relationship with the CIA, as of February 1976. At that time the CIA, under mounting pressure from Congress, announced it would no longer use "accredited" American journalists as spies. But, the committee pointed out, this tricky proviso did not apply to unaffiliated, independent journalists or news executives. As a result, less than half of the CIA journalists were affected by the new policy.* As the committee noted, "All American journalists... may be suspects when any are engaged in covert activities."

The CIA also planted stories in the foreign press, some of which were played back to American audiences. Colby assured the House intelligence committee that the CIA would never manipulate AP, since it was an American wire service, but felt free to plant stories with Reuters, the British wire service. In addition, the CIA operated two news services of its own in Europe. These "proprietaries," or CIA cover companies, serviced American newspapers; one had more than thirty U.S. subscribers. The Agency's penetration of the news media was, of course, an insidious and very possibly unconstitutional practice, since it ran counter to the First Amendment. It could only increase public distrust of the press and cause American reporters overseas to be suspected as spies. The CIA had polluted the public's major source of information about its government, the foundation upon which democracy rests.

And it was not only the press and publishing world that the CIA infiltrated. As of 1976, the Senate intelligence committee reported, the CIA maintained contact or operational relationships with "many thousands of United States academics at hundreds of U.S. academic institutions." Of these, "several hundred" in more than a hundred institutions actively work for the CIA, often without the knowledge of the college or university administration. Sometimes at least one university official is aware of which professors are CIA.

In addition, the CIA has sometimes used American clergy or mis-

---

* The Agency, reacting to the controversy over CIA use of journalistic cover, announced that it would no longer employ or use any journalist "accredited by" a U.S. news organization. A CIA spokesman said this policy applied both to journalists working for the CIA and to CIA officers working under journalistic cover.

sionaries for intelligence purposes. At least twenty-one members of the clergy had secret agreements with the CIA, according to figures the Agency provided to the Senate committee. In February 1976 the CIA said it would no longer have "secret" relationships with the clergy.

Besides infiltrating existing institutions, the CIA operates a complex network of its own business proprietaries. Through Air America, Southern Air Transport, and other airlines, it has been heavily involved in the aviation business over the years. It also runs a secret insurance complex, a security firm in Virginia with three subsidiaries, and a travel service. The private security firm performs commercial investigative work in the Washington area, but of course its clients do not know that they have hired the CIA.

So there were enough CIA domestic and foreign operations for Congress to investigate. Early in 1975, even before the Rockefeller Commission had reported, Seymour Hersh's story resulted in a full-scale Senate inquiry. Senator Charles McC. Mathias of Maryland had for some months been urging such a probe, and the *Times* story, Colby's admissions of domestic spying, and the appointment of a presidential commission created the necessary political climate for a Senate investigation. On January 27 the Senate voted to create the eleven-member Select Committee to Study Governmental Operations with Respect to Intelligence Activities, and the Senate Majority Leader, Mike Mansfield, named Senator Frank Church of Idaho as chairman.° The House launched a parallel investigation, at the outset under Lucien N. Nedzi of Michigan, who headed the existing House subcommittee on CIA activities. In June it was revealed that Nedzi had been briefed a year earlier on CIA domestic operations and overseas assassination plots but had failed to inform the House. Nedzi was forced to step down. The House select committee was reconstituted with Representative Otis G. Pike, a Democrat from Suffolk County, Long Island, as the new chairman. Pike, a congressional veteran, had earned wide respect in 1969 when he conducted a House subcommittee investigation of the capture of the intelligence ship *Pueblo* by North Korea.†

° The other Democrats were Senators Philip A. Hart of Michigan, Walter F. Mondale of Minnesota, Walter D. Huddleston of Kentucky, Robert Morgan of North Carolina, and Gary Hart of Colorado. The Republican vice chairman was John Tower of Texas, and the other Republican members were Howard H. Baker, Jr., of Tennessee, Barry Goldwater of Arizona, Mathias, and Richard S. Schweiker of Pennsylvania.

† In January 1976 the House intelligence committee drafted a devastating report that concluded the federal intelligence agencies were then "beyond the lawmaker's scrutiny." The solidly documented report was particularly critical of Kissinger. At one point the report noted that Kissinger had been given three Oriental rugs and a gold-and-pearl necklace for his wife from the leader of the Kurds, who was

But a Senate investigation normally commands more public attention than its counterpart in the House, and the spotlight of national publicity swung to the Senate select committee and its chairman, Frank Church. An outspoken opponent of the Vietnam war, Church had difficulty shaking the image of the boy orator—which he had been—even though he had by 1975 served almost two decades in the Senate. Church did sound rather like a preacher as he remonstrated with CIA or FBI witnesses, but the comments delivered from the senatorial pulpit were always incisive, he had an excellent grasp of the issues involved, and a deep concern over the danger of "Big Brother government" posed by America's intelligence agencies.

At age fifty, Church's hair was streaked with gray, he really no longer looked boyish, his face had grown full, and he wore glasses. He was well aware of the political risks of investigating secret agencies that many Americans seemed to equate with their personal safety and the nation's security. He was cautious, not sure even now that the political climate was right. He did not know how the public would react to a Senate investigation. As a boy he had listened to radio programs about the fine work done by the FBI, he had been brought up to believe these things, and perhaps the country was not ready yet for the idols to be shattered.

Church had another problem; he harbored presidential ambitions, and no matter how he handled the intelligence investigation, his critics would charge that he had used it as a political springboard. Despite these difficulties, Church and his committee dug deeper than any congressional panel had done before into the dark underbrush of the intelligence apparatus. Church recruited a large experienced staff under William G. Miller, a former assistant to Senator John Sherman Cooper, and hired Frederick A. O. Schwarz, Jr., a Man-

---

receiving millions in CIA funds. The Nixon Administration supported the Kurds for two years but then Washington double-crossed them; despite pleas to Ford and Kissinger, the United States in March 1975 permitted the Kurdish forces to be overrun by Iraqi troops. The report was full of other embarrassments for the CIA, including the revelation that the Agency had procured women for foreign leaders and made porno movies. Perhaps the most devastating conclusion of the Pike report was that despite the vast sums spent on U.S. intelligence, the CIA had failed in several instances to give precisely the kind of advance warning of events that led to its establishment in the first place. The report pointed to the failure to predict the Tet offensive in Vietnam in January 1968, the Soviet invasion of Czechoslovakia in August, the Middle East war in October 1973, the coup in Portugal in April 1974, the explosion of a nuclear device by India in May, and the coup on Cyprus in July. When the substance of the report leaked to the New York Times on January 25, 1976, the full House, responding to a political backlash against disclosure of classified information, voted to suppress the report. Daniel Schorr of CBS News, who had a copy, then provided it to the Village Voice, which published major segments on February 16 and 23.

hattan attorney (and the grandson of the toy merchant), to serve as chief counsel. A number of the hearings were carried on public television, and over four months during the fall of 1975, for the first time the public got a detailed look at the officials, their mindsets, and some of the inner workings of the nation's intelligence agencies. The hearings forced some officials long accustomed to working mole-like in the shadows to step forward into the bright television lights where their fellow citizens could get a good look at them. Among them were such men as the CIA's wizened James Angleton, and Thomas H. Karamessines, the Agency's former deputy director for operations. "Tom K," as he was known inside the CIA, had never before been seen in public; he was one of the more mysterious of the CIA's "black," i.e. covert, operators. Blinking under the lights, Karamessines, a short pompous man with heavy horn-rimmed glasses, looked no more ominous than a high school mathematics teacher.

To dramatize the abuses under investigation, the Senate select committee deliberately chose to open its public hearings with an inquiry into why the CIA, despite a presidential order, had failed to destroy its supplies of deadly shellfish toxin and cobra venom.° William Colby, then the CIA Director, former Director Richard Helms, and other Agency officials were summoned to testify about the CIA poisons. The toxin and snake venom were only two items in the Agency's lethal stockpile of biochemical weapons.† President Nixon had ordered toxins destroyed in 1970, in accordance with the United States decision to renounce the development or use of biological weapons.

During the hearings, the existence of various lethal and exotic CIA assassination weapons was revealed. Colby, for example, dis-

---

° During a press conference in September 1975, Church confirmed to reporters that the committee would investigate the CIA's retention of the shellfish toxin and snake venom. This exchange took place:

Q. Can you tell us a little about the cobra venom? . . . Do they inject it into individuals? Is it for mass use or what?

SENATOR CHURCH: Cobras inject it directly through their fangs. I don't know what methods the CIA has devised.

† The other CIA substances were destroyed in accord with the presidential order. The stockpile included germs to cause anthrax, rabbit fever, encephalitis, TB, botulism, intestinal flu, and paralysis. The CIA medicine chest, according to the official inventory, also contained "2-4 pyrolo," which "causes temporary amnesia"; something known as "M-246," which produces paralysis; Cogentin, "wide range of debilitative, physiological effects"; colchicine, which in overdoses "leads to death via paralysis and respiratory failure"; dehydroacetic acid, "impairs kidney function and causes vomiting and convulsions"; phencyclidine, "causes disorientation. High dosage leads to convulsions and death"; and neurokinin, an incapacitant that "produces severe pain."

closed that the CIA had developed "a nondiscernible microbioinoculator"—in plain English, a poison dart—to inject its victims. The darts were so tiny that a person would feel nothing as one penetrated his clothing and entered his skin; no trace of the dart or the poison would be found in a later medical examination of the dead person. The poisons and special weapons were developed and stockpiled under the CIA's top-secret Project Naomi.

Colby said the CIA had also developed a special silent gun to shoot the poison darts, and he displayed one to the committee.* A memorandum to the chief of the CIA's Technical Services Division, which handles such matters, referred to the dart gun as "a noise-free disseminator." The memo explained: "A nondiscernible microbioinoculator has been developed especially for use by the Clandestine Services and has been demonstrated successfully. The ... device is accurate at ranges up to 250 feet and has a very low sound level."

An Army scientist who had worked on joint research programs with the CIA at Fort Detrick, Maryland, testified that about 1967 he and other scientists rode the subways in Manhattan and simulated a biological warfare attack on New York City. Charles Senseney, the project engineer, said he dropped bulbs containing the simulated poison on the subway tracks. The bulbs broke and within minutes the substance had spread through the air over forty-three blocks of tracks. Senseney also told the Senate committee that he had developed poison-dart launchers concealed in umbrellas, walking canes, and fountain pens, as well as a fluorescent bulb that spread a lethal poison when the light was switched on by the unsuspecting victim.

Colby and Helms could offer no real explanation of why the CIA failed to destroy the shellfish toxin. The testimony of the CIA witnesses conflicted and was unpersuasive. Colby said the CIA scientist responsible had explained that he hated to destroy the poison because it had cost so much to extract and distill it. Dr. Nathan Gordon, the CIA official who had preserved the shellfish poison, told the committee that he didn't think that the President's order really applied to the CIA. Karamessines, who had been Helms's deputy for covert operations, said it was his "understanding" with Dr. Sidney Gottlieb, head of the CIA's Technical Services Division, that all toxins had been returned to the Army to be destroyed. But Dr. Gordon said he kept the toxin and never told Gottlieb.

Senator Church said he had been told by the CIA that the eleven grams of shellfish toxin, which were stored in a CIA building near the

---

* The committee insisted that Colby bring the dart gun to the hearings. He had little choice but to comply. When Church held up the weapon, it made a dramatic front-page photograph in newspapers across the country the next morning, much to the dismay of the White House.

State Department in downtown Washington, could kill "at least 14,000 people" if given orally. Administered externally, he said, by poison dart guns or other sophisticated CIA equipment, the toxin would kill a great many more, with estimates varying up to "hundreds of thousands." This was so because if the poison was injected intramuscularly, only a microscopic amount would be needed to kill a human being. Dr. Edward Schantz, the gray-haired scientist who developed the method of brewing the toxin, testified that, for example, only two tenths of a milligram on the end of a dart would be sufficient to kill. Schantz estimated that the amount retained by the CIA, if injected by darts, could kill "55,000 people." Schantz explained that he had himself dug the Alaskan butter clams from which the toxin was extracted; the clams became poisonous, he said, when they ate the same microorganisms that cause the deadly "red tide."

It remained for CIA Director Colby, however, to put the entire matter in proper perspective. The amount of lethal shellfish toxin hidden by the CIA, he testified, was really very small. It was, he assured the select committee of the United States Senate, just "a couple of teaspoons."

For all of the Church committee's substantive disclosures, its most important contribution may have been its exposure to the public of the mind of the CIA. In the end, the committee's most valuable service was simply to put officials of the CIA, the FBI, and other intelligence agencies at the witness table and let them talk.

The best and most instructive example was James Angleton. The feared former chief of the CIA's Counterintelligence Staff looked for all the world like someone who had emerged from a damp underground cave where he had spent three decades of Cold War creeping among the stalagmites. Eased out of the CIA by Colby amidst the disclosures of Seymour Hersh, Angleton had been portrayed in the media as a mysterious character out of Graham Greene or John Le Carré, and indeed, in some respects he was.

A tall, stooped, very thin man—he was known inside the CIA as "the Gray Ghost"—Angleton was portrayed in news accounts as a superb, patient trout fisherman who tied his own flies; the implication was, of course, that he was equally adept at reeling in Soviet agents as his catch. His hobby was raising prize-winning orchids, another touch out of British spy fiction, whose heroes are generally upper-class Oxbridge men puttering about in their gardens or engaging in other incongruous pastimes in delicious contrast to their sinister occupations.

Angleton's father served in Mexico in 1916 under General John J. Pershing, pursuing Pancho Villa. He courted a young Mexican girl, married her, and returned to Idaho, where their son, whom the couple named James Jesus, was born in 1917. Angleton's father became an executive of the National Cash Register Company in charge of European operations, and Angleton grew up in Rome. He went to Yale, edited the poetry quarterly, and became a friend and admirer of Ezra Pound. He attended Harvard Law School and served in the OSS in Italy during World War II. After the war, he joined the CIA. As chief of counterintelligence, it was Angleton's job within the CIA to suspect everybody, even the Director, even his closest friends. He lived in a world populated by real and imaginary KGB agents.° The thaw in the Cold War in the early seventies defoliated his world and threatened the Angletons on both sides with obsolescence. To Angleton, a détente was a trick, and the Soviet Union and the Chinese still a monolithic enemy in 1975. The job and its incredible psychological demands had taken its toll after three decades. Angleton, according to one close associate, had ulcers and emphysema. "He killed himself working," the friend said. "He must have smoked three or four packs of cigarettes a day. I've been in a car with him when he could hardly breathe. He'd turn on the air conditioner to try to get his breath." It was rumored—and no doubt exaggerated—that Angleton had wiretaps all over town, that he knew everything going on in whichever salons and bedrooms of Washington were of intelligence interest.

On television before the Church committee, the sinister aura that had enveloped Angleton evaporated. In the reality of the brightly lit, chandeliered Senate caucus room, he came on like a thinner Lionel Barrymore, a slightly cantankerous old man who might, at any moment, clamor for his Ovaltine. He peered at the documents offered to him by the committee counsel and seemed to have difficulty reading them and in hearing the senators' questions. Suddenly Angleton, the man, was no longer frightening. What was absolutely chilling, however, was the realization that such a man could have held a high position for so long in so powerful an agency of the government.

Angleton was questioned by Senator Church, who noted that as part of the Huston Plan, Nixon had been asked in 1970 to approve the opening of first-class mail; the President was told the practice had been discontinued, when in fact it was still going on.

° Ironically, Angleton apparently did not suspect a real KGB agent, Kim Philby, with whom he dined regularly at Harvey's, a Washington restaurant also favored by J. Edgar Hoover. Philby, assigned to Washington in 1949 by MI-6, the British secret intelligence service, was actually working for the Soviet Union, to which he defected in 1963. Philby later wrote of his lunches with Angleton: "He was one of the thinnest men I have ever met, and one of the biggest eaters." See Kim Philby, *My Silent War* (New York: Grove Press, 1968), pp. 190–91.

"You have referred to the President as the Commander in Chief," Church said. "What possible justification was there to misrepresent a matter of such importance to the Commander in Chief?"

"I would say that your question was very well put, Mr. Chairman," Angleton mumbled, his words barely audible. "...I have no satisfactory answer to your question." The senator pursued the point, in rising anger:

> CHURCH: The fact that illegal operations were being conducted by the very agencies we entrust to uphold and enforce the law makes it all the more incumbent that the President be informed of what's going on doesn't it? ...You have said there was an affirmative duty on the part of CIA to inform the President?
>
> ANGLETON: I don't dispute that.
>
> CHURCH: And he was not informed...he was misinformed. Not only was he misinformed, but when he reconsidered authorizing the opening of the mail five days later and revoked it, the CIA didn't pay the slightest bit of attention to him, did it, the Commander in Chief as you say?
>
> ANGLETON: I have no answer to that.
>
> CHURCH: Well, I don't think there is a satisfactory answer.... So the Commander in Chief isn't the Commander in Chief at all. He's just the problem. You don't want to inform him in the first place because he might say no. That's the truth of it. And when he did say no, you disregard it. And then you call him the Commander in Chief!
>
> I have no further questions.

That was only a warm-up for an even more revealing dialogue a few moments later between Angleton and Senator Schweiker. The senator pointed out that in an executive session of the committee Angleton, when questioned about the CIA's failure to destroy the shellfish toxin, had replied: "It's inconceivable that a secret intelligence arm of the government has to comply with all the overt orders of the government."

Had Angleton *really* said that? Schweiker asked in disbelief. Was it an accurate quote?

"Well, if it's accurate," Angleton replied, "it shouldn't have been said."

"Do you believe that statement that you made then, or don't you believe it?" Schweiker asked. "What's your belief of whether a secret intelligence agency has the right to contradict a direct order of a President?"

There was a very long pause. It was a moment of excruciating tension in the hearing room. Spectators began to stir and whisper as they waited for Angleton to answer. Finally he managed a reply: "I had been rather imprudent in making those remarks."

"I think it's indicative of what this committee has to deal with," Schweiker snapped. "It's indicative of what the Congress has to deal with when you feel, or the [intelligence] community feels that even a direct order of the President they're removed from. I think it does come to the heart of the issue. I think you were honest in your statement."

Church bored in. Did Angleton wish to withdraw his statement?

"I do," said the ex-counterintelligence chief.

"Didn't you mean it when you said it the first time?" Church asked.

"I don't know how to respond to that question," Angleton replied. ". . . I said that I withdrew the statement."

"But you're unwilling to say whether or not you meant it when you said it."

"I would say that the entire speculation should not have been indulged in."

Thus far and no further; in effect, all Angleton would admit was that he had talked too much. He never specifically disavowed his belief that the CIA did not have to obey the orders of the President.

Later in the hearing Angleton cast aside his humble-pie manner and revealed his philosophy. Even though the CIA had committed a crime by opening the mail, Angleton defended it as "an indispensable means of collecting foreign intelligence on the Soviets who regard this country to be the main enemy." He added, "This is very persuasive for someone who has given up 31 years of their life with certain very high ideals for this country. When I left the army, as many of us did, I believed that we were in the dawn of the millennium. When I look at the map today and the weakness of power of this country, that is what shocks me."

"Mr. Angleton," Senator Robert Morgan responded slowly in the soft accents of North Carolina, "the thing that shocks me is that these actions could be carried on contrary to the constitutional rights of the citizens of this country."

And Morgan went to the core of the problem. He wanted to know if Angleton had any suggestions on "how the actions of the Central Intelligence Agency can be monitored in such a way as to protect the fundamental rights of American citizens in this country? . . . How can we act when . . . if we do act the intelligence agencies refuse to obey the guidelines or ordinances? In other words . . . you were doing all these things before the Huston Plan was devised, you continued to do them after the President rejected the report. So what assurances do we have that the intelligence agency would follow any mandate of the congress or of the President?"

"I have nothing to contribute to that, sir," James Jesus Angleton replied.

If there was no way to be sure that the CIA would obey the President, there were some orders that the CIA seemed to understand whether or not it had explicitly received them.

"Nobody wants to embarrass a President of the United States by discussing the assassination of foreign leaders in his presence," former CIA Director Richard Helms told the Church committee at a closed session on June 13, 1975. "I just think we all had the feeling that we were hired . . . to keep those things out of the Oval Office."

Helms's explanation is quoted in the course of the Church committee's 347-page report on CIA assassination plots, which became the centerpiece of the Senate investigation. The committee report made it clear that the CIA had, directly or indirectly, been involved in assassination plots, coups, or attempted coups against eight foreign leaders: Premier Fidel Castro of Cuba, Patrice Lumumba of the Congo, Rafael Trujillo of the Dominican Republic, President Salvador Allende and General René Schneider of Chile, President Ngo Dinh Diem of South Vietnam, President François Duvalier of Haiti, and President Sukarno of Indonesia.°

The committee, originally created in the wake of published revelations about CIA domestic spying, had not, at the outset, expected to devote the major share of its energies investigating CIA assassination plots. Colby's written report to Ford, delivered to the President at Vail the day before Christmas 1974, made no mention of such plots. But when Colby met with Ford at the White House ten days later, on January 3, he told the President there was something worse than domestic spying that Ford might have to cope with—CIA assas-

---

° The main sections of the report deal with five leaders: Castro, Lumumba, Trujillo, Schneider, and Diem. However, CIA plots against Duvalier and Sukarno are mentioned in a footnote. The actions taken against Allende are encompassed in the section on Schneider and in a separate report by the Church committee on covert operations in Chile. Of the eight leaders, five—Lumumba, Trujillo, Allende, Schneider, and Diem—died violently, with the CIA's role in plots against them varying in each case. The report concluded that "officials of the United States government initiated and participated in plots to assassinate" Lumumba and Castro and "encouraged or were privy to coup plots which resulted in the deaths of Trujillo, Diem, and Schneider." The CIA failed to poison Lumumba and Castro. Duvalier died in April 1971 after a long illness described as heart disease and diabetes. Sukarno died in June 1971; he was under house arrest at the time and had been admitted to a hospital in Jakarta for high blood pressure and kidney disease.

sination plots going back fifteen years, including the use of two mob-sters in attempts to kill Fidel Castro.

On January 16 the senior executives of the *New York Times* met with President Ford at the White House. The visitors were Clifton Daniel and James Reston from the Washington bureau, and publisher Arthur O. Sulzberger, A. M. Rosenthal, Max Frankel, John Oakes, and Tom Wicker from New York. Over lamb chops in the smaller, family dining room on the second floor, Ford chatted informally with the *Times* editors; his press secretary, Ron Nessen, and two other presidential aides, Alan Greenspan and Robert A. Goldwin, also attended the luncheon. Most of the conversation concerned the sorry state of the economy, but near the end, the subject of the Rockefeller Commission's investigation of CIA arose. There are somewhat varying recollections of the President's remarks, but in essence, Ford said he had, with great care, deliberately picked a responsible group of members to serve on the commission; he had given it a mandate to confine itself to domestic operations of the CIA because he did not wish the panel to exceed its charter and stray into the area of covert operations abroad. For if the commission dug too deeply, it would break disturbing ground. He had been surprised himself to learn of things that could blacken the reputation of every President after Harry Truman. He was talking, Ford added, about the assassinations of foreign leaders.

The President's listeners were stunned. "As I was listening to the President," Wicker said, "I had the definite impression he was dropping a story on us. I've been around too long to think that that kind of information would hold. That kind of stuff is dynamite, it's going to come out."

Max Frankel, the *Times*' Sunday editor, returned to New York immediately after the lunch. The rest of the newspaper's executives adjourned to the Washington bureau, where Reston told Daniel, the chief of the bureau, that he felt the President's remarks were privileged; Ford had been sharing his problems with them and, Reston said, obviously had not meant his words to be reported. A debate over what to do then took place in Daniel's office. Wicker pushed hard to publish the story, but the other participants were, in varying degree, hesitant to print Ford's seemingly indiscreet remark. It developed that no ground rules governing publication had been agreed upon with the White House in advance of the luncheon. Nevertheless, Daniel considered the meeting off the record—in the nature of a return engagement for a private luncheon given by the *Times* for Ford when he was Vice President. Rosenthal, the *Times*' managing editor, also concluded that the remark could not be published. "At some point," he said, "the President used the words 'off the record,'" which left fuzzy the question of what if any material from the interview could be used. "It was one of those ambiguous things," he said. The discussion went around and around and finally, to Wicker's dismay, Daniel called Ron Nessen, who naturally insisted that Ford's comments were off the record.

But as Wicker had recognized, information of that magnitude is very hard to keep quiet; one or more of the *Times* executives talked about it, and eventually word of the President's remark filtered back to a TV network reporter, Daniel Schorr of the CBS Washington bureau. On February 28 Schorr broke the story on the CBS Evening News. Ford, he reported, had warned "associates" that "if current investigations go too far, they could uncover several assassinations of foreign officials in which the CIA was involved."° Schorr added that the assassinations, "believed to have numbered at least three," had been uncovered by an internal CIA investigation.†

The leak from the *Times*' lamb-chop luncheon had far-reaching and unforeseen consequences. Following the Schorr broadcast, a spate of stories appeared linking the CIA to assassination plots, including a report that the agency had hired Mafia figures to kill Fidel Castro. The cap was off the bottle, and Ford was under growing pressure to

---

° The *Times*, tied up on a major news story, was nevertheless free to report what Schorr had said, and the following morning it carried a dispatch from Washington quoting the CBS correspondent. Wicker, angry at being scooped by CBS on his own story, wrote a column reporting on Schorr's broadcast. Wicker added that it could be "unequivocally confirmed" by him that Ford was indeed worried that a close investigation of covert operations abroad would disclose "assassinations." Wicker was obviously signaling furiously to his more alert readers that he knew something. Then events took a surreal turn. The next day, March 2, in the same Sunday paper in which Wicker's column appeared, the *Times* ran an Associated Press dispatch *denying* the CBS broadcast. AP quoted an unnamed former CIA official as saying that some "eager beavers down the line talked about these things, but none was ever carried out." Another ex-CIA official was quoted as saying he had heard a lot of "loose talk" about killing Castro "but never by a person in a position of authority." AP even found a third obliging former CIA official who said: "This is dream department stuff." Finally, Schorr took the *Times* off the hook. In an article published in the newspaper's "Week in Review" section on May 4, Schorr noted that Ford had first mentioned his concern over assassinations at a luncheon with *Times* executives.

† On April 28, after being grilled by the Rockefeller Commission for three hours, former CIA Director Richard Helms lost his temper when he encountered Schorr in a corridor. "Killer Schorr! Killer Schorr!" Helms cried in a loud voice as he walked down the hall. Helms told newsmen he knew of no foreign leader "ever assassinated by the CIA." However, when the Senate committee's assassination report was made public seven months later, in November 1975, the committee noted that Diem, Trujillo, and Schneider had died in plots in which the CIA was in some fashion involved. As the report made abundantly clear, the CIA's failure to poison Lumumba and Castro was not for want of trying.

respond in some way to the allegations. It was a dilemma of his own making.

On Sunday, March 16, the *Times*, in a front-page story by Nicholas Horrock, reported that Ford, concerned over the news reports about CIA assassination plots, had decided to turn the issue over to the Rockefeller Commission, after all. Schorr, who was in New York, sped back to Washington that night just in time to catch Rockefeller arriving at National Airport in his private plane. Rockefeller told Schorr that it was true; he had talked with Ford and had been asked to edge into the area of foreign assassinations, at least as far as they involved domestic planning.

The next day the story came full circle for President Ford. At a news conference in South Bend, Indiana, he acknowledged that he has discussed the subject of assassinations with Rockefeller and would decide in a few days how best to handle the problem. His Administration, he said, did "not condone ... any assassination attempts."

Clouds of mist closed in thereafter; the Rockefeller Commission said in its report that *it* had made the decision to investigate assassinations, and that the President "concurred." But at a press conference Ford insisted that the panel had investigated assassinations "at my request." Ford also explained that the matter was "sensitive," and since the commission's assassination inquiry was incomplete, he had decided it was "not in the national interest" to release the assassination material along with the rest of the report. Instead, he was making it available to Congress.

Ford was thereby lobbing the explosive assassination grenade into the hands of Senator Church. In a narrow sense, it was an astute political move by Ford; he had transferred a nettlesome issue from the Republican White House to a Democratic Congress. But the President's action left the Church committee with little choice but to conduct a comprehensive investigation of CIA assassination plots. If Ford's purpose had been to keep the issue safely submerged, if he had wanted no assassination probe, then the remarks he blurted out to the *Times* executives and his decision to hand off the problem to Congress had brought about the opposite result.

It was fortunate for the country, for the Church committee's assassination report was one of the most chilling and important documents ever made public by a committee of Congress. In addition to detailing specific assassination plots, it disclosed that the CIA had developed an "Executive Action" unit capable of carrying out the assassination of foreign officials. The report also disclosed that the CIA had a panel with the ghastly name of the "Health Alteration Committee"—which was exactly what it sounded like. The hideous nature and tone of some of the details revealed in the report can be illustrated by one quote from the section on the effort to kill Lumumba: the CIA station officer in the Congo, the report said, testified that he had received "rubber gloves, a mask, and a syringe" along with lethal poison from a CIA scientist "who also instructed him in their use."

The Church committee professed to be totally frustrated in its efforts to determine if any President had explicitly authorized an assassination. It found the system so "inherently ambiguous" that it was unable "to draw firm conclusions concerning who authorized assassination plots." The committee said it could therefore make no finding "implicating Presidents." CIA officials testified that in discussing assassinations they spoke even to one another in riddles and "circumlocutions," like characters in Lewis Carroll.

It was as though a committee of the Congress had been turned loose in a funhouse, in which the images it found were grotesque and distorted, and somewhat beyond its comprehension. One can hear throughout the wheeze of the calliope, and the CIA shouting, "Hey, Rube!" The senators, after all, were not used to operating in a bizarre, secret world of Ivy League gentlemen killers who dealt in poison and euphemism.

"It is like trying to nail jello to the wall," Senator Mondale said at a press conference when the report was released, "and I believe the system was intended to work that way: namely, that things would be ordered to be done that should it be made public, no one could be held accountable." Mondale came closest to understanding what the committee was dealing with.

So did Senator Mathias. At one point while questioning Helms, Mathias invoked Henry II, who, without issuing a specific order, had Thomas à Becket assassinated by asking, "Will no one rid me of this turbulent priest?"* Helms agreed that the historical reference was apt:

> SENATOR MATHIAS: You feel that spans the generations and the centuries?
> MR. HELMS: I think it does, sir.

CIA Directors and supporters of the Agency have maintained for years that the CIA always operates under strict presidential control. Yet not a single CIA witness testified to receiving or having direct knowledge of an assassination order issued by a President.

* Becket, the Archbishop of Canterbury, had suspended the bishops who took part in the coronation of Henry II's son. Four knights who heard the King's plea thought they understood him, went to Canterbury on December 29, 1170, and murdered Becket in the cathedral.

The Church committee report disclosed that there were eight CIA plots against Castro, including poison pills, a poison pen, a diving suit contaminated with disease-bearing fungus, and "an exotic seashell, rigged to explode ... in an area where Castro commonly went skin diving." In addition, the CIA planned to destroy Castro's bearded image by dusting his shoes with thallium salts so that eventually his beard would fall out.°

According to the report, the main CIA plot began during the Eisenhower Administration in August 1960, when Richard Bissell, the deputy director for plans (later renamed operations), asked Colonel Sheffield Edwards, the CIA director of security, to find someone to murder Castro. Edwards and another CIA official (identified in news accounts as James O'Connell) contacted Robert A. Maheu, a former FBI agent and lieutenant of Howard Hughes, and asked him to recruit John Rosselli, a mobster whose real name was Filippo Saco, for the hit. The CIA offered $150,000 for Castro's assassination.

Rosselli in turn brought in Momo Salvatore (Sam) Giancana, a Chicago gangster, and Santos Trafficante, who had been the top Mafia don in Cuba. The mob's interest in killing Castro was obvious: the Cuban Premier had thrown the syndicate out of the lucrative gambling casinos of Havana. With Castro removed, the syndicate might be able to move back in.

The poison pills, actually six gelatin capsules filled with a liquid botulinum toxin, were prepared by the CIA. The poison had first been tested on monkeys. The monkeys died. Rosselli arranged for the pills to be delivered to Cuba, where the plan was for someone close to Castro to slip the poison into the Cuban leader's drink or food.† In two or three days Castro would be dead and an autopsy would reveal no trace of the poison. Rosselli remembered Maheu explaining that the capsules could not be used in "boiling soups," but would work in water or other liquids. The plan failed, however; phase one of the plot fizzled sometime around the Bay of Pigs invasion in April 1961, by which time John F. Kennedy was President.

But the plotting against Castro continued, and late in 1961 the assassination operation was transferred to William Harvey, a senior CIA operative, who got back in touch with Rosselli. In April 1962,

---

° "The depilatory was to be administered during a trip outside Cuba," the report said, "when it was anticipated Castro would leave his shoes outside the door of his hotel room to be shined."

† The pills were passed to a Cuban exile in Miami who claimed to have a contact inside a restaurant frequented by Castro. One witness said he was present when the poison was given to the Cuban exile outside the Boom Boom Room of the Fontainebleau Hotel in Miami Beach. The poison was never administered; one CIA official said Castro stopped going to the restaurant.

four more pills were given to the gangster, who had them delivered to Cuba. Once again, the plot failed and had been abandoned by mid-February 1963.

In yet another plot, a high official of the Castro government code-named AM/LASH by the CIA, was given a poison pen for use against Castro. A CIA case officer serving under Desmond Fitzgerald, a top CIA covert operator, met with the Cuban in Paris and handed him the poison pen at about the moment that President Kennedy was assassinated in Dallas on November 22, 1963.

The committee's efforts to pin down the origins of the Castro assassination plots was typical of the "jello to the wall" problem of which Senator Mondale had complained. Richard Bissell said Sheffield Edwards in his presence had briefed CIA Director Allen Dulles in "circumlocutious terms" about the plan to use the "syndicate representatives." Referring to Dulles, Bissell said, "he knew."

John McCone, who had succeeded Dulles in 1961, swore he knew nothing of any plots to kill Castro. But Richard Helms, providing a bit of B-movie dialogue, said bluntly of McCone: "He was involved in this up to his scuppers just the way everybody else was that was in it, and . . . I don't understand how it was he didn't hear about some of these things that he claims that he didn't."

William Harvey stated that at an August 10, 1962, meeting of the Special Group—the interagency committee that was supposed to approve CIA covert operations°—Defense Secretary Robert McNamara suggested that the panel consider the "elimination or assassination of Fidel." Harvey said McCone, a prominent Catholic, told him afterward that if he got involved "in something like this, I might end up getting myself excommunicated."

The assassination report revealed that CIA officials met with Attorney General Robert F. Kennedy on May 7, 1962, and informed him

° Since 1948, a secret interagency committee has had responsibility for controlling covert operations. Basically the same agencies have been represented on the committee, although of course the names of the players—and often the name of the committee—has changed with succeeding Administrations. The membership has usually comprised the President's National Security Adviser, the Director of the CIA, the Deputy Secretary of Defense, the Under Secretary of State for Political Affairs, and the Chairman of the Joint Chiefs of Staff. The committee has taken its name from successive directives of the National Security Council: The 10/2 Panel (later the 10/5 Panel), June 18, 1948; the 5412 Group (also called the Special Group), March 1954; the 303 Committee, June 1964; the Forty Committee, February 1970; and the Operations Advisory Group, February 1976. According to the final report of the Church committee, the 1964 NSC directive changing the panel's name to the 303 Committee occurred because "the name of the Special Group had become public as a result of the publication of the book, *The Invisible Government*, and, therefore, it was felt that the name of the covert action approval committee should be changed."

of the CIA's 1960–61 plot to use Rosselli and Giancana to assassinate Castro. But the CIA witnesses said they assured Kennedy the scheme had ended, although in fact it had been reactivated. Here matters get very complicated.

Apparently Giancana, while plotting with the CIA in Miami in 1960, fretted that in his absence his girl friend, singer Phyllis Maguire, might be having an affair with entertainer Dan Rowan. The CIA through Maheu obligingly paid a private detective to bug or wiretap Rowan's hotel room in Las Vegas; a maid discovered the private eye's equipment and he was arrested on October 31. Two weeks earlier Hoover, doubtless through FBI wiretaps of crime figures, had discovered that Giancana was boasting to friends that Castro would soon be eliminated. After the arrest of the private detective in Las Vegas, the FBI began to figure out what was going on. In April of 1961 it learned from Maheu that the Las Vegas tap was part of a CIA anti-Castro plot. In May, Hoover sent Robert Kennedy a memo which did not mention assassination but said the CIA was using Giancana in an "operation" against Castro.

A year later, on May 9, 1962—two days after the CIA informed Robert Kennedy of the assassination plot against Castro—Kennedy met with Hoover. According to Hoover's memo of that meeting, Kennedy told him that the CIA had admitted arranging for the Las Vegas tap, and that the Agency had put itself in a position where "it could not afford" to have Giancana or Maheu prosecuted for the tap—for prosecution might reveal the CIA plot to murder Castro.

Ironically, within the underworld another reason may have been whispered. Hoover said he told Kennedy that there was "gutter gossip" around that the reason Giancana had escaped prosecution was "because of Giancana's close relationship with Frank Sinatra, who, in turn, claimed to be a close friend of the Kennedy family. The Attorney General stated he realized this and it was for that reason that he was quite concerned when he received this information from CIA about Giancana and Maheu."

Hoover, the old spider, must hardly have been able to believe the parade of flies now blundering into his web. First, he had caught his hated rival, the CIA, dealing with the underworld. Second, he had uncovered a secret CIA operation against Castro.[*] Third, he had caught the CIA helping to install a wiretap for a Chicago mobster;

---

[*] Documents unearthed by the Senate committee do not specifically show that Hoover knew the CIA had hired Giancana to kill Castro. But the FBI knew that Giancana was saying Castro would be assassinated, and it also knew that the CIA was using the mobster in an "operation" against Castro. It would not be unreasonable to assume that the FBI could manage to put those two facts together and deduce the nature of the "operation."

he now had the CIA squirming with apprehension over the possibility of a prosecution that would reveal its role. Fourth, he was able to remind Bobby Kennedy, his archenemy, of the uncomfortable fact that his friend Sinatra was also a friend of Sam Giancana, who was not being prosecuted. As had been highly publicized, both Robert Kennedy and his brother the President knew Sinatra well; the crooner was a charter member of the Hollywood "Rat Pack" along with Peter Lawford, the actor then married to the Kennedys' sister, Pat. Fifth, and best of all, the FBI chief had by now discovered Judith Campbell, the prize, the heaven-sent crown jewel for Hoover, who specialized in blackmailing Presidents as his best possible form of job security.

According to the Church committee, FBI reports indicate that "a close friend" of President Kennedy who had "frequent contact" with him during this period was also a close friend of Rosselli and Giancana. The committee report noted there had been seventy calls between "the President's friend" and the White House. It did not identify the friend by name or gender, but Laurence Stern of the Washington *Post* soon learned and reported that the woman was Judith Campbell. Wearing large sunglasses, and looking rather tough but still attractive fifteen years later, Mrs. Judith Campbell Exner (she had since remarried) stepped before network TV cameras in December 1975 and claimed a "close, personal" relationship with President Kennedy. She said she had met with him frequently in the White House and elsewhere, including Palm Beach. She also said a "mutual friend" had introduced her to Kennedy and later to Giancana, who in turn had introduced her to Rosselli. She declined to name the friend, but news accounts soon identified him as Frank Sinatra.

The FBI had learned of Judith Campbell early in 1962. Hoover could hardly wait to break the good news to President Kennedy. On March 22 he went to the White House for lunch with the President, taking with him a memo about Mrs. Campbell and her mobster friends.* It must have been some lunch. No record of it survives. It was usually Hoover's style on such occasions, however, to describe in great detail what the FBI had learned and then assure the political figure involved that he could rest easy, the information would never get out. "The last telephone contact between the White House and

---

* Hoover discovered Mrs. Campbell in the course of a crash FBI investigation of Rosselli. While Giancana and Rosselli were plotting the Castro assassination, the FBI bugged both their homes in Florida. Before Hoover's lunch with President Kennedy, he sent a memo to the White House which, in the words of the Church committee, said that "a review of the telephone toll calls" from Mrs. Campbell's residence "revealed calls to the White House." That language could mean that the FBI had simply checked her long-distance toll slips, but it could also be construed to mean that the FBI had bugged or tapped Mrs. Campbell and learned of her calls to President Kennedy that way.

the President's friend occurred a few hours after the luncheon," the report said.°

The committee's assassination report drew no conclusion as to whether President Kennedy had been told of the plot against Castro by Mrs. Exner; both Rosselli and Mrs. Exner testified that she did not know about the CIA operation. Giancana could not be heard on this point; he was shot to death at his home in a Chicago suburb before the Church committee had completed arrangements to question him.†
The committee gingerly suggested that Hoover might have realized that the CIA had plotted Castro's assassination, and could have so informed Kennedy at lunch, but it was unable to establish that Hoover had done so. The report concluded that there was "insufficient evidence" to establish whether Eisenhower or Kennedy had "authorized the assassination of Castro."

The CIA plot against Lumumba also read like some fictional invention of Ian Fleming. In 1960 Bissell, one of the fathers of the U-2 spy plane and later an architect of the Bay of Pigs invasion, asked the head of CIA's Africa Division, Bronson Tweedy, to explore the feasibility of killing the Congolese leader. Bissell, the report said, also asked a CIA scientist to make preparations to assassinate or incapacitate an unnamed African leader. The committee report used the pseudonym "Joseph Scheider" for the scientist, but "Scheider" was

° The day after the luncheon, Hoover took steps that led to the final decision to drop any federal prosecution of those involved in the Las Vegas wiretap. The CIA had previously warned the FBI that prosecution would reveal an intelligence project. The decision not to prosecute thus prevented exposure of the CIA's involvement with mobsters in a plot to kill Castro. It may also, of course, have prevented the surfacing of Judith Campbell.

† The Church committee had planned to question Giancana, according to chief counsel F. A. O. Schwarz, Jr., and had taken preliminary steps toward that end when Giancana was shot seven times in the head and neck at his home in Oak Park, Illinois, on the evening of June 19, 1975. Michael J. Madigan of the committee staff, who was assigned the task of finding Giancana, told the author that the committee had not yet talked to Giancana or his attorney at the time of the mobster's death. But he said the committee had located Giancana in a hospital in Houston (where heart surgeon Dr. Michael DeBakey had removed his gall bladder) and later in a hotel there, and had obtained his addresses and telephone numbers in Chicago and Los Angeles. "We wanted to contact Giancana to find out who his lawyer was and then interview Giancana," he said. Madigan said he made several calls to Giancana's home in Chicago, including one on June 19. He raised the possibility that the telephone may have been ringing, with the Senate committee attorney calling from Washington, as Giancana lay sprawled on the floor of his basement kitchen. "One of the calls," Madigan said, "may have been made when he was dead."

A little more than a year later on August 8, 1976, Rosselli too was found murdered apparently in gangland style. Fishermen discovered his body stuffed inside a 55-gallon oil drum floating in the ocean near Miami.

identified in the press as none other than the ubiquitous Dr. Sidney Gottlieb, the same Dr. Gottlieb who, as a scientist working in Operation Artichoke in the early fifties, was a principal figure in the CIA's LSD-testing program that resulted in the death of Frank Olson.°

Gottlieb, who had a degree in chemistry, reviewed the list of CIA biological materials, which included germs to cause diseases ranging from smallpox to sleeping sickness. He selected a disease that could be fatal and was indigenous to Africa, bottled the lethal biological material, personally delivered it to the CIA station officer in Leopoldville, "and instructed him to assassinate Patrice Lumumba."† Gottlieb explained to the CIA agent that the toxic material should be put on Lumumba's "food or a toothbrush," anything that would "get to his mouth."

The poison was never administered to Lumumba. He was captured by the troops of Joseph Mobutu in December, imprisoned in Katanga province, and killed there on January 17, 1961, three days before President Eisenhower left office.

Had the CIA acted under orders? The Church committee reached no definite conclusion but said the evidence supported a "reasonable inference that the plot to assassinate Lumumba was authorized by President Eisenhower."

Guns, not poison, were the CIA's weapons of choice against Generalissimo Rafael Trujillo, the brutal dictator of the Dominican Republic. In August of 1960 the United States broke off relations with the Dominican Republic and pulled out most of its diplomatic person-

---

° Olson, a civilian employee of the Army, was one of a group of ten CIA officials and Army researchers who attended a dinner meeting in November 1953 in a cabin at Deer Creek Lake in western Maryland. As part of Operation Artichoke, Olson and some of the others were given LSD in their after-dinner liqueurs.

Dr. Gottlieb did not tell them that they had taken the drug until twenty minutes later. In 1975 Gottlieb, claiming his life was endangered, went into federal court attempting to have his name stricken from the Senate assassination report, although he had already been prominently identified in news reports as the CIA scientist who testified about the poison sent to the Congo for use against Lumumba. Gottlieb lost in the district court, but appealed; rather than delay publication of the report, the Church committee voluntarily deleted his name. The name "Joseph Scheider" was chosen by the committee and was not an operational alias used by Gottlieb in the CIA; it was selected because the committee wanted a Germanic-sounding name consistent with the real name, and also because it had the same number of letters—fourteen—to make it easy for the Government Printing Office to substitute the pseudonym at the last moment.

† The CIA also recruited and dispatched to the Congo a *Day of the Jackal* type agent, a European criminal who considered himself a member of an "execution squad." Before sending the agent to the Congo, the CIA provided him "with plastic surgery and a toupee so that Europeans travelling in the Congo would not recognize him." The agent was given the CIA code name WI/ROGUE.

nel, leaving Henry Dearborn, a career foreign service officer, as the senior American diplomat and *de facto* CIA chief of station. Dearborn was in close touch with Dominican dissidents who, he advised Washington, were ready to assassinate Trujillo. The mild-mannered and soft-spoken Dearborn wrote to the State Department that if he were a Dominican, he would favor the destruction of Trujillo "as my Christian duty." He added: "If you recall Dracula, you will remember it was necessary to drive a stake through his heart to prevent a continuation of his crimes."

In March of 1961 Dearborn asked Washington for three pistols; they were sent in the diplomatic pouch and passed to the dissidents, as were three carbines already in the U.S. consulate. After the failure of the Bay of Pigs invasion in April, Washington tried to apply the brakes to the dissidents plotting against Trujillo. But Dearborn warned the State Department that it was "too late" to stop things now. On May 29 President Kennedy sent Dearborn a cable warning that the United States could not be associated with political assassination. The next day Trujillo's car was ambushed and the dictator was shot to death. Handguns were used; whether these were the same pistols sent to Dearborn and passed to the plotters could not be pinned down by the Church committee.

The committee was very cautious in its conclusions about U.S. responsibility for the deaths of President Ngo Dinh Diem of South Vietnam and his brother Ngo Dinh Nhu. But the report noted that Lucien Conein, the CIA agent working with the generals plotting against Diem, had been assured by General Tran Van Don that the general "would make the plans for the coup available to the Ambassador [Henry Cabot Lodge] four hours before it took place." The coup began on November 1, and Diem and his brother were murdered the next day. General Duong Van (Big) Minh offered to show Conein the bodies, but he declined. He did not want to involve the United States.

General René Schneider, the commander in chief of the Chilean army, was shot and killed during a kidnap attempt on October 22, 1970. President Nixon had ordered that Salvador Allende be blocked from taking office as President of Chile, and Schneider was a definite obstacle; he believed strongly in his country's constitution, which provided for free elections. Early on the morning of October 22 the CIA provided machine guns and ammunition to a group of Chilean military officers. The CIA knew the arms were to be used by the officers in an attempt to kidnap Schneider. The CIA also authorized a payment of $50,000 to the military plotters. But, the Senate report said, as it turned out, Schneider was killed by a different group of conspirators.

The murder failed to stop Allende from taking office. But the CIA continued to work against Allende, and he died in a military coup three years later.

These were the specific case studies selected by the Senate committee for detailed treatment, but there were other plots sprinkled in the footnotes. In February 1960, for example, the CIA's Health Alteration Committee approved a proposal by the Near East Division to "incapacitate" an Iraqi colonel who was believed to be promoting Soviet interests. The Health Alteration Committee recommended to Richard Bissell that a "disabling operation" be undertaken. Bissell's deputy, Tracy Barnes, approved the plan, which was "to mail a monogrammed handkerchief containing an incapacitating agent to the colonel from an Asian country." Sidney Gottlieb remembered mailing such a handkerchief, but the colonel never had a chance to use it. The CIA informed the Church committee that the Iraqi, at about that time, had "suffered a terminal illness before a firing squad in Baghdad."

Art imitates life, or death. A few years ago Americans saw a motion picture called *Executive Action*, about a right-wing plot to assassinate an American president. The Senate report disclosed that the CIA actually had a special unit named Executive Action. It was organized in 1961 to develop "a capability to assassinate foreign leaders."

A foreign criminal (code name QJ/WIN) was recruited in Europe to be the unit's hit man. As Helms explained it to the Church committee, "If you needed somebody to carry out murder, I guess you had a man who might be prepared to carry it out." Richard Bissell, who had authorized the Executive Action unit, characterized it as "purely preparatory." William Harvey, the same agent who had taken over the Mafia assassination plot against Castro in 1961, was placed in charge of Executive Action.

Bissell testified that he informed McGeorge Bundy, President Kennedy's national security adviser, about the CIA's Executive Action capability and might have mentioned the names of Castro, Lumumba, and Trujillo. Bundy did not seem to remember the conversation as well as Bissell; he thought that Executive Action involved what the Senate report called an "untargeted capability." But Bundy, now head of the Ford Foundation, which finances various humanitarian projects around the world, said he had plainly understood that Executive Action involved "killing the individual." He said he neither approved nor tried to stop the CIA plan because he did not consider that it called for the assassination of a specific individual. As Bissell had put it so felicitously, Executive Action was "purely preparatory."

The assassination report opened a chamber of horrors and confirmed the very worst fears about what the CIA had been doing. Yet its publication resulted in no immediate, broad-based move to end covert political operations, of which assassination was an extreme form.

Although a decade after leaving the White House President Truman denounced covert CIA operations, they had begun during his Administration under National Security Council directive 10/2 of June 18, 1948. Congress, in passing the National Security Act of 1947, establishing the CIA, did not authorize covert political operations. Indeed, CIA's general counsel, Lawrence Houston, wrote a memo that year stating "we do not believe that there was any thought in the minds of Congress that the CIA under the act would take positive action for subversion and sabotage." Truman's order was based on the clause in the 1947 act which said the Agency shall perform such "other functions and duties" as the NSC might from time to time direct.

The "other functions" loophole became the eye of the needle through which, over the years, CIA covert operations were threaded around the globe. The CIA helped to overthrow the government of Iran in 1953 and Guatemala in 1954; it secretly trained Tibetans in Colorado in the late fifties to infiltrate their homeland and fight the Chinese Communists. It supported the rebels fighting Sukarno in 1958. It invaded Cuba at the Bay of Pigs in 1961. It operated a 30,000 man army in Laos in the sixties. It poured millions of dollars into Italy and other Western European countries to support moderate political parties. And it encouraged the military coups in Vietnam and Chile in which the leaders of those countries were killed.

The American public was assured that these activities were tightly controlled by the President through the Forty Committee and its predecessors.° But the Church committee was unable to pin down clear authority for any of the CIA's murder plots. Moreover, Richard Helms bluntly testified that the Forty Committee was set up "as a circuit

° In February 1976 President Ford announced that the Forty Committee would be reorganized as part of his general plan to restructure American intelligence. Ford named George Bush, who had succeeded Colby in January as CIA Director, to head a three-man Committee on Foreign Intelligence to direct U.S. intelligence. He also named Ambassador Robert D. Murphy to head a three-member Intelligence Oversight Board. He announced that the Forty Committee would become the Operations Advisory Group and expanded to include the Attorney General and the director of the Office of Management and Budget as "observers." He said he would also support legislation to outlaw assassinations in peacetime. In addition, Ford issued a set of guidelines governing physical and electronic surveillance, break-ins, and infiltration of domestic groups by the CIA or other foreign intelligence agencies, but these were hedged in with exceptions that still permitted the agencies wide latitude.

Ford coupled these changes with a proposal that Congress pass a virtual Official Secrets Act, making it a crime for a government official to reveal certain classified intelligence information to the press and the public.

breaker so that these things [assassinations] did not explode in the President's face and that he was not held responsible for them."

The House intelligence committee, in its final report, said that under Henry Kissinger, the Forty Committee "fell into virtual disuse," with telephone approvals the usual rule. "One formal meeting was held in 1972, none in 1973 and 1974." The report concluded: "In practice, the Forty Committee has often been little more than a rubber stamp."

And the Pike committee also noted that only "politically sensitive" covert operations required review by the Forty Committee. Since there was no "clear definition" of what constituted a politically sensitive operation, covert projects were often approved within the CIA, at the level of the deputy director for operations, without ever reaching the Forty Committee. The head of the CIA could decide which covert operations should be submitted to the Forty Committee for review.° And CIA Directors made sure the Forty Committee was not overly burdened with work. "By CIA statistics," the Church committee reported, "only about one-fourth of all covert action projects are considered by the 40 Committee."

The Church committee also provided specific examples of the lack of control exercised over the CIA by the Forty Committee. The Senate panel's assassination report noted that Richard Bissell testified he never told the Forty Committee (then the Special Group) of the plan to murder Castro. The report also disclosed that when Nixon in 1970 ordered the CIA to block Allende, he specifically ordered that the Agency by-pass the Forty Committee and report directly to Kissinger. Another example was revealed in the House report; when Nixon approved what eventually totaled $16 million in aid to Kurdish rebels in Iraq, the Forty Committee was told about it after the decision had been made.

What had long been suspected was finally clear; the Forty Committee was mere window dressing, a mechanism designed to give the appearance of presidential control over covert operations without the reality. It was equally clear that the well-bred old boys of the CIA, the adenoidal gentlemen at the top, with their reversible names and consciences to match, did not stop at murder.

Living in their own clandestine world, safe in the dark, weird cocoon of Langley, accountable only to themselves, they had been

---

° The House intelligence committee report also provided the first analysis of types of covert operations undertaken by the CIA. From 1965 to 1975, of projects approved by the Forty Committee, 32 percent were to influence foreign elections (the United States poured $65 million into Italy over twenty years, for example), 29 percent were media and propaganda projects, and 23 percent were to finance secret armies, or to transfer arms, ammunition, or military equipment.

schooled at St. Grottlesex but learned their political morality from Eichmann. In their ignorance of the very system of government they professed to serve, they confused their arrogance with patriotism. It was put quite plainly by Richard Helms when he appeared before the Church committee in an executive session. "I believe it was the policy at the time to get rid of Castro," he said, "and if killing him was one of the things that was to be done in this connection, that was within what was expected."

*Colby said he had danced around the room several times
for ten minutes to try to avoid becoming specific on this.*

—CIA memorandum,
December 18, 1972

7
CIA:
The Watergate Connection

A year after the Watergate break-in James R. Schlesinger, the new
Director of Central Intelligence, was asked by a House subcommittee
whether he was certain he really knew everything about the Agency's
role in the affair.

"I believe I have a fair degree of confidence we have all of the
information now," Schlesinger replied carefully, "but there are many
rocks and there are many things crawling out from under the rocks."

During Watergate the central drama revolved around whether
Richard Nixon would survive in office, be impeached, or resign, and
whether the nation's constitutional system would be equal to the challenge it faced. And there was, not far below the surface, some fear
that however unlikely the possibility, Nixon might seize power, defy
Congress if impeached, or take some precipitous military action—
perhaps even push the nuclear button. Nor was this merely the stuff
of novels. James Schlesinger, Secretary of Defense when Nixon quit,
admitted to reporters at a background luncheon in Washington two
weeks later that he had taken precautions to keep an eye on both
Nixon and U.S. military commanders in the President's final days in

office.* These primary concerns over Nixon and the Presidency tended to overshadow questions about the CIA's Watergate role.

In retrospect, however, it is plain that the CIA was not only entangled in many of the events that led up to Watergate but was an active, even eager participant in the cover-up that followed.

The CIA's cover-up role was a triple one. First, the Agency cooperated with Richard Nixon in obstructing justice by assisting the President in his attempt to stop the FBI investigation from going any higher than the men arrested in Democratic headquarters. Second, the CIA attempted in a variety of ways to conceal from the prosecutors, the FBI, the Justice Department, the press, and the public its own relationship to Watergate and the burglars. Third, the CIA attempted to hide its own participation in the Nixon cover-up.

The CIA's efforts to cover its own tracks after Watergate is a complex story—men concealing the truth do not act openly, the more so when they are trained in the arts of deception—but the details can be geologically reconstructed by a careful examination of Schlesinger's rocks. The result is as disturbing as the Watergate break-in itself, for what happened illustrates the dangerous degree to which the CIA has become an actor in the American political process.

None of the congressional investigations concluded that the CIA planned, approved, or had any advance knowledge of the Watergate break-in. In the absence of hard persuasive evidence, no assumptions can be made that the CIA did have such knowledge. Yet there remain tantalizing facts and lingering, unanswered questions about what the CIA might have known. Certainly it had at least three channels of information available to it prior to the break-in, as will be seen.

Of the seven original Watergate burglars, all but two had worked for the CIA.† One of the seven, Eugenio Martinez, was on a $100-a-month CIA retainer at the time of his arrest in the Watergate. Two of the team's leaders, Hunt and McCord, were twenty-year veterans of

---

* Half a dozen reporters attended the luncheon, organized by Alan L. Otten, chief of the Washington bureau of the *Wall Street Journal.* Under the ground rules Schlesinger could not be quoted by name, but he was soon identified as the source of the stories written after the luncheon. In a story in the Miami *News* of August 24, 1974, Andrew J. Glass, who was present at the luncheon in the Sheraton-Carlton Hotel, reported that Schlesinger—whom he identified as a "senior Pentagon official," in keeping with the ground rules—had said he "felt it prudent to keep a close watch on the President and on his commanders" and also said he had been concerned about the effect that a long impeachment trial in the Senate might have on "a man with the capability of ordering a nuclear attack on the nation's enemies."

† The exceptions were G. Gordon Liddy, who had been an FBI agent, and Virgilio Gonzales, the Watergate team's locksmith.

the Agency. The CIA background of the burglars did not, of course, prove CIA involvement in the burglary.*

Howard Hunt, at least according to the official record, retired from the CIA in April 1970. For aid in finding a job, he turned to CIA's External Employment Assistance Branch, one of whose officials, Francis A. O'Malley, helped to place him on the payroll of the Robert R. Mullen Company. Apparently Richard Helms was also of some help.† Hunt had not traveled very far; the Mullen Company was, after all, a CIA front.

Early in July of 1971 Charles Colson, who knew Hunt, brought him into the Nixon White House as a consultant. On July 7 Ehrlichman telephoned General Robert Cushman, the Deputy Director of the CIA, informed him that Hunt had been ordered "by the President" to work on security problems and would be asking CIA's assistance. "You should consider he has pretty much carte blanche," Ehrlichman said.

The choice of Cushman as the CIA official to be approached by the White House was not accidental, for Cushman owed much of his rapid advancement in the military to Richard Nixon. A four-star general in the Marine Corps, Cushman had been given a major command in the Vietnam war. When Nixon became President, he brought Cushman home to be the number-two man in the CIA.

---

* But it did illustrate the easy availability of at least some former CIA men for criminal political activity. Retired spies must find work somewhere.

In this connection, one of the more fascinating, if little-noticed, news reports of the Watergate period was a story on page 11 of the New York Times of May 2, 1973, headlined: "'AGING' OF STAFF A C.I.A. PROBLEM; SPIES ARE TOO OLD AND TOO NUMEROUS, DIRECTOR SAYS." The dispatch explained that James Schlesinger, then Director of the CIA, was asking Congress to increase from 830 to 1,200 the number of overseas CIA agents who could retire at age fifty after twenty years of service. Schlesinger put droves of aging spies, including many influential senior officers, out in the cold, which embittered the Agency's old boys. As more CIA men reach retirement age, the possibility exists that, heaven forbid, increasing numbers of Howard Hunts may be offering their services to political candidates.

† Robert F. Bennett, the son of Senator Wallace Bennett, a Utah Republican, took over the Mullen Company while Hunt was employed there. Bennett testified that Mullen in his presence had once reminded a CIA official that he had a letter in his files from Richard Helms recommending Howard Hunt and that Hunt had been hired "because the CIA had recommended him." Helms testified he could well have written such a letter to Mullen but did not recall it. Mullen testified he had said at one time that he had a letter from Helms but "when I actually looked into it, it was not a letter to me . . . it was a letter that Helms had written to, as I recall, some chemical company in the Middle West, somebody else. It was a reference for Howard . . . I cannot say the Agency leaned on me in any way to hire him. I am the one that did it."

Cushman's association with Nixon went back more than a decade. When Nixon was Vice President, Cushman served as his national security aide for four years, from 1957 to 1961. As it happened, in that job Cushman had been Nixon's liaison with the CIA; in particular he monitored for Nixon the CIA's progress in planning the Bay of Pigs operation. Nixon had a vital interest in that operation—he had hoped that the invasion of Cuba and the overthrow of Castro would take place before November 8, 1960, for he believed this would guarantee his election to the Presidency.

On July 22, 1971, Hunt met with Cushman. The two men knew each other; years earlier, when Cushman had done a previous tour of duty at the CIA, from 1949 to 1951, they had, at least according to Hunt, shared an office.° And Hunt had met Cushman during the planning of the Bay of Pigs, at a time when Cushman watched the operation for Nixon, and Hunt, under the code name Eduardo, served as the CIA's political action chief among the Cuban exiles. Now the two men greeted each other familiarly.

Unknown to Hunt, however, Cushman secretly recorded their conversation, so that their chit-chat about Cushman's weight problem ("I go on the wagon . . . the only way I can lose weight is to be miserable") is preserved for posterity, along with Hunt's demands for CIA spy equipment.

"I've been charged with quite a highly sensitive mission by the White House," Hunt said after they got down to business, "to visit and elicit information from an individual whose ideology we aren't entirely sure of, and for that purpose they asked me to come over here and see if you could get me two things: flash alias documentation, which wouldn't have to be backstopped at all, and some degree of physical disguise, for a one-time op—in and out."†

"I don't see why we can't," replied General Cushman.

Hunt explained he would need a false "driver's license" from "any state at all," and some "pocket litter," by which he meant business cards or other material to back up his new identity. He specified only that the first name used in the documents should be "Edward." The

---

° "In the early 1950's," Hunt testified to a House subcommittee, "then Colonel Cushman and I found ourselves sharing an office at the Central Intelligence Agency. I was then detailed by the Marine Corps to a brief tour of the Agency. We were working for the same supervisor and got to know each other on a first-name basis."

† By "flash alias documentation" Hunt, using CIA jargon, meant credit cards or other false identification that could be displayed—"flashed"—to someone but not used for other purposes. A credit card actually used to pay for anything would have to be "backstopped" by a real account opened with the credit-card company under a false name.

conversation was outwardly friendly, but there were half-hidden un-dercurrents. Cushman handled his White House visitor gingerly, with hearty, rather forced cordiality, and Hunt, on his part, obviously relished lording it over the Deputy Director of the secret agency in which he had so recently been a mere operative in the ranks.

Both men understood the change in their power relationship; as soon as Hunt had left, Cushman snapped to and ordered that the false identification documents and disguises be prepared.° The task was turned over to the CIA's Technical Services Division, or TSD, which, in addition to handling poisons—it will be recalled that Dr. Sidney Gottlieb was its former chief—was also in charge of fake mustaches and similar matters.

The same day, Stephen Carter Greenwood, a twenty-six-year-old specialist with the Technical Services Division, was summoned to the office of Dick Krueger, the deputy chief of the division, and instructed to provide someone named "Edward" with the materials Hunt had requested. The following day, Greenwood met with Hunt at a CIA "safehouse" near the Washington Cathedral.† It was the first of several meetings at the safehouse between Greenwood and Hunt. The young CIA technician provided Hunt with his famous wig, a pair of glasses, a speech-alteration device which resembled a set of dentures and caused Hunt to lisp, and a second set of false teeth, with one missing tooth. It was a Technical Services Division safehouse, rather like a theatrical costumer's shop, so the wigs and false teeth and other disguises were right there in stock. Greenwood also gave Hunt various alias documents, including a Social Security card, a New York State driver's license, and several association membership cards—including one for the Hot Rod Club of America—all in the name of Edward Joseph Warren. Hunt now had two sets of false CIA credentials, for in 1960 he had been assigned the alias Edward J. Hamilton and issued various membership cards and a District of Columbia driver's permit, which through an apparent clerical error was made out to Edward V.

° Richard Helms, at the time Director of the CIA, later conceded that he was aware that materials were being supplied by the CIA to Howard Hunt because Cushman had told him so. Cushman also testified he had notified Helms.
† Hunt later told a federal grand jury that the safehouse was located "on upper Massachusetts Avenue near the cathedral, on the west side of the street" in a "modest apartment building." The CIA maintains many unmarked safehouses in Washington and elsewhere. Hunt provided a succinct definition of the term to the grand jury: "A safehouse is . . . where people on clandestine business are able to meet and transact their business without fear of interruption, or being identi-fied, or being overheard." The CIA's safehouses are not always Spartan. The report of the House intelligence committee noted that in addition to "refrigerators, ranges, and living room furniture," the CIA in decorating its safehouses "at times provides luxury items, such as china or crystal."

Hamilton. When Hunt left the CIA in 1970, he held on to some of the Hamilton credentials.°

A week later Greenwood met Hunt at the safehouse again to adjust his glasses. The glasses were a special super-duper CIA item; they had no effect on the wearer's vision, but were ground so that to anyone else they appeared to be thick prescription lenses.

But the first use that Hunt made of his fancy CIA disguise gear and documentation had nothing to do with national security. It had everything to do with Senator Edward Kennedy.

Earlier that month Hunt's employer at the Mullen Company, Robert Bennett, told Hunt that he knew of a General Services Administration employee in Rhode Island, one Clifton De Motte, who might know something about the Kennedys in general and Chappaquiddick in particular. De Motte had worked for Bennett at the Department of Transportation. Hunt later testified that Charles Colson asked him to see De Motte after he told him of Bennett's suggestion. Hunt said he would need a disguise. Colson, Hunt testified, then said he would see about getting help from the CIA. The evidence indicates, therefore, that Ehrlichman's call to Cushman and the approach to the CIA was, initially at least, designed to outfit Hunt to go to Rhode Island to dig up dirt about Chappaquiddick. It was the old Ulasewicz assignment in CIA clothing.†

On July 28, wearing his wig, his thick glasses, and possibly lisping through his CIA dentures, Hunt flew to Providence and checked into a motel room. There, with the lights dim—to enhance his disguise—he tape-recorded an interview with De Motte. In 1960 De Motte had been public relations director of the Yachtsman motel, in Hyannisport, where members of President Kennedy's staff and the press stayed during the campaign. He knew tidbits about the Kennedys, but his knowledge of the accident at Chappaquiddick was zilch. Hunt's one-time op, in and out, was a dismal failure.

But Hunt, meeting at safehouses in the shadow of the Washington Cathedral, wearing his disguises, zooming around in jet planes, masquerading as Edward Warren, was back in business. He was *operating* again. In some inner recess of his heart, he must have secretly indulged, if only for a moment, in the luxury of comparing himself favorably to Peter Ward, the fictional CIA hero of his own spy novels.

Soon Hunt was escalating his demands on the CIA. On August 18

° In preparing for the Watergate break-in, both Hunt and McCord used the alias Edward Warren, and Hunt and Sturgis both used the alias Edward J. Hamilton.
† Hunt was crestfallen when Colson penetrated his disguise. At one point, Colson said, Hunt showed him a Polaroid photograph and asked, "Can you tell who this is? And he showed me the photograph. And I said, yes, it is you." Colson added, "He seemed to be disappointed."

he requested that the Agency bring back to Washington a CIA secretary, then assigned to the Paris station, to work with him. Cushman balked at that, but in the meantime Hunt was demanding and getting more equipment and services from the CIA.

Cleo Gephart, a CIA electronics engineer, met three times with Hunt and supplied him with a Uher tape recorder disguised in a battered typewriter case. Hunt was given a "sterile" CIA telephone number, 965-9598, to dial when he wished to contact Gephart.° Hunt used the number twice to get in touch with him.

Around the same time Hunt demanded a "backstopped" telephone number in New York; what Hunt had in mind was a special CIA hookup so that when the number rang in New York, it' would be answered in Washington—unknown to the caller.† He also demanded a backstopped driver's license, and real Hertz and Avis credit cards under his alias.

On August 25 Greenwood met Hunt again at another safehouse, and delivered the tape recorder and some business cards. This time "Edward" unexpectedly brought with him a man for whom he requested a disguise and alias documents in the name of "George F. Leonard." The newcomer was none other than G. Gordon Liddy. Liddy, too, was outfitted with glasses and a wig. The CIA technician also provided a heel lift designed to make the wearer limp. At the same meeting Hunt asked for, and later in the day was given, a small Tessina camera disguised in a tobacco pouch, which he claimed he needed to photograph someone in a poorly lit corridor. Greenwood heard the two men talk about catching a plane.

Later that day Hunt and Liddy flew to Los Angeles to case Dr. Fielding's office.‡ On the evening of August 26 Hunt called Greenwood from the West Coast and asked him to meet him at Dulles Airport at six o'clock the next morning. At Dulles, Hunt handed the CIA man the camera in the tobacco pouch and a roll of exposed film. He asked that the film be developed and printed and delivered to him later in the day, which was done. But before bringing the photographs to Hunt at a safehouse, Greenwood showed them to Dick Krueger, the deputy chief of the Technical Services Division.

Krueger recognized the location as Southern California and ordered one of the prints blown up. In the enlarged picture he could

---

° The number could not be traced back to the CIA. The 965 exchange covers a portion of northwest Washington, including Wisconsin Avenue in upper Georgetown.

† Hunt later explained that he wanted a "sterile telephone" to "ring in New York, since the documentation that had been provided to me provided for an address on, I believe, West 73d Street."

‡ Liddy wore the heel lift to Los Angeles, according to Hunt, but it was so painful that he threw it away in disgust.

make out the name "Dr. Fielding" in the parking lot next to his office. On Krueger's instructions, Greenwood made a set of Xerox copies of the photographs before delivering them to Hunt at the safehouse. Another CIA official who saw the prints recognized them as "casing photos," according to a report on CIA links to Watergate issued by Senator Howard Baker during the Senate Watergate investigation.

By now red flags were beginning to go up inside the CIA. Krueger, in still-secret Senate testimony, admitted having the photos enlarged, seeing Dr. Fielding's name, and reporting the contents of the photos to his CIA superiors. But Krueger denied mentioning the name of Dr. Fielding when he did so. On August 26, however, Krueger had called Cushman's assistant, Karl Wagner, to complain that Hunt's demands were getting out of hand and that he now had a considerable amount of CIA equipment, some of which could be traced back to the Agency. The next day Krueger telephoned Wagner again, reporting that the CIA had developed the films for Hunt.

Wagner, in a prescient note to Cushman, said, "Hunt has brought a stranger into the picture who is now privy to TSD's role in this affair. The White House should have cleared this with us and we must be told who this fellow is. He could embarrass us later." Moreover, Wagner warned, "Hunt's use of unique clandestine equipment in domestic activity of an uncertain nature also has potential for trouble. The Agency could suffer if its clandestine gear were discovered to be used in domestic secret operations."

The game was getting too risky now. On August 27 Cushman telephoned Ehrlichman and complained that the CIA could not continue to meet Hunt's demands. Ehrlichman agreed. Richard Helms testified that he was the one who instructed Cushman to get in touch with Ehrlichman and "have this whole thing stopped."

Lieutenant General Vernon A. Walters, who succeeded Cushman as Helms's deputy, later insisted that the Agency "had no contact whatsoever" with Hunt after August 31, 1971, which is a significant date in that the Fielding burglary took place three days later. By claiming it had already severed relations with Hunt, the CIA sought to distance itself from the break-in. The trouble with the CIA's claim was that it was not true.

In July the White House had asked that the CIA prepare a psychological profile of Daniel Ellsberg. Helms gave his approval. On August 12 Hunt, Liddy, and David Young met with Dr. Bernard Mathis Malloy, the CIA's chief psychiatrist, in Room 16, the Plumbers' basement headquarters, to discuss the CIA's draft profile.° The White

---

° At this meeting, Dr. Malloy later said, Hunt said he wanted to "try Dr. Ellsberg in public" and render him "the object of pity as a broken man." He said Hunt also hoped to be able to refer to "Dr. Ellsberg's oedipal conflicts or castration

House was not satisfied with the CIA's first effort and instructed Malloy to try harder. In October, *after* the Fielding break-in, more information was sent to the psychiatrist by the Plumbers. Malloy met with Hunt once more, and a new profile was prepared. Helms sent it to David Young with a covering note warning that the CIA's involvement "should not be revealed in any context, formal or informal. I am sure that you appreciate our concern."

So Hunt was still working with the CIA on the Ellsberg profile months after August 31, 1971, and he had numerous other contacts with the Agency after that date. Later in the year he approached a CIA agent about a break-in job, and in December he asked for and got a CIA computer name trace on a Latin American political figure. Hunt also approached CIA's placement bureau early in 1972 and asked Francis O'Malley, the same official who had placed him at the Mullen Company, to locate a "retired lockpicker." Hunt had several times asked for the names of retired CIA agents. O'Malley obligingly sent Hunt a number of résumés, including that of Thomas C. Amato, who had recently retired and was living in Florida. Amato, a violinist, photoengraver, and skilled metalworker, was also a locksmith with, his résumé advertised, a "good working knowledge of tumbler, lever, wafer disc, warded and combination locks."

And Hunt continued to use his CIA disguises and credentials right up to and including Watergate. Early in 1972 columnist Jack Anderson publicized a memo allegedly written by Dita Beard, a Washington lobbyist for ITT, suggesting that the government might drop an antitrust action against the multinational firm in exchange for a $400,000 contribution to the Republican National Convention. It became vitally important to the White House to discredit Dita Beard and the explosive memo. Hunt was assigned the job. Wearing his wig, he flew to Denver as Edward Hamilton, and interviewed Mrs. Beard in her hospital room. Afterward Mrs. Beard issued a statement claiming her memo was a fake.

Later Mrs. Beard's son Robert told Bob Woodward of the Washington *Post* that a mystery man had indeed visited his mother in the hospital, and "he did have a red wig on, cockeyed, as if he'd put it on in a dark car." The *Post* story was the origin of the most famous prop of Watergate, what was forever afterward described as Howard Hunt's "ill-fitting red wig."*

---

fears." When the Plumbers asked Malloy what materials he needed, he said he replied that "data from early life from nurses or close relatives would be useful." Malloy said he was also assured at the meeting that "the first Mrs. Ellsberg would be cooperative."

* There is, however, some dispute over the color of the wig. In a television interview on November 14, 1974, Hunt said he wore a "brown wig" when he inter-

Senator Howard Baker and his committee staff, including Fred D. Thompson, minority counsel to the Senate Watergate committee, and two assistant minority counsel, Howard S. Liebengood and Michael J. Madigan, dug deeply into the CIA's ties to Watergate. Their investigation did not establish that the agency knew about the Watergate break-in before it occurred. But they did find intriguing evidence of possible CIA advance knowledge.

Late in 1971, months before the Watergate break-in, the CIA learned that Hunt had been in touch with Eugenio Martinez, who was later arrested in the Watergate. Martinez was an interesting figure, a Cuban who became a naturalized U.S. citizen and was recruited by the Agency in January 1961, before the Bay of Pigs. Martinez earned $8,100 a year as a full-time CIA employee until 1969, when he went on the $100-a-month retainer to report on the Cuban exile community in Miami. While on the CIA retainer he was also a partner in Bernard Barker's real-estate business.

In November 1971, two months after Martinez took part in the Fielding break-in, he told his CIA case officer in Miami, and Jacob D. Esterline, the Miami station chief, that he had been in contact with Howard Hunt. There is evidence that he had also mentioned Hunt to the case officer some months earlier. Then, in March of 1972, Martinez told Esterline that Hunt was working for the White House and was active in Miami. He also asked pointedly whether Esterline was sure he knew of all Agency operations in the Miami area.

Alarmed that something was going on that he had not been told about, Esterline queried Langley asking for information on Hunt's alleged White House status. The CIA, of course, knew very well that Hunt was working for the White House; the Agency had outfitted him with all his spy equipment and it was by now acutely uncomfortable about its relationship with E. Howard Hunt, Jr. On March 27 the assistant deputy director of the Plans Directorate advised Esterline not to concern himself with Hunt's activities in Miami; Hunt, Esterline was told, was on an unknown domestic assignment for the White House, and

---

viewed Mrs. Beard. But when Helms was questioned about "the red wig" by a House Armed Services subcommittee he replied: "The wig given to Hunt by the Agency was a black wig. Where he got the red wig, I don't know." Testifying a few months later, in August 1973, before the Senate Watergate committee, Helms said it was "a brunette wig" and "the Agency technicians rather resented the fact that the red wig had been tied in with the CIA because it was such a lousy fit." Hunt testified that he and Liddy wore their wigs on the reconnaissance trip to California for the Fielding break-in, at least during the daylight hours.

MR. NEDZI: You wore the wig?
MR. HUNT: During the daytime, I believe so, yes, sir. It was very sunny out there.

Hunt also complained that the wig "was very hot" and uncomfortable.

the station chief should "cool it." Esterline, angry and uneasy, ordered Martinez to prepare a report in Spanish on his contacts with Hunt. But Martinez, warned by his case officer that anything he put in the report might bounce back and cause him trouble, wrote an innocuous cover story which went into the files.

The day after the Watergate break-in, Esterline cabled CIA headquarters with a background report on Martinez, since he had been arrested and was in the pay of the CIA. But having been told to "cool it," the station chief's memo omitted any mention of Howard Hunt. Headquarters acidly advised Esterline to keep in better touch with his operatives in Miami, advice that must have sent Esterline right up the wall.*

Martinez had two case officers, one named Gonzales and another named Richie, according to a document filed in federal court.† The second case officer took over in March or April of 1972.

But when Senator Baker attempted to question the first case officer, the CIA said he had been on "African safari" during all of June 1972, and had since been transferred to Indochina. He was never produced by the CIA. The second CIA officer did give testimony that remained classified; he said he had been rushed back to headquarters right after the Watergate break-in and told he would have to remain there all summer because of his knowledge about Martinez. A year later he was still assigned to CIA headquarters.

A second channel of possible CIA advance knowledge centered on the mysterious figure of Arthur James Woolstan-Smith, a private investigator in Manhattan with vague, shadowy ties to the CIA. A short, stocky, bald man who smoked a pipe, Woolstan-Smith was a

---

* In secret testimony to the Watergate committee, the assistant deputy director of plans said he had assumed in March 1972 that Hunt was involved in partisan political work for the White House, and that this is why he told Esterline to "cool it." After the Watergate break-in Esterline confronted his superior; he wanted to know why, if the CIA suspected Hunt of partisan activity, he, Esterline, had not been told to fire Martinez.

† Case officer Gonzales was the third Gonzales to flit through matters connected with Watergate. Virgilio Gonzales, the locksmith, was one of the original Watergate burglars. On May 30, 1975, John Reynolds, a member of the Canadian Parliament, reported that a Mexican named Virginio Gonzales said he had worked for the CIA from 1959 to 1964 and had, under CIA orders, tailed John Meier, a former employee of Howard Hughes, in Canada. Reynolds made his statement at a time when Canadian government officials were becoming increasingly concerned over charges that the CIA was running covert operations in Canada without Ottawa's permission. The day after Reynolds named Gonzales, the CIA issued a statement denying that Virginio Gonzales had "ever been connected" with the CIA. However, it should be noted that this was the same statement in which the Agency denied that Frank Sturgis had "ever been connected" with the CIA.

citizen of New Zealand with rumored links to both Canadian and British intelligence. He was a member of that hidden fraternity of private investigators who perform work for the large law firms in New York and Washington and for corporate clients. Many are graduates of federal intelligence agencies. They tend to know one another, and they have ways of knowing what is going on in their profession. It is not impossible to suppose, for example, that dealers in wiretap equipment might, after selling a large quantity of electronic devices to one investigator, mention that fact to another.

At any rate, on March 23, 1972, William F. Haddad, former Peace Corps official, former investigative reporter for the New York *Post* and a well-connected figure in New York Democratic circles, wrote to Lawrence O'Brien. Haddad informed the Democratic National Chairman that he was hearing "some very disturbing stories about GOP sophisticated surveillance techniques," and would O'Brien like to know more? O'Brien instructed an assistant, John Stewart, to get in touch with Haddad.

Haddad later testified in closed session before the Watergate committee that his information had come from Woolstan-Smith, who told him the Democratic National Committee headquarters was about to be or had been bugged, and that this activity was linked to the November Group, the advertising men handling Nixon's media campaign, and to "Cuban people." Haddad said he met at his office, 1 Columbus Circle, with Stewart and Woolstan-Smith sometime before the Watergate break-in. Haddad said that at the same time that he was alerting the Democratic National Committee, he also sent his information to Jack Anderson.

Stewart confirmed that he had talked to Woolstan-Smith by telephone in April about wiretapping attempts against the Democrats, but thought that the New York meeting with Haddad and Woolstan-Smith had taken place after Watergate, not before. But Woolstan-Smith, in his testimony, placed the date at April 26, 1972. Woolstan-Smith confirmed that he had warned Haddad about possible bugging attempts against the Democrats. He said it was Haddad, not he, who had brought up the possibility that Cubans were involved, and he said Haddad added that the Republicans might try to prove that the Democratic party was getting money from Cuba.

Woolstan-Smith said that he was a private investigator in Manhattan with excellent intelligence contacts, and that his New York offices had been used by the CIA to screen returning members of the Cuban brigade after the Bay of Pigs.* So he had done some work for

---

* Woolstan-Smith operated from offices at 441 Lexington Avenue under two names, Science Security Associates and Confidential Investigation Bureau. Each had a separate phone number.

the CIA, but when he was questioned by Senate investigators, he said he had no relationship with the Agency in April 1974.

He also said he had discovered that Gordon Liddy was a powerful figure in the November Group, which was accurate. He was extremely vague about how he had learned of the planned bugging attempt against the Democrats. But he said he had noted that some very odd things were going on at the local level; retail credit agencies were getting a lot of inquiries about political figures, for example, and a New York City policeman with a name "like Lasewitz" was everywhere.* He had also heard that James McCord was purchasing electronic equipment. Woolstan-Smith also said he knew that John Ragan was a Republican security officer and that he had learned sometime before March 1972 that McCord had replaced Ragan. He also said he knew that Ragan had worked for ITT in Chile.

So Arthur James Woolstan-Smith knew a great deal. He had ties to the CIA, and the CIA had a file on Woolstan-Smith. But the source of his information that the Democrats would be bugged, whether the CIA could have told him this, or whether Woolstan-Smith told the CIA—none of those questions were answered.

The Mullen Company and its president, Robert F. Bennett, provided a third possible channel of CIA knowledge about Watergate. Robert Bennett bought the Mullen firm early in 1971. He continued the company's cover relationship with the CIA and was introduced in April to the Mullen CIA case officer, Martin J. Lukoskie, to whom he reported thereafter. In July, Howard Hunt, who was already a Mullen employee, began working part-time for the White House Plumbers and part-time for Bennett and the Mullen Company.

About the time that Bennett took over the Mullen firm, fortune, in the guise of Howard Hughes, smiled upon him. From 1969 until February 1971 Lawrence O'Brien, later a target of the Watergate break-in, had been receiving $15,000 a month (which is $180,000 a year) as a Washington consultant to Hughes. O'Brien landed this plum through Hughes lieutenant Robert Maheu, who a decade earlier had been the CIA's liaison with the Mafia in the Agency's attempt to hit Fidel Castro. When Hughes broke with Maheu in November 1970, O'Brien soon lost the account. It went to Bob Bennett, who had come in contact with the Hughes organization in his job as an official of the Department of Transportation in the Nixon Administration.† Since Bennett was director of congressional liaison for the Transportation

---

* An apparent reference to Anthony Ulasewicz.

† In the summer of 1970 Frank W. (Bill) Gay, a top Hughes aide, contacted Bennett at the Department of Transportation to seek his help in blocking the dumping of nerve gas by the government near the Bahamas. Bennett was unable to stop the dumping, but he apparently impressed the Hughes people.

Department, Charles Colson at the White House kept in close touch with him. Colson encouraged Bennett to make the move to the Mullen Company.

Thus, Bennett brought the Hughes Tool Company account with him to the Mullen Company, which he had purchased from Robert Mullen, a Washington public relations man well known in Republican political circles. Mullen had done PR work for, among others, Henry Cabot Lodge in his bid for the Republican presidential nomination in 1964, and his company had flourished during the Eisenhower Administration. He had many friends in Washington, among them Richard Helms. Under the arrangements between the CIA and the Mullen Company, CIA agents worked overseas under deep cover in the Mullen offices in Europe and Asia. The benefits were mutual, since the CIA obtained commercial cover for its operations in places like Stockholm and Amsterdam, and the Mullen Company enjoyed the prestige of overseas offices with which to impress its clients.

In his book *Undercover*, Hunt claimed Mullen had promised to sell him an interest in the company. As a result, Hunt said, he was angered when Mullen sold the firm to Bennett instead.

As it turned out, according to the Baker report, the man who served Bennett as the Washington lobbyist for Hughes Tool was none other than Robert Oliver, the father of R. Spencer Oliver, the Democratic party official whose telephone was tapped by Howard Hunt's Watergate burglars.

In his book Hunt claimed that sometime after he had joined the Mullen firm, he dined one night with Mullen, Bennett, and Spencer Oliver. Hunt said that Mullen and Bennett had asked what he thought of Spencer Oliver as a possible partner, but that he had opposed Oliver, a Democrat, on the grounds that he would dilute the firm's Republican image.

Oliver disputed Hunt's version of these events in an interview early in 1976 in Washington. Watergate had complicated his life. He was a victim of the break-in and bugging of Democratic headquarters, and the episode had caused him a variety of personal and professional problems in the four years since his phone was tapped. Oliver had gone to work for the Democratic National Committee in 1967; he was soon elected president of the Young Democrats and became director of the committee's youth division. About the same time, he became active in organizing exchange programs of young political leaders in the NATO countries.

Oliver said that he had never had dinner with Howard Hunt. In the spring of 1970 "I had lunch with Mullen only, at the Metropolitan Club." He said his father had asked him to see Mullen, who "wanted to bring in Bennett and me as vice presidents." Oliver said he picked up Mullen at his office, and on the way out to go to lunch, Mullen may have introduced him briefly to Howard Hunt.

Oliver was not interested in the position because at the time he had already negotiated a grant from the Ford Foundation to fund the American Council of Young Political Leaders and to organize international exchange programs. By 1976, he said, the council was being funded at the rate of $250,000 a year by the State Department; Oliver was executive director.

In an interview with the author on November 15, 1974, Hunt was questioned about the coincidence that he knew or had met the man whose telephone he and his confederates had bugged in the Watergate. He confirmed that he had gone to Bennett at one point and objected to the talk of bringing Spencer Oliver into the Mullen Company.

"Was Spencer Oliver a specific target of the Watergate bugs?" Hunt was asked.

"He was not," Hunt replied, "because I did not know he was employed by the Democratic National Committee" at the time of the break-in. Hunt insisted, therefore, that he did not know that Oliver's telephone had been bugged.*

In the fall of 1971 Oliver had returned to the Democratic National Committee to serve as liaison with the party's state chairmen. He said the tap on his phone would have given the Republicans valuable political intelligence in June of 1972, including an up-to-the-minute delegate count.

If, despite Howard Hunt's denials, he did know that Spencer Oliver's phone had been tapped, that would in turn at least raise the question of whether Hunt had hoped for some reason to gain information that would discredit Oliver. The tap did in fact lead to results that were embarrassing to Oliver. When the White House transcripts were released, they included an April 14, 1973, conversation in which Ehrlichman told Nixon: "They—what they were getting was mostly this fellow Oliver phoning his girl friends all over the country lining up assignations."

Oliver said that this was untrue, but that his wife of course read about it and that it contributed to his marital difficulties and eventual separation. Although Oliver's telephone at the Democratic headquarters was connected to the switchboard—he did not have a private line —apparently its location afforded privacy. Secretaries at the committee therefore considered it "safe," because they used it for personal conversations. Alfred Baldwin, the former FBI man hired by McCord to listen in at Howard Johnson's across the street, said in an interview

---

* However, Oliver said that some months after the burglary, he met James McCord, who told him, "You were one of our secondary targets."

with the Los Angeles *Times* in October 1972 that some of these conversations were "explicitly intimate." "We can talk," a secretary would say; "I'm on Spencer Oliver's phone."

Almost everywhere one looked in the Watergate affair, there were ties to Robert Bennett and the Mullen Company. In the months before the break-in, Bennett was deeply involved with Hunt's White House political spying. It was Bennett who suggested that Hunt see Clifton De Motte about Chappaquiddick, and Bennett who handled the release of Dita Beard's statement from Denver disavowing her memo.

Although Bennett has denied that he knew in advance of the plan to break into the Watergate, he has testified that three days before the burglary, he was told that Howard Hunt wanted to bug George McGovern's headquarters. Bennett said he learned this from Thomas Gregory, a student whom Hunt had planted as a spy in Muskie headquarters and later in McGovern's entourage. Gregory had developed "moral uneasiness" about this work, Bennett said, and around June 14 came to him and said, "Well, they want to bug Frank Mankiewicz's office. They want me to help them." And Gregory, he said, was fearful of saying no to Hunt. Bennett apparently felt some personal responsibility for Gregory, who had been recruited by Hunt through Bennett's nephew. Bennett said that since Gregory was uncomfortable as a spy, he persuaded the young man to quit and delivered a letter of explanation from Gregory to Hunt.

After the Watergate break-in, Bennett was still in the thick of things; he served as a point of contact for Hunt and Liddy in the two weeks after the burglary, and on July 10 he reported his knowledge of Watergate in detail to his case officer, Martin Lukoskie, who submitted a long handwritten report to the CIA.

Bennett had also met Eric W. Eisenstadt, Lukoskie's superior at the CIA and chief of the Central Cover Staff. In a memo dated March 1, 1973, Eisenstadt said: "Mr. Bennett said also that he has been feeding stories to Bob Woodward of the Washington *Post* with the understanding that there be no attribution to Bennett. Woodward is suitably grateful for the fine stories and by-lines which he gets and protects Bennett (and the Mullen Company)."*

---

* Inevitably this led to wide speculation in Washington that Robert Bennett was Woodward and Bernstein's legendary "Deep Throat." "I have told Woodward everything I know about the Watergate case," Bennett later testified to a House subcommittee. Bennett claimed he helped Woodward because he wanted the Watergate story to come out, but he also emphasized to the CIA that Woodward's stories had not exposed the Mullen Company's relationship with the CIA. Bennett thus seemed to be trying to impress his CIA case officer with the idea that by serving as a source for Woodward, he had diverted the *Post* reporter from investigating or blowing the Mullen firm's cover.

In sum, the CIA provided extensive operational support to Howard Hunt in the months before Watergate, and during those months it learned through its agent Martinez that Hunt had been in contact with him in Miami and was up to something. It had a past relationship with Woolstan-Smith, who seemed to know that the Democrats would be bugged. And it was deeply involved with the Mullen Company, which employed Hunt and whose president, Robert Bennett, reported at intervals to his CIA case officer.

If despite all this the CIA had no specific advance knowledge of the Watergate break-in, it was certainly complaisant in helping the White House conceal the crime. Six days after the break-in, on the morning of June 23, 1972, Haldeman explained to Nixon that "the FBI is not under control,"—it was actually investigating the break-in—but the problem could be solved if Vernon Walters, the CIA's Deputy Director, called Acting FBI Director Patrick Gray and said "Stay to hell out of this . . . we don't want you to go any further on it."

"And you seem to think the thing to do is get them [the FBI] to stop?" asked Haldeman.

"Right, fine." Those two words, spoken by Richard Nixon and recorded by his own taping system in time became the "smoking gun," the incontrovertible piece of evidence that blasted him out of the White House fourteen months later.[*]

The conversation continued, sealing Nixon's doom:

H—They say the only way to do that is from White House instructions. And it's got to be Helms and to— ah, what's his name . . .? Walters.

P—Walters.

H—And the proposal would be that Ehrlichman and I call them in, and say, ah—

P—All right, fine. How do you call him in— I mean you just— well, we protected Helms from one hell of a lot of things.

The nature of those "things" remained a matter of speculation after the transcript was released, but the President, at least, felt that Helms was obligated to him.[†] And Nixon agreed to what Haldeman bluntly termed "the CIA turnoff" as the way to end Watergate.

---

[*] The United States Supreme Court ruled 8–0 on July 24, 1974, that Nixon must yield up sixty-four tapes demanded by Watergate Special Prosecutor Leon Jaworski. Among these were the June 23 tapes, which were released by Nixon on August 5; four days later he resigned.

[†] In a series of written answers to the Church committee, made public in March 1976, Nixon gave his own explanation of his mysterious remark. Nixon stated that early in 1972—which would have been about the time that the CIA was moving against Victor Marchetti—Helms had told him that a former CIA employee was planning a book that would expose a great deal of classified information about

Vernon Anthony Walters, the key figure in all of this, was no run-of-the-mill Army general; an impressively large, hawk-faced man in the Sidney Greenstreet tradition, he was an accomplished raconteur, fluent in seven languages. He had served as an interpreter to Presidents Truman, Eisenhower, and Nixon at numerous high-level diplomatic conferences, and he had a gift for moving nimbly down the corridors of power. As in the case of General Cushman, whom he succeeded, his career was closely linked with that of Richard Nixon. When Nixon's limousine was stoned and spat upon in Caracas, Walters was in the car with him. In his book *Six Crises*, Nixon recalled: "The shatterproof glass did not break but it splattered into the car. Walters got a mouthful and I thought for an instant, 'There goes my interpreter.'" In March 1972 Nixon had summoned Walters back from Paris, where he was senior U.S. military attaché, nominated him for three stars, and named him Helms's deputy.

Once Nixon had agreed to "the CIA turnoff," events moved swiftly. The Nixon-Haldeman meeting on June 23 ended at 11:39 A.M. Less than two hours later, at 1:30 P.M., Haldeman, Ehrlichman, Helms, and Walters were meeting in Ehrlichman's office in the White House. Later Walters wrote in a memo of the conversation that Haldeman explained that "the investigation was leading to a lot of important people and this could get worse." Haldeman, Walters wrote, then asked what connection the CIA had to the break-in, and Helms said none. Walters added: "Haldeman said that the whole affair was getting embarrassing and it was the President's wish that Walters call on Acting FBI Director Patrick Gray and suggest to him that since the five

---

the Agency. Nixon assured Helms of his "full support" for any CIA legal actions against the book. "As I recall," Nixon added, "it was in the light of this incident" that he had made his remark on June 23, 1972.

Nixon's explanation was not overwhelmingly persuasive. Nor was it the only cryptic remark he had made on June 23. In instructing Haldeman to have the CIA stop the FBI, Nixon said he should explain that "the President believes that it is going to open the whole Bay of Pigs thing up again" and "that they should call the FBI in and [unintelligible] don't go any further into this case period!" The strange reference to the Bay of Pigs arose later in the day during a second Nixon conversation with Haldeman. This time Nixon said, ". . . Hunt, ah, he knows too damned much . . . If it gets out that this is all involved, the Cuba thing it would be a fiasco. It would make the CIA look bad, it's going to make Hunt look bad, and it is likely to blow the whole Bay of Pigs thing which we think would be very unfortunate—both for CIA and for the country, at this time, and for American foreign policy. Just tell him to lay off. Don't you?" Since the Bay of Pigs had taken place eleven years earlier and was ancient history, it was rather puzzling. It was possible, of course that "Bay of Pigs" was a euphemism for CIA plots to murder Castro. There is some evidence, although inconclusive, that Helms may have told Nixon about the Castro murder plots in a White House conversation.

suspects had been arrested that this should be sufficient and that it was not advantageous to have the enquiry pushed, especially in Mexico, etc."* Helms, Walters wrote, said he had already talked to Gray the day before and assured him that the CIA was not involved and that no covert operations were jeopardized by the FBI investigation.

Despite this, Walters did exactly what he was told; he sped to the FBI, met with Gray only moments later, at 2:34 P.M., and informed him—in Walters own words—that while the FBI investigation "had not touched any current or ongoing covert projects of the Agency, its continuation might lead to some projects."

Gray seemed to get the message. The FBI chief said his problem was how to "low-key this matter" now that the investigation had already been launched. The quote is from another Walters memo, one of a series he wrote as a record of his conversations at the White House and at the FBI during this period. According to Walters, Gray added that "this was a most awkward matter to come up during an election year and he would see what he could do."† Walters then repeated his plea, warning that FBI probing "south of the border" could endanger "covert projects." Since five men had been arrested, Walters said—following his instructions from Haldeman precisely— it would be best to stop there.

A year later, when these events surfaced in May of 1973, the CIA with the help of Senator Stuart Symington managed to sell the idea to the news media and the public that the CIA had stoutly refused to assist the White House in blocking the FBI investigation of Watergate. Symington released a summary but not the text of the Walters memos. ("CIA RESISTED LENGTHY COVER-UP EFFORT BY WHITE HOUSE, HILL ACCOUNT REVEALS," the Washington *Post* bannered across eight columns on May 16.)‡

Walters' actions hardly seemed like standing up to the White House, but the Symington-CIA version died hard. The fact is, however, that on June 23, 1972, within a few hours of Nixon's order to use the CIA to turn off the Watergate investigation, the CIA's Deputy Director had delivered the message to the Director of the FBI. And

---

* Nixon and his men were worried about Mexico because, as Haldeman had informed Nixon that morning, some of the Nixon campaign money used to finance the break-in had been laundered through a Mexican bank.
† In *Rashomon* fashion, Gray placed a different interpretation on his conversations with Walters. He submitted his own memos to the House Armed Services subcommittee, disputing various points in the Walters memos.
‡ Three weeks later, however, Symour M. Hersh of the *New York Times* obtained and published the actual texts of the Walters memos, and they revealed a rather different picture of the CIA's role.

according to Walters, Gray said "he understood" and would study the problem to "see how it could best be done."

On Monday morning, June 26, Walters was back at the White House, meeting this time with John Dean. Walters, who had in the meantime talked with Helms, said the CIA was not involved in Watergate and "the Director wished to distance himself and the Agency from the matter." Dean said some of the burglars were getting scared and "wobbling," and he wondered if the CIA could pay their bail money. Walters argued that the scandal could become "ten times greater" if that were done.

Later John Dean was to shed interesting light on why the White House was dealing through Walters, not Helms. Ehrlichman, Dean testified, "told me that I should deal with General Walters because he was a good friend of the White House and the White House had put him in the Deputy Director position so they could have some influence over the Agency." When Dean reported back to Ehrlichman following his unsuccessful effort to get the CIA to pay the bail of the Watergate defendants, Ehrlichman, Dean recalled, said "something to the effect that General Walters seems to have forgotten how he got where he is today."

Two days after his first talk with Dean, Walters returned for a second meeting. Dean said bluntly that the problem was how to stop the FBI. Did Walters have any suggestions? Caught between Helms and Nixon, Walters walked the tightrope. He warned that Watergate was a "high-explosive bomb" that could, by involving the CIA now, become "a megaton hydrogen bomb." But he then volunteered that Watergate "already had a strong Cuban flavor and everyone knew the Cubans were conspiratorial" and interested in the attitude of both major parties toward Castro. The Cuban story might be "costly," Walters told Dean, but "plausible." Dean liked the Cuban suggestion, but said "it might cost half a million dollars."

Although Walters apparently did his best in these later meetings to fend off further misuse of the CIA by the White House, he had already delivered the crucial message to Gray. And although Walters warned Dean of the political dangers of dragging in the CIA, he did not convey these warnings to Gray. On the key issue, thus far the CIA was playing ball.

On the same day, June 28, Helms asked Gray not to interview two CIA officials, who as it happened knew a great deal about Howard Hunt's dealings with the CIA prior to the Watergate break-in. They were Karl Wagner, Cushman's assistant and a key figure, since he had sent up the red flags on Hunt just before the Fielding break-in, and John Caswell, executive officer of the Agency's European Division. In

October 1971 Hunt had telephoned Caswell and arranged to obtain CIA files relating to L'Affaire des Fuites, a leak of documents about Indochina from the French government in 1954. Hunt, pursuing the Ellsberg leak, apparently wanted to brush up on this French version of the Pentagon Papers.

In a memo to Walters on the afternoon of June 28, Helms wrote the most damning words of all. Repeating CIA policy toward the FBI investigation, he instructed his deputy: "In addition, we still adhere to the request that they confine themselves to the personalities already arrested or directly under suspicion and that they desist from expanding this investigation into other areas which may well, eventually, run afoul of our operations."

By early July, however, both Gray and Walters had become alarmed; they were being asked to cover up a crime and their own position had become precarious. In time-honored bureaucratic fashion Walters and Gray closed ranks to protect themselves and their respective agencies. On July 5 Gray telephoned Walters; he could not, he said craftily, stall the investigation unless the CIA put its request in writing. The next morning Walters went to see the FBI Director. He could not possibly write such a "spurious" letter, Walters explained. "Gray thanked me for my frankness and said that this opened the way for fruitful cooperation between us." There was safety in numbers; Gray made it clear that he and Walters would now stand together, for Gray could not "sit on this matter," it was too risky.

So it was not until July 6, two weeks after the first White House meeting attended by Helms and Walters, and almost three weeks after the Watergate burglary, that the CIA refused to go further in blocking the FBI probe—and this only after Gray had demanded something in writing. And at no point did Helms or Walters retract the initial warning to Gray to stop the investigation with the five arrested burglars. Instead, Helms reiterated this position in his June 28 memo to Walters.

So much for the CIA's resistance to Nixon's Watergate cover-up. Walters understood that the CIA was enmeshed in a cover-up; he admitted as much under oath to the House Armed Services subcommittee. John Dean, he said, "was obviously trying to cover up something, sir ... he was exploring the possibility of doing something illegal." Despite this, Walters admitted that it was not until May 1973, almost a full *year* later, that he informed the Department of Justice of the White House efforts to have the CIA stop the FBI investigation.

Helms insisted to the same subcommittee that he did not know the White House had asked him to lie to Gray. Yet he conceded he had already told Gray, before June 23, that the investigation did not endanger any CIA activities in Mexico. "I had no way of knowing I was being asked to lie," he said. ". . , I realize in hindsight it makes me look like a boob. I am sorry."

And Helms, with a straight face, assured the subcommittee that he and Walters had stood firm against the White House. "We held the line together all through these various feelers that were put out," he said.

In fact, the CIA continued to assist the White House cover-up of Watergate for another seven months. But in addition, the Agency consistently sought to conceal its *own* involvement, particularly the assistance it had given to Hunt.

The CIA's own cover-up had begun very quickly. The five Watergate burglars were arrested shortly after 2 A.M. on June 17, 1972. By nightfall the CIA knew that several of its former employees were involved. At 7:45 P.M. Arnold L. Parham, an FBI agent assigned to the Alexandria field office, called the CIA to ask for a name trace on "James Martin," who had been arrested while "demonstrating at the Watergate." This was undoubtedly a garbled version of the name Edward Martin, which McCord used as an alias. An hour later Howard J. Osborn, CIA director of security, was alerted by his deputy, who told him of the FBI call and of the fact that McCord's name was being mentioned in news reports of the break-in. Osborn went to his office at the CIA, although it was now about 9 P.M., and at 9:45 he called Parham back, who provided the names of McCord and the four other burglars. Parham also had more bad news; one of the burglars had a check in his hotel room signed by Howard Hunt. At 10 P.M., within twenty hours of the arrests, Osborn called Richard Helms and informed him that former CIA men Hunt and McCord appeared to be involved in the break-in.

It must have made Helms queasy to hear the news, for he knew that with his approval the CIA had been providing Hunt with spy equipment. Moreover, Helms knew what the press and public did not; Hunt's name did not surface publicly until two days later.°

On June 19 Helms discussed the Watergate burglary at his morning staff meeting at the CIA, and briefed his subordinates on the involvement of former CIA men in the break-in. From that day on, the Agency worked toward the twin goals of protecting the White House and itself. It systematically concealed evidence from U.S. At-

---

° Testifying before the Senate Watergate committee in August 1973, Helms was asked when he first got the news of the burglary and replied, "It is my impression that I heard about it, read about it in the newspapers and heard it on the radio." But it was so long ago, he added, he was not sure "just exactly who might have told me or how I might have heard it."

torney Earl Silbert, who was handling the Watergate prosecution, from
FBI agents investigating the case, and from the Justice Department. It
destroyed tapes. And it sought desperately to mislead Silbert about
the crucial fact that the White House had asked the CIA to aid Hunt.

On June 28, after Helms had dictated his memo to General Walters
urging the FBI to confine its investigation to the five suspects, he got
out of town. Helms left the country, and by design or not, went about
as far away as he could, to Australia. He stayed abroad for three weeks,
and during his absence—and in the months that followed—the CIA's
Watergate cover-up was handled by William Egan Colby.

Colby had returned to Washington from Vietnam in July 1971, the
same month that Howard Hunt was hired by the White House and
began getting his equipment from the CIA. In September, Colby was
named Executive Director of the CIA, directly under Helms. Colby
confirmed to the Senate Armed Services Committee in 1973 that he had
been put in charge of Watergate matters by Helms. "I was sort of the
chief of staff," he said, in answer to questions by Senator Edward M.
Kennedy, "drawing the staff together to produce the papers and take
the actions appropriate at the time, after June 1972, in the Watergate
affairs." Colby, in short, was the mechanic, the man who tried to contain Watergate for the CIA.

One of his first moves was to stiff-arm the FBI agents in Alexandria, in whose jurisdiction CIA headquarters is located. Arnold Parham, the agent who had telephoned the CIA the night of the burglary,
was running into a stone wall in his efforts to penetrate the CIA's
relationship to Hunt before the break-in. Unknown to Parham, Helms
and Colby had decided to hold back information from the Alexandria
field office, and deal only with the reliable Patrick Gray, who, after all,
understood that Watergate was an awkward problem in an election
year.

But Parham was persistent. Somewhere along the line he learned
about a mysterious "Mr. Cleo" who had been involved in some way,
and he began pressing the Agency for information. He didn't get any.
Finally, on July 28, Walters called on Gray and met with him alone.
He handed him a memo explaining that "Mr. Cleo" was Cleo Gephart,
the electronics engineer who had provided Hunt with the tape recorder
in August of 1971.

Colby later explained that the CIA had withheld information
from the investigating FBI agents about the help given to Hunt because "we were trying to keep CIA's name out of the publicity." The
best way to do that, he thought, was to provide reports only "at the
top level to Mr. Gray."

Howard Osborn, the CIA's security chief, testified that he prepared the memos for the FBI but that everything that was sent to the

FBI had to be cleared first with Colby. At one point, Osborn said, he got a call from Helms, who gave him a cryptic message: "About Karl Wagner, you forget about that, I will handle that. You take care of the rest of it." At the time he was puzzled, Osborn said, but later the pieces fell into place. "It was the business of the wig, the recorder, and the whole bit," he said. Helms, in short—according to Osborn— had instructed him to "forget about" reporting to the FBI that Hunt had received equipment from the CIA.

Sometime afterward, Osborn testified, Colby telephoned him to ask if he had a senior security officer " 'who I would put my hand in the fire for,' who is capable, discreet, that could work for him directly on a special phase of the Watergate incident." Osborn assigned Leo H. (Skip) Dunn, who "worked like hell" for Colby on Watergate but never, Osborn said, told him exactly what he had been doing.

The CIA and Colby went to incredible lengths to conceal the most dangerous truth of all—that it was the White House and John Ehrlichman specifically who had asked the CIA to assist Hunt. On July 7 Colby drafted a disingenuous memo to Gray, which went out over Walters' signature. The FBI had been asking about the CIA alias documents found on the burglars, and the Walters memo very briefly and sketchily confirmed that documents and "certain other operational support items" were given to Hunt in response to "a duly authorized extra-Agency request." The latter phrase was gobbledegook for the White House and John Ehrlichman, but Colby hoped to slip it by Gray, a fast ball that might just nip the inside corner.

"It was not believed necessary to volunteer to Mr. Gray how that authorization came about," Colby later explained to the Senate Armed Services Committee. But Earl Silbert wanted to know more; he feared that the burglars would claim that they were acting under CIA orders, and for that reason he needed to know precisely what relationship the defendants had had with the CIA.

In October, Silbert put a series of questions to the Agency's general counsel, and later that month Helms handed over a series of CIA memos and documents concerning Watergate to Attorney General Richard Kleindienst. But the memos did not reveal the White House role in asking help for Hunt. On November 27 Colby and John S. Warner, the CIA's general counsel, met with Silbert and Henry E. Petersen, the Assistant Attorney General in charge of the Criminal Division.

Silbert zeroed in on the "extra-Agency request" that had been made to the CIA to outfit Howard Hunt. What agency was involved? The CIA was the agency that had furnished the equipment to Hunt, Colby replied, with all the innocence of the kid who asks, "What spitball?" But that wasn't the question. Silbert wondered mildly if the CIA hadn't at least checked with anyone in the White House when the request was made. Colby stalled, ducked, and in his own words, "danced around the room several times for ten minutes to avoid becoming specific on this." Finally Colby admitted that the White House itself was the source of the "extra-agency" request that the CIA help Hunt. Colby said he "was then pinned by Silbert with a demand for the name," and he offered up the name of John Ehrlichman.

U.S. Attorney Silbert asked a lot of other questions, and the CIA prepared some more answers. On December 13, in the course of readying those answers, Colby paid a visit on General Cushman, who by now was Commandant of the United States Marine Corps. Colby brought with him the transcript of Cushman's original tape recording of his conversation with Hunt on July 22, 1971. At one point, the transcript showed, Hunt had dropped Ehrlichman's name and Cushman had said, "Yes, he called me." Shown the transcript, Cushman confirmed to Colby that the request to aid Hunt had indeed come from Ehrlichman.

Colby had not informed Ehrlichman that he had fingered him to Silbert. But somehow, Ehrlichman found out. On December 15, Helms and Colby were summoned to the White House for a meeting with Ehrlichman and Dean. Colby said he got the impression at the meeting "that Mr. Ehrlichman had heard that his name had been used in my conversation with Mr. Silbert, and I was the source of using his name."

At the White House meeting Colby explained how the CIA was handling the FBI by dealing only with Gray. Colby then related the details of his unfortunate meeting with Silbert; he had "danced around the room" to avoid mentioning Ehrlichman, but was finally "pinned" and provided the name. Colby tried very hard to convince Ehrlichman that he had not lightly yielded up his name.

But Ehrlichman clearly regarded Colby as a canary; he ordered that the CIA's written answers to Silbert, which the CIA officials showed to him and Dean, be delayed until he could have a little chat with General Cushman. Colby was instructed to have Cushman call Ehrlichman so that they could discuss the problem of the "alleged" telephone call requesting aid to Hunt. According to Colby, Ehrlichman said he could not remember calling Cushman; in fact, Colby thought Ehrlichman appeared "genuinely perplexed."

Colby later testified that he thought there might be some "legitimate confusion here between General Cushman and Mr. Ehrlichman, and that was a problem that could best be worked out between them." He added, "It was not all that important who made the phone call from the White House to General Cushman about this one little assistance for Mr. Hunt."

After the meeting Colby immediately called Cushman, as Ehrlichman had instructed. He told the general that Ehrlichman "did not remember" the 1971 telephone call. Colby suggested that Cushman call Ehrlichman "and reconstruct the event."

Cushman explained at a press conference in May 1973 that Colby had told him to write a memo about how the request was made to the CIA to aid Hunt "and send it *to Mr. Ehrlichman*, which I did." (Italics added.) It seemed an odd way to route the memo to Silbert. Colby thoughtfully provided his own secretary, Barbara Pinder, who had been Cushman's secretary, to type it. Cushman dutifully prepared a memo, dated January 8, 1973. In July 1971, it said, "I received a call over the White House line from either Mr. Ehrlichman, Mr. Colson, or perhaps Mr. Dean (I simply cannot recall at this late date just which one it was) stating that Mr. Hunt would call on me to ask for some support..."

Three names! Cushman was not getting the idea. Ehrlichman immediately telephoned the general after receiving the memorandum. As Cushman put it at his press conference, "he [Ehrlichman] said: 'I don't have any record of the call and I don't think we made one—I don't recollect it.' I said: Well, I don't have a piece of paper at this time to prove it so, out of fairness, I'll just say I don't recollect."

As for the first memo, Cushman said, "I tore it up at his [Ehrlichman's] request. It was agreed I couldn't recollect and I wrote one which just said I couldn't recollect."°

In the old movies about the United States Marines, Wallace Beery always saves the regiment and the honor of the Corps at the last moment, but this was real life, and the Commandant of the U.S. Marines picked up the telephone and called Colby's secretary again. It was back to the old drawing board. As the secretary's stenographic notes later recorded, Cushman told her: "I had a call from the White House, and they suggested that, since I do not know what name I am talking about, I simply state that."

Cushman, ever obliging, then prepared a second memo to Ehrlichman, dated January 10. "I cannot recollect at this late date who placed the call," Cushman wrote, "but it was someone with whom I was acquainted, as opposed to a stranger."†

° Cushman also got a phone call from John Dean, to whom Ehrlichman had shown the memo. Dean assumed that Ehrlichman had craftily arranged to insert Dean's name in the memo to help make sure that all three names would be taken out. Dean told Cushman he was "somewhat surprised" to find his name in the memo, since he had never before spoken to Cushman. Dean also said that Ehrlichman had suggested if Cushman could not remember who had called him, perhaps he should not mention anyone.

† Not until May 11, 1973, eleven months after Watergate, did General Cushman finally provide accurate testimony about who had telephoned him to assist Hunt:

This was more like it, and the second, no-names memo eventually made its way to Silbert. Colby's sworn explanations to the Senate Armed Services Committee of this whole sequence of events is surreal. It was up to Ehrlichman and Cushman to work out the problem of the telephone call, he testified. Yet, all along Colby had the transcript of the Cushman-Hunt meeting of July 22, 1971, in which Cushman explicitly stated that he had received a call from Ehrlichman.* Not only that, at the end of the transcript Cushman engages in a little ingratiating chit chat about Ehrlichman. "If you see John Ehrlichman, say hello for me," he trills at Hunt. "I will indeed," Hunt replies, "I expect to see him tomorrow." The chatter about Ehrlichman goes on for some time, with Cushman claiming at one point that Ehrlichman was "an old friend of mine."

Moreover, before Hunt met with Cushman, Cushman had informed Helms of the White House request and said the telephone call had come from Ehrlichman. Helms knew that, of course, because when he eventually instructed Cushman to cut off the aid to Hunt, it was Ehrlichman whom he told Cushman to call.

Despite his personal knowledge of the assistance given to Hunt, Helms, in his own Senate testimony, displayed marvelous vagueness about it all. When Senator Baker asked Helms whether he had known that the CIA gave Hunt alias documents and a disguise, Helms replied innocently, "Yes. There was a voice changer, wasn't it, and a wig?"

Helms even tried to convince Senator Sam Ervin that when Hunt asked for the disguise, "there was no intimation that this was undercover work." Ervin became somewhat agitated:

SENATOR ERVIN: Well, when a man undertakes to disguise himself as someone else, he is engaged in undercover work, isn't he?
MR. HELMS: Well, we run into a definitional problem, sir.
SENATOR ERVIN: Well, you didn't think that he applied for this voice alteration device in order to sing a different part in the choir, did you?

"About 7 July 1971, Mr. John Ehrlichman of the White House called me..." Cushman explained that earlier in May, the CIA had located the minutes of a staff meeting of July 8, 1971, in which Cushman had reported the call from Ehrlichman. It was the discovery of the minutes that led him to change his testimony again, Cushman explained. On February 5, 1974, Karl Wagner stated that he had finally located the actual transcript of Ehrlichman's call to Cushman, in a "brown folder containing ten stenographic notes" of Cushman's telephone conversations with members of the White House staff. Wagner said he discovered the notes at the bottom of the second drawer of his office safe.

* Helms and Colby were well aware of the existence of the transcript; it was specifically discussed at the June 19 morning staff meeting at which Helms briefed his senior aides on Watergate.

It was good theater, but the testimony tended to obscure a central point: for five months, with Helms and Colby pulling the levers, the CIA had managed to conceal from the FBI and the federal prosecutors the fact that it was the White House—and specifically the President's Assistant for Domestic Affairs—that had ordered the Agency to outfit Howard Hunt.

The casing photos of Dr. Fielding's office, Xerox copies of which rested in the CIA's files since August 1971, made even more snail-like progress in reaching the prosecutors. It was not, apparently, until January of 1973 that the photographs were turned over to the Justice Department. At that time the CIA also finally provided copies of the alias documents that had been given to Hunt.

The Xerox copies were obviously of excellent quality, for Henry Petersen, examining them before the Senate Watergate committee, said, "I recognize one which is a picture of Mr. Liddy in front of a stationery store which has the sign on the window 'Xerox copies while you wait.' I recognize that one. I recognize another one in which there is an address 11923 on the building, a car outside. I recognize another one in which there is written on it—two automobiles—reserved Dr. Fielding, reserved Dr. Rothberg."

Petersen insisted that the Justice Department, then prosecuting Daniel Ellsberg, did not know who "Dr. Fielding" was and did not connect the photos to the Ellsberg case. But Ehrlichman and Dean feared that someone *might* make the connection, and early in 1973 Dean asked Petersen whether the package could be returned to the CIA. Petersen said if that were done, a card would have to be left in the files stating that the material had been returned to the CIA.

Dean persisted, and on February 9 he telephoned James Schlesinger, who had replaced Helms a week earlier. Dean asked the CIA Director to retrieve the package of photos from Justice. Schlesinger huddled with Colby and Walters and decided it could not be done, and Walters so informed Dean. For one thing, Schlesinger felt it might violate a letter sent to federal agencies by Senate Democratic leader Mike Mansfield, asking that all material in their files relating to Watergate be preserved for the pending investigation of the Ervin committee. Returning the material to the CIA, and leaving a card in the files saying where it had gone, would, Schlesinger later testified, "quite obviously point an arrow at Langley."

Mansfield's letter, dated January 16, 1973, had reached the CIA while Helms was still Director. At the time, Helms and his secretary were busily cleaning out his files prior to his departure to be ambassador to Iran.

Although it was a closely held secret, the CIA Director had a taping system similar to the more famous one installed in the Oval Office by Richard Nixon. The CIA's system, in existence for about ten years, clandestinely recorded telephone and room conversations in the office of the Director, the Deputy Director, and an adjoining conference room known as the French Room.* The taping system was not automatic; a button had to be pushed to activate it. Seven floors down in the CIA building, the tapes would then begin to roll in a special recording room. The tapes were routinely transcribed, the transcripts filed, and the tapes reused. About a week after Mansfield's letter had been received, Helms's secretary asked him what should be done about the tapes and three file drawers full of transcripts covering his seven years as Director. "I said, 'Let's get rid of them,' " Helms testified.

Before doing so, Helms said, he and his secretary spot-checked the transcripts. Helms could not recall any relating to Watergate, although there is evidence that the transcripts included conversations with the President, Haldeman, and Ehrlichman. So everything was destroyed.† The Rockefeller Commission concluded that Helms had used "poor judgment" in destroying the tapes, but it may have been wrong about that. As the commission noted, "there is no way in which it can ever be established whether relevant evidence has been destroyed."

But there were other instances in which it was definitely established that Watergate evidence was in fact withheld by the CIA. From July to December 1972, McCord sent a series of letters to the Agency. The first letter, addressed to Helms and signed "Jim," was shown to the CIA Director by Howard Osborn early in August. Osborn told Helms he was not positive but was fairly sure the letter had come from McCord. Osborn testified he "felt very strongly that the letter should be turned over to the Federal Bureau of Investigation" but that Helms and Lawrence Houston, the Agency's general counsel, decided not to do so. Osborn said he was instructed to keep the letter in a secure place in his office and do nothing more.

In December, McCord sent several letters to Paul F. Gaynor, one of Osborn's assistants on the CIA's security staff. McCord warned that there was "tremendous pressure" to blame the Watergate operation on "the company," a euphemism for the CIA. Another letter, a copy of one

---

* When Cushman left and General Walters arrived to replace him as CIA Deputy Director in May 1972, Helms quietly removed the taping mechanism from Walters' office. "I didn't know Walters very well; I wouldn't have any control over it," Helms explained. "I didn't think it was necessary to him and I just had it taken out."

† The CIA, like the Pentagon and the State Department, destroys tons of secret papers each day. The tapes were shredded, pulverized, burned, or otherwise disposed of in a destruction area deep inside the CIA known as "the pit."

McCord sent to Jack Caulfield, warned: "If Helms goes and the Watergate operation is laid at CIA's feet, where it does not belong, every tree in the forest will fall. It will be a scorched desert."

A third missive from McCord, dated December 29, said: "I have evidence of the involvement of Mitchell and others, sufficient to convince a jury, the Congress, and the Press." This was rather interesting news, but it remained bottled up in the CIA. Houston later testified to the Nedzi subcommittee that he had advised Helms in August, after the first note was received, "that we had no legal responsibility to pass the letter on to any other authorities . . ."

MR. NEDZI: Isn't this really suppressing evidence?
MR. HOUSTON: No, sir, I did not consider it evidence at all.

Not until May of 1973, when CIA Director Schlesinger ordered his inspector general to investigate the Agency's handling of Watergate, did the McCord letters come to light. Osborn then told the inspector general about the letters.

Perhaps the most blatant example of the CIA's suppression of evidence occurred in what became known as "the Pennington affair." In August of 1972 the FBI's patient agent Parham in Alexandria asked the CIA for information about a man named Pennington who had once been McCord's supervisor. The CIA cheerfully forwarded a file on a former employee named Cecil H. Pennington who had no connection with McCord. It was some time, almost a year and a half, in fact, before the FBI learned that the man they wanted was one Lee Pennington, a close friend of McCord's.

And there was good reason for the CIA's throwing sand in the eyes of agent Parham. Lee Pennington, who had been a paid informant for the CIA's Office of Security for years, had gone to McCord's home shortly after the Watergate burglary and helped to burn documents linking McCord to the CIA. In the panic to destroy the documents someone forgot to open the flue, causing extensive smoke damage to McCord's home; one CIA witness said that "three rooms had to be repainted" afterward.

Pennington was an unlikely figure to be on a CIA retainer. Then close to eighty, but presumably still spry, he had retired from the FBI in 1953. He then went to work compiling files on domestic "subversives" for the American Legion's "National Americanism Commission," later moving to a job with the American Security Council. While with the American Legion, Pennington claimed to have "developed contacts throughout the United States who would feed information in to me." He said he had "70,000 confidential contacts" across the country, and often passed information along to the House Un-American Activities Committee. He was receiving $250 a month from the CIA, by "sterile" check, which could not be traced back to the government, apparently to pick up congressional hearings, press releases, and other openly available material, which was a very strange arrangement. Once a month Pennington would report to his case officer, Louis W. Vasaly, at the Burgundy Room, a restaurant in Chevy Chase.

While helping Mrs. McCord burn the documents, Pennington saw at least one that said "CIA" on the cover. When he returned to his own home, Pennington later claimed, he immediately telephoned the CIA to report what he had seen.

In January 1974 John Richards of the CIA inspector general's office was reviewing Watergate files in the Office of Security. Sooner or later he was bound to come across the Pennington file. So Osborn, according to subsequent testimony, issued instructions to remove the Pennington file. Two subordinates on Osborn's staff objected strenuously, and the decision was reversed.° The files were made available to Richards.

In November 1975 President Ford, as part of a larger shake-up of his Administration, suddenly dismissed Colby as CIA Director. But he asked Colby to stay on until his successor, former Republican National Chairman George Bush, could be confirmed. Having fired Colby, Ford then presented him with a medal.† The consensus in Washington was that Ford replaced Colby because the White House believed he had been too cooperative with the House and Senate committees investigating the CIA. In fact, given the revelations of domestic spying and foreign assassination plots, and the crunching pressures on the CIA, Colby had done a clever public relations job of defending the Agency. With his ice-blue eyes, and tightly contained manner—he seldom showed anger in public—Colby sat for hours, days, and weeks, testifying, answering the questions of congressional committees, and making speeches around the country. His strategy was to minimize; the domestic spying was not massive, the shellfish poison was only two teaspoons, and so on.

But the CIA's stock in trade is concealment and deception, and it was not surprising that the Director of the CIA, in answering his critics, consistently sought to mislead the public. To the CIA, it was just another operation. Within the basic framework of deception, Colby did a rather good job of it.

Colby was fired for the wrong reasons. He could justifiably have

---

° Prosaically, the two security officers reached their decision of conscience over cones at Gifford's, an old-fashioned local ice cream parlor.

† On January 26, 1976, as Colby was leaving office, Ford presented him with the National Security Medal, the nation's highest intelligence award. The White House, however, made no advance announcement of the ceremony, so reporters and photographers were unable to cover it.

been dismissed much earlier for the deliberate cover-up of the CIA's links to Watergate and the burglars, which he personally managed under Helms's direction, for approximately eight months.

The CIA's fingerprints were all over Watergate, even though it may have had no advance knowledge of the break-in. Afterward, however, the CIA did its best to cover up the burglary, the White House role, its assistance to Hunt, Nixon's misuse of the Agency to block the FBI investigation, and the CIA's own cooperation in that effort.

Like the CIA's own "Hydra" computer system, Watergate had a hundred tiny tentacles connecting the burglary and its central actors to Langley. Finding itself enmeshed in the worst political scandal in American history—no President resigned over Teapot Dome, after all —the CIA chose to do what would lead an ordinary citizen to jail. It concealed its knowledge of a crime.

"Mr. Hoover had no close regard for the Central Intelligence Agency."

—Charles D. Brennan, former
assistant director, FBI,
September 25, 1975

8
Vanished

The gray wooden house on Sixth Street had a spacious picture window in the living room, but there was little to distinguish it from the others on the block. It stood in a quiet upper-middle-class neighborhood of college professors and their families near the campus of the University of Colorado at Boulder, a peaceful place of bicycles, children, and shade trees. If the neighborhood was ordinary, the scenery was breathtaking, for the foothills of the Rocky Mountains rose majestically in the background.

The first trace of spring had come to the Rockies by mid-March 1969, when Thomas Riha, thirty-nine, professor of Russian history at the University of Colorado, vanished from this house. Before it was over, the repercussions of this fact had left the two most powerful secret agencies of the United States government locked in a bizarre controversy, and helped to set in motion a chain of events that ended, ultimately, in the resignation of the President of the United States.

From surface appearances, there was every reason to assume that Thomas Riha was a happy man. He was a published scholar and a respected member of the university faculty. Only five months earlier he had married Hana Hrushkovna, a twenty-four-year-old Czech who had been visiting the United States on a student visa. Riha, like his wife, had been born in Czechoslovakia. He emigrated to the United States after World War II and became a naturalized American citizen. He earned a Ph.D. at Harvard and taught at the University of Chicago before moving west to Colorado in 1967.

At the wedding reception at the Black Bear Inn, near Boulder, Riha had seemed ecstatic over his young bride. But some of the guests later remembered that there had been another, older and rather mysterious woman at the reception whom Riha referred to as "the Colonel."

Just after midnight on the morning of March 9, a week before Thomas Riha vanished, guests were leaving a party next door to the Rihas at the home of Professor Richard Wilson. One of the guests, Professor Robert Hanson, saw Mrs. Riha standing at a first-floor window in her house, screaming for help. He ran through the snow and pulled her out through the window. Hanson smelled a strong odor of what he thought was chloroform. Hana Riha, sobbing, took shelter with the Wilsons.

When the police arrived to investigate the trouble, they were met at the Rihas' house by the professor and a woman. The woman, whose manner was both forceful and imperious, loudly claimed to be connected with U.S. Immigration—although she could produce no official identification—and told the police that Mrs. Riha's visa had expired. The police found a jar of ether and several ether-soaked gauze pads in Mrs. Riha's bedroom, but concluded, rather sappily, that there was "no evidence of foul play."

But Hana Riha did not move back into her house after that night. The new life she had started in Boulder with her American husband had turned into a nightmare, the house a grotesque stage setting for a horror story directed by the woman her husband called "the Colonel." For weeks the woman, who used the name Galya Tannenbaum, had been pressuring Hana to sign "immigration" papers. A month earlier Thomas Riha had quietly filed for a divorce. He also told a few friends that his wife's visa had expired and that she was about to be deported.

Earlier on the night that she was pulled screaming from her window, Mrs. Riha had come home after staying at a hotel all day to avoid seeing Mrs. Tannenbaum. She heard whispered voices in the study, and perhaps sensing danger, went directly to her bedroom and locked the door. During the night she awoke to a strange odor wafting into the room. There was a hissing sound, and strong fumes were coming in either from a furnace vent or from under the bedroom door. She felt dizzy, opened a window, broke the screen, and cried for help.

That night from the neighbors' house she telephoned New York and spoke to David Regosin, a lawyer who had helped her aunt and uncle bring her to America. Regosin later said Mrs. Riha was frightened and told him "was very much concerned about her personal safety in the presence of Mrs. Tannenbaum." Soon afterward, through arrangements made with Regosin's help, Hana Riha safely left Boulder for New York City, where she remained and got a job in a bank.

On March 14, a week after Mrs. Riha had escaped from her bedroom, Professor Riha attended a party at the home of a friend in Boulder. He left about 12:20 A.M., climbed into his small foreign car, and drove off. The next day was Sunday, and friends of Riha's came looking for him when he failed to keep a dinner engagement. They found no one at home, but they peered through a window and saw the kitchen table set with a cereal bowl, dishes, and silverware, apparently put there for a breakfast that Riha never ate. At noon on Monday, Riha failed to attend a faculty meeting; on Tuesday he did not show up for his classes.

As Riha's friends became increasingly worried about his disappearance, strange things began to happen to his possessions. What looked like the missing man's signature showed up on documents authorizing the sale of his car and house. His art works, appraised at almost $20,000, were donated to the Denver Art Museum by a Mrs. Galya Tannenbaum.

Five months after Riha's disappearance, royalty checks from the University of Chicago for Riha's three-volume work *Readings in Russian Civilization* were deposited by Mrs. Tannenbaum in a Denver bank. The checks were endorsed to her with the signature "Thomas Riha."

Whether or not Riha was still alive, it was by now apparent that Mrs. Tannenbaum had exercised a strange and sinister influence on the Czech-born college professor. Riha had told friends that she was a "colonel" in Army intelligence, a masquerade that Mrs. Tannenbaum encouraged by wearing a trench coat with eagles on the shoulders and swooping into houses through the window rather than by the front door. Those who came in contact with "the Colonel" apparently shared a common emotion; they feared her.

And possibly with good reason, for on June 18 one of her friends, Gustav F. Ingwersen, seventy-eight, a Denver inventor and plastics engineer, was found dead in his home of potassium cyanide poisoning. In his will Ingwersen left Mrs. Tannenbaum a cuckoo clock, a color television, and a dinosaur bone.

On September 13, another friend of "the Colonel's," Mrs. Barbara Egbert, fifty-one, was found dead in her Denver apartment. An autopsy was performed. It disclosed traces of cyanide in her body.

In October Mrs. Tannenbaum was charged with forging Gustav

Ingwersen's will. Over the next several months she was arrested and jailed twice on charges of forging Riha's name on the deeds for the sale of his car and home, and on a check she used to pay for a charter airplane flight to Texas more than four months after Riha had vanished. In March 1970 the case took an even more ominous turn. Denver District Attorney James D. (Mike) McKevitt revealed that a gold wedding ring had been found in the home of Gustav Ingwersen. It belonged to Thomas Riha.*

In July Mrs. Tannenbaum was committed to the Colorado State Hospital at Pueblo by a court that found her mentally ill. And who was this woman who had apparently convinced an intelligent man, an associate professor at the University of Colorado, that she was an officer in Army intelligence? One psychiatrist testified that Mrs. Tannenbaum claimed to have had a dozen identities in her lifetime. He said she professed to be a retired intelligence officer, with the rank of colonel, who had made false passports and spirited persons out of Czechoslovakia to the West. She also claimed to have worked for the CIA and the FBI.

At her sanity trial in December her eleven-year-old son testified that he understood his mother was a general in the Army who often went to Vietnam. The boy also said his mother told him that she had designed the Mercury spacecraft and had a car with bulletproof glass, reinforced steel, and guns.

It was a sad story, but what made Mrs. Tannenbaum's influence over Riha all the more puzzling was that she was hardly an attractive woman or a likely candidate for a Mata Hari. Although a year or two younger than Riha, she was dumpy, gray-haired, and dowdy, and wore unflattering butterfly glasses. She was born, or so it appeared from her police record, as Gloria Forest. She had served two prison terms in Illinois in the sixties, including one for forgery, and had been arrested a decade earlier in Texas using the name Gloria Ann McPherson. She had been married in Chicago, and later lived there with a man named Leo Tannenbaum, a commercial artist whose last name she was now using. She had four children. She claimed to have known Thomas Riha in Chicago and to have followed him to Colorado.

But what was particularly disturbing, maddening, about the case to Riha's friends was that official agencies seemed to take little interest in his disappearance. And Dr. Joseph R. Smiley, the president of the University of Colorado, seemed oddly complacent about the fact that Riha had vanished from the face of the earth.

About a month after Riha disappeared Dr. Smiley announced

---

* The ring was inscribed "To Tomas from Hana." Mrs. Riha said she had made the wedding band herself in the summer of 1968 at a relative's dental laboratory in New York City. She had met and become engaged to Riha early that summer.

that he had been told by "reliable sources" in Washington that Riha was "alive and well." Smiley repeatedly refused to say what agency of the federal government had given him this assurance. In his smooth Southern accent, he would only repeat, "A confidence is a confidence."

It was all so clandestine and spooky that it was not too difficult to figure out which agency of the federal government had passed along this assurance to Dr. Smiley and buttoned him up so tightly. Only the CIA would have sufficient cloak-and-dagger mystique to make a Smiley come in from the cold.

The Boulder police appeared to share Dr. Smiley's lack of concern. Lieutenant Ralph Ruzicka, who eventually did investigate Riha's disappearance, at first explained to the press that "an agency" had told the Boulder police "not to worry." He declined to identify the agency. A group of Riha's colleagues on the university faculty filed a formal report on his disappearance with the police, but heard nothing more. Captain Willard Spier of the Boulder police said some months later that his "understanding" was that Riha had "disappeared of his own accord" and there was "no use wasting time looking for him just as a missing person."

The reason that Dr. Smiley had issued his public statement was that the CIA had in fact quietly told him that Thomas Riha was alive and well. The man who had acted as the conduit for that assurance was Michael M. Todorovich, the CIA's station chief in Denver.°

Not all of the facts in the complex case are clear even now, but the available evidence suggests that Todorovich, in turn, later claimed to have received his information about Riha's being safe from an agent in the FBI's Denver office. In any event, by early 1970 Todorovich found himself in the eye of a hurricane, the key figure in a confrontation that was fast building over the case between the CIA and the FBI in Washington.

In Colorado, pressure had been mounting on public officials to disclose what they knew about the disappearance of an American citizen from his home. Riha's friends were asking how this could happen in the United States and demanding that Smiley explain himself. Reporter Fred Gillies of the Denver *Post* was doggedly pursuing the story, and publishing stories suggesting that both the CIA and the FBI were somehow mixed up in the affair.† The fears of Riha's friends

---

° Then in his early fifties, Todorovich was a career intelligence operator who had served in the Balkans during World War II with the Office of Naval Intelligence. He had also been in the Soviet Union for ONI. He had an ideal job in Denver, the prestige of a big-city domestic CIA station without the pressures of a Los Angeles or a New York, and the climate was nice.

† Denver police said that the police in Boulder, quoting the FBI, had told them not to worry about Riha. Denver police detective Mike Allegretto said, "Boulder

for his safety were not assuaged when in January 1970 Mrs. Tannen-baum told Gillies in an interview that Riha was fine and would be returning to Denver later that month. He didn't. Gillies also reported that Riha might have some intelligence connection—that while on a visit to Prague in 1958, he had been approached by a Communist-bloc intelligence agent named Mr. Chrpa (Mr. Cornflower in Czech) who had attempted to recruit him.

By early 1970 Denver District Attorney Mike McKevitt had moved into the case. McKevitt, a combat intelligence officer in the Air Force during the Korean War, was a short pudgy man with glasses who affected a sort of Irish-tough-cop image. He was slightly pugnacious, even a little theatrical, but he knew a good case when he saw one. (Later in the year McKevitt, a Republican, ran for Congress, was elected, and served one term in the House.) McKevitt also knew where to begin: he would ask Smiley to disclose which agency had told him Riha was "alive and well."

Todorovich was alarmed; under subpoena, Smiley might be forced to reveal his source. Todorovich went to the Denver FBI office and urged that an FBI agent accompany him to McKevitt's office to attempt to persuade the DA not to subpoena Smiley. A heated argument erupted in which an FBI agent apparently denied that the Bureau had ever given the CIA the assurances that were passed to Smiley. The FBI agent refused to accompany Todorovich to the DA's office.

So he went alone. When Todorovich walked in the door, it was Mike McKevitt's first contact ever with the CIA. Six years later McKevitt, practicing law in Washington, remembered the meeting vividly. "The local CIA guy [Todorovich] knew all about me," he said. "The CIA brought in a guy who knew my dad. It was spooky; of course it could have been a coincidence, but he knew my dad." Todorovich, McKevitt recalled, was "stocky, five-foot-ten, partially bald. He looked like an ex-football player, which he had been. He had played at Gonzaga with my dad. He was a pleasant guy; he seemed to have grown up in North Spokane, because he knew the Boone Avenue gang. That's where the Irish were in North Spokane."

"'We're both Mikes,'" McKevitt remembered his visitor saying, "'but I knew you as Jim.'" That, said McKevitt, "really impressed me," since very few people knew him as Jim, a name he had dropped when

---

police told us that the FBI told them to forget about Riha, because they knew where he was and that he was alive and well." But the FBI flatly denied that it had ever told any such thing to police either in Boulder or in Denver. The CIA denied knowing anything about Riha. But Professor Stephen Fischer-Galati of the University of Colorado said he had been told by the CIA in April 1969, soon after his colleague had vanished, that Riha was safe and had left Boulder voluntarily.

he picked up the nickname Mike in the Air Force. Todorovich, Mc-Kevitt said, explained that there had been a "misunderstanding" between the CIA and the FBI over the Riha case but would not go into details. "He said it would not benefit cooperation between these two national security agencies if I dug into this aspect." McKevitt said his visitor warned that if he persisted, the result would be "jeopardy of the ongoing relationship between those two agencies." He said Todorovich never asked him to "stop investigating or to lay off" but "he appealed to my national concern." McKevitt added, "He wanted me to talk to Smiley and have Smiley say that it was all a mistake when he [Smiley] said that Riha was alive and well." The district attorney was impressed with his visitor's arguments.

McKevitt had previously been unsuccessful in his efforts to talk to Smiley, who by this time had left Colorado and become president of the University of Texas at El Paso. But sometime after the meeting he got Smiley on the phone. And on February 12 McKevitt issued a public statement saying that there was "no substantial basis in fact" for Smiley's April statement. It had all been the result of "a misunderstanding and an honest mistake," he said. Because he had promised Smiley, McKevitt added, "I cannot identify the national agency" that had supposedly given the assurance about Riha to Smiley.[*]

The Boone Avenue gang had done its work well, but it was too late. By this time, a rip-roaring feud had broken out in Washington between the CIA and the FBI. The noise was so loud that it soon reached the ears of J. Edgar Hoover. Furious, Hoover demanded that the CIA disclose the identity of the FBI agent who had allegedly told Todorovich that Riha was "alive and well." Todorovich, knowing that any FBI man he named would be banished to some FBI Siberia, refused to name the agent. Summoned home by Richard Helms, Todorovich still declined to name his source and offered to resign.

Helms then wrote a three-page letter to Hoover on February 26, 1970, noting that "you wish to have the identity of the FBI agent who was the source of certain information communicated to an employee of this Agency." Helms then assured Hoover he had ordered Todorovich "to report to me in person" about the Riha case. Helms said he

---

[*] As McKevitt dug into Riha's background, he developed something less than an admiration for the missing professor. At the time of Riha's disappearance, McKevitt said, he was having an affair with a faculty wife. McKevitt clearly disapproved of Riha's life style; he saw him as a ladies' man with Continental manners who took advantage of professors' wives. He would, McKevitt said, pretend an interest in them only to get them in bed. He would play the piano and read poetry to them by candlelight. It was not, McKevitt said, the way Americans lived. I asked McKevitt what he thought had happened to Riha. "He's dead," McKevitt replied. But he added that he was only speculating.

had requested Todorovich "to reveal the identity of his source," but that "as a point of honor and personal integrity" Todorovich was "adamant that he could not disclose the identity of his source."

The purpose of Todorovich's visit to the district attorney, Helms told Hoover, was to "remove pressures" on Smiley and to prevent the possible serving of a subpoena on the university president. The CIA agent also hoped to correct the DA's "erroneous impression of the roles of the CIA and the FBI, thereby eliminating further adverse publicity."

Helms noted that Todorovich had called on the FBI office in Denver to try to get an FBI agent to accompany him, but that an "oral exchange" took place in which an FBI man "proceeded to challenge the veracity of Mr. Todorovich." But, Helms pointed out, Todorovich had gone on to see McKevitt alone and had persuaded the DA to issue a statement that had calmed the public.

Then, attempting to placate Hoover, Helms added that "poor judgment" had been employed in passing the information about Riha to Smiley and McKevitt without "specific FBI approval." It would not happen again, Helms said. Although he was sure Todorovich had "acted honestly" and in the interest of preserving CIA-FBI relations, Helms said he was "taking administrative action" against him.

Helms closed by hoping "this recent incident" would not impair vital cooperation between the two intelligence agencies. And he pleaded with Hoover to continue to work with the CIA "in an atmosphere of mutual respect."

The Director was not appeased. He scribbled various acerbic comments in the margin of the letter. At the bottom, under Helms's signature, Hoover wrote magisterially: "This is not satisfactory. I want our Denver office to have absolutely no contacts with CIA. I want direct liaison here with CIA to be terminated and any contact with CIA in the future to be by letter only. H."

With a stroke of the pen, because of a dispute that grew out of the disappearance of a college professor, J. Edgar Hoover had broken off liaison with the CIA. It meant that Sam Papich, the respected FBI official in Washington who had long served as liaison with the CIA, was virtually out of a job.° Some months later, around July of 1970, Hoover cut off liaison with all other intelligence agencies; according to William Sullivan, Hoover did this so he could not be accused of discriminating against the CIA.†

° The break was not total; secure telephones were installed and some contacts continued on the working level. But formal liaison between the FBI and the CIA was not restored until after Hoover's death in 1972.

† Sullivan told the author, "Here's what happened: We used to say nobody will ever believe this. When he cut off relations with CIA it was very damaging. You

Without mentioning any names or the location, Helms obliquely referred to the Denver case and its aftermath in testimony to the Senate Foreign Relations Committee in 1973. But his version differed significantly from the account he had given to Hoover: "He [Hoover] became irritated with me because I would not oblige a member of the Agency to inform him which one of his agents in Denver, Colorado, had given our man some information. I saw no reason to put my fellow in this position. Mr. Hoover could very well have investigated his own office and asked his own employees who had talked to a fellow from the CIA, but in any event he declined to do it and I stood my ground at which point apparently in a fit of pique he simply said, 'Well, my liaison officer isn't coming over to the CIA any more.' "

Like so many facets of the Riha case, the basis of the information that the CIA passed on to Smiley remains cloudy. One possibility, of course, is that the FBI was relying on information from the Boulder police—who in turn may have relied on the word of Galya Tannenbaum.

Sam Papich had good reason to know the facts of the Riha case, since he retired from the FBI in its wake. Before leaving the FBI, Papich pleaded fervently with Hoover to restore liaison with the CIA. Hoover refused.

"I think it was one of the university officials who came to the CIA man—the overt man who was stationed out there—and asked him if he could find out through his government contacts what may have happened to the fellow," Papich said. "And the CIA man called one of his FBI friends and asked him if he knew anything about the case. I think one of the FBI agents checked with the Denver Police Department and got the story that the man had been having some wife problems and decided to get away for a while. That was passed back to the CIA man. He gave it to the university official without disclosing his source, and the official thereupon gave it to the press. The Denver DA went to the university official and asked him for the identity of his source. The university official came back to the CIA man—the Marx Brothers could have handled this one—then the CIA man goes to the FBI chief out there and suggests they both go to

---

have to have on a working level a good relationship, so we continued surreptitiously, underneath the table, to do business as well as we could. Nevertheless, criticism reached Hoover that he was discriminating against CIA. So you know what he did? One bright morning he just issued an edict to abolish the entire liaison with the Army, the Navy, the Air Force, Internal Revenue, and everybody else. He retained only one liaison, with the White House. Then he was in a position to say, 'I'm not discriminating against the CIA. I've cut out liaison with everybody except the White House.' It was one of those unbelievable damn things. It was a nightmare."

the Denver DA and tell them neither one is investigating, they don't know where the guy is, and all they knew they got out of the Denver Police Department. Thereupon the FBI man took another tack; he wanted to know who was the FBI agent who gave him the story. The CIA man refuses; that becomes a heated issue, goes back to Washington and is reported to Mr. Hoover. Mr. Hoover demands the identity of the FBI agent, the CIA refuses to identify the man, Mr. Hoover breaks off the relationship."

Scott Werner, a gray-haired, mustached, and distinguished-looking man who headed the FBI Denver office when Riha vanished, had retired to California by 1976. He refused to discuss the case.°

Michael Todorovich retired from the CIA after the Riha case, but remained in Colorado. He denied that he had left the CIA because of the controversy over his role. He said he had retired because of "bad arthritis," and described it as "a medically mandatory retirement." Todorovich declined, however, to discuss the case, or to answer questions about his own actions or about what happened to Riha. He referred questions to the CIA. "The story is there," he said. "If they put me in an unfavorable light, then that's how it will be. I did my job in terms of the best interests of the country. I have no compunctions about what I've done. I've closed the book on the Riha case."

Senator Gary Hart of Colorado questioned Charles Brennan, the former head of domestic intelligence for the FBI, about Riha when Brennan appeared before the Church committee. "My recollection is that he left this country voluntarily," Brennan said. There was no indication that Riha had been "spirited off by Communist agents." The CIA's James Angleton told the committee he "heard speculation" that Riha "was in Czechoslovakia."

Galya Tannenbaum could not testify. On March 7, 1971, in the Colorado State Hospital at Pueblo, she swallowed sodium cyanide and died. A male patient at the mental hospital claimed she told him she had used cyanide to kill three persons, including Riha, and that she had wrapped his body in a plastic bag and placed it in a Denver sewer. Just before she died, Mrs. Tannenbaum said to her doctor, "Of everything I've done, I didn't kill Riha." She was also quoted as saying, "I didn't kill him. That son of a bitch—he's in Russia. He just made it."

° Todorovich never disclosed the name of the FBI agent who was allegedly his source. However, at least one FBI agent who reportedly gave assurances about Riha's well-being was partially identified. Ralph Ruzicka, who was with the Colorado Bureau of Investigation in 1976, said in an interview that an FBI agent named "Smithie" had told him, while he was still with Boulder police, "Don't worry about Riha." Ruzicka said "Smithie" later denied making this statement and said, "Don't quote me."

As a senator from Colorado and a member of the Church committee, Gary Hart pressed the CIA, the FBI, and other U.S. intelligence agencies for information about Riha and the CIA-FBI dispute that followed his disappearance. The CIA provided both classified and unclassified answers to Hart. On the basis of reviewing both the secret and open material, Hart concluded that neither Riha nor Tannenbaum had ever worked for or been in contact with the CIA, FBI, Army intelligence or any other U.S. intelligence agency. Hart added, "Thomas Riha is, most probably, living somewhere today in Eastern Europe, possibly in Czechoslovakia. He was sighted there in 1973."

The CIA released to Hart a heavily censored memo from the Domestic Collection Division dated March 13, 1974, and captioned "Sighting of Thomas Riha." The document, with all names of individuals masked out, said that a CIA source told the Agency that he had learned from another person that Riha had been seen in Czechoslovakia. The other person, whom the CIA called "Ident 3," had "learned of Riha's presence in Czechoslovakia from the person who actually sighted him, Ident 4. . . . According to Ident 4 after sighting Riha Ident 4 checked with a friend and confirmed that Riha was actually in Czechoslovakia."

Rick Inderfurth, Hart's legislative assistant, who pulled together the material on Riha from the intelligence agencies, was asked why, on the basis of the CIA report, the senator had issued the unqualified statement that "Riha was sighted" in Czechoslovakia in 1973. Inderfurth said the identities of the three individuals cited in the classified version of the CIA report were persuasive.

There the matter rested until July of 1976 when Dr. Robert F. Byrnes, professor of Russian history at the University of Indiana, at Bloomington, told the Denver *Post* that the supposed sighting of Thomas Riha had occurred in a hotel in Bratislava, Slovakia. Byrnes elaborated in an interview with the author. "A former student of mine, a Czech living in America now, told me that a friend of his had seen Riha. The former student is perfectly reliable; the friend, also a former Czech, had been visiting Czechoslovakia and saw Riha in a hotel. He told my former student, who told me."

Byrnes said his former student asked that "his name be kept confidential," and that he, Byrnes, did not even know the name of the person who supposedly spotted Riha. The Indiana professor said that in 1973 he had told a number of Riha's friends about the reported sighting. One, Donald Fanger, a professor of Russian literature at Harvard, sent him a photograph of Riha and asked that it be passed along to the person who supposedly saw the missing scholar. "I turned it over to my former student, who turned it over to his friend, who said it was Riha," Byrnes said.

Nevertheless, Byrnes expressed some skepticism about the report. The person who claimed to have encountered Riha had not seen him "for twenty to twenty-five years. Also, I don't know how far away he was. He didn't talk to him [Riha]."

Although it seemed apparent that the CIA document released by Senator Gary Hart referred to Byrnes, his former student and the latter's friend, Byrnes denied that he was the direct source of the CIA file. Since he had mentioned the matter to many friends, "others may have been the source of that," he said. "A great many people knew about the sighting. I didn't go to CIA and tell them about the sighting." In fact, Byrnes insisted, "I have not passed on the name of the student to anyone, including the government." That only served to compound the mystery, since the CIA document suggested that the Agency knew the name of the former student *and* his friend.

The world of intelligence was not entirely unfamiliar to Byrnes; he said that he had worked for the CIA from 1951 to 1954 during the Korean War in the Office of National Estimates, which performs intelligence analysis rather than covert operations. He said he had had no "particular" relationship with the CIA since that time, although he occasionally lectured there.

The irony of all this is that in 1969, when the CIA informed Joseph Smiley that Thomas Riha was alive and well, it apparently had no such information in its files. It was not until four years later, in 1973, that Riha was allegedly seen in Czechoslovakia by the friend of a friend of Dr. Robert F. Byrnes.

On June 5, 1970, only a little more than three months after Hoover broke off liaison with the CIA over the Riha case, Richard Nixon summoned the chiefs of all U.S. intelligence agencies to his office in the White House and read them the riot act: they were failing to provide the information he wanted on the antiwar movement and domestic dissent. Those present, in addition to Nixon, were Haldeman and Ehrlichman; Hoover and Helms; Vice Admiral Noel Gayler, director of the National Security Agency; Lieutenant General Donald V. Bennett, director of the Defense Intelligence Agency; and Tom Charles Huston of the President's staff. "The President," General Bennett later testified, "chewed our butts."

The FBI-CIA breach over the Riha case was apparently on Nixon's mind. In later testimony to Senate and House committees, Huston described the meeting. The President, Huston said, expressed his concern about the lack of coordination between the intelligence agencies. Helms and Hoover explicitly assured the President there was good coordination. Huston sat there silently seething, knowing that Hoover had cut off liaison with the CIA.

Nixon told his intelligence chiefs he wanted a plan to improve the collection of intelligence about radicals and protesters.* The tone of the session can be gleaned from a portion of the talking paper that Huston prepared for Nixon for use at the meeting:

"We are now confronted with a new and grave crisis in our country—one which we know too little about. Certainly hundreds, perhaps thousands, of Americans—mostly under 30—are determined to destroy our society."

The President named Hoover chairman of a new committee to draft an intelligence plan. And he appointed Tom Charles Huston to oversee its work.

William Sullivan, who headed the FBI's domestic intelligence efforts, said there was "a direct relationship" between Hoover's decision to cut off relations with the CIA and the drafting of the Huston Plan. The break in relations over the Riha case, he said, was one factor that led to the White House meeting.

But Sullivan downgraded Huston's role. "He didn't conceive any plan. All the committee did was draw up a document recommending the reinstitution of FBI programs that had been in effect for years"—programs that Hoover had curtailed since the mid-sixties. After the June 5 meeting, Sullivan said, "Hoover came back and called me in. He was very distressed." Hoover considered the meeting critical of both the FBI and himself, and "he was very upset. He didn't want any part of this thing. But here he had been made chairman and he couldn't avoid it."

On June 8 Hoover met with the other intelligence directors in his office; he said it seemed that President Nixon wanted an historical summary of unrest in the country. Huston responded that Hoover had misunderstood; Nixon wanted changes in methods of intelligence col-

---

* In a statement on May 22, 1973, Nixon offered his rationale for the Huston Plan. In the spring of 1970, he said, "a wave of bombings and explosions struck college campuses. . . . Rioting and violence on college campuses reached a new peak after the Cambodian operation and the tragedies at Kent State and Jackson State . . . Gun battles between guerrilla-style groups and police were taking place."

In an oblique reference to FBI "black bag" jobs, Nixon added, "Complicating the task of maintaining security was the fact that, in 1966, certain types of undercover FBI operations that had been conducted for many years had been suspended." Then Nixon made a cryptic reference to the conflict that had developed over the Riha case, but he did not mention it by name and provided no details: "At the same time, the relationships between the FBI and other intelligence agencies had been deteriorating. By May, 1970, FBI Director Hoover shut off his agency's liaison with the CIA altogether."

lection. The others supported Huston. Hoover, irritated—the meeting was getting away from him—finally agreed and abruptly adjourned the session. Huston, he later observed to Sullivan, was a "hippie intellectual."

Hoover named Sullivan his representative on a drafting subcommittee whose members included Huston, James Angleton from the CIA, Benson K. Buffham of NSA, and James E. Stilwell from DIA. The subcommittee held a series of meetings at CIA headquarters. Huston, then twenty-nine, had been assigned to the Defense Intelligence Agency while in the Army for two years, and had dealt mostly with information from reconnaissance satellites. He had no other intelligence experience.

Huston knew generally what had happened in Denver to cause the break in relations between the FBI and the CIA, and at one point he buttonholed Helms before a meeting of the committee to plead that the CIA Director apologize to Hoover over the Denver case. "We're getting along all right," Helms blandly told Huston.*

Within three weeks the committee drew up a 43-page report recommending that most restraints on intelligence-gathering be taken off or relaxed; break-ins, wiretaps, bugs, mail opening, and other police-state methods were to be given presidential approval. But Hoover sprinkled the report with footnotes, registering the FBI's objections to several of these proposals.

At a final meeting in Hoover's office, at which all the intelligence directors signed the report, Hoover went through the document page by page, asking for comments. He showed his contempt for Huston by consistently getting his name wrong: "Any comments, Mr. Hoffman?" "Any comments, Mr. Hutchinson?"

But Huston, despite the FBI's reservations, had his report. As already noted (in chapter 5), Huston—ignoring Hoover—drew up a memo recommending that the plan be put into effect. Nixon, through Haldeman, approved the Huston Plan.† But Tom Charles Huston was over his head in trying to outflank the likes of Hoover and Helms.

---

* But Huston wasn't so sure. At one meeting in Hoover's office, Huston was wide-eyed when he witnessed the CIA chief walk into Hoover's office. "Good morning, Mr. Hoover," Helms said. "Good morning, Mr. Helms," Hoover said. Since the two men obviously had known each other for years, Huston had expected a "Dick" and "Edgar" routine. It was not to be.

† Haldeman called it "the thing." In an effort to keep Nixon one step removed from approving state burglary and other facets of the plan, Haldeman wrote a top-secret memo to Huston on July 14: "The recommendations you have proposed as a result of the review have been approved by the President. He does not, however, want to follow the procedure you outlined . . . regarding implementation. He would prefer that the thing simply be put into motion on the basis of this approval."

Hoover complained to Mitchell, and five days later the plan was withdrawn.

Sullivan has shed some light on why Hoover was so adamant against the plan. When the committee had completed its draft, he said, Hoover called him in. "'I have taken responsibility for these programs in the past,'" Sullivan quoted Hoover as saying, "'but I'm not going to take responsibility in the future because it's getting too dangerous.'" According to Sullivan, Hoover raised no objection that the plan was illegal or violated individual rights; he simply argued that with "more policemen on the streets the danger of getting caught was getting much greater." Hoover, Sullivan said, noted that the committee set up by the White House could not take responsibility, since it would go out of business when its work was done, and Attorney General Mitchell could not take responsibility because he had not been invited to serve as a member of the committee that drew up the plan. Hoover suggested that Sullivan write a long memo voicing his objections, but Sullivan thought there was an easier way—the series of footnotes taking exception to parts of the plan.

Huston was no match for Hoover, but the young White House assistant did not know when he had been beaten. On August 5, 1970, a week after his plan had been pulled back, he wrote a frustrated memo to Haldeman. "At some point, Hoover has to be told who is President," he said. "He has become totally unreasonable..." Hoover, Huston pointed out, had cut off liaison with the CIA and later with all the other intelligence agencies. This was bound to have "a crippling effect" on U.S. intelligence. If Hoover "gets his way it is going to look like he is more powerful than the President... all of us are going to look damn silly in the eyes of Helms, Gayler, Bennett, and the military chiefs if Hoover can unilaterally reverse a Presidential decision based on a report that many people worked their asses off to prepare..."

But that is exactly what Hoover had done. Huston finally got the message around September. "I heard nothing from anybody, frankly," he testified to a House subcommittee. "I was writing memorandums and nobody was responding." Eleven months later, with Hoover refusing to participate in the Huston Plan, the Nixon White House created a police force of its own—the Plumbers. In less than a year, the Plumbers had turned into the Watergate burglars.

The ripples caused by Thomas Riha's disappearance from the house on Sixth Street had moved outward to an astonishing point. Even so, public references to the case were often obscure. During the Church hearings, for example, Senator Walter D. Huddleston of Kentucky asked James Angleton whether Hoover had been concerned that "informants" inside the FBI were telling the CIA things that Hoover did not want told to the CIA. "Sir," Angleton replied, "I think you're referring directly to the one straw that broke the camel's back."

But Hoover could do as he wished. Like a sovereign, he broke off relations with the rest of the United States government when it suited his whim. He died four weeks before Howard Hunt's burglars made their first entry into the Watergate. At the time, Hoover's power was secure, his reputation still relatively intact. The deluge was coming.

> *"We must be willing to surrender a small measure of our liberties to preserve the great bulk of them."*

> —Clarence M. Kelley, Director,
> Federal Bureau of Investigation,
> August 9, 1975

9
FBI:
The Lawbreakers

On September 30, 1975, some 7,000 employees of the Federal Bureau of Investigation attended dedication ceremonies in the courtyard of the Bureau's massive new headquarters on Pennsylvania Avenue. As the FBI agents and tourists craned their necks, the United States Marine Band struck up the specially composed "J. Edgar Hoover March," and President Ford briskly entered the courtyard.

The President praised Hoover as "a pioneering public servant," and revealed that he himself had at one time wanted to become an FBI agent. With unintended irony—in view of the FBI abuses then coming to the surface—Ford took the occasion to call for a renewed commitment "to the rule of law in America." He did not, of course, mention lawbreaking by the FBI.

It was entirely fitting that even three years after Hoover's death, the President literally marched to his tune. Ford's predecessors had done the same, all eight Presidents under whom Hoover had served. For forty-eight years, from 1924 until his death in 1972 at the age of seventy-seven, from Coolidge through Nixon, Hoover had been Director of the FBI. No President dared to remove him from the job—only death could do that.

The words "J. Edgar Hoover F.B.I. Building" glittered in huge golden letters on the front of the $126 million building, the most expensive ever built by the federal government.° Eleven stories high, the structure suggests a medieval fortress done in modern buff-colored concrete. A gravel moat along one side adds to the impression that the new FBI headquarters was designed to withstand a siege; at any moment, a mounted knight may sally forth and pull up the drawbridge. The thousands of tourists who stream through the building still get the standard FBI guided tour that ends with an exhibition of FBI marksmanship, but a new feature has been added. A portion of J. Edgar Hoover's office, with his own desk and other original furnishings, has been reproduced for the multitudes to gape at.

The headquarters, occupying an entire city block, is almost twice as large as the Justice Department across the street, of which the FBI is technically a part. The symbolism could not have been lost on Hoover, who worried and fussed over the blueprints of the new building in the fading days of his life. The monument would have to be appropriately huge, for Hoover's power had often exceeded that of the Attorneys General, whom he nominally served.

In large measure Hoover's power rested on the information he had squirreled away in his secret files. Put simply, the famous Director of the FBI, the cereal-boxtop, G-man hero of generations of American youth, was a blackmailer. Hoover collected and filed away facts, tidbits, gossip, scandal, and dark secrets that gave him leverage over members of Congress, the Cabinet, even Presidents. He knew it and they knew it. He counted his secrets the way old men count their gold. If information was power, Hoover was J. P. Morgan; to vulnerable political leaders, the midget of their fear sat permanently upon his knee. At any moment it might become a giant, destroying their reputations, their careers, their families. The night with the hooker in Baltimore, the financial indiscretion, the motel dalliance, the long-forgotten arrest record, these were the coin of Hoover's political riches.

"He has a file on everybody," Richard Nixon told John Dean as the Watergate enveloped him.

Hoover even investigated Jesus. Early in 1966 Mitchell Rogovin, then Assistant Attorney General in charge of the Tax Division, learned that the FBI had bugged the hotel room of Washington lobbyist Fred B. Black, Jr., a business associate of wheeler-dealer Bobby Baker. The transcripts had turned up while government attorneys were preparing to bring Baker to trial. At the time, Black was petitioning the Supreme Court to review his tax conviction.

° The Pentagon cost $83 million, the CIA's headquarters $46 million. After the Church committee revealed FBI outrages against Dr. Martin Luther King, Jr., and other targets, Congressman Gilbert Gude, a Maryland Republican, introduced a bill to change the name of the FBI Building. Congress did not rush to pass it.

"Holy shit!" was Rogovin's remembered response when informed of the bug. He sped to the office of Attorney General Katzenbach and persuaded him that the government would have to confess error, which it did in the Supreme Court. Hoover was extremely displeased, and Rogovin much out of favor with the FBI chief. Later, when Ramsey Clark replaced Katzenbach, he arranged a lunch with Hoover to mollify the Director.

Hoover began, not very subtly, by reminding Rogovin that one of his predecessors had gone to jail. Then Hoover reminisced about the time that President Truman had summoned him to the White House and instructed him, "I want you to investigate the Justice Department and the IRS." Hoover tried to discourage the Administration from investigating itself. "Mr. President," he said, according to Rogovin, "wouldn't it be better to have a congressional inquiry rather than an executive-branch inquiry of the executive branch? For as you will recall, our Lord had a disciple who was unfaithful."

Truman turned to Hoover. "I think you'll find that three of Jesus' disciples were unfaithful."

"I asked the research people to check it out," Hoover told Clark and Rogovin. "You know, the President was right—there *were* three unfaithful to Jesus."

William Sullivan, who served Hoover for thirty years and rose to the number-three position in the Bureau before his fall from grace, has described how Hoover used the information he collected.

"That fellow was a master blackmailer," Sullivan told Jack Nelson of the Los Angeles *Times* in 1973. "The moment he would get something on a senator he'd send one of the errand boys up and advise the senator that we're in the course of an investigation and by chance happened to come up with this data on your daughter. But we wanted you to know this—we realize you'd want to know it. But don't have any concern, no one will ever learn about it. Well, Jesus, what does that tell the senator? From that time on, the senator's right in his pocket."

One of the incongruous aspects of Hoover's talent for political blackmail was that his own life style inevitably gave rise to whispers about his sexual preferences, if any. Hoover was born on New Year's Day, 1895, in Washington, where his father, Dickerson Naylor Hoover, was a minor employee of the Coast and Geodetic Survey. His mother, Anna Marie Scheitlin, was a niece of Switzerland's first consul general in the United States, and by most accounts a stern Calvinist who imposed a strict discipline on her son. Perhaps no one could replace her in Hoover's life, for he never married. He lived with his mother from the time her husband died in 1922, until her own death sixteen years later.* By then Hoover was in his forty-third year. Two years after his mother's death, Hoover bought the red brick house near Rock Creek Park. He lived alone, except for his cook-housekeeper, but spent most of his free time with Clyde A. Tolson, his top deputy at the FBI, and his constant companion after hours. Tolson, too, remained a bachelor. The two men dined together frequently, went to the race track together, and vacationed together.

There was something of Neil Simon's Odd Couple about them. A glimpse of their life together was provided by former FBI agent Joseph L. Schott, in *No Left Turns*, published in 1975. The title of the book was taken from the fact that in 1959 Schott helped arrange a 200-mile auto trip for Hoover and Tolson from Dallas to Austin, in which the FBI driver was forbidden to turn left. A few months earlier in California, Hoover's car had been hit from the rear while his chauffeur was making a left turn. Hoover had forbidden any more left turns.

According to Schott, the special agent arranging hotel accommodations for Hoover and Tolson had been given detailed notes. The suite was to consist of a living room and two bedrooms, each with private bath, each with a double bed. Mattresses not too hard, not too soft, exactly four down pillows on each bed. The special agent in charge emphasized *down* pillows. As Schott recalled it, the instructions continued this way:

> All appliances in rooms, such as radios and television sets, must have typed instructions explaining how to turn on and turn off. Typing must be neat. Check closely for misspelling and typographical errors. Decorative flowers may be placed in suite living room but not in bedrooms. Basket full of fruit may be placed on coffee table of living room. If liquor placed in suite, Director drinks Jack Daniel's . . .

Gossiping about the relationship between Hoover and Tolson was sheer insanity for FBI agents to indulge in, a sure transfer to Butte, Montana, if not outright dismissal, but apparently speculation on that subject went back decades. Washington attorney James H. Rowe, who had been a White House assistant to Franklin D. Roosevelt, recalled that when he later served under Francis Biddle at Justice, he would sometimes walk down the hall past Hoover's office with the Attorney General. As they passed Hoover's office, Biddle would ask in a loud voice, "Jim, do you think Hoover is a homosexual?"

---

* Hoover listed his mother's maiden name in *Who's Who in America* as "Annie M. Scheitlin." He called his housekeeper "Annie" Fields. By coincidence or not, there was always an "Annie" around to take care of Hoover.

Rowe would die, and try to hush the Attorney General; this, he would tell Biddle, was not the place to discuss it.

"Oh," Biddle would boom out, "I only mean a LATENT homosexual!"

Hoover's autocratic leadership of the FBI, the strait-laced standards he decreed for Bureau agents in their mode of dress and personal morality, his crotchets, likes and dislikes, have all passed into legend. For example, Hoover insisted that FBI trainees have dry palms when they shook hands with him at graduation, so each new agent as he stood in line gripped a handkerchief, to be discarded surreptitiously at the last second.° Hoover also insisted that in their memos agents always refer to Washington as the SOG, which stood, majestically, for Seat of Government. Just as Hoover used fear as a weapon against congressmen and others outside the FBI, he used it to preserve his absolute dictatorship within the Bureau.

The result is nowhere better illustrated than in an exchange of memoranda between Hoover and Sullivan in August 1963, shortly before Martin Luther King's March on Washington. Sullivan was then the head of the Domestic Intelligence Division, which prepared a memo for Hoover on the efforts of the Communist party to exploit American blacks. The memo concluded: "The Communist Party in the next few years may fail dismally with the American Negroes as it has in the past."

This analysis was correct, of course, but it was not what Hoover wanted to hear. Irritated, Hoover wrote on the memo: "This memo reminds me vividly of those I received when Castro took over Cuba. You contended then that Castro and his cohorts were not Communists and not influenced by Communists. Time alone proved you wrong. I for one can't ignore memos about [various names deleted] as having only an infinitesimal effect on the efforts to exploit the American Negro by the Communists."

Michael Epstein, a staff attorney for the Church committee, testified that Sullivan then about-faced and wrote another memo. Sullivan now concluded: "The Director is correct. We were completely wrong about . . . Fidel Castro . . . On investigating and writing about Communism and the American Negro, we had better remember this and

---

° According to Joseph Schott, as the last graduate filed out the door after one such handshaking ceremony for new agents, Hoover turned to their counselor and barked, "One of them is a pinhead. Get rid of him!" The luckless FBI man, after unsuccessfully trying to spot the pinhead, finally had an inspiration. At the time, all FBI agents were required to wear hats. While the men were on the firing range at the FBI Academy in Quantico, Virginia, the counselor went through each man's clothing locker and checked hat sizes. The smallest size was 6⅞. Unfortunately, *three* trainees wore that size. There was nothing that could be done; all three were fired.

profit by the lessons that it should teach us." Sullivan added that it may be "unrealistic to limit ourselves as we have been doing to legalistic proofs or definitely conclusive evidence that would stand up in testimony in court . . . that the Communist Party, USA, does wield substantial influence over Negroes which one day could become decisive."

"The memorandum which the Director penetratively questioned," Sullivan went on, "while showing in the details the Communist impact on Negroes, did suffer from such limitations." Finally, he wrote: "We regret greatly that the memorandum did not measure up to what the Director has a right to expect from our analysis." Then, in September 1963, Sullivan told Hoover that FBI field offices were being ordered to intensify their coverage of Communist influence on blacks and to adopt "aggressive tactics" through COINTELPRO, the counterintelligence program.

Despite this sycophancy, Sullivan could not pacify Hoover, who now wrote back: "No. I cannot understand how you can so agilely switch your thinking and evaluation. Just a few weeks ago you contended that the Communist influence in the racial movement was ineffective and infinitesimal. This notwithstanding many memos of specific instances of infiltration. Now you want to load the field down with more coverage, in spite of your recent memo deprecating CP influence in racial movement. I don't intend to waste time and money until you can make up your minds what the situation really is."

It was enough to drive strong men to distraction, but Sullivan swallowed hard and wrote another memo: "It is obvious that we did not put the proper interpretation upon the facts which we gave to the Director." He then renewed his request for increased field coverage, adding: "May I repeat that our failure to measure up to what the Director expected of us in the area of Communist-Negro relations is a subject of very deep concern to us . . . We are disturbed by this and ought to be. I want him to know that we will do everything that is humanly possible to develop all of the facts." A few months later the FBI planted its first bug against Dr. Martin Luther King, Jr., ostensibly because he had come under the influence of a "Communist" attorney in New York.

Fear of Hoover's wrath distorted the FBI's operations in large ways and small. In 1970 Charles Brennan succeeded Sullivan as assistant FBI director for domestic intelligence; when the Pentagon Papers were leaked to the *New York Times* the following year, FBI agents sought to interview Louis Marx, the toy manufacturer, who was Daniel Ellsberg's father-in-law. Brennan well knew that Marx was a personal friend of Hoover's, so he sent a memo up to the Director asking for his approval.

"It came back with a small blue ink note saying 'NO,' " Brennan recalled. "I couldn't conceive that J. Edgar Hoover would not approve the interview. When I saw the notation I thought it said 'OK.' I told New York to go ahead and interview Marx. Then an assistant asked me if I had seen the notation. I looked again, and it said 'NO.' My assistant suggested we call New York and stop the teletype report of the interview. I said no, Marx might tell Hoover he had been interviewed and then I'd have a problem."

When the teletype came in and Hoover saw it, he hit the roof. Brennan was demoted to a meaningless job as chief inspector in charge of special investigations. He remained in the deep freeze for months, although "I even recommended myself for censure." This was a common procedure in the Byzantine bureaucracy of the FBI, according to Brennan. "I had taken many of these over the years," he said. "It was routine to blame someone. But this time some SOB agreed but added that I should be put on probation. So I was censured *and* put on probation." Eventually Brennan was resurrected by L. Patrick Gray III, and placed in charge of the Alexandria office.

In governing the FBI, Hoover had one controlling standard: "Don't embarrass the Bureau." The rule prevailed even—or perhaps especially—when charges were brought against FBI agents for misconduct. As late as 1975, the FBI manual of rules and regulations, under the heading "Disciplinary Matters," contained this instruction:

Any investigation necessary to develop complete essential facts regarding any allegation against Bureau employees must be instituted promptly, and *every logical lead which will establish the true facts should be completely run out unless such action would embarrass the Bureau* or might prejudice pending investigations or prosecutions . . ."* (Italics added.)

Hoover's first federal job, at age eighteen, was that of a lowly messenger in the Library of Congress. At night he studied law at George Washington University and earned a bachelor's and a master's degree. He joined the Justice Department in 1917. He soon became a special assistant to Attorney General A. Mitchell Palmer, who rounded up thousands of suspected Communists in 1919. In April of 1924, in the wake of the Teapot Dome Scandal, Coolidge named Harlan Fiske Stone as the new Attorney General. On May 10, 1924, Stone called in Hoover, then twenty-nine, and named him head of the Bureau of Investigation.†

---

* This instruction is contained in Part 1, Section 9, of the FBI manual. The FBI claimed in 1975 that this was no longer its policy, but the rule nevertheless remained in print in the manual.
† The Bureau of Investigation was established in 1908 by President Theodore Roosevelt. The word "Federal" was added in 1935.

It was in the thirties that Hoover built his reputation as gang-buster and super G-man. The phrase "G-man" (for government man), which became synonymous with Hoover and the FBI, has been attributed to George "Machine Gun" Kelly, a desperado who surrendered to the FBI in 1933 begging, "Don't shoot, G-men, don't shoot." Pretty Boy Floyd, Ma and Fred Barker, Baby Face Nelson, and in 1934 John Dillinger himself were all killed in gun battles with the FBI. Two years later, in New Orleans, Hoover personally captured Alvin Karpis, then "Public Enemy No. 1," who had sneeringly referred to Hoover as a "rat." During World War II the FBI chased Nazi spies and saboteurs. After the war, it was Communists and "subversives."

If Hoover's power rested on the secrets in his dossiers, it was based as well on his sure instinct for public relations and the support he was able to generate among the public and in Congress. On films, on radio and television, in the guided tours for the visitors, the FBI image was huckstered and sold as an incorruptible band of clean-cut heroes, led by their bulldog-faced master J. Edgar Hoover. Hoover loved to settle down in his armchair and watch *The FBI*, starring Efrem Zimbalist, Jr., the popular TV series produced under the FBI's careful scrutiny.

It was only in the sixties that criticism of Hoover and the FBI began to surface widely. A series of disenchanted former agents began talking, and writers of the stature of Tom Wicker examined the Bureau and found it wanting. It began to dawn on the public that Hoover's concentration on Communists had obscured the fact the FBI had done very little to break up organized crime.

But it was not until 1971, when FBI files were stolen from a Bureau office in Media, Pennsylvania, and later released to the press, that the full scope of the FBI's secret-police activities began to emerge. As the documents made clear, the FBI was snooping on college campuses, gathering intelligence in black neighborhoods, and harassing the New Left and other dissident groups through its COINTELPRO operations. Watergate and the Church committee investigations completed the process of de-mythification of the FBI. The mask had finally been pulled off Hoover and Bureau. And it all came tumbling out almost too fast to absorb—the bugs, the bag jobs, the wiretaps, the harassment of citizens and groups, Hoover's outrageous attempt to destroy Martin Luther King, Jr., the greatest civil rights leader in America's history. Suddenly the FBI was revealed as potentially more dangerous than its adversaries. It had become a lawless political police, led by an aging, tyrannical Director who was feared even by the Presidents he supposedly served. The situation was all the more disturbing because the Bureau still, despite all, enjoyed a strong reservoir of public support, a secret police benignly protected by its own legend, by the national memory of junior G-man badges and the Lady in Red.

But it was still the secret files that gave Hoover his enormous power in Washington, and when he died on May 2, 1972, mysterious games began to be played with the files. Attorney General Richard Kleindienst has testified that when he learned of Hoover's death early that morning he issued orders "that the offices of the Director be locked and secured." But instead, the contents of about thirty-five file cabinet drawers containing Hoover's "personal file" were shipped to his house near Rock Creek Park. John P. Mohr, a senior FBI official, blandly insisted his instructions from Kleindienst had been to "secure his [Hoover's] personal office," which he had done. Only, it contained no files at all. Mohr assured the Attorney General he had sealed Hoover's office and that "I had the keys." In the meantime the files were on their way to Hoover's house; once there, his secretary of fifty years, Helen Gandy, insisted she had them destroyed. "I tore them up, put them in boxes and they were taken away to be shredded," she said. "I have no reason to lie." Some of the material might have had historic value, she conceded, "but I had my instructions." According to an internal FBI investigation, these personal files, after being reviewed by Miss Gandy, "were picked up at the house on several occasions and destroyed by personnel of the Washington Field Office."

In 1975 Attorney General Edward Levi revealed that another set of Hoover's files, 164 folders labeled "Official and Confidential," had suddenly been discovered by the Justice Department. The files, Levi said, had been kept in Hoover's office suite, and included forty-eight folders dealing with "public figures or prominent persons," including "Presidents, Executive Branch officers and 17 individuals who were members of Congress."°

In a conversation with the author, William Sullivan claimed that "Mohr has removed very mysterious files . . . documents that were in Hoover's office, very sensitive and explosive files, containing political information, derogatory information on key figures in the country." It was pointed out to Sullivan that Levi said he had located 164 such files in the Justice Department.

"Yeah," Sullivan responded, "but he didn't locate the gold. He didn't locate the gold."

° Although the FBI investigation of what happened to Hoover's secret files made a distinction between his personal files and the "Official and Confidential" (OC) files, the two sets of files intersected. Investigators for the Church committee, who discovered the FBI "black bag" memo in the OC files, noticed that the letters PF (for Personal File) had been crossed out. Checking further, they learned that before his death Hoover had begun reviewing his secret files and had transferred some of the personal files into the OC files. But he only did so for letters A through C. Helen Gandy said she reviewed every document from C to Z and found not a single piece of paper that was not personal. "As I say, you just have my word," the seventy-eight-year-old secretary testified.

Mohr, who denied to reporters that he had removed any files, played a key role in the struggle over the fruits of Hoover's estate. In 1972, when Hoover's will was filed for probate in Washington, it was revealed that he had left almost all of the estate of $551,000 to Clyde Tolson, who moved into his house after Hoover died. Three years later, in April 1975, Tolson died at the age of seventy-four.

Within three months his brother, Hillory Tolson, also a former FBI agent, filed a petition challenging Tolson's will and charging that he had disinherited his own brother at the suggestion of Mohr, to whom Tolson left $26,000. Hillory Tolson said Mohr had used "fraud and deceit" to exclude him from the will. There were thirteen beneficiaries of Tolson's $500,000 estate, most of which presumably represented the money and holdings left to him by Hoover.

Six months later it was revealed that Nicholas P. Callahan, Associate Director of the FBI under Clarence Kelley, and a former aide to Mohr, admitted that Clyde Tolson's signature on a document giving Tolson's power of attorney to Mohr was probably not authentic. Callahan conceded he had witnessed Tolson's signature without actually seeing Tolson sign the document. James B. Adams, the number-three man in the FBI under Kelley, had also witnessed the document.

All three men obviously had wielded great power in the upper reaches of the FBI. Mohr had been Tolson's aide for more than twenty-five years, Callahan worked under Mohr, and Adams below Callahan. Mohr retired in June 1972 after Hoover's death, but Kelley retained the rest of the old Hoover-Tolson team and promoted them, although he dismissed Callahan in 1976.° Even in death, the Hoover stamp remained on the top echelon of the FBI.

If Hoover intimidated Presidents with his secret files, he also used the same techniques to serve Presidents by gathering information about their adversaries. In the symbiosis of political blackmail, the process gave Hoover even more power, for when Presidents misused the FBI against their opponents, they paid a price by giving Hoover even greater subtle leverage over the White House. A President wanted the information, the FBI provided it, but by ordering Hoover to get it, a President placed himself in further hostage to Hoover's power.

° Mohr was under fire on another front. Until his retirement in 1972, Mohr had been assistant director of the FBI for administration. The House intelligence committee discovered that the FBI purchased its bugging and tapping equipment at high markups from the U.S. Recording Company, which served as an FBI "cutout" to disguise the identity of the manufacturers. The president of U.S. Recording, Joseph Tait, was a frequent poker partner of Mohr's during weekends at the Blue Ridge Club, near Harpers Ferry, West Virginia. For a decade, top FBI and CIA officials had played poker at the retreat. It burned down the night before investigators from the House intelligence committee were scheduled to inspect its books.

Early in 1973, as Richard Nixon sweated privately in the White House with his guilty knowledge of Watergate and related crimes, it occurred both to him and to John Dean that a way out, one possible way to release the enormous pressure that was building would be to uncover abuses of the FBI by other Presidents. If "they all do it"— the cynic's standard reaction to Watergate—could be documented, perhaps it would deflect public criticism and expiate Nixon's sins.

But, alas, Hoover was dead and couldn't help, a fact that Nixon lamented. "Hoover was my crony," Nixon said to Dean in February 1973. "He was closer to me than Johnson, actually although Johnson used him more ... I think we would have been a lot better off during this whole Watergate thing if he had been alive. Because he knew how to handle that Bureau. ... Hoover performed. He would have fought. He would have scared them to death."

But who would know Hoover's secrets now that he was gone? One possibility was Deke DeLoach, formerly the FBI's top public relations man who had risen to the post of Assistant to the Director but retired to take a corporate job. His name had already come up. Months earlier, in September, Nixon had told Dean: "We were bugged in '68 on the [campaign] plane ... God Damnedest thing you ever saw." It was a shame, said Dean, that only Hoover could have proved that. "Others know it," Nixon responded.

"DeLoach?" Dean asked.

"DeLoach, right."

By then DeLoach was working for Nixon's friend Donald Kendall as chief of public relations for Pepsi-Cola. Dean later swore that Nixon instructed him to telephone Kendall "and tell him that DeLoach had better start telling the truth because 'the boys are coming out of the woodwork.' He said this ploy may smoke DeLoach out."* Dean said he never called Kendall. But apparently John Mitchell called DeLoach, at least twice, fishing for information. DeLoach told Mitchell that Nixon's plane had not been bugged, but that the FBI had checked Agnew's phone calls from Albuquerque in 1968, including some from the Republican vice-presidential candidate's campaign plane during a stopover in that city.

If DeLoach would not help, then who? Dean suggested William Sullivan, who had clashed with Hoover, left the FBI and "has a world of information." But, he told Nixon, he was keeping Sullivan at arm's

---

* Dean's testimony on this point was buttressed by a memo Haldeman had sent to him on February 9, 1973. Haldeman told Dean to have Attorney General Kleindienst order the FBI to find out all possible information "on the 1968 bugging." The memo then added: "Mitchell should probably have Kendall call DeLoach in and say that if this project turns up anything that DeLoach hasn't covered with us, he will, of course, have to fire him."

length, treating him warily until he was sure "he is safe." Nixon was eager to approach Sullivan. "You still think Sullivan is basically reliable?" he asked.

Two weeks later Nixon and Dean again toyed with the question of how to get Sullivan to unlock the past secrets of the FBI. Why would Sullivan play ball? Nixon asked. Because he badly wanted to get back into the FBI, Dean replied.° "That's easy," Nixon said. Dean then told Nixon that Sullivan's real desire was to set up a domestic intelligence system, but the Huston Plan had crumbled over Hoover's opposition; perhaps "we could put him out in the CIA" for a while.

"Put him there; we'll do it," Nixon responded. Anything.

But Dean was still cautious about Sullivan. "I don't know if he's given me his best yet. I don't know if he's got more ammunition . . . than he has already told me." But, Dean added, Sullivan might be prepared to "tell everything he knows . . . he's a bomb."

Dean said he had instructed Sullivan to write a memo on what he knew, "just put it together on a pad." (Obviously the White House did not want Sullivan's trip down memory lane seen even by the FBI secretary or typist.) "So he is doing that," Dean said.

But the problem was how to get the information out publicly once Sullivan provided it, and Dean and Nixon fretted about that at some length. "If we are involved in pissing on Johnson," Nixon said, "that concerns me." If Sullivan took his memo to Kleindienst, Dean said, the Attorney General would discourage him and say, "you are going to take DeLoach's name down with it, and DeLoach is a friend of ours."

PRESIDENT: Bull shit.
DEAN: Something I have always questioned.
PRESIDENT: Nobody is a friend of ours. Let's face it.

Dean had called Sullivan to the White House late in February. According to Sullivan, Dean wanted to discuss the Kissinger taps, but then moved into a discussion of how the White House might cope with Watergate. Sullivan said he had no ideas about that. Dean told him to think it over. On a subsequent visit to the White House, Dean asked Sullivan point-blank to prepare a memo listing examples of political use of the FBI by previous Presidents.

Sullivan prepared two memos, which Dean later turned over to the Senate Watergate committee. The committee never published the

---

° When the White House transcripts were made public in 1974, Sullivan claimed that Dean had lied to Nixon in suggesting that Sullivan would exchange secrets for a federal job. If anyone had offered him a job as a payoff, Sullivan said, it would have violated federal law and "I'd have taken steps to have him arrested . . . I didn't want a damn thing from them. I never asked Dean or anyone else in the White House for anything."

Sullivan memos, however. The first, which Sullivan labeled SECRET, was a single page accompanied by a note in which Sullivan offered "to testify in behalf of the Administration." The facts, he said, "would put the current Administration in a very favorable light." The second, longer memo ran to four pages and was marked TOP SECRET. Both documents appeared to have been typed by Sullivan himself.

The memos mentioned Roosevelt briefly, but otherwise dealt entirely with Lyndon Johnson's use of the FBI. "To my memory the two Administrations which used the FBI the most for political purposes," he wrote, "were Mr. Roosevelt's and Mr. Johnson's. Complete and willing cooperation was given to both. For example, Mr. Roosevelt requested us to look into the backgrounds of those who opposed his Lend-Lease Bill . . . Mrs. Roosevelt would also make some unusual requests. The contrary was also true in that the Roosevelts would indicate to FBI they were not interested in FBI pushing certain investigations too far if the subjects were ones the Roosevelts did not want derogatory information developed on . . ." One example, Sullivan wrote, occurred when Sumner Welles served as FDR's Under Secretary of State "and information had been received that he was a homosexual." Welles had clashed with Secretary of State Cordell Hull, who bitterly resented him as FDR's agent in the State Department. Rumors circulated in Washington that Welles had made advances to a black porter on a railroad train.

Sullivan elaborated on the FBI's role in an interview with Donald G. Sanders, deputy minority counsel to the Watergate committee. "In the matter of Sumner Welles," Sanders wrote in a memo of the interview, "Cordell Hull desired to get rid of him. The FBI developed information that he was a homosexual, and Attorney General Biddle told Roosevelt that the FBI had the facts. Sullivan heard at the time that Roosevelt listened without responding, that Biddle repeated the information and that Roosevelt said, 'Well, he's not doing this on government time, is he?'"

But Welles's usefulness was over and he resigned in 1943 at Roosevelt's request. Sullivan also claimed in his memos to Dean and in a subsequent interview with Sanders that Mrs. Roosevelt had once intervened with the FBI in behalf of author Joseph P. Lash in regard to a security clearance.*

---

* Sullivan kept referring to "Don Lash" but it was clear from the context that he meant Joseph P. Lash, who was a friend of Mrs. Roosevelt's and later author of the best-selling book *Eleanor and Franklin*. Sullivan told Sanders that "Lash tried to get a commission in the U.S. Navy. There was derogatory information developed about him with regard to security clearance, and Mrs. Roosevelt interceded in his behalf. She seemed interested in his future." In a book published in

Questioned by Sanders about Roosevelt's request that the FBI investigate opponents of his Lend-Lease program, Sullivan, who was a supervisor at FBI headquarters at the time, recalled "that a physical surveillance, a telephone tap, and a microphone surveillance were placed upon one of these opponents."

In his memos Sullivan pointed out that Hoover always tried to develop "a close unilateral relationship with Presidents" and their key aides. "Once established, the Attorney-Generals were ignored." Congressmen and Cabinet members of both parties were carefully cultivated with such skill "that each usually thought he was alone getting the special and helpful treatment."

But at times, he said, "President Johnson would ask the FBI for derogatory information . . . on Senators in his own Democratic Party who were opposing him." Johnson would then leak the derogatory information to Everett M. Dirksen, the Republican leader of the Senate, "who would use it with telling effect against President Johnson's opponents."

Sullivan noted in his memos that Johnson had been close to Hoover for some years, which may have "facilitated" LBJ's use of the FBI. He pointed out they had once been neighbors. But Sullivan indicated that Johnson always had a reservoir of suspicion about Hoover; as President, whenever Johnson called Hoover, he kept repeating one question: "Did you have a telephone tap on me when I was in the Senate?"

"He was always told we did not, which was the truth, but he never seemed to believe it."

Sullivan also disclosed that the FBI, at Johnson's request, had sent a special squad to Atlantic City for the 1964 Democratic National Convention that renominated him. "The 'cover' would be that it was a security squad to guard against militants, etc.," Sullivan wrote. But the squad also developed "political information useful to President Johnson."

The man whom Hoover chose to head the special squad was Deke DeLoach. Tough and smooth—he almost purred when he talked—DeLoach still retained the accents of his native rural Georgia. He joined the FBI in 1942, quickly became a Hoover favorite, and rose

---

1964, Lash wrote that in 1941, after he had applied for a Navy commission and been rejected, Mrs. Roosevelt met with Martin Dies, chairman of the House Un-American Activities Committee, to protest the harassment of persons like Lash who had renounced the radical views they had held in the thirties. Mrs. Roosevelt arranged for Lash to appear before the committee in executive session. But Lash said he had no thought of re-applying for his Navy commission. See *Eleanor Roosevelt: A Friend's Memoir* (New York: Doubleday, 1964), pp. 276–87.

rapidly through the ranks to become the Bureau's top PR man in 1959. That post put him in contact with the Washington press corps and senior figures in Congress, including Lyndon Johnson.°

DeLoach, accompanied by his assistant, Harold P. Leinbaugh, and half a dozen FBI agents from Washington, traveled to Atlantic City in two FBI automobiles. Agents from Atlantic City and other FBI offices joined them. Altogether, more than twenty-five FBI agents and technicians served on the secret squad. DeLoach's agents blanketed the convention. The FBI bugged and tapped Martin Luther King's hotel rooms in Atlantic City and a storefront office used by black groups. They monitored the two-way radios used by the civil rights groups, set up a network of informers to infiltrate various factions at the convention, and using press credentials, posed as newsmen.

From all these sources, DeLoach kept a steady stream of information flowing to Lyndon Johnson in the White House. Afterward, in a memo to Mohr, DeLoach said: "During our Convention coverage, we disseminated 44 pages of intelligence data to Walter Jenkins. . . . Additionally, I kept Jenkins and [Bill D.] Moyers constantly advised by telephone of minute-by-minute developments. This enabled them to make spot decisions and to adjust Convention plans to meet potential problems before serious trouble developed."

To the Church committee, DeLoach insisted that his team had been instructed to gather "intelligence concerning matters of strife, violence, etc." and not political information. But in fact the FBI squad provided Johnson with information that gave him complete political and physical control of the convention. Johnson—literally—had the convention wired.†

The political value of the reports flowing to the President was illustrated by a typical haul from the electronic surveillance on Dr. King. Leaders of the Mississippi Freedom Democratic party, the FBI informed Johnson, "have asked Reverend King to call Governor Egan of Alaska and Governor Burns of Hawaii in an attempt to enlist their

° Sullivan, too, had become a powerful figure within the FBI during those years, and he and DeLoach were rivals. Even after both men had left the FBI, there were discernible DeLoach and Sullivan factions within the Bureau. DeLoach became Assistant to Hoover in 1965, the number-three job in the FBI. He left in 1970 to go with Pepsi-Cola (by then it was apparent that Hoover would never retire and DeLoach would not become FBI chief), but he remained basically loyal to Hoover. Hoover named Sullivan to replace DeLoach as Assistant to the Director, but Sullivan fought with Hoover and was forced out in 1971.

† Political commentators at the time remarked on how masterfully Johnson had controlled the convention from the White House. Only columnist Walter Lippmann appeared to smell a rat. "The interesting question is why he had such a complete control," he wrote. "Quite evidently he is a great politician but what is the secret of his greatness as a politician?"

support. According to the MFDP spokesmen, the Negro Mississippi Party needs these two states plus California and New York for the roll call tonight."

The only dissident note in Johnson's carefully orchestrated convention was the fight by the Mississippi Freedom Democratic party to be seated as convention delegates. DeLoach's post-convention memo sheds further light on how the FBI was used by Johnson to political advantage:

"By counseling Messrs. Jenkins, Carter and Moyers, we convinced them that they must make major changes in controlling admissions into the Convention Hall and thereby preclude infiltration of the illegal Mississippi Freedom Democratic Party (MFDP) delegates in large numbers into the space reserved for the regular Mississippi delegates. Through our counterintelligence efforts, Jenkins, et al., were able to advise the President in advance regarding major plans of the MFDP delegates. The White House considered this of prime importance."

What Johnson really feared the most at Atlantic City was a runaway convention that would, in a surge of emotion, reject his renomination and choose Attorney General Robert F. Kennedy, the brother of the martyred President whom Johnson had replaced. Johnson, in an elaborate maneuver, had already ruled out Robert Kennedy as his running mate, but the visceral fear remained. And the FBI squad kept close watch on Kennedy, reporting his contacts with King.

Leo T. Clark, the senior FBI agent in the Atlantic City office, provided a detailed account of the FBI's convention activities in an interview with the staff of the Senate Watergate committee. Clark told the committee that he overheard DeLoach speaking on the phone to both President Johnson and Hoover, reporting information coming from the bugs and taps.° A staff summary of Clark's testimony reported:

"In a DeLoach conversation with the President, Clark heard mention of discussions concerning the seating of delegates or delegations, of vice presidential candidate possibilities and the identities of congressmen and Senators going in and out of King's quarters. Robert Kennedy's activities were of special interest, including his contacts

---

° Special agent Bill D. Williams also recalled hearing a DeLoach conversation. In 1975 the FBI conducted an internal inquiry into the Atlantic City operation. Williams, who was Special Agent in Charge of the Kansas City office in 1975, denied that the FBI had been used politically, but added, "I do recall, however, that on one occasion I was present when DeLoach held a lengthy telephone conversation with Walter Jenkins. They appeared to be discussing the President's 'image.' At the end of the conversation DeLoach told us something to the effect, 'that may have sounded a little political to you but this doesn't do the Bureau any harm.'"

with King." Clark said DeLoach told him he had not discussed the bugs and wiretaps of King with Kennedy.*

Three days before the convention began on August 24, Clark found out that King and his group would be staying at the Claridge Hotel in Atlantic City. Clark rented room 1821 and arranged with the hotel to give King three rooms on the floor above. Two agents from Newark planted the bugs and taps. "With the cooperation of the Claridge Hotel management," the summary said, "these men were given the keys to King's rooms which they then surveyed.

"Room 1821 in the Claridge Hotel was used for monitoring the installations in King's rooms as well as to monitor an installation in a storefront at 2414 Atlantic Avenue which was rented by CORE.... A wiretap and microphone were installed in 2414 Atlantic Avenue which eventually became a central headquarters for several groups." The civil rights groups two-way radios were monitored by the FBI "in one of the rooms in the Post Office Building.

"Special agents John P. Devlin and John J. Connolly worked in room 1821 monitoring King and John J. Cramer and Billy D. Williams worked in 1821 monitoring the CORE installation. All of these men were from Newark. There were no typewriters in room 1821 to the recollection of Clark, but conversations were taped." From the monitoring center, the agents called DeLoach, Leinbaugh, or other senior agents, who dictated to stenographers.

Robert Wick, DeLoach's top assistant at the time, remained in Washington. When calls came in from the convention, stenographers at FBI headquarters took down and transcribed the bulletins. According to Wick, reports would then be typed on plain bond paper with no markings to indicate who had prepared them or that they came from the FBI. These would then be rushed by messenger to the White House.

Leo Clark also disclosed that the FBI had used a "considerable number of live informants" who "came to Atlantic City from all around the nation." The informants were given the number of a special phone in DeLoach's office in the Post Office Building, Clark said. They were instructed to identify themselves by saying, "This is Elmer."

According to the staff summary of the Clark interview, one agent, "Lloyd Nelson, posed as a news photographer" and was able to photograph "individuals and groups" when the FBI wanted a photographic record.

Then Clark provided a startling bit of information. One FBI man, he said, had posed as an NBC correspondent. To the delegates and other newsmen, he looked like a typical television reporter laden down with electronic gear. The Clark interview summary states: "Special

---

* Kennedy, however, had approved FBI wiretapping of King in October 1963.

agent Ben Hale had credentials as an NBC correspondent. He conducted interviews with key persons in various groups, using walkie-talkie equipment..." The agent was broadcasting not to NBC, however, but to DeLoach and the FBI agents in the Post Office control center.

When reports first surfaced in 1975 that NBC press credentials had been used by FBI agents at the Atlantic City convention, Julian Goodman, the board chairman of NBC, said the network had investigated "as thoroughly as we know how and we still don't know what it's all about or why NBC has been implicated in this way."

However, on August 29, 1964, after the convention, DeLoach wrote a memo describing how agents, "using appropriate cover as reporters," were able to keep the White House informed. A later FBI document said DeLoach had reported that "through cooperation with the management of NBC News our Agents were furnished NBC press credentials."

"I selected several members of the squad to utilize this cover," DeLoach wrote. "As an example, one of our 'reporters' was able to gain the confidence of [deleted]. Our 'reporter' was so successful, in fact, that [deleted] was giving him 'off the record information' for background purposes, which he requested our 'reporter' not to print.... During the period when the Convention was actually in progress, we established a secondary command post at the Convention Hall Rotunda operated by an agent using his 'reporter' cover."

Although DeLoach's memo said that "several" agents had used NBC press credentials, he mentioned only two press passes when he testified to the Church committee in 1975. "There was one agent that accompanied me to Atlantic City from FBI headquarters who had a friend among the employees of NBC who were attending the convention," DeLoach said. The agent was given "a couple of pieces of cardboard where you filled in your own name." DeLoach said he did not know the extent to which the credentials were used. In his testimony DeLoach did not identify the FBI man who obtained the passes. But away from the witness table, in answer to a question, he identified him as Harold (Bud) Leinbaugh, his assistant.°

In 1975 special agent Ben Hale, identified by Leo Clark as the FBI man who used NBC press credentials, was assigned to the FBI office in Memphis. In a telephone interview he declined to confirm

° Leinbaugh, who retired from the FBI in 1973, declined comment. "It's been so long a time I don't think I can be of any help," he said. Leo Clark, also retired, declined to comment when asked to clarify how many FBI men had posed as NBC reporters. But he did not retract his identification of Ben Hale and Lloyd Nelson as agents who had posed, respectively, as an NBC correspondent and a press photographer. "I gave my testimony under subpoena and I stand by my testimony," he said.

292 / THE AMERICAN POLICE STATE

or deny that he was at the Atlantic City convention or had used NBC credentials. "I can't make any comment," he said.°

Hoover was well pleased with the work of the FBI at the Democratic convention. At the bottom of DeLoach's memo summarizing the work of the special squad at Atlantic City, the FBI director scrawled: "DeLoach should receive a meritorious award."

In his memos to the Nixon White House, Sullivan said that President Johnson had also brought political pressures on the FBI in the Walter Jenkins case. In the midst of the 1964 presidential campaign, it was revealed that Jenkins, one of Johnson's top aides, had been arrested along with another man on a morals charge. The arrest took place in a men's washroom in the basement of the YMCA a block from the White House. How word leaked from the police blotter to the press remained a mystery, although the Republican National Committee seemed to have some knowledge of the facts before they were publicized.

The incident threatened to affect Johnson's re-election campaign against Senator Barry Goldwater, the Republican nominee. Furious, and suspecting a Republican plot, Johnson, according to Sullivan, issued instructions that the man arrested with Jenkins be "pinned down more fully" by the FBI and specifically asked whether he knew two Republican officials—Dean Burch, then Republican National Chairman and manager of Goldwater's presidential campaign, and John E. Grenier, executive director of the Republican National Committee and Goldwater's campaign manager in the South.

On October 19, five days after the Jenkins story broke in the press, Sullivan said, Supreme Court Justice Abe Fortas, Johnson's confidant, telephoned the FBI to say that Jenkins was suffering from a serious disease that caused "disintegration of the brain." Sullivan said the FBI visited Jenkins' doctor seeking a public statement to this effect, "but the doctor refused, saying his examination showed no brain injury or disease."

According to Sullivan, Johnson called the FBI the next day and

° Hale said he could talk to the author only if FBI headquarters in Washington approved. A request for clearance to speak to Hale about the use of NBC press credentials at the 1964 convention was submitted to Tom Harrington of the FBI press office in December 1975. A few days later Harrington said the request had been denied and that Hale would be told not to discuss the matter with the author.

The Justice Department announced in 1968 that the FBI had been instructed not to impersonate newsmen. The three television networks received that assurance from Attorney General Ramsey Clark. The networks had complained that FBI agents had apparently posed as newsmen at a draft-card-burning ceremony in Washington. Reporters noticed that some of the questions being asked seemed very peculiar. Challenged, one of the "newsmen" identified himself as a reporter from the International News Service, which had not existed for years.

gave instructions that the FBI report on Jenkins should state that "Jenkins had engaged in no other incidents of homosexuality," that of the hundreds of people interviewed by the FBI "no one spoke derogatorily of Jenkins," that Jenkins had been "a devoted government servant in peace and war" and that the FBI probe "had failed to show any breach of security whatsoever."°

There was more to come in the Jenkins episode, for Johnson suspected that Goldwater was somehow involved. In a column in *Newsweek* in March 1975 Bill Moyers, then Johnson's assistant, wrote that he had asked the FBI for a name check on members of Goldwater's Senate staff. Moyers said Johnson told him that Hoover believed "some of Goldwater's people may have trapped Walter—set him up."

Johnson, according to Moyers, said he wanted an FBI check on "every one of Goldwater's people who could have done this thing . . . You call DeLoach and tell him if he wants to keep that nice house in Virginia, and that soft job he's got here, his boys had better find those bastards." Using the U.S. Senate telephone directory to obtain the list of names, the FBI checked fifteen persons on Goldwater's staff; minor derogatory information was found in the FBI files on one staff member, and a traffic violation was unearthed in the files of a second staff assistant. DeLoach hand-delivered a letter to Moyers on October 27, containing the disappointing results of the name checks.

As Sullivan also noted, there was a sequel to Atlantic City four years later, in 1968. According to FBI documents, William Connell, an assistant to Vice President Humphrey, called DeLoach in August, before the Democratic National Convention in Chicago. President Johnson, Connell said, had told Humphrey about the "great service" rendered by the FBI's "special team" at Atlantic City four years earlier, and "the Vice President hoped the Director would extend to him the same service during the forthcoming Democratic National Convention in Chicago."

DeLoach told Humphrey's assistant that the Chicago FBI office "is very well prepared to gather intelligence" at the convention. He recommended to Hoover that Humphrey's office be told there was no need for another special squad. The following week Hoover told Connell that there would be no special team sent to Chicago but that the FBI's Chicago office would give Humphrey "any kind of assistance he wants." Hoover then telephoned Chicago to explain that Humphrey wanted "an operation similar to what we did down at Atlantic City"

° Sullivan added: "This latter point was of grave concern to some men in the FBI. Jenkins could have seriously compromised our national security, for he had access to the most sensitive secrets. Nothing could be proven one way or the other."

for Johnson. Hoover said Humphrey's assistant "would like to have us furnish the same type of information and be in contact with him, Connell, on any so-called intelligence we might get. I stated I told Mr. Connell we would do that."

Sullivan also reported that Johnson, during the 1968 campaign, had requested physical surveillance of Mrs. Anna Chennault, the Chinese-born widow of General Claire Chennault. On October 31, in the closing days of the presidential campaign, Johnson announced a halt to the bombing of North Vietnam, a move designed to produce a negotiated end to the war. Johnson's timing was obviously designed to help Hubert Humphrey in his presidential campaign against Richard Nixon. But a day later the South Vietnamese government announced it would boycott the Paris peace talks. Johnson was enraged, convinced that the Republicans had influenced Saigon and were undermining his peace plan. Some days earlier the National Security Agency had intercepted a cable from the South Vietnamese embassy in Washington to Saigon. The message convinced Johnson that Mrs. Chennault was using her influence to persuade Saigon to resist a peace agreement. Johnson's suspicions were inflamed by the fact that Mrs. Chennault was an open and ardent Nixon supporter and fund-raiser.

On October 29, even before Saigon announced it would not participate in the Paris talks, Johnson had ordered an FBI wiretap placed on the Washington embassy of South Vietnam. The order was relayed to DeLoach by J. Bromley Smith, executive secretary of the NSC. Smith said the White House also wanted to know about everyone going in or out of the embassy over a three-day period, and the FBI conducted physical surveillance of the embassy in addition to the wiretap. Attorney General Ramsey Clark approved the wiretap the same day.

The next day Smith again called DeLoach and said Johnson wanted immediate FBI surveillance of Mrs. Chennault. Asked what this included, DeLoach testified: "The usual physical surveillance as I recall . . . following her to places where she went in the city of Washington, and as I recall . . . also a trip that she made to New York." DeLoach said he also believed that "a wiretap was placed on her telephone."

On November 4, the day before the election, according to the Sullivan memos, Bromley Smith called the FBI again to say that Johnson wanted all messages dealing with the Chennault surveillance completely "protected and secured." Smith, Sullivan said, added that "this situation may very well blow the roof off the political race yet."

On November 7, two days after Nixon's election victory, Smith called the FBI and spoke to DeLoach again. According to Sullivan,

Smith said he had just talked with Johnson, who wanted the surveillance of Mrs. Chennault discontinued but the embassy wiretap maintained. Smith, Sullivan wrote, said "the President was of the opinion that the intelligence obtained by the FBI in this operation was of the highest order. He stated that the facts furnished by the FBI had been exactly what had been needed by the White House and that he and the President were very grateful."

But Johnson was determined to prove that the Republicans and the widow of the famed Flying Tigers general had conspired to wreck his peace plan. A full week after the election, on November 12, he called DeLoach. "It was late at night when Johnson called me," DeLoach said in an interview. "It was the worst dressing-down I ever got. He wanted to know what calls Agnew made from his campaign plane in Albuquerque" during a stop there on November 2. DeLoach suggested to Johnson that it was very late at night and "it would be wrong to get the telephone company people up out of bed." In the back of his mind, DeLoach said, was the fact that President Kennedy had been criticized for having FBI agents rout newsmen out of bed to question them during the steel crisis.

"Do you know who I am?" Johnson roared, according to DeLoach. "I am the commander in chief of the United States." DeLoach said he told the President it was still awfully late to call up the telephone-company executives. Finally "Johnson said, 'All right, get it in the morning.' And he hung up."

In the morning the FBI checked telephone toll-call records in Albuquerque. "There were five phone calls made," Sullivan wrote in his memos. "Three of the calls were from a phone on the plane and two were made from a pay station at the airport near by. Johnson was advised that Mr. Agnew talked to Secretary of State Rusk. Kent Crane [an Agnew aide] made one call to a Cal Purdy in Texas. A third call was made by Kent Crane to this number in New York (212-288-8444). The FBI office in New York was requested to check it out and found it was listed to Bruce Friedle, a sculptor.* A fourth call was made to Jim Miller of New York City. A fifth call was made by Mr. Crane to Mr. Hitt in Washington, D.C. It was a call to the Nixon-Agnew campaign Headquarters."

At 4 P.M. Johnson called to ask what progress the FBI was making, Sullivan said. Given the information obtained by the FBI, John-

---

* Friedle, who still had the same telephone listing in Manhattan in 1976, said Kent Crane had previously bought some sculpture from his New York studio. "He called from the plane because he had seen in the window of my shop a piece of Nixon, wearing a tuxedo, leading an elephant—like a circus barker." Crane, as Friedle recalled it, said that some group wanted to buy the sculpture to give to Nixon as an inaugural gift. But, Friedle said, the sale never took place.

son "then instructed that a check be made to determine if the fifth
call could have been to Mrs. Chennault. This was done." Johnson then
ordered the FBI to see if Mrs. Chennault had telephoned New
Mexico, Texas, or Los Angeles on November 2. "This was done with
negative results."

As President, Johnson was frequently in touch with DeLoach,
a fellow Southerner with whom he felt comfortable. But Johnson insisted on instant access to Hoover's assistant. "I have seven children,"
DeLoach testified to the Church committee, "and it was necessary for
me to put a rule in my own home that no child could talk on the
phone for over three minutes. . . . I had a teenager who talked one
night for 18 minutes to one of her friends. The President was trying
to get me to discuss an applicant type investigation concerning an
appointment he wanted to make. He became very irate. The next
morning when my family and I were trying to go to church, we were
met in the driveway of my home by two men from the White House.
They told me they had instructions from the President to put a direct
line in my home. I told them to go ahead and put it in the den, and
they said no, the President said put it in your bedroom."

Although Sullivan's memos were fascinating, they focused for the
most part on Lyndon Johnson. A broader picture of past misuse of the
FBI was provided in testimony to the Church committee by John T.
Elliff, a professor of political science at Brandeis who headed the Senate select committee's task force on the FBI. Elliff noted that FDR
forwarded to Hoover hundreds of telegrams that he had received in
opposition to his request to Congress in May 1940 for additional funds
for national defense. Stephen Early, Roosevelt's secretary, told Hoover:
"It was the President's idea that you might like to go over these, noting the names and addresses of the senders." The following month,
telegrams approving of a speech by Colonel Charles Lindbergh, in
which he was critical of Roosevelt, were also forwarded to Hoover
by the White House.

Truman regularly received letters from Hoover marked "Personal
and Confidential," and containing information of political value. One
letter, dated June 25, 1947, warned that "a scandal pertaining to sugar"
was brewing and "will be very embarrassing to the Democratic Administration." Another reported on the efforts of Thomas (Tommy the
Cork) Corcoran, a former Roosevelt aide, to influence high-level appointments in the Truman Administration. The reports Truman received on Corcoran were from an FBI wiretap that was kept on for
almost three years beginning in June 1945.

In 1961 and 1962, during the Kennedy Administration, Attorney
General Robert F. Kennedy authorized FBI wiretaps in an investigation
of sugar lobbying by the Dominican Republic and other countries. In

the course of the investigation, the FBI bugged the New York City hotel room of Congressman Harold D. Cooley, a North Carolina Democrat and the powerful chairman of the House Agriculture Committee. It was Cooley who controlled the crucial sugar-quota legislation that determined how much sugar each foreign country could sell in the United States. In all, there were twelve wiretaps, three bugs, and physical surveillance of eleven persons. The targets of the wiretaps included three Administration officials, a congressional staff member,* and two registered lobbyists, one the Washington law firm of Surrey & Karasik.

According to the Church committee, in 1961 Robert Kennedy also authorized an FBI wiretap on Lloyd Norman, *Newsweek*'s Pentagon correspondent, during an investigation of a leak of classified documents. The following year Kennedy authorized taps on Hanson Baldwin, the military correspondent of the *New York Times* and his secretary, again to find the source of a news leak. And the committee found evidence that President Eisenhower and his aides had also received from Hoover the usual tidbits of information from "confidential" sources, some of it useful politically.

One of the disadvantages faced by Nixon in calling on William Sullivan to dredge up past misuse of the FBI was that he knew too much about Nixon's own dealings with the Bureau.† Sullivan knew of the wiretaps of seventeen Administration officials and newsmen, for example, because he administered the program for Hoover and sent the logs in a satchel to Robert Mardian. But Sullivan did not include Nixon's dealings with the FBI in his memos; instead he offered to testify publicly and place Nixon in "a very favorable light."

Nixon's own misuse of the FBI for political purposes has already been documented here and elsewhere. In addition to the seventeen wiretaps, for which no normal FBI records were kept, Nixon sought, through the CIA, to limit the FBI investigation of the Watergate burglary. His appointee to head the Bureau after Hoover's death, Patrick Gray, destroyed crucial Watergate evidence on White House orders. His chief of staff, H. R. Haldeman, had the FBI run a full-field investigation of CBS correspondent Daniel Schorr when his broadcasts displeased the Administration. The White House then lied, and with the President's approval, claimed that the investigation had been

---

* The Washington *Post* reported that the tapped congressional employee was Christine Gallagher, chief clerk of the House Agriculture Committee.
† It was a point that Nixon and John Dean worried about.

DEAN: ... there's one liability in Sullivan here, is that's his knowledge of the earlier things that occurred, uh—
PRESIDENT: That we did?
DEAN: That we did.

ordered because Schorr was under consideration for an environmental post. Milking William Sullivan for past political secrets was, in itself, a form of political misuse of the FBI.

But if the FBI was ready to be misused, it was equally capable of abusing the power entrusted to it by the people and the law. Perhaps the most shocking example of FBI abuse of power was its campaign of unrelenting surveillance and harassment of Martin Luther King, Jr.

Hoover set out to destroy King by using the full powers of the FBI against him. There have been various theories offered for Hoover's motive, and there may have been a combination of factors involved. Hoover was enraged when King criticized the FBI. The FBI's stated rationale for bugging and tapping King was to uncover ostensible "Communist" influence on the civil rights leader. Nor was Hoover pleased with King's growing success in the use of nonviolent confrontation. The police dogs of Birmingham snarling and ripping at black men and women in the summer of 1963 made for a bad image for law enforcement generally. The strains of "We Shall Overcome" fell harshly on Hoover's ears.

William Sullivan said that Hoover's view of blacks was the root cause of the campaign against King. "The real reason was that Hoover disliked blacks," Sullivan said in an interview. "He disliked Negroes. All you have to do is see how many he hired before Bobby came in. None. He told me himself he would never have one so long as he was FBI Director.° He disliked the civil rights movement. You had a black of national prominence heading the movement. He gave Hoover a peg by criticizing the FBI. And King upset Hoover's nice cozy relationship with Southern sheriffs and police. They helped us on bank robberies and such and they kept the black man in his place. Hoover didn't want anything to upset that relationship with law-enforcement authorities in the South."

In the end, one is forced to the conclusion that the FBI sought to discredit King because J. Edgar Hoover was a racist. Ultimately, Hoover battled King because King was black, and powerful, and his power was growing. He had the gift of poetry in his speech, he could mesmerize a nation with the lyricism of his dream. Who could foretell what might happen if the black people of America mobilized behind

---

° After Robert Kennedy became Attorney General, he asked Hoover how many black agents the FBI had, Sullivan testified to the Church committee. Hoover replied that the Bureau did not categorize people by race, creed, or color. That was laudatory, Kennedy said, but he still needed to know how many black agents there were in the FBI. Hoover had five black chauffeurs in the Bureau, Sullivan said, "so he automatically made them special agents." In 1975 there were 8,000 FBI special agents, of whom 103 were black—still far below the percentage of blacks in the U.S. population as a whole.

such a leader? To Hoover, Martin Luther King was uppity and biggity and he had to be stopped.

The FBI's fear that King might become a black "messiah" was expressed in precisely these words in a memo from headquarters to field offices on March 4, 1968, one month before King's death. The memo said one of the goals of COINTELPRO against "Black Nationalist-Hate Groups" would be to prevent the rise of a 'messiah' who could unify, and electrify, the militant black nationalist movement." Martin Luther King might "aspire to this position," the memo added. "King could be a very real contender for this position should he abandon his supposed 'obedience' to 'white, liberal doctrines' (nonviolence) and embrace black nationalism."

It was just before King's March on Washington in August 1963 that Sullivan and Hoover began their exchange of memos about the degree of Communist influence among blacks in the civil rights movement. And it is significant that when Sullivan about-faced and corrected his thinking on this subject, he told Hoover what he knew Hoover wanted to hear: ". . . we regard Martin Luther King to be the most dangerous and effective Negro leader in the country."

The FBI had begun surveillance of King's civil rights activities in the late fifties. In January of 1962 the FBI warned Attorney General Robert Kennedy that one of King's senior advisers was a "member" of the Communist party, and later that year a formal FBI investigation was opened into alleged "Communist infiltration" of King's movement. The FBI bombarded Robert Kennedy with memos warning of King's continued contacts with the adviser and with a second associate who the FBI said had strong ties to the Communist party. In February 1963, after the FBI warned that King would be meeting with the two advisers, Kennedy wrote a note to Assistant Attorney General Burke Marshall: "Burke—this is not getting any better."

The FBI's alleged concern over Communist influence on King centered on the figure of Stanley Levison, a New York attorney long close to the civil rights leader. In his 1971 book *Kennedy Justice*, Victor Navasky reported that Robert Kennedy gave his approval to tap King after receiving FBI allegations that Levison and Jack O'Dell, a member of the staff of King's Southern Christian Leadership Conference had "Communist" backgrounds. By Navasky's account, both President Kennedy and Robert Kennedy warned King about Levison and O'Dell in June 1963, and King then agreed to sever relations with the two men. O'Dell was eased out of the SCLC, Navasky wrote, but King after a time resumed his friendship with Levison, convincing Hoover that King was under Communist control and leading Hoover to increase his pressure on Robert Kennedy to approve the wiretapping of King.

The FBI warnings that King had "Communist" advisers placed both President Kennedy and his brother in a vulnerable political position. The Administration was closely identified with King and had publicly defended the civil rights leader. The President did not want him tarred as a Communist; on the other hand, if the Administration failed to act, the FBI might leak the allegations to the press, which could damage not only King but the Kennedys. It was, in short, another form of Hoover blackmail.

And both Bobby Kennedy and the President understood the internal dynamics of the situation clearly; two tidbits churned up by the Senate intelligence committee illustrate what steps the Kennedys took to counter Hoover. According to Congressman Andrew Young, who had been an aide to King, after King met with the President in June 1963, the civil rights leader quoted Kennedy as saying "there was an attempt [by the FBI] to smear the movement on the basis of Communist influence." By Young's account, the President had also warned King: "I assume you know you're under very close surveillance."

The following month Hoover sent Robert Kennedy another memo charging that King was affiliated with Communists. Courtney Evans, the FBI's liaison man with the Justice Department, described Kennedy's reaction in a memo: "The Attorney General stated that if this report got up to the Hill at this time, he would be impeached."

One way to determine if Hoover's charges about King were true, of course, was to tap King's telephone. Evans testified that Robert Kennedy raised the question in a meeting with him in July of 1963.

Evans told his FBI superior he had advised Kennedy that King traveled a great deal and that he doubted that "surveillance of his home or office would be very productive." Evans also suggested that if a tap on King ever became known, it could have unpleasant repercussions. "The AG said this did not concern him at all; that in view of the possible Communist influence in the racial situation, he thought it advisable to have as complete coverage as possible." Evans advised Kennedy he would check into the possibility of a wiretap, but within a week, on July 25, Kennedy informed Evans that he had decided against tapping King.

Early in September, Sullivan recommended to Hoover that the FBI wiretap King. It was only a week after Sullivan had admitted to Hoover that he had been sadly mistaken in failing to perceive the Communist threat in the racial movement. Hoover approved, although he scrawled he was still "dizzy over vacillation" about the degree of Communist influence in the civil rights movement.

On October 7 Hoover formally requested Robert Kennedy's approval of wiretaps on King's home and office, citing "possible Communist influence in the racial situation." On October 10 Evans and

Kennedy conferred about Hoover's request. This time, according to the FBI memo of their meeting, Kennedy approved the taps on King "on a trial basis, and to continue it if productive results were forthcoming." On October 21 Kennedy told the FBI that by a trial basis he meant thirty days, after which the taps would have to be evaluated before any decision was made to continue them.

But the tap installed on King's home in Atlanta remained in place for one year and six months, until April 1965.* In addition to the tap on King's home, the FBI wiretapped his hotel rooms in Los Angeles and Atlantic City, and SCLC headquarters in both Atlanta and New York. The longest tap, on the Atlanta office, lasted two years and eight months, from November 1963 until June 1966.

Three years later Hoover charged that the impetus to tap King had come from Robert Kennedy. By then Robert Kennedy had been assassinated. But Kennedy's associates claimed that the pressure to tap King had come from Hoover, and that Kennedy had gone along with it to disprove FBI suspicions of King's alleged Communist ties. Support for this version came from William Sullivan, who headed the FBI division that handled the wiretapping. Asked whether the idea of tapping King came from the Attorney General or from Hoover, Sullivan told the author, "Not from Bobby. It came from Hoover. He sent down a memo. He wanted King given the full treatment. The whole impetus came from us."

And Sullivan added, "I do know that Bobby Kennedy resisted, resisted, and resisted tapping King. Finally we twisted the arm of the Attorney General to the point where he had to go. I guess he feared we would let that stuff go in the press if he said no. I know he resisted the electronic coverage. He didn't want to put it on."

In December 1963, after William Sullivan had agreed that King was "the most dangerous and effective Negro leader in the country," a meeting was convened at FBI headquarters in Washington to plan the FBI's war on the civil rights leader. Among the tactics and subjects discussed was whether black FBI agents in the Atlanta area might be used, and how many would be needed, and whether TELSURS and MISURS (telephone and microphone surveillance) might be used against King's associates. The agenda drawn up for the meeting asked:

"What are the possibilities of using this [electronic surveillance]? Are there any disgruntled employees at SCLC and/or former employees who may be disgruntled, or disgruntled acquaintances? Does

---

* Asked whether it had been re-evaluated after thirty days, as Kennedy had instructed, Courtney Evans told the Church committee, "I have no personal knowledge in this regard but I would point out for the information of the committee that the assassination of President Kennedy occurred within that 30-day period and that this had a great effect on what Robert Kennedy was doing."

the office have any contacts among ministers, both colored and white, who are in a position to be of assistance, and if so, in what manner could we use them?

"Do we have any information concerning any shady financial dealings of King which could be explored to our advantage? Was this point ever explored before? And what are the possibilities of placing a good looking female plant in King's office?" A total of twenty-one such ideas was contained in the FBI agenda.

It was after this meeting that the FBI began bugging King's hotel and motel rooms, in addition to wiretapping his telephone conversations. The first bug was placed in the Willard Hotel, a block from the White House, when King stayed there in January 1964. In all, the FBI bugged sixteen of King's hotel rooms in Washington and six states.°

Although Robert Kennedy approved the wiretaps, there is no evidence that he ever knew of or approved the FBI's use of bugs against King. When asked by the Church committee whether Kennedy had ever authorized the bugs or been told about them, Courtney Evans replied, "Not to my knowledge."† Kennedy received FBI memoranda based on the King bugs, but not so labeled; it is possible, however, that he guessed or suspected that the information came from hidden microphones.

On January 8, 1964, two days after the FBI began bugging King's hotel rooms, Sullivan wrote a memo to Hoover. The time was approaching, he wrote, to take King "off his pedestal and reduce him completely in influence." But if the FBI succeeded in that objective,

---

° The FBI bugs were placed in King's hotel rooms in Washington, D.C., Milwaukee, Honolulu, Los Angeles, Detroit, Sacramento, Savannah, and New York City, between January 1964 and November 1965.

New York and Miami police, and probably others, bugged King—even in church. Andrew Young testified before the Senate intelligence committee: "We found a bug in the pulpit in a church in Selma, Alabama, in 1965 . . . We took it out from under the pulpit, taped it on top of the pulpit, and Reverend Abernathy called it 'this little do-hickey,' and he said, 'I want to tell Mr. Hoover, I don't want it under here where there is a whole lot of static, I want him to get it straight,' and he preached to the little bug."

† On March 30, 1965, after Nicholas Katzenbach had become Attorney General, he required that the FBI seek prior written approval of the Attorney General before planting any bugs; later that summer Katzenbach gave Hoover permission to move without advance approval in "emergency circumstances." The Church committee obtained from FBI files four memos stating that King's hotel rooms in New York City had been bugged in May, October, and November of 1965, with approval after the fact. Although Katzenbach conceded that each memo "bears my initials in what appears to be my handwriting," he professed to have no memory of reading or receiving them. Under questioning, however, Katzenbach declined to characterize them as forgeries.

the Negroes will be left without a national leader of sufficiently compelling personality to steer them in the proper direction. This is what could happen, but need not happen if the right kind of a national Negro leader could at this time be gradually developed so as to overshadow Dr. King and be in the position to assume the role of the leadership of the Negro people when King has been completely discredited.

For some months I have been thinking about this matter. One day I had an opportunity to explore this from a philosophical and sociological standpoint with [name deleted] whom I have known for some years ... I asked him ... if he knew any Negro of outstanding intelligence or ability ... [He] has submitted to me the name of the above-captioned person. Enclosed with this memorandum is an outline of [deleted] biography, which is truly remarkable ... On scanning this biography, it will be seen that [deleted] does have all the qualifications of the kind of a Negro I have in mind to advance to positions of national leadership.

I want to make it clear at once that I don't propose that the FBI in any way become involved openly as the sponsor of a Negro leader to overshadow Martin Luther King. If this thing can be set up properly without the Bureau in any way becoming directly involved, I think it would be not only a great help to the FBI, but would be a fine thing for the country at large.

Hoover was pleased. "I am glad to see that 'light' has finally, though dismally delayed, come to the Domestic Intelligence Division," he responded. "I struggled for months to get over the fact that the Communists were taking over the racial movement, but our experts here couldn't or wouldn't see it. H."

By the fall of 1964 the FBI's campaign against King had become full-scale war. For months the Bureau had been bugging King's hotel rooms, and now it began to whisper stories to newsmen in Washington about the alleged sexual practices of the civil rights leader. King, the FBI told reporters, cavorted with women in his hotel rooms; explicit details were available to newsmen willing to listen to the FBI's *Decameron.* The purpose of the FBI whispers was to publicize stories that King, whose power rested upon his moral authority, had a lively extramarital sex life, which the FBI considered inconsistent with his public reputation and his profession as a minister. The FBI coupled these stories with unsupported claims that King was under the complete control of the Communist party.

Rumors circulated in Washington that the FBI had offered to let trusted reporters either see the transcripts of the bugging of King's hotel rooms or listen to the actual tapes. In 1976 Benjamin C. Bradlee, the editor of the Washington *Post,* said that he had been offered a transcript of a King tape by Deke DeLoach in the fall of 1964. At the time, Bradlee was chief of *Newsweek*'s Washington bureau. "The circumstances involved a cover story we were doing on Hoover," Bradlee said. "I had finally succeeded in getting an interview with Hoover. It was to be me, Jay Iselin, and Dwight Martin from New York. On the morning of the interview we all had breakfast together to plan the interview, and then went back to the office around nine-thirty. The phone rings and it's DeLoach. Martin is not acceptable to the Director. In an act I regret, we [Bradlee and Iselin] went over alone. We went in and saw Hoover and asked one question and he talked for thirty minutes." According to Bradlee, the interview was worthless. Afterward, Bradlee said, he met with DeLoach, who had promised to explain why Martin was barred. "He [DeLoach] showed me the file. He said Martin's wife had been under some suspicion. It turned out to be his ex-wife, who was apparently an Oriental. During World War II she had seen a lot of military people. Since she worked for a Chinese tailor, it wasn't surprising—her customers were military people."

At this point, Bradlee went on, the only persons present were "DeLoach and me. He offered a transcript of Martin Luther King. No, I said, I did not want to see it." Bradlee said it was made clear to him that the transcript was from the bugging of King's hotel rooms. "I said I thought it was a tape, I know of a journalist in Atlanta who heard the tape." But, he said, "it was a transcript he was offering, and I had the impression that he had the transcript on his desk next to the file on Dwight Martin's ex-wife. He kind of hustled it—saying King made unpleasant references to the Kennedy family." Asked whether the alleged remark by King referred to Jacqueline Kennedy, Bradlee replied, "Yes."*

Jay Iselin, who accompanied Bradlee to the FBI, vividly remembered the circumstances. In the cab going back to the *Newsweek* office, Bradlee filled him in. Iselin said Bradlee told him the conversation with DeLoach had been along the lines of "What do you think of a black man fooling around with white women?" He added, "Ben was offered the tapes. I remember my slack-jawed astonishment. We obviously declined to have anything to do with it." Bradlee, as Iselin recalled it, said the tapes had been described to him as "based on the bugging of hotel rooms of King. They would get white girls in the rooms . . . that sort of thing."

---

* Since it was well known that Bradlee had been a close personal friend of the late President Kennedy, he said he assumed the derogatory reference to Jacqueline Kennedy was mentioned in an effort to pique his interest in looking at the transcript. That, he said, is what he meant by saying that DeLoach had "kind of hustled" the transcript.

In October, *Newsweek* gave a large party to celebrate the open-ing of its new offices on the twelfth floor of an office building a block from the White House. Attorney General Katzenbach was there, and Iselin remembers needling Katzenbach and Burke Marshall, the As-sistant Attorney General in charge of the Civil Rights Division, asking them what kind of operation they were running, peddling smut.

Katzenbach said that at the *Newsweek* offices Bradlee told him that the tapes he had been offered were "from hotel rooms and in-volved sexual activities... Bradlee said DeLoach had offered 'inter-esting' tapes, with a leer."

Katzenbach described the incident in general terms to the Church committee, without revealing the names of Bradlee and Iselin. He testified that he was dismayed "and felt that the President should be advised immediately." Katzenbach said he flew with Burke Marshall to the LBJ Ranch to see President Johnson. Katzenbach told Johnson of his conversation with Bradlee and, he said, warned "that this was shocking conduct and politically extremely dangerous to the Presi-dency. I told the President my view that it should be stopped imme-diately and that he should personally contact Mr. Hoover."

Katzenbach said he got the "impression" that Johnson would do so. The President, Katzenbach said in an interview, "sat in a rocker by the fire and pretty much listened. He didn't comment one way or the other. But I had the distinct impression that he was going to do something about it to stop it."° Back in Washington on Monday, Katzenbach said, he was told by one or two other newsmen of similar offers by the FBI.† The same day, Katzenbach said, he confronted

---

° But the FBI did not stop spreading rumors to newsmen about King's alleged extramarital activities. If Johnson did speak to Hoover, there is no record of it; what evidence does exist suggests that LBJ was annoyed not with the FBI, but with Bradlee for talking to Katzenbach. According to a DeLoach memo of Decem-ber 1, 1964, Bill Moyers told him Johnson had heard that a newsman (whose name was deleted from the memo as published by the Senate intelligence com-mittee) was "telling all over town" about the FBI bugging King. Moyers said "the President wanted to get this word to us so we would know not to trust" the newsman, DeLoach wrote.

† Various newsmen were apparently offered transcripts of the King bugs by the FBI. David Kraslow, chief of the Washington bureau of the Cox newspapers, said that an FBI source had telephoned him—he thought it was late in 1964 or early in 1965—to offer a transcript of an interesting tape. At the time, Kraslow was a reporter for the Los Angeles *Times* in Washington. Kraslow said the FBI official began reading from a purported transcript of King allegedly participating in a sex orgy. Kraslow interrupted the FBI man and said he did not wish to listen to any more. He declined to identify his FBI source.

In February 1976 writer Paul Clancy reported in *Quill* magazine, a journalism trade publication, that James McCartney, while a reporter for the Chicago *Daily News*, had been offered a photograph by an FBI official supposedly showing King

DeLoach. "He rather angrily denied it," Katzenbach said. "I didn't believe him."

In an interview DeLoach disputed the accounts by Bradlee, Iselin, and Katzenbach. DeLoach said he had arranged an interview for Bradlee "with Mr. Hoover. The day before, Bradlee said he wanted to bring the man who would write the story. When he asked to bring the additional man, Mr. Hoover said have a file check. As a result of the file check, Mr. Hoover said he did not want to see the man." DeLoach added, "At no point did I ever offer Bradlee the transcripts or to play the tape." DeLoach also denied that Katzenbach had questioned him about making such an offer to Bradlee. "Absolutely not," he said. "He did not ask about the transcripts."

On November 18 Hoover met with a group of women reporters in Washington and pronounced King "the most notorious liar in the country."* Specifically, Hoover criticized King for telling his followers not to bother to report acts of violence to the FBI office in Albany, Georgia, because the agents were Southerners who would take no action on civil rights violations. Hoover claimed that "70 per cent" of agents assigned to the South were born in the North.

Hoover's astonishing attack on King received extensive coverage in the news media. In contrast, the prurient stories that the FBI had whispered to the press about King's sex life were not achieving their purpose, for nobody would print them. Hoover apparently decided to take a more direct approach. On November 21, three days after Hoover's remarks to the women journalists, the FBI mailed an anonymous letter and a tape of the King hotel-room bugs to King and his wife, Coretta.

"King, there is only one thing left for you to do," the letter said. "You know what it is. You have just 34 days in which to do it. This exact number has been selected for a specific reason. It has definite practical significance. You are done."†

---

leaving a motel with a white woman. Clancy also said that Eugene C. Patterson, while editor of the Atlanta *Constitution*, had been approached by an FBI agent in Atlanta and offered similar material.

* The FBI's top public relations man was unhappy at Hoover's comment. "I was with Hoover at the time," DeLoach testified. ". . . I passed Mr. Hoover a note indicating that in my opinion he should either retract that statement or indicate that it was off-the-record. He threw the note in the trash. I sent him another note. He threw that in the trash. I sent a third note, and at that time he told me to mind my own business."

† Who wrote the letter was a matter of dispute. The text quoted at the Church committee hearings was, according to the FBI, found in the files of William Sullivan sometime after he was forced out by Hoover. Sullivan claimed that the draft was a plant written by someone else and placed in his files to embarrass him. The significance of the "thirty-four days" was not clarified by the Senate intel-

The letter was mailed three weeks before King was due to receive the Nobel prize in Oslo, on December 10. Since it was accompanied by a tape which the FBI considered compromising, the letter might have been interpreted as an invitation to King to kill himself. Apparently that is how King construed it, for Congressman Young, King's former assistant, told the Church committee that when King received the tape and the letter, "he felt somebody was trying to get him to commit suicide."

William Sullivan said in an interview that he had, on orders from Hoover, arranged to have a tape mailed to Mrs. King. He said he received the order from Hoover's assistant, Alan H. Belmont.°

"Belmont called me. We met at his request and he said Hoover and Tolson wanted certain tapes sent to Coretta King. I objected, not on moral groups, but on practical grounds. I said, 'She'll know immediately that the FBI made the tapes.'

"Belmont said King has been critical of Hoover and Hoover wants to stop that, and the tapes will blackmail him [King] into stopping. And Belmont said he was going to have the tapes sanitized so that Mrs. King will not know that they came from the FBI. He said, 'I'll arrange to have the tapes selected and I'll have them sent to you in a box.'" In due course, Sullivan said, the box arrived, and he had the impression the tape it contained was "a composite of three tapes."

Had the FBI put together a composite in order to select what it considered the most damaging parts of the various hotel room tapes to send to Mrs. King? "Probably," Sullivan said, "but I understood it was to sanitize, to disguise the FBI origin. Perhaps it was a composite of more than three tapes, I don't know." The work was done by the FBI laboratory, the same one extolled to the thousands of tourists who visit FBI headquarters each year in Washington. "I think Belmont called the lab," Sullivan said. "I don't know how it was done.

"Hoover called me on the phone and said he wanted it mailed from a Southern city. I picked an agent who was a very close-mouthed fellow; I picked him because I knew he wouldn't talk about it. I never told him what was in the box. I told him what the assignment was. 'Take this down to Tampa and mail it,' and he did. He came back and

---

ligence committee. But from November 21, the date the tape was mailed, it would have been exactly thirty-four days to Christmas Day.

James B. Adams, Deputy Associate Director of the FBI, testified he could not "find any basis" on which the committee staff had concluded the letter was "a suicide urging." That annoyed Senator Church:

THE CHAIRMAN: It is certainly no Christmas card, is it?
MR. ADAMS: It is certainly no Christmas card.
° Sullivan testified he was told by Belmont that Hoover wanted the tape mailed to Mrs. King to break up her marriage and diminish King's stature.

told me it had been done. I never discussed it with Hoover afterward. He never mentioned it to me."[*]

With the Hoover-King controversy now threatening to undermine King's leadership and endanger the civil rights movement, other black leaders urged King to meet with the FBI Director. King, the Reverend Ralph Abernathy, and other SCLC leaders met with Hoover and DeLoach in Hoover's office on December 1. Precisely what was said is not clear, but there is some reason to believe the meeting may not have been unlike Hoover's chat with President Kennedy about Judith Campbell. DeLoach has described it as "a very amicable meeting, a pleasant meeting between two great symbols of leadership." Hoover, he said, told King "that, in view of your stature and reputation and your leadership with the black community, you should do everything possible to be careful of your associates and be careful of your personal life, so that no question will be raised concerning your character at any time."

This at a time when the FBI was actively bugging and wiretapping King's hotel rooms—which King now knew, since he had received the tape—and telling newsmen all about King's sex life. For the moment, Hoover's tried-and-true blackmail techniques seemed to work. A subdued King said after the meeting that he and Hoover had reached "new levels of understanding."

The tape, the apparent suicide letter, and the attempt to impugn King's moral character were the most vicious aspects of the FBI's campaign. But the FBI's harassment of King reached as well into pettier areas. According to Frederick Schwarz, the Church committee's counsel, the FBI in 1964 sought to block Marquette University from giving King an honorary degree "because it was thought unseemly," since the university had once granted an honorary degree to Hoover. Later that year the FBI learned that King planned to visit Pope Paul VI. John Malone, the head of the FBI's New York office, was dispatched to see

[*] Although the whole purpose of the exercise was to mail the tape to Coretta King, the FBI agent who went to Florida told the Senate intelligence committee that he had mailed it to "Martin Luther King, Jr." on Sullivan's instructions. Andrew Young said the tape was received at SCLC headquarters in Atlanta and later sent to King's home.

The tape, regardless of the FBI's motive in sending it, apparently had very little effect. In an interview in the *New York Times* on March 9, 1975, Mrs. King acknowledged to correspondent Nicholas Horrock that she had listened to such a tape. "I received a tape that was rather curious, unlabeled," she said. "As a matter of fact, Martin and I listened to the tape and we found much of it unintelligible. We concluded there was nothing in the tape to discredit him." Mrs. King also said that she and her husband realized the tape had been made covertly and "presumed" it had been done by the FBI.

Francis Cardinal Spellman to persuade him to intervene with the Pope and prevent the audience. Malone thought he had succeeded, but the Pope met with King anyhow. "Astounding," Hoover wrote on a memo. "I am amazed . . ."

Four years later King was in Memphis to participate in a strike of city garbage workers. The FBI campaign had not abated, for on March 28, 1968, the FBI drafted a blind memo—bearing no FBI markings—for distribution to "cooperative news media." "The fine Hotel Lorraine in Memphis is owned and patronized exclusively by Negroes," the memo said, "but King did not go there." Instead, King was staying at "a plush Holiday Inn Motel, white-owned, operated, and almost exclusively white patronized." The purpose of the proposed planted news item, the FBI documents said, was "to publicize hypocrisy on the part of Martin Luther King." Hoover signed the FBI memo, "Okay, H." It was not established whether the memo was leaked to the press, but King did change hotels. He went home to Atlanta, and when he returned to Memphis the following week, he moved into the Lorraine. Standing there on the balcony outside his room, he was shot and killed on April 4, 1968. James Earl Ray, a small-time escaped convict, pleaded guilty to the crime a year later and was sentenced to ninety-nine years in prison. But whether he acted alone or was part of a conspiracy remained an open question.

When the Church committee disclosed details of the FBI's campaign against King, including the "suicide" letter, questions were publicly raised about whether the FBI's actions against King could conceivably have extended to complicity in his murder. On November 26, 1975, Attorney General Edward H. Levi ordered a review of the FBI's investigation into the death of Martin Luther King.

For more than forty years, the FBI has engaged in the collection of domestic intelligence about individual Americans and groups. Most citizens, Congress, and the press assumed that somehow, somewhere, there existed a law that gave the FBI the right to do so. Not until the seventies, when the Bureau came under serious scrutiny for the first time, was it realized that the FBI had *no* clear legal authority to gather intelligence at home; the entire FBI effort against "subversives" and "extremists" was legally a house of cards.

One of the first to question the FBI's authority in the domestic intelligence field was Frank Donner, a Yale Law School professor and expert on the FBI. In an article in the *Nation* in June 1974, Donner wrote: ". . . for more than three decades a secret police force has spied into and kept records on the lives of Americans, without authority from either Congress or the Executive."

Little more than a year later, an official government study reached almost the same conclusion. The study, by the General Accounting Office, Congress' watchdog agency, found that the FBI's authority to conduct domestic intelligence investigations was "vague and ambiguous." Cautiously, the GAO stopped short of concluding that "the authority claimed does not exist." But the GAO was unable to point to any executive order or statute of the United States giving the FBI the right to pry into the lives of Americans.

The first indication of a presidential request to the FBI to gather such intelligence is contained in a memo written by Hoover on August 25, 1936. Reporting on a meeting with President Roosevelt, Hoover said FDR had expressed concern about "the movement of the Communists and of Fascism in the United States" and was interested in a "broad picture" of such activity.

On September 6, 1939, Roosevelt issued the first public directive; he instructed the Justice Department to have the FBI take charge of "investigative work in matters relating to espionage, sabotage, and violation of the neutrality regulations." Roosevelt also asked that local police furnish the FBI with any information they had on "subversive activities." But the FBI later claimed that the peripheral reference to "subversive activities" gave it broad power to snoop at home. Roosevelt, Truman, and Eisenhower subsequently issued similar directives. The Bureau also claimed legal authority from a section of the Internal Security Act of 1950 making it a crime to conspire to establish a totalitarian form of government in the United States.

The FBI also pointed to a law giving the Attorney General power to appoint officials "to detect and prosecute" crimes against the United States. But, as the GAO study noted, the coupling of those two words suggests that the FBI may only "detect" crimes that are to be prosecuted, and not engage in general intelligence-gathering or fishing expeditions.

The strongest argument made by the FBI in favor of the need for general intelligence-gathering is that the Bureau should not have to wait to act until a bomb goes off or a plane is hijacked, for then it is too late. In times of political stress, when bombings or other forms of violence are taking place, most citizens probably support this argument. The public expects the FBI to prevent such violent crimes if it can.

The difficulty is that the FBI, by infiltrating and spying on selected groups in American society, arrogated to itself the role of a thought police. It decided which groups were legitimate, and which were a danger—by FBI standards—to the Republic. It took sides in the social and political conflicts of the fifties and sixties, deciding, for example, that those who opposed the war in Vietnam, or whose skin was black, should be targets of FBI attention. Since the FBI acted secretly, it distorted the normal political process by covertly acting against certain groups and individuals. In short, the FBI filled the classic role of a secret political police.

"The inescapable message of much of the material we have covered," Yale law professor Thomas I. Emerson said at a 1971 conference on the FBI, "is that the FBI jeopardizes the whole system of freedom of expression which is the cornerstone of an open society . . . At worst it raises the specter of a police state . . . in essence the FBI conceives of itself as an instrument to prevent radical social change in America. . . . throughout most of its history the FBI has taken on the task not only of investigating specific violations of federal laws, but gathering general intelligence in the national security field . . . the Bureau's view of its function leads it beyond data collection and into political warfare."

As Emerson suggested, the FBI did not confine itself to spying on domestic groups and individuals whom it considered to be suspect, but engaged in active disruption of such groups through COINTEL-PRO. A secret and powerful government hand moved behind the scenes to harass and destroy organizations and individuals, in some cases to break up marriages, to cause people to be fired from their jobs, and even to foment violence.

The FBI often gathers domestic intelligence by infiltrating groups and using paid informers. One such informant, Sara Jane Moore, was sentenced to life imprisonment in January 1976 for attempting to shoot President Ford. In case after case it was disclosed that many an FBI informant was playing the role of *agent provocateur*, often teaching activist groups how to use explosives, and urging that the members commit specific crimes. For example, Robert Hardy, an FBI informant, testified that he actually led a group of thirty antiwar activists in a raid on the Camden, New Jersey, draft board in 1971. "I taught them everything they knew," he said, "how to cut glass and open windows without making any noise . . . how to open file cabinets without a key."

In choosing sides in the domestic political process, the FBI saw itself on the ramparts, as the guardian of the status quo and the established order. The prevailing political view within the FBI is starkly etched in internal memoranda that were never expected to leak out.

For example, a May 1968 message from FBI headquarters to all field offices referred to recent attempts by students to seize control of college and university buildings. These outbreaks, the message said, were "a direct challenge to law and order and a substantial threat to the stability of society in general."

In September 1970 W. Mark Felt, a high-ranking FBI official, recommended that the age for FBI campus informants be lowered from twenty-one to eighteen:

"Never in our history have we been confronted with as critical a need for informant coverage. Terrorist violence is all around us and more has been threatened. Even our own doors are being threatened by Weatherman fanatics. Bombings, assassination of police officers, kidnapping and torture murder are all part of the picture. These violence-oriented black and white savages are at war with the Government and the American people."

Felt argued that eighteen was none too soon to recruit college students to the ranks of FBI informers. "By the time they are 21 years of age they are almost ready to leave college and have been subjected to the corrosive influence and brainwashing of ultra-liberal and radical professors."

Another 1970 FBI memo typified the tone of the Bureau's intelligence-gathering program. It recommended that each FBI field office set up a "Key Black Extremist (KBE) Program" to identify and increase "coverage" of Black Panther and other black nationalist leaders. Each KBE, the memo said, "must be included in the Black Nationalist Photograph Album (BNPA) . . . all aspects of the finances of a KBE must be determined. Bank accounts must be monitored. Safe deposit boxes, investments, and hidden assets must be located . . . obtain suitable handwriting specimens of each KBE to be placed in the National Security File in the Laboratory."

Under Richard Nixon, the FBI even started an intelligence newsletter with a very select audience—initially only Nixon himself and Attorney General Mitchell. Later Vice President Spiro Agnew was added to the list. The project was code-named INLET. The nature of the items that Hoover peddled to the White House can best be gleaned by the instructions to agents in the field, who were told to be on the alert for "items with an unusual twist or concerning prominent personalities which may be of special interest to the President or the Attorney General." According to the Church committee, one of the tidbits sent to the White House via INLET dealt with "the personal life" of a prominent actress.

But it was not only campus radicals and black activists who were investigated by the FBI. The Bureau also found time to spy on such dangerous groups as the Women's Liberation Movement. FBI files include reports on the release of white mice by women at a protest demonstration, and the sensational news that women's lib was opposed to the Miss America Pageant at Atlantic City.

By assuming that the moribund Communist party *might* try to influence the "New Left," the FBI was able to cast its intelligence net so wide as to encompass virtually every kind of legitimate political group in America. A message from FBI headquarters to field offices on January 30, 1967, laid this out in unmistakable terms:

> Each office must remain constantly alert to the existence of organizations which have aims and objectives coinciding with those of the Communist Party and are likely to be susceptible to communist influence. This necessarily includes antiwar and pacifist groups, civil rights groups, and other radical groups which advocate civil disobedience and oppose the exercise of authority by duly constituted Government officials.

One purpose of the FBI intelligence program was to determine which of us to lock up in the event of war or a presidentially decreed "emergency." In 1939 the FBI established a Security Index, a list of names of persons "on whom there is information available to indicate that their presence at liberty in this country in time of war or national emergency would be dangerous to the public peace and safety of the United States government." Then, in 1950, Congress passed the Internal Security Act, which provided for the confinement of suspected citizens in detention camps in time of emergency or insurrection. Six camps were actually established but never used. The FBI complained to the Justice Department that the act provided for individual arrest warrants in time of emergency, "a time-consuming procedure compared to the use of one master arrest warrant for all subjects apprehended," as planned under the Security Index. Since the act in other ways set stricter standards for rounding people up, the FBI with the approval of the Attorney General simply ignored the law and continued to keep its own list. But the FBI in 1951 urged that the Justice Department review the names on the Security Index so that, in the words of one memo, "the Bureau would not be open to an allegation of using Police State tactics."

Finally, in 1968, the Justice Department issued revised criteria for listing people on the index; it included any person who, although not a member of a suspect organization, had "revolutionary beliefs," and might, in time of trouble, attempt to interfere with the operations of the government. Even if a person did not meet the specific criteria, he could be listed if the FBI had information that he was a "dangerous individual."

Because of a public outcry over the existence of concentration camps in America, unused or not, the emergency detention provision of the 1950 law was repealed in 1971. At one time, however, the FBI Security Index listed 26,174 Americans who might be locked up in time of war or emergency. Thousands were especially targeted for "priority apprehension." Although Clarence Kelley assured Congress that the Security Index had been discontinued in 1971, it was revealed in 1975 that the FBI still maintained an Administrative Index (ADEX), a list of 1,200 Americans "who would merit close investigative attention" if the balloon went up; moreover, the FBI reportedly never destroyed some 15,000 cards that comprised its Security Index.°

In addition to the various security indices, the FBI maintains intelligence dossiers on hundreds of thousands of American citizens, and the files keep growing. Since 1939 the FBI has compiled more than 500,000 dossiers on Americans.

Quite aside from the fact that the FBI's intelligence-gathering program rests on the shakiest of legal foundations, the evidence suggests that it has not been very effective. The GAO found that only 3 percent of the FBI's domestic intelligence investigations resulted in prosecutions, with only 1.3 percent leading to convictions. Only 2 percent resulted in advance warning of "extremist acts or . . . violent acts."

The most outrageous of the FBI's activities was its COINTELPRO operation, which the Bureau admitted it had conducted for fifteen years, between 1956 and 1971.† Under this program, a secret arm of the United States government, using taxpayers' funds, harassed American citizens and disrupted their organizations, using a wide variety of covert techniques. As the House intelligence committee concluded in its own study of COINTELPRO, "Careers were ruined, friendships severed, reputations sullied, businesses bankrupted and, in some cases, lives endangered."

Attorney General William B. Saxbe announced in 1974 that there were seven counterintelligence programs. Five were against the "Communist Party, USA, Socialist Workers Party, White Hate Groups, New Left, Black Extremists." Two others, entitled "Espionage or Soviet-Satellite Intelligence" and "Special Operations," both classified secret,

---

° Through the sixties, in addition to the Security Index the FBI maintained a Reserve Index of persons who did not meet the criteria of the Security Index but who would still get special FBI attention in an emergency. The Church committee reported: "In 1962, there were approximately 10,000 names in the Reserve Index. A special section of that list was reserved for educators, labor union organizers and leaders, media personnel, lawyers, doctors, scientists and other potentially influential people." In 1967, on Hoover's orders, the FBI also created a Rabble Rouser Index of persons who might cause racial discord. A year later it was renamed the Agitator Index, and FBI field offices were directed to obtain photographs of each person on the list. In January 1976 the FBI announced that it would no longer keep its 1,200-name Administrative Index. But who knows.

† In a memo dated April 28, 1971, Hoover officially ended the program—but only because its existence had been revealed in the documents stolen on March 8, 1971, from an FBI office in Media, Pennsylvania. There were published reports that the FBI continued to use the same technique against domestic political groups, without using the name COINTELPRO.

were aimed at "hostile foreign intelligence sources, foreign Communist organizations and individuals connected with them." But six months later Attorney General Levi suddenly found five more; these were called the Puerto Rican Bomber Program (1966), Operation Hoodwink (1966), Operation Border Coverage (1961), the Cuban Program (1961), and the Yugoslav Program (1969). One of the largest of these was the Puerto Rican program, in which the FBI took thirty-seven separate actions to disrupt groups seeking Puerto Rican independence. Hoodwink sought to pit the Mafia against the Communist party. "A dispute between the Communist Party, USA, and La Cosa Nostra would cause disruption of both groups," a 1966 FBI memo said. As part of Hoodwink, the FBI wrote a letter to the *Daily Worker*, noting that the mob was seeking a successor to the deceased Mafia leader Thomas (Three Finger Brown) Luchese. The letter charged that the Mafia enriched itself at the expense of "the working and oppressed classes." Levi identified the Puerto Rican program and Operation Hoodwink, but said the other three programs were "classified." In one of the classified programs the FBI told local authorities that members of a group had met with prostitutes. In another program the FBI saw to it that the wife of a foreign Communist had her visa revoked. The FBI also leaked stories that members of a foreign Communist embassy who were supposedly traveling to investigate "fishing sites" were really engaged in economic espionage. Over a fifteen-year period, the FBI admitted to proposing a total of 3,247 "dirty tricks" against citizens and groups, of which 2,370 actions were actually approved and carried out.

Saxbe issued a report saying that COINTELPRO involved "practices that can only be considered abhorrent in a free society." But Clarence M. Kelley openly and publicly disagreed. At a joint press conference with Saxbe, Kelley said the FBI admittedly took actions "to disrupt the anarchistic plans and activities of violence-prone groups whose publicly announced goal was to bring America to its knees. For the FBI to have done less under the circumstances would have been an abdication of its responsibilities to the American people." Despite his public endorsement of COINTELPRO, Kelley was permitted to remain in his post as Director of the FBI.°

To hear Kelley tell it, COINTELPRO saved the Republic from the Visigoths. The facts are somewhat different, as Maude Wilkinson— and many other Americans—can attest. In 1969, while a college student at American University in Washington, she joined a student affiliate of the Socialist Workers party, attracted by the group's opposi-

---

° Levi, to his credit, characterized COINTELPRO as "foolish" and "outrageous." But he continued to work with an FBI Director who thought the illegal harassment of American citizens by their government was just peachy—necessary, in fact.

tion to the war in Vietnam. Mrs. Wilkinson, the daughter of a Methodist minister, was teaching four-year-old black schoolchildren in Washington's inner city a year later when the FBI's Washington field office, filling its quota of COINTELPRO actions, sent an anonymous letter to William Manning, school superintendent of the District of Columbia. The FBI letter said the writer was acting "in order to protect the D.C. school system from the menace of a teacher who does not have the interests of the children or the country at heart." A gentle and popular teacher, Mrs. Wilkinson was not fired.

But the FBI had better luck in Austin, Texas, where Mrs. Evelyn Rose Sell was hired in 1969 as a teacher in the city's federally funded Head Start program. The FBI informed the Austin Police Department that Mrs. Sell was a member of the Socialist Workers party and urged that the information be passed on to the local school board. Although Mrs. Sell was a highly qualified teacher, the Austin school board failed to renew her contract in 1970. Later FBI agents visited her new employer, the Human Opportunities Commission, in an effort to get her fired from *that* job.

The FBI scored again when it encouraged Arizona State University to dismiss Dr. Morris Starsky, an antiwar activist on the campus and a member of the Socialist Workers party. The FBI mailed anonymous letters denouncing Starsky to the faculty members who were reviewing his teaching contract. Soon after, the board of regents arranged to send Starsky on a one-year sabbatical from which "he would not return." Starsky later sued, contending that he had been unable to get a college teaching job since then.

Hoover's COINTELPRO even reached out to try to discredit actress Jane Fonda, who became a prime target because of her antiwar and other activist stands. In 1970 the FBI sent a letter from a nonexistent "Morris" to Hollywood gossip columnist Army Archerd. The fictitious letter writer said he had attended a Black Panther rally at which he claimed to have been shocked to see Miss Fonda lead the audience in chanting: "We will kill Richard Nixon, and any other m . . . . . f . . . . . who stands in our way." Wesley G. Grapp, in charge of the Los Angeles FBI office, messaged Hoover: "It is felt that knowledge of FONDA's involvement would cause her embarrassment and detract from her status with the general public." Hoover agreed, cautioning Grapp to "insure that mailing cannot be traced to the Bureau." Miss Fonda, who filed a $2.8 million lawsuit against the federal government for spying on and maligning her, said she had attended the rally but never made the statements attributed to her.

The FBI's COINTELPRO operatives devoted a considerable portion of their energies against the New Left. The program against the movement was established in May 1968, after Charles Brennan wrote a memo to Sullivan noting that among other things, "The New Left has on many occasions viciously and scurrilously attacked the Director and the Bureau in an attempt to hamper our investigation of it and to drive us off the college campuses." The purpose of the new program, the memo added, "is to expose, disrupt and otherwise neutralize the activities of this group and persons connected with it."

The FBI's COINTELPRO operators formed social and moral as well as political judgments. The Newark FBI office was upset that students at Rutgers University were distributing *Screw*, a newspaper "containing a type of filth that could only originate in a depraved mind. . . . The paper is being given away and sold inside Conklin Hall, Rutgers University, Newark by 'hippie' types in unkempt clothes, with wild beards, shoulder-length hair and other examples of their non-conformity."

Nonconformity! It had to be stamped out and the Newark office drafted an anonymous letter. Signed by "A Concerned Student," it was mailed to the New Jersey state legislator in charge of the Senate Education Committee. ("Would you want your children or grandchildren, especially young girls, subjected to such depravity? . . . this is becoming a way of campus life. Poison the minds of the young, destroy their moral being and in less than one generation this country will be ripe for its downfall. Rutgers is supported by public funds . . .") The letter was written in pure Hooverese, but it worked; the New Jersey Senate Education Committee launched an investigation.

If the FBI professed that its moral sensibilities were offended by *Screw*, it was nevertheless willing to use crudities when it suited its purpose. One COINTELPRO handbill, designed to split the peace movement from the Socialist Workers party, was headlined, in large capital letters: "BALLS!" Another FBI flyer announced a "Pick the Fag Contest" and displayed pictures of four left-wing figures and a list of mock prizes. The FBI's disruption specialists also wrote salacious anonymous letters when it was deemed useful.

In one classic case the FBI early in 1970 targeted a white woman who was active in ACTION, a biracial group in St. Louis. The FBI scrawled a letter to her husband signed "A Soul Sister." It said: "Dear Mr. [name deleted]: Look man, I guess your old lady doesn't get enough at home or she wouldn't be shucking and jiving with our black men in ACTION, you dig? Like all she wants to intergrate [*sic*] is the bed room and us Black Sisters ain't gonna take no second best from our men. So lay it on her, man—or get the hell off [blank]." The letter may have contributed to the couple's marital difficulties and separation of the woman and her husband that soon followed.°

° The FBI took credit; in June, four months after the "Soul Sister" letter had been sent, the St. Louis office messaged Hoover that the white woman "and her hus-

There were endless examples of FBI outrages involving such "disinformation" and misinformation. During the 1968 Democratic National Convention in Chicago, the National Mobilization Committee to End the War in Vietnam attempted to find housing for demonstrators who had come to the convention. The FBI field office obtained 217 housing forms and filled them out with false names and addresses, each supposedly representing persons who were willing to offer housing to the demonstrators. As the FBI later reported, the young people who went to look for these houses made "long and useless journeys to locate the addresses and the efforts to find housing were cancelled." The identical tactic was used by the FBI to disrupt demonstrators who came to Washington when Nixon was inaugurated in January 1969. On that occasion the FBI also found out what citizen's band was being used by the marshals in charge of the demonstrators and used those channels to feed the marshals false information and to countermand their orders.

In 1967 a New York City newspaper, the *East Village Other*, announced it would bomb the Pentagon with flowers as its contribution to a peace rally planned in Washington to protest the Vietnam war. The paper ran an ad asking for a pilot. The FBI answered the ad and strung the game along until the last moment. When the publisher showed up at the airport with two hundred pounds of flowers, there was no pilot to fly the plane. In another case the FBI decided to sabotage the Radical Education Project, a group in Detroit that published pamphlets and newspapers. The Detroit office asked the FBI lab to prepare a quart of a solution "capable of duplicating a scent of the most foul-smelling feces available."*

In yet another COINTELPRO case, the FBI's Newark office suggested that it would lead to "confusion and suspicion" within the Black Panther party if the Bureau sent a false telegram warning that food donated to a party convention "contains poison" of which one symptom was stomach cramps. "It is suggested that the Bureau then consider having the Laboratory treat fruit such as oranges with a

---

band had recently separated, following a series of marital arguments. [Deleted] has taken an apartment during this separation, which might become a permanent arrangement. This matrimonial stress and strain should cause her to function much less effectively in ACTION.

"While the letter sent by the St. Louis Division was probably not the sole cause of this separation it certainly contributed very strongly."

* It was not clear whether the FBI intended to break a bottle of the foul liquid in the REP offices, or to mix it with the ink used in printing the organization's publications. The Church committee was unable to discover whether the liquid was ever used, but the record "indicates clearly that [the request] was not disapproved."

mild laxative-type drug by hypodermic needle or other appropriate method."°

And the FBI, which set itself up as the foe of violence and "violence-prone" groups, at times fomented violence through its own COINTELPRO operations. A secret 1969 memo to Hoover from the San Diego field office said: "Shootings, beatings and a high degree of unrest continues [sic] to prevail in the ghetto area of southeast San Diego. Although no specific counterintelligence action can be credited with contributing to this overall situation, it is felt that a substantial amount of the unrest is directly attributable to this program."

At the time, the FBI sought to encourage armed warfare between the Black Panther party in San Diego and a rival organization known as US. Two persons were killed and four wounded during fighting between the two groups over the summer, and there were shotgun and rifle attacks and a bombing. In San Diego two years later, according to a report of the American Civil Liberties Union, the FBI organized and recruited the Secret Army Organization, a right-wing terrorist group, and paid it to attack antiwar activists. The FBI's key informant in the terrorist group, Howard B. Godfrey, later admitted that he was in an automobile with another member of the organization who fired a shot through the window of the home of Peter G. Bohmer, an economics professor at San Diego State University, and a Marxist. Bohmer was not at home but the shot hit a friend, Paula Tharp, wounding her in the elbow. For almost six months Steven L. Christiansen, an FBI agent working with the group, hid the pistol in his home while police were searching for it. Christiansen later resigned from the FBI.

Some of the targets of FBI disruption naturally knew or suspected what was going on long before the press or the general public. One of the most poignant moments in the Church committee hearings came when Senator Philip A. Hart of Michigan, gravely ill of cancer, made a brief statement after listening to a recitation by staff attorneys of FBI counterintelligence programs:

"I have been told for years by among others, some of my own family, that this is exactly what the Bureau was doing all of the time, and in my great wisdom and high office, I assured them that . . . it just wasn't true. It couldn't happen. They wouldn't do it.

"What you have described is a series of illegal actions intended squarely to deny First Amendment rights to some Americans. That is

---

° Hoover drew the line at injecting oranges, but only because the FBI would have no control over fruit while it was being shipped and there would be some risk that the hypoed oranges would fall into the wrong hands. But he thought the telegram ruse "has merit."

what my children have told me was going on. Now, I did not believe it.

"The trick now . . . as I see it, Mr. Chairman, is for this Committee to be able to figure out how to persuade the people of this country that indeed it did go on. And how shall we insure that it will never happen again? But it will happen repeatedly unless we can bring ourselves to understand and accept that it did go on.

"And now my last note. Over the years we have been warned about the danger of subversive organizations, organizations that would threaten our liberties, subvert our system, would encourage its members to take further illegal action to advance their views, organizations that would incite and promote violence, putting one American group against another.

"And I think the story you have told us today shows us that there is an organization that does fit those descriptions, and it is the organization, the leadership of which has been most constant in its warning to us to be on guard against such harm. The Bureau did all of those things."

William Sullivan, the key FBI figure in COINTELPRO and the Bureau's intelligence-gathering programs in the turbulent sixties, later tried very hard to defend his actions. "COINTELPRO was under my control," he admitted. "I would never say otherwise." But Sullivan insisted that COINTELPRO had not been evil. For example, he said, as part of COINTELPRO he had directed the FBI's efforts against the Ku Klux Klan.

"My father fought the Klan in Massachusetts," Sullivan said. "I always used to be frightened when I was a kid and I saw the fiery cross burning in the hillside near our farm. When the Klan reached fourteen thousand in the mid-sixties, I asked to take over the investigation of the Klan. Hoover agreed and the whole responsibility for the Klan became mine. When I left the Bureau in 1971 the Klan was down to a completely disorganized forty-three hundred. It was broken. They were dirty, rough fellows, and we went after them with rough, tough methods." But, he said, "a lot of things done in COINTELPRO shouldn't have been done."

Sullivan emerged as a bitter critic of Hoover after being eased out of the FBI in 1971. He was an ambiguous figure, warning in 1974 that the Bureau was "a potential threat to our civil liberties," and urging that it be relieved of all authority over domestic security.

How, I asked Sullivan, if he later came to hold such views, could he have sent the tape to Coretta King? How could he do it? What went through his mind at the time?

"It would take hours to explain," he said. But through the years, as he rose within the FBI, "I was so inured and accustomed to any damn thing I was told to do I just carried it out and kept my resentment to myself. I was married and trying to buy a house with a big mortgage and raise a family.

"You know," the man who had headed the FBI's Domestic Intelligence Division for a decade added, "you know, Marx was right. Economics determine a lot of things in this life."

> *"He [George Shultz] didn't get Secretary of the Treasury because he has nice blue eyes. It was a goddamn favor to him to get that job."*
>
> —Richard Nixon, September 15, 1972

10
IRS:
The Abuse of Power

On September 15, 1972, three months after the Watergate burglary but well before the presidential election, Richard Nixon talked to his advisers about how to make better use of the Internal Revenue Service against his political enemies.

Only four days earlier John Dean had handed an Enemies List of 490 McGovern aides and supporters to Johnnie M. Walters, the IRS commissioner. Now, in the meeting in the Oval Office, H. R. Haldeman assured the President that Dean was "moving ruthlessly on the investigation of McGovern people . . . working the thing through IRS."

A bit more than two weeks before this discussion, Secretary of the Treasury George P. Shultz had relayed disappointing news to the White House: the IRS had gone over the tax returns of Lawrence O'Brien, chairman of the Democratic National Committee, and they seemed in order. Now, late in the afternoon of this September day Nixon made it clear that he did not want to hear any protests by his Treasury Secretary against the political use of the IRS.

". . . I don't want George Shultz to ever raise the question because it would put me in the position of having to throw him out of the office," Nixon told Haldeman and Dean. "He didn't get Secretary of the Treasury because he has nice blue eyes. It was a goddamn favor to him to get that job."

Nixon ruminated that things would be different after his re-election. He would take control of the IRS. "We have to do it artfully so that we don't create an issue that we are using the IRS politically. And there are ways to do it, goddamn it. Sneak in one of our political appointees."

He added, "I look forward to the time that we have the agents in the Department of Justice and the IRS under our control after November 7." After the election, Nixon said, "the whole bunch go out and if he [Shultz] doesn't do it he is out as Secretary of the Treasury and that is the way it is going to be played."

In the course of the meeting Dean complained to Nixon that he was having trouble obtaining tax information from the IRS about Henry Kimelman, George McGovern's chief fund-raiser and finance chairman.

"Well, goddamn, they ought to give it to you," Nixon replied.*

It was earlier in this same conversation that Dean had assured the President he was keeping lists of enemies: ". . . one of the things I've tried to do, is just keep notes on a lot of the people who are emerging as less than our friends."

"Great," Nixon replied.

Dean added, "Because this is going to be over some day and they're— We shouldn't forget the way some of them have treated us."

Nixon then instructed Dean to write it all down. "I want the most, I want the most comprehensive notes on all of those that have tried to do us in," he said. "Because they didn't have to do it. . . . and they are asking for it and they are going to get it. We have not used the power in the first four years as you know. We have never used it. We have not used the Bureau and we have not used the Justice Department but things are going to change now. And they are either going to do it right or go."

"What an exciting prospect," John Dean replied.

. . .

* Nixon's comments about Shultz and the IRS were contained in a thirteen-minute segment of tape that Nixon refused to release to the House Judiciary Committee considering his impeachment. On June 14, 1974, Judge John J. Sirica ordered the segment turned over to the Watergate Special Prosecutor, but it was not made public. However, on July 26, 1974, excerpts were published in a story by Eugene V. Risher, then a Washington correspondent for the Cox newspapers. Risher said in an interview that he had been allowed to read the transcript and take verbatim notes. "The document I saw was a transcript of the entire conversation," not just the thirteen-minute segment, he said. "My source was a Nixon loyalist who had been helpful to me in the past and was outraged because he knew Nixon had lied." The Nixon quotes are from Risher's story in the Atlanta *Journal* of July 26.

The Internal Revenue Service, with more than 88,000 employees, 700 offices across the country, and a budget of more than $2 billion, is one of the most powerful and feared of all federal agencies. The average American may never have any dealings with the FBI, the CIA, the DIA, or the NSA, but he comes in contact at least once a year with the IRS, on April 15.

Americans have never been notably enthusiastic about paying taxes. British attempts to collect revenue from the Colonies led to the Boston Tea Party and, ultimately, to the American Revolution. The new nation needed revenue, however, and Article I of the Constitution provides: "*Sect. 8.* The Congress shall have power to lay and collect taxes . . ."

President Lincoln signed the first income-tax law in 1862 to help finance the Civil War, but it was repealed after the war. Congress passed another income-tax law in 1894, but the Supreme Court declared it unconstitutional the following year.[*] In 1913 the states ratified the Sixteenth Amendment, permitting Congress to impose a federal income tax, which it did later that year.

When Americans file their tax returns, they often provide the federal government with enormous amounts of personal information—not only about their finances, sources of income, borrowing and spending habits, but also about what physicians they have seen, whether they purchased a pair of eyeglasses in the past year, where and when they traveled, whether they bought or sold a house, and for how much. The more than 80 million individual income-tax forms filed each year comprise a vast data bank of detailed personal information in the hands of federal authorities. All of this information is centralized and stored on tapes in a bank of IRS computers in Martinsburg, West Virginia.

Individual income taxes are the government's largest single source of revenue—estimated to bring in $153.6 billion in 1977—and the IRS has extraordinary powers to collect that money. It can demand to see all kinds of personal and financial records and it can and does, if necessary, seize a taxpayer's assets—his home, automobile, bank account, salary, furniture, paintings, or other property—through something known as a "jeopardy assessment."

In recent years, federal officials have with good reason worried about a "taxpayer revolt" by middle-class Americans repelled by the loopholes, gimmicks, and tax shelters that benefit the rich, permitting some millionaires to pay no taxes at all. The tax dollars poured into the war in Vietnam, and continuing high defense budgets have

[*] The Court held that a direct tax on incomes was not apportioned by population as the Constitution required.

added to taxpayer disenchantment. Even so, most citizens, through a combination of respect for the law, fear, and patriotism, continue to pay up. Since the IRS has only 2,600 special agents to investigate suspected criminal tax evasion, the tax system essentially rests on voluntary compliance.° At the heart of this system is the citizens' trust and belief that the government will not use the vast powers of the IRS to punish citizens for their political views.

That confidence was rudely shattered by Watergate. The congressional investigations that followed, and the White House tapes, disclosed that the Nixon Administration blatantly attempted—and in some cases did—use the IRS for political purposes. Richard Nixon well understood that the power to tax is the power to destroy; he wanted to use that power to crush his enemies. And he succeeded to some extent, although as his conversation with Haldeman and Dean indicated, not as much as he would have liked.

The bureaucracy resisted, in part because it feared complicity in the abuses ordered by Nixon and his Gauleiters. But the White House nevertheless enjoyed considerable success, and the record of Nixon's misuse of the IRS is possibly the most shocking aspect of the sordid years of his Presidency.

Nixon had no fewer than three IRS commissioners in five years, a fact that was directly related to his unrelenting efforts to gain political control of the tax agency. His first appointee was Randolph W. Thrower, a prominent Atlanta tax lawyer and former FBI agent who for eight years had been the city's Republican chairman. Thrower, then fifty-five, had the right political and professional credentials. But to watch over the IRS (and Thrower) the White House also placed its own political operative inside the revenue service.

Roger Vincent Barth was only half a dozen years out of law school when he found himself operating as the President's mechanic in one of the most sensitive of all government agencies. A tax lawyer in Buffalo, Barth in 1968 had landed a job with the Nixon campaign that opened up swift and unexpected access to power; he was assigned to be the advance man for Julie and Tricia Nixon and David Eisenhower. As such, he worked directly under John Ehrlichman; after the election Roger Barth became special assistant to the commissioner of Internal Revenue—often reporting to his sponsor, Ehrlichman.

A short unprepossessing man with glasses, Barth, despite his youth, was almost completely bald. During Watergate he had the rare distinction of appearing as a character witness for G. Gordon

---

° Special agents are assigned to criminal cases; the IRS also has more than 15,000 revenue agents who handle ordinary audits.

Liddy. If Barth lacked experience as a high-level federal official, he nevertheless knew the right people—he boasted openly of his White House connections. And one of his tasks at the IRS was of particular interest to Ehrlichman, Dean, and the others around Nixon. It was Barth who handled the "sensitive case reports." The IRS kept a special file of prominent citizens—senators, congressmen, friends of the President, celebrities, and others whose tax problems had a potential for political embarrassment. About twenty-five such reports a month made their way up to the head of the IRS. If any of these cases seemed important enough to bring to the attention of the President, Barth would call Ehrlichman or Dean.

In the summer of 1969 Tom Charles Huston—not yet famous for his plan; that came along a year later—had been meeting with a group of conservative White House staff members known, somewhat ominously, as the "Committee of Six." Among the group's recommendations to Nixon was that the IRS investigate the tax exemptions of left-wing organizations.

On June 16, 1969, Dr. Arthur Burns, then Nixon's economic counselor and later chairman of the Federal Reserve Board, met with Randolph Thrower and Huston in the Executive Office Building. Burns later claimed to have no memory of the meeting, but Thrower's memorandum for the files said that Burns had expressed Nixon's "great concern" that tax-exempt activist groups might be "stimulating riots both on the campus and within our inner cities."

At the meeting Huston gave several specific examples to the IRS chief of tax-exempt organizations that he thought might be investigated. Thrower's memo said he would have Barth "get in touch with Mr. Huston and advise him that we would be pleased to receive" more information of the sort that Huston had supplied at the meeting. Four days later Huston wrote a follow-up memo to Barth on the subject of tax exempt groups. "I have advised the President that Mr. Thrower is aware of his personal interest in this subject," Huston wrote pointedly. "The President . . . is anxious to see some positive action taken . . ."

Five days later the Senate permanent subcommittee on investigations held a hearing on tax-exempt activist organizations. After the hearings Huston, keeping the pressure on, telephoned Barth and asked what the IRS was doing about radicals and activists. On July 2, the day after Huston's call, the IRS convened a top-level meeting to consider the problem. Later that month it established a secret section that eventually became known as the Special Service Staff (SSS).

Operating under what was called "red seal" security and hidden away in the basement of IRS headquarters in Washington, SSS ultimately compiled 11,458 files on 8,585 persons and 2,873 organizations. It amounted to a clandestine intelligence unit within the IRS, the tax collector's version of CIA's Operation CHAOS. The SSS staff had close liaison with the FBI, regularly receiving COINTELPRO reports, and it was in contact with Army intelligence and other federal intelligence units. Before it was disbanded in 1973, SSS had received more than 11,000 FBI reports. Former SSS employees interviewed by congressional committee reported that the FBI reports were a "Niagara Falls," coming in by the "armload" and by the "pound."

SSS was given responsibility for investigating and collecting intelligence on "ideological, militant, subversive, radical and similar type organizations" and individuals. An official IRS document said the unit's targets were "violent groups" including bombers, arsonists, and skyjackers, and "non-violent" groups and individuals, including draftcard burners, peace demonstrators, and persons who "organize and attend rock festivals which attract youth and narcotics." Like the FBI, the IRS had become an instrument for social control, making its own judgments about what political views and cultural preferences were acceptable. And SSS operated in the shadows, literally in the basement.

Among the suspicious characters and groups that SSS found appropriate to list in its files were Jimmy Breslin, Mayor John Lindsay of New York, Shirley MacLaine, Coretta King, columnist Joseph Alsop, the American Library Association, the Ford Foundation, the Head Start program, the American Civil Liberties Union, the National Urban League, and the entire University of North Carolina.

The IRS opened files on each of the taxpayers whose names were considered by SSS and more than 200 were later subjected to audit and in some cases criminal fraud investigation. SSS received about 10,000 names on computer print-outs from a Justice Department intelligence panel, the Interdivisional Information Unit (IDIU). In its final report, the Church committee concluded that the names provided by the computer and the FBI were not those of suspected tax violators. "Rather, these groups and individuals were targeted because of their political and ideological beliefs and activities."

It was not, however, the first time that the White House had used the IRS against political targets. During the Kennedy Administration a somewhat similar, albeit much more limited investigation of rightwing organizations was conducted by the IRS. Later, some left-wing groups were added. The program never involved more than a total of forty-seven organizations, according to a study by the Joint Committee on Internal Revenue Taxation. Although it never reached the size and scope of SSS, it was an earlier example of political use of the IRS.

Randolph Thrower had earned good marks in cooperating with the White House and setting up SSS, but in the summer of 1970 he showed unwelcome signs of independence that may have hastened his departure from Washington. A plum had opened up in the IRS, the position of director of the Alcohol, Tobacco, and Firearms division, and Thrower was advised that the White House wanted John Caulfield in the post. The White House pressured Thrower through Charls Walker, the Under Secretary of the Treasury, and as such, one of Thrower's bosses. The IRS commissioner told Walker he did not consider Caulfield qualified for the post, and countered by offering him the job of chief of enforcement for the division rather than director.

Caulfield turned that down, but soon afterward the persistent Walker was on the telephone again to tell Thrower he had a new candidate for division director—G. Gordon Liddy. At the time, Liddy was a Treasury Department official, but he had already established a reputation as a violent opponent of gun control, and Thrower pointed out that Liddy might not be just the right person to head the Alcohol, Tobacco, and Firearms division.

Meanwhile Walker had a new suggestion for moving Caulfield into the IRS; he would take the enforcement post, after all, but would report directly to Thrower. The IRS chief opposed that, too. Ultimately, according to an affidavit by Thrower, Walker told him that the White House had considered his views but was ordering Thrower to make the personnel changes it wanted. When Thrower threatened to quit, the White House backed down.

In January 1971, however, Thrower resigned. He asked to see the President to discuss his concern over White House interference with the IRS, but was told it could not be arranged. Finally Thrower went to see Mitchell, of all people, to warn that "the introduction of political influence into the IRS would be very damaging." Then he went back to Atlanta.

On August 16, 1971, John Dean, at the request of Haldeman and Ehrlichman, wrote the memo that became the classic expression of the philosophy of the Nixon Administration.

"This memorandum addresses the matter of how we can maximize the fact of our incumbency in dealing with persons known to be active in their opposition to our Administration. Stated a bit more bluntly— how we can use the available federal machinery to screw our political enemies."

Dean went on to say that he had reviewed the matter "with a number of persons possessed of expertise, in the field," and concluded that the White House did not need an elaborate mechanism or "game plan" to go after its enemies, merely a "project coordinator." Key staff members should be asked to "inform us as to who they feel we should be giving a hard time." The project coordinator, Dean said, could then find out what dealings the enemies had with the federal government "and how we can best screw them (e.g., grant availability, federal contracts, litigation, *prosecution*, etc.)." (Italics added.) The project coordinator, Dean said, must have access to and "full support" of the top officials of the federal agency working against a political enemy.

Although Dean later played a crucial role in exposing the crimes of the Nixon Administration, his memo takes its place alongside the Huston Plan as one of the most chilling documents in modern American history. The President had been elected by the people, but his men were moving to corrupt the government entrusted to them in order to perpetuate their own political power.

In response to Dean's memo, Charles Colson sent him an "opponents list" compiled on June 24 by George T. Bell, a White House staff member. The list had twenty names, and Colson noted "I have checked in blue those to whom I would give top priority." The list included Edwin O. Guthman, an editor of the Los Angeles *Times*, "a highly sophisticated hatchetman. ... It is time to give him the message"; Morton Halperin, "A scandal would be most helpful here"; Sidney Davidoff, Mayor Lindsay's aide, "A first class S.O.B., wheeler-dealer and suspected bagman"; Congressman John Conyers of Detroit, "Coming on fast. Emerging as a leading black anti-Nixon spokesman. Has known weakness for white females"; Daniel Schorr of CBS, "A real media enemy"; and Mary McGrory of the Washington *Star*, "Daily hate Nixon articles."

From June of 1971 through Watergate, literally scores of enemies lists circulated through the White House. "This list," John Dean later testified, "was continually being updated, and the file was several inches thick." When Dean first revealed the existence of the Enemies List in his testimony before the Senate Watergate committee in June of 1973, Colson wrote a letter to Senator Ervin blandly explaining that the White House indeed had a list but it was "primarily intended for the use of the social office" to exclude political opponents from White House dinners and teas.

This was prenatal Colson, before he got religion and was Born Again. His transparently phony explanation failed to clarify why he had suggested the names he checked in blue be given "top priority."

Although John Dean is generally credited with originating the Enemies List, William Sullivan has insisted that the FBI is entitled to that dubious distinction. "It originated in the Bureau. In the Bureau it was called the 'No Contact List.' Hoover had established it years ago. And on the No Contact List went all individuals who had criticized the FBI or Hoover personally. And in particular he disliked intellectuals, so you had Dr. Robert Maynard Hutchins, Henry Steele Commager, and Arthur M. Schlesinger, Jr., and a host of others. You weren't supposed to have anything to do with the people on the list. And then the White House got the idea and picked it up and called it, for their purpose, the Enemies List."

In any event, and regardless of its creator, the Enemies List project occupied the time of a considerable number of White House aides. And during the same period that Dean, Colson, and others were compiling their lists, the White House was increasing its pressures "to make IRS politically responsive," as Dean put it in a memo in November 1971. Dean testified that he and Caulfield prepared the memo for a meeting that Haldeman was to have with the head of the IRS or Secretary of the Treasury John B. Connally.

In August, Thrower had been replaced as IRS commissioner by Johnnie Walters, a Republican lawyer from Greenville, South Carolina. Apparently he failed to display a sufficient degree of subservience to the White House, for Dean complained that the Administration was not making much progress in harassing tax-exempt foundations, and "We have been unable to obtain information in the possession of IRS regarding our political enemies . . . We have been unable to stimulate audits."

"Walters *must* be more responsive," Dean wrote. "Walters should be told that discreet political action and investigations are a firm requirement and responsibility on his part." A "talking paper" that accompanied Dean's memo called the IRS "a monstrous bureaucracy . . . controlled by Democrats." Randolph Thrower, it added, had become "a total captive of the democratic assistant commissioners. In the end, he was actively fighting both Treasury and the White House." What was worse, the paper added, Johnnie Walters appeared to be developing some of the same tendencies.

In fact, Dean's complaints were overstated—the IRS for some months had been cooperating with the White House in a number of specific cases, providing tax returns, investigating enemies, and assisting friends of the White House. But it wasn't enough.

On September 11, 1972, less than three months after the Watergate break-in, Walters was summoned to John Dean's office. The meeting took place in the midst of the presidential election. The President's counsel handed the IRS commissioner a list of 490 staff members and contributors to George McGovern, the Democratic candidate opposing Richard Nixon, who, as the incumbent, had ultimate authority over the IRS.

Johnnie Walters had been considered reliable. In 1969 he was recruited for the Justice Department by John Alexander, a senior partner in Nixon's old law firm in New York with whom Walters had once worked on a major tax case a decade earlier. For two years, Walters had served under John Mitchell as Assistant Attorney General in charge of the Tax Division. In August 1971, Walters had moved over to the IRS.

Walters later swore that Dean, at their White House meeting, gave him the Enemies List and asked the IRS to "undertake examinations or investigations of the people named on the list." Dean confirmed this; and he told the House Judiciary Committee considering Nixon's impeachment that the list had been prepared by Nixon's old backstage political manager, Murray Chotiner. Dean said that after discussing the list with Haldeman's assistant, Larry Higby, and with Chotiner and Ehrlichman, his instructions were to "ask Mr. Walters to have Internal Revenue Service audits conducted on these people."

This group of names, by far the longest of the White House lists, included Representative Bella Abzug; Mortimer Caplin, a former Democratic head of the IRS; Clark Clifford; Richard Dougherty, McGovern's campaign press secretary; Henry Kimelman; Shirley MacLaine; Lawrence O'Brien; Pierre Salinger; actress Polly Bergen; John Kenneth Galbraith; Gene Hackman; Gilman Kraft, of Los Angeles (the brother of Joseph Kraft); Burt Lancaster; Norman Lear; Paul Newman, and his wife, Joanne Woodward, and hundreds of other McGovern supporters.

Walters said he warned Dean that auditing the McGovern enemies would make Watergate look like a "Sunday school picnic." But two days later Walters discussed the picnic with Secretary Shultz, who had replaced John Connally in June at Treasury. According to Walters, Shultz told him to "do nothing," so he placed the list in a sealed envelope inside his office safe. Walters believed he told Dean of Shultz's reaction.

On September 15 Nixon had his conversation with Dean and Haldeman about the IRS, enemies, and George Shultz's blue eyes, the conversation in which he warned that Shultz would be thrown out after the election if he didn't play ball. Ten days later Dean called Walters demanding to know what progress the IRS had made on auditing the President's enemies, and could they at least go after fifty to seventy of the names? Once more, Walters said, he protested but promised to take up the problem again with Shultz, which he did on September 29. And again, Walters said, they agreed to do nothing.

In 1973, when Wilbur Mills was still chairman of the Joint Committee on Internal Revenue Taxation—it was well before his companion, stripper Fanne Foxe, had dived into the Tidal Basin—the staff of the committee investigated whether the IRS had punished taxpayers on the enemies lists or, conversely, helped Nixon's friends. The staff could find "no indication" that those on the list who were audited were examined more vigorously than other taxpayers who were audited. But it conceded that the enemies had been audited "significantly more frequently" than other citizens in similar income brackets.

That conclusion was, to put it charitably, an understatement. About 2.3 percent, or fewer than 2 million of the 82 million Americans who file individual income-tax returns are audited each year. The joint committee combined and analyzed 216 names on various lists turned over to Dean when he testified to the Ervin committee, and it examined the 490 names on the Enemies List of McGovern supporters. It found that 22 percent of the names on the first list and 26 percent on the second list had been audited by the IRS. But the committee noted that many enemies were "a relatively affluent group," and that just over half of the persons on the first list had reported incomes of over $50,000. Persons in that bracket were audited about 14 percent of the time, the committee said, a conclusion designed to minimize the greater percentage of enemies who were audited compared to other citizens with high incomes. But the committee omitted a vital statistic; almost half of the persons on the first list had incomes of between $10,000 and $50,000 a year, and of persons in that bracket only 2.5 percent, a hair more than the general taxpaying population, are audited. Yet 22 percent of all the 216 enemies on the first list were audited.

Quite aside from these statistics, there were numerous specific examples of White House pressure on the IRS, with varying results. In addition to the Ehrlichman-Barth channel, the Nixon team had developed another pipeline into the IRS through the relationship of Jack Caulfield with Vernon "Mike" Acree, the assistant commissioner of the IRS. Acree, an impressive-looking, heavy-set man in his fifties and a natty dresser, was a thirty-year veteran of the federal law-enforcement bureaucracy. He knew his way around, and soon, according to Caulfield, was providing him with IRS information.[*]

When Dean was instructed to arrange tax problems for Robert Greene, the *Newsday* reporter who had done the series on Bebe Rebozo, Nixon's closest friend, he turned to Caulfield for assistance. Caulfield testified that he called Mike Acree "and he indicated that a means of accomplishing an audit was sometimes undertaken through the— what is known as an anonymous letter being written." Caulfield said Acree later told him that the letter had been sent. This nice process is known in the back rooms of the IRS as the "squeal."[†] Greene

---

[*] In April 1972, before John Connally left office, he named Acree commissioner of the U.S. Bureau of Customs.

[†] Each year as many as 100,000 Americans volunteer information about other taxpayers to the IRS, either because they bear a grudge against someone or because they hope to collect a reward. The law permits the IRS to pay rewards of up to 10 percent of taxes collected as a result of a tip. In 1974 the IRS paid $467,952 to informants; 4,421 claims for rewards were filed, but only 13 percent were allowed. To collect his blood money, an informant must file a Form 211,

was indeed audited. The Joint Committee on Internal Revenue Taxation, bending over backwards to protect its IRS constituency, noted that the audit was carried out by New York State under a federal/state exchange program and concluded that the audit was "unrelated" to his status as a White House enemy. However, the committee glossed over the fact that the state conducted the audit of Greene *for* the federal government—it was not, after all, an audit of Greene's state taxes but of his federal return. Moreover, the committee staff either did not know or did not choose to report that the decision to audit Greene had been made by the IRS office in Brooklyn.

Dean also testified that Haldeman had requested "that certain individuals have audits commenced on them." Caulfield testified that at Dean's request, he once brought Acree to the White House because Dean "wanted to see if Mr. Acree could initiate audits on four individuals, three or four individuals." Acree, Caulfield said, "indicated that he would give it his attention." But Caulfield claimed that Acree was reluctant to follow through and that the matter was dropped.

In another case, Caulfield was assigned to investigate Stewart Udall, former Secretary of the Interior, and the Overview Corporation, of which Udall was board chairman. Caulfield submitted a biography of Udall to Dean which noted, among other things, that "He has climbed Mount Fuji (in winter)." Caulfield also told Dean that he had "asked for an IRS check." The White House was particularly interested in Overview because its president was McGovern's fundraiser, Henry Kimelman. W. Richard Howard, a White House aide to Charles Colson, wrote a memo to Dean's office in May of 1972, suggesting that Kimelman, a Virgin Islands businessman, had "wheeled and dealed" when Udall was in the Cabinet and the Virgin Islands were under his jurisdiction as Secretary of the Interior. "We believe there must be material at Justice and Interior on this sleazy [*sic*] character that we would like to obtain through your fantastic sources," Howard wrote.

In October 1971 Caulfield suggested to Dean that the White House initiate "discreet IRS audits" of Emile de Antonio, producer of *Millhouse*, a satirical film about Nixon, as well as the company that made the film and the distributor. Caulfield said his suggestion was not acted upon.

The same month, Lawrence Yale Goldberg, a toy manufacturer and prominent Republican in Rhode Island, was under consideration by the White House to be chairman of the Jewish Citizens for the Re-election of the President. Caulfield said he obtained copies of

---

Application and Public Voucher for Reward for Original Information. But a word of caution is in order; the IRS carefully audits the returns of informers to make sure they report their IRS rewards on their own returns.

portions of Goldberg's tax returns from Acree. The returns listed Goldberg's charitable contributions for 1968, and Caulfield cautioned in a memo that they reflected "an extremely heavy involvement in Jewish organizational activity." Caulfield also warned that Goldberg had been working to get the State Department to modify its policy toward Israel, and he questioned his "loyalty" to CREEP. Acree said he could not remember sending the copies of Goldberg's tax returns to Caulfield.

About the same time, one Anthony Cortese, an Oldsmobile dealer from El Cerrito, California, wanted to donate a wine storage vault to Nixon (who fancied 1966 Château Margaux at $30 a bottle). Caulfield said he obtained tax information about Cortese from Mike Acree, who had only a hazy memory of their conversation.*

There were other instances of the White House pulling tax returns or obtaining confidential tax information from the IRS. In 1970 Clark Mollenhoff, an investigative reporter serving as special counsel to Nixon, was instructed by Haldeman to obtain a report on the tax investigation of Gerald Wallace, brother of Alabama Governor George C. Wallace. The report noted that the IRS was investigating charges of corruption in the Wallace administration, involving hundreds of thousands of dollars in alleged kickbacks and commissions to Gerald Wallace in state highway contracts and liquor sales. Less than a month after the report was delivered by Mollenhoff to Haldeman, the details appeared in Jack Anderson's column. Mollenhoff denied leaking the IRS material and blamed the leak on "the highest White House level." Nixon feared a challenge by Wallace in 1972. At the time of the leak, Wallace was locked in a close primary race for governor against Albert Brewer; the Anderson column had an enormous impact and almost cost Wallace the election.

Although Nixon sought to use the IRS to punish his enemies, his friends were another story entirely. And no White House friend fared better than Nixon himself. In October 1973 the Providence *Journal* revealed that Nixon had paid only $792 in taxes in 1970 and $873 in 1971. Amid the Watergate disclosures, the full story emerged: Nixon had paid virtually no taxes because he had taken a whopping $576,000 tax deduction for donating his vice-presidential papers to the government. But the deed for the gift, signed on April 10, 1970, by his attorney, had been backdated a year, since Congress had prohibited such deductions for gifts made after July 25, 1969. Before Nixon

---

* Acree, it will be recalled, was proposed by Caulfield as a principal in his ill-fated Operation Sandwedge. "He is a strong Nixon loyalist and has so proved it to me, personally, on a number of occasions," Caulfield wrote in his Sandwedge proposal. Acree, he added, would retire from the government but somehow provide "IRS information input" to Sandwedge.

resigned, the IRS informed him he owed $467,000 in back taxes, penalties, and interest, but that conclusion was reached by the IRS only after Nixon's incredibly low tax payments had been publicized in the press.°

Friends of the Administration got special attention. John Dean testified that he had been asked to "do something" about the audits of evangelist Billy Graham and actor John Wayne. "I was told that I was to do something about these audits that were being performed on two friends of the President," he said. "They felt they were being harassed . . ." In September of 1971 Caulfield reported to Dean that Graham's tax returns for four years were being "scrutinized" by the IRS, possibly as a result of an anonymous telephone call. A "back door" copy of an IRS sensitive case report had been "viewed" and indicated that the IRS's Atlanta office was checking into allegations that Graham had received free construction work and gifts of clothing. "The material requested regarding John Wayne is not in yet," Caulfield added. He later said he had been shown the sensitive case report, or told about it, by Mike Acree. Dean forwarded Caulfield's memo to Haldeman, with a note asking, "can we do anything to help." Haldeman scribbled back: "NO—it's already covered."

A much more elaborate procedure was arranged in the case of John Wayne. Caulfield asked the IRS to select some Hollywood stars who had been politically active and compare their audits to Wayne's. The IRS dutifully compiled a detailed history of audits performed on Richard Boone, Sammy Davis Jr., Jerry Lewis, Peter Lawford, Fred MacMurray, Lucille Ball, Ronald Reagan, and Frank Sinatra. The figures did not help Wayne very much. The Duke had been found to owe the IRS a whopping $237,331 in one year, but then, Jerry Lewis had been socked for almost half a million dollars in a series of audits. In view of the IRS figures, Caulfield reported, "the Wayne complaint" did not appear to be strong enough to pursue. Again, Caulfield said he had obtained the analysis of the taxes of the other eight entertainers from Mike Acree, who, he said, delivered the figures to his White House office.

But the starkest example of the contrast in the IRS's handling of Nixon's enemies and friends was provided by the incredible disparity in the treatment given Lawrence O'Brien and Bebe Rebozo.

In the spring of 1972, in the course of a major investigation into

---

° When the story leaked out, the IRS concealed Nixon's returns. Francis I. Geibel, a retired IRS official, said in 1975 that he had ordered Nixon's name eradicated from the IRS indexes after his low payments were publicized. Ralph F. Lacross, a retired IRS auditor, said he had participated in "burning off" Nixon's name from microfilmed indexes in order to make it impossible for anyone to locate the President's tax returns.

the affairs of Howard Hughes, the IRS discovered that the billionaire had made huge payments to O'Brien to represent him in Washington. O'Brien had formed a consulting firm, O'Brien Associates, in October 1969; the company received $15,000 a month from Hughes until February 1971. O'Brien performed various services for Hughes; he tried to arrange an out-of-court settlement between the Hughes organization and Trans World Airlines, and he helped select attorneys to represent Hughes in the TWA case. He also provided public rela- tions suggestions to Hughes and his companies. In March 1970 O'Brien became chairman of the Democratic National Committee, so for almost a year he received the consulting fees from Hughes while simultaneously serving as Democratic chairman.

The IRS prepared a sensitive case report on the Hughes investiga- tion, which must have been of more than passing interest to the White House, for it revealed the payments to O'Brien but also referred to possible improprieties by Rebozo, Donald Nixon, and others.

Roger Barth took this sensitive case report to Treasury Secretary Shultz, and a copy went to Ehrlichman at the White House. Barth, meanwhile, was not getting on well with Johnnie Walters. "Through- out IRS, maybe with minor exceptions," Walters later testified, "he [Barth] was thought to be a White House spy." Walters said that when his own name had surfaced as a likely possibility for IRS chief, Barth had come to his office at the Justice Department and asked to be named deputy commissioner of the IRS. Walters told the White House he would not go along with that "and that if the Administration felt that they needed someone at IRS in the role of a spy that they did not want me as Commissioner." So Barth's power play was blocked, but the episode did not make for warm relations in the executive suite between Walters and his young special assistant.

After reading the sensitive case report, Ehrlichman ordered Shultz to investigate O'Brien's tax returns. Shultz, in turn, passed the order down to Walters.

The Treasury Secretary, according to Walters, told him that the White House "had information that Mr. O'Brien had received large amounts of income which might not have been reported properly. The Secretary asked whether IRS could check on the matter, and I advised that IRS could."

But Ehrlichman, hedging his bets, also called in Barth and told *him* to get after O'Brien's returns. Barth knew how the IRS worked; if he asked the audit people to pull the returns of the chief of the Democratic party, it would make waves, perhaps leak to the press and cause embarrassment. But the IRS Inspection Service, an internal watchdog for the IRS, had access to any files in the agency. So Barth went to them.

"I did not want to make any contact with our field personnel through normal channels," he said, "because I did not want to give the impression I was [acting] on behalf of the Commissioner ... I asked for Lawrence O'Brien's tax returns and asked that they get them in a way that the agents working on the case in the field wouldn't know that I had requested them. And they did this, and what I did, I just looked at the tax returns of Mr. O'Brien and his consulting firm and made sure that there was enough gross income reported for those years, the two years involved, to cover the $300,000 and whatever it was."

In the meantime Walters asked an assistant to find out if O'Brien had filed returns and whether he had been audited. A few days later Walters got back word that O'Brien had filed his returns and reported large amounts of income. He had been audited, asked to pay a relatively small amount more, he had paid, and the audit was closed. Walters reported this to Shultz, who relayed the sad news to Ehrlichman.

Ehrlichman was not happy, because some time afterward, Walters said, Shultz informed him of Ehrlichman's displeasure. The IRS chief then pointed out to the Secretary of the Treasury that, after all, Hughes was under investigation, so "we could interview Mr. O'Brien and just be sure that the amounts reflected in the return covered the particular amounts from the Hughes organization." That was creative thinking on Walters' part, and IRS agents were dispatched to interview the Democratic leader. O'Brien was busy trying to elect George McGovern, who had won the Democratic nomination on July 12. O'Brien was by now McGovern's campaign manager, and the IRS agents had trouble making an appointment to see him. They talked to O'Brien's son, but Secretary Shultz told Walters that was not good enough, and on August 17, 1972, the agents interviewed O'Brien. He cooperated with the IRS men, but suggested that any further conferences be postponed until after the election.

In fact, according to Walters, the IRS had already decided months before that with the 1972 election approaching, any politically sensitive interviews would be postponed until after Election Day. The interview with O'Brien in August, under strong White House pressure, violated that unwritten IRS policy.

"We didn't want to make either side mad," Walters told the Senate Watergate committee in explaining the IRS decision to delay election-year interviews. "With that policy in mind it's obvious that in any pursuit, or interview, if that's a good word—maybe I shouldn't use the word 'pursuit' of Larry O'Brien ... would have been postponed until after the election. So, I think IRS would not have conducted that interview until after the election had it not been for the generation of pressure from the White House, Ehrlichman."

Perhaps Walters should not have used the word "pursuit"—it just slipped out—but certainly there was extraordinary activity going on at the IRS in connection with the O'Brien investigation during the month of August. At one point O'Brien's tax returns were flown down to Washington from the IRS office in New York.

The investigation was coldly political. Haldeman told Senate investigators that O'Brien was considered the only effective Democratic politician in the country, and the White House wanted to curtail his power. Both Ehrlichman and Haldeman hoped to embarrass O'Brien by publicizing the fact that he had been on a retainer from Hughes while serving as Democratic chairman.

The report of the IRS interview with O'Brien was delivered to Ehrlichman, but it did not satisfy him. Once again, Shultz told Walters that Ehrlichman wanted more information. On August 29, at Shultz's request, Walters and Barth called on the Treasury Secretary at his office. They discussed O'Brien's taxes, and decided that nothing more could really be done. The Secretary of the Treasury then placed a conference call to Ehrlichman at the White House, with Shultz, Walters, and Barth each on a different telephone extension. Walters gingerly told Ehrlichman that O'Brien's tax returns were in order.

"I'm goddamn tired of your foot-dragging tactics," Ehrlichman snapped.

Walters, who later testified that Ehrlichman had made this comment, added, "I hung up the phone . . . because I felt if I didn't, I might say something I shouldn't."

Ehrlichman, too, remembered he had been angry. "My concern," he later testified, "was throughout, that the IRS down in the woodwork was delaying the audit until after the election . . . . that there was a stall on . . . because when the sensitive case report came in I said 'Aha, when are you going to audit him?' Well they had 75 well-selected reasons why they should not audit him . . ." Ehrlichman said he told Shultz, "George, your guys are being lopsided. Here is a probable cause for auditing O'Brien and it's apparently not going forward."

Then Ehrlichman explained his motive for ordering the O'Brien audit in terms that left no one confused. "I wanted them to turn up something and send him to jail before the election," he said, "and unfortunately it didn't materialize."

Ehrlichman said he had indeed bawled out Walters. "You are darn right," he testified. "It was my first crack at him. George wouldn't let me at him. George wanted to stand between him and his Commissioner and this was the first time it—I had a chance to tell the Commissioner what a crappy job he had done."

That did not end the matter. A few days later Walters apparently relayed more figures on O'Brien's taxes to Shultz. The notes Walters made of a telephone conversation with the Treasury Secretary on September 5 stated: "Delivered figures to Shultz, and he will call Ehrlichman."

It was only a week later that Dean summoned Walters to his office and handed him the list of 490 McGovern enemies (including O'Brien), and asked that they be audited. Four days afterward, on September 15, Nixon met with Dean and Haldeman and complained about Shultz and the IRS. There is some evidence that on the thirteen-minute segment of tape that was not made public, the IRS investigation of O'Brien was specifically discussed.[*]

And it was against the background of the IRS's failure to manufacture a tax case against O'Brien that Nixon raged against Shultz and his blue eyes, and promised that things would be different at the IRS after the election. But it was clear by then that Ehrlichman's plan to put the campaign manager for Nixon's presidential opponent in jail before Election Day had failed.[†]

Roger Barth, as much as anyone, knew the game was over. He took his copies of O'Brien's tax returns, the ones he had obtained from the inspection division, and put them through his office shredder.

Although the identical sensitive case report that had triggered the vendetta against O'Brien had also mentioned Bebe Rebozo, the White House and the IRS reacted very differently in the case of the President's closest friend.

The IRS first learned of a relationship between Rebozo and the Hughes interests in December 1971. The revenue service was investigating John Meier, who had allegedly received millions from the fradulent sale of mining claims to Hughes. That month the IRS learned that Rebozo had reputedly advised Meier to make himself unavailable to the IRS. Rebozo may have feared the interview would reveal that Meier had been wheeling and dealing with Donald Nixon.

---

[*] In June of 1973 Fred Thompson, the minority counsel to the Ervin committee, received a call from J. Fred Buzhardt at the White House reporting on various Dean conversations with Nixon. Immediately afterward Thompson prepared a memo of their conversation. The first entry reads: "September 15 1972 Dean reported on IRS investigation of Larry O'Brien."

[†] The IRS was not through with O'Brien, however. Early in 1973, after the presidential election, the O'Brien case was reopened. During 1969, before he formed his own consulting firm, O'Brien had gone to New York to serve as president of McDonnell and Company, a Wall Street investment banking firm. O'Brien, according to one federal investigator, claimed a loss on his McDonnell stock, and the IRS once again audited his returns.

In March of 1972 Johnnie Walters relayed this information to John Connally, then the Secretary of the Treasury.

On May 15, special agents of the IRS interviewed Richard Danner, a Hughes lieutenant, at the offices of the Hughes Tool Company in Houston, Texas. Danner had been the FBI's special agent in charge in Miami in the early 1940's. He resigned to manage George Smathers' first primary campaign for Congress in 1946, a campaign in which Bebe Rebozo also played an active part. Smathers and Nixon were both elected to Congress that year and became friends. After the 1950 election, when both were elected to the Senate, Nixon went to Florida, where he stayed with Danner, who introduced him to Rebozo. Nixon and Rebozo became close friends; long before he enjoyed the isolation of cruises down the Potomac on the presidential yacht *Sequoia*, Nixon used to relax in Florida waters aboard Rebozo's houseboat, the *Cocolobo*.

Now Danner had startling news for the IRS agents. Under oath, he swore he had delivered two packages containing a total of $100,000 in cash to Rebozo, an alleged political contribution from Howard Hughes that later became the subject of much conflicting testimony. Although word of O'Brien's financial relationship with Hughes had galvanized the White House and the IRS, no effort was made during 1972 to question Rebozo about all that Hughes cash. (Walters later explained this by citing the IRS policy of delaying politically sensitive interviews during the election year. But it had only worked for Rebozo, not O'Brien.)

Not until nine months later, on February 23, 1973, did Walters tell Shultz that the IRS had concluded it really ought to interview Rebozo about the $100,000. Walters sent his memo to Shultz after discussing the Rebozo case with William E. Simon, then Deputy Secretary of the Treasury, later Shultz's successor. Walters said Simon told him that Shultz would be meeting with President Nixon at Camp David later that day and that the IRS request to interview Rebozo could be brought to his attention then.

But Walters did not receive approval to interview Rebozo until April 7. By this time Walters was on his way out, serving his time for another month until he could be replaced by yet another IRS commissioner, Donald C. Alexander, a Cincinnati tax attorney whom Nixon had appointed on March 19.

Shultz approved the Rebozo interview by returning Walters' memo with the notation: "Go ahead with Bebe and Don N. Keep DA [Donald Alexander] informed so no gaps when JMW goes." Walters, walking on eggs, asked Barth to notify Rebozo that the IRS was coming to call. Barth telephoned Ehrlichman, who testified that Barth said he needed a "green light" to interview Rebozo. Barth said Ehrlichman gave the green light, and approved the interview, but only after he assured Ehrlichman that Rebozo was not in any trouble with the IRS. Ehrlichman then telephoned Rebozo to say that the IRS would be asking him about the Hughes money.

"I told him what the agent would be interested in," Ehrlichman said. It was a singular service that the White House was providing, alerting a private citizen to the fact that the IRS would be visiting him, and pinpointing the subject that the tax men would be asking about.

As soon as Rebozo was tipped off by Ehrlichman, he began making frantic efforts to return the $100,000 to Howard Hughes. But the money was like flypaper; Hughes didn't want it back. Danner wouldn't hear of it.

Rebozo's efforts to unload the $100,000 would have been hilarious in a less desperate setting. "Well, of course I was surprised," Danner testified, when Rebozo offered to return the cash. But Danner said it was not his money, "it was Mr. Hughes' money," and there was no way he was about to accept it. One can almost hear faint echoes of the chorus line in *Guys and Dolls* singing "Take Back Your Mink."

Rebozo later testified that he twice discussed the return of the money with Nixon, once after the 1972 election and a second time after Ehrlichman had alerted him that the IRS would be contacting him. On April 30 Rebozo met with Herbert Kalmbach at the White House; later the two disagreed on what was said, but Kalmbach testified that Rebozo told him he had received the $100,000 from Hughes, that the IRS was coming to question him about it, and unfortunately he had already given some of the money to Rose Mary Woods, Nixon's secretary, and the President's brothers, Donald and Edward Nixon.* "This touches the President's family," Rebozo said, according to Kalmbach, "and I just can't do anything to add to his problems at this time, Herb." Kalmbach said he advised Rebozo to get himself the best tax lawyer he could find and turn over the balance of the cash to the attorney.

On May 10, 1973, Rebozo was interviewed by two IRS agents,

---

* All three denied receiving money from Rebozo, and the circumstances surrounding the $100,000 and its travels remained rather mysterious. However, the Senate Watergate committee developed evidence suggesting that Rebozo could have used some of the money to pay for Nixon's personal expenses. The committee found that Rebozo had paid out $50,000 in various expenses for Nixon, including an "Arnold Palmer Putting Green," a pool table, a fireplace, and other improvements to Nixon's property at Key Biscayne, and $4,562.38 for a pair of platinum diamond earrings for Mrs. Nixon (containing eighteen pear-shaped and two baguette diamonds), purchased at Harry Winston, the New York jeweler, and presented by Nixon to his wife on her sixtieth birthday in 1972.

Donald Skelton and Albert Keeney.[*] The agents explained they were investigating Howard Hughes and his associates and simply wished to verify Danner's testimony about a campaign contribution to Rebozo. Rebozo said he had indeed received the contribution and still had the money, untouched, in a safe-deposit box.

Then Rebozo made a startling suggestion. According to the Senate Watergate committee, which obtained a copy of the IRS report of this interview, Rebozo asked the agents "what he should do with the money—whether he should give it to us [the agents]."

Ten days later Rebozo and Danner met with Nixon at Camp David. Rebozo said he had discussed the return of the Hughes money with Danner at Camp David, but insisted they did not discuss it with Nixon. What *did* they discuss? According to Rebozo, the purpose of the meeting with the President was to enable Danner to convey to Nixon his impressions of political sentiment in Las Vegas. "Danner spent a lot of time telling me about the pulse of the people he meets out there," Rebozo assured an executive session of the Senate Watergate committee. "In Vegas, he meets people from all over the country." Danner felt that out West, Watergate was less of an issue than in the East, and since Watergate was then coming down around Nixon's ears, Rebozo said he thought the news might cheer Nixon up a bit.

Soon after this chat with the President about political sentiment in Las Vegas, Rebozo saw fit to tell Nixon's chief of staff, General Alexander Haig, about the Hughes money. On May 23 Haig telephoned William Simon, who called Donald Alexander asking for the latest on the IRS investigation. Alexander immediately dispatched a memo up to Simon, and after that, Haig met with three White House lawyers, Len Garment, Chapman Rose, and Fred Buzhardt, to be briefed on the Rebozo affair. Thereafter Haig briefed Nixon on the IRS investigation of Rebozo. "I don't think it was news to him," Haig recalled later.

Nixon instructed Haig to give Rebozo the name of Kenneth Gemmill, a Philadelphia tax attorney and an old friend of Nixon's. Gemmill advised Rebozo to go to his bank right away and count the money in front of a government official. Rebozo called Kenneth Whittaker, the FBI agent in charge in Miami, who came to Rebozo's Key Biscayne Bank and watched as Rebozo counted out a thousand $100 bills.[†]

Several seriocomic meetings then ensued, with Rebozo still plead-

---

[*] Rebozo said he remembered that one of the agents was named Skelton because "Red Skelton is a friend of mine and he comes from the same town in Indiana that Skelton came from," although, Rebozo added, the IRS agent was not related to the comedian.

[†] There was one slight embarrassment. After counting the money, Rebozo discovered there was an extra $100 bill.

ing with the Hughes organization to take back their $100,000. In June, Rebozo met Gemmill in Philadelphia, but Danner failed to show. Gemmill refused to take the money, so Rebozo with the cash still stuffed in his briefcase, proceeded to Yonkers, New York. There he met with William E. Griffin, corporate secretary of the Precision Valve Company, owned by Nixon's millionaire friend Robert Abplanalp. Rebozo explained he, uh, had this $100,000 with him that he had expected to offload in Philly, but he had not been able to do so, and could he leave it with Griffin? Griffin agreed to hold the money in *his* safe-deposit vault in Yonkers. Finally, on June 27, at the Marine Midland bank in lower Manhattan, Griffin turned the $100,000 over to Walter Glaeser, a representative of Howard Hughes.

Meanwhile Troy Register, IRS district director for intelligence in Jacksonville, Florida, assigned two more agents to the Rebozo matter. They were John Bartlett, of the intelligence division—which handles criminal-fraud cases—and Burt Webb, of the audit division. The IRS men initially said they would review Rebozo's taxes for the past five years, but when Gemmill objected, they waived three of the years. The IRS also agreed not to contact any other persons who might have relevant information, but to let Gemmill and Rebozo obtain any data needed by the IRS from third parties.

The IRS agents met several times over that summer and fall with Rebozo, who lost no opportunity to remind them of his close friendship with the President. At Gemmill's request, the IRS provided him with a copy of the IRS's May 10 interview with Rebozo. Later, agent Bartlett told Rebozo he did not expect there would be any continued criminal investigation by the IRS of the matter. In other ways, the IRS was very nice to Rebozo.

On October 18 Haig called Attorney General Elliot Richardson to complain that Archibald Cox, the Watergate Special Prosecutor, was going too far. Haig, according to Richardson, said "he didn't see what Mr. Cox's charter had to do with the activities of Mr. Rebozo, especially when there had already been an investigation of the whole matter by the Internal Revenue Service."

On Saturday night, two days later, the President fired Cox, Richardson resigned, and Nixon began the descent into San Clemente. The massacre was triggered by the dispute over the White House tapes that Judge Sirica had ordered Nixon to turn over to the court. General Haig later insisted that it had nothing to do with Archibald Cox's investigation of Bebe Rebozo's $100,000.

The two-story building in a rundown area of N.W. Fifth Street in Miami was surrounded by a barbed wire fence and overlooked an empty lot overgrown with weeds. A sign outside revolved constantly, flashing the temperature and the time of day and proclaiming that the building was the Franklin Federal Savings and Loan Association.

It wasn't. The building was actually the secret headquarters of the federal government's organized-crime strike force in Miami, one of seventeen such units around the country.

On March 15, 1975, Mrs. Elsa Gutierrez, a beautiful and voluptuous dark-haired woman of thirty-three, born in Havana, revealed that she had been working as a paid spy for the Miami office of the IRS. The cases were part of the work of the Miami strike force. Mrs. Gutierrez, a divorcée, said IRS intelligence agents had instructed her to gather information about thirty prominent Dade County public officials. In particular, she said, she was told to find out about their sex and drinking habits. Her code name was Carmen. The IRS project for which she worked, she said, was called Operation Leprechaun.

Mrs. Gutierrez's revelations rocked the IRS, touched off several congressional investigations, an in-house probe by the IRS, and focused widespread public attention on the fact that the IRS does more than collect taxes. It is also an intelligence-gathering agency, just like the FBI, the CIA, or the NSA. And it spies on American citizens.

The woman who surfaced Operation Leprechaun was an intriguing figure. She lived in a pleasant Spanish-style house in Coral Gables with her three teen-aged daughters and Rommel, a large dog trained to attack any strangers. Since 1968, it was reported, she had worked as a paid informant for the Secret Service, the Miami Strike Force, and the Drug Enforcement Agency (DEA), as well as the IRS.

The Miami newspapers exploded with stories about Operation Leprechaun. According to Mrs. Gutierrez, she met in a Miami motel with IRS intelligence agents, who showed her some thirty surveillance photos of her targets, prominent public figures reported to include two women judges, Ellen Morphonios and Rhea Grossman; a federal judge, the late Emett Choate; and State Attorney Richard Gerstein.

Mrs. Gutierrez said the IRS paid her $200 a week. Since the best place to mingle with her affluent targets was in the confines of a private club, the IRS paid for her memberships in the Playboy Club and the Mutiny Club.

As the revelations mounted, they focused on the man who ran and had christened Operation Leprechaun, a veteran IRS intelligence agent named John T. Harrison. Mrs. Gutierrez said she feared her boss, better known (behind his back) as "the Bald Eagle" or "Yul Brynner," since he had not a hair on his head. She said he sometimes wore a wig, had a gold tooth, a scar on his right forearm, and was "very tough."

Testifying before a House Ways and Means subcommittee, Harrison was asked by Representative J. J. Pickle of Texas whether his network of informants in Florida had used a "sex and booze" approach to tax collecting. Pickle cited news reports that the IRS had employed informants "to have drinks and sexual relations with individuals for the purpose of gathering tax information." He asked, "Do you think that is a proper function of the IRS?"

> MR. HARRISON: Mr. Pickle, as you put it, I deny it. That is not to say that one or more informants did or did not have sexual relations with one or more subjects . . . I never asked one of my informants to have sexual relations with a subject to gain information or for any other reason. . . . In the case of Elsa Gutierrez, . . . also known as Carmen, the code name, she claimed to have had sexual relations in the performance of her information-gathering activities.
> I did not condemn her for it. I did not encourage it and I did not discourage it.
> MR. PICKLE: I assume this trick took place. Do you think that was helpful in developing the tax case?
> MR. HARRISON: I would have to say that it was helpful if it was her way of getting information and if that is the way she got her information.

If Harrison was to be believed, Mrs. Gutierrez had taken John Dean's advice about screwing enemies rather literally. But Harrison denied that he had given any "blanket instruction" to his informants to "go out and seek sexual and drinking habits of suspected tax violators." He conceded, however, that on more than one occasion he had asked for information on girl friends being kept in expensive apartments. "I do not recall ever requesting information concerning sex lives and drinking habits . . . or any other personal information of anyone that was not related to obtaining information . . . regarding suspected tax evaders or avoiders," Harrison added. The personal information, he said, all had "potential tax value."

Harrison created Operation Leprechaun in 1972, and in time built up a network of sixty-two IRS informants, according to the IRS's internal investigation. The best description of how Leprechaun got its name was provided by Jeffrey A. Shapiro, an IRS official who later testified before the subcommittee.

Harrison, he said, selected the name Operation Leprechaun "because he viewed his web of confidential informants as little people who would delve in all sorts of matters. Additionally, he happened to be using a green pen at the time he was assigned to engage in what became known as Operation Leprechaun and combining the green ink with his view of these wee, little people, he coined the terminology Operation Leprechaun." Shapiro made it sound like *Brigadoon*. Harrison said he picked up Elsa Gutierrez from the Florida Department of Law Enforcement, which owed him a favor. Until their falling-out, he said, she provided excellent information. "Yes, sir. She certainly did," Harrison told Congressman Charles A. Vanik of Ohio, the subcommittee chairman, ". . . she even turned her own father in."

This is the kind of dedication that made America great, and the Vanik subcommittee, a friendly protector of the IRS bureaucracy, could find little to criticize about either Operation Leprechaun or agent Harrison. This despite Harrison's description of the trouble he had with some of his other wee people. Among them were two "loyal informants," Nelson Vega and Roberto Novoa, who knew Elsa Gutierrez before she joined the Leprechaun team. He was "shocked," Harrison testified, to learn that the pair had burglarized the office of a Republican congressional candidate, Evelio Estrella, in November 1972.*

Vega also told the Miami *Herald* that he had participated in a scheme to disable the car of Judge Ellen Morphonios outside the studios of WKAT, where she was the hostess of a radio talk show. Vega said the plan then called for him to happen along, offer to help, and "charm her, get in close to her." The seduction scheme was dropped, Vega said, but instead he and Novoa staked out her home, for as long as five hours at a time, to see who came and went.

Judge Morphonios said she was "flabbergasted" to learn she was a target of Leprechaun. "It's nothing more than Hitlerism, fascism," she commented. Richard Gerstein, the Florida prosecutor who gained national attention for his investigation of aspects of Watergate, had much the same reaction. "They're [IRS] working for the wrong government," he said. "They should be working for Castro's Cuba or Soviet Russia. This information demands a full-fledged congressional investigation."

There were investigations, but not very full-fledged. Ten days after the story broke in the Miami papers, IRS chief Donald Alexander testified before the Vanik subcommittee that Leprechaun had been "ill-advised." In June the IRS put out a cautious 28-page report on Leprechaun concluding that the "free rein" given to Harrison and lack of supervisory control led to the "problems" that had arisen. By December, when the Vanik subcommittee held hearings on Operation Leprechaun, it had cast its protective net around both the intelligence division and Harrison.

As the hearings revealed, to ferret out any wrongdoing by the Leprechaun network the IRS dispatched Jeffrey Shapiro, a twenty-eight-year-old hawkshaw whose tenacity and experience as an investigator fell somewhat short of Inspector Maigret or Bulldog Drummond. Vanik, setting the tone for the proceedings, declared, "It had been our

---

* Estrella lost the election to Representative Claude Pepper.

hope to have as a witness, along with Mr. Shapiro, his supervisor, Mrs. Lucille Smoot, better known as PeeZee Smoot. However, we understand that Mrs. Smoot is ill, and we all wish her a speedy recovery."

With PeeZee on the bench, Shapiro was pitching for the IRS. He explained how he had been sent down to the regional office in Jacksonville to read the Leprechaun files, where he met another IRS official, Martha Broxton, who accompanied him to Miami. Describing the encounter in Stanley and Livingston terms, he testified, "My meeting with Martha was really more or less of an introductory meeting, 'I am Shapiro,' 'I am Martha Broxton.'"

Together they produced what became known in the IRS as the Broxton-Shapiro report. It concluded, the witness said, that except for a bit of carelessness with the funds used by the IRS to pay informers (who received close to $50,000), Operation Leprechaun had not broken the rules. "Martha and I reviewed the various primary source documents that were in existence in Miami," he said, and "we did not think the documents were all that oriented toward sexual and/or drinking information."*

Representative Pickle, who did not appear convinced, wanted to know if collecting such information about citizens was a "proper procedure" for the IRS.

> MR. SHAPIRO: Proper, to the extent that excesses in the sex or drinking area could presumably convey the picture that an individual under investigation was spending more than his or her net worth. This would seem to indicate, to that extent, there could conceivably be some kind of tax-relatedness issue.
>
> MR. PICKLE: Was the Operation Leprechaun then a usual or ordinary type of procedure to be followed by Internal Revenue Service?
>
> MR. SHAPIRO: Yes, sir, I would say so.

Shapiro also made it clear that he felt the newspapers had exaggerated their reports about Operation Leprechaun. But to Harlem Congressman Charles B. Rangel, Shapiro conceded that he had interviewed no one in Jacksonville or Miami in the course of his investigation; as instructed, he had merely reviewed the IRS's own reports.

"So all you did was go through some papers and reach a conclusion?" Rangel asked incredulously.

"Yes."

---

* However, the separate IRS internal study made public on June 23, 1975, found that 23 percent of Leprechaun informants' reports dealt with "sexual and/or drinking activities."

"You spoke with nobody? You merely went through papers and reached a conclusion?"

"Per our normal procedures, that was exactly what I did."

During Watergate, the controversy over the IRS centered on misuse of the tax agency against political enemies. But in the wake of Leprechaun and the Church committee investigation, the focus moved to IRS intelligence-gathering. Rather suddenly the public learned the extent to which the IRS, no less than other federal intelligence agencies, was engaged in covert operations and spying.

Leprechaun itself turned out to be only part of a secret, large-scale IRS intelligence program called the Intelligence Gathering and Retrieval System (IGRS), which by 1975 had an astonishing 465,442 individuals and companies listed in its indexes across the country. As part of its investigation of Leprechaun, the IRS also concluded that IGRS was collecting and indexing information that did not meet the IRS's own criteria of relevance to tax questions. It was embarrassed to find that the IGRS files even contained the names of "former Commissioners of IRS, Regional Commissioners, Senators and IRS itself merely because the names appeared in the same news article or documents in which a potential subject's name appeared." In January of 1975 Alexander shut down IGRS.

But even as the Leprechaun headlines faded, the names of other IRS cover operations began surfacing one after another in congressional investigations and news stories. The code names sounded more like CIA than IRS, as this sampling suggests:

Project Haven: Aimed at trust accounts established overseas by U.S. citizens to avoid paying taxes. The operation began in 1973 when Richard Jaffe, an IRS agent in Miami, obtained from an informant photographs of 450 pages of the records of a bank in the Bahamas. IRS agents were apparently able to photograph the records secretly when a bank official visited Miami and went off to dinner with a woman friend of the informant.

In the fall of 1975 the IRS, under Alexander, suspended Project Haven, reportedly because of concern over the methods used by Jaffe and his informant, code-named TW-24. Alexander also sharply reduced IRS participation in the Justice Department's seventeen organized-crime strike forces and slashed the IRS budget for general intelligence gathering by several million dollars over a two-year period. This and other actions left many IRS intelligence agents embittered at Alexander, whom they blamed for undermining the agency's intelligence efforts.

The intelligence operators at the IRS were dangerous opponents, even for the head of the IRS. Soon stories were leaked from the IRS discrediting Alexander. First, it was revealed that the records of the bank in the Bahamas included the name of Alexander's old law firm in Cincinnati, although the IRS said the commissioner did not know this when Project Haven was suspended. Next, there were allegations that Alexander had planned to meet aboard a yacht in Florida with Mark H. Kroll, a convicted real-estate swindler from Cincinnati. A federal grand jury called Alexander to testify; in April 1976 the Justice Department announced it could find "no evidence" to support these allegations.

Operation Tradewinds: Tied to Project Haven, and also run by agent Jaffe, Tradewinds was a nine-year effort to obtain the names of U.S. citizens who made secret deposits in Bahamian banks. Alexander curtailed this operation at the same time that he suspended Project Haven.

Operation Sunshine: The IRS authorized payments of almost $55,000 to Harry C. Woodington, an undercover agent who hung around bars in Miami and Fort Lauderdale for a year and a half and gathered allegations on 913 persons, supposedly to try to identify patrons who might be bribing IRS officials. But IRS officials admitted that not a single case of corruption was uncovered through Woodington's barfly efforts. Woodington told a House subcommittee that his job was to make friends in bars and take notes on fellow drinkers. There were, of course, occupational hazards; one confidential Operation Sunshine memo suggests that Woodington's superiors were worried that he was drinking too much. The officials concluded that the agent was not a drunk, but "he has been working very hard." He was diligent; the same memo, signed by IRS official D. A. Raffel, said that Woodington had compiled "probably the most extensive notes and logs that I have ever seen."

And like Leprechaun, Operation Sunshine gathered information on sex and drinking habits of private citizens. A three-man panel of IRS officials who reviewed the files in 1975 concluded that some of the Sunshine data was "non-tax information on the private lives of individuals of no particular interest to the Service. For example, the files contain gossip learned . . . in the Juggler Lounge, Airliner Motel, that P frequents the Lounge with his secretary (blonde girl) and that their relationship is more than a normal business relationship." Another memo reported that an Operation Sunshine target "frequents a motel" and it was common knowledge that the "manager supplies this official with all the booze and broads he wants." Woodington had been assigned to the project by Mike Acree, before Acree moved from the IRS to Customs. In 1976, when Woodington testified, he was an enforcement agent for the Customs bureau.

Operation Harry the Hat and *Operation Banana Boat*: Both were additional undercover operations in Florida in which Woodington participated. One official indicated that "Harry the Hat" was simply a code name for Woodington. Operation Banana Boat, despite its romantic sound, was not nautical in nature. Woodington testified in Fort Lauderdale that he "visited the Diplomat Hotel, the Banana Boat Lounge, and I refer to this mission for lack of a better name as... Banana Boat, because that was the principal target of the mission."

Operation W and *Operation Rosebud*: Two secret operations in the Miami area about which the IRS would say little. But Alexander admitted that one informant in Operation W was paid $100 a day by the IRS.

Operation Mercury: In the sixties, according to testimony before the Church committee, when anyone sent a money order of over $1,000 through Western Union, the IRS was alerted. In many cases, the IRS investigated the person's tax status.*

In June of 1975, a House subcommittee headed by Representative Benjamin Rosenthal, a New York Democrat, released IRS documents disclosing that IRS undercover agents were "major participants" in illegal activities that included extortion, fraud, fencing, gambling, bootlegging, and bugging.† These were no free-lance informants like Elsa Gutierrez but trained IRS agents who were provided with deep cover in the manner of CIA agents in the Clandestine Services. The IRS agents had "an assumed name including a social security card, driver's license, military background, automobile registration and license, and prior employment history and references." Howard Hunt could not have asked for more.

The IRS scandals led to renewed debate over whether the agency should be used as tool for criminal law enforcement or whether it should devote itself to administering and enforcing the tax laws. While it was true that in the past, the IRS had been effective in organized-crime prosecutions, the abuses turned up during and after Leprechaun fit an all too familiar pattern; once again a federal intelligence agency had engaged in police-state tactics against its citizens, paying out hundreds of thousands of dollars to spies and informants, gathering information on the sex lives of public officials, and turning loose un-

---

* An official list of IRS intelligence operations includes other cloak-and-dagger projects including Scorpio ("Profit from irregular practices of political figures"), Operation P ("Pimps, panderers, prostitutes, pornography, massage parlors"), Project Claw and Project Chewing Gum (no explanation provided by the IRS), Project à Go-Go ("Compliance check of go-go dancers"), Jewel Thieves Project ("Compliance check of jewel thieves"), Chain Link ("Identify and determine compliance of local fences"), Operation Rabbit ("Investigations of police shake-downs in Chicago"), and Scalpel ("Compliance of physicians").

† Although eighteen IRS agents had engaged in one or more such crimes, only one was prosecuted.

dercover agents with false identities who themselves engaged in serious criminal activity. In short, it broke the law to enforce the law.

Its various secret intelligence units, from SSS to IGRS, compiled dossiers on or indexed the names of hundreds of thousands of individuals and groups. The tax collector sat in judgment on the political reliability of American citizens.

Moreover, the privacy of tax returns—which most taxpayers assumed to be carefully protected by federal law—was largely a delusion. In 1974 the IRS turned over 29,520 tax returns to other agencies of the federal government. In at least fourteen cases, the IRS gave returns to the CIA via back-door channels. In addition, in 1974 the IRS turned over computer tapes containing 63 million individual returns to the states. (The IRS has written pacts to share tax information with forty-eight states—all but Texas and Nevada.)

The frightening mindset of the IRS intelligence apparatus was perhaps nowhere so well revealed as in the testimony of E. J. Vitkus, who, as regional commissioner for intelligence in Atlanta, had supervisory responsibility over Operation Leprechaun. "I can honestly say," Vitkus told the Vanik subcommittee, "that I don't know of a single instance of an abuse that grew out of Leprechaun." Enthusiastically, he estimated that Leprechaun's informants had been responsible for recovering $7 million in taxes for the government. He had approved payments to informants over the years, Vitkus said, and "I think it was money well spent." He then engaged in a colloquy with Representative Pickle:

> MR. PICKLE: If that is the case and if it is so, then the type of operation carried on under Leprechaun is in your opinion the type of operation that should be carried on in any part of the United States, if it is justified?
>
> MR. VITKUS: Yes, sir. I believe that we ought to have that.

—President Richard Nixon,
July 24, 1971

11
1984

On the afternoon of Tuesday, July 27, 1971, William R. Van Cleave, a thirty-five-year-old expert on strategic weapons for the Department of Defense and a member of the U.S. delegation to the SALT talks, sat in a small barren room in Washington as a CIA technician attached wires and tubes to his body.

The CIA man, who was gray-haired and wore glasses, carefully explained each step to Van Cleave. The corrugated rubber tube strapped around his chest was called a pneumograph; it would expand and contract as he breathed and measure his respiration rate. The technician wound an inflatable pressure cuff around Van Cleave's arm, a cardio-sphygmomanometer that would, the CIA agent explained, record Van Cleave's blood pressure and pulse. Finally, the most frightening objects of all—two metal electrodes. The CIA man swiftly attached them to Van Cleave's palm with surgical tape. A psychogalvanometer, he explained, to measure his galvanic skin response (GSR) to electric current. To measure, in other words, how much Bill Van Cleave would sweat when the inevitable questions began.

Two years earlier, Van Cleave had taken a leave of absence from the faculty of the University of Southern California to come to Washington. He had never expected to find himself in this bare little room. Nor did he know, as the CIA man switched on the machine and methodically began asking questions, that this lie-detector test had been personally ordered by the President of the United States.

"I don't know anything about polygraphs," Richard Nixon had said when he issued that order, "and I don't know how accurate they are, but I know they'll scare the hell out of people."

William Van Cleave's ordeal, which could have come from the pages of George Orwell, was rooted in an event that had taken place more than a month earlier. On June 13, 1971, the *New York Times* began publishing the Pentagon Papers, the classified history of the Vietnam war. To stop the series, Nixon turned to the federal courts, where he lost. But in the meantime he secretly took other steps.

Nixon had tried before to foil news leaks, principally through the wiretapping and surveillance of Joseph Kraft and through the Kissinger taps. But these measures had failed to give Nixon the control and the degree of secrecy he coveted. Now he tried a new scheme.

"During the week following the Pentagon Papers publication," Nixon later explained, "I approved the creation of a Special Investigations Unit within the White House—which later came to be known as the 'Plumbers.'"

Nixon gave John Ehrlichman the responsibility of supervising the Plumbers, with some help from Charles Colson. Egil "Bud" Krogh, Jr., Ehrlichman's young assistant, the square-jawed Mr. Clean of the Nixon White House, and David Young of Kissinger's office were placed in charge of the Plumbers' day-to-day operations. Howard Hunt and G. Gordon Liddy were assigned to their staff. The Plumbers moved into Room 16 of the Executive Office Building. A secretary, Kathleen A. Chenow, sat in a reception room, providing the suite with an outward appearance of normalcy. But in the inner offices, Krogh and Young presided over a Plumbers "Situation Room" and—typical of the management-oriented Nixon White House—even had "flow charts" to keep track of their various cloak-and-dagger projects.

Thus the Plumbers were already in place and busily at work when on Friday, July 23, 1971, the *New York Times* published a page-one story which, coming on the heels of the Pentagon Papers, caused a state bordering on apoplexy within the White House. The article described in detail the reported position of the U.S. negotiators at the Strategic Arms Limitation Talks that had resumed in Helsinki two weeks earlier. The agreement that Nixon and Soviet party chief Leonid Brezhnev signed in Moscow ten months later varied in some respects from the details reported in the *Times*, but most of the essentials were the same: a freeze in the construction of offensive missiles and a limit on the number of antiballistic missiles that could be built by the United States and the Soviet Union.

Nixon and his advisers were furious at the leak, the more so because the story carried the by-line of William Beecher, the newspaper's Pentagon correspondent. It was Beecher's article of May 9, 1969, reporting the secret bombing of Cambodia, that had triggered Kissinger's calls to Hoover from Key Biscayne, the tapping of Morton Halperin and, eventually, sixteen others including Beecher himself.[*]

So Nixon was ready for blood when he met at the White House early on the afternoon of July 24 with Ehrlichman and Krogh. While the President was out of the room for a moment, Krogh confided to Ehrlichman that Al Haig had predicted that if matters were handled right, "twenty or thirty people" might be forced to resign over the SALT-leak story. It would be the kind of massive purge that the President and his men were itching for—to show the liberal press, the Beechers, the Ellsbergs.

" 'We've got a prime suspect,' " Krogh quoted Haig as saying. "Fine," Krogh had replied to Haig, "let's start there and let's just grill the hell out of that guy and people around him in that one unit."

The House Judiciary Committee's transcript of the taped conversation then reveals the name of Haig's suspect:

KROGH: It's Van Cleve [*sic*] right now.

A moment later Nixon re-entered the room, and Krogh filled him in:

KROGH: Well, we've got one person that comes out of DOD [the Department of Defense] according to Al Haig who is the prime suspect right now. A man by the name of Van Cleve who, they feel, is very much the guy that did it. He spent two hours with Beecher, apparently, this week. He had access to the document. Uh, he apparently has views very similar to those which were reflected in the Beecher article. And, it would be my feeling that we should begin with him and those immediately around him before going to a dragnet polygraph.

PRESIDENT: Okay.

KROGH: ... If he doesn't pan out—then to move on to the rest.

PRESIDENT: Polygraph him.

KROGH: Yes, sir.

PRESIDENT: You understand.

KROGH: Yes sir, I do.

---

[*] Beecher was tapped for nine months, from May 4, 1970, in the wake of the Cambodian invasion, until February 10, 1971, when the last of the Kissinger taps was removed.

Nixon then asked whether the suspect's views were "hawkish or dovish." Krogh said Haig did not know. But, Krogh added, "they've got this man nailed down." Nixon was angry:

PRESIDENT: I don't care whether he's a hawk or a dove or a— If the son-of-a-bitch leaked, he's not for the government.

KROGH: Sir.

PRESIDENT: . . . All right. Now I want you to get over there . . . I don't want any ifs, ands or buts. . . . if Van Cleave answers questions you can say, "All right, we're going to give you a polygraph." That's orders . . . I've decided something on the polygraph thing, John, today, and it makes more sense. Trying to get a million people— Are there a million that have TOP SECRET clearances in government?

EHRLICHMAN: No. Not that many.

PRESIDENT: Well—four hundred thousand?

KROGH: Yeah. Yeah.

PRESIDENT: . . . Here's what I want . . . I've studied these cases long enough, and it's always a son-of-a-bitch that leaks. . . . So, what I plan to do is to have everybody down through GS something or other, you know in the foreign service and so forth. . . . Here, in Washington, and just in Washington, I want all of them who have TOP SECRET clearances. It means if we can get them to, to agree to take a polygraph. . . .

Nixon seemed to be proposing that thousands of government officials take lie detector tests, but then he scaled down his vision somewhat:

PRESIDENT: . . . Bud, I want that to be done now with about four or five hundred people in State, Defense and so forth, so that we can . . . immediately scare the bastards. Don't you agree?

KROGH: Right.

PRESIDENT: . . . I mean, just say . . . the top executives in government, who have access to TOP SECRET things. That should include everybody in the NSC staff, for example. You start with them. It should include about, uh, a hundred people. But, uh, probably four or five hundred at State; four or five hundred at Defense, and uh, two or three hundred over at, uh, CIA. And uh, that's it.°

° During the discussion of polygraphing large numbers of officials Nixon got sidetracked into a hilarious discussion of the classification system. Perhaps another approach to stop leaks, Nixon said, would be "to set up a new classification. . . . Which we would call what? . . . Don't use TOP SECRET for me ever again. I never want to see TOP SECRET in this God damn office. . . . John, what would be a good name? 'President's Secure—' Or, uh— 'Eyes Only' is a silly thing too. It doesn't mean anything anymore."

Ehrlichman then suggested it be called "Privilege." The suggestion did not

It was at this point that Nixon observed he didn't know anything about polygraphs but he knew "they'll scare the hell out of people." Krogh agreed; the operators often asked "a lot of tough questions, personal questions about a man's sex life. About what his mother was like, and things like that."

"We're going to start shaking them," Nixon assured his lieutenants, "shaking the trees around here." He added, "And if we catch the guy his resignation is speedy, and, and, and that's what I like. Not quietly."

EHRLICHMAN: Right.
PRESIDENT: Understand, any person. On one condition. You catch anybody, it's not going to be quiet. I'm going to— we're going to put the God damn story out and he's going to be dismissed and prosecuted.

Richard Nixon had made his position clear. He did not want any wrongdoer to resign from the government and escape prosecution.

William Van Cleave did not, at that moment, have any sense of impending disaster. A short man with strong square features, Van Cleave had already established a considerable reputation as a conservative thinker in strategic studies. He was born in Missouri, but had been educated in California, where he earned his Ph.D., and he was plugged into the military-industrial–university–think-tank complex that flourished there. His consultancies told the story: the Stanford Research Institute, the RAND Corporation, the Los Alamos Laboratory, the Defense Department, the Atomic Energy Commission, the Army, the Air Force, and the Lawrence Radiation Laboratory.

He was one of a legion of scholars trained to think rationally about the irrational, those experts on intercontinental nuclear weapons who spoke to each other in a language of their own, wrangling over mutual assured destruction (MAD), counterforce, throw weight, MIRVs, SLBMs, ABMs, payloads, essential equivalence, and first-strike capability. They played war games, had access to highly classified information, and constructed hypothetical models for Armageddon.

---

please Nixon, however.
PRESIDENT: "Privilege" is, is not strong.
EHRLICHMAN: [instantly agreeing] Too soft. Too soft.
PRESIDENT: Right. "National Security—" and, uh— I agree to "National, Na—, National Security—"
EHRLICHMAN: "Restriction"?
PRESIDENT: "Priority."
EHRLICHMAN: "Controlled"?
PRESIDENT: Or "National Security"—"Priority"—"Restricted"—"Controlled."

They were the priests of the nuclear temple; and if theologians and scientists pondered the beginning of the world, the defense intellectuals pondered its end. Everything in its place.

He had left Los Angeles, where he was associate professor of international relations at USC, to become a member of the SALT delegation and a special assistant in the Pentagon's office of International Security Affairs. ISA was the military's "little State Department," the foreign policy planning arm of the Pentagon. When not in Europe with the delegation, Van Cleave sat in an office in the E ring and toiled in the SALT mines.

Van Cleave, however, was no friend of SALT. He was an articulate spokesman for the antidisarmament elements within the government and the academic community. He made no secret of the fact that he was opposed to the U.S. negotiating approach and suspicious of Soviet motives and tactics.

"My position," Van Cleave said in an interview with the author, "was that we were leaping to the conclusion that Soviet objectives in SALT talks were the same as our own. That we were not trying to look at SALT as a negotiating, competitive endeavor, that we were concentrating all of our attentions on getting an agreement without enough attention being paid to what the agreement should do or what it should be like; that I was very skeptical of Soviet motivations in SALT and very critical of what I thought was our failure to negotiate very well." The Soviets, in Van Cleave's view, were using the SALT talks to "mask the momentum of their own strategic-force development."*

On Friday morning, July 23, when the Beecher story was published, Van Cleave had discussed it with two of his colleagues in the Defense Department, Gardiner L. Tucker, Assistant Secretary of Defense for Systems Analysis, and Archie L. Wood, a Deputy Assistant Secretary for Strategic Planning. The story had an enormous impact all over Washington.

On Saturday morning, as scheduled, he had gone to the State Department to attend a meeting of the "Backstop Committee," a support group for the negotiators in Helsinki. Normally Van Cleave would have been in Helsinki with the delegation, but he was back home because he had planned to leave the Pentagon the following month and return to the University of Southern California. Philip J.

---

* Later he was critical of the agreements that were signed; it was not surprising that in July of 1972, Van Cleave was a key witness before Senator Henry M. Jackson's Senate Subcommittee on National Security and International Operations. By then Jackson had emerged as the most vocal American critic of the SALT agreements.

Farley, deputy director of the Arms Control and Disarmament Agency, opened the meeting by reading an irate cable from Gerard Smith, the chairman of the U.S. delegation, in which Smith complained bitterly about the leak and the leaker.

After the meeting Van Cleave returned to his home in Virginia, at Middle River House, one of those high-rise apartment buildings within walking distance of the Pentagon, where he lived with his wife, Jeanne. They were preparing to go out to a dinner party that evening. About midafternoon, some two hours after Nixon had issued his terse order to Egil Krogh—"Polygraph him"—Van Cleave's telephone rang. It was his boss, Armistead Selden, Jr., the Deputy Assistant Secretary of Defense for ISA. Selden told Van Cleave "that Doc Cooke wished to talk to me." David O. Cooke, the Pentagon's chief administrator, was, among other things, in charge of security.

Van Cleave telephoned Cooke "and I was asked to come in and see him. I was informed it had to do with the Beecher story. I was told to come directly to his office as soon as I could and not to bother going by my office. It seemed a little fishy."

Van Cleave went to the Pentagon. But instead of reporting to Cooke, he made a beeline for his own office, Room 4E843. It was a frightening sight; Pentagon security agents were already there. They had, in effect, seized his office. "There were two people in my office going through my safe, my appointment records and my desk, and they had brought in my secretary, Mrs. Margaret Byers, to assist them. I asked them what was going on and they told me that they had nothing to say to me and that I would not be allowed in the office while they were conducting this search. They told me to go see Doc Cooke, which I then did."

As Van Cleave made his way to Cooke's office two floors below in the E ring he realized his position was precarious. In his office there were several four-drawer safes for guarding top-secret material, but it was in the two-drawer safe by his desk that he kept his most current documents and it was this safe that the security men were going through. In that safe, Van Cleave knew, the security agents would find or might already have discovered a top-secret document containing the President's latest instructions to the SALT delegation. Van Cleave was on the access list for the document and therefore entitled to have it. But the *Times* story appeared to reflect information in the document. And earlier that week, in his Pentagon office, Van Cleave had had a long discussion with William Beecher.

Four men confronted Van Cleave in Cooke's office. Besides Cooke, there were W. Donald Stewart, an ex-FBI man who was then chief of the Pentagon's investigative division, and two men whose names Van Cleave could not recall, but who almost certainly were Nixon's Plumbers, Egil Krogh and David Young.°

The officials questioned Van Cleave for about an hour. They were, he said, "pretty heavy-handed, as if they were convinced that I was guilty. They were quite accusatory. It was very clear they weren't just after evidence, they were trying to make a case which they had already prejudged." Van Cleave protested the fact that his office had been taken over by the security men. But he said the investigators told him they knew he had met with Beecher because they had already seen it "on my appointments calendar" when going through his desk.

That was not surprising, Van Cleave replied; he was acquainted with Beecher, whose regular beat was the Pentagon, and saw him from time to time. His questioners then pointed out that he had seen Beecher alone, a technical violation of Pentagon rules that required a press officer to be present when a reporter interviewed an official.†

"They said that I had the document, they had found the document with my marks on it in the top drawer of my safe.‡ I said that was scarcely anything out of the ordinary since I had just had a meeting based on the document that morning. They felt strongly the story had to have come from the Defense Department because the story was based on the DOD's position. They said I was known to be a critic within the government of SALT and suggested I might have some purpose in leaking SALT positions, as if I were out to sabotage it."

The investigators wanted to know if Van Cleave considered Beecher's story detrimental to national security. His reply did not make

° In an interview with the Senate Watergate committee, Stewart said he was called to Cooke's office on July 24, 1971. "Egil Krogh and David Young were there," the interview report stated. "The purpose of the conference was the SALT leak. The primary objective was to find Beecher's source."

† The rule is obviously designed to inhibit officials from speaking freely to newsmen.

‡ Van Cleave said he could not recall the precise appearance and format of the document, although he was certain it was "a set of instructions to the SALT delegation. Whether it was an NSDM (National Security Decision Memorandum) actually signed by the President or Henry Kissinger . . . I don't recall. But I believe it was an NSDM, top-secret, and stamped, generally, 'Sensitive, Eyes Only' and limited to an access list, a very limited access list."

In his book *Cold Dawn*, author John Newhouse reported that Nixon had signed NSDM 117 on July 2, 1971, proposing a freezing of ICBMs at the end of that year. According to Newhouse, the SALT bureaucracy appealed and challenged many points in the document, and on July 20 a revised version, NSDM 120, was distributed. Very likely, the document Van Cleave was questioned about was one of these NSDMs.

his position any easier, since he felt the story had not harmed security. In the first place, Van Cleave told his inquisitors, the story was "not entirely accurate." Second, he argued, "all it did was tell the American people what we were then telling the Russians. Third, SALT was so far along by then, the idea of being sabotaged didn't seem very likely to me."

Asked by the investigators whether he favored making the SALT record public, Van Cleave replied that he did. "But I said I had accepted security clearances with the government and assumed a responsibility I took very seriously not to leak or talk to unauthorized people about classified material. That I did not and would not."

Van Cleave's interrogators then accused him of playing politics. "They had seen on my calendar that I had had breakfast that week with Congressman Craig Hosmer. I pointed out he was from my area of Southern California and that we had been friends for a number of years. They said from my appointment calendar I had seen Senator Goldwater that week. I said that was entirely coincidental; a mutual acquaintance had suggested I might like to meet the senator and have a chat, which I did.

"They made some very thinly veiled threats about my security clearances, about my position. They said I would not be given access to my office or to classified material until this was cleared up. They wanted me to take a polygraph exam that night. They let me know that either I took the polygraph examination or I was assumed to be the guilty person and that I would not have access to my classified materials and my working papers again—until and unless I was cleared by the polygraph examination."

Clearances are the passkeys to power for the defense intellectuals; without them their careers, their federal grants, and government jobs would wither on the vine and die. So threats, thinly veiled or not, to withdraw clearances or cut off access to classified documents can have drastic economic and career consequences.

Van Cleave had no intention of taking a lie-detector test until he could consult a lawyer, so he stalled. He pointed out that he had a dinner engagement that night and could not be expected to take a polygraph exam on Sunday.

The investigators shifted gears and asked Van Cleave directly if he had leaked the story. "And I told them no. They asked me if I had shown documents to Beecher and I said no. They wanted to know what we talked about and I told them just chatty conversation about Bill's vacation, which he had just returned from." Toward the end of their conversation, Van Cleave told the investigators, Beecher had pulled out his notebook "and said he had some information on SALT he'd like to check out with me. I told them I responded to Bill that he knew I did not discuss details of SALT. He [Beecher] then read off some items on SALT and asked if I had any response. I said I had no comment whatever to make on what he had read off."

On the defensive now, Van Cleave went so far as to admit to the investigators that there was "some possibility that I might have said something that could be taken to be an indiscretion—but I didn't think so." Van Cleave said he wanted time to think more about his conversation with Beecher.

Before the interrogation ended, he said, "there were attempts to badger me into an admission." There was also an implied hint of surveillance. "They assured me I would be watched very closely until this was taken care of." Van Cleave was not prohibited from going to his office, but he was told he would not have access to his files; the security people would change the combinations on the locks to all his safes.

The interrogation broke off, Van Cleave went home, got his wife, and went to the dinner party. "I tried to act natural," he recalled. "My wife was scared to death." Van Cleave was shaken as well.

On Sunday he went to his office in the nearly deserted Pentagon. He spent a good part of the day attempting to reconstruct his conversation with Beecher. There was no one else around, and in the empty office Van Cleave typed out a two-page memo to Selden summarizing his meeting with the *Times* correspondent. "By that time I was confident that I had not committed an indiscretion, and on Monday I gave him the memo telling precisely what I had talked over with Bill. I emphatically denied that I had been the source of the story in any way. That is the truth."

On Monday, Van Cleave also talked with Cooke and Stewart again. This time, he said, they explained he would not be assumed guilty if he refused the lie-detector test. "But there was the hint there, since it was left undisclosed how I would ever get access to my materials. There was the hint my job and clearances were at stake."

He consulted Harry Almond, a Defense Department attorney on the staff of the Pentagon's general counsel, J. Fred Buzhardt, who, ironically, two years later emerged as counsel to Richard Nixon in the final throes of the impeachment summer.

Again Van Cleave was told that the Department did not insist that he take the lie-detector test. It must be "voluntary" on his part. "I finally decided that I really had no choice. I made it clear that I didn't like it, that I objected in principle to the polygraph, but that I would take it."

Having crossed the Rubicon and come to terms with The Machine, Van Cleave tried to strike as good a bargain as he could. As a condition of taking the test he demanded that if he were cleared by it, the matter be ended immediately with no further attempt to make him a scapegoat. He said he would only answer questions about the Beecher leak. He would answer no question about his sex life or other personal or irrelevant subjects. Finally, he insisted he be permitted to see the questions in advance to make sure they were worded precisely. He set these conditions in the course of two more meetings on Monday with Cooke and Selden.

Tuesday was polygraph day. Van Cleave spent the morning in his office, went home for a quick lunch with his wife, returned to the Pentagon and reported to Donald Stewart's office. Unknown to Van Cleave, the Plumbers were encountering difficulty in carrying out Nixon's orders. The Plumbers had no lie detectors of their own, and the FBI had declined to polygraph officials of other federal agencies. Howard Hunt then volunteered that the CIA had the finest polygraph operators in the world and plenty of lie detectors.

Krogh acted on Hunt's suggestion; he telephoned Howard Osborn, the CIA's director of security, and ordered him to provide a polygraph machine and an operator.° Krogh decided the lie-detector tests would be done at the State Department rather than at the CIA, and he alerted G. Marvin Gentile, chief of State Department security, to expect the CIA man and his machine.

Donald Stewart assigned an escort to drive Van Cleave to the security area of the State Department. Van Cleave, given to understatement, said he felt some "trepidation." He added, "I was naturally concerned. I felt there was no question of guilt but still I was concerned about the ordeal that was coming. I had the normal person's apprehension of polygraphs and being taped up to machines and asked questions. I was taken to an office and allowed to cool my heels —that must be part of the approach—for maybe half an hour while my escort went off somewhere. I sat there apparently being given every chance in the world to become more nervous." Finally Van Cleave was summoned to the little room and introduced to the polygraph operator. The escort left and they were alone.

"It was a very plain room, as if it were used regularly for this type of activity. It was a very small room off a suite of offices, very sparsely furnished." There was a table, a couple of chairs, nothing on the walls.

Van Cleave and the CIA technician checked the questions before they began the text. When they came to one that asked whether he had ever revealed classified information, Van Cleave suggested that it be reworded to cover consultants. The phrase "other than those cleared" was added.

° "I was just giving them the equipment—the paint and the brush," Osborn later explained. At least three State Department employees were also polygraphed.

The time had come to begin. The rubber tube was strapped around his chest, the pressure cuff was slipped around his arm, and the electrodes were taped to his palm. "The operator sat sort of behind me and to the side. He explained all the technical registering of the machine, pulse rate, respiration, sweat, heartbeat. He explained the little anodes that they attach to you to check these types of things. They try to establish my normal pattern and then measure deviations that they regard as falsification, lies."

The polygraph operator went through all the questions while a pen wired to each device recorded Van Cleave's reactions on a moving sheet of graph paper.° Van Cleave repeated his denials. The operator checked the graphs.

"It looks clear, but I'm having problems with one question."

"Which one?"

The CIA man wouldn't say. He ran the entire test again, with the same results.

"I'm still getting a slight irregularity on one question," he said.

This time he told Van Cleave the question. "It was one of the general ones," Van Cleave recalled, " 'have you ever discussed anything classified with anyone.' I said, 'Look, why don't you add my wife to the list of exceptions?' He added that and then ran that and a couple of other questions by me."

The CIA man called in Van Cleave's Pentagon escort and another official, who was introduced as a State Department security agent.

"They closeted themselves," Van Cleave said, "and came out and said as far as they were concerned I had passed the polygraph exam. They said it did not reveal any guilt on my part and they would immediately notify the office of the Secretary of Defense."

They must have telephoned while Van Cleave was being driven back across the Potomac to Virginia, because Cooke knew the results by the time Van Cleave reached the Pentagon around three o'clock. "They took immediate measures to restore my access to classified material," he said. "I was given the new combinations on the locks."

For the first time since his ordeal had begun four days earlier, Van Cleave saw G. Warren Nutter, the Assistant Secretary in charge of ISA, who admonished him for speaking to Beecher without a PR

° A polygraph machine does not detect lies; what it does is measure physiological changes that may accompany emotion. The usual procedure is for the operator to ask innocuous questions, which provide a base line for comparison with the answers to the "critical" questions. But studies have suggested at least three ways to "beat" the machine: some form of yoga or meditation to maintain a detached emotional state, tensing one's toes or other muscles, or thinking of some exciting or upsetting images.

man present. Van Cleave was also warned that he had erred in keeping an NSDM in his office safe instead of a central security area, although Van Cleave insisted this was common practice.

That, as far as Van Cleave knew, would be the end of it. But it wasn't.

After being cleared by the lie-detector test, Van Cleave was told that he would be continued as an active Pentagon consultant after returning to his teaching post in California. But on one of his early trips back to Washington, "Sometime in the early fall I was contacted by two young FBI men who said they had been handed this whole can of worms and wanted to discuss it. I told them I doubted they would ever find the culpable person. The FBI men said, 'Despite the fact that you were cleared by the polygraph, all the circumstantial evidence, particularly your attitudes, tend to point to you.' Later they told me they had been unable to find anybody."[*]

Late in 1971 the FBI also contacted Beecher. The call came to Beecher's home in Bethesda (at that time his phone was no longer being wiretapped by the FBI) and the FBI agent asked if he could interview the *Times* reporter. Beecher politely said he assumed the FBI man wished to discuss the SALT story and his sources, and since he could not talk about sources, he regretted to say there would be

---

[*] In *Cold Dawn*, John Newhouse reported that the Beecher story had a devastating and divisive effect among the officials dealing with SALT. "The FBI spent four months trying to run down the source of the leak. Its agents questioned many people known to have talked to Beecher, whose contacts extend beyond the Pentagon. . . . Unless the President and Attorney General have information available to no one else, the daring culprit is still unknown."

There was great irony in Newhouse's discussing the SALT leak. His own book —a fine job of reporting on the complex subject of the SALT negotiations—was clearly based on extraordinary access to secret material, access which he had gained with the help of Henry Kissinger. Kissinger testified to the Senate that he had met with Newhouse and instructed his aides to assist him. But, Kissinger insisted, he told his people that Newhouse was to be given "no access to specific NSDM's or internal memorandum."

A rather similar situation developed in 1976 when Edward R. F. Sheehan, a Harvard research fellow, published an account of Kissinger's Middle East diplomacy in *Foreign Policy* magazine purporting to contain "verbatim" quotes of Kissinger's conversations with Arab leaders. Kissinger again disclaimed responsibility and gave a farcical "reprimand" to Alfred L. Atherton, Jr., the Assistant Secretary of State for Near Eastern and South Asian Affairs.

The outraged reactions of the government to the Beecher leak, and to the leak of the Pike committee report to Daniel Schorr, compared to the phlegmatic response to *Cold Dawn* or the Sheehan article, pointed up the hypocrisy of official hand-wringing over "national security" secrets leaking to the press. It is only the embarrassing leak that bothers the men in power. Unlike Van Cleave, Alfred Atherton was not taped to a lie detector. After his reprimand, he went off to a luncheon with Henry Kissinger.

no point to the interview. The FBI man, equally polite, said he understood and hung up.

Toward the end of November, Van Cleave said, he was preparing to return to Washington to serve as chairman of a panel of outside consultants for ISA when he got a call from Lawrence S. Eagleburger, then an ISA official and later Kissinger's top aide at the NSC and the State Department.

"Larry Eagleburger told me not to come," Van Cleave said. "He said I was in trouble and my consultancy was going to be canceled. He said he could not tell me why."

Soon afterward Van Cleave came to Washington for another meeting. "When the meeting broke up, they asked me to stay and closed the door. They asked me if I knew that a rumor was being circulated that I had been adjudged guilty and that was the reason that my consultancy was being terminated." Angry, Van Cleave called on Selden, who said he knew nothing of the rumor but would check into it. "He was unable to find out anything," Van Cleave said, "but my consultancies were dropped, and the rumor continued to circulate."

Van Cleave added, "Whether I was dropped because they wanted a scapegoat, or because I had just given a public statement on SALT to the first international conference on arms control in Philadelphia—and Mr. Kissinger sent a couple of representatives of his office to that meeting to listen to what I had to say—I don't know. I've never been able to find that out."

Van Cleave was dropped as a Pentagon consultant in November 1971.° He was never told why. The SALT leak controversy continued to affect his career. Three years later he was under consideration for another Defense Department post. "I was the leading candidate, and in discussions at the secretary's level this was brought out and used. And I think, I just have to face it."

William Van Cleave was polygraphed on the direct orders of the President of the United States. Regardless of the circumstantial evidence against him, he was deprived of constitutional due process of law and forced to submit to a lie-detector test because of the economic and professional stakes involved; to have refused would have jeopardized his career. Even though he was cleared by the polygraph, he lost his consultancy and was stigmatized within the defense bureaucracy.

On July 19, 1974, almost three years to the day after Van Cleave's ordeal, Representative Peter W. Rodino, Jr., chairman of the House Judiciary Committee, released the transcript of the twelve-minute Nixon conversation. Van Cleave was stunned to learn for the first time that

---

° He was rehired as a consultant in the summer of 1973, after James Schlesinger, who shared some of Van Cleave's strategic views, moved to the Pentagon as Secretary of Defense.

on that Saturday afternoon in 1971, as he lazily prepared to go out to the dinner party with his wife, the President had personally ordered him polygraphed.

There is a point on the tape where Krogh cautioned the President that the results of the lie-detector test could not be used to prosecute the leaker. The President's hidden tape recorders were whirring, and they captured his reply:

> PRESIDENT: Doesn't make any difference. If it's taken, we're going to catch him and he needs to be prosecuted.
> EHRLICHMAN or KROGH: Doesn't make any difference.

12
CAPBOM

At 12:59 A.M. on March 1, 1971, the night switchboard at the United States Capitol received a warning from an anonymous caller: "This building will blow up in thirty minutes. You will get many calls like this but this one is real. Evacuate the building. This is in protest of the Nixon involvement in Laos."

Thirty-three minutes later, at 1:32 A.M., a powerful bomb went off in a men's room on the ground floor of the Capitol across the corridor from the Senate barbershop. The men's room was destroyed. The blast shattered windows in the Senate dining room and damaged the barbershop as well as a number of unmarked "hideaway" offices used by senators to snooze, relax, or hold meetings in privacy, away from the high visibility of their public offices. No one was injured by the explosion, but damage was estimated at $300,000.

The bombing caused widespread revulsion among the public, since the Capitol is not only a beautiful building but a symbol of American democracy. The nation's political leaders vigorously denounced the bombing. President Nixon called it a "shocking act of violence." Spiro Agnew said much the same. Senator George McGovern, while denouncing the explosion as "barbaric act," saw a direct link to the war in Vietnam. The United States, he noted, had been conducting massive bombardment in Indochina. "It is not possible to teach an entire generation to bomb and destroy others in an undeclared, unjustified, unending war abroad without paying the price in the derangement of our own society," he observed.

Because the bombing had occurred inside the Capitol, the Federal Bureau of Investigation was given responsibility for investigating the explosion and finding the perpetrators. J. Edgar Hoover assigned literally hundreds of FBI agents to the case. Within the FBI, the investigation was given the code name CAPBOM.

It was a time of violence in America. In 1970 there had been thirty-two bombings or attempted bombings of federal buildings, usually at night when they were unoccupied. The violence abroad in the land had reached its height that year; in March a town house on New York's West Eleventh Street in Greenwich Village had blown up and three young radicals, who had been making bombs in the basement, were killed. At Kent State University in May, after Nixon's invasion of Cambodia, four students were shot and killed by national guardsmen; at Jackson State College in Mississippi ten days later, two students were killed by police. In August, Robert Fassnacht, a young physicist, was killed when a bomb went off in an Army research laboratory on the campus of the University of Wisconsin. The explosion rocked the building at 3:42 A.M., two minutes after police had received an anonymous telephoned warning; the call came too late to save Fassnacht, who had stayed late to work on a research project.

Some of the bombings across the country were attributed to the Weathermen, an offshoot of Students for a Democratic Society. They took their name from a line in a Bob Dylan song, "You don't need a weatherman to know which way the wind blows." Some of the Weatherpeople went underground in 1970, and the FBI could not find them.

Within twenty-four hours of the Capitol bombing, the Associated Press received a letter signed "The Weather Underground" and claiming credit for the explosion. A typed communiqué attacked the Nixon Administration's "criminal invasion of Laos.*"

The bombing of the Capitol caused consternation inside the White House. Not only was the war in Laos going badly, the Weatherpeople, or whoever was responsible, had walked right into the United States Capitol, planted explosives, and gotten away scot-free. The FBI was under tremendous pressure to solve the bombing, but it appeared to have absolutely no clues. The pressure on the FBI came not only from the Nixon White House but from members of the House

---

* On February 8 South Vietnamese troops, supported by massive U.S. artillery and air strikes, had invaded Laos. The South Vietnamese forces were routed by the end of March.

and Senate, who, understandably, did not like the prospect of being blown up.

April brought a new round of antiwar demonstrations in Washington. The Vietnam Veterans Against the War were encamped on the Mall, throwing their combat ribbons and helmets on the Capitol steps. On April 24 some 200,000 persons gathered for a peaceful rally at the Capitol. But more ominous events were afoot; the vanguard of the militant May Day Tribe was already in the capital, planning, they said, to block traffic and cut off access to government buildings during the week of May 1. Their objective, their leaders said, was to "shut the government down."

On April 29, two months after the bombing of the Capitol and only forty-eight hours before May Day, readers of the Washington *Post* learned of the first break in the Capitol bombing case. The page-one headline read:

GIRL ARRESTED
AS WITNESS IN
CAPITOL BLAST

The story explained that Leslie Bacon, a nineteen-year-old girl who was in Washington for the May Day protests, had been arrested by the FBI as a material witness "with personal knowledge" of the Capitol bombing. Agents had seized her after raiding a commune in which she had been living in northwest Washington. She was being held in $100,000 bail for an appearance before a grand jury in Seattle that was investigating the bombing. There had been numerous bombings of federal buildings in that city, but the government did not explain, then or later, why the bombing of the U.S. Capitol was being investigated in Seattle. The story said that Miss Bacon came from Atherton, California, a community of expensive homes thirty miles south of San Francisco, and that her father was a lumber-company executive. It quoted her mother, Mrs. John W. Bacon, as saying her daughter had denied any connection with the bombing in a telephone conversation they had after her arrest.

Few details of the young woman's alleged involvement in the bombing were available, but Daniel C. Mahan, a square-jawed FBI agent, had testified at a federal court hearing in Washington before Judge John Sirica that an undercover informant, identified only as "S-1," had identified Bacon as someone who had knowledge of the bombing, who had associated with fugitives having received "widespread publicity"—an obvious reference to the Weather Underground —and who had carried messages between various unidentified persons.

Although the girl was being held only as a material witness, there was a hint that the FBI had solved the bombing itself.

At the court hearing, agent Mahan was asked, "Is she [Bacon] suspected of having participated in the bombing of the Capitol?"

After a momentary pause Mahan replied, "Yes."

Late in March, Leslie Bacon had moved into the house on Lanier Place, a polyglot white-black-Hispanic neighborhood near Columbia Road, east of Rock Creek Park. She had come to Washington a month earlier to work on a newspaper that the May Day Tribe was publishing to help organize the antiwar demonstrations. "On April 27," she said in an interview, "I was standing in line to take a shower, there were so many people staying in the house. All of a sudden a friend of mine came running into the bathroom, saying 'Leslie, get the fuck out of here, the FBI's here, they're after you!' They'd torn the front door off the front of the house. I had heard someone, this woman downstairs, screaming, 'You'll pay for this, you'll pay for this!' The babies started to cry—there were three, like one-and-a-half, two-year-olds lived in the house—and the kids were screaming and somebody was yelling and there was all this noise. So I just threw on my skirt and sweater and went running up to the roof. They were on the second floor when I was in the attic, and I pulled myself up through the skylight and to this day I'll never figure out how I did it. I mean, I wasn't that strong. But I pulled myself onto the roof and went down the skylight into the house next door where these students lived that we kind of knew, but not very well. And I stayed there the rest of the day. There were twelve to fifteen FBI cars in front of the house and behind the house in an alley. I stayed in that house. I finished taking a shower and listened to some music, ate some granola, and smoked some pot." Someone had telephoned Philip Hirschkop, a movement lawyer, and later that day he showed up at the house where Bacon was hiding, accompanied by a young assistant, Michael Fayad. "Hirschkop came in and he goes, 'Boy, you must really be heavy, man, you wouldn't believe the way they are trying to get you!' He had been talking to some Justice Department guy."

Hirschkop had been dickering with Harold Sullivan, the United States Attorney for the District of Columbia. "They wanted to take me to a grand jury in Seattle, they weren't indicting me, they were going to arrest me to subpoena me. I was relieved that I wasn't being indicted about something, because I really didn't understand what the grand jury stuff was about. And maybe I was sort of flattered, you know, that they thought that I was a big enough fish to do something about, you know. He [Hirschkop] told me all this stuff and then he said, 'Look, do you know anything about this?' And I said no, man, I don't know shit about these things, it's ridiculous. If I had something to do with that bombing, I never would have been in Washington, obviously, you know. I mean, I am not that stupid that if I had had something to do with it I would have been sitting around. I didn't know anything about it."

Meanwhile the FBI was still out on the street. "Almost during that entire month they'd been out in front of the house. And it was stupid, the lawyers left to go talk to this Justice Department guy again. But it was so obvious when those two lawyers were leaving the house next door. They would have no reason to be there unless I was there. They left, and about ten minutes later the Feds were looking in the window and they came in the door of the house, and I was up on the roof again. And I thought, Oh fuck, this is ridiculous, but I just don't want to get nabbed for something I didn't do. And at the same time I thought, I am not going underground. Why am I going to go underground for something I didn't do? I had never been arrested before. I was nineteen years old. You know, it was stupid. So I am running up on the roof, hiding behind this chimney, and this Fed comes, coming up through the skylight, he's got a gun in his hand and he's just walking on the roof. There's all this gravel on the roof. I could hear crunching. And this guy is going, 'Miss Bacon? Miss Bacon? Miss Bacon?' You know. And so then he came and he saw me and he pulls out his ID and he says he's FBI, and he starts screaming that he's got me, and like three or four more of them come up on the roof and they take me down through the skylight and down the stairs of the house and throw me in this FBI car. And they picked up the microphone and they said —you know one of those walkie-talkie things in the car—and they go, 'We picked up that object we were looking for.' And I said, 'Thanks a lot.' "

John S. Hughes was the assistant chief in charge of intelligence for the Washington, D.C., police force at the time. A white-haired, stocky man with a Johnny Cash face, he was tough-looking but friendly, a streetwise veteran of the Metropolitan Police Department. "We were having demonstrations every day in 1971," he recalled. "We was blessed; we had one operative who could get in everywhere. All we wanted to know was what demonstrations were coming and where." To Hughes it was a simple question of money and manpower. If you knew where the trouble was coming and when, you knew how to deploy your men to meet it.

The informant in whom Hughes placed such a high degree of confidence was a young woman who had infiltrated the antiwar movement. She had apparently come to Washington about six months before that troubled spring of 1971, and now she was in the pay of the MPD, reporting to the intelligence division and Hughes.

"Almost immediately after the Capitol bombing"—within forty-eight hours, Hughes thought—"our operative got in touch with us and said Leslie Bacon knows something about the Capitol bombing." What happened next, he said, "was all that Kunkel's fault."

"That Kunkel" was Robert G. Kunkel, a short, thin, sandy-haired man with horn-rimmed glasses who in 1971 was Special Agent in Charge of the FBI's Washington Field Office. WFO was considered a plum within the FBI; it was obviously a very sensitive post, since the White House, the Congress, and almost the entire United States government was located within the jurisdiction of this particular field office, and those SACs who did well in the job generally moved up within the Bureau hierarchy. In the FBI it was whispered that Kunkel owed his progress in part to his ties to Hoover's powerful secretary, Helen Gandy; he was one of that coterie of favored FBI agents known by their colleagues, with a mixture of contempt and jealousy, as "the Gandy dancers."

The number-two man in WFO under Kunkel was Courtland Jones (the same FBI supervisor who had brought over the first four names to the FBI listening post in May of 1969, when the Kissinger wiretaps began). According to Assistant Chief Hughes, Kunkel, Jones, and a third FBI agent came to his office "and stated they wanted to talk to the operative." The FBI knew her name, Hughes explained, since the MPD worked closely with the FBI's Washington field office.

"We wanted her to remain undercover," Hughes said. "With May Day coming up, we thought that was more important than the Capitol bombing. We didn't want to turn her loose. Hoover really blew his cork over it."

William Sullivan, then Hoover's assistant, also remembered the dispute over the informant who had named Leslie Bacon. "We were never able to prove anything," he said. "One thing that hampered the investigation was that there was a girl who was an informant of the Metropolitan Police Department. Hoover was so jealous, he said to have nothing to do with the case. They had the informant, we didn't. Because they had the informant, Hoover took the position 'Well, let them solve the case, we don't want to be bothered.'"

Of J. Edgar Hoover's irritation and the mounting tension between the MPD and the FBI over her, Leslie Bacon knew nothing. She had been living in Boston, early in 1971, active in the antiwar movement, when the talk had begun about the May Day demonstration in Washington. "Rennie Davis had asked some of us to come to Washington to work on putting out a one-issue paper, like an underground paper, to be distributed all over the United States to help organize for May Day. Our tactic was to be civil disobedience, but it was really a different thing than what had happened in the past when there had been these mass—you know sit around and sing 'We Shall Overcome' with Peter Yarrow and Pete Seeger. I mean, the alternative had been 'Let's trash in the streets and run around' and, you know, smash imperialism by smashing windows. The tactics to be used here were a real change. It was to be an actual exercise of power. But not by flipping out and trashing things. We were going to shut the city down. We were going to try. In some ways the trashing is a much more personal thing, like an emotional release. And that violence really scares people, who don't understand why you're doing it, and then it can be used by the government to really sway people's emotions and to justify whatever repression they want to use. At least the way I saw May Day it was like people really could have learned from it about how to use power, and the thing about community, and doing things together. But no matter what we would have done would have been symbolic, because we weren't going to shut down the city forever. It was really an exercise of another kind of power. We really could have affected things."

So toward the end of February, Leslie Bacon and her friends had come to Washington to publish the newspaper. They had moved into a house on M Street in Georgetown, across from a fire station. "So we were working on this paper, we sat around talking about what it should be about. We worked together, wrote articles, different people took different responsibilities, we criticized each other's articles, and then it was typeset and laid out with photographs and graphics and then off it went to the printer."

By Friday, February 26, the work was done and they were ready to leave. "Except Judy Gumbo, whose car we had come to Washington in, her car was being fixed. It was a VW and the clutch was fucked up." So Bacon had spent the weekend in Washington, and on Monday morning "we woke up and I just remember coming downstairs and somebody saying, 'Guess what, the Capitol building was bombed!' We all kind of laughed and thought, you know, How weird . . . Out of sight . . . I wonder why? I don't remember what we thought. We were waiting for Judy Gumbo's clutch on her green Volkswagen. And I decided I didn't want to go back to Boston, and I would stay in Washington and work.

"The morning the Capitol was bombed, March 1, I went outside and there was an FBI car sitting there. The car was unmarked, but I don't need a marked FBI car to say that it's an FBI car. They were all brand-new Fords, air-conditioned, with antennas, metallic green or light green, light metallic blue, and they're really just obvious. From the time I began to be involved in the antiwar movement there was always this paranoid, ego-tripping fantasy about how the Feds were following us and the phone was tapped. We were sure that we were always seeing lenses through the venetian blinds of the firehouse across the street on M Street. I now know we probably were.

"I guess the group that came to Washington was suspect, so of course they were watching us. But after the Capitol was bombed, we were being followed by the FBI in a really threatening manner. We were driving around Dupont Circle, we would just keep driving around the circle, you know, to freak them out, and they would keep driving around the circle, and they were tailgating us and it was like rush hour and they kept bumping into us, hitting the car. Just to scare us. I mean, we thought it was funny. They thought they were going to terrify us. Meanwhile Stewart Albert, Judy Gumbo, and two other people who had been working on the newspaper had left Washington and they were driving back to Boston in Judy Gumbo's little Volkswagen. They were in Pennsylvania—I guess they had been followed all the way from Washington—when all of a sudden there were like the highway patrol and ten cars of FBI agents pulling them over. I think they made them lay down on the concrete, frisked them all, and searched the car and held them there for a number of hours. They didn't find anything. And then it turned out they were really after this green like Army knapsack. The FBI was looking for dynamite in this green knapsack. But it had been filled with dope. We had gone to Washington before Stu did, and we complained that we had this really shitty pot and we needed some good dope if we were going to save the war, and if we were going to let loose our imaginations to figure out a really great way to do this newspaper, good graphics and all that. So Stu brought some good dope in a green knapsack, it was really good pot, and I remember saying, 'Dynamite weed, dynamite weed.' The FBI got the knapsack but there was nothing in it then.° There's a part I am leaving out; we were going to rent this land and a few houses in Harpers Ferry and set up like this tribal community. We spent a lot of time talking about it and fantasizing about it, because of John Brown, and it's a

---

° On May 25 Judy Gumbo, Stewart Albert, and Jerry Rubin held a press conference on the Capitol steps. Rubin and Albert were officials of the Youth International party (Yippie), and Gumbo described herself as a WITCH, a member of the Woman's International Terrorist Conspiracy from Hell. Although known in the radical movement as Judy Gumbo, she had been identified by the *New York Times* a week earlier as Judith L. Clavir, a former activist at the University of California at Berkeley and a friend of Eldridge Cleaver, the Black Panther leader. At the press conference Gumbo praised the Capitol bombing but denied any role in it. Albert said he did indeed have a knapsack, "but it wasn't full of dynamite. It was full of marijuana. It was Colombia marijuana—the best."

beautiful place, you know, three states come together, the Shenandoah and the Potomac merge there, and John Brown, there's definitely revolutionary karma about the place, you know. The idea of all these people living on the land together and building some kind of community, only a week or two before we went into Washington to do this mass civil disobedience, was really exciting. We were all taking a lot of acid then, and our perception of what was happening was really involved in that, just like striking down this enormous beast. We were just the rumbling of this thing that was rising up in America."

If what J. Edgar Hoover liked to call the New Left had an official nemesis in the early seventies, a devil figure universally loathed and feared, it would have been the chief of the Special Litigation section of the Internal Security Division of the Justice Department, Guy L. Goodwin. With his meticulously styled, blown-dry gray pompadour and his immaculate clothes, Goodwin might have been mistaken for a particularly successful and expensive hairdresser, or perhaps a television anchorman. Variously described in news accounts as "imperious" and "sarcastic," Goodwin certainly made no effort to mask the distaste in which he held the radical targets he so relentlessly pursued. For years his visage had stared out of a "Wanted" poster popular among youthful members of the antiwar movement. Goodwin seemed to like that, and he put one of the posters, identifying him as "special prosecutor for the Nixon-Mitchell gang," on the wall of his office in the Department of Justice. He came out of Kansas, a former Assistant U.S. Attorney in Wichita who had moved to Washington and the Justice Department soon after Nixon took office. The Special Litigation section quickly emerged as the Administration's spearhead against the movement, the Weatherpeople, and a broad range of militants on the political left. Guy Goodwin was Nixon's point man in the battle against the counterculture. "Goodwin's somewhat prissy manner—his coiffured hair, manicured nails and precise, high-registered tone of voice—makes his image as a dedicated terrorist-buster a little incongruous," the *New York Times* reported in 1973. "Yet he pursues his quarry with a vengence. He has memorized the biographies and backgrounds of scores of radicals."

Goodwin was working in an entirely comfortable environment in Richard Nixon's Justice Department. It was headed by John Mitchell, that cold-eyed, jowly symbol of "law and order," and his deputy, Richard Kleindienst, the Arizona conservative who had managed Barry Goldwater's presidential campaign in 1964. At the time that the explosion blew up the men's room in the Senate wing of the United States Capitol, the Assistant Attorney General in charge of the Internal Security Division was Robert Mardian, another Goldwater Republican whose closest friend was Richard Kleindienst.

Mardian's father was an Armenian refugee from the Turks, an immigrant whose four sons had built up a construction business in Phoenix with $25 million a year in sales. The country had indeed been good to the Mardians, and now one of them, Robert, was in charge of protecting the country. He was responsible for nothing less than the internal security of the United States, a task that he approached with great zeal. Mardian cracked down on the revolutionaries and radicals, but he did so with such enthusiasm that he even frightened Tom Charles Huston, who once remarked, "Mardian didn't know the difference between a kid with a beard and a kid with a bomb."

There were conspirators everywhere, and Mardian apparently installed a secret debugging device in his office, for fear that even within the confines of the Department of Justice the enemy might be listening.° And it was to Mardian that Guy Goodwin reported.

In retrospect, it is ironic to consider that all three of those senior Justice Department officials, Mitchell, Kleindienst, and Mardian, were themselves convicted of Watergate crimes. But in March of 1971 they were the hunters and not the hunted.

If the FBI had the task of tracking down the radicals who had presumably bombed the Capitol, within the Department of Justice the bombing case was the direct responsibility of Goodwin and Mardian. They wanted to crack it, but the FBI official on whom they relied for leads had disappointing news about the MPD's prize informant.

Charles Brennan, assistant director of the FBI, had succeeded William Sullivan as head of the Domestic Intelligence Division in 1970. To Chick Brennan, Kunkel's fight with John Hughes over the girl informant was an irrelevant exercise; he, too, wished to solve CAPBOM, but he knew something that he hastened to share with Mardian.

"The girl had previously cooperated with the Bureau in the Midwest," he said in an interview. "She was originally active in the student movement in the Cincinnati area. She was attracted to the life style of the movement. She was a little kooky, unreliable. So we dropped her. Then she turned up here and was milking the MPD,

---

° The anti-bugging device was discovered after Mardian left, in 1972, when CBS attempted to interview his successor, A. William Olson, who did not know the device was still in the office. CBS kept getting mysterious feedback on the microphone, an inexplicable hum; finally someone called a Justice Department security man who found the gadget and turned it off.

and they paid her a goodly sum, maybe a thousand dollars a month.

"Mardian gigged me that the MPD was outshining us in collecting intelligence." But, Brennan added, he had made it clear to Mardian that the FBI considered the woman unreliable. "I told Mardian we had that turkey and we dropped her. She put Bacon in a meeting where Bacon said something that indicated an awareness of the planning of the Capitol bombing. She said she lived in one of the pads with Bacon. The nature of the conversation led her to believe Bacon knew about it. I think she [the informant] was puffing."

Brennan agreed in the interview that an unreliable informant can still provide accurate information. But he added, "The heat was really on to nail this case. MPD was hooked into this broad. There is no way to tell if it [her information] was any good. There's a fifty-fifty chance. I never saw anything she had to offer that enabled you to get hard, factual information. I think they went on a pretty weak case. I was telling Mardian that she was unreliable. But the heat was on."

The heat was indeed on, and the antiwar activists who remained in Washington felt it. "We were followed more and more," Leslie Bacon recalled. "The Feds came to a lot of different people's apartments in the middle of the night with keys. They grabbed people as they were getting into their cars in parking lots and threw them into the car and drove around for a few hours, bribing them, telling them they'd give them thousands of dollars and a new passport if they'd only sing a song. And it didn't make any difference whether they did or not, 'cause their goose was cooked, they had information on us—it just went on and on."

A few days after her friends had left for Boston, she moved into the house at 1747 Lanier Place. Early in April her personal nightmare began. "One night I'd been tripping as usual and I went off to sleep about six in the morning. I was not really asleep, I was just kind of in a trance, spaced-out in my bed, on the verge of being asleep but still awake. We had taken acid. We were tripping out about once a week. And I looked up and there were these twelve FBI agents standing next to my bed. They pulled the covers off my bed, so there I am completely naked with twelve FBI agents. I was still tripping, your mind is really vulnerable then and I didn't know what to do. Because, I mean, it's one thing when they're knocking on your door, you know how to say, 'Fuck you, get outta here,' and close the door, but when you're laying there naked in your bed and they're standing there staring at you . . . So then they went into the next room and pulled the covers off this bed, and there were these two gay guys and they were sleeping. The FBI agents, they thought they would see a hot scene between some man and woman. They freaked out and they went running up the stairs yelling, 'They're just faggots!'

"There was one FBI agent that was older than the others, that was still kind of the G-man type, you know. All the rest of them were younger, to me they were slimy. The older guy was like my grandfather or something. The rest of them were like Nixonoids to me and the other guy looked like a remnant of another era. So they went up the stairs. I got dressed and I went upstairs and the whole house had been awakened by then. I don't know how they got into the house; I don't think anybody let them in. They stood there talking to us and somebody was saying, 'Don't you know you have to have a warrant? I mean, who the hell do you think you are, sneaking around somebody's house?' and they said, 'Oh yeah, all we need is one more big bang in this town and you'll see what repression is really like.' I remember them saying, 'All we really need is one more big bang in this town.'

"They kept saying stuff like 'Oh, Leslie, I thought you and I would get along better, we're both from the same hometown.' This was like to get you to go, 'Oh, you're from there, too,' but I didn't say anything because I knew what kind of tricks they used. They tried to get me to come outside with them, they said they just wanted to ask me a few questions. I said, 'You can ask me any questions you want to right here in front of all these people. I'm not saying I'll say a fuckin' word to you but if you want to ask me anything, you can do it here.' Then someone called a lawyer, and they left.

"I stayed in the house for a couple more hours and left with a friend of mine to go to our office. As I tried to get in the car we were surrounded by D.C. police, in uniform. They were asking me my name, and I wouldn't tell them, so they threw me in a police car and took me to the police station. They wouldn't tell me if I was under arrest. They wouldn't tell me why they busted me. But they didn't put me in a cell, they didn't book me, they didn't question me. They just called up the FBI on the telephone and tried to get me to talk to them. They kept trying to get me to talk to the FBI on the phone. The FBI had told them to pick me up and the FBI, I assume, felt a little awkward about it because they had nothing to pick me up about. They held me about four hours at the station. They didn't question me. Then somebody called a lawyer and they just let me go. So then I split for about a week. Actually for about four days I stayed in the Howard Johnson's motel across from the Watergate, where Gordon Liddy was [later] bugging. Out the window of my room I could see Martha Mitchell's plants."

Guy Goodwin was getting ready to pounce. He had overcome a major obstacle. Assistant Chief Hughes had stuck to his guns, refusing to permit the FBI to interview the woman informant. So Goodwin himself had managed to see her. "The unusual aspect," Chick Brennan recalled, "was that Justice involved itself directly. Goodwin actually sat in with this woman in a motel and conducted an interview with her for several hours. Mardian asked me to come in and listen to the tape. I did." Nothing Brennan heard on the tape of the motel interview, however, changed his mind about the reliability of the informant.

As chief of the FBI's Domestic Intelligence Division, Brennan was the principal investigative official responsible for gathering and evaluating information about the bombing of the U.S. Capitol. Although Brennan warned Mardian, head of the Justice Department's Internal Security Division, that the MPD informant had been dropped by the FBI *because* she was considered unreliable, the government nevertheless ordered the Washington field office to arrest Leslie Bacon. On the morning of April 27, as Leslie Bacon was preparing to take her shower, Kunkel's men surrounded the commune on Lanier Place.

When Bacon was captured in the room that evening, several hours after she had found refuge with the students next door, she was taken directly to FBI headquarters. "They booked me and fingerprinted me a thousand times. Hirschkop comes in and was yelling about how they weren't supposed to fingerprint witnesses. And they said, 'Oh yeah, you're right, you're right, we'll destroy the prints.' We were sitting around this office, and they were asking me about, what did I think about those faggots—there was a lot of the same guys that had come that time to the house. I made some snide remark about J. Edgar Hoover and they were like sitting on the side of the desk, these cowboys, and telling me that J. Edgar Hoover was always going to be there, and when he died there would be another boss.

"They turned me over to the custody of federal marshals, two men and two women. They were black. They said, 'Oh, we better get something to eat,' so we went to McDonald's, riding in this guy's pink Cadillac, with this little tape deck with Aretha Franklin, you know, it was weird. It was really weird because I am thinking, These people are lackeys, these people are being so co-opted. Here I am, sitting in the middle of these four black people who are smoking Kools and talking about Aretha Franklin. And they're keeping me captive. It's ridiculous, you know.

"So we went to the hotel right near the Capitol grounds, it was kind of a new plastic hotel. The feeling I had was that the hotel staff really knew what was going on and they had seen this scenario before. Two marshals stayed in the room awake all night and one was out in the hall. And there were guns and radios, and they were talking in code on these radios all the time. And then in the morning, I realized there had been a lot more of them there than I thought. Because the restaurant in the hotel was just cluttered with Feds and all with their little radios. And then I had a court hearing that day, in front of Judge Sirica, who everyone thinks he's a really nice guy, right? I just remember that he had these eyebrows.

"And the same Fed that had served me with some paper in the Fed car took the stand [agent Mahan] and testified that there was a grand jury sitting in Seattle and a subpoena had been issued by that grand jury for me, and that the judge in Seattle, Judge George Boldt, had issued a warrant for my arrest. The FBI agent said an informant had overheard a conversation and my name had been mentioned in connection with the bombing, no specifics, and the agent's name was S-1. That's the only evidence that has ever been given against me in a courtroom, that was all. And they set my bail at a hundred thousand dollars." Sirica refused to delay her removal to Seattle, but Hirschkop raced down to the clerk of the court and filed a handwritten writ of habeas corpus, and the court of appeals agreed to hear the case the next day. The marshals moved Bacon to another motel, but at the hearing the next morning, the two appeals-court judges denied the motion that she be released from custody. Chief Judge David L. Bazelon and Circuit Judge Spottswood W. Robinson III ruled that there was "substantial doubt" whether the court had jurisdiction; Bacon, they said, "can raise any and all of the issues" in the district court in Seattle, and she would have "ample opportunity to do so prior to any appearance before the grand jury." As soon as the appeals court had ruled, the marshals rushed her to the airport.

"So they were going to take me to Seattle, and we went on the freeway in Washington to the airport. The May Day stuff was happening then, and we drove past West Potomac Park and I could see all these people, all these tents with flags and stuff. When we got to the airport, they were lost. I was always amazed at how inept the FBI and the marshals were because they could never find each other, and they never really knew what they were supposed to be doing, and they spent a lot of time in airports trying to find each other. They took me in through some luggage-compartment place, some little warehouse, to the plane, surrounded by like twelve FBI agents. It was insane. All of a sudden from nowhere comes this TV camera and all these lights, and all these reporters going, 'Did you do it, Leslie? Did ya do it? Did you do it, Leslie? Did ya do it?' And I just kept walking; I mean, it was pathetic, you know, it was really pathetic. That was the story they wanted, you know, that they'd solved the Capitol bombing. And it was absurd, it was kind of beyond their scope to understand that that wasn't what was happening at all.

"So I got on this plane, just a regular passenger plane, and we were flying for a few hours and then all of a sudden we were landing, and I was thinking, We are not in Seattle yet; it takes longer to go across country than this. And I said, 'What's going on? Where are we landing?' And at first they wouldn't tell me. Then they said we are landing at O'Hare Airport. So we landed in Chicago, and the other passengers got off and they kept me on the plane. They had about four or five marshals surrounding me. And then, all of these Chicago Feds or marshals came on and they were just the most gruesome-looking bunch I had ever seen, they were awful. I just remember this one guy with the most enormous yellow teeth I could imagine. And so they took me off the plane and put me in a car, and we drove over to the other side of the airport and they put me on another plane. And from up above where they had the observation thing, through this glass you could see all the TV cameras and all these lights, and they were trying to—they were filming me changing planes. I mean, it was just so amazing, you know. There were all these lights flashing and stuff, and so then we got on this plane. And the only other passengers were all these young men who had just had their heads shaved, and I couldn't figure out whether they had all been drafted or whether they were a football team.

"So we flew for a couple of hours and this stewardess came in. She was giving people ginger ale and drinks, and I said I wanted a ginger ale. So she hands me this warm ginger ale, and I said, 'Could you put some ice in it, please?' And the marshal said, 'No, she can't have any ice. You can't have any ice.' So I said, 'What do I want warm ginger ale for? What's going on?' Later I got it from another marshal that it was in their little manual that they think that if they give you ice that either you will try to commit suicide by trying to choke on it or that it will make you pee more, so then you will go into the bathroom and get the razor-blade dispenser and take a razor blade out and either slash your wrist or try to hijack the plane with a razor blade, right? That was the reason for not letting me have ice in my ginger ale. I mean, it was absurd, but at that moment it was really heavy, like they were playing one more game with me, you know.

"So we landed in Seattle and the next day they took me into a court. The judge said he wouldn't rule on the warrants and on me being in custody because there had already been a hearing about it in Washington. And my lawyers were saying—but at the other hearing, the judge said he couldn't rule because it was out of his jurisdiction. It was Catch-22. Then they took me in front of the grand jury."

The institution of the grand jury is older than the Magna Carta. It first appeared in 1166 under King Henry II, when the Assize of Clarendon ordered that "inquiry be made in each county" by "men sworn to say truly" whether any "robber, or a murderer or a thief" lived among them. In time, the grand jury became a cornerstone of English law, and it was adopted by the new American nation. The Fifth Amendment of the United States Constitution provides that no person shall be held to answer "for a capital or otherwise infamous crime, unless on a presentment or indictment of a Grand Jury." That language applies to federal cases, but not to the states, where defendants are more often brought to trial on an information issued by a judge. The grand jury (which gets its name because it is larger than a trial jury), does not determine guilt or innocence. It seeks to establish whether enough evidence exists to warrant a criminal trial. If so, it can vote an indictment, or true bill. If it decides there is insufficient evidence, it issues a no bill.

The Fifth Amendment provision for indictment by grand jury was included in the Bill of Rights to protect individuals against federal power. But in recent years it has taken on another, opposite role. Increasingly, and disturbingly, the grand jury has been used by the federal government as an intelligence-gathering and political weapon. The process was developed to an art during the Nixon Administration.

The Justice Department's use of the grand jury against both political dissenters and organized crime was buttressed in 1970 by the passage of the Organized Crime Control Act, which for the first time provided for a narrow "use" immunity for witnesses before grand juries. The new procedure means that a witness forced to accept immunity before a grand jury can still be indicted later if the government is able to obtain incriminating information independent of the testimony of the witness. In a number of cases the government has granted immunity to potential defendants to force them to testify; when they refused, they were sent to jail for contempt during the life of the grand jury, which is eighteen months. After that, they could be hauled back before the grand jury and if they again refused to testify, sent back to jail for another eighteen months, and so on.

No one made more controversial use of the grand jury as a weapon against the political left than Guy Goodwin. Between 1970 and January 1973, the *New York Times* reported, Goodwin and his assistants presented evidence to more than a hundred grand juries in thirty-six states and eighty-four cities, subpoenaing up to two thousand witnesses, who were directed to testify under oath. Several hundred refused to testify and about thirty were cited for contempt.

It was Goodwin who played the leading role in virtually all the big federal indictments against antiwar radicals. He presented the evidence to the grand jury in Harrisburg, Pennsylvania, that indicted the Reverend Philip Berrigan and five others for allegedly planning to kidnap Henry Kissinger. And he presided over the indictment of fifteen Weathermen in Detroit, a case that eventually involved thirty-nine alleged conspirators in ten different states and twenty-two cities from Southern California to northern Vermont.

The Goodwin grand juries produced more than four hundred indictments and a good many unhappy U.S. attorneys who were left to try the cases after Goodwin left town. Activists, civil libertarians, and many liberals charged that Goodwin was on a fishing expedition, attempting to gather intelligence on the New Left and suppress dissent by creating a climate of fear. Frank Donner, director of the American Civil Liberties Union research project on political surveillance at Yale, suggested that Goodwin used grand juries to collect data on the travels and associations of activists; these, Donner and others said, were fed into a computer to form a "sociogram," a chart tracing the structure and relationships among members of a group. Goodwin denied all this. He called it "complete garbage."

On Friday, April 30, the day after Leslie Bacon arrived in Seattle she appeared before the grand jury to be questioned by Guy Goodwin. Her attorneys were Michael Fayad, Hirschkop's young associate, and Jeffrey Steinborn, a local attorney who had recently defended members of the "Seattle 7," a group of antiwar activists indicted for conspiracy to destroy federal property. Both attorneys advised her to testify rather than to invoke her constitutional right to remain silent. Steinborn told reporters that he represented "a very frightened nineteen-year-old girl." After each question she was allowed to come out into the hall to consult her attorneys. But Steinborn was worried. "She's no match for Guy Goodwin, I think," he said.

Leslie Bacon did not like Goodwin. "He's sitting in there and he's really kind of reptilian, you know, and a lot of it kind of shows in his face, and the kind of self-satisfied, kind of sadistic vibes he puts out." But she was surprised that Goodwin did not, at first, seem interested in the bombing of the Capitol. "He didn't say, 'Tell us what you know about the Capitol bombing and who you know that was involved.' They got to that about the third day. The first two days he asked, 'Tell us everywhere you've been in the last two years, and how you got there, and why you went there, and who you went with, and where the money had come from, and when you got there who did you talk to, and what did you say or do, and tell us everyone you've ever lived with, and tell us where they lived before they ever lived with you, and where did you get your money, and who sleeps with who, and have you ever been in a room with a gun?' and just everything. It wasn't about the Capitol bombing. It was about how does the movement function. And they asked me everything from Eldridge Cleaver to Timothy Leary, to the Chinese, to all kinds of stuff; I mean, it was like they just went down everything that has happened in the movement in the last three years and asked about it. Most of the stuff I knew nothing about. And the thing is, most of the stuff that you tell them they already know, but it legitimizes their knowledge to have it come out of your mouth rather than out of an FBI log.

"A lot of the time Goodwin would just sit there and ask me questions and all I could say was no. I mean, he would read off a whole list of names. Do you know this person and this person, do you know this person, and I would just say no. The grand jury was sitting there and nodding out the whole time, doing crossword puzzles and falling asleep, you know. I mean, the whole thing was really very boring. The questions were very interesting, but the answers were nothing." Since her attorneys had advised her to testify, Leslie Bacon did name a number of names to the grand jury—a candor, however, for which she was later criticized by other antiwar activists.*

On Saturday, May 1, Bacon was not in Washington for May Day. Once again she was taken before the grand jury in Seattle and questioned by Goodwin for six and a half hours. This time she was asked about the bombing of the Capitol. "I said, 'I don't know. I wasn't there that day. I didn't know anything about it.' "

She was also asked by the grand jury whether she had been inside the Capitol building in February of 1971, prior to the explosion, or on the Capitol grounds, and she replied that she had not. "I was in Washington," she recalled, "but I wasn't in the Capitol building. I had never been in the Capitol building. I had never been near the Capitol in my life. I mean, about four years earlier I had been in the Library of Congress or something like that with my cousin, who is a lawyer, in the summer.

"I mean, this is absurd. I told Guy Goodwin, when he was

---

* In his book, *Political Prisoners in America* (New York: Random House, 1973), former Senator Charles Goodell reported that on the basis of Leslie Bacon's testimony, Guy Goodwin launched grand jury investigations in New York, Washington, and Detroit and questioned a score of witnesses.

interrogating me, he said, 'Tell us every time you have been in a room with explosives.' And I said, 'Well...on the Fourth of July, my father always used to get cherry bombs and a little package of firecrackers, you know?' "

To the American public, which did not always make the nice distinction between a material witness and a convicted criminal, Leslie Bacon was coming across on the TV screens and in print as a dangerous radical, possibly the person who had bombed the Capitol. Why else would she be held in $100,000 bail and whisked across the continent to Seattle before a federal grand jury? With her long blond hair, her maxi-skirts, clogs, and beads, and no make-up, she easily fit the image of a pot-smoking, rock-loving, acid-dropping, hippie-peacenik.

She was all of these things. She was also a highly intelligent, articulate, and perceptive young woman, from an affluent family, with an *I Am a Camera* gift for capturing and comprehending what she had experienced. She was a child of the sixties, almost the arche-type of a generation. The journey from the wealthy suburbs of San Francisco to the commune on Lanier Place followed a familiar path. With thousands of others she had been caught up in 'the movement,' in the rebellion against the war, against authority, against the American life style. Leslie Bacon did not grow up in a vacuum; she was very much a product of her time.

And she knew who she was. "You see, when I was in front of the grand jury, I realized by the fact of who I was, the kind of person I was, the culture I was involved in, and my feelings about the war, that those people sitting on the grand jury, and also people reading about it in the newspapers—there was nothing really to contradict that. I fit most of the same images as most of the underground Weatherwomen did; I came from the same kind of bourgeois back-ground and, I mean, a spoiled brat, you know, who gets impatient with the way the world is going and they flip out and start doing these crazy things. The fact that I could run in the streets with an NLF flag in a demonstration would make it look very feasible that I was also bombing buildings at the same time. They didn't under-stand that there could be a distinction between those two things."

She was born on September 7, 1951, and grew up on the Pen-insula, in San Mateo and Atherton, the eldest of eight children in a noisily exuberant Catholic family of Irish-English extraction. On her mother's side the family had been in California for five generations. The Bacons were well-to-do, although perhaps a shade less wealthy than their neighbors.

"I went to Catholic schools. I went to the same school Patty

Hearst did. We had to curtsy to the nuns. I have six younger brothers. I have a mother and a father and a sister. And we always had three or four dogs, three or four snakes, and four or five enormous turtles, and we bred mice and rats, and iguanas we had, and birds, and ducks in the swimming pool. We did have a swimming pool. What can I say? It was a madhouse. My family was like always outcast in our neighborhood, too. I remember that my friends' mothers didn't like me because I was always barefoot. And I was only a kid of twelve, you know, and in the summer on the peninsula it was like a hundred degrees. And I would always say 'Hi,' instead of saying 'Good afternoon.' The neighborhood was sort of—well, I keep thinking, tight-assed. We always made too much noise. There were always people yelling in our backyard, our dogs were always barking.

"When we moved to Atherton, I went to the Convent of the Sacred Heart, and then I went to public high school. That was like 1965 and 1966 and I started playing folk music and listening to Bob Dylan and taking LSD, and going to the Fillmore to listen to the Grateful Dead. And reading books about Buddhism. So my parents took me out of that school and put me in private school. Then I started running away to the Haight-Ashbury and hanging around the San Francisco *Oracle* that was an underground paper in the Haight, and there was this like community group, and like the Diggers Store and the people in the Psychedelic Shop, and I used to hang around there and be this little fifteen-year-old groupie. I was a Haight-Ashbury runaway.

"I guess the longest I was gone ever was a couple of weeks. I hated school. I went to demonstrations, I went to antiwar marches in the city and wore peace buttons. I would never do my homework. I never did what the teachers told me to, but I was always reading constantly. The last time that I ran away, which was like in 1967, I got hit by a car, and I was on crutches for six or seven months, and I was really trapped then. I couldn't go anywhere, and they stuck me back in Catholic school. And the nuns didn't know what to do with me at all because there I was, this cripple, this gimp on these crutches. First I was on two crutches, and then I was on one crutch, and then I walked like Quasimodo for months and months. I was really this weird case and they wouldn't be mean to me, you know, but I was always arguing with them. And the nuns would always make these comments about Vietnam. Once somebody asked something about napalm, and this nun she said, 'One thing I know is that napalm has no lasting harmful effects on the human body.' Those were her exact words. And I was just seething, and usually I was always really good at taunting from the back of the classroom with wise remarks, but this time I thought I'm going to be polite because there's something of substance here. So I raised my hand, and I said, 'Excuse me, Sister, but I was under the impression that napalm is jellied gasoline that they dropped from bombs and it clings to your body, and if you don't die from burns, you die from suffocation. What do you *mean* it has no lasting harmful effects on the human body?' And I stormed out of class, and within about three months I was thrown out of school.

"I guess I was just always rebelling and I was always asking the wrong questions. I mean, I always kind of trusted my own insight and my own opinions then, and I—and there wasn't space for them. And in America, in most schools, you learn by rote and not by curiosity, they stifle curiosity."

But it was while she was in high school, while she was running away to the Fillmore and wearing the peace buttons, around the time that Lyndon Johnson was escalating the war, and bombing the North, that she began to think about politics.

If Leslie Bacon was rebelling in her attitudes toward school, politically there was less to rebel against, for she came from a rather liberal family. Both of her parents were opposed to the war. "The first time I had ever heard anything about Vietnam and all the horror that was going on was from my father talking about it. My father used to get into fights about it, you know, at cocktail parties. And my mother worked for Pete McCloskey in the beginning when he was running against Shirley Temple Black, and in the next election."

Her odyssey began when she left high school. "I hitchhiked to Vancouver, and I hitchhiked across Canada, and I traveled back and forth across the country ten times, hitchhiking, just roaming around. I lived in New York for a while in a kind of youth hostel for European students. I lied and said I was Canadian, so they let me stay. I had a job walking dogs. Then I went to live in Washington around September of 1969. These relatives of mine had been sent by my parents to rescue me from the squalor, and so I went to Washington to stay with them. I went to cocktail parties and ate in restaurants." As it happened, she was in Washington when the New Mobilization Committee to End the War in Vietnam held its mass rally on the grounds of the Washington Monument on November 15. "I was in enormous fights with all my relatives about whether they were going to allow me to go there. That was kind of how I ended up leaving. I went to the Moratorium and got gassed, and got my head busted. I was chasing back and forth around the Smithsonian and I got the shit knocked out of me by this cop because I was carrying buckets of, you know, milk and water, to put on your skin to keep tear gas from burning. I was just by myself, I didn't know any of the people that were there. Then I came back to California, went to Mexico, and then I started going to a junior college, Canada College, on the peninsula. I guess I got bored, so I left and went to Yosemite for a month. I was really getting into being isolated and then one day, it had been winter and there was snow all over the place and all of a sudden that spring thaw happened, and like all the snow was gone, and the rivers were full and the waterfalls were rushing, and I had been really isolated and away from everything. And I was sitting by this fire one night, and by this river that was rushing, and it was really dark, you know, and someone said, 'Nixon invaded Cambodia last night.' And it just seemed like this totally cannibalistic thing because we were in the middle of this total serenity. About two days later, I was sitting in the middle of this field and someone just came and threw a newspaper down and they just kept walking. It was a *Chronicle* and it wasn't filled with the usual 'East Bay Heiress Commits Suicide While Tripping on LSD,' it was the shootings at Kent State and Nixon invades Cambodia and just all of this horror all over the front page. So I left Yosemite and went back to the college I had been going to and got involved in the strike there."

In the summer of 1970, she went to New York again, lived in a loft on Seventeenth Street, and worked for the Underground Press Syndicate. She became deeply involved in planning a rock concert on Randall's Island and the concert took place, but "it was a bummer. Then I met a lot of people that were involved in politics. I started working with the Yippies, but they were trying to change the image of that word from just being outrageous appendages of Abbie Hoffman or Jerry Rubin into a more serious kind of thing."

That fall she also became involved with a group of radicals, later known as the Piggy Bank Six, who decided that the way to protest against the established order was to firebomb the branch of the First National City Bank of New York at Ninety-first Street and Madison Avenue. The attack on the bank was planned to coincide with the anniversary of the death of Fred Hampton, the Chicago Black Panther leader who was killed in a police raid on December 4, 1969. A New York City undercover policeman, Steven Weiner, who worked for BOSSI, had infiltrated the group, and on December 4 three men and three women were arrested at the bank with the fire bombs in their possession. Leslie Bacon was not among them, however; more than a month earlier, she had withdrawn from the group entirely and left New York for Boston.

On the first day that Bacon testified before the grand jury she was advised by Stan Pitkin, the United States Attorney in Seattle, of the "remote possibilities" that her testimony might be used against her someday in a criminal proceeding. Since the issue seemed to be the bombing of the Capitol, about which Bacon said she had no knowledge, she testified freely. After two days of questioning, the government attorneys suddenly began asking Bacon about "her participation" in plans to bomb the bank in New York. On the advice of her attorneys, she invoked the Fifth Amendment. On Monday the government sought to compel her to testify; the Justice Department argued that she had already answered some questions about the New York case and had waived her right to claim the constitutional privilege against self-incrimination.

By now Leslie Bacon had been in custody of the United States government for a week, although charged with no crime. For two more weeks, while refusing to answer further questions, she remained captive of the federal marshals. Meanwhile on May 7, in New York City, five of the persons arrested in the bank plot appeared before a state court; they had earlier pleaded guilty and were given prison sentences ranging up to four years. On May 14 a federal warrant was issued in New York for the arrest of Leslie Bacon on a charge of conspiring with six others to firebomb the bank on Madison Avenue. Stan Pitkin said it meant that Bacon could be transferred to New York as soon as the grand jury in Seattle was through with her.

On May 18 the government forced Bacon to accept "use" immunity to compel her testimony in Seattle. She rejected the grant of immunity, again refused to testify, and was sent to jail for contempt the next night. She informed the judge who sentenced her that she had no intention of answering any more questions. "I answered some of them over and over again," she said. As she was led off to jail, she accused the government prosecutors of having "paranoid fantasies" about the Capitol bombing. She remained in jail from May 19 until June 16, when the federal appeals court in San Francisco ordered her released on $10,000 bail.

Counting the time that she had been held by the U.S. marshals, moving from one motel to another, Leslie Bacon had been in the custody of the federal government from April 27 to June 16, a period of more than seven weeks. She had not been charged with any crime.

Finally, on June 24, Bacon was indicted by a federal grand jury in New York on the bank firebombing charge. But there was about this indictment the redolent odor of rotten fish. All of the other persons involved in the case had been arrested by New York City police more than six months before, on December 4, and indicted by a local grand jury in Manhattan four days later. Since the group had been completely infiltrated, the police, and the New York County District Attorney, Frank Hogan, obviously knew about Leslie Bacon's association with the defendants earlier that fall. But Bacon had not been indicted or prosecuted in the bank case. All the others were prosecuted by local authorities in New York. Bacon was the *only* federal defendant, and the federal charges were brought only after her arrest in the Capitol bombing case and after she balked at testifying further in Seattle.

Kenneth Conboy, Assistant District Attorney under Hogan in Manhattan, remembered that he thought it "curious" when the federal indictment of Bacon came down. "The conspiracy ran from early September to December. Sometime in October her boyfriend decided to move to Boston. He was a hippie type. She left town with him. She withdrew from the conspiracy and was not even physically in the state at the time of the arrests. She was in Massachusetts. The evidence against Miss Bacon was extremely thin. She had not been part of the conspiracy when the target was selected. She was not present when they detonated explosives in Dutchess County, which was a dry run. There was a lot of very radical talk by the group about Nixon's law firm, Rockefeller's yacht. They actually went to Nixon's law firm to see if it had Coke machines because that would be a good place to put a bomb. But the conspiracy here was to blow up a bank. Bacon withdrew from it, in my judgment. The grand jury voted a no bill as to her." Conboy said Hogan had agreed with his judgment that Bacon should not be prosecuted.[*]

On the day the Piggy Bank Six were sentenced in the State Supreme Court, Conboy said, Hogan had told him he had received a call from the United States Attorney's office inquiring about whether there might be a New York State warrant for the arrest of Leslie Bacon. "I said, 'Chief, we do have her on tape talking about shaking up the establishment.[†] But she did not participate in the Dutchess County dry run and there is absolutely no basis for a warrant. She is not in any way criminally liable or culpable.' "

Whitney North Seymour, Jr., was the United States Attorney for the Southern District of New York at the time. The prestigious Southern District has traditionally had a high degree of independence, and in a book published in 1975,[‡] Seymour emphasized that he had carried on in this mold, more than once rejecting orders from Robert Mardian and the Nixon Justice Department. Was it possible that the indictment of Leslie Bacon was an exception?

[*] Conboy said that the federal government, too, had known about Bacon's role. "When she went to Massachusetts, BOSSI communicated that information to the FBI," he said.

[†] Steven Weiner, the undercover cop who infiltrated the group, had been secretly wired and had tape-recorded the members' conversations.

[‡] *United States Attorney: An Inside View of "Justice" in America Under the Nixon Administration* (New York: Morrow, 1975).

"I have no hesitation in telling you about it," Seymour said. "The indictment was brought over our objection on the personal order of the Attorney General of the United States." He added, "We had told Mardian we would not file the indictment. Mardian took it upstairs and the Attorney General ordered us to file. It is the only time where the Attorney General ordered us to institute a criminal proceeding."

Seymour said that although Attorney General Mitchell had ordered the indictment of Leslie Bacon on the bank conspiracy charges, the order had come down "by telephone from Kleindienst." Wasn't it unusual, Seymour was asked, that the federal government would act when New York County authorities, who knew about Bacon's role, had not prosecuted her? "That was one of the reasons we didn't want to bring the case," Seymour said. He added, "We did not feel a jury would convict on the facts."

Why had Mitchell ordered the indictment? "It doesn't take much of a genius to reconstruct it," he said. "They were dragging her in and out of the grand jury at the time. It seemed to me this was a device to show that this was a serious business they were engaged in." Was it a political indictment, then? "Depends on your definition of political. But we thought it was ill-advised and we said so very forcefully at the time."

Leslie Bacon seemed to sense a lack of enthusiasm on the part of the federal prosecutors in New York. "I went to New York, and we had numerous pre-trial hearings, and they kept putting it off. They didn't want a trial. The guy who was first prosecuting it, I remember the day I walked into the courtroom, he was looking at me, and I knew that he didn't want to be prosecuting that case. I just knew by the way he was looking at me. He looked like one of my brothers. He just looked a little too clean and Irish, if I can throw in one of my own prejudices, you know. I think I went through three prosecutors, and two of them quit working for the U.S. Attorney's office while they were supposed to be prosecuting me. The prosecution was being ordered from Washington, and the people in New York weren't putting any energy into it, but I had to stay in Manhattan for five months. I couldn't leave Manhattan. I couldn't go to Brooklyn; I couldn't go to New Jersey. I had no way to support myself. I existed by bumming ten dollars off of this lawyer and ten dollars off of that lawyer. I mean, New York in the summertime is a real drag, especially if you don't have an air conditioner or enough money to ride in a cab. Finally I left in the fall. I went to San Francisco State and took a class on Kafka. I read *The Trial*. I just couldn't believe it. It was just so appropriate, you know, especially in the end where these two guys come to take him away and he goes, 'Who sent you, why did you come for me?' and they said, well, 'We are not prepared to answer questions.' That was just—that really rang a bell somewhere, you know. I really could say this was written for me."

On September 30, 1971, the United States Appeals Court for the Ninth Circuit, sitting in San Francisco, held that the federal government had acted illegally when it arrested Leslie Bacon as a material witness and took her to Seattle. The court held that the arrest warrant signed by Judge Boldt on April 22 was illegal because there had not been sufficient evidence to show that Bacon would have avoided a subpoena if one had been served.° The government provided no proof that she would flee to avoid testifying. "Mere assertion will not do," the court ruled. "As a basis for Bacon's arrest, the warrant was invalid." The three-judge panel did not rule on the validity of her citation for contempt of court.

Pitkin had left the day before on a fishing trip to Kamloops, British Columbia. But Guy Goodwin was reached by the press and asked for comment. "Miss Bacon's status hasn't changed at all in regard to the contempt citation," he said. "She is still under order of contempt . . . and that order still will have to be satisfied."

The New York bank conspiracy charges were also pending, but in Manhattan, Federal Judge Sylvester J. Ryan postponed a pre-trial hearing because of the decision against the government in San Francisco. In March of 1972 Bacon had been studying at the college library all day, and when she returned to her home she found a note from her father to call William H. Schaap, a friend and attorney who had represented her in New York. "So I went across the street to a phone booth and I called Schaap. 'Well, how do you feel,' he says. And I said, 'I feel all right, what do you mean how do I feel?' So he said, 'Don't you know you've been indicted again?' I asked what for, and he says 'Perjury.' And it was like if they couldn't indict me for bombing the Capitol, they indicted me for saying that I didn't do it." Actually the perjury indictment was based on her answers to five questions before the Seattle grand jury in which she denied having been in or near the Capitol during the month before it was bombed. The indictment, dated March 24, was signed by the grand jury foreman and Stan Pitkin.

In June, two days after the Watergate break-in, the Supreme

° Judge Boldt presided over the controversial trial of the "Seattle 7" in December 1970, and accused Jeffrey Steinborn—who became one of Leslie Bacon's attorneys—of failing to stop his clients from engaging in "misconduct" during that trial. Boldt later went to Washington to become chairman of the Pay Board in President Nixon's economic stabilization program.

Court in the *Keith* case held that John Mitchell did not have power to wiretap domestic groups without a warrant. A week later the Court ruled that grand jury witnesses could refuse to answer questions based on illegal government wiretapping or bugging. The ruling had the effect of overturning the contempt citation against Leslie Bacon.°

On August 4, while Bacon was in Miami shortly before the Republican National Convention met to renominate Richard Nixon, the government dropped its perjury case against her. After the *Keith* decision, the Justice Department was dropping cases against radicals one after another rather than disclose the contents of illegal wiretaps. On November 3, 1972, Richard J. Davis, an Assistant U.S. Attorney in New York, arose in Judge Ryan's courtroom and announced that the government was dropping the bank conspiracy case against Leslie Bacon rather than disclose the content of sealed wiretaps that the government had filed with the court. The Attorney General of the United States, Davis said, believed that disclosure of the sealed exhibit would prejudice the national interest.† No one listening to Davis knew it, but Whitney North Seymour had—with great poetic justice—refused to *nolle prosequi* the indictment, that is, to drop it, unless he could state publicly that he was doing so on Mitchell's orders. "We would not dismiss the case until we were able to say that the *nolle pros* was filed at the direction of the Attorney General," he said. Mitchell had ordered the prosecution; now Mitchell would have to dismiss it.

With the dropping of the bank case, the federal government had removed the last of its charges against Leslie Bacon, eighteen months after her arrest on the roof in Lanier Place. She had been arrested as a material witness in the Capitol bombing, jailed for contempt of court, indicted for conspiring to commit arson against a bank, and indicted again for perjury. She was deprived of her liberty for almost two months. Yet she was never tried or found guilty of

° In October of 1971 the Justice Department had admitted to Leslie Bacon's defense attorneys that she had been placed under electronic surveillance by the government and overheard at various times and places, but it provided no details. As a result of the Supreme Court decision, the federal appeals court in San Francisco formally dropped the contempt case against Bacon in August of 1972. † There was indeed a sealed exhibit in the case, but Davis, a lawyer in private practice in 1976, indicated that the Justice Department must have had some other reason for dropping the case. "There was no way in hell that electronic surveillance could have tainted our case," he said, because it rested entirely on the evidence gathered by Steven Weiner, the New York undercover police officer. Weiner had taped the Piggy Bank group, but since the recorder was concealed on his own person, the bugging was "consensual," and therefore legal.

anything. One by one, the government dropped every charge against her. An appeals court ruled that the government had broken the law in arresting her in the first place.

She had been arrested by the Nixon Justice Department in the Capitol bombing case despite the strong warning by the head of the FBI's Domestic Intelligence Division that the Bureau considered the informant who had provided the information against her to be unreliable. Later, in an effort to further damage her reputation in the eyes of the public, or to compel her to testify, or both, the Attorney General—over the strong objection of the United States Attorney in Manhattan—personally ordered her indicted. The full, lawless power of the federal government had been brought to bear against a nineteen-year-old girl who in the end was convicted of nothing. Despite this, many Americans, if they remember Leslie Bacon at all, probably have the vague idea that she is "the girl who bombed the Capitol."

Leslie Bacon was remarkably objective about her experience. "My reasoning is that they probably knew the Weather Underground did it when it happened, and when they got their communiqué, they knew for sure.° J. Edgar Hoover was under a lot of pressure to resign then, and the fact that they hadn't come up with anyone about this bombing added to it. They knew the Weather Underground had done it, and they also knew they had been looking for those people for three years and they couldn't find them, so the easiest way to deal with it was just to pretend that these people didn't really do it and we'll nab this one here and that made the connection with the May

° As of mid-1976, the Capitol bombing was still an open and unsolved case. Although the five-year statute of limitations for the bombing had passed in March of that year, in effect there is no statute of limitations to prevent prosecution in a federal conspiracy case. Although by law a conspiracy, too, must be prosecuted within five years, the government could take the position that the Capitol bombing was part of a larger and continuing conspiracy; by this reasoning, the case was virtually open-ended.

On November 6, 1975, *Rolling Stone* quoted Jeff Jones, a member of the Weather Underground, describing in detail how "several" Weatherpeople allegedly carried out the Capitol bombing. According to the article, by Peter Biskind and Marc N. Weiss, Jones talked about the bombing in a documentary film on the Weather Underground produced by Emile de Antonio. Jones said the Weatherpeople carried the explosives on their bodies to get past security, then assembled the bomb in "an obscure room behind a barbershop." As they were putting the bomb in place, he said, it fell but did not explode. But that night it failed to go off as scheduled. The next day the Weatherpeople returned to the men's room and planted a smaller device atop the larger bomb, to act as a trigger. "It worked," he said. "It ignited the big one."

Day demonstrations that were just verging on happening. And they could slur us with this violence.

"During that whole almost month before I went to jail, I had been in custody in hotels. I got about five hours sleep a night. They watched me twenty-four hours a day. They watched me piss. I was almost never alone. I would wake up in the middle of the night and there would be this zombie sitting there watching me. Sometimes a woman, sometimes a man, sometimes a man and his wife. By then I told my lawyers I *wanted* to go to jail. I wanted to be in a jail cell. I didn't want to be sitting in this fucking hotel any more.

"Look, I think that the Capitol building deserved to be blown up. I don't know what damage it really did. But politically, I wouldn't do that, that kind of bombing. It gives legitimacy to the government's repression. People end up thinking that the person who did the bombing is their enemy, and they feel threatened by it. But the Capitol bombing, who was really hurt by that? Probably I'm the only person who was really hurt by that."*

She had, as one result of it all, gained a somewhat different perspective toward her family. Her parents had supported her when she was arrested. "My father even said that J. Edgar Hoover was senile, when the press came to him. My mother said, 'Who cares about somebody blowing up the Capitol when the government is blowing up people?' And I just couldn't *believe* my mother saying that. My mother is a rebel in her own right, too. I mean, people who came to California, they started out on the other side of this country and kept flipping out and thinking it will be better if we just go over the next hill, you know. I mean, that's the kind of thing that America was built on. So there's like a certain kind of madness and also a kind of strength about your own opinions and stuff that I think my parents are kind of into, you know, American individualism."

Four years after her name had made headlines across the country, Leslie Bacon was living quietly in Berkeley. She wanted no more than to raise her young daughter, Ariel, and stay out of the limelight. "I don't believe in anything," she said. "I believe in freedom, composting my garbage, and feeding my baby."

But she did observe that almost everything that happened to

* Two years after the last of the charges against her had been dropped, Leslie Bacon sued the federal government for false arrest and illegal wiretapping. She asked damages of $3 million, plus the statutory provision of $100 a day for the wiretapping. Michael Kennedy, the San Francisco lawyer who had defended her against the perjury charges, also represented her in the damage suit. Later, he said, "she changed her mind and decided not to go through with it. She didn't want the hassle, she didn't want to give another deposition. She didn't want the exposure. She wanted no more."

her would not have happened if the American political and legal system had functioned the way it is supposed to. "Look," she said, "I'm not going to hold up the Constitution and say this is the greatest thing that ever happened in the history of the world, but they were violating the Constitution in doing the things they did to me. They were breaking their own laws, you know, their own rules. I mean, I don't know what the system would be like if it worked."

> *"I cannot say that our country could have no central police without becoming totalitarian, but I can say with great conviction that it cannot become totalitarian without a centralized national police ... a national police ... will have enough on enough people, even if it does not elect to prosecute them, so that it will find no opposition to its policies."*
>
> —Supreme Court Justice Robert H. Jackson,
> *The Supreme Court in the American System of Government* (1955)

13
Restoring the Balance

The headquarters entrance is a store front on the street level ... The door is locked with a Master padlock only ... There is a street light located on the north side of the street, approximately five store fronts east of the headquarters. Inasmuch as the nearest other street light is located on the southeast corner ... the immediate area of the headquarters is reasonably dark in evening hours.

Previous spot checks on numerous occasions have shown that there is a very limited amount of pedestrian and automobile traffic after 12 midnight. These spot checks have also shown that the lights of the apartments in the building are darkened.

Entrance will be made between the hours of 12 midnight and 4 A.M.

The language is instantly recognizable as that of a casing report. But the burglar in the night, the intruder who celebrated the darkness, was no common criminal; it was the government of the United States. The words are those of an official memo from FBI headquarters in Washington to the FBI's Manhattan field office. The target was the office of the Young Socialist Alliance, an affiliate of the Socialist Workers party, groups which the FBI burglarized on an average of every three weeks for six years.°

For some four decades, a period roughly spanning seven Administrations, the government's intelligence and police agencies have broken the law and violated the Constitution. They have done so secretly, out of view of the governed, often under cover of the darkness at midnight.

The techniques used by the government against the people have included, but are not limited to, wiretapping, bugging, break-ins, burglaries, opening of mail, cable interception, physical surveillance, clandestine harassment, widespread use of informants, detention lists, and political tax audits. Some of these activities have been organized under rubrics that have become familiar: the Huston Plan, the Enemies List, Operation CHAOS, the Plumbers, the Watergate burglars, COINTELPRO.

An American police state has evolved, operating in the shadows side by side with the legitimate system of government. It has emerged in spite of the Bill of Rights and the protections of the law and the Constitution. We have created a uniquely *American* police state, one that has managed to grow and operate within, or at least alongside, the democratic system. Naturally, by Nazi or Soviet standards, America is not a police state. But the dictionary definition does not require the extremes of a Gestapo, or a KGB; it defines a police state as "a government that seeks to intimidate and suppress political opposition by means of police, especially a secret national police organization." The FBI and the CIA have done precisely that.

It is unnerving to think that a kind of totalitarianism has taken root in America, but if we shrink from recognizing it, we shall not remove it. One of the characteristics of a police state is the use by political leaders of the apparatus of the government to perpetuate their own power. When the President's assistant, John Ehrlichman, ordered the IRS to audit Larry O'Brien, the chief of the opposition party, he was candid about his motive: "I wanted them to turn up something and send him to jail before the election."

Tom Charles Huston, whose blueprint for a police state was approved for a time by Richard Nixon, was equally candid when he

---

° This particular casing memo was dated June 23, 1960. FBI agents broke into the New York City offices of the Socialist Workers party and its affiliates at least 92 times between 1960 and 1966; the agents took photographs of about 10,000 documents. The party sued the government for damages because of the break-ins, and one agent, George P. Baxtrum, Jr., testified that between 1958 and 1965 he participated in "between 50 and 90" break-ins at party headquarters in Manhattan to search desks, photograph documents, and on occasion, plant microphones. And FBI informant Timothy Redfearn had burglarized the party's offices in Denver as recently as July 7, 1976.

explained his motives to the Senate intelligence committee: "We faced an extraordinary situation requiring an extraordinary response, and you don't want a constitutional, legal mandate for that kind of thing. You don't want to institutionalize the excesses required to meet extraordinary threats."

Other officials have spoken in a similar vein; we have but to listen. The Director of the FBI, Clarence M. Kelley, has openly advocated that we "surrender" some of our liberties to preserve the rest. To those in charge of federal intelligence agencies, the limits of power appear to be pragmatic rather than constitutional; the best system for catching foreign spies would be "one FBI agent for each espionage agent," Kelley once told reporters, but "our budget doesn't allow it."

The director of the passport office of the Department of State, Frances G. Knight, has advocated that each American citizen be fingerprinted and required to carry a government identity card. She said this would deter fraud and other crimes, and added that "an insignificant number of our citizens would be opposed to national registration and being issued a national identity card." She predicted it will eventually be done.

Sometimes evidence of the scope of the government's domestic intelligence activity surfaces unexpectedly, in odd places. In July of 1975 the *New York Times* published a story about the city's problems with parking violators. The federal government, the article noted, was refusing to pay about $6 million a year in parking tickets in New York City. Down in the story there appeared a startling figure: *more than 10,000* undercover cars were operated by the federal government in New York City on any given day.°

The enormous degree of intrusion into our lives by the police and intelligence agencies of the government cannot adequately be portrayed by statistics, but the figures are numbing. The intelligence establishment was powerful enough to delete the total size of its budget from the final report of the Church committee, but enough clues were provided so that the figure can be calculated at $12 billion a year. The number of persons spied upon in one fashion or another, or made the subject of government dossiers, is not as easily arrived at, but certainly it runs into the millions.

According to the Senate intelligence committee, for example, the CIA, which opened first-class mail for twenty years, screened 28 million letters, photographed the outside of 2.7 million, and opened al-

---

° The story included this quote from a frustrated city official: ". . . the FBI, the CIA, Customs, Treasury, the Drug Enforcement Administration and other agencies have cars registered to fictitious names and addresses. We don't know whether it's an undercover vehicle unless it's towed away. We find out when someone comes to pick it up."

most 215,000. For more than two decades, with the collusion of the communications companies, the NSA in Operation Shamrock received copies of literally millions of cables sent from, to, or through the United States. From 1955 to 1975, the FBI investigated 740,000 "subversive" targets. The CIA indexed 300,000 names in its "Hydra" computer during Operation CHAOS and compiled separate files on 7,200 Americans. The Army kept files on some 100,000 Americans, including members of Congress and other civilians. The FBI as late as 1972 had 7,482 "ghetto informants" on its payroll; it still maintains a network of 1,500 "domestic intelligence" informants whom it pays $7.4 million a year. The IRS had more than 465,000 Americans and organizations in its IGRS intelligence files, and another 11,500 in the basement files of the Special Service Staff.

But statistics do not fully convey the loving attention to detail with which the intelligence agencies went about their appointed rounds. When Dr. Martin Luther King, Jr., visited Honolulu in 1964, an entire squad of FBI wiretappers and electronic-bugging experts was flown in from San Francisco. Forty reels of tape were obtained from that trip and the bug in Washington's Willard Hotel alone. J. Edgar Hoover personally ordered that a transcript be prepared of the King hotel room bugs. "I think it should be done now while it is fresh in the minds of the specially trained agents," he instructed his subordinates. The transcript came to 321 pages.

So inured had the CIA become to its unlawful opening of first-class mail that at one point in the sixties, the Agency developed a steam oven for use by its team of agents at Kennedy International Airport, where the mail-opening physically took place in a secret office. The oven could handle about a hundred letters simultaneously, but it was undependable. The agents soon returned to a simpler method: steaming the letters open with a tea kettle. The CIA men who performed this illegal work were graduates of a one-week course in mail-opening at CIA headquarters. It was called "flaps and seals."

The government, through the intelligence agencies, created a system of institutionalized lawbreaking. For years RCA, ITT, and Western Union made available copies of international cables to the National Security Agency in Operation Shamrock. In the sixties, when some of the communications companies switched to storing their cables on magnetic tape, NSA transported the tapes daily to its headquarters at Fort Meade, Maryland, for copying and back to New York City the same day. By 1966, the round trips had become burdensome, and Louis Tordella, the deputy director of NSA, asked the CIA to provide a secret location in New York where the tapes could be duplicated. The CIA, in the guise of a television-tape processing company, accommodated NSA by renting office space in lower Manhattan for seven years; at Langley, Virginia, the project was tunefully code-named LPMEDLEY.

Much of what has happened in America, the shape and details of the abuses committed against the people, are now known, through a progression of circumstances: Vietnam; the Pentagon Papers; the theft of FBI documents at Media, Pennsylvania; Watergate, which sliced open the intelligence melon, revealing much of the rot within; some vigorous investigative reporting; and finally, the congressional probes, especially the thousands of pages of testimony and documents compiled by the Church committee.

But why did it happen? Undoubtedly a combination of factors was responsible, but perhaps the most important element was fear— fear of external enemies that might destroy our freedoms, fear that led government officials to the surreal rationale that it was necessary to preserve the law by breaking it.

"Perhaps it is a universal truth," James Madison wrote to Thomas Jefferson in May of 1798, "that the loss of liberty at home is to be charged to provisions against danger real or pretended from abroad."

Emerging from World War II into an era of Cold War and global responsibility, the United States rapidly created a vast military and intelligence machine. "National security" became the catch phrase to justify massive defense spending, a secret army of CIA covert operators abroad, and a carte blanche for J. Edgar Hoover to root out "subversives" at home. McCarthyism flourished, then faded, but the fear remained.

In the name of national security, the government broke the law repeatedly, methodically, even routinely. National security was the justification for COINTELPRO, for chaos, for the mail-opening, the bugging of Martin Luther King, Jr., for the Kissinger wiretaps, and for the surveillance of Joseph Kraft in a Paris hotel room. The FBI's burglars broke into homes and offices of Americans in the name of national security. One remembers Nixon, Dean, and Haldeman seizing on the phrase gratefully as they struggled to find a retrospective rationale for the burglary of a psychiatrist's office. Yes, said John Dean, I think we can get by on that.

One FBI agent who performed many "black bag" jobs told the Church committee that it was not always necessary to break in. If a building owner appeared to be "patriotic," he said, the agents would ask him for help in entering an apartment—"show our credentials and wave the flag."

In the beginning, much of the machinery of national security was directed at adversaries abroad. The CIA, in particular, was given the mission of manipulating the internal affairs of other countries, from rigging elections to engineering coups. But it is not possible to create an invisible government, a world of secret agents and covert operators, without using those resources sooner or later against the American people. In a sense, Howard Hunt was inevitable.

On the "spillover" effect from covert operations abroad to domestic politics, the testimony of the FBI's William Sullivan to the Church committee is instructive. Questioned by Senator Walter Mondale about the techniques used against Martin Luther King, such as the scheme to use a female "plant" in his office, Sullivan defended them as "common practice among intelligence services all over the world . . . This is a common practice, rough, tough, dirty business. Whether we should be in it or not, that is for you folks to decide. We are in it . . . no holds were barred. We have used that technique against Soviet agents. They have used it against us."

"The same methods were brought home?" Mondale asked.

"Brought home against any organization against which we were targeted."

Although national security is the most familiar rationale for the abuses of the police and intelligence agencies, it has frequently been used as a cloak for political activity. Thus, Lyndon Johnson used a national security agency, the FBI, to wiretap the 1964 Democratic National Convention. Richard Nixon wiretapped newsmen and officials after government secrets leaked to the press, but when two of the targets went to work for Senator Muskie, the taps remained on their home telephones, producing valuable political intelligence.

Nixon's Plumbers were the classic illustration of the blending of national security and political motives. Howard Hunt was hired to find leaks, but his first act, in his CIA disguise, was to interview someone who might have dirt on Teddy Kennedy. Almost the identical team of Plumbers that burglarized Dr. Fielding's office for alleged national security purposes later broke into the headquarters of the opposition party at the Watergate for partisan political reasons. There was no need to change the players.

And it was natural for Nixon to use the CIA to block the FBI investigation of the burglary—the act that ultimately sealed his doom as President. Particularly in the Nixon White House, national security concerns became indistinguishable from political concerns. This was so because Nixon and the men around him equated their own power with the power of the state. They believed themselves to *be* the government, rather than the temporary trustees of the government for the people. From this it easily followed that they saw no difference, and made no distinction, between their own political security and the national security.

There were other reasons why the normal checks and balances of the American constitutional system failed to prevent the intelligence agencies from breaking the law and violating basic rights. In any democratic society there is a tension between liberty and order, between individual freedom and the requirements of society as a whole. Normally, however, such conflicts are resolved within the framework of law and the judicial system. But the intelligence operators believed in a higher morality. They persuaded themselves that they had the right to use any means in the pursuit of the ends of national security.

A 1954 report of the Hoover commission on government reorganization set the tone: "It is now clear that we are facing an implacable enemy whose avowed objective is world domination by whatever means and at whatever cost. There are no rules in such a game. Hitherto acceptable norms of human conduct do not apply. If the U.S. is to survive, long-standing American concepts of 'fair play' must be reconsidered."

William Sullivan told the Senate intelligence committee, "... never once did I hear anybody, including myself, raise the question: 'Is this course of action which we have agreed upon lawful, is it legal, is it ethical or moral?' ... We never gave any thought to this line of reasoning, because we were just naturally pragmatists. The one thing we were concerned about was this: Will this course of action work, will it get us what we want ... ? As far as legality is concerned, morals or ethics, [it] was never raised ... I think this suggests really in government that we are amoral. In government—I am not speaking for everybody—the general atmosphere is one of amorality."

Another FBI official, William Branigan, put it succinctly, "It was my assumption that what we were doing was justified by what we had to do ... the greater good, the national security."

When G. Gordon Liddy was masterminding the Nixon Administration's covert campaign against Daniel Ellsberg under the code name Project Odessa, he wrote a memo to Egil Krogh and David Young warning that "Odessa must be closely held" or the press would have a field day. "The only overt program should be that involving criminal prosecution under the appropriate federal statutes. The remaining malefactors should be identified and dealt with no less severely, but *by alternative means* [italics added]." "Alternative means" —the phrase captures the essence of the police state.

In a democracy, official amorality and lawbreaking take place in secret. The intelligence abuses have been able to flourish because of a pervasive system of official secrecy that has permitted the lawbreakers to conceal their illegal acts by stamping them "Top Secret." The government's classification system, which has existed for civilian agencies only since 1951, has thus provided a vital cocoon of secrecy to mask the illegalities from the public, the press, and the Congress. What has surfaced has been disclosed in spite of this system, partly through the accident of Watergate. How much is still going on today we do not know.

Government secrecy has in some cases resulted in the intelligence agencies' concealing information from Presidents, and from one another. For a long time the FBI, which had its own illegal program of mail-opening, did not know that the CIA was doing the same thing.

The secrecy helps to confuse the public. An odd, almost theological debate has taken place in recent years over whether the police and intelligence agencies have been misused by Presidents, or whether the agencies are out of control and have themselves engaged in abuse of power. The answer is both. The two problems are not mutually exclusive. At times Presidents have misused the intelligence agencies, as Nixon did in Watergate. At other times, the agencies have acted, in varying degree, on their own. Senator Church phrased it the most dramatically; in its assassination plots, he suggested, the CIA was "a rogue elephant on a rampage." Indeed, the CIA, according to Richard Helms, did not think it appropriate to discuss murder plots with the President of the United States. The FBI did not bother to inform Presidents that it was harassing American citizens, even endangering their lives at times, through COINTELPRO. But the agencies have obeyed White House orders as well. Senator Frank Church's "rogue elephant" is also a trained elephant that can sit up and perform dirty tricks when called upon.

The growth of presidential power in the past four decades has of course been a significant factor in unleashing the intelligence apparatus against the electorate. The increase in the size, budget, and sheer power of the intelligence establishment has paralleled the growth of the executive branch as a whole.

As a result, the bureaucratic requirements of the agencies have, at times, proved as important, or perhaps even more important, than ideology. Within the FBI, Hoover kept the pressure constantly on the agents in the field to come up with more ingenious suggestions for harassing the "New Left," and "Black Nationalist" groups. To the FBI man who could dream up the better stink bomb, the more insidious poison-pen letter, the most nauseating doctored fruit, went the approval of headquarters and the Director.

Often presidential demands have fueled illegal or improper acts by the agencies of the government: Lyndon Johnson demanded the surveillance of Anna Chennault and the inquiry into Spiro Agnew's toll calls in 1968; Richard Nixon ordered the polygraphing of William Van Cleave, the wiretapping of his own White House aides, the CIA cover-up in Watergate. Moreover, the executive has utterly failed to institute effective internal checks on the intelligence apparatus. The much-vaunted Forty Committee, which was supposed to control covert operations abroad, proved nothing but a sham—high-level window dressing, a "circuit-breaker," as Helms described it, to insulate the President from responsibility for crimes up to and including murder.

Until the scandal could no longer be ignored, Congress preferred not to know. The traditional attitude of the shadow committees that watched over the CIA for many years was personified by Senator John C. Stennis of Mississippi, chairman of the Armed Services Committee and its CIA subcommittee. "Spying is spying," he told the Senate a few years ago, ". . . you have to shut your eyes some and take what is coming."

In 1975 Stennis unsuccessfully opposed the establishment of a permanent Senate committee on intelligence. "I'm ashamed of what CIA had done at home in one of its bad moments," Stennis said, "but of course I knew nothing about it." There was marvelous irony in Stennis' comment, since it was precisely his job, of course, to know everything about it.

It was not only institutions that failed. There was, as well, a failure of leaders and of officials to understand that American democracy can survive only if it obeys the dictates of the Constitution, the law, and its conscience.

The long-range results of this failure have not yet been fully measured. If one may borrow a phrase from the language of the intelligence operators, the damage assessment is not complete. It is not at all clear whether the people can ever regain control of the secret instruments of government that supposedly serve them.

What is clear is that democracy has been diminished and individual freedom curtailed without the nation's knowing what was happening. Even the victims of FBI harassment seldom suspected that the government was behind their difficulties. A police state, American style, has developed, not by the choice of the voters, or by the legislative process, but by erosion.

The trust between the people and the government, on which democracy depends, has also been eroded by the wide-ranging disclosures of improper activities and official lawbreaking. When that trust is weakened or destroyed, it is not easily restored.

In fact, the revelations tend to breed and reinforce paranoia, since they confirm our worst suspicions and fears. The political dissident, the news reporter, or the black leader who fears that his telephone is tapped, or his hotel room bugged, or his office broken into, or his tax return politically audited, may well be right.

Perhaps the most dramatic example of how the abuses feed our darkest instincts was provided by the actions of the intelligence agencies before and after the assassination of President Kennedy. As the

Senate intelligence committee documented, both the CIA and the FBI withheld vital information from the Warren Commission. The CIA, whose Director, Allen Dulles, was a member of the commission, did not disclose that it had plotted to poison Fidel Castro—who might thus have had a motive to retaliate against Kennedy. The CIA did not tell the commission that at the very moment when the President was shot in Dallas, a CIA case officer in Paris was handing a high Cuban official a ball-point pen, especially equipped with a poison needle, for use against Castro. Nor did the commission know that the Cuban, Rolando Cubela, code-named AMLASH, may have been a double agent, reporting the entire plot back to Castro. Similarly, the FBI did not confide to the Warren Commission that a few weeks before November 22, 1963, Lee Harvey Oswald had visited the FBI office in Dallas and left a note—apparently threatening the FBI—that was destroyed after Kennedy's murder.

The fact that the CIA and the FBI covered up relevant information after the assassination of the President of the United States did not prove that Kennedy's death was the result of a conspiracy. Nor did it necessarily follow that because the CIA tried to kill Castro, the Cuban leader retaliated by having Kennedy assassinated.* But if the intelligence agencies could not be trusted in their investigation of the single most traumatic political event of recent years, can they justifiably ever expect the confidence of the people?

The misused power of the intelligence establishment has warped and distorted the political process itself. The Kissinger taps of Muskie advisers or the bugging of the 1964 Democratic convention by Lyndon Johnson were not exceptional examples of political use of the "national security" machinery. Army intelligence agents, besides spying on a number of civilian political leaders, eavesdropped on radio communications at the 1968 Democratic National Convention from three locations in Chicago. The FBI's repeated burglaries of a leftist political party, the referral of the names of political opponents to the FBI during the Roosevelt Administration, the operational support given by the CIA to Howard Hunt's political investigations—the list is long. The entire FBI COINTELPRO operation was, in its deepest sense, a violation of First Amendment rights, since it was fundamentally designed to stifle free expression.

Beyond that, many of the government's actions amounted to an assault on the dignity of the individual, on the right of privacy, and

---

* On September 12, 1963, two months before Kennedy's death, the government's interagency Cuban Coordinating Committee met to consider what steps Castro might take to retaliate against the covert activities directed at him by the CIA. Listing Castro's options, the committee concluded: "Attacks against U.S. officials. (Unlikely)."

the right to be oneself in a free society. The outrageous FBI letters to black militants, accusing spouses of adultery, were designed to break up marriages (as was the mailing of the FBI tape to Coretta King). In San Diego and Chicago, the FBI encouraged black militants to kill one another. Martin Luther King was apparently urged to kill himself.

Although the fact has been little publicized, the CIA did not confine its tests of LSD to government officials such as Frank Olson, who committed suicide after being drugged. Even after Olson's death, the CIA continued its tests on unwitting subjects. A favorite technique used by the CIA was to pick up people in bars at random, invite them back to a CIA safehouse for a friendly drink, and then drug them while agents in an adjoining room switched on tape recorders and observed their reactions through two-way mirrors. The victims, of course, never knew that their host was the Central Intelligence Agency. Some of the subjects became ill for hours or days, and at least one required hospitalization. The CIA was hardly in a position to conduct follow-up medical checks on the health of these subjects, so there is no way of knowing whether the victims, as a group, suffered long-range effects.

As far back as 1953, Richard Helms informed Allen Dulles that the CIA was looking into the development of a chemical to cause a "reversible non-toxic aberrant mental state, the specific nature of which can be reasonably well predicted for each individual. This material could potentially aid in discrediting individuals, eliciting information, and implanting suggestions and other forms of mental control."

And it is not generally known that the ill-fated Huston Plan at one point included the use of truth serum along with the other techniques to be used against politically unreliable citizens. All of these hideous methods had a common strand running through them—their effect was to reduce the individual to an object, and to strip him of his humanity, the more easily to be manipulated by the state.

Since technology has outpaced efforts at political control of the intelligence agencies—indeed until quite recently there were virtually no such efforts at all—the prospects for the future are not pleasant. The super-sophisticated techniques developed by the National Security Agency to intercept telephone or other conversations, or to tap, uninvited, into computers, may mean that in the not too distant future those who dissent from established policy may literally have no place to hide.

Another danger—one that merits independent journalistic investigation or congressional inquiry—is the growing linkage between the federal intelligence agencies and local police forces. For years, Army intelligence in Chicago received copies of almost every intelligence report by Mayor Richard Daley's police. The federal government's prosecution of Leslie Bacon was based on the assertions of a local police informant in Washington, D.C. The FBI provided, in its own words, "a detailed floor plan" of the residence of Black Panther leader Fred Hampton to Chicago police, who proceeded to raid the apartment and kill Hampton. The CIA trained local police from several cities and rewarded cooperative chiefs with gifts and free vacations. The federal intelligence bureaucracy's ties to local police raises the specter of an eventual national network of police capable of spying on citizens at any level of government.

We are, as a nation, susceptible to the idea that for each problem there is a solution. As soon as the outrages of the intelligence operators were revealed, there were demands for new laws. Guidelines were promulgated, promises made, and Gerald Ford issued an executive order designed to give the appearance, if not the reality, of tightening control over the police agencies.

Certainly new laws are needed, and guidelines may help, but ultimately the outcome will depend more on whether, as a nation, we believe in freedom or fear it. Legislation cannot, by itself, ensure control, accountability, and legality for the intelligence agencies. No amount of institutional or bureaucratic reform, or legislative remedies, can protect us against an evil President. We have created powerful intelligence mechanisms, and they will be misused if a President, in seeking to ensure domestic tranquillity, abandons the blessings of liberty.

Existing laws have repeatedly been broken. The law says it is illegal to open first-class mail. The CIA and the FBI both opened first-class mail. The law says burglary is illegal; the Fourth Amendment says it is also unconstitutional. The FBI and other agencies, including the White House, the CIA, the NSA, and the IRS (through hirelings) nevertheless committed burglaries. The law says murder is illegal; the CIA plotted murders. Richard Nixon approved the Huston Plan despite a written reminder that the break-in features were "clearly illegal."

Nevertheless, a government of laws requires a legal framework if there is any hope that powerful agencies are to be controlled, and the basic laws governing the CIA and the FBI have been shockingly vague. The National Security Act of 1947 should be rewritten or replaced to prohibit the CIA from engaging in domestic spying. The CIA's entire network of shadowy domestic divisions should be shut down and the Agency confined to gathering intelligence overseas— which was Congress' intention when it created the intelligence agency.

CIA covert operations, from rigging elections abroad to overthrowing governments and instituting political assassinations, should be specifically barred by law in peacetime. It has been amply demonstrated by now that the cost of covert operations to our own system is too high.

The myth that covert operations can be employed sparingly, only when necessary, and then carefully controlled, has long since exploded. Richard Bissell testified to the Senate intelligence committee that he never told the Special Group—the predecessor of the Forty Committee—about the CIA's plots to use underworld figures to kill Castro. Richard Nixon instructed the CIA not to tell the Forty Committee about its operations against the Allende government. In the end, the committee was reduced to meeting on the telephone.

The operation in Chile is perhaps the most striking recent example of the bizarre logic of covert operations. Nixon made $10 million available to the CIA to block Allende's election, yet a contemporaneous CIA document concluded that the United States "has no vital interests within Chile." A month later the CIA cabled the Chile station that the coup plot had "no pretext or justification" to make it acceptable to the Chilean military. Langley then offered its own suggestions. The CIA not only worked toward a coup, it provided the reasons for one, since the Chileans apparently did not have any.

In addition to new laws, Congress should set its own house in order by establishing a joint committee on intelligence agencies, an instrument that has worked well in the equally sensitive field of atomic energy. The permanent Senate Select Committee on Intelligence, an outgrowth of the Church committee investigation, is a step in the right direction. At a minimum, the House should set up a companion committee. But the House has demonstrated little enthusiasm for controlling intelligence; having established a committee to investigate the agencies, at a cost of almost half a million dollars, it proceeded to suppress the committee's report, preferring to investigate the leaking of the document to Daniel Schorr.

The tendency of Congress to fret about leaks of classified information, instead of the abuses by the agencies whose secrets have leaked, is not an encouraging sign. It is the activities of the CIA and other intelligence agencies that have injured the United States, not the leaking of a report that admirably detailed those activities in the expectation that the public might have a chance to read about them.

Limiting the CIA to intelligence-gathering abroad does not resolve a troublesome question of whether, or to what extent, the FBI should be permitted to gather intelligence at home. "There is always the possibility," Attorney General Harlan Fiske Stone warned in 1924, "that a secret police may become a menace to free government and free institutions, because it carries with it the possibility of abuses of power which are not always quickly apprehended or understood. . . . The Bureau of Investigation is not concerned with political or other opinions of individuals. It is concerned only with their conduct and then only with such conduct as is forbidden by the laws of the United States. When a police system passes beyond these limits, it is dangerous to the proper administration of justice and to human liberty, which it should be our first concern to cherish."

When Stone appointed Hoover to head the FBI, he ordered him to limit his investigations "to violations of law." It was only later, during the Roosevelt Administration, that the FBI branched out into intelligence-gathering, with only a misty legal basis.

Stone was right, both about the proper role of the FBI and about the dangers of passing beyond those limits. In an era when the United States, as a highly industrialized society, is increasingly vulnerable to terrorists, it is tempting to argue—as the FBI does—that it must be permitted to infiltrate all kinds of groups to prevent violence before it occurs.

The difficulty is that once infiltration begins, it never ends. The necessity of gathering intelligence on "subversives" was used by the FBI for decades as justification for all sorts of illegal or dubious acts. It was an easy next step to harassing individuals and groups who did not conform. Gradually the FBI became an arbiter of orthodoxy, an instrument of social and political control.

America's traditions and ideals suggest that we should prefer the risks of freedom to spying on groups and citizens because of their political views. The FBI should be limited to investigation of crimes or of conspiracy to commit crimes. It is in this latter area that the FBI must be closely watched, for in the past the Bureau has argued that the possibility that a crime may be committed mandates broadly based "preventive intelligence." Congress can and should draw very careful standards so that the FBI is permitted to investigate potential terrorist acts only when there is probable cause to believe that such acts are being planned. A bombing by a radical group, or a skyjacking, need not become an umbrella for indiscriminate infiltration of society as a whole.

Moreover, such investigations should be for a limited time period —not open-ended, as has often been the case—and they should require approval of the Attorney General, perhaps even of the President. All government wiretapping, bugging, or searches should require a court warrant that meets the standards of the Fourth Amendment. There should be no exception for "national security."

Quite aside from the dangers, and the violations of individual rights, the FBI's preventive intelligence-gathering has resulted in few convictions. The FBI has seldom prevented a bombing, and in the case of political radicals, it has had great difficulty in finding the bombers—for all of its intelligence programs and informants. And all too often, the FBI informant has become the criminal who encourages or leads the violent act. The informants, in preserving their cover or gathering intelligence have committed government-sanctioned crimes.

The Internal Revenue Service should be confined to collecting taxes—and dealing equally with friends and enemies. Congress should take a close look at the National Security Agency, which it has never done, and sharply restrict its domestic activities, if it can.

The list of possible reforms is almost endless, but the right answers are not easily found. Where to draw the line in controlling secret power is enormously complex, particularly since in times of social turmoil, the people demand more vigorous government action against those who dissent or turn to violence.

But at least the debate is out in the open, and the nation has been forced to recognize that the government has, in the name of the people, violated the fundamental rights of the people. The problem is not a new one. "You must first enable the government to control the governed," James Madison wrote in *The Federalist*, "and in the next place oblige it to control itself."

In monitoring the police agencies, the press has perhaps the most crucial role of all. With some exceptions, the press for many years failed to focus on the activities of the police arms of the government. The hidden intelligence abuses went ignored and unreported for too long. Like other segments of society, the press can be gulled by the "national security" slogan.

When the press exposes government lawbreaking it is not harming our security, it is fulfilling its constitutionally protected role. As for the danger of news "leaks," the government leaks selectively all the time. President Ford's indiscreet luncheon remarks to the editors of the *New York Times* amounted to one of the major leaks of recent years, but it was of great benefit to the country, for it forced out into the sunlight the fact that the CIA had planned the assassination of foreign leaders.

What vital secrets does the government protect? In the case of the Pike committee report, the secrets included the fact that three rugs had been given to Henry Kissinger, that his wife had received a necklace, that the United States had double-crossed the Kurdish rebels, that the CIA had provided women to King Hussein and other leaders and had produced porno movies, and that the intelligence agencies had a budget many billions of dollars higher than Congress had ever been told. Some secrets.

In the end, laws can be broken, guidelines evaded. It is what all of us as a people want America to be that will determine whether the machinery of the police state can be controlled or whether it will grow and eventually pervade and take over the legitimate state.

Fifty years ago Justice Brandeis saw it all coming: "Our government is the potent, the omnipresent, teacher. For good or for ill, it teaches the whole people by its example. Crime is contagious. If the government becomes a law-breaker, it breeds contempt for law; it invites every man to become a law unto himself; it invites anarchy. To declare that in the administration of the criminal law the end justifies the means—to declare that the government may commit crimes in order to secure the conviction of a private criminal—would bring terrible retribution."

Agencies created to uphold and enforce the law, to protect our liberties and preserve democracy, have broken the law, violated the Constitution, and threatened our freedom. Often they have done so in the name of protecting our security, to save us from our enemies.

But by adopting the methods of the enemy, we change the very nature of the system we are trying to preserve. We lose by winning. For, in time, if we accept the values of the enemy as our own, we will become the enemy. If government in America is different from that of our adversaries, we must preserve the difference. We cannot uphold the law by breaking it, we cannot defend the Constitution by violating it, and we cannot survive as a democracy by adopting the police-state methods of totalitarianism.

In Vietnam, during the Tet offensive of February 1968, American troops caught in the town of Bentre called in heavy-artillery support close to their own positions. The bombardment left much of the village in rubble and led to the most famous quote of the Vietnam war, by an unidentified United States major: "It became necessary to destroy the town to save it."

What is true of a village can also be true of a nation.

I began work on this book in the impeachment summer of 1974, soon after Richard Nixon resigned the presidency, accused by the House Judiciary Committee of abusing the powers of his office. It seemed to me, then and now, that the deeper significance of Watergate lay not in the questions about the cover-up and the President's complicity, but in the larger issue of the misuse of the police power of the state against individuals who dissent from established policy.

The book begins with the story of the wiretapping of Joseph Kraft because, whether or not there actually was "a ladder against the bedroom window," the case to me symbolized the problem. If the President of the United States can secretly order the wiretapping of a prominent newspaper columnist who has displeased him, is any citizen safe?

The fact that the clandestine machinery of the government could be used against individual opponents of the President or his policies seemed to me the essence of a police state, and a corruption of democracy. The governed had become the enemy, the people the targets.

It seemed equally apparent that many of the abuses of the intelligence agencies had roots that reached back many years to previous Administrations. To recognize this is not to exonerate Richard Nixon.

When I commenced my research two years ago there was not yet a Rockefeller Commission, a Church committee, or a Pike committee. On December 22, 1974, Seymour M. Hersh disclosed the CIA's domestic spying operations in the *New York Times*. The official investigations that followed revealed the dimensions of the intelligence abuses, and I have attempted to describe and summarize the major official findings.

But much of the material contained here has not been published before. The book is based, in addition to official records, upon more than two hundred interviews conducted by the author from 1974 to 1976. The persons interviewed include many present and former government intelligence officials and the targets of their wiretapping, break-ins, and other operations. A number of these individuals were interviewed more than once; some were seen several times. Most of the interviews were conducted in person; others were accomplished by telephone. I have tried to indicate in the text of the book wherever material is based upon, or quotes directly from, these interviews. In a very few cases, the persons interviewed asked that the material not be attributed to them by name, and I have respected their wishes.

Wherever possible, I attempted to interview primary sources involved in the events described in the book. Thus, in dealing with the Nixon era, I interviewed, among others, John Ehrlichman, E. Howard Hunt, Jr., John Caulfield, John Ragan, and by telephone, Anthony T. Ulasewicz and Charles W. Colson. During the spring and summer of 1974, in researching articles for the *New York Times Magazine*, I was able to talk at length with Alexander Haig, James D. St. Clair, J. Fred Buzhardt, and many of Nixon's other senior advisers, and with Peter W. Rodino, Jr., chairman of the House Judiciary Committee, all of which provided valuable background.

In reconstructing the seventeen "Kissinger wiretaps" and the surveillance of Joseph Kraft, I interviewed William C. Sullivan, the FBI official who supervised these activities, at length. I did so in a series of telephone interviews over a period of several months, supplemented by detailed exchanges of correspondence. I also talked with Joseph Kraft several times, and I interviewed a majority of the seventeen targets of the Kissinger taps: William Beecher, Henry Brandon, Daniel Davidson, Morton Halperin, Marvin Kalb, Anthony Lake, James McLane, Richard Moose, Robert Pursley, William Safire, and John Sears. Roger Morris and William Watts, among others, enhanced my understanding of the Kissinger staff system. To all go my thanks, with a special word of appreciation for the assistance given by Morton Halperin and his attorney, Walter B. Slocombe.

On questions concerning the technical and other aspects of wiretapping and bugging, I am particularly indebted to Michael J. Hershman, a former investigator of the Senate Watergate committee and later chief investigator for the National Commission for the Review of Federal and State Laws Relating to Wiretapping and Electronic Surveillance. On Watergate matters and the activities of Caulfield and Ulasewicz, I wish to express my thanks to Senator Lowell P. Weicker, a member of the Ervin committee, and to his staff, and also to Terry F. Lenzner, who served as assistant chief counsel of the committee, and Marc E. Lackritz, who was assistant majority counsel, both of whom were extremely helpful. So were Nick Akerman, Charles F. Ruff, Philip A. Lacovara, Peter M. Kreindler, Daniel N. Rosenblatt, and other present and former members of the staff of the Watergate Special Prosecutor.

For the chapter on break-ins, I am indebted to Robert Fink, whose article "The Unsolved Break-ins, 1970–1974" (*Rolling Stone*, October 10, 1974), provided essential background. I appreciate as well the cooperation of the victims of break-ins who were willing to talk with me, and who are identified and quoted in the chapter, as well the assistance of Mitchell Rogovin and Patrick F. J. Macrory, the attorneys for the plaintiffs in a number of these cases.

Senator Frank Church and the staff of the Senate intelligence committee were helpful in the chapters dealing with the CIA and the FBI, and I should thank in particular Spencer Davis, press secretary of the committee; Deborah Herbst, the assistant press secretary, whose patience and efficiency were unfailing; Frederick A. O. Schwarz, Jr., chief counsel; and John Elliff, leader of the task force on domestic intelligence. Senator Gary Hart, a member of the committee, and his assistant, Rick Inderfurth, assisted in the chapter dealing with the break in CIA-FBI relations over the disappearance of Professor Thomas Riha.

Senator Howard H. Baker, Jr., and his staff were of help in my research on the relationship of the CIA to Watergate. Louise Brown of the Tax Reform Research Group provided useful data on IRS intelligence-gathering. The case studies on William R. Van Cleave and Leslie Bacon could not have been written without the extensive cooperation of both, and I appreciate their willingness to talk at length with me.

The list of helpful friends and colleagues in the press corps in Washington and elsewhere is long, but it must include Seymour M. Hersh of the *New York Times*, who has contributed greatly to alerting the American public to the dangers discussed in this book; as well as Tom Wicker, James B. Reston, E. Clifton Daniel, A. M. Rosenthal, and E. W. Kenworthy, of the *Times*; Robert J. Donovan of the Los Angeles *Times*; Thomas B. Ross of the Chicago *Sun-Times*; Laurence M. Stern and Benjamin C. Bradlee of the Washington *Post*; David Kraslow and Andrew J. Glass of the Cox Newspapers; Michael J. O'Neill of the New York *Daily News*; Tad Szulc and Marianne Szulc; Dan Rather, Daniel Schorr, and Marvin Kalb of CBS; Martin J. Schram of *Newsday*; John Jay Iselin of WNET, New York; Eugene V. Risher; and Victor Marchetti and John D. Marks, the authors of *The CIA and the Cult of Intelligence*.

Others who were generous with their time and aid include attorneys Melvin L. Wulf, John H. F. Shattuck, and Hope Eastman, of the American Civil Liberties Union; Michael Kennedy, Gerald B. Lefcourt, and William H. Schaap; Marcus Raskin of the Institute for Policy Studies; Sam Papich and Charles D. Brennan, formerly of the FBI; and Margaret Carroll and Esther Newberg.

In addition, many published and unpublished documents, court records, hearings, congressional reports and similar records were consulted. The most useful congressional documents on the intelligence agencies are the hearings and reports of the Church committee, *Hearings Before the Select Committee to Study Governmental Operations* with Respect to Intelligence Activities, United States Senate, 94th Congress, Volumes 1–7, and the committee's *Final Report*, Books 1–5. The final report of the House Select Committee on Intelligence was suppressed by a vote of the House, but may be read in the *Village Voice*, February 16 and 23, 1976. The CIA's domestic spying is discussed in the *Report to the President by the Commission on CIA Activities Within the United States*, June 1975 (the Rockefeller Report).

A great store of information is contained in the thirty-nine volumes compiled in the Nixon impeachment investigation, *Hearings* Before the Committee on the Judiciary, House of Representatives, 93d Congress, 2d Session. Of the twelve volumes comprising the committee's *Statement of Information*, Book VII, Parts 1–4, deal with White House surveillance activities, including the Kissinger wiretaps. For details of these wiretaps, see also "Dr. Kissinger's Role in Wiretapping," *Hearings* of the Committee on Foreign Relations, United States Senate, 93d Congress, 2d Session, 1974, and the committee's *Hearings*, "Nomination of Henry A. Kissinger," Parts 1 and 2, 1973. The records of the Senate Watergate committee were another basic source; see "Presidential Campaign Activities of 1972," *Hearings*, Executive Sessions, and Appendices of the Select Committee on Presidential Campaign Activities of the United States Senate, 93d Congress, 2d Session, and the committee's *Final Report*, June 1974. Certain unpublished files of the Senate Watergate committee were also consulted by the author.

Quotations from the White House tapes are from both the edited version released by Nixon, *Submission of Recorded Presidential Conversations*, April 30, 1974, and the House Judiciary Committee's version, *Transcripts of Eight Recorded Presidential Conversations*.

A number of libraries and reference sources were helpful to me, including William A. Hifner of the Washington *Post*; David A. Brewster of the Washington bureau of the *New York Times*; Leslie Parsley of the Denver *Post*; Evelyn Collobert of the *Rocky Mountain News*; Joseph F. McCarthy of the New York *Daily News*; James R. Berger and the research staff of *Congressional Quarterly*; Wayne Kelley, the executive editor of CQ, and John Fox Sullivan, publisher, and Dom Bonafede, senior editor of the *National Journal*.

My debt is especially great to the persons directly involved in the preparation of this book: first and foremost, Nancy D. Beers, who assisted me with the research and interviewing, and whose insights into the subject matter were invaluable over many long months, and deeply appreciated by me. My thanks go as well to Judith Kolberg, who helped in the early stages of the research, and to Gwen Gibson and Mordecai Lee, who assisted with special research; to S. L. Carson, who provided staff assistance; to Anne Jorgensen and Judith Grogan, who kept the newspaper clipping files up to date, and to Mrs. Connie de Launay, who typed the manuscript.

This book took more than two years to research and write, as my wife, Joan, and my children, Christopher and Jonathan, well know. As much as for anyone, this book was written for my sons, in the belief that telling what has happened in our country will help to make it less likely to continue or recur. I hope that they will also understand that despite what this book is about, America has been, and can again be, a place of freedom.

Washington, D.C.   David Wise
July 29, 1976

Index

About the Author

DAVID WISE is a political writer based in Washington. He is the author of *The Politics of Lying* and the co-author of *The Invisible Government*, the book about the Central Intelligence Agency which became the nation's number-one best seller and was widely credited with bringing about a reappraisal of the role of the CIA in a democratic society. He is former chief of the Washington bureau of the New York *Herald Tribune*. A native New Yorker and graduate of Columbia College, he joined the *Herald Tribune* in 1951, served as the newspaper's White House correspondent during the Kennedy Administration and as chief of the Washington bureau from 1963 to 1966. During 1970–71 he was a Fellow of the Woodrow Wilson International Center for Scholars in Washington, D.C. During 1977–78, he lectured in political science at the University of California at Santa Barbara. With Thomas B. Ross, he is co-author of *The U-2 Affair* (Random House, 1962), *The Invisible Government* (Random House, 1964), and *The Espionage Establishment* (Random House, 1967). He has also contributed articles on government and politics to *The New York Times Magazine*, the *New Republic*, *Esquire*, and other national magazines. In 1969 he received the Page One Award of the Newspaper Guild of New York for best magazine writing. In 1974 he received the George Polk Memorial Award for *The Politics of Lying*. He is married and has two children.